P9-DYD-942

PERGAMON GENERAL PSYCHOLOGY SERIES
EDITORS
Arnold P. Goldstein, Syracuse University
Leonard Krasner, Stanford University & SUNY at Stony Brook

HELPING PEOPLE CHANGE
(PGPS-52)

Pergamon Titles of Related Interest

Barlow/Hayes/Nelson THE SCIENTIST PRACTITIONER: Research and Accountability in Clinical and Educational Settings
Barlow/Hersen SINGLE CASE EXPERIMENTAL DESIGNS: Strategies for Studying Behavior Change, Second Edition
Bellack/Hersen BEHAVIORAL ASSESSMENT: A Practical Handbook, Third Edition
Hersen/Bellack DICTIONARY OF BEHAVIORAL ASSESSMENT TECHNIQUES
Higginbotham/West/Forsyth PSYCHOTHERAPY AND BEHAVIOR CHANGE: Social, Cultural and Methodological Perspectives
Wolpe THE PRACTICE OF BEHAVIOR THERAPY, Fourth Edition

Related Journals
(Free sample copies available on request.)

ADVANCES IN BEHAVIOUR RESEARCH AND THERAPY
BEHAVIORAL ASSESSMENT
BEHAVIOUR CHANGE
BEHAVIOUR RESEARCH AND THERAPY
JOURNAL OF BEHAVIOR THERAPY AND EXPERIMENTAL
  PSYCHIATRY
CLINICAL PSYCHOLOGY REVIEW

HELPING
PEOPLE CHANGE
A Textbook of Methods
Fourth Edition

Edited by

FREDERICK H. KANFER
University of Illinois at Urbana-Champaign

ARNOLD P. GOLDSTEIN
Syracuse University

PERGAMON PRESS
Member of Maxwell Macmillan Pergamon Publishing Corporation
New York • Oxford • Beijing • Frankfurt
São Paulo • Sydney • Tokyo • Toronto

Pergamon Press Offices:

U.S.A.	Pergamon Press, Inc., Maxwell House, Fairview Park, Elmsford, New York 10523, U.S.A.
U.K.	Pergamon Press plc, Headington Hill Hall, Oxford OX3 0BW, England
PEOPLE'S REPUBLIC OF CHINA	Pergamon Press, 0909 China World Tower No. 1 Jian Guo Men Wei Avenue, Beijing, 100004, People's Republic of China
FEDERAL REPUBLIC OF GERMANY	Pergamon Press GmbH, Hammerweg 6, D-6242 Kronberg, Federal Republic of Germany
BRAZIL	Pergamon Editora Ltda, Rua Eça de Queiros, 346, CEP 04011, Paraiso, São Paulo, Brazil
AUSTRALIA	Pergamon Press Australia Pty Ltd., P.O. Box 544, Potts Point, NSW 2011, Australia
JAPAN	Pergamon Press, 8th Floor, Matsuoka Central Building, 1-7-1 Nishishinjuku, Shinjuku-ku, Tokyo 160, Japan
CANADA	Pergamon Press Canada Ltd., Suite 271, 253 College Street, Toronto, Ontario M5T 1R5, Canada

Copyright © 1991 Pergamon Press, Inc.

All rights reserved. No part of this publication may be reproduced, stored in a retrieval system or transmitted in any form or by any means: electronic, electrostatic, magnetic tape, mechanical, photocopying, recording or otherwise, without permission in writing from the publishers.

Library of Congress Cataloging in Publication Data

Helping people change : a textbook of methods / edited by Frederick H. Kanfer, Arnold P. Goldstein. -- 4th ed.
    p. cm. -- (Pergamon general psychology series : 52)
    Includes bibliographical references.
    ISBN 0-08-037893-5 : -- ISBN 0-08-037892-7 (pbk.) :
    1. Behavior therapy. 2. Adjustment (Psychology) 3. Change (Psychology) 4. Community mental health services. I. Kanfer, Frederick H., 1925— . II. Goldstein, Arnold P. III. Series.
    RC489.B4H45 1991
    158--dc20
                                          90-32185
                                                      CIP

Printing: 1 2 3 4 5 6 7 8 9   Year: 1 2 3 4 5 6 7 8 9

Printed in the United States of America

The paper used in this publication meets the minimum requirements of American National Standard for Information Sciences -- Permanence of Paper for Printed Library Materials, ANSI Z39.48-1984

To Ruby, Ruth, and Larry for their infinite patience,
encouragement, and affection

and

To Susan with love and admiration for her concern
with helping others

Contents

Preface to the Fourth Edition

Effective means for helping people change continue to evolve, and we have sought to reflect such intervention progress in this fourth edition. Current approaches whose efficacy is well demonstrated are again strongly represented in the chapters which follow, as are newer developments in the domains presented. Chapter coverage is both extensive and intensive; that is, each intervention method examined is placed in a broad context, yet described in sufficient detail for direct use by practitioners. Even more than in past editions, we have sought to make this truly a textbook of methods.

Several of the intervention-relevant trends that have helped to shape the contents of previous editions of this book have continued, and even grown. These include efforts to individualize treatments, integrate seemingly disparate treatment strategies, construct new treatments and combine them in different ways, and to offer interventions targeted to problems currently evidencing high levels of incidence in American society. Eating disorders, marital concerns, body image distortions, stress-management difficulties, the desire to enhance interpersonal competence, and biopsychological wellness are frequent examples.

In our view, it appears that the professional community's utilization of diverse intervention approaches has changed in several regards, and we have sought to reflect such shifts in our chapter coverage. For example, biofeedback procedures as major therapy strategies seem to be in declining use. Therefore, we have eliminated the material that highlighted them.

Operant and aversion methods are still widely used, and their presentation has been retained. But neither area appears to be expanding in application or innovative research. In contrast, cognitive-behavioral intervention is coming into growing professional use, and most of four chapters (7, 8, 9, 11) are devoted to methods that broadly fall into this category. We have also added a new chapter (10) dealing with topics that go beyond targeting the individual for change, focusing instead on external resources available to clients, such as social support, empowerment, and self-help groups. These themes draw heavily from modern community psychology and social psychology.

In all, we have sought to provide a comprehensive, empirically supported, practitioner-oriented presentation of currently employed and effective methods of psychological intervention. As this book's editors, we especially wish to express our high regard and appreciation to its chapter authors. Their considerable expertise as scientist–practitioners, and their high levels of concern regarding means for increasing human satisfaction and effectiveness have given this book both its spirit and its substance.

Frederick H. Kanfer
Arnold P. Goldstein

HELPING PEOPLE CHANGE

1
Introduction

Frederick H. Kanfer
Arnold P. Goldstein

Perhaps the most characteristic feature of our lives during the last few decades has been the rapid increase in the rate of change—in the physical environment, in our technology, and in our social, political, and moral institutions. Bombarded by mass media, by a wealth of available goods and ideas, and by the ever-changing scene to which our senses are exposed, each of us finishes the day having changed for better or worse, even if ever so slightly. A conversation with a friend, an interesting movie or book, a political rally, a work of art, or a breathtaking natural scene may all make a deep impression on us and can alter our attitudes about ourselves and about the world. If an experience is sufficiently intense, it can alter our behavior to the extent that our families and friends are surprised at the change. Yet, many persons go through their daily routine given the same exposure to ideas, images, and people as others but remain unable to change their view of themselves or others and unable to give up self-defeating patterns of behavior, even though solutions and opportunities for growth are at an arm's length. Others meet their world in rigid, fearful, or aggressive ways, finding little happiness or satisfaction, yet unable to break the vicious circles they seem to engender. It is these populations, persons who are stymied in resolving their personal and interpersonal problems, who are the focus of our attention as professional helpers.

This book is about psychological methods designed to help people change for the better, so that they can fully develop their potentials and capitalize on the opportunities available in their social environment, or change their attitudes to accept what is beyond their power to change. The helping methods we will examine share the common goal of promoting change in ways that can lead to greater personal happiness, competence, and satisfaction. Our point of view stresses that a professsional or paraprofessional helper can serve as both a consultant and an expert teacher or guide to persons whose discomforts, psychological disabilities, and social inefficiencies have been of sufficient concern to them, or to others in their environment, that the assistance of a trained outsider is deemed necessary.

People help one another in numerous ways in everyday life and, indeed, people do change as a result of such informal assistance. However, several distinct characteristics consistently differentiate the professional or paraprofessional helping relationship from friendship or other helpful interactions. Whether the helping relationship is called psychotherapy, counseling, guidance, behavior modification, or Gestalt therapy, and whether it is conducted by a physician, a psychiatrist, a psychologist, a social worker, a child case worker, a mental health technician, or a hospital nurse or aide, the same features are found in all professional or paraprofessional helping relationships: They are unilateral, systematic, formal, and time limited.

The *unilateral* aspect of the helping relationship reflects that the participants agree that one person is defined as the helper and the other as the client. It is also agreed, explicitly or implicitly, that the focus of the relationship and all its activities is on solving the problems of the client. In this respect, the change process is unlike most other interpersonal interactions. The personal problems, the private affairs, the worries and the wishes of one person, the helper, are intentionally not focused on. Treatment, therapy, or whatever the helping relationship is called is one-sided. It concentrates exclusively on the client.

The professional or paraprofessional helping relationship is *systematic* in that the participants typically agree at the outset on the purposes and objectives of their interaction. The helper attempts to plan and carry out procedures that move in an organized fashion from a description of therapeutic goals toward resolution of the client's problems.

The relationship is *formal*, in that the interaction between helper and client is usually confined to specified times and places. Although the interaction need not always be conducted at the same time of day and in the same office, clinic or hospital, this usually is the case. The times and places are arranged in such a way that the helper has no other role or duty during meetings with the client. At times, the helper might intentionally create an informal atmosphere. For example, a helping interaction can occur when a child care worker plays checkers or Ping-Pong or takes a walk with a child, or when an adult client is seen in his or her home. However, under these circumstances the child care worker's concern in not with winning the game or getting physical exercise during the walk, nor is the visit in a client's home a social occasion for mutual enjoyment. These are, instead, examples of formal treatment in an informal setting.

Helping relationships are *time limited*. The relationship terminates when the stated objectives and goals are reached. The termination is always considered the final outcome of the relationship and can be based on mutual agreement or on either the helper's or the client's initiative. Despite the task orientation of the therapeutic interaction, both participants are influenced by the other's personal characteristics, empathy, and apparent depth of involvement in the relationship. The *therapeutic bond* (Orlinsky, 1989) affects the course of therapy and requires deliberate structure and evaluation (Beutler, Crago, & Arizmendi, 1986; Morris & Magrath, 1983; Sweet, 1984). In chapter 2 some of its components and its impact on treatment are discussed in detail.

If you consider a friendship or an interaction with a colleague or a neighbor for a moment, it will become clear that few of the features listed in such relationships are the same as those characterizing the helper–client relationship. Social relationships are formed for mutual benefit of the participants, there is usually no fixed agenda for what is to be accomplished, the relationship is typically enjoyed for what it is rather than for what it may accomplish, and it is terminated for numerous reasons other than completion of a task.

The presence of common elements in most psychotherapies has raised interesting questions about the equivalence of therapies that are based on quite different theories, use different techniques, and even differ in training requirements of helpers. Several reviews of psychotherapy outcome studies have concluded that there is little difference in treatment effectiveness, even when they are alternatively based on psychodynamic, behavioral, cognitive, humanistic, or eclectic conceptual frameworks (Luborsky, Singer, & Luborsky, 1975; Smith, Glass, & Miller, 1980). The apparent equivalence of outcome has been attributed to various factors; among them: flaws in research design, poor selection of studies in meta-analyses, use of global rather than case-specific outcome criteria, and focus on final outcome rather than microanalysis of within-session effects (Stiles, Shapiro, & Elliott, 1986). Numerous authors have suggested that these equivalent outcome results are due to the common features that characterize all therapies, including the aforementioned core characteristics of helping relationships as well as personality characteristics of the helper and the positive expectations of clients and the treatment rationale either brought with them or conveyed by the helper throughout the therapy process (Brewin, 1988; Goldstein, 1962).

These problems in determining what are the effective ingredients responsible for positive therapeutic outcomes have led to attempts to describe generic models of therapy process (e.g., Kanfer & Grimm, 1980; Orlinsky, 1989; Prochaska & DiClemente, 1986) and to integrate different approaches at various levels of abstraction. This *eclectic* approach has many variations but the most common is a "technical eclecticism" (Lazarus, 1967) that endorses the use of a variety of techniques, regardless of their conceptual origin, but combines them in the context of a single theory. A recently organized society (SEPI, Society for the Exploration of Psychotherapy Interaction) has devoted itself to the study and advancement of various integrative perspectives.

From a viewpoint that stresses the pragmatic nature of the therapeutic change process and views it as a problem-solving enterprise jointly carried out by client and helper, the *events paradigm* is especially appealing as a tool for effectiveness evaluation. It suggests that techniques be examined for their utility in a specific problem context, that is, by asking whether they achieve the desired effect, as measured by the client's response or the consequences of the client's actions, at a particular time in therapy (Rice & Greenberg, 1984). This approach maximizes the availability of various strategies for the individual client's particular needs. It is consistent with the presentation of a range of trans-theoretical methods that could be combined with strategies from different schools of therapy.

The history of professional helpers goes back over many centuries. In each age, the predominant theory of human nature determined which professional group was considered the most competent to relieve people's discomforts and psychological problems. In societies in which theological explanations of humans dominated, priests, shamans, or witch doctors were given the task of assisting people with their personal problems or rectifying behavioral deviations. More recently, the assumption was accepted in Western societies that behavioral disorders were manifestations of disturbances of the nervous system or the biological structure of the individual. As a result, major responsibility for dealing with psychological problems was given to physicians and, in particular, psychiatrists. Indeed, early suspicions that brain damage or weak nervous system structures were the causes of many behavior disorders resulted in rigorous search for the specific roots of what were then called "mental diseases." Even Freud's comprehensive theory of human behavior was based on the assumption that the driving energy underlying human activity, psychic libido, developed by conversion from physical energy via the nervous system.

In the last 3 decades there has been increasing disenchantment with the view that behavioral problems represent mental illnesses associated with the organisms's biological or psychic structures. Alternate models of psychological disturbances have been based on ideas derived from philosophical systems and, increasingly, from scientific psychology. While earlier scientific models posed relatively simple linear, single-level models of pathology and treatment, more recently theorists have emphasized the multilevel, iterative nature of human actions and experiences. To understand and treat psychological dysfunctions, one must recognize their biological and social context and their self-modifying effect in sustaining or changing their nature as a function of time. Congruent with this trend, there has also been the recognition that relief of psychological problems can be offered by persons with expertise in nonmedical specialties. Further, the erosion of belief in the infallibility of the authoritative professional has hastened the development of brief training programs that permit many laypersons to participate in the treatment or behavior change process. This expansion of the helper pool has helped reduce the scarcity of assistance available, caused by the small number of highly trained professionals and the large number of persons in need of help. The contributions of paraprofessionals have ranged from work in prevention and temporary assistance to persons under stress to long-term counseling and support of persons with physical and psychological disabilities.

But there has also been a recent change in the potential contributions of various professions to different populations. For example, as a result of developments in research and methods in the health sciences, psychologists participate increasingly in the care of physically ill persons and in the prevention and rehabilitation of incapacitating medical problems. Treatment programs for diabetics, postsurgical cancer and heart patients, and for persons with hypertension and many other illnesses include a strong psychological component.

There has also been a recent increase in the utilization of drugs for the treatment of behavioral dysfunctions. For some clients' problems, the specific effects of some medical interventions and drug prescriptions dictate the desirability of combining psychological and pharmacological interventions. Some dysfunctions respond well to initial drug interventions and, at the time, may represent the best available treatment. Further, some psychological disturbances or distress are caused mainly by biological factors, and a differential diagnosis is essential to plan treatment. Therefore, it is important for any therapist to recognize the need for a collaborative program with a physician and to be familiar with some of the conditions and treatments available for different complaints. In a combined therapeutic effort, it is also essential that both professionals inform each other of the actions and intended effect of the interventions to achieve the maximum benefits of the integrated program. The differing competencies of various professionals represent an advantage in planning an intervention program when the helper is familiar with both the skills and limitations of his or her own profession and is aware what contributions persons in other professions can make in the diagnosis and treatment of various components of the client's problem.

WHO IS QUALIFIED TO HELP?

Many different professions have as one of their goals the accomplishment of behavior change in their clients. Teachers, physicians, clergy, social workers, psychologists, and probation officers are among the professionals who offer services designed to change human behavior. Even if enduring changes in the client's behavior are not the immediate focus of the professional service, they can still play a role in the total context of the services offered. Attorneys, nurses, dentists, and financial advisors are among those who can achieve their specifically stated goals more easily if they can influence their clients to change in ways ranging from minor accommodations to sweeping changes in their life patterns. For example, the more effective dentist is one who not only restores tooth damage or applies preventive treatment in the office, but who is also able to persuade the patient to alter daily oral hygiene behaviors and, perhaps, even eating habits sufficiently so that future damage is prevented or retarded. However, not all professionals are equally qualified to deal effectively with psychological problems. Currently, the most acceptable criterion for qualification in the helping professions has been evidence of successsful completion of specified training programs. Generally, the successful completion of a study program is certified by a degree, and the holder is regarded as competent to carry out a specified range of professional duties. Of course, the distinction between meeting requirements in academic courses and showing the skills needed for professional practice is not clearly made by degree-granting institutions. In fact, frequent and heated debates have centered on the type of training that qualifies persons best for helping professions.

The most widely accepted criteria of professional-level competence are doctoral degrees with specialties in clinical psychology or counseling psychology, medical degrees with residency training in psychiatry, or advanced degrees in social work. However, there has been a growing recognition that the management of behavior change programs is not the province of any single discipline, nor is it necessary to expect every practitioner to be able to function in all areas within the given discipline. In fact, as treatment methods for psychological problems have moved away from their earlier foundations in religious, philosophical, or biological concepts of humans, to encompass psychological, social, economic, and political components as well, there has been a parallel development that has facilitated the delivery of effective behavior change programs by persons with much shorter and less complex formal training than the mastery of 4 to 6 years of postgraduate training that is required of psychologists or psychiatrists. As noted earlier, such persons can and do make significant contributions to helping people change. In part, this change in requirements is a result of the division of labor now possible because of clearer specification of the ways in which behavior change techniques can be applied. Traditional psychotherapeutic techniques were based primarily on complex and abstract personality theories, and the interpersonal relationship between helper and client was considered to be the primary instrument of change. As a result, it was necessary to train a person first, in depth, in the theories and assumptions of the therapy system. The development of treatment skills was a slow process, mainly by apprenticeship and close individual supervision. In many disciplines—for example, psychoanalysis—the training period might extend until the trainee was in his or her 40s. With the realization that many components of a behavior change program can be learned rather quickly and that complete mastery of the entire field is not essential for participating in some stages of the total program, there has been the increased effort noted earlier to train persons with limited knowledge of change methods (paraprofessionals) to work under the direction of more extensively trained persons.

Although in some clinical activities helpers with limited training and experience may not differ substantially from trained clinicians, research is needed to clarify exactly for which therapeutic activities paraprofessionals are most effectively employed (Garb, 1989). Earlier studies (e.g., Durlak, 1979) have shown that paraprofessionals were generally most effective when working in narrowly defined roles with specific client populations. To assume responsibility for orchestrating and conducting a full therapy program, clinicians must have skills in evaluating the nature and scope or a person's problems in social, biological, and psychological contexts. They must have skills in making decisions that would permit them to select among available helping techniques in order to construct a therapeutic program. They must know the methods by which progress in a program can be monitored and under what conditions the helping program can be changed. Finally, they must know the limitations of both their own skills and those of other helpers, and they must have knowledge of resources that can be called on when the problem falls beyond the limits of their own competence or the resources of their agencies. In this sense, a pyramid operation can be developed with a supervisor or consultant whose role is greatest at the beginning of treatment, who can monitor progress or treatment, and who can offer to the paraprofessional any supervision and advice needed. This concept of a therapeutic team of helpers varying in skill and competence is also useful because it permits the delivery of psychological services to large numbers of people who previously could not have afforded expensive individual psychotherapy.

A totally different qualification for a helper concerns personal characteristics. As already indicated, and as discussed in detail in a following section on ethics, it is essential that the helper be motivated primarily by the goal of helping the client rather than furthering his or her own interest. In addition, the helper must be able to discern cues about the impact of his or her own behavior on the client. Since clients have been unable to resolve their problems on their own and may suffer distress, they often show helplessness, pessimism, or even despondency. It is therefore critical that clinicians have an optimistic outlook, believing that some positive changes are possible in almost all cases. A strong belief in the value of human life, in the potential for some personal control, and in the possibility of developing some positive goals in every person that facilitate both personal and social growth is essential for the clinician's capacity to instill hope in clients and to motivate them to overcome the obstacles to change. Which other particular helper characteristics are desirable has been the subject of research and theory for many years. They seem to include, at minimum, helper empathy, warmth, honesty, and expertness. These and other apparently desirable helper characteristics are examined in depth in chapter 2.

Although the helping methods described in the following chapters have been tested and validated to some extent, it cannot be stressed too often that the methods themselves do not guarantee success. It is both skillful *application* (i.e., the judgment of when to apply what methods to which clients) and knowledge about when to *change* a technique or an objective that are essential for successful helping programs. Most of the techniques described in the following chapters are not tied to specific client problems. Thus, they can be used in ameliorating a wide variety of personal and social problems. When skillfully applied, they are likely to bring about beneficial changes in the client's behavior. But mere acquaintance with a catalog of available therapeutic techniques is insufficient preparation for competent psychological helping.

The problems and dangers of use of psychological helping techniques by persons without proper qualifications are legion. For example, operant techniques applied to continuing physical complaints could reduce the frequency of the complaints. However, such a change could also mask the inroads of a serious medical illness. Increasing assertiveness or feelings of independence in one marriage partner could indeed change the partner's behavior. However, without a thorough assessment and appreciation of the interpersonal context of the problem, an unskilled therapist could also find himself or herself contributing to increasing problems between marriage partners, and perhaps divorce or abandonment by a partner. The helper must have full awareness of the range of factors that go into designing a treatment program, be aware of his or her own limitations, and work closely with others who can provide the necessary guidance. Premature, clumsy, or ignorant application of behavior change techniques is wasteful and inefficient at best, and harmful at worst.

Summarizing our discussion on the necessary qualifications of the helper, it should be clear that paraprofessionals, students, human service aides, mental health technicians, attendants, nurses, and many other persons without prolonged professional training in psychological services can make major contributions to helping people change. In many settings, a paraprofessional worker spends more time with a client than any professional and has, by far, more influence in his or her extensive contact with the client than a senior professional might have in the short time of a diagnostic or therapeutic interview. However, execution and not design is the task of the paraprofessional. Continuous self-monitoring and feedback to a consultant or supervisor are necessary to maintain the efficiency of the program and to protect the client.

WHAT IS A PSYCHOLOGICAL PROBLEM?

Psychological problems, in general terms, are difficulties in a person's relations with others, in his or her perception of the world about him or her, or in his or her attitudes toward himself or herself. Psychological problems can be characterized by a person's feelings of anxiety or tension, dissatisfaction with his or her own behavior, excessive attention to the problem, inefficiency in reaching desired goals, or inability to control emotions or actions or to function effectively in psychological areas. Psychological problems can at times also be characterized by a situation in which the client has no complaint but others in his or her social environment are adversely affected by his or her behavior or judge him or her to be ineffective, destructive, unhappy, disruptive, or in some other way acting contrary to the best self-interest or the best interest of the social community in which he or she lives. Thus, the major characteristics of a psychological problem are in evidence when (a) the client suffers subjective discomfort, worry, or fears that are not easily removable by some action that he or she can perform without assistance; (b) the client shows a behavioral deficiency or excessively engages in some behavior that interferes with functioning described as adequate either by himself or herself or by others; (c) the client engages in activities that are objectionable to those around and that lead to negative consequences either for himself or herself or for others; and (d) the client shows behavioral deviations that result in severe social sanctions by those in the immediate environment.

Psychological problems sometimes are related to problems in other areas. For example, an automobile accident can cause physical disability that in turn leads to psychological difficulties. A person who has lost a job, marital partner, or life savings might temporarily face psychological difficulties. Discriminatory practices against a minority member, economic problems, sexual, moral, or religious demands by the environment that are inconsistent with the person's past history, all can cause psychological problems. Frequently, transient psychological problems can be resolved not by psychological helpers but by resolution of the "source" problem. For example, concern about a medical disability or serious illness is better treated, if treatable, by medical care than by psychological help. Unhappiness over loss of a job is more easily remedied by finding a new job than by resolving psychological problems about the loss. It is incumbent on the psychological helper, therefore, to analyze the total problem to determine if dealing successfully with at least some aspects of it can be more effectively carried out by someone who is not a psychological helper, whereas those components that comprise the person's attitudes, behaviors, or interactions remain the proper domain for mental health helpers. In this task it is useful to differentiate between the client's *complaint*, often a description of a current situation, such as the loss of a partner or recurrent night terrors, and the *problem* formulation. The latter involves relating the complaint to some actions that would eventuate in changing the present situation to a more desirable one (Kanfer & Schefft, 1988; Nezu & Nezu, 1989). Client complaints often represent unalterable facts, byproducts or consequences of the client's or others' behavior. For example, for the person who complains that his partner has left him, the goal may be formulated as focusing on accepting the loss and finding another partner, attempting to restore the broken relationship, or examine and improve the client's social skills. The definition of the central problem and selection of a therapeutic goal, gradually shaped from the client's complaint, is an early task in the helping relationship.

GOALS AND OBJECTIVES OF HELPING RELATIONSHIPS

A good treatment program is built with a clear conception of treatment goals, developed jointly by the helper and the client. It is possible to differentiate among five long-term treatment objectives: (a) change of a particular problem behavior, such as poor interpersonal skills; (b) insight or a clear rational and emotional understanding of one's problems; (c) change in one's subjective emotional comfort, including changes in anxiety or tension; (d) change in one's self-perceptions, including goals, self-confidence, and sense of adequacy; and (e) change in one's lifestyle, or "personality restructuring," an objective aimed at a sweeping change in the client's way of living. The selection of any one of these goals does not eliminate the secondary achievement of other objectives. For example, although many of the techniques described in this book are oriented toward change of particular behaviors, such changes often bring with them changes in the person's insights into his or her own actions, modification of attitudes toward himself or herself, and in some cases, a rather sweeping alteration of the person's total life-style. At the same time, therapists who aim for improved insight and major personality changes in their clients might also achieve, during the helping process, change in social behaviors or self-reactions. Thus, treatment objectives are not mutually exclusive, and the foregoing list is simply intended to indicate that primary emphasis can be given to a particular goal without sacrificing the achievement of others as byproducts or secondary outcomes of the change process.

Behavior Change

If the goal of a helping effort is to change a particular behavior, a thorough evaluation of the person's life circumstances is required to be sure not only that the target behavior is amenable to change, but also that such a change will lead to a significant improvement in the person's total life situation. Frequently, both interpersonal and cognitive behavior changes are needed. Standardized training programs exist for specific skills (e.g., enhancing assertiveness, overcoming fear, phobia, and panic, and increasing prosocial behavior). In the following chapters, techniques are also described for modifying more general strategies (e.g., coping with stress, developing self-management skills, and maintaining treatment gains to avoid relapse) that equip the client to cope effectively with future difficulties, rather than to alter only current symptomatic behaviors. A more detailed description of the steps necessary prior to beginning the change program follows in our discussion of the diagnostic process.

Insight

Insight as a goal has been most characteristic of psychoanalysis and its variations. These helping methods are not covered in the present volume, first because the assumptions underlying psychoanalytic therapy are extensive, and thorough training of therapists in psychoanalytic methods, including personal analysis and long supervision of cases, is usually required. Second, the therapeutic benefits of psychoanalytic and other insight-seeking methods are currently not well substantiated by empirical research and laboratory findings. They are excessively time consuming and, in our view, rarely represent the treatment of choice. The arguments in the psychological and psychiatric literature concerning the utility of insight versus behavior change, however, have sometimes been overstated. When a motivated client establishes a relationship between current behavior problems and past history, whether or not such a relationship is in fact accurate, the satisfaction of having achieved an explanation for his or her own behavior and the new labels he or she can then attach to emotional experiences can serve as a beginning for change in actual daily behaviors.

Emotional Relief

The reduction of anxiety has long been considered a central problem in the management of neurotic disorders. In general, when anxiety reduction or relief of chronic emotional tension is the primary objective of a helping effort, it is assumed that the client will later be able to conduct himself or herself more effectively because (a) he or she already has a repertoire of skills necessary to deal with life situations, and (b) his or her use of these skills was previously inhibited by anxiety. If this is not the case (i.e., if the problem involves not only inhibition due to anxiety, but also incompetence due to skill deficiency), changes in particular skill behaviors might be set up as the next goal in the change program. If the problem is both partly emotional and partly related to particular behavior deficiencies, then both the reduction of emotional tension and behavioral skill training could be dual treatment objectives.

Change in the Client's Self-Perception

Techniques for changing a person's self-perceptions and evaluations of his or her own behavior are found in several chapters in this volume. In general, the application of such procedures assumes that a person's improved self-image is sufficient to help him or her perform the constructive behaviors of which he or she is capable. For example, once a person sees himself or herself as competent or perceives himself or herself more realistically in relation to others, he or she might be able to plan and act with greater self-confidence, a greater sense of direction, and greater social effectiveness.

Lifestyle Changes

The most ambitious objective for a change program is the attempt to alter the person's total pattern of living. Frequently, this requires not only a change in the client's behavior, but also plans for changing the environment in which he or she lives, his or her circle of friends, his or her place of employment, and so forth. One example might be the client who is a drug addict and whose entire daily routine is subordinated to the procurement of an illegal narcotic. But every change process results in some changes of the person's daily life pattern, if it is at all successful. In some instances, the clarification of the lifestyle to which the person aspires can itself be a preparatory part of the change process. In other cases the main objective of treatment is the development of goals in a person who feels "alienated" or complains of a lack of direction and purpose. Thus, all change programs include consideration of the extent to which treatment success would alter the client's life. However, the extent to which these considerations are focal varies from minimal, as in correcting a study habit problem, to maximal, as in treating drug addiction or agoraphobia.

A PRESCRIPTIVE CAUTION

In the early years of psychotherapy research, investigators concerned with its effectiveness typically framed their research questions in global outcome terms, for instance, Does treatment A work? or Is treatment A superior to Treatment B? Such questions could be answered affirmatively only in those exceptional instances in which the treatment(s) studied were sufficiently powerful to override the high degree of between-patient, within-conditions heterogeneity. Even then, the generality of such questions often provided little information either about how to improve the effectiveness of the treatment (because the treatment as a whole had been studied, with little or no concern for its separate components) or about how to use the outcome information to help any *individual* patient (because only between-*group* effects were examined). In attempts to alleviate these weaknesses and to broaden the criteria for assessing treatment effectiveness, researchers now use statistical methods and evaluation procedures that permit examination of the *process* of change in individuals (Barlow, Hayes, & Nelson, 1984) and meta-analyses that evaluate the magnitude of treatment effects across many studies (Glass, McGraw, & Smith, 1981). Analysis of cost-effectiveness is also included in developing guidelines for mental health policies (Kiesler, 1980, 1982). But innovations in statistical techniques still leave unanswered the critical question about what specific mechanisms of change are embedded in various therapies and how their effectiveness is related to specific patient categories and problems (Parloff, 1984).

Investigators now seek to discern which type of patient, meeting with which type of therapist, using which type of treatment, will yield what outcome? This is a prescriptive view of psychotherapy. It holds that most treatments cannot be classified as "good" or "bad" in any comprehensive sense. Instead, this view holds that different treatments and therapists are appropriate for some patients but not for others. This prescriptive view of the therapy enterprise looks toward identifying optimal patient × therapist × treatment matches in designing treatment plans. In both research and practice, a conscious and consistent effort is made to avoid the patient, therapist, or treatment uniformity myths against which Kiesler (1966) has warned.

The implications of this viewpoint for the use of the present book are both clear and major. In each of the following chapters, many behavior change procedures are described and explicitly and implicitly recommended for clinical use. Our prescriptive view cautions us that, although each procedure rests, at least to some extent, on supportive empirical research, almost none should be expected to lead to behavior change in all patients, or for all problems of one patient, or at all stages of the treatment process. In the next chapter, for example, the nature and value of therapist empathy is examined. The position taken is that patient perception of therapist-offered empathy is a significant influence on certain aspects of a positive therapeutic relationship and eventual patient change. Yet we must not assume this to be the case for all patients or at all times. We agree with Mitchell, Bozarth, and Krauft (1977), who commented that

> empathy, warmth, and genuineness might be used differentially depending on client diagnosis. Clinical wisdom suggests that high levels of empathy might overwhelm a schizophrenic client early in therapy and that, instead, empathy might best be increased slowly over time within the context of uniformly high levels of warmth. On the other hand, with a neurotic, initially high levels of warmth might best be lowered somewhat in the middle phase of therapy in order to heighten negative aspects of the "transference" and increase anxiety sufficiently so it becomes an excellent stimulus for change. (p. 490)

We and others have developed this prescriptive view of psychotherapy in detail elsewhere (Goldstein, 1978; Goldstein & Stein, 1976) for those interested in pursuing its implications further. For our present purpose, its import is to caution the helper that optimal utilization of a technique requires consideration of the joint characteristics of patient, therapist, and technique.

DESIGNING A CHANGE PROGRAM

This volume is not intended to provide the helper with in-depth knowledge about diagnostic methods for analyzing the client's problem and designing a treatment program on the basis of this assessment. Nevertheless, the reader should be aware of the importance of an early analysis of the problem as the absolutely essential foundation for the application of any treatment technique. At this time, there are few widely accepted principles that can guide a helper through the evaluation and assessment process. There are many books and articles that summarize available psychological tests. Some also discuss the most critical features of the person's life situation that should be examined and the strategies to be used in arriving at a therapy goal and its associated treatment technique (Ciminero, Calhoun, & Adams, 1986; Goldstein & Hersen, 1984; Kanfer, 1985; Kanfer & Nay, 1982; Kanfer & Schefft, 1988; Karoly, 1985; Nelson & Hayes, 1986). As a minimum requirement for deciding on the choice of helping methods, the helper must make a thorough analysis of the context in which the problem behavior occurs, the form and severity of the problem behavior, the consequences both to the client and to his or her environment of the problem behavior, the resources of the client and of his or her environment for the promotion of change, and the effects which a change in behavior would have on the client and others. These and other factors comprise the content of what has been called a *functional analysis* of the problem situation. The information necessary to complete such an analysis may come from interviews, from observations, from knowledge of the client's past history, from reports of other persons who know the client, or from any other source that yields reliable information. In some cases, especially when the problem behavior has some physiological components, information about the medical status and physical health of the client is absolutely necessary.

A good functional analysis reveals factors that have contributed to the problem behavior and those that currently maintain it. It also gives some information about what particular stresses and demands are placed on the client by the environment in which he or she lives. For example, for a complete assessment it is not sufficient to know what a person does and what effects his or her actions have. It is also necessary to have an understanding of what requirements are placed on him or her by his or her immediate circle of friends, job situation, community, and persons who are important in his or her life. Further, a good functional analysis also yields a list of problematic behaviors that might require attention and information that would assist the helper to set priorities so that he or she can better decide which particular problem(s) to attack. Which items are placed high on the priority list would depend on the individual's life circumstances and initial responses to the change program. For example, any behavior that is self-destructive or has serious social consequences would be the most central initial target. However, in some cases, several problems might have equal priority. In this instance, a decision might rest on which of these problem behaviors are more amenable to solution by the available techniques. The client's conviction that he or she can change and the degree of support from other persons in his or her environment to assist in the change program must also be taken into account.

Another important aspect of the assessment procedure lies in the establishment of some methods and criteria for assessing the client's progress throughout the program. For example, the operant behavior change methods described in chapter 4 are usually applied in conjunction with quantitative records of the frequency, intensity, or duration of the behavior being changed before, during, and after the change program. With other techniques, the evaluation component is not so readily built into the treatment program. For example, relationship methods, group techniques, and attitude change methods often aim to alter more complex behavior patterns and typically do not incorporate a quantitative measurement or monitoring process into the treatment. Nevertheless, the helper should have some record of the patient's problem behaviors, complaints, and expectations prior to the onset of any change program. It is only with such documentation that helper and client can decide whether the change program has been effective, and further decisions about shifting to other objectives or terminating the relationship can be made (Kanfer & Busemeyer, 1982). The evaluation component of the treatment program is of importance not only for assisting the helper and the client in making decisions about progress and termination. It also serves as an incentive for both client and helper by giving them some objective evidence of the progress that has been achieved, and it enables the helper to specify more clearly the areas in which the program may have failed and the reasons for this failure.

ETHICAL CONSIDERATIONS

A helper makes a number of demands on her or his clients, expecting them to be frank in discussing their problems, to be involved in the change program, and to commit themselves to certain requirements of the program such as keeping appointments, paying bills, and carrying out contracted exercises or activities. Because of the very nature of the helping relationship, it is obvious that the client's interests must be protected to avoid damage or grief resulting from a helper's ignorance, unscrupulousness, self-serving manipulation of the client, or exploitation of the client's vulnerability. The ethical responsibilities of the helper, both to society and to the client, have been outlined in publications by various professional organizations. Helpers should be familiar with the criteria for ethical conduct that prevail in their respective professional group.

The use of the helping techniques described in this book should be restricted to situations in which a person *seeks* help from others in a formal way. Thus, the change techniques should not be applied in informal settings in which a person is unaware that attempts are being made to change his or her behavior; they should not be applied casually in personal relationships with friends or family members; they should not be applied when a client denies the existence of a problem even though it has been pointed out by others. In the latter case, more complex treatment programs would have to be used, even though the change techniques presented here could ultimately comprise part of the total treatment package.

In our discussion of professional qualifications, we pointed to the importance of the helper's training and background for the protection of the client. In this section we will look at a series of ethical considerations that a helper must abide by if he or she is to be helpful to the client and to be accepted by the community in which he or she practices. On some of the matters that follow, there is debate concerning the breadth of action open to the helper. Therefore, the following items range in importance from those for which a breach of ethics can lead to expulsion from professional societies to those items that are primarily a matter of individual conscience.

Exploitation by the Helper

There is no disagreement concerning the absolute requirement that the helper must not utilize the relationship in order to gain social, sexual, or other personal advantage. The self-serving functions of a helper, however, can extend from the slight extension of a treatment program beyond its absolutely necessary duration, in order to provide a helper with financial resources, to the flagrant financial, moral, or sexual exploitation of a client. The helper has access to confidential information that could embarrass or hurt the client. Even subtle pressure implying the use of such information for self-serving purposes is equivalent to blackmail and is clearly unethical.

Deception

The purposes and goals of the interaction should be clear to the client or her or his guardian. The client or guardian should be informed of any hazards or potential aversive consequences that are involved in a treatment procedure, and no exaggerated promises should be made about the likelihood of successful treatment outcome. It is improper to discuss the achievements or objectives of a change program with a third party, be it a marital partner, a parent, or an employer, without communicating such intentions to the client. Similarly, advice and guidance that would force the client into a situation over which she or he has no control would constitute unethical behavior. Advice to engage in illegal behaviors or suggestions of actions that would expose the client to hazards or predictable untoward consequences are examples of deceptive helper maneuvers.

Competence and Appropriate Treatment

It is the responsibility of the helper not only to offer the highest level of service, but also to be aware of his or her own limitations so that he or she can refer the client to someone else when necessary. In addition to referrals to others in the mental health field, it is also the helper's responsibility to be certain that problems outside the area of psychological treatment be properly referred. For example, referral to a physician for medical difficulties, to an attorney for legal problems, or to a social service agency for economic assistance should be made when these problems are evident or likely. Because the helper sometimes is not fully aware of the limitations in his or her own training, it is advisable for a helper to have some professional affiliation that will enable him or her to obtain assistance from colleagues regarding difficult cases. Persons who have paraprofessional training should discuss such problems with their supervisors, under whose direction the change program is conducted.

Principle of Least Intervention

Although it is obvious that almost any person might benefit from psychological counseling or a helping relationship, it is essentially the task of the helper to intervene in the client's everyday life only to the extent that the client desires a change. Once the jointly agreed on objective is reached, the helper should either terminate the relationship or discuss in detail with the client the possibility of future change programs. Only if the client agrees to additional programs should they be undertaken. A prior problem concerns the question of whether any treatment should take place at all. In some instances, clients seek assistance for problems that actually turn out to be common difficulties in everyday life. In such cases, for example, when a client is experiencing a grief reaction after the death of a close relative, information and reassurance could be sufficient. Similarly, parents might refer a child for assistance when, in fact, the child's behavior is not unusual for his or her age group. In such instances, behavior change programs would not be undertaken, and it could be possible to terminate the interaction when reassurance and information are given to the client.

Some techniques of behavior change, especially those that rest heavily on the alteration of the client's social environment (discussed in chapter 4), could involve the participation of other persons in channeling the client's behavior in a desired direction through the use of rewards and punishments. Programs in institutions such as hospitals, schools, or prisons might involve deprivation of certain privileges in order that they could be used later as rewards for appropriate behaviors. There is intense dispute concerning the appropriateness of such techniques because of their nonvolitional and manipulative aspects. As a result, special caution must be exercised to assure that the client's civil rights are not infringed on and that the client can make the kinds of choices about participating in a program that would normally be considered reasonable in the institutional setting in which they are introduced. The utilization of aversive stimuli is considered unethical when permission by the client or his or her guardian is not obtained. Other ethical problems associated with this method are discussed in detail in chapter 6.

In general, the helper needs to assure himself or herself continuously that she or he is maintaining the dignity of the client and guarding the confidentiality of information obtained in the helping relationship and that the therapeutic program does not have detrimental effects on either the client or others. It is the helper's responsibility to protect the client's rights and interests so that the change program clearly contributes to the client's welfare, rather than creates new problems and conflicts for her or him.

WHAT IS IN THE FOLLOWING CHAPTERS?

The chapters in this book provide detailed descriptions of different behavior change techniques by professionals who are expert in their respective fields. The techniques are generally appropriate for treatment of persons who show no gross social disorganization or such serious disturbances in their social or personal behavior that they require institutionalization. The techniques are, therefore, most applicable to persons who have difficulties in some areas of their lives but who can function at least marginally well in other areas. The techniques presented here are by no means exhaustive of the field of behavior change. They do constitute the most important methods that have been applied in the treatment of psychological problems. In selecting treatment approaches and techniques, we have chosen only those that are based on psychological theory that is widely accepted and that have as their foundation at least some laboratory research and evidence of effectiveness in application. Many of the methods mentioned here are quite new or still in the exploratory stage. However, we have eliminated from presentation a large number of methods now practiced that are based only on the belief of the practitioner that they are effective but that have no other empirical evidence or theoretical rationale behind them. Anecdotal observation or limited clinical experience that has not been substantiated by research or field studies is insufficient grounds for use of a method. We have eliminated techniques that clients have reported have made them feel better, unless some independent evidence of change is also available. All of the methods that are discussed in the following chapters have been described at considerable length in the professional literature. The reader will find references at the end of each chapter that will guide him or her to additional reading in order to strengthen his or her knowledge of each technique and, consistent with the ultimate goal of this book, more fully aid the helper in helping people change.

REFERENCES

Barlow, D. H., Hayes, S. C., & Nelson, R. O. (1984). *The scientist-practitioner.* Elmsford, NY: Pergamon Press.

Beutler, L., Crago, M., & Azrimendi, T. (1986). Research on therapist variables in psychotherapy. In S. L. Garfield & A. E. Bergin (Eds.), *Handbook of psychotherapy and behavior change* (3rd ed., pp. 257–310). New York: John Wiley & Sons.

Brewin, C. R. (1988). *Cognitive foundations of clinical psychology.* Hillsdale, NJ: Lawrence Erlbaum Associates.

Ciminero, A. R., Calhoun, K. S., & Adams, H. E. (Eds.). (1986). *Handbook of behavioral assessment* (2nd ed.). New York: John Wiley & Sons.

Durlak, J. A. (1979). Comparative effectiveness of paraprofessional and professional helpers. *Psychological Bulletin, 86,* 80–92.

Garb, H. N. (1989). Clinical judgment, clinical training and professional experience. *Psychological Bulletin, 105,* 387–396.

Glass, G. V., McGraw, B., & Smith, M. (1981). *Meta-analysis in social research.* Beverly Hills, CA: Sage Publications.

Goldstein, A. P. (1962). *Therapist-patient expectancies in psychotherapy.* New York: Macmillan.

Goldstein, A. P. (Ed.). (1978). *Prescriptions for child mental health and education.* Elmsford, NY: Pergamon Press.

Goldstein, A. P., & Stein, N. (1976). *Prescriptive psychotherapies.* Elmsford, NY: Pergamon Press.

Goldstein, G., & Hersen, M. (Eds.). (1984). *Handbook of psychological assessment.* Elmsford, NY: Pergamon Press.

Kanfer, F. H. (1985). Target selection for clinical change programs. *Behavioral Assessment, 7,* 7–20.

Kanfer, F. H., & Busemeyer, J. P. (1982). The use of problem-solving and decision-making in behavioral therapy. *Clinical Psychology Review, 2*, 239–266.

Kanfer, F. H., & Grimm, L. G. (1980). Managing clinical change: A process model of therapy. *Behavior Therapy, 4*, 419–444.

Kanfer, F. H., & Nay, W. R. (1982). Behavioral assessment. In G. T. Wilson & C. M. Franks (Eds.), *Contemporary behavior therapy: Conceptual and empirical foundations of clinical practice* (pp. 367–402). New York: Guilford Press.

Kanfer, F. H., & Schefft, B. K. (1988). *Guiding the process of therapeutic change.* Champaign, IL: Research Press.

Karoly, P. (Ed.). (1985). *Measurement strategies in health psychology.* New York: John Wiley & Sons.

Kiesler, C. A. (1980). Mental health policy as a field of inquiry for psychology. *American Psychologist, 35*, 1066–1080.

Kiesler, C. A. (1982). Public and professional myths about mental hospitalization. *American Psychologist, 37*, 1323–1339.

Kiesler, D. J. (1966). Some myths of psychotherapy research and the search for a paradigm. *Psychological Bulletin, 65*, 110–136.

Lazarus, A. A. (1967). In support of technical eclecticism. *Psychological Reports, 21*, 415–416.

Luborsky, L., Singer, B., & Luborsky, L. (1975). Comparative studies of psychotherapy. *Archives of General Psychiatry, 32*, 995–1008.

Mitchell, K. M., Bozarth, J. C., & Krauft, C. C. (1977). A reappraisal of the therapeutic effectiveness of accurate empathy, nonpossessive warmth, and genuineness. In A. S. Gurman & A. M. Razin (Eds.), *Effective psychotherapy: A handbook of research.* Elmsford, NY: Pergamon Press.

Morris, R. J., & Magrath, K. H. (1983). The therapeutic relationship in behavior therapy. In M. J. Lambert (Ed.), *Psychotherapy and patient relationships.* Homewood, IL: Dorsey-Jones-Irwin.

Nelson, R. O., & Hayes, S. C. (Eds.). (1986). *Conceptual foundations of behavioral assessment.* New York: Guilford Press.

Nezu, A. M., Nezu, C. M. (Eds.). (1989). *Clinical decision making in behavior therapy: A problem-solving perspective.* Champaign, IL: Research Press.

Orlinsky, D. E. (1989). Researchers' images of psychotherapy: Their origins and influence on research. *Clinical Psychology Review, 9*, 413–441.

Parloff, M. B. (1984). Psychotherapy research and its incredible credibility crisis. *Clinical Psychology Review, 4*, 95–109.

Prochaska, J. O., & DiClemente, C. C. (1986). The transtheoretical approach. In J. C. Norcross (Ed.), *Handbook of eclectic psychotherapy* (pp. 163–200). New York: Brunner/Mazel.

Rice, L., & Greenberg, L. S. (1984). *Patterns of change: Intensive analysis of psychotherapeutic process.* New York: Guilford Press.

Smith, M. L., Glass, G. V., & Miller, T. I. (1980). *The benefits of psychotherapy.* Baltimore: Johns Hopkins University Press.

Stiles, W. B., Shapiro, D. A., & Elliott, R. (1986). Are all psychotherapies equivalent? *American Psychologist, 41*, 165–180.

Sweet, A. A. (1984). The therapeutic relationship in behavior therapy. *Clinical Psychology Review, 4*, 253–272.

2

Relationship-Enhancement Methods

Arnold P. Goldstein
H. Nick Higginbotham

Barbara Harris is a 34-year-old woman, a wife, the mother of two children, a part-time office receptionist and, every Tuesday at 10:00 a.m., a psychotherapy patient. Over the course of the past few years, Barbara developed a number of concerns that more and more were interfering with her comfort and happiness. Backaches and a series of vague physical symptoms that seemed hard to cure were the apparent beginning of her change from a relatively problem-free and fully functioning person. Conflicts with her husband began around this time—about money, about sex, and about raising their children. Barbara's physical discomfort, her irritability, and her difficulty in getting along with people all increased as time passed. Eventually, these concerns and behaviors became so troublesome to Barbara and those around her that she contacted a psychotherapist recommended by her physician. She has been meeting with him for about a year now, and both feel she has made substantial progress in dealing effectively with her problems. Her physical complaints have decreased markedly, her relations with others are considerably more satisfying and, in general, Barbara seems well on her way to joining the two-thirds of all psychotherapy patients who apparently benefit from treatment.

In the same city in which Barbara lives there are four other women who have gone through similar difficulties and similar recovery from these difficulties. Yet none of them has ever met with a psychotherapist. What did they do? Pressed by the stress each was experiencing, each sought out a "good listener" or a "friendly problem solver" with whom she felt she could share her burdens. For one, it was a friend; for the second, her minister; for the third, her family physician; and for the last, a "paraprofessional" helper called a "home aide." All five women changed for the better, apparently in large part because of whatever occurred between each and her helper. Barbara's recovery might or might not have been somewhat more complete, or somewhat more rapid, but, for our present purposes, the significant fact is that all the women improved.

These mini-case histories are fictitious, but the facts they portray are all established. Many people do find problem relief, personal growth, and self-understanding as a result of participating in some form of psychotherapy. But many people obtain similar benefits as a result of their interactions with a wide variety of other types of helpers—friends, clergy, bartenders, relatives, counselors, nurses, and so forth. These facts have long intrigued researchers interested in what it is that causes people to change their behavior, emotions, and attitudes. Perhaps, many of these researchers have proposed, some of the causes of such changes can be identified by determining what ingredients successful psychotherapy and successful help from others have in common. If certain procedures, circumstances, or events are clearly characteristic of successful helping of different kinds, then we have the opportunity to use them most effectively in helping others.

Dr. Jerome Frank, in his important book, *Persuasion and Healing* (1961), has made a similar point. He compared psychotherapy, "informal" psychotherapy (from a friend, clergy person, etc.), faith healing, religious revivalism, placebo effects in medical practice, and a host of other activities in which two people, a helper and a client, collaborate to bring about some sort of psychological change in the client. According to Frank, perhaps the major responsible ingredient in determining whether such change occurs is the quality of the helper-client relationship. The same conclusion emerges if one examines descriptions of almost all of the many different approaches to formal psychotherapy. These several approaches vary in many respects—therapist activity and directiveness, how much this focus is on behavior versus the patient's inner world of feelings and attitudes, whether emphasis is placed on the patient's present life or childhood history, which aspects of his or her current difficulties are examined, and in a host of procedural ways. Yet, almost every approach to psychotherapy emphasizes the importance of the therapist-patient relationship for patient change. The better the relationship (a) the more open is the patient about this feeling, (b) the more likely he or she is to explore these feelings deeply with the helper, and (c) the more likely he or she is to listen fully to and act on his or her own insights, or advice offered by the helper; that is, the more likely the patient is to change.

This remarkably consistent viewpoint, in the psychotherapies and in other approaches to psychological change, has also found consistent support in other fields. How well a variety of medications serve their intended purpose has been shown to be partly a result of the relationship between the drug giver and the drug receiver. Learning in school has been demonstrated to depend in part on the teacher-pupil relationship. The subject's behavior in the experimental laboratory can also be readily influenced by the experimenter-subject relationship. In brief, there now exists a wide variety of research evidence, from several different types of two-person interactions, to indicate that the quality of the helper-client relationship can serve as a powerful positive influence on communication, openness, persuasibility and, ultimately, positive change in the client. This evidence is also useful in providing information that helps define the term relationship. Our definition, it will be noted, emphasizes positive feelings and interpersonal attitudes reciprocally held by the helper and the client: A positive or "therapeutic" relationship can be defined as feelings of liking, respect, and trust by a client toward the helper from whom she or he is seeking assistance, combined with similar feelings of liking, respect, and trust on the part of the helper toward the client.

HELPER BEHAVIORS AND THE THERAPEUTIC RELATIONSHIP

Richard and Elaine are final year counseling graduate students about to have their first "solo" session, each with a male minority student complaining of test anxiety. Their supervisor rates both of them as excellent in their theoretical understanding of systematic desensitization, the procedure each will use with the client over five sessions. As we watch the sessions unfold, we see that both initially greet the client warmly and sit comfortably facing him in an armchair. After opening statements, Richard steers the conversation toward aspects of test situations which produce anxiety in his client, and begins to formulate a hierarchy of such situations in his own mind.

Elaine moves much more slowly, finding things that she has in common with her client, and talking a bit about herself, and her own concerns about exams when she first started university studies. At one point when her client was fidgeting a bit in his seat, Elaine asked him if coming to the counseling center was a bit scary, and if talking to someone with a different ethnic background about personal matters was awkward or uncomfortable. The client agreed. The rest of the session was spent exploring what it was like to be a minority student on campus, what words the student used to talk about his feelings of insecurity regarding success, and how his body felt when he was under tension. Richard, on the other hand, had been able to get his client to list 10 situations linked to test anxiety, and to rank them from highest to lowest anxiety provoking.

When Elaine and Richard met to compare notes later, Richard complained that there were a lot of pauses in his conversation and felt that the client was not highly motivated to improve because he seemed disinterested in the hierarchy development process. At the next session, wishing to build better rapport and enhance motivation, Richard leaned forward a lot more as he spoke. He also borrowed a strategy from Elaine—as the session opened, Richard began to tell his client about how upset and fearful he used to be when taking exams, to the point of being physically sick before going in to take the test. Richard looked out the window as he talked about his memories, then came back to the present, and began to explain the principles of deep muscle relaxation. Elaine spent most of her second session exploring how the client viewed his problem; why it might be happening, and what actions the client saw as reasonable for diminishing the problem. At the end of the second session, Elaine made a small confession: "You know, when we first met last week I had real doubts that we'd be able to work well together. Now it is clear to me that you really want to work hard on this, and I'm right behind you one hundred percent!"

Over the next three sessions, Elaine translated the ideas and methods of systematic desensitization into the client's own language and understanding of the problem. At the end of the five sessions, the client reported being able to cope much better with tests. He also asked to continue seeing Elaine in counseling, as there was something much more important he wanted to deal with—problems of intimacy with his girlfriend. Richard was rather disappointed that his client did not return for the third session. When the Center secretary contacted him by phone, the client said he stopped coming because he had joined a counseling group at his church.

Why did the helping relationship unfold productively for Elaine but not for Richard, given similar clients and the counselors' equivalent level of training? It followed from differences in the use of specific relationship-enhancement methods. Elaine spent time initially using "small talk" to identify commonalities with her minority client, including well-timed and appropriate level of self-disclosure. She learned the client's language system for expressing and interpreting test anxiety, and used this information to negotiate successfully a meaningful application of systematic desensitization. Richard, in contrast, was technique oriented, failed to translate the treatment procedure into language his client would understand, and violated an unspoken equilibrium of intimacy between himself and the client by self-disclosing too much at the wrong time.

A number of methods have been identified as ways of making the helper-client relationship a more positive one. Each of these relationship-enhancement methods has been the subject of considerable research. Each has both added to our understanding of what the relationship is and helped explain the usefulness of the relationship for helping people change. These several methods, therefore, form the framework for the remainder of this chapter. We will, in turn, consider several concrete examples of each method, focusing on how the relationship can be enhanced or improved to the benefit of client change. Figure 2.1 provides an overview of our viewpoints.

The relationship enhancers listed are the major means currently available for improving the quality of the helper-client interaction. This interaction or relationship can be defined in terms of the three components indicated: liking, respect, and trust. Successful enhancement of these components, in turn, has been shown to lead to greater influenceability and, subsequently, to greater client change. Most

Relationship Enhancers	Relationship Components	Relationship Consequences	Outcome

Client structuring
Client imitation
Client conformity
Helper expertness
Helper credibility
Helper empathy
Helper warmth
Helper self-disclosure
Helper-client matching
Helper-client physical closeness
  and posture
Helper-client negotiation of
  meaning
Overcoming helper-client cultural
  mismatch
	Liking
	
	Respect
	
	Trust
		Communication
		
		Openness
		
		Persuasibility
			Client change

Figure 2.1. Progression from relationship-enhancement to client change.

psychotherapists and psychotherapy researchers view a positive relationship between helper and client as necessary, but not sufficient, for client change. Without such a relationship, change is very unlikely. With it, the foundation exists for other more specific change procedures (such as those described in subsequent chapters) to yield their intended effects.

ATTRACTION

Laboratory research has developed several procedures for successfully increasing attraction of the experiment's subjects to their experimenter. The present writer (Goldstein, 1971) has shown that many of these attraction-increasing procedures are highly effective in enhancing the helper-client relationship, especially the client's liking of the helper. Three such procedures are: structuring, imitation, and conformity pressure.

Structuring

It is perhaps fitting, in this book in which several dozen procedures for helping people change will be described, that the first procedure to be illustrated is probably one of the least complex. Structuring a client so that he or she will like or be attracted to his or her helper is, quite simply, a matter of (a) telling him or her that he or she will like the helper ("direct" structuring), (b) briefly describing certain positive characteristics of the helper ("trait" structuring), or (c) clarifying what he or she can realistically anticipate will go on in meetings with the helper (role expectancy structuring). Each of these three structuring procedures seeks to mold the client's expectations and feelings about his or her relationship with the helper. Relationship researchers have shown that what partners believe about each other may be more important than objective reality in influencing relationship satisfaction (Hendrick, Hendrick, & Adler, 1988). In one of the first uses of direct structuring to strengthen client attraction to the helper, new clients at a counseling center were first given certain tests that asked information about the kind of helper they would prefer to meet with—his or her behavior, expectations, goals, and so on. Shortly after this testing, clients were told by the tester:

> We have carefully examined the tests you took in order to assign you to a therapist whom you would like to work with most. We usually can't match a patient and therapist the way they want most, but for you we have almost exactly the kind of therapist you described. [The tester then showed the client how well his test results describing his preferred helper apparently matched other information purportedly indicating the actual behavior, expectations and goals of the helper with whom he would be meeting.] As a matter of fact, the matching of the kind of person you wanted to work with and the kind of person Mr. _____ is, is so close that it hardly ever happens. What's even more, he has often described the kind of patient he likes to work with most as someone just like you in many respects. You two should get along extremely well. (Goldstein, 1971, p. 21)

No actual matching of client preferences with helper characteristics was done here. Clients participated in the structuring procedure we have just described, and then each was assigned to a therapist whose turn it was for a new patient. Nevertheless, such structuring led clients to show increased liking of their helpers and increased openness about their problems. Thus, clients' belief that helpers would be the kinds of people they would like was enough to influence their actual attraction toward them and to facilitate the therapy process.

The enhancing effect on both attraction and openness has been shown to be even stronger when trait structuring of the client is conducted. These are instances in which specific, important qualities of the helper are described to the client before they actually meet, by persons such as the referring source or agency intake workers. Once again, the effect of these procedures on the actual attraction that develops is quite strong, even though the helper characteristics described might in fact not be present. Which particular helper characteristics are selected to be described to the client is an important matter. In most uses of trait structuring, the two helper traits chosen have been "warmth" and "experience"—the first of which tells the client something important about how comfortable she or he is likely to feel during the helping process, the second of which gives her or him information about the likely positive outcome of this process. Both items of information, therefore, enhance client attraction to the helper. The statement that follows is an example of trait structuring of helper warmth and experience:

> The therapist has been engaged in the practice of therapy for over 20 years and has lectured and taught at some of the country's leading universities and medical schools. Questionnaries submitted to the therapists's colleagues seem to reveal that he is a rather warm person, industrious, critical, practical and determined. (Goldstein, 1971, p. 50)

Trait structuring has also been used successfully "in reverse" to increase helper attraction toward the client. With this, qualities of the client are emphasized that lead the helper to anticipate that the client will be "a good patient." The type of problem the client supposedly has, the diagnosis, and his or her motivation to work hard to improve are some examples of positively structured traits of the client that have been communicated to the helper. Indeed, as we describe later, it is probably even more important for the therapist to perceive the help-seeker as an attractive client, given the relatively greater power of the helper's expectations to influence eventual treatment outcome.

A great deal of psychological research has been conducted on the effects of leading a person to believe she or he is similar to a stranger in important attitudes, background, or values and on her or his liking that person when they meet. This research convincingly shows that the greater the structured similarity, the greater the attraction to the other person. When other people's beliefs or attitudes agree with our own, it may satisfy our motive to be logical and interpret the environment correctly. Or, similarity may produce attraction because we assume that people who agree with us will also like us; and we tend to like those who like us (Condon & Crano, 1988). Nevertheless, this positive effect of structured similarity on attraction has also been found to operate in the helper-client relationship. It is largely for this reason that great use has been made in recent years of certain types of paraprofessional helpers, that is, persons who are lacking in certain formal training or degrees but who possess beliefs, personal backgrounds, and lifestyles similar to those of the persons they are seeking to help. These similarities between paraprofessional helpers and the people they serve, like structured similarity, enhance the quality of the therapeutic relationship.

We have seen thus far that direct structuring and trait structuring for warmth, experience, and similarity can each have attraction-increasing effects. So, too, can the final type of structuring we present—role expectancy structuring. Whereas direct and trait structuring mostly concern telling the client something about the kind of person the helper *is*, role expectancy structuring focuses on what the helper (and what the client) actually will *do* when they meet. If, because of misinformation or lack of information about what to expect, the client later experiences events during these meetings with the helper that surprise or confuse him or her, negative feelings will result. Events that confirm his or her expectancies serve to increase his or her attraction to the helper. For example, many new psychotherapy patients come to therapy with expectations based primarily on their past experiences in what they judge to be similar relationships, such as what happens when they meet with their medical doctors. During those visits, the patient typically presented a physical problem briefly, was asked a series of questions by the physician, and was then authoritatively told what to do. Now, however, when the client with such "medical expectations" starts psychotherapy, he or she is in for some surprises. The client describes a psychological problem and sits back awaiting the helper's questions and eventual advice. The helper, unlike the general physician, wants the client to explore his or her feelings, to examine his or her history, to speculate about the causes of the problem. These are not the client's role expectations, and when such important expectations differ, the relationship clearly suffers. These are but a few of the several ways in which client and helper can differ in their anticipations of how each will behave.

Prior structuring of such expectations has been shown to be an important contributor to increased attraction and a more lasting and fruitful helper-client relationship. This structuring can be provided by having new clients listen to a tape recording of a typical helper-client meeting. More commonly, role expectancy structuring has been accomplished by providing the client with a structuring interview (also called an *anticipatory socialization interview* or a *role induction interview*) before the first meeting with the helper. In this interview, a helper provides specific information about what the prospective client can expect to occur in psychotherapy. Topics covered include how much talking the client is expected to do; how the problem will be assessed; whether or not to expect direct advice; the amount of responsibility assigned the client in the "work" of therapy; potential emotional discomfort; and so forth. The following is an excerpt from such an interview in which a helper explains to the prospective client what he or she can expect to occur in psychotherapy:

> Now, what is therapy about? What is going on? Well, for one thing, I have been talking a great deal; in treatment your doctor won't talk very much. The reason I am talking now is that I want to explain these things to you. There is equally good reason that the doctor in treatment does not say much. Everyone expects to tell the psychiatrist about his problem and then have him give advice which will solve everything just like that. This isn't true; it just doesn't work like that. . . . Before you came here you got advice from all kinds of people. . . . If all of the advice you have received had helped, odds are that you wouldn't be here. Your doctor wants to help you to figure out what you really want to do—what the best solution is for you. It's his job not to give advice but to help you find out for yourself how you are going to solve your problem.
>
> Now, what goes on in treatment itself? What is it that you talk about? What is it that you do? How does it work? Well, for one thing, you will talk about your wishes, both now and in the past. . . . You will find that with your doctor you will be able to talk about anything that comes to your mind. He won't have any preconceived notions about what is right or what is wrong for you or what the best solution would be. Talking is very important because he wants to help you get at what you really want. . . . The doctor's job is to help *you* make the decision. . . . Most of us are not honest with ourselves. We try to kid ourselves, and it's your doctor's job to make you aware of when you are kidding yourself. He is not going to try to tell you what he thinks but he will point out to you how two things you are saying just don't fit together.
>
> The patient . . . sometimes feels worse and discouraged at some stages of treatment. You know, you'll feel you're not getting anywhere, your doctor is a fool, and there's no point in this, and so on. These very feelings are often good indications that you are working and that it's uncomfortable. It is very important that you don't give in to these temporary feelings when they come up.

Say whatever comes to your mind, even if you think it is trivial or unimportant. It doesn't matter. It is still important to say it. And if you think it is going to bother your doctor, that doesn't matter either; you still say it.

So, just like the [keeping of] appointments, we make an absolute rule not to think ahead about what you'll say and therefore protect yourself from facing important things. Say whatever is on the top of your mind, no matter what. (From "Anticipatory socialization for psychotherapy" by M. T. Orne and P. H. Wender, 1968. *American Journal of Psychiatry, 124,* pp. 1202–1212. Copyright 1968 by the American Psychiatric Association. Reprinted by permission.)

The way in which helper-client perceptions of each other are structured is important because it produces expectations about the benefits of the helping relationship that will ultimately determine treatment results. For example, a client entering treatment may not initially view the helper as having sufficiently attractive qualities to produce problem improvement, and will thus be reluctant to make a commitment to therapy. However, it is the interplay of both client and helper expectations about the benefits of treatment that affects how hard each will work and the mobilization of positive or negative emotions. Most probably, though, the therapist's expectancies are more powerful determinants of counseling events and outcomes than those of the client. When helper-client beliefs are discrepant, the therapist's expectancies will nullify the effects of the initial expectancies of those clients who remain in therapy (Higginbotham, West, & Forsyth, 1988, 150–165).

When a helper learns that the client perceives poor chances for problem solving in the relationship, several strategies can be applied to overcome the low success expectancy. First, the helper can draw on his or her status as an "expert" with certain credibility in such matters and explicity state a positive prediction of treatment outcome. Second, a helper can elicit and actively discuss any discrepant expectations. The helper will then either accommodate to client expectations, or initiate the negotiations of alternative client beliefs aligned more with the professional's perspective. Therapist-offered conditions will seldom violate all of the client's preferences. Gladstein (1969) found that disconfirmation of role expectations results in client dissatisfaction only when *none* of the various expectations are confirmed. Preferred events that both participants hold in common can be pinpointed and emphasized.

Client assimilation of the helper's positive expectation can occur if the therapy rationale presented is believable and couched in metaphors familiar to the client. Beliefs are likely to shift when the client receives hopeful assurances of change, clear homework instructions, and an immediate experience during therapy implying improvement, such as proprioceptive feedback from muscle relaxation (e.g., Kazdin, 1979). Helpers who are able to encode subtle messages of affiliation, encouragement, involvement, and concern simultaneously through several nonverbal channels will probably elicit higher ratings of credibility and be able more dependably to raise expectations (Berman, personal communication,

September, 1979). Nonverbal cues expressing affiliation in counseling have been found to include smiling, positive head nods, animated hand movements, high eye contact, a direct angle of shoulder orientation, and slight forward body lean (Hermansson, Webster, & McFarland, 1988; LaCrosse, 1975).

We may note then, in summary of our presentation thus far, that structuring can lead to increased attraction of the client toward the helper, whether such structuring is a simple matter of a straightforward statement of probable liking (direct structuring), a description of certain of the helper's positive qualities or of helper-client similarity (trait structuring), or an explanation of the events and behaviors one should expect in the relationship (role expectancy structuring). Whether a given structuring statement of any of these kinds actually does increase client attraction depends in part on matters other than the structuring itself. These statements tend to be most effective when the person doing the structuring is perceived as trustworthy, and when the client is experiencing distress or discomfort from her or his problems.

Helper-client attraction generated by structuring closely relates to the perception of benefits expected from the therapeutic relationship. However, even when the client initially does not foresee the possibility of treatment gains through the helping relationship, the therapist is in a strong position to overcome low expectations among those clients who return for additional sessions. Strategies for doing so involve dealing directly with discrepant expectations, offering highly plausible alternative beliefs, and use of nonverbal messages of affiliation.

Helper-Client Negotiation of Meaning

Another method to enhance helping relationships involves purposeful negotiation of the inevitable differences that exist between client and helper. Differences in social status, gender, age, values, ethnicity, and so forth may come to subvert the development of the therapeutic alliance unless resolved in the initial meetings. Such differences are not trivial because they influence fundamental helping processes, such as the language forms people use to communicate, and the meaning attached to the presenting problem. This section explains how cooperative conversation is created and sustained, particularly when helper and client are of unequal status or culturally dissimilar. Three points are made. First, speakers must negotiate access to culture-specific knowledge if they are to interpret accurately and respond to the social meaning of spoken information. Second, the meaning of client nonverbal communications must be explained, given what they reveal about client feelings toward the helping relationship. Third, the interpretation of the illness event or problem should also be negotiated in order to set a mutually agreeable course of treatment.

When client and therapist face one another at their first session, each brings linguistic abilities tuned to the conventions of his or her own speech community.

Mutually understood conversation becomes possible only when the speakers are able to negotiate a common interpretation of the signals used in their verbal and nonverbal exchanges. Gumprez (1982) found that people socialized in different speech communities will signal the intended meaning of what is said by following different unspoken ground rules. Cues to signal the meaning of speech include eye contact; gestures; posture shifts; changes in voice tone and loudness; how questions are posed; and other subtleties. In our highly mobile and urbanized society, communication with speakers of differing sociocultural backgrounds is the rule rather than the exception (Gumprez, 1982). Clinicians must identify breakdowns in conversational coordination, and deftly negotiate with the client accurate interpretations of speech signals in order to reestablish fluent conversation.

Higginbotham et al. (1988) describe how helpers may overcome language barriers with clients and gain conversational cooperation. First, the clinician carefully monitors initial verbal exchanges with the client, and listens for an uneven flow of talk, hesitant pauses, or abrupt changes in sentence rhythm, pitch level, and intonation. These uncomfortable moments alert the listener to the breakdown in rhythmic exchange of signals between self and speech partner. When partners miss each other's cues regarding how what is said is to be understood, it is clear that they have not yet agreed on what activity is unfolding and the ground rules by which it is carried out.

When the clinician detects uncomfortable moments, he or she refrains from placing blame for the poor communication because it is understood that troublesome interactions are jointly produced by the speech partners. Instead of viewing the client as uncooperative, hostile, or of low intelligence, other reasons are explored. It may be that there are cultural differences in speech conventions. The client may feel that the relationship is accelerating too quickly with too much self-disclosure demanded. Discomfort is expressed through hesitant speech and anxious gestures as the client acts to avoid intimacy. Or, despite good intentions, the helper and client may not have negotiated a common framework for agreeing on the nature of their conversation and where it is going. Thus, the clinician needs to be prepared with each client to undertake a momentary diagnosis of the conversation—in the midst of an uncomfortable moment *as it happens*.

How can the helper and client better decipher each other's messages? One strategy is through "small talk"; active searching for personal similarities, mutual interests, or experiences. Self-disclosure appropriate to the partner's expectations helps identify background commonalities. However, active listening and self-disclosure, which enhance feelings of commonality and help coordinate interactions, are generalized insights rather than discrete skills. Erickson and Shultz (1982) point out that clinical training which approaches cross-cultural communications as simply skills training—that is, how to talk with blacks, Asians, Chicanos, and other minorities—will only reinforce racial, ethnic, and social class stereotypes (see also Pederson, Draguns, Lonner, & Trimble, 1989). Moreover, if helpers attempt too quickly to elicit personal dialogue from the clients by offering self-revealing statements or asking intimate questions, then clients are apt to feel threatened and to compensate by decreasing affiliation with the helper (Capella, 1981; Derlega & Chaikin, 1975). Therapist openness, steady gaze, forward body lean, and other nonverbal gestures to increase contact may actually prompt reactions of extreme avoidance among some psychiatric patients. Such therapist approaches were found to increase delusional activity and negative self-disclosure, postural rigidity, and nonfunctional nervous movements among psychiatric inpatients (e.g., Fairbanks, McGuire, & Harris, 1982).

Clinicians strain not only to interpret accurately spoken messages, but to read the client's face and body for nonverbal cues that reveal the affect, intensity, and sincerity of the accompanying words. The helping relationship is enhanced when the helper assumes the role of "discrepancy detector" and becomes sensitive to discrepancies between nonverbal and verbal communication channels, as well as inconsistencies among the nonverbal channels themselves—face, body, and voice quality. The face is not the place to look for the speaker's true feelings, because we learn to monitor and control emotional expression in that channel. People are less aware of the information they convey through body channels—hands, feet, and legs. Consequently, the affect sent is less disguised or controlled (DePaulo, Zuckerman, & Rosenthal, 1980; Ekman & Friesen, 1969). Experimental studies of deception also show that subjects induced to lie will blink at a higher rate, hesitate longer before answering, groom and touch themselves more frequently, and have more frequent errors and hesitations in speech (Kraut, 1980).

Just as uncomfortable moments of conversation alert the therapist that mutual understanding is deteriorating, so too discrepant nonverbal cues and cues of deception signal moments when clients' unspoken emotions more accurately describe their experience of the therapeutic relationship than does the verbal content of their speech. When these inconsistencies remain hidden, unsatisfying patterns of communication result. Therefore, the therapeutic task is to pinpoint these moments, and then to negotiate with the client his or her definition of the situational and affective meaning associated with those unspoken reactions. A therapist sensitive to nonverbal communication will penetrate the client's masked and unspoken emotions, and will strive to coordinate his or her rhythm of therapeutic communication with the system of cues sent by the client (see Higginbotham et al., 1988, 93–103).

The third area of negotiation in the helper-client relationship concerns how the presenting problem will be interpreted and managed. Cognitive therapists in the tradition of George Kelly and Jerome Frank endorse as a universal condition of healing the sufferer's and therapist's willingness to share a conceptual framework. Healing transpires when the therapist helps sufferers draw on this conceptual framework, to translate the cognitive expressions of their demoralization into verbal referents and assumptions that are more meaningful and therefore more manageable. Meichenbaum (1977) states that helper and client together fabricate a new explanation for the etiology and maintenance of maladaptive behavior, and that the client *implicitly* accepts this new conceptualization as a byproduct of therapeutic interaction.

We propose that the construction of a new problem interpretation be made an *explicit* aim of the negotiation cycle. Therapist and help-seeker will undertake four clinical steps to arrive at a mutually validated understanding of the problem and a treatment plan. First, the helper draws out the client's implicit theory or explanation of the problem. Probes are made of the client's specific propositions about the dysfunction: (a) why it is happening; (b) why the symptoms have assumed a particular form; (c) how the dysfunction works psychologically or physically to produce its effects; (d) how long it will last; and (e) the most suitable treatment and expected benefits (see Kleinman, 1980, 105–106).

The second step involves therapist self-disclosure of selected portions of the clinical theory with which he or she interprets the client's presenting problem. The professional's model should be conveyed in nontechnical and direct terms for each of the aforementioned five propositions about the problem (Kleinman, Eisenberg, & Good, 1978). Third, client and therapist examine the discrepancies and "fit" between their respective problem explanations. This examination brings into sharp focus any conflicts in problem conception which will require either clarification and further explanation or frank negotiation to resolve (Kleinman et al., 1978). However, clinicians should keep in mind that clients may use the same term but define its meaning differently, may have the same problem definition but infer that it has different causes, or may steadfastly avoid using a term because of social stigma associated with it by their social group (Harwood, 1981).

The fourth step requires helper and client to either bridge the differences in their understanding and expectations or break off the relationship. A further circular exchange of information, clarifying terms and concepts, may prove differences to be more apparent than real. "Conceptual translation" may be required, where one speaker explains the meaning of his or her concepts through the use of metaphors, images, or idioms which the listener is known to understand. For example, Nichter described lithium's effects to a "manic" patient by using the patient's own image of her nervous system as a network of electrical wires (Nichter & Trockman, 1983). Ultimately, the client may adopt the helper's explanation in addition to (or instead of) his or her original model; retain the original model; or devise a totally new explanation (Kleinman, 1980). Successful negotiation produces a satisfying working relationship and agreement about the most effective treatment method and what comprises a beneficial outcome. Failure to agree on a common problem conception may best be handled through referral to another care provider who may be able to produce a closer match with the client's orientation.

Client Self-Monitoring and Perceptions of the Helper

Recent studies of "self-monitoring" provide helpers with predictions about how client personality differences could affect the helper-client relationship. Snyder

(1987) shows that high self-monitors strive to be the kind of person called for by social and interpersonal cues. Low self-monitors, on the other hand, typically try to express their own attitudes and traits regardless of the situation. Hence, the behavior of high self-monitors varies from situation to situation, whereas low self-monitors behave across situations in close correspondence with their own attitudes (Clark & Reis, 1988).

Research shows that choice of interaction partner (such as a therapist) is broadly influenced by self-monitoring tendencies (see Clark & Reis, 1988). High self-monitors tend to select partners skilled at the activity in question regardless of how well liked those partners were, whereas low self-monitors tended to select well-liked partners regardless of their abilities in particular activities (Snyder, Gangestad, & Simpson, 1983). Friendship is generally preferred with others of similar self-monitoring levels. High self-monitors describe friendships in terms of shared activities, whereas low self-monitors stress mutual nurturance and compatibility (Snyder & Smith, 1986). Low self-monitors may less frequently form close, enduring, romantic relationships, and change partners more often. Of significance to the counseling relationship, Snyder, Berscheid, and Glick (1985) found that low self-monitoring individuals paid a greater amount of attention to and placed greater weight on information about interior personal attributes when choosing a partner. High self-monitors, in contrast, paid more attention to and put greater weight on exterior physical appearance.

In summary, we expect that high self-monitors will be more swayed by physical appearances when evaluating therapist qualities and may have more difficulty establishing an enduring therapeutic alliance. The low self-monitors will be moved by relevant information about the therapist's personality characteristics, will take the relationship more seriously, but hold firmer to their preexisting attitudes which become targets of change (Snyder et al., 1988).

Imitation

A fourth approach to attraction enhancement, that is, to the liking component of the helper-client relationship, has relied on different procedures, those based on research concerned with imitation. Essentially, increasing attraction to the helper through imitation involves exposing the client to a person (the *model*) who plays the part of a client who likes the helper and clearly says so. This approach is also called *modeling* or *observational learning*. In the typical use of imitation, an audiotape or videotape of the attracted model client is played to the real client. The content of such tapes is usually part of an actual or constructed counseling or psychotherapy session between the model and the helper. The client simply listens to or observes the tape(s) and then later meets with the helper. The following is an excerpt from such an attraction-imitation tape, a tape that in its entirety contained a dozen such high-attraction statements by the model client:

> How would I like my parents to be different? Well, I think mostly in the fact that they could've cared more, that they could have showed it, you know, been warmer and not

so cold. That's mainly it. . . . You know, I guess I said this before, but *even though all you've been doing the past 5 or 10 minutes is asking me questions, I still for some reason or another feel comfortable talking to you and being honest about myself. I feel that you're warm and that you care.* (Goldstein, 1973, p. 216)

As suggested in our discussion of structuring, a change-enhacing relationship involved *both* client attraction toward the helper and helper attraction toward the client. The more reciprocal or mutual the positive feelings, the more likely the progress toward rapid client change. For this reason, imitation has also been used to increase helper attraction to the client. The following transcript is part of a modeling tape designed for this purpose, a tape used successfully with helpers of several kinds. Each statement in italics depicts a model helper expressing attraction, liking, or positive evaluation toward a client, that is, expressing the behaviors we were training the listening helpers to imitate.

Therapist: Since this is our first interview, I'll be asking you about a number of different areas of your life. Why don't we start off by your telling me about your family?

Patient: My family. Well, you know sometimes—sometimes I think my family could do—just as well without me. You know. Like I'm a—a useless sort of object that sort of sits around the house. When I—come home from work it's like—like there's nothing there.

Therapist: You don't feel that your family looks forward to your coming home at night?

Patient: Sometimes it—sometimes it seems that they don't even know when I'm home. Kids'll be running around and—my wife—well sometimes the way she acts it would be better if I just stayed out. Some of the things that she gets into—MMMMMMMMMM.

Therapist: I'm not clear why your wife would act that way. I find you a rather easy person to talk with. . . . What kind of things does your wife get into?

Patient:—I don't know. She's always yelling and screaming—wants me to do things when I come inside—always telling me I have this to do and that to do. She doesn't realize I just wanna come home and I wanna relax a little bit. Nah—I don't know how she can push me all the time—do this—do that—all the time.

Therapist: Sounds like marriage has been a lot of trouble for you.

Patient:—Yeah. Yeah—really it—it was different before. When we first got married it was—it was nice. We went out and saw different people, did . . . did some things together. Got along pretty good too. Didn't have all this that's going on now.

Therapist: From our meeting so far, I'm finding it rather easy to get along with you too. . . . I guess things aren't going very well with your wife now.

Patient: No—my wife changed. She got—she got different. Things started—you know—she started not to care about things. We couldn't go out as much. Then—then the babies came and then—wow—feeding them and taking care of them and doing all those things. Never had any time to do the things that we used to do together.—You know, it's usually hard for me to talk about things like this, but it's easy talking to you. Like—you know when I'd come home from work—my wife—she'd be running around the house after the kids—and when I'd come in the door I'd get ignored you know. No one says hello—no one asks you how you are.

Therapist:—Somehow all this seemed to happen around the time the children came?

Patient: It—seems that way. Before we had the kids we didn't have these problems. Now it—it's just not the same.

Therapist: What about your parents, did your father—drink?

Patient: Oh, yeah. He—could down them with the best of them. My old lady will tell you that. Yeah, he really knew how to drink. Used to get into some terrible fights with my old lady though. Boy—he'd come home—have a little too much in him—she'd really let him have it. I'd have to—pull the pillow up over my head so I wouldn't hear the noise. Couldn't get to sleep.

Therapist: Your mother was very hard on your father then.

Patient: Yeah. She really used to get mad at him. You know, for drinking and all that. She used to yell at him. Get on his back all the time. Really be nasty to him. Maybe that's one of the reasons why he's six feet under right now.

Therapist: Sort of like the same thing your wife is doing to you?

Patient: Yeah. You're right. You really hit the nail on the head. You really understand what's going on. There's a lot of things about the two that are kind of the same. I think she's trying to do the same thing to me that my mother did to my father.—Yell and fight—the yelling and carrying on. They'll both do it. Scream at you—and call you a drunk. Telling me I can't take on any responsibility. Always yelling about something. Money. Why don't you have more of it? Why can't we buy this? Why can't we buy that? I'm working—as hard as I can—and she does—she doesn't realize that. She thinks all I have to do is work—all the time. She thinks it's—it's easy for me to—to work every day.—Always pushing me. I don't like to be pushed. I get—I'll get things done. But I have to work—at my own pace, otherwise—it just doesn't matter if I work or not, if I can't work at my own pace.

Therapist: You seem to be really trying to make your marriage work. I respect people who really try like that. . . . It sounds like your wife and you just—don't do things the same way.

Patient: Yeah. She's in her own world.—She doesn't care about anything that I do—or say. She doesn't care about me or anyone else. Sometimes I just feel like getting up and leaving. There's nothing there any more.

Therapist: You'd like to just go away?

Patient: Mmhmm.

Therapist: Have you ever done this?

Patient: Not for any long time. Used to—get away for a couple of days by myself. But I always ended up coming back because I had no one else to go to.

Therapist: Well, now when you feel like that you can come see me. . . . You don't like being alone.

Thus, imitation is a second established path to attraction enhancement. Yet matters are not quite this simple. Each of us observes many people every day, but most of what we observe we do not imitate. We see expensively produced and expertly acted modeling displays of people buying things on television commercials, but much more often than not we do not imitate. People imitate others only under certain circumstances. We tend to imitate others with whom we can identify; thus, to encourage imitation, the taped model should be the same sex and approximate age as the viewing client whose attraction we are seeking to increase. We are especially prone to imitate behavior we see leading to rewards that we too desire. Therefore, the most successful attraction-enhancing modeling tapes are those on which the attracted model is rewarded by having his or her problems resolved. Further, it is not by accident that television commercials so frequently involve extensive repetition (particularly of the product's name), because imitation often increases with the repetition of the modeling display. Finally, imitation will be more likely if the viewer is encouraged to rehearse or practice what he or she has seen. In short, repetitive watching of a rewarded model of the viewer's age and sex, and rehearsing the observed behaviors, will all increase the amount of imitation that occurs.

Conformity Pressure

People with problems often have problems with people. Clients often seek help in the first place because of difficulty in getting along with others, and this difficulty can be reflected in *low* attraction (dislike, suspiciousness, ambivalence) toward the helper. Under such circumstances, trying to increase attraction by telling (structuring) or showing (imitation) him or her appropriate materials might not work. More powerful procedures could be required. If so, conformity pressure is one such possibility. In the typical use of conformity pressure in the research laboratory, a group of individuals meet and each member in turn is required to make a judgment aloud—about which of two lines is longer, or whether a dot of light moved, or which social or political viewpoint is more correct, or some other matter of judgment. However, unknown to one member of the group, all the other members are actually accomplices of the group leader and are told in advance to respond to his or her requests for their judgments in a predetermined and usually unanimous or near-unanimous manner. In at least a third of the groups arranged in this manner, the nonaccomplice member conforms to the majority judgment— even when it is (to the outsider) obviously incorrect. Research conducted by one of the present writers in counseling settings indicates that similar use of conformity pressure can indeed serve as a powerful attraction-enhancer. After hearing a taped session between a helper and client, three members (accomplices) of a group of four "clients" rated aloud the helper as attractive in a variety of ways. The real client conformed to this pressure and did likewise. Of greatest interest, in other groups, different real clients also rated the taped helper as highly attractive after conformity pressure from accomplices, even when the taped helper being rated was (again to outside observers) highly *un*attractive in several important respects.

HELPER CHARACTERISTICS

Expertness and Status

Our definition of relationship emphasized reciprocal liking, respect, and trust. Seeking to improve the relationship by focus on attraction enhancement is equivalent to emphasizing the liking component of this definition. Relationship can also be enhanced by procedures relevant to the respect component. A major means of enhancing client respect for the helper concerns the helper's real or apparent expertness and status. In general, we may assume that the greater the helper's expertness, the greater the client's respect for her or him.

In psychotherapy, there is much about the psychotherapist, his or her behavior, and his or her physical surroundings that testifies to his or her apparent expertness and authority. Haley (1963) commented in this regard:

> The context of the relationship emphasizes the therapist's position. . . . Patients are usually referred to him by people who point out what a capable authority he is and how much the patient needs help. Some therapists have a waiting list, so that the patient is impressed by standing in line to be treated, while others may imply that patients with similar symptoms were successfully treated. Furthermore, the patient must be willing to pay money even to talk to the therapist, and the therapist can either treat him or dismiss him, and so controls whether or not there is going to be a relationship. Not only the therapist's prestige is emphasized in the initial meeting, but also the patient's inadequacy is made clear. The patient . . . must emphasize his difficulties in life to a man who apparently has none. The physical settings in which most therapists function also reinforce their superior position. In many instances the therapist sits at a desk, the symbol of authority, while the patient sits in a chair, the position of the suppliant. In psychoanalytic therapy the arrangement is more extreme. The patient lies down while the therapist sits up. His chair is also placed so that he can observe the patient's reactions, but the patient cannot observe him. Finally, the initial interview in therapy usually makes quite explicit the fact that the therapist is in charge of the relationship by the rules for treatment he lays down. He suggests the frequency of interviews, implies he will be the one who decides when treatment will end, and he usually instructs the patient how to behave in the office. He may make a general statement about how the patient is to express himself there, or he may provide specific instructions as in the analytic situation where the patient is told he must lie down and say whatever comes to mind. (pp. 71–73) (From *Strategies of psychotherapy* by J. Haley, 1963. New York: Grune & Stratton. Copyright 1963 by Grune & Stratton, Inc. Reprinted by permission.)

What else is there that distinguishes the expert helper from the inexpert? In our own research, as will be seen shortly, the level of apparent helper expertness was varied by altering the external trappings surrounding the helper—his or her title, books, office, diploma, and so on. Research reported by Schmidt and Strong (1970) showed that clients also judge expertness to a large extent from the observable behavior of their helpers. According to their results, college students describe the expert and inexpert counselor quite differently:

> *The expert* shakes the student's hand, aligning the student with himself, and greets him with his first name. He seems interested and relaxed. He has a neat appearance but is not stuffy . . . . He talks at the student's level and is not arrogant toward him. The expert assumes a comfortable but attentive sitting position. He focuses his attention on the student and carefully listens to him. He has a warm facial expression and is reactive to the student. His voice is inflective and lively, he changes his facial expressions, and uses hand gestures. He speaks fluently with confidence and sureness. The expert has prepared for the interview. He is informed as to why the

student is there and is familiar with the student's test scores, grades, and background. . . . He asks direct and to-the-point questions. His questions are thought-provoking and follow an apparently logical progression. They seem spontaneous and conversational. The expert is willing to help determine if the student's decisions are right, but does not try to change the student's ideas forcefully. He lets the student do most of the talking and does not interrupt him. The expert moves quickly to the root of the problem. He points out contradictions in reasoning, and restates the student's statements as they bear on the problem. . . . He makes recommendations and suggests possible solutions.

The *inexpert* is awkward, tense, and uneasy. He seems to be afraid of the student. He does not greet the student by name to put him at ease. . . . He is not quite sure of himself or of some of his remarks. He seems too cold, strict and dominating, and too formal in attitude and action. His gestures are stiff and overdone. . . . The inexpert slouches in his chair. He is too casual and relaxed. . . . His voice is flat and without inflection, appearing to show disinterest and boredom. . . . The inexpert comes to the interview cold. He has not cared enough about the student to acquaint himself with the student's records. The inexpert asks vague questions which are trivial and irrelevant and have no common thread or aim. His questioning is abrupt and tactless with poor transitions. He asks too many questions like a quiz session, giving the student the third degree. . . . The inexpert is slow in getting his point across and is confusing in his discussion of what the student should do. . . . The inexpert does not get to the core of the problem. . . . He just doesn't seem to be getting anywhere. (p. 117) (From "Expert and inexpert counselors" by L. D. Schmidt and S. R. Strong, 1970. *Journal of Counseling Psychology, 17,* pp. 115–118. Copyright 1970 by the American Psychological Association. Reprinted by permission.)

These descriptions were then used by the investigators (Strong & Schmidt, 1970) as the script outline in a study examining the effects of status on a helper's influence. Counselors taking the role of expert and inexpert were thoroughly rehearsed in the aforementioned behaviors. The former were introduced to clients with the statement

The person you will be talking with is Dr. _____ , a psychologist who has had several years of experience interviewing students.

The inexpert helper was, contrastingly, introduced with the statement

We had originally scheduled Dr. _____ to talk with you but unfortunately he notified us that he wouldn't be able to make it today. In his place we have Mr. _____ , a student, who unfortunately has had no interviewing experience and has been given only a brief explanation of the purpose of this study. I think he should work out all right, though. (Strong & Schmidt, 1970. p. 83)

Analysis of the helper-client interviews that were then held revealed, as predicted, greater positive change in those clients structured and in fact seen by the "expert" helper.

It thus seems that the greater the change-agent's expertness, the greater his or her effectiveness in altering the behavior and beliefs of the target. Laboratory research strongly supports this contention. A substantial number of investigations confirm that a statement is more fully accepted and acted on when the recipient believes it comes from an expert or high-status person than when its apparent source is a person of low or unknown expertise.

The first evidence we obtained in support of the relationship aspect of this finding was obtained almost accidentally (Goldstein, 1971). We conducted a study whose purpose was to determine if client attraction to the helper would increase if the helper went out of his way to do a small favor or extend an extra courtesy to the client. The courtesy involved was offering the client coffee and a doughnut, not a usual event in counseling or psychotherapy. Although this procedure did improve their relationship, attraction increased even more at those times when the helper made it clear that the coffee and doughnut were for himself, and not for the client! We had not predicted this result, and only half-jokingly speculated that perhaps attraction increased because anyone behaving so boorishly must be an important person. That is, perhaps attraction increased here because, in the client's eyes, the helper had increased his status. We tested this notion more directly in our next investigation (Sabalis, 1969). Sabalis had four groups of clients, two of whom were seen by what appeared to be a high-status helper, two by a low-status helper. Not all persons, we predicted, are attracted to high-status persons. Authoritarian persons, those rigidly respectful of authority, seem to be highly responsive and attracted to such persons, whereas more equalitarian individuals are less drawn to experts and similar sources. Thus, in this study, it was predicted that a high-status helper would increase the attraction-to-helper of high authoritarian clients but not of equalitarian clients.

The clients (of both kinds) in the high-status groups each received a postcard indicating the time of the interview. The interviewer was "Dr. Robert Sabalis." When each client arrived for the interview, the interviewer introduced himself as "Dr. Sabalis, a member of the faculty of the Psychology Department." A "Dr. Robert Sabalis" nameplate was on the interviewer's desk, and the office itself was a large, well-furnished one belonging to a faculty member. The interviewer was neatly dressed in a business suit. The session began with some test taking by the client, which the interviewer described as tests on which he was doing research. As the client filled out the test forms, the interviewer opened a text and began to jot down notes from it, indicating to the client as he did that he was preparing an examination for one of the classes he taught.

For the low-status groups, the interviewer's name on the postcard and in his introduction on meeting was "Bob Sabalis." He described himself to clients as a senior undergraduate psychology major who was meeting with them as a requirement for one of his own courses. His attire was consistent with the typical undergraduate's. The interview office was quite small and sparsely furnished. As the test taking commenced, he began note taking from a text again, but this time indicated he was preparing for an examination he had to take.

The predicted effect of status on attraction was obtained. That is, high authoritarian clients became significantly more attracted to the interviewer after the high-status, but not the low-status, procedures.

As described earlier, Strong and Schmidt showed the positive effect of expertness by training counselors to behave as either expert or inexpert. Sabalis used one interviewer, who served as both the high- and the low-status helper. The positive effect on the helper-client relationship was obtained again. Streltzer and Koch (1968) implemented expertness in yet another way. Their research concerned the effects role-playing the part of lung cancer patients would have on persons needing to reduce their smoking. Participating "patients" role-played a series of scenes involving meeting the doctor, the doctor's giving the diagnosis, treatment plans, and advice to quit smoking immediately. Half of the "patients" enacted their role with a "doctor" who was a 21-year-old female psychology major. She used no title. The other smokers met with a 32-year-old male physician who introduced himself as "Doctor." Both types of smokers decreased in smoking more than persons not participating in the role-playing. Those role-playing with the real expert, furthermore, showed by far the greatest negative change in their attitudes toward smoking.

Similar findings have been reported by other researchers. Corrigan, Dell, Lewis, and Schmidt (1980) have provided an especially comprehensive review of these recent studies, examining the array of evidential, reputational, and behavioral cues to helper expertness and status that have been shown with reliability to have substantial attraction-enhancing potency. In general, it may be concluded that helper expertness and status serve to increase client respect, which in turn leads to the client's being more open to the helper's attempts to influence him or her and, subsequently, more likelihood of client change.

Credibility

The respect component of the helper-client relationship is also influenced by helper credibility. The greater the level of credibility, the greater the client's respect for the helper. Johnson and Matross (1977) defined helper credibility as his or her perceived ability to know valid information and his or her motivation to communicate this knowledge without bias. As Johnson (1972) observed, empirical evidence exists demonstrating that credibility is determined by several helper characteristics: (a) *expertness* as defined earlier, and as signified by title, institutional affiliation, and other indexes of academic and professional achievement; (b) *reliability* as an information source, that is, dependability, predictability, and consistency; (c) *motives and intentions* of the helper—the clearer it is to the client that it is his or her interests, and not the helper's own, toward which the helper is working, the greater the helper's credibility; and (d) *dynamism* of the helper, his or her apparent confidence, forcefulness, and activity level.

Empathy

We have just examined the positive effects on the helper-client relationship of the real or apparent expertness and status of the helper, as well as her or his perceived credibility. There are several other helper qualities of importance in this regard, and the present section will focus on one of these—empathy. The level of empathy offered by the helper and its effects on the client has been the object of considerable research and theory. This research has consistently shown that a helper's empathy with the client's feelings strongly influences the quality of the helper-client relationship that develops and, subsequently, the degree of client change, at least with a substantial proportion of psychotherapy clients.

Truax and Carkhuff (1967) have been quite active in studying the effects of empathy on the helper-client relationship. They commented, as a beginning definition of *empathy,*

> As we come to know some of his wants, some of his needs, some of his achievements and some of his failures, we find ourselves as therapists "living" with the patient much as we do with the central figure of a novel. . . . Just as with the character in the novel, we come to know the person from his own internal frame of reference, gaining some flavor of his moment-by-moment experience. We see events and significant people in his life as they appear to him—not as they "objectively are" but as he experiences them. As we come to know him from his personal vantage point we automatically come to value and like him. . . . We begin to perceive the events and experiences of his life "as if" they were parts of our own life. It is through this process that we come to feel warmth, respect and liking. . . . (p. 42)

These same researchers have also developed a more detailed definition of empathy, which follows in full. Described in the statement that follows is their Empathy Scale, consisting of levels of empathy that a helper can provide a client—graduated from very low (level 1) to very high (level 5).

EMPATHIC UNDERSTANDING IN INTERPERSONAL PROCESSES

A Scale for Measurement

Level 1
The verbal and behavioral expressions of the helper either do not attend to or detract significantly from the verbal and behavioral expressions of the client(s) in that they communicate significantly less of the client's feelings and experiences than the client has communicated himself.

Example. The helper communicates no awareness of even the most obvious, expressed surface feelings of the client. The helper may be bored or disinterested or simply operating from a preconceived frame of reference which totally excludes that of the client(s).

In summary, the helper does everything but express that he is listening, understanding, or being sensitive to even the most obvious feelings of the client in such a way as to detract significantly from the communications of the client.

Level 2
While the helper responds to the expressed feelings of the client(s), he does so in such a way that he subtracts noticeable affect from the communications of the client.

Example. The helper may communicate some awareness of obvious, surface feelings of the client, but his communications drain off a level of the affect and distort the level of meaning. The helper may communicate his own ideas of what may be going on, but these are not congruent with the expressions of the client.

In summary, the helper tends to respond to other than what the client is expressing or indicating.

Level 3

The expressions of the helper in response to the expressions of the client(s) are essentially interchangeable with those of the client in that they express essentially the same affect and meaning.

Example. The helper responds with accurate understandings of the surface feelings of the client but may not respond to or may misinterpret the deeper feelings.

In summary, the helper is responding so as to neither subtract from nor add to the expressions of the client. He does not respond accurately to how that person really feels beneath the surface feelings; but he indicates a willingness and openness to do so. Level 3 constitutes the minimal level of facilitative interpersonal functioning.

Level 4

The responses of the helper add noticeably to the expressions of the client(s) in such a way as to express feelings a level deeper than the client was able to express himself.

Example. The helper communicates his understanding of the expressions of the client at a level deeper than they were expressed and thus enables the client to experience and/or express feelings he was unable to express previously.

In summary, the helper's responses add deeper feeling and meaning to the expressions of the client.

Level 5

The helper's responses add significantly to the feeling and meaning of the expressions of the client(s) in such a way as to accurately express feelings levels below what the client himself was able to express or, in the event of ongoing, deep self-exploration on the client's part, to be fully with him in his deepest moments.

Example. The helper responds with accuracy to all of the client's deeper as well as surface feelings. He is "tuned in" on the client's wave length. The helper and the client might proceed together to explore previously unexplored areas of human existence.

In summary, the helper is responding with a full awareness of who the other person is and with a comprehensive and accurate empathic understanding of that individual's deepest feelings. (pp. 174–175) (From *Toward Effective Counseling and Psychotherapy* by Charles B. Truax and Robert R. Carkhuff, 1967, Chicago: Aldine. Copyright © by Charles B. Truax and Robert R. Carkhuff. Reprinted by permission of the authors and Aldine Publishing Company.)

A great deal of research has been done on the effects of high levels of helper empathy in counseling, guidance, and psychotherapy. Certain effects on the client regularly occur in these studies. Feeling understood, that someone has been able to truly perceive his or her deeper feelings, the client's liking of the helper increases. In a sense, the client also comes to trust himself or herself more under these circumstances, for one regular result of high helper empathy is deeper and more persevering *self*-exploration by the client. In several of these studies, greater client change is a clear result. High levels of helper empathic responding can, therefore, be viewed as a necessary (but probably not sufficient) condition for client change. Carkhuff (1969) is, we feel, largely correct in his comment:

> Empathy is the key ingredient of helping. Its explicit communication, particularly during early phases of helping, is critical. Without an empathic understanding of the helpee's world and his difficulties as he sees them there is no basis for helping. (p. 173)

A more concrete understanding of helper empathy, and its effects on client behavior, is provided by the specific examples that follow. The first is drawn from a psychotherapy session. Note how all helper statements are at least level 3, and often higher:

Helpee: Um. I don't know whether, whether I'm right or wrong in feeling the way I do, but, uh, I find myself withdrawing from people. I don't care to go out and socialize and play their stupid little games any more. Um, I get very anxious and come home depressed and have headaches—it seems all so superficial. There was a time when I used to get along with everybody; everybody said, "Oh, isn't she wonderful! She gets along with everybody; she's so nice and everybody likes her," and I used to think that was . . . that was something to be really proud of, but, oh, but, I think that only told how I, or who I was at that time, that I had no depth. I was sort of whatever the crowd wanted me to be, or the particular group I was with at the time. Um, I know it's important for my husband's business that we go out and socialize and meet people and make a good impression and join clubs and play all those stupid little games—Elks, and, you know, bowling banquets, and, uh, fishing trips and fraternity-type gatherings. Um, I . . . I just don't care to do it any more, and, um, I don't know if that means that I'm a . . . that there's something wrong with me psychologically, or, uh, or is this normal. I mean . . . uh . . . people don't really know who I am and they really don't care who one another, who the other person is. They . . . it's all at such a superficial level.

Helper: You're darn sure of how you feel, but you really don't know what it all adds up to. Is it you? Is it the other people? What are the implications of your husband's business? You? Where is it all going?

Helpee: Uh, huh. It's an empty life. It's, um, there's, uh, no depth to it at all. I mean, you just talk about very, very superficial things, and the first few times, it's O.K. But then after that, there's nothing to talk about. So you drink and you pretend to be happy over silly jokes and silly things that people do when they all, uh, are trying to impress one another, and they're very materialistic, and, uh, it's just not the route I want to go.

Helper: So your feelings are so strong now that you just can't fake it any more.

Helpee: That's right, so what do you do? People say, "Oh, there's something wrong with you," then, "You need to see a psychiatrist or something," because you . . . you know the thing in society is that the normal person gets along with people, and uh, can adjust to any situation. And when you . . . when you're a little discriminating, maybe very discriminating or critical, then that means there's something wrong with you.

Helper: While you know how strongly you feel about all these things, you're not sure you can really act in terms of them and be free.

Helpee: I don't know if I'm strong enough. The implications are great. It may mean, uh, a break up of the marriage, uh, and it means going it alone, and that's too frightening. I don't think I have the courage. But I do feel like I'm in sort of a trap.

Helper: You know you can't pretend, yet your're really fearful of going it alone.

Helpee: Yes, there's nobody I can really talk to, I mean, you know, it's one thing if you have a . . . like your husband . . . if you can share these things, if he can understand it at some level, but . . . um . . . he can't.

Helper: It's like, "If I act on how I really feel, though, it frightens the people who mean most to me. They won't understand it, and I sure can't share that with them."

Helpee: (Pause) So what do you do. (Pause) I mean . . . I . . . you know. I find myself going out and telling the people who I really feel about, about different topics and getting into controversial issues, and, uh, and that's, that's too anxiety provoking for me. I can't, because then you get into arguments and I don't want to do that either, that leads nowhere. I just get frustrated and anxious and upset and angry with myself for getting myself into the situation.

Helper: You know that doesn't set you free, you know. . .

Helpee: No, it bottles me up.

Helper: That only causes you more problems, and what you're really asking about is, how you can move toward greater freedom and greater fulfillment in your own life.

Helpee: I . . . I think I know who I am now, independent of other people, and, uh, which people aren't and . . . um . . . there's no room for that kind of person in this society.

Helper: There's no room for me out there!

Helpee: (Pause) So what do I do?

Helper: We run over and over the questions that . . . you end up with. "Where do I go from here? How do I act on this? I know how I feel, but I don't know what'll happen if I act on how I feel."

Helpee: I . . . have an idea of what'll happen.

Helper: And it's not good!

Helpee: No! It means almost starting a whole new life.

Helper: And you don't know if you can make it.

Helpee: Right, I know what I've got here, and if I don't make it all the way with the other, then I'm in trouble.

Helper: While you don't know what'll happen if you act on your feelings, you know what the alternatives are if you don't. And they're not good either. They're worse.

Helpee: I . . . I don't have much choice. (pp. 219–220) (From *Helping and human relations* by R. R. Carkhuff, 1969, New York: Holt, Rinehart & Winston. Copyright 1969 by Holt, Rinehart & Winston. Reprinted by permission.)

A second series of examples is drawn from our own research (Goldstein, 1973), in which we sought successfully to increase helper empathy by a set of training procedures rather different from Truax and Carkhuff's. Our trainees were nurses and attendants employed in state mental hospitals. Part of our training sequence involved exposing them to a number of different examples of highly empathic responses to difficult or problematic patient behaviors and statements. These examples included (From *Structured learning therapy* by A. P. Goldstein, 1973, New York: Academic. Copyright 1973 by Academic Press. Reprinted by permission.)

1. *Nurse:* Here is your medicine, Mr. _____ .
   Patient: I don't want it. People here are always telling me to do this, do that, do the other thing. I'll take the medicine when *I* want to.
   Nurse: So it's not so much the medicine itself, but you feel you're bossed around all the time. You're tired of people giving you orders.
2. *Patient:* I can't leave the hospital, I'm still sick. What will I do when I get home?
   Nurse: You just don't feel ready to go yet, and wonder if you're up to being home.
3. *Patient:* I don't know why they keep giving me this medicine. I've taken it for weeks and I don't feel any better. I've told this to Dr._____ twice already.
   Nurse: Not only doesn't the medicine seem to work, but the doctor doesn't seem interested in doing anything about it.
4. *Patient:* I was in the hospital before. Things were really bothering me. Finally, I just couldn't take it anymore. I left home, didn't show up at work, and somehow ended up in the hospital.
   Nurse: Things just piled up and up, from bad to worse, and you wound up here.
5. *Patient:* Sometimes I think my family could do just as well without me. It's like I almost don't exist as far as they're concerned. they almost never come to see me.
   Nurse: You'd really like them to visit, but they don't really seem to care about you.
6. *Patient:* My father and mother used to get into terrible fights. He'd come home and they'd really go at it. I'd have to pull the pillow over my head so I wouldn't hear the noise.
   Nurse: It sounds like something that would be really upsetting, especially to a child.
7. *Patient:* I'd really like to know about their school, their friends, things like that. You know, the things a father is interested in. My youngest son, he's on a football team, but he never invited me to a game. He never cared if I was there or not. I don't understand it.
   Nurse: It must hurt very deeply when he doesn't let you be a part of his life.
8. *Patient;* I don't like talking to the psychologist. He's OK but I've been asked *all* the questions many times already.
   Nurse: You're just good and tired of going through the whole procedure.
9. *Patient;* It's just not fair that I have to stay on the ward because of last weekend. My husband was nasty. He made me very nervous. It wasn't my fault. Can't I please go off the ward?
   Nurse: You feel the trouble at home was really your husband's fault, and now you're being punished for it.
10. *Patient:* I can't stand her anymore. She never shuts up, talk, talk, talk. She talks more than any other patient here. I don't want to sit near her or be near her.
    Nurse: She's really very annoying to you. You'd like to have nothing to do with her.

A similar set of high-empathy examples was used to train a different type of helper, home aides. These are persons trained to provide psychological and physical assistance to elderly, disabled, psychiatric outpatients, and similar persons in their own homes. Some of these examples were

1. *Patient:* The old age home was really different from this apartment building. All my friends are still there. I don't even know anyone here.

Home Aide: Sounds like you're lonely in your new home. Kind of like a stranger in a new place. I can see how it's pretty depressing missing all your friends.

Patient: I sure *am* lonely. Every friend I have is still at the home. And it's so hard living all alone with three whole rooms to myself. I even get sad listening to people's voices in the other apartments.

Home Aide: You like to get out of your three lonely rooms and meet some of the other people in the building. You'd be happier if you made some new friends.

2. *Patient:* I don't like. . . . It makes me feel silly for you to wash and feed me.

   Home Aide: It makes you uncomfortable when someone takes care of you. You feel like you should be doing things on your own and you shouldn't need me.

   Patient: Mm hm. I feel like a baby when someone's helping me. But I know I can't do stuff myself now 'cause I've tried.

   Home Aide: You feel foolish when you have to rely on other people since you should be helping yourself. But you know that you need other people's help now for you own well-being.

3. *Patient:* I think about things like falling down the stairs, or dropping my cigarette in bed, or a stranger coming to my house late at night. . . . I don't really know what I'd do. . .

   Home Aide: You're worried about whether you could handle an emergency all alone.

   Patient: Yeah, I worry, *a lot.* . . . I remember how scary it was the time I fainted and nobody was here to help me.

   Home Aide: It would be nice to be able to count on somebody's help when something goes wrong, and you're not sure you can take care of things all by yourself.

4. *Patient:* All I seem to do is care for these kids 25 hours a day! Which is a lot for a mother to do by herself!

   Home Aide: Sounds as if you'd like more time to yourself or someone to help you. That's a lot for one person to do and you seem angry about it.

   Patient: Why shouldn't I be angry! It's a lot to expect one person to change diapers, tie shoelaces, fix meals, yank the kids out of the mud, wash their filthy faces, constantly run to drag their stupid toys out of the road. . .

   Home Aide: You get pretty angry when you constantly have to watch over those kids. It's like the more demands they make on you, the less time you have to do things for yourself.

5. *Patient:* My kids couldn't care less if I exist. They're only in Rochester, but somehow that's too far away to visit me.

   Home Aide: You'd like them to visit, but somehow they don't seem interested enough.

   Patient: Yeah, you got the idea. If they were interested in me they'd made the short trip to come to see me. But they don't even call. And I'll be damned if I'll invite them one more time.

   Home Aide: You're not about to beg them to visit you if they aren't interested. But you seem pretty hurt that your own children don't seem to care about you.

6. *Patient:* (Bashfully looking down) Do you think you could maybe show me how to, um, wash myself alone, instead of you helping me. The nurses helped me in the hospital when I had arthritis. . . . Well . . . I still shake so much I'm afraid I'll drop the soap or fall down.

   Home Aide: It's kind of embarrassing to need someone to help you wash. Even though right now it's probably safer that way, you'd really rather do it yourself.

   Patient: You're not kidding. I can't tell you how I hated bathtime in the hospital.

It was so embarrassing to have the nurse see me, you know, naked. But maybe it had to be that way. Like you say, it was safer. And also a lot cleaner than if I did it myself.

Home Aide: So even though you don't like people to see you naked, maybe it would make you feel more comfortable if I helped you while the arthritis is still bothering you.

7. *Patient:* This apartment's *nothing* like the old age home. There I had people to take care of me, and there was always something to do, and my room was arranged differently there. . .

   Home Aide: It's hard getting used to a brand new home which doesn't even seem like your home yet.

   Patient: But you know, I remember being afraid I wouldn't get used to the old age home, and I did. So, even if it's hard now in this new place, I guess I'll get used to it.

   Home Aide: Even though it's a little hard and scary at first, it's comforting to know you got used to a new home before and you can probably do it again.

8. *Patient:* (Annoyed) I wish you wouldn't put things away in my house any way you feel like it!

   Home Aide: I'm just barging right into your home, doing whatever I want with your things—as though I don't respect you.

   Patient: Yeah! I keep my things in certain places for certain reasons and I don't like anyone moving them without asking me.

   Home Aide: You're used to living a certain way and all of a sudden I come in and put things where *I* think they should go. I can understand that you'd be angry with me for barging in.

9. *Patient:* (Hectically) Oh! I'm really sorry about that chair! I was planning to reupholster it last week! And that lightbulb just blew out yesterday. (Heavily, shaking head in hand) Oh-h-h I'm sorry. . . . This place is a rathole.

   Home Aide: It's kind of embarrassing when someone comes to your house for the first time and sees it looking like a mess.

   Patient: Well, *you'd* be embarrassed, wouldn't you? The furniture is a wreck, the walls are shabby, some of the lights don't work. . . . I don't even want you to see the kitchen. . . . I feel terrible that you have to see everything like this!

   Home Aide: You're ashamed that everything in your house seems to be dirty or broken and you feel like apologizing for the mess.

10. *Patient:* The only reason I called Home Aides is that the doctor recommended it and he was standing right there. I really don't want you to take care of me. I don't need help.

    Home Aide: You feel that you can take care of yourself, and you resent it when I come in and start doing things for you.

    Patient: Yes, I *can* take care of myself! . . . Except, I guess I could use some help now that I don't see so good.

    Home Aide: You still feel up to taking care of things like before, but you realize it's a little harder now. . . . Even so, you don't like to ask for help.

The significance of helper empathy in the helping enterprise has been emphasized in our earlier discussion, and we have now provided several examples. It will be useful to close this section with a listing of the guidelines, provided by Carkhuff (1969), for helpers wishing to become proficient in offering these levels of empathic responses to clients.

1. The helper will find that he is most effective in communicating an empathic understanding when he concentrates with intensity upon the client's expressions, both verbal and nonverbal.
2. The helper will find that initially he is most effective in communicating empathic understanding when he concentrates upon responses that are interchangeable with those of the client (Level 3).
3. The helper will find that he is most effective in communicating empathic understanding when he formulates his responses in language that is most attuned to the client.
4. The helper will find that he is most effective in communicating empathic understanding when he responds in a feeling tone similar to that communicated by the client.
5. The helper will find that he is most effective in communicating empathic understanding when he is most responsive.
6. The helper will find that he is most effective in communicating empathic understanding when, having established an interchangeable base of communication (Level 3), he moves tentatively toward expanding and clarifying the client's experiences at higher levels (Levels 4 and 5).
7. The helper will find that he is most effective in communicating empathic understanding when he concentrates upon what is not being expressed by the client, and, in a sense, seeks to fill in what is missing rather than simply dealing with what is present.
8. The helper will find that he is most effective in communicating empathic understanding when he employs the client's behavior as the best guideline to assess the effectiveness of his responses.

Further useful rules for the effective communication of helper empathy, and examples thereof, are presented in the work of Egan (1976), Goldstein (1981), Goldstein and Michaels (1985), Guerney (1977), and Ivey and Authier (1971).

Warmth

As was true of empathy, warmth is appropriately considered a central ingredient of the helping relationship. Whatever specific change methods the helper uses, their likelihood of success seems in large measure to be a result of the relationship base on which she or he and the client are interacting. Helper warmth is a highly important aspect of this base. Without it, specific helping procedures can be technically correct but therapeutically impotent.

Helper warmth is also important in relationship terms because it appears to beget reciprocal warmth from the client. Truax and Carkhuff (1967), in fact, commented that "It is a rare human being who does not respond to warmth with warmth and to hostility with hostility. It is probably the most important principle for the beginning therapist to understand if he is to be successful in the therapeutic relationship." This contention received ample support in a research program conducted by one of the present writers (Goldstein, 1971). When liking of A toward B (helper or client) was increased by structuring, status-enhancement, or other procedures, B's liking of A reciprocally increased—even though we had applied no procedures whatsoever to B directly. Several other researchers have reported the same reciprocal result. The Truax and Carkhuff definition of this helper quality, and their examples of its occurrence in counseling and psychotherapy, help clarify the nature and significance of helper warmth.

The dimension of nonpossessive warmth or unconditional positive regard ranges from a high level, where the therapist warmly accepts the patient's experience as part of that person without imposing conditions, to a low level, where the therapist evaluates a patient or his or her feelings, expresses dislike or disapproval, or expresses warmth in a selective and evaluative way.

Level 1. The therapist is actively offering advice or giving clear negative regard. He or she could be telling the patient what would be "best" for him or her, or in other ways actively approving or disapproving of his or her behavior. The therapist's actions make him or her the locus of evaluation; he or she sees himself or herself as responsible for the patient.

Example.

> *Patient:* . . .and I don't. I don't know what sort of a job will be offered me, but—eh . . .
>
> *Therapist:* It might not be the best in the world.
>
> *Patient:* I'm sure it won't.
>
> *Therapist:* And, uh . . .
>
> *Patient:* . . . but . . .
>
> *Therapist:* But if you can make up your mind to stomach some of the unpleasantness of things.
>
> *Patient:* Um hm.
>
> *Therapist:* . . . you have to go through—you'll get through it.
>
> *Patient:* Yeah, I know I will.
>
> *Therapist:* And, ah, you'll get out of here.
>
> *Patient:* I certainly, uh, I just, I just know that I have to do it, so I'm going to do it but—it's awfully easy for me, Doctor, to (sighs) well, more than pull in my shell. I—I just hibernate. I just, uh, well, just don't do a darn thing.
>
> *Therapist:* It's your own fault. (Severely)
>
> *Patient:* Sure it is. I know it is. (Pause) But it seems like whenever I—here—here's the thing. Whenever I get to the stage where I'm making active plans for myself, they say I'm high. An . . .
>
> *Therapist:* In other words they criticize you that . . .
>
> *Patient:* Yeah.
>
> *Therapist:* So tender little lady is gonna really crawl into her shell.
>
> *Patient:* Well, I—I'll say "okay."
>
> *Therapist:* If they're gonna throw, if they're goona shoot arrows at me, I'll just crawl behind my shell and I won't come out of it. (Forcefully)
>
> *Patient:* That's right. (Sadly)
>
> *Therapist:* And that's worse. (Quickly)
>
> *Patient:* (Pause) But why don't they let me be a little bit high? Why—right now I'm taking . . .
>
> *Therapist:* (Interrupting) Because some people . . .

Patient: (Talking with him) . . . 600 milligrams of malorin, whatever that is, malorin.

Therapist: . . . because a lot of people here don't know you very well at all. And because people in general, at times, you have to allow that they could be stupid. You too. I mean you're stupid sometimes, so why can't other people . . .

Patient: So much of the time.

Therapist: Why can't other people? I mean, you're an intelligent person and are stupid. Why, why can't you allow that other intelligent people can also be stupid? When it comes to you they don't know very much.

Patient: Mmm. (Muttering)

Level 2. The therapist responds mechanically to the client, indicating little positive regard and hence little nonpossessive warmth. He or she might ignore the patient or his or her feelings or display a lack of concern or interest. The therapist ignores the client at times when a nonpossessively warm response would be expected; he or she shows a complete passivity that communicates almost unconditional lack of regard.

Example.

Patient: (Speaking throughout in a woebegone voice) You don't have to sit down and, and, and write like that but I thought he'd answer my letter. I thought, I didn't think he'd answer the letter, I thought he'd come up.

Therapist: Um,hm.

Patient: . . . and, and visit me; it's only 50, he hasn't been to visit me yet. It's only been about, uh, it's only about 50, 60 miles from here.

Therapist: Uh, hm.

Patient: And I kind of expected him last Sunday but he didn't . . .

Therapist: You were just sort of looking for him but he . . .

Patient: (Interrupting insistently) Well, I wasn't, I wasn't, I was looking for him, I wasn't looking for him. I had a kind of a half-the-way feeling that he wouldn't be up here. I know him pretty well and he's—walks around, you know, and thinks and thinks and thinks and—maybe it'll take him two or three weeks an' all of a sudden he—he'll walk in the house (laughs)—"Let's go see—so and so." (Nervous laughter) He's a—he's a lot like I am—we're all the same, I guess. He probably—read the letter and—probably never said very much, walked out, forgot about it (laughing nervously), then all of a sudden it dawned on 'im (nervous laughter) and, ah, that's, ah, that's about, about the size of it, as far as that goes. And, uh, uh, so as I say, I—I wouldn't be, I wasn't—too overly disappointed when he, when he didn't ah, ah, ah, ah, answer it or come to see me. He probably will yet. (Laughs) I'm an optimist, I always have been, he'll probably come and visit me some day. Maybe he'll come and let me go down there 'n live. Maybe he won't, won't make much difference (laughs) one way or another.

Therapist: Hmmm. You can sort of . . .

Patient: Yeah.

Therapist: . . . take things as they come. (Brightly)

Level 3. The therapist indicates a positive caring for the patient or client, but it is a semipossessive caring in the sense that she or he communicates to the client that her or his behavior matters to the therapist. That is, the therapist communicates such things as "It is not all right if you act immorally," "I want you to get along at work," or "It's important to me that you get along with the ward staff." The therapist sees herself or himself as responsible for the client.

Example.

> *Patient:* I still, you sorta hate to give up something that you know that you've made something out of, and, and, uh, in fact, it amounts to, uh, at least, uh, what you would, uh, earn working for somebody else, so . . .
>
> *Therapist:* (Enthusiastically) O.K. What, well, eh, why don't—why don't we do it this way? That, uh I'll kind of give you some homework to do. (Laughs) And when you're going home these weekends, um, really talk to your wife, and, ah, think yourself about pretty specific possibilities for you, considering the location and considering what time of year it is and, what you can do and things like this, and eh, then we can talk it out here and really do some, some working on this in earnest, and not just talk plans . . . (Patient answers "yeah" after every phrase or so.)
>
> *Patient:* (Interrupting) Well, I actually, I'd almost feel gettin' out right away but I, somethin' sort of holds me back, yet the season isn't—there (*Therapist:* Uh, huh) and I don't know if it's good for me or not (*Therapist:* Uh, huh), but I, ah . . .
>
> *Therapist:* O.K., but at least this next couple of months we can use in—trying at least to set something up or, or . . .
>
> *Patient:* Cuz I feel that I, I don't know, I—feel I just want to do things again.
>
> *Therapist:* (Um, hm). Uh, 'cuz the longer you stay away from work, I was just reading about that psychologist James here the other day, an' it seems like if once you get into things and work, you feel better (*Patient:* Sure) . . . and you don't uh, it seems like, uh the further you stay away from things, eh, you, well, eh, you sort'a think about it, put it that way. Um, hm. O.K. So, ah—in our thinking about it, though, that next few weeks, let's get closer to the doing of them. O.K.? (Warmly)
>
> *Patient:* Well, yes, that's—what . . .
>
> *Therapist:* Sounds okay to you?
>
> *Patient:* Yes, It sounds okay to me.
>
> *Therapist:* Good enough. (Amiably)

Level 4. The therapist clearly communicates a very deep interest and concern for the welfare of the patient, showing a nonevaluative and unconditional warmth in almost all areas of functioning. Although there remains some conditionality in the more personal and private areas, the patient is given freedom to be himself or herself and to be liked as himself or herself. There is little evaluation of thoughts and behaviors. In deeply personal areas, however, the therapist might be conditional and communicate the idea that the client may act in any way he or she wishes—except that it is important to the therapist that he or she be more mature, or not regress in therapy, or accept and like the therapist. In all other areas, however, nonpossessive warmth is communicated. The therapist sees himself or herself as responsible to the client.

Example.

> *Therapist:* One thing that occurs to me is I'm so glad you came. I was afraid you wouldn't come. I had everything prepared, but I was afraid you wouldn't come. (Pause)

Patient: What—would you have thought of me then? I guess maybe I shouldn't have, but I did anyway. (Rapidly)

Therapist: Is that—like saying, "Why or What?" But, partly you feel—maybe you shouldn't have come—or don't know if you shouldn't or "not should." There's something about—feeling bad that could make you—not want to come. I don't know if I got that right, but—because if you feel very bad then—then, I don't know. Is there anything in that?

Patient: Well—I've told you before, I mean, you know, two things that, when I feel bad. I mean one that always—I feel that there's a possibility, I suppose, that you know, that they might put me back in the hospital for getting that bad.

Therapist: Oh, I'd completely forgotten about that, yeah—yet, and that's one thing—But there is another?

Patient: Yeah, I already told you that, too.

Therapist: Oh, yeah, you sure did—I'd forgotten about it—and the other you've already said, too?

Patient: I'm sure I did tell it. (Pause)

Therapist: It doesn't come. All I have when I try to think of it is just the general sense that if you feel—very bad, then it's hard or unpleasant to—but I don't know—so I may have forgotten something—must have. (Pause)

Patient: You talk—you always, hear what I'm saying now, are so good at evading me, you always end up making me talk anyway.

Therapist: You're right.

Patient: You always comment on the question or something, and it just doesn't tell me.

Therapist: (Interjecting) Right, I just instinctively came back—to you when I wondered—what, I, well like saying, because—that's what I felt like saying. You mean to—you mean to say that a few minutes ago we had decided that I would talk . . .

Patient: Well, you—you mentioned it, but (*Therapist:* Right) that's as far as it got.

Therapist: Your're right—and I just—was thinking of what you're asking—I'm more interested in you right now than anything else.

Level 5. At stage 5, the therapist communicates warmth without restriction. There is a deep respect for the patient's worth as a person and his or her rights as a free individual. At this level the patient is free to be himself or herself even if this means that he or she is regressing, being defensive, or even disliking or rejecting the therapist. At this stage the therapist cares deeply for the patient as a person, but it does not matter to him or her how the patient chooses to behave. The therapist genuinely cares for and deeply prizes the patient for his or her human potentials, apart from evaluations of his or her behavior or thoughts. The therapist is willing to share equally the patient's joys and aspirations or depressions and failures. The only channeling by the therapist might be the demand that the patient communicate personally relevant material (Truax & Carkhuff, 1967, pp. 58–68).

Example.

Patient: . . . ever recovering to the extent where I could become self-supporting and live alone. I thought that I was doomed to hospitalization for the rest of my life and seeing some of the people over in, in the main building, some of those old people who are, who need a lot of attention and all that sort of thing, is the only picture I could see of my own future. Just one of (*Therapist:* Mhm) complete hopelessness, that there was any—

Therapist: (Interrupting) You didn't see any hope at all, did you?

Patient: Not, not in the least, I thought no one really cared and I didn't care myself, and I seriously—uh—thought of suicide; if there'd been any way that I could end it all completely and not become just a burden or an extra care, I would have committed suicide, I was that low. I didn't want to live. In fact, I hoped that I—I would go to sleep at night and not wake up, because I, I really felt there was nothing to live for. (*Therapist:* Uh, huh [very softly]) Now I, I truly believe that this drug they are giving me helps me a lot, I think, I think it is one drug that really does me good. (*Therapist:* Uh, hm).

Therapist: But you say that, that during this time you, you felt as though no one at all cared, as to what (*Patient:* That's right) . . . what happened to you.

Patient: And, not only that, but I hated myself so that I didn't, I, I felt that I didn't deserve to have anyone care for me. I hated myself so that I, I, I not only felt that no one did, but I didn't see any reason why they should.

Therapist: I guess that makes some sense to me now. I was wondering why it was that you were shutting other people off. You weren't letting anyone else care.

Patient: I didn't think I was worth caring for.

Therapist: So you didn't ev- maybe you not only thought you were—hopeless, but you wouldn't allow people . . . (Therapist statement is drowned out by patient.)

Patient: (Interrupting and very loud) I closed the door on everyone. Yah, I closed the door on everyone because I thought I just wasn't worth bothering with. I didn't think it was worthwhile for you to bother with me. "Just let me alone and—and let me rot that's all I'm worth." I mean, that was my thought. And I, I, uh, will frankly admit that when the doctors were making the rounds on the ward, I mean the routine rounds, I tried to be where they wouldn't see me. The doctor often goes there on the ward and asks how everyone is and when she'd get about to me, I'd move to a spot that she's already covered . . .

Therapist: You really avoided people.

Patient: So that, so that she wouldn't, uh, talk with me (*Therapist:* Uh, hm) and when—the few times that I refused to see you, it was for the same reason. I didn't think I was worth bothering with, so why waste your time—let's just . . .

Therapist: Let me ask you, ask you something about that. Do you think it would have been, uh, better if I had insisted that, uh, uh, you come and talk with me?

Patient: No, I don't believe so, doctor. (They speak simultaneously.)

Therapist: I wondered about that; I wasn't sure . . . (Softly)

Patient: I don't—I, I, I . . .

Raush and Bordin (1957) helped define warmth further. Helper warmth they held, has three components.

Commitment. The therapist demonstrates some degree of willingness to be of assistance to the patient. This assistance may vary in degree of activity and concreteness. For example, the therapist may offer help in the form of setting limits, breaking limits, or actively collaborating with the patient in the solution of an external problem, or he may offer help only by committing his time. At any given moment, the therapist occupies some point along a continuum representing degree of commitment. . . . The therapist most typically commits a specified amount of time to the patient; he commits, for the patient's use at those times, a private meeting place which will remain relatively undisturbed by extraneous factors, he commits his skills and his efforts at understanding and aiding the patient; he also commits to the patient a relationship in which the patient's needs and interests are dominant, and in which the therapist's personal demands and minimized. For the patient also there are commitments: to honor appointments, to pay fees regularly, to avoid conscious inhibitions of associations, to discuss impending decisions, and so forth.

Effort to understand. The therapist shows his effort to understand by asking questions designed to elicit the patient's view of himself and the world, by testing with the patient the impressions that he, the therapist, has gained of these views, and by indicating, by comments or other forms of action, his interest in understanding the patient's views. At the other extreme, aside from absence of the kind of behavior we have just described, the therapist tends to act as though he had a preconceived view of the patient, his actions, and his feelings. . . . Certainly, it is the therapist's efforts at understanding which produce the first major emotional tie between patient and therapist in most forms of psychotherapy . . . this effort on the part of the therapist will be a major determinant of "rapport" and of communication between patient and therapist. Such an effort on the part of the therapist may be communicated in many ways: by attentive and unintrusive listening, by questions indicative of interest, by sounds of encouragement, by any of the verbal or nonverbal cues which say in effect, "I am interested in what you are saying and feeling—go on." But whatever the manner of communication, the effort at understanding on the part of the therapist is communication of warmth. . . . The patient's gratification and his willingness to communicate more freely under these circumstances . . . are "natural" responses to warmth, in the sense that both children and adults feel gratified when their serious communications are listened to seriously.

Spontaneity. The least spontaneous therapist is guarded, either consciously or unconsciously masking all of his feelings. These masked feelings may be intimately related to the underlying needs and feelings of the patient, or they may be those which occur as part of the natural interaction between any two people. Such a therapist maintains an impressive mien and is likely to be inhibited in all of his motor expressions, such as gestures. His verbal communications are marked by stereotype, formalism, and stiffness. The least spontaneous therapist may, however, seem to act impulsively. Such impulsivity will have a compelled, unnatural quality. . . . "Simply going through the motions of psychotherapy is not enough," is, and must be, emphasized by supervisors of students of the process. The therapist must be capable of expressing something of himself. . . . Observation of different therapists indicates considerable variability in the amount of affect expressed. Some therapists seem always to have a tight rein on themselves; they are or seem to be emotionless. Others seem to feel much freer to express themselves; they seem more "natural." (p. 352) (From "Warmth in personality development and in psychotherapy" by H. L. Raush and E. S. Bordin, 1957, *Psychiatry, 20,* pp. 351–363. Copyright 1957 by *Psychiatry.* Used with permission.)

Similar behaviors represent warmth in yet another research. In one we read: "During a warm interview the interviewer smiled, nodded her head, and spoke warmly. During a cold interview she spoke unsmilingly, she did not nod her head; and she kept her voice drab and cold." As in much of this type of research, these investigators found that interviewees talked significantly more to the warm interviewer. (The term *significantly* will be used throughout this book in its common statistical usage, that is, a statistically significant result is a "real" one, one that might happen by chance only 5 times in 100.) Another study with a similar result used a helper speaking in a "soft, melodic and pleasant voice" versus speaking in a "harsh, impersonal, and business-like voice" for the comparison of warm versus cold helpers. In a successful repeat study, the same researcher elaborated his definition of warmth in a manner akin to Raush and Bordin's "commitment" and "effort to understand." Specifically, in addition to the voice qualities, the warm helper "showed interest, concern, and attention," whereas his "cold" counterpart displayed "disinterest, unconcern, and nonattentiveness."

Though it is clear that helpers can be trained to show reliably the aforementioned behavior, and these helper behaviors have been shown to affect what the client does, the reader must be cautioned against a too rigid adoption of "a warm stance." Smiling, a pleasant voice, and the like can indeed represent warmth. But if warmth at root is, as Raush and Bordin suggested, commitment, effort to understand, and spontaneity, warmth can also be represented behaviorally by directiveness, assertiveness, autonomy-enhancing distancing, and even anger. To a large extent, it is the context and content of the helper-client interaction that will determine if a given instance of helper behavior is perceived by the client as warmth. Carkhuff and Berenson (1967) made a similar observation when they commented: ". . . it is not always communicated in warm, modulated tones of voice; it may be communicated, for example, in anger. In the final analysis, it is the client's experience of the expression that counts" (p. 28).

Self-Disclosure

The trust component of the helper-client relationship (see Figure 2.1) can be positively influenced by helper self-disclosure (Bierman, 1969; Johnson, 1972). Johnson and Matross (1977) described a trust-enhancing, self-disclosure sequence in which (a) the client disclosed personal information about his needs, problems, history, relationships; and (b) the helper responded by offering facilitative conditions and reciprocated in self-disclosure by revealing such information as his views of the client, his reactions to the unfolding therapy situation, and information about himself.

A number of investigations have consistently shown that helper self-disclosure does function to elicit reciprocal client self-disclosure and ratings of greater helper trustworthiness (Bierman, 1969; Drag, 1968; Sermat & Smyth, 1973). Simonson has shown in a number of studies that these positive effects are optimized when the content of what the helper discloses about himself or herself is private (background, preferences, views) but not relevant to the helper's own, personal problems (Simonson & Apter, 1969; Simonson & Bahr, 1974).

MISCELLANEOUS METHODS

We have seen so far in this chapter that the helper-client relationship can be enhanced by direct statements to the client about the helper's likability (structuring); by the client's observation of a counterpart expressing attraction to a helper, or helper observation of a counterpart expressing attraction to a client (imitation); by a client's hearing other clients rate a helper as attractive (conformity pressure); by describing the helper to the client as someone of considerable expertness, experience, and accomplishment, or by surrounding the helper with various signs and symbols of such expertness and achievement (status); by helper believability and openness about himself or herself; by helper credibility and self-disclosure; or by the facilitative conditions of helping behaviors actually offered the client by the helper (e.g., empathy and warmth). These several approaches can be considered the major methods of relationship enhancement currently available, because of the amount and conclusiveness of research on each. However, certain other means of improving the nature of the helper-client interaction have also appeared in the professional literature. Each of these should be viewed by the reader as somewhat more tentative or speculative than those just considered, because the amount of quality or supporting research evidence for each is still rather small.

Helper-Client Matching

This approach to the helping relationship, in contrast with those just considered, typically does not seek to alter anything in the helper or client in order to enhance the goodness of their fit. Instead, an effort is made to (a) identify real characteristics of helpers and clients that are relevant to how well they relate, (b) measure helpers and clients on these characteristics, and (c) match helpers and clients into optimal (for client change) pairs based on these measurements. Much of the research on matching is conflicting or inconclusive, but some of it does lead to useful, if tentative, conclusions. The following are frequent characteristics of an optimal helper-client match.

1. Helper and client hold congruent expectations of the role each is to play in the relationship. They understand and agree on their respective rights and obligations regarding what each is expected to do and not to do during their interactions.
2. Helper and client are both confident of positive results from their meetings. Each anticipates at least a reasonably high likelihood of client change.
3. Helper and client come from similar social, cultural, racial, and economic backgrounds.
4. Helper and client are similar in their use of language, conceptual complexity, extroversion–introversion, objectivity–subjectivity, flexibility, and social awareness.
5. Helper and client are complementary or reciprocal in their need to offer and receive inclusion, control, and affection. The need for inclusion is related to associating, belonging, and companionship versus isolation, detachment, and

aloneness. Control is a power or influence dimension, and affection refers to emotional closeness, friendliness, and the like. Helper and client are complementary or reciprocal on these dimensions if the level of inclusion, affection, or control that one member needs to offer approximates the level of that dimension that the other member needs to receive.

Obviously, no given helper and client can be paired on all of these dimensions. However, the greater the number of them reflected in a particular pairing, the more likely that a favorable relationship will develop.

Proxemics

Proxemics is the study of personal space and interpersonal distance. Is there a connection between how far apart two persons sit and their posture, on the one hand, and the favorableness of their relationship on the other hand? First, it does appear that liking in an interview setting leads to physical closeness and a particular type of posture. In an experiment by Leipold (1963), one group of college students were told, "We feel that your course grade is quite poor and that you have not tried your best. Please take a seat in the next room and Mr. Leipold will be in shortly to discuss this with you." Other groups heard neutral or positive statements about their course performance. Those receiving praise subsequently sat significantly closer to the interviewer; those who were criticized chose to sit farther away.

A second study also suggests that increased liking leads to decreased physical distance. Walsh (1971) used imitation procedures to increase successfully how attracted a group of patients was to an interviewer. Before each interview, the office was arranged so that the patient's chair was physically light, on wheels, and located at the other end of the room 8 feet from where the interviewer would be sitting. On entering the room, the interviewer suggested to the patient that he "pull up the chair." Attracted patients pulled the chair significantly closer to the interviewer than did unattracted patients.

Our concern, of course, is the other way around, that is, relationship enhancement. Does close sitting and certain posturing *lead to* a favorable relationship? This notion was tested in one of our modeling studies. For some patients, the interviewer not only sat close by (27 inches), but also assumed a posture shown in other research to reflect liking. Specifically, he leaned forward (20°) toward the patient, maintained eye contact 90% of the time, and faced the patient directly (shoulder orientation of 0°). Very different distance and posture were involved in the contrasting condition. The interviewer was 81 inches from the patient, leaned backward 30°, showed eye contact 10% of the time, and faced partially away from the patient with a shoulder orientation of 30°. Results of this research did in part show that distance and posture can indeed influence the patient liking that develops. As was true in the case of helper-client matching, relevant proxemic research is not great. Tentatively, however, we may begin to view close distance and "interested" posture as probable relationship enhancers.

Conversational "Dos" and "Don'ts"

A step-by-step, relationship-building "cookbook" is neither possible nor desirable. Obviously, each helper-client pair is different enough from others, so that what we have provided in this chapter should be read and used as *general* suggestions only. How, when, and where a given procedure is used and what specific form it takes must be left to the good judgment of each helper. This same proviso applies to the material that follows. Wolberg (1967) has provided a listing of what he views as helper behaviors to include or avoid when trying to build a favorable helper-client relationship. Most of this listing, and the examples he provided, follow. His suggestions should be taken as guidelines only, and not as a recipe to be applied verbatim.

Avoid exclamations of surprise.
Patient: I never go out on a date without wanting to scream.
Unsuitable responses.
Therapist: Well, for heaven's sake!
Therapist: That's awful!
Therapist: Of all things to happen!
Suitable responses.
Therapist: I wonder why?
Therapist: Scream?
Therapist: There must be a reason for this.
Avoid expressions of overconcern.
Patient: I often feel as if I'm going to die.
Unsuitable responses.
Therapist: Well, we'll have to do something about that right away.
Therapist: Why, you poor thing!
Therapist: Goodness, that's a horrible thing to go through.
Suitable responses.
Therapist: That must be upsetting to you.
Therapist: Do you have any idea why?
Therapist: What brings on this feeling most commonly?
Avoid moralistic judgments.
Patient: I get an uncontrollable impulse to steal.
Unsuitable responses.
Therapist: This can get you into a lot of trouble.
Therapist: You're going to have to put a stop to that.
Therapist: That's bad.
Suitable responses.
Therapist: Do you have any idea of what's behind this impulse?
Therapist: How far back does this impulse go?
Therapist: How does that make you feel?
Avoid being punitive under all circumstances.
Patient: I don't think you are helping me at all.
Unsuitable responses.
Therapist: Maybe we ought to stop therapy.

Therapist: That's because you aren't cooperating.
Therapist: If you don't do better, I'll have to stop seeing you.
Suitable responses.
Therapist: Let's talk about this; what do you think is happening?
Therapist: Perhaps you feel I can't help you.
Therapist: Is there anything I am doing or fail to do that upsets you?
Avoid criticizing the patient.
Patient: I just refuse to bathe and get my hair fixed.
Unsuitable responses.
Therapist: Are you aware of how unkempt you look?
Therapist: You just don't give a darn about yourself, do you?
Therapist: That's like cutting off your nose to spite your face.
Suitable responses.
Therapist: There must be a reason why.
Therapist: Do you have any ideas about that?
Therapist: How does that make you feel?
Avoid making false promises.
Patient: Do you think I'll ever be normal?
Unsuitable responses.
Therapist: Oh, sure, there's no question about that.
Therapist: In a short while you're going to see a difference.
Therapist: I have great hopes for you.
Suitable responses.
Therapist: A good deal will depend on how well we work together.
Therapist: You seem to have some doubts about that.
Therapist: Let's talk about what you mean by normal.
Avoid threatening the patient.
Patient: I don't think I can keep our next two appointments, because I want to go to a concert on those days.
Unsuitable responses.
Therapist: You don't seem to take your therapy seriously.
Therapist: If you think more of concerts than coming here, you might as well not come at all.
Therapist: Maybe you'd better start treatments with another therapist.
Suitable responses.
Therapist: I wonder why the concerts seem more important than coming here.
Therapist: Maybe it's more pleasurable going to the concerts than coming here.
Therapist: What do you feel about coming here for therapy?
Avoid burdening the patient with your own difficulties.
Patient: You look very tired today.
Unsuitable responses.
Therapist: Yes I've been having plenty of trouble with sickness in my family.
Therapist: This sinus of mine is killing me.
Therapist: I just haven't been able to sleep lately.
Suitable responses.
Therapist: I wouldn't be surprised, since I had to stay up late last night. But that shouldn't interfere with our session.
Therapist: I've had a touch of sinus, but it's not serious and shouldn't interfere with our session.
Therapist: That comes from keeping late hours with meetings and things. But that shouldn't interfere with our session.
Avoid displays of impatience.

Patient: I feel helpless and think I ought to end it all.
Unsuitable responses.
Therapist: You better "snap out of it" soon.
Therapist: Well, that's a nice attitude, I must say.
Therapist: Maybe we had better end treatment right now.
Suitable responses.
Therapist: I wonder what is behind this feeling.
Therapist: Perhaps there's another solution for your problems.
Therapist: You sound as if you think you're at the end of your rope.
Avoid political or religious discussions.
Patient: Are you going to vote Republican or Democratic?
Unsuitable responses.
Therapist: Republican, of course; the country needs good government.
Therapist: I'm a Democrat and would naturally vote Democratic.
Suitable responses.
Therapist: Which party do you think I will vote for?
Therapist: Have you been wondering about me?
Therapist: I wonder what you'd feel if I told you I was either Republican or Democrat. Would either make a difference to you?
Therapist: I vote for whoever I think is the best person, irrespective of party, but why do you ask?
Avoid arguing with the patient.
Patient: I refuse to budge an inch as far as my husband is concerned.
Unsuitable responses.
Therapist: It's unreasonable for you to act this way.
Therapist: Don't you think you are acting selfishly?
Therapist: How can you expect your husband to do anything for you if you don't do anything for him?
Suitable responses.
Therapist: You feel that there is no purpose in doing anything for him?
Therapist: Perhaps you're afraid to give in to him?
Therapist: How do you actually feel about your husband right now?
Avoid ridiculing the patient.
Patient: There isn't much I can't do, once I set my mind on it.
Unsuitable responses.
Therapist: You don't think much of yourself, do you?
Therapist: Maybe you exaggerate your abilities.
Therapist: It sounds like you're boasting.
Suitable responses.
Therapist: That puts kind of a strain on you.
Therapist: Have you set your mind on overcoming this emotional problem?
Therapist: You feel pretty confident once your mind is made up.
Avoid belittling the patient.
Patient: I am considered very intelligent.
Unsuitable responses.
Therapist: An opinion with which you undoubtedly concur.
Therapist: The troubles you've gotten into don't sound intelligent to me.
Therapist: Even a moron sometimes thinks he's intelligent.
Suitable responses.
Therapist: How do you feel about that?
Therapist: That's all the more reason for working hard at your therapy.
Therapist: That sounds as if you aren't sure of your intelligence.

Avoid blaming the patient for his failures.
Patient: I again forgot to bring my doctor's report with me.
Unsuitable responses.
Therapist: Don't you think that's irresponsible?
Therapist: There you go again.
Therapist: When I tell you the report is important, I mean it.
Suitable responses.
Therapist: I wonder why?
Therapist: Do you know why?
Therapist: Perhaps you don't want to bring it.
Avoid rejecting the patient.
Patient: I want you to like me better than any of your other patients.
Unsuitable responses.
Therapist: Why should I?
Therapist: I don't play favorites.
Therapist: I simply don't like a person like you.
Suitable responses.
Therapist: I wonder why you'd like to be preferred by me.
Therapist: Perhaps you'd feel more secure if I told you I liked you best.
Therapist: What do you think I feel about you?
Avoid displays of intolerance.
Patient: My wife got into another auto accident last week.
Unsuitable responses.
Therapist: Those women drivers.
Therapist: Women are sometimes tough to live with.
Therapist: The female of the species is the most deadly of the two.
Suitable responses.
Therapist: How does that make you feel?
Therapist: What do you think goes on?
Therapist: How did you react when you got this news?
Avoid dogmatic utterances.
Patient: I feel cold and detached in the presence of women.
Unsuitable responses.
Therapist: That's because you're afraid of women.
Therapist: You must want to detach yourself.
Therapist: You want to destroy women and have to protect yourself.
Suitable responses.
Therapist: That's interesting; why do you think you feel this way?
Therapist: How far back does this go?
Therapist: What feelings do you have when you are with women?
Avoid premature deep interpretations.
Patient: I've told you what bothers me. Now what do you think is behind it all?
Unsuitable responses.
Therapist: Well, you seem to be a dependent person and want to collapse on a parent
figure.
Therapist: You're got an inferiority complex.
Therapist: You never resolved your Oedipus complex.
Suitable responses.
Therapist: It will be necessary to find out more about the problem before I can offer
a valid opinion of it.
Therapist: We'll continue to discuss your attitudes, values and particularly your
feelings, and before long we should discover what is behind your trouble.

Therapist: That's for us to work on together. If I gave you the answers, it wouldn't be of help to you.

Avoid the probing of traumatic material when there is too great resistance.

Patient: I just don't want to talk about sex.

Unsuitable responses.

Therapist: You'll get nowhere by avoiding this.

Therapist: You must force yourself to talk about unpleasant things.

Therapist: What about your sex life?

Suitable responses.

Therapist: It must be hard for you to talk about sex.

Therapist: All right, you can talk about anything else you feel is important.

Therapist: Sex is always a painful subject to talk about.

Avoid unnecessary reassurance.

Patient: I think I'm the most terrible, ugly, weak, most contemptible person in the world.

Unsuitable responses.

Therapist: That's silly. I think you're very good looking and a wonderful person in many ways.

Therapist: Take it from me, you are not.

Therapist: You are one of the nicest people I know.

Suitable responses.

Therapist: Why do you think you feel that way?

Therapist: How does it make you feel to think that of yourself?

Therapist: Do others think the same way about you?

Express open-mindedness, even toward irrational attitudes.

Patient: I think that all men are jerks.

Unsuitable responses.

Therapist: That's a prejudiced attitude to hold.

Therapist: You ought to be more tolerant.

Therapist: With such attitudes you'll get nowhere.

Suitable responses.

Therapist: What makes you feel that way?

Therapist: Your experiences with men must have been disagreeable for you to have this feeling.

Therapist: Understandably you might feel this way right now, but there may be other ways of looking at the situation that may reveal themselves later on.

Respect the right of the patient to express different values and preferences from yours.

Patient: I don't like the pictures on your walls.

Unsuitable responses.

Therapist: Well, that's just too bad.

Therapist: They are considered excellent pictures by those who know.

Therapist: Maybe your taste will improve as we go on in therapy.

Suitable responses.

Therapist: Why?

Therapist: What type of pictures do you like?

Therapist: What do you think of me for having such pictures?

Make sympathetic remarks where indicated.

Patient: My husband keeps drinking and then gets violently abusive in front of the children.

Unsuitable responses.

Therapist: Why do you continue living with him?

Therapist: Maybe you do your share in driving him to drink.

Therapist: He's a no-good scoundrel.

Suitable responses.

Therapist: This must be very upsetting to you.

Therapist: It must be very difficult to live with him under these circumstances.

Therapist: You must find it hard to go on with this kind of threat over you. (pp. 584–590) (From *The technique of psychotherapy.* 2nd ed. by L. R. Wolberg 1967. New York: Grune & Stratton. Reprinted by permission of Grune & Stratton, Inc. and the author.)

The "Resistive" Client

In chapter 1 we entered a prescriptive caution, holding that the diverse change procedures examined in this book are optimally implemented in a differential, tailored, or prescriptive manner. No change-relevant procedures fit all clients; all change-relevant procedures fit some clients. The same statements are also true of relationship-enhancing techniques. The several procedures described and illustrated in the present chapter as potentially relationship enhancing should be viewed as potentially powerful interventions that, nevertheless, are in no instance applicable to all clients. A ready example of this prescriptive perspective concerns empathy. Research of the past decade confirms not only that high levels of perceived helper empathy are facilitative with some client subsamples and irrelevant with certain others, but also that such helper behaviors can function as a negative influence on the therapeutic relationship in certain other samples of clients. As we have recently noted elsewhere,

> While it is perhaps the most widely held (non-prescriptive) belief in contemporary psychotherapies of all types that an empathic and genuine therapist-patient relationship is a necessary and at times even sufficient facilitator of patient change (Patterson, 1966; Rogers, 1957; Truax & Carkhuff, 1967), the possibility that this generalization might not hold with at least some subtypes of juvenile delinquents has appeared sporadically in the delinquency literature for at least the last 25 years (Edelman & Goldstein, 1984; Goldstein, Heller, & Sechrest, 1966; Redl & Wineman, 1957; Schwitzgebel, 1961; Slack, 1960). Characteristic of this perspective is the early statement by Redl and Wineman (1957) specifically warning against overwhelming the delinquent with a close therapeutic relationship and recommending instead that a benevolent but somewhat impersonal and objective style of interaction might more likely lead to favorable therapeutic events, especially in the early stages of treatment. An identical perspective has been operationalized in such therapies as "experimenter-subject psychotherapy," Slack's (1960) "streetcorner research," (Schwitzgebel, 1961; Stollak and Guerney's, 1964 "minimal contact therapy," Sechrest and Strowig's (1962) recommended use of teaching machines, and our own suggestions in this context regarding the likely prescriptive utility of impersonal, machine, and action therapies. (Goldstein, Heller, & Sechrest, 1966)

It is not only the delinquent youngster for whom less, or at least different, might be better than more for relationship-enhancement purposes. DeVoge and Beck

(1978) described a broad range of potential clients for whom the closeness, friendliness, and submissiveness of a "typical" therapist-patient relationship could be highly aversive.

> We contend that with many clients, the therapeutic situation is a more complex, perhaps even a grim atmosphere which neither elicits nor offers support for such behaviors from a therapist. We refer to persons predisposed toward hostility, people who tend to prefer noncompliance or resistance toward a therapist. (p. 235)

Munjack and Oziel (1978) assumed a similar position in their valuable explication of diverse types of resistive client behavior. From them, as well as from the several sources mentioned in the last Goldstein et al. quote, it seems clear that substantial numbers of clients exist who, from one perspective, can be viewed as resistive to typical therapist relationship-enhancing behaviors. Rather than view such thwarting as "resistive," we prefer to conclude that such relationship offerings are simply prescriptively less than optimal and often functionally counterproductive. What then ought to be offered to such clients, beyond the aforementioned general "impersonal and objective" stance? Stated otherwise, are there currently available, prescriptively useful means of enhancing the quality of the therapeutic relationship with what might be termed "low relatability" clients? Although this is clearly not a matter that has received considerable empirical scrutiny, given the sheer numbers of such persons, it clearly should. Potentially effective relationship-enhancing techniques for use with such persons are already apparent, and they include employing a less authoritative structure, maintaining patient permission, and acceding to patient need for autonomy and even power (Beutler, 1982); providing patients with a high degree of choice with minimal justification, seeking initial compliance under conditions of low external pressure, and using reattributional training to enhance self-attribution to responsibility (Willis, 1982); using interpretive modeling, antisabotage procedures, paradoxical prescriptions (Spinks & Birchler, 1982); building on patient variability, acknowledging patient beliefs while challenging them, selectively using initial overnurturance (Wachtel, 1980); and other social-psychological (Higginbotham et al., 1989), paradoxical (Bogden, 1982), and eclectic (Lambert, 1982) procedures. Again we stress: The need is considerable, the potential relationship-enhancement technology for such clients contains many good leads at present, and the empirical work remains largely undone.

Negative Effects

In recent years, research on possible "deterioration effects" in psychotherapy has increasingly verified that such intervention cannot only be for better, but also for worse (Lambert, Bergin, & Collins, 1977; Mays & Franks, 1985; Strupp, Hadley, & Gomes–Schwartz, 1977). Participation in psychodynamic (Colson, Lewis, & Horwitz, 1985), behavioral (Barbrack, 1985), group (Dies & Teleska,

1985), or marital or family therapy (Kinskern & Gurman, 1985) may, and in some instances demonstrably does, cause clients to become worse. Strupp and Hadley (1976) surveyed a large national sample of prominent psychotherapists for their views on the causes and correlates of such negative effects. The several factors identified, many of which find concrete expression within the therapeutic experience via therapist-patient relationship qualities, include:

1. therapist coldness, ignorance, seductiveness, pessimism, sadism, or absence of genuineness;
2. misapplication and deficiences of technique, such as holding in oneself or structuring in the client inappropriate prognostic expectancies, failure to reach mutual agreement on treatment goals, prescriptively inappropriate matching of particular techniques with a given client, and various types of technical rigidity;
3. faulty understanding and management of counter-transference manifestations; and
4. diverse therapist-patient communication problems, involving either or both the clarity of messages delivered by the therapist and distortions in the message as heard by the client.

It is clear that expert opinion holds therapist inadequacies, and their relationship consequences, as largely responsible for therapeutic deterioration effects. Both early and more recent research on this matter, in the context of diverse psycho-therapies, confirms this perspective. Reviewing much of the earlier relevant research, Lambert (1982) comments:

> These reviews are unanimous in their opinion that the therapist-patient relationship is critical. . . . The first well-accepted and experimentally substantiated finding is that the quality of the relationship, as defined by this therapist-offered conditions (empathy, warmth, and genuineness) and as experienced by the patient, correlates with and perhaps produces positive outcomes. A corollary finding is that low levels of these relationship variables are associated with patient deterioration. (p. 25)

Lieberman, Yalom, and Miles (1973), analogously implying an array of relationship-relevant "don'ts," found negative effects in the context of group psychotherapy to be produced by therapists who were excessively controlling, overly impersonal, and too laissez-faire. And in marital and family therapies, Kinskern and Gurman (1985) observe:

> Therapist variables appear to play a central role . . . in the worsening which occurs in marital-family therapy. A particular therapist style appears to increase the probability of negative effects. This style is best described as one in which the therapist does relatively little to structure and guide early treatment sessions; uses frontal confrontations of highly affective material very early in therapy, rather than reflection of feeling; labels unconscious motivation early in therapy rather than stimulating interaction, gathering data, or giving support . . . (p. 108)

Clearly, good psychotherapeutic relationships and outcomes are as much a matter of errors avoided as competencies utilized.

SUMMARY

For whom is this chapter written? Who should our helpers be? Relationship-enhancing procedures, as well as the many helper methods described in the chapters that follow, are not the private property of a chosen few who happen to have earned certain professional credentials. Certainly, such training can lead to skills of considerable positive consequence for client change. But at least as important is the kind of person the helper is. We are in strong agreement with Strupp (1973), who observed:

> It seems that there is nothing esoteric or superhuman about the qualities needed by a good therapist! They are the attributes of a good parent and a decent human being who has a fair degree of understanding of himself and his interpersonal relations so that his own problems do not interfere, who is reasonably warm and empathic, not unduly hostile or destructive, and who has the talent, dedication, and compassion to work cooperatively with others. (p. 2)

Thus, the potential helper's personal background, degree of self-understanding, maturity, typical ways of relating, and concern for others are all as crucial to the outcome of her or his helping effort as is her or his formal training as a helper.

We have held throughout this chapter that, without a favorable helper-client relationship, client change will rarely occur. With such a relationship, client change is possible, or even probable, but not inevitable. Other, more specific, change measures must typically be utilized in addition. We leave to the chapters that follow the task of fully describing and illustrating these specific procedures.

REFERENCES

Barbrack, B. (1985). Negative outcome in behavior therapy. In D. T. Mays & C. M. Franks (Eds.), *Negative outcome in psychotherapy and what to do about it*. New York: Springer Publishing Co.

Beutler, L. E. (1982). *Eclectic psychotherapy*. Elmsford, NY: Pergamon Press.

Bierman, R. (1969). Dimensions for interpersonal facilitation in psychotherapy and child development. *Psychological Bulletin, 72*, 338–352.

Bogden, J. L. (1982). Paradoxical communication as interpersonal influence. *Family Process, 21*, 443–452.

Capella, J. N. (1981). Mutual influence in expressive behavior: Adult–adult and infant–adult dyadic interaction. *Psychological Bulletin, 89*, 101–132.

Carkhuff, R. R. (1969). *Helping and human relations*. New York: Holt, Rinehart & Winston.

Carkhuff, R. R., & Berenson, B. G. (1967). *Beyond counseling and therapy*. New York: Holt, Rinehart & Winston.

Clark, M. S., & Reis, H. T. (1988). Interpersonal processes in close relationships. *Annual Review of Psychology, 39*, 609–672.

Colson, D., Lewis, L., & Horwitz, L. (1985). Negative outcome in psychotherapy and psychoanalysis. In D. T. Mays & C. M. Franks (Eds.), *Negative outcome in psychotherapy and what to do about it*. New York: Springer.

Condon, J. W., & Crano, W. D. (1988). Inferred evaluation and the relation between attitude similarity and interpersonal attraction. *Journal of Personality and Social Psychology, 54*, 789–797.

Corrigan, J. D., Dell, D. M., Lewis, K. N., & Schmidt, L. D. (1980). Counseling as social influence process: A review. *Journal of Counseling Psychology, 27*, 395–441.

DePaulo, B. M., Zuckerman, M., & Rosenthal, R. (1980). Humans as lie detectors. *Journal of Communication, 30*, 129–139.

Derlega, V. J., & Chaikin, A. L. (1975). *Sharing intimacy*. Englewood Cliffs, NJ: Prentice-Hall.

DeVoge, J. T., & Beck, S. (1978). The therapist-client relationship in behavior therapy. *Progress in Behavior Modification, 6*, 203–248.

Dies, R. R., & Teleska, P. A. (1985). Negative outcome in group psychotherapy. In D. T. Mays & C. M. Franks (Eds.), *Negative outcome in psychotherapy and what to do about it*. New York: Springer.

Drag, L. R. (1968). *Experimenter-subject interaction: A situational determinant of differential levels of self-disclosure*. Unpublished master's thesis, University of Florida, Gainesville, FL.

Edelman, E., & Goldstein, A. P. (1984). Prescriptive relationship levels for juvenile delinquents in a psychotherapy analog. *Aggressive Behavior, 10*, 269–298.

Egan, G. (1976). *Interpersonal living*. Monterey, CA: Brooks/Cole.

Ekman, P., & Friesen, W. V. (1969). Nonverbal leakage and cues to deception. *Psychiatry, 32*, 88–106.

Erickson, F., & Shultz, J. (1982). *The counselor as gatekeeper: Social interaction in interviews*. New York: Academic Press.

Fairbanks, L. A., McGuire, M. T., & Harris, C. J. (1982). Nonverbal interaction of patients and therapists during psychiatric interviews. *Journal of Abnormal Psychology, 91*, 109–119.

Frank, J. D. (1961). *Persuasion and healing*. Baltimore: Johns Hopkins Press.

Gladstein, G. (1969). Client expectations, counseling experience, and satisfaction. *Journal of Counseling Psychology, 16*, 476–481.

Goldstein, A. P. (1971). *Psychotherapeutic attraction*. Elmsford, NY: Pergamon Press.

Goldstein, A. P. (1973). *Structured learning therapy toward a psychotherapy for the poor*. New York: Academic Press.

Goldstein, A. P. (1981). *Psychological skill training*. Elmsford, NY: Pergamon Press.

Goldstein, A. P., Heller, K., & Sechrest, L. B. (1966). *Psychotherapy and the psychology of behavior change*. New York: John Wiley & Sons.

Goldstein, A. P., & Michaels, G. Y. (1985). *Empathy: Development, training and consequences*. Hillsdale, NJ: Lawrence Erlbaum Associates.

Guerney, B. G. (1977). *Relationship enhancement: Skill training program for therapy, problem-prevention, and enrichment*. San Francisco, CA: Jossey-Bass.

Gumprez, J. J. (1982). *Discourse strategies*. New York: Cambridge University Press.

Haley, J. (1963). *Strategies of psychotherapy*. New York: Grune & Stratton.

Harwood, A. (1981). Communicating about disease: Clinical implications of divergent concepts among patients and physicians. In A. Harwood (Ed.), *Ethnicity and medical care*. Cambridge, MA: Harvard University Press.

Hendrick, S. S., Hendrick, C., & Adler, N. L. (1988). Romantic relationships: Love, satisfaction, and staying together. *Journal of Personality and Social Psychology, 54*, 980–988.

Hermansson, G. L., Webster, A. C., & McFarland, K. (1988). Counselor deliberate postural lean and communication of facilitative conditions. *Journal of Counseling Psychology, 35,* 149–153.

Higginbotham, H. N., West, S. G., & Forsyth, D. R. (1988). *Psychotherapy and behavior change: Social, cultural and methodological perspectives.* New York: Pergamon Press.

Ivey, A. E., & Authier, J. (1971). *Microcounseling.* Springfield, IL: Charles C Thomas.

Johnson, D. W. (1972). *Reaching out: Interpersonal effectiveness and self-actualization.* Englewood Cliffs, NJ: Prentice-Hall.

Johnson, D. W., & Matross, R. (1977). Interpersonal influence in psychotherapy: A social psychological view. In A. S. Gurman & A. M. Razin (Eds.), *Effective psychotherapy: A handbook of research* (pp. 395–432). Elmsford, NY: Pergamon Press.

Kazdin, A. (1979). Nonspecific treatment factors in psychotherapy outcome research. *Journal of Consulting and Clinical Psychology, 47,* 846–851.

Kinskern, D. P., & Gurman, A. S. (1985). A marital and family therapy perspective on deterioration in psychotherapy. In D. T. Mays & C. M. Franks (Eds.), *Negative outcome in psychotherapy and what to do about it.* New York: Springer.

Kleinman, A. (1980). *Patients and healers in the context of culture.* Berkeley, CA: University of California Press.

Kleinman, A., Eisenberg, L., & Good, B. (1978). Culture, illness and care: Clinical lessons from anthropologic and cross-cultural research. *Annals of Internal Medicine, 88,* 251–258.

Kraut, R. (1980). Humans as lie detectors: Some second thoughts. *Journal of Communication, 30,* 209–216.

LaCrosse, M. B. (1975). Nonverbal behavior and perceived counselor attractiveness and persuasiveness. *Journal of Counseling Psychology, 22,* 563–566.

Lambert, M. J. (1982). *Psychotherapy and patient relationships.* Homewood, IL: Dow Jones-Irwin.

Lambert, M. J., Bergin, M. E., & Collins, J. L. (1977). Therapist induced deterioration in psychotherapy. In A. S. Gurman & A. M. Razin (Eds.), *Effective psychotherapy: The therapist's contribution.* Elmsford, NY: Pergamon Press.

Leipold, W. E. (1963). *Psychological distance in a dyadic interview.* Unpublished doctoral dissertation. University of North Dakota, Grand Forks, ND.

Lieberman, M. A., Yalom, I., & Miles, M. B. (1973). *Encounter groups: First facts.* New York: Basic Books.

Mays, D. T., & Fanks, C. M. (1985). *Negative outcome in psychotherapy and what to do about it.* New York: Springer.

Meichenbaum, D. (1977). *Cognitive-behavior modification: An integrated approach.* New York: Plenum Press.

Munjack, D., & Oziel, J. L. (1978) Resistance in the behavioral treatment of sexual dysfunctions. *Journal of Sex and Marital Therapy, 42,* 122–138.

Nichter, M., & Trockman, G. (1983). *Toward a psychosociocultural evaluation of the psychiatric patient: Contributions from clinical anthropology.* Unpublished manuscript, Department of Psychiatry, School of Medicine, University of Hawaii, Honolulu.

Orne, M. T., & Wender, P. H. (1968). Anticipatory socialization for psychotherapy. *American Journal of Psychiatry, 124,* 1202–1212.

Patterson, C. H. (1966). *Theories of counseling and psychotherapy.* New York: Harper & Row.

Raush, H. L., & Bordin, E. S. (1957). Warmth in personality development and in psychotherapy. *Psychiatry, 20,* 351–363.

Redl, F., & Wineman, D. (1957). *The aggressive child.* Glencoe, IL: Free Press.

Rogers, C. R. (1957). The necessary and sufficient conditions of therapeutic personality change. *Journal of Consulting Psychology, 21,* 95–103.

Sabalis, R. F. (1969). *Subject authoritarianism, interviewer status, and interpersonal attraction.* Unpublished master's thesis, Syracuse University, Syracuse, NY.

Schmidt, L. D., & Strong, S. R. (1970). Expert and inexpert counselors. *Journal of Counseling Psychology, 17,* 115–118.

Schwitzgebel, R. (1961). *Streetcorner research: An experimental approach to the juvenile delinquent.* Cambridge, MA: Harvard University Press.

Sechrest, L. B., & Strowig, R. W. (1962). Teaching machines and the individual learner. *Educational Theory, 12,* 157–169.

Sermat, V., & Smyth, M. (1973). Content analysis of verbal communication in the development of a relationship: Conditions influencing self-disclosure. *Journal of Personality and Social Psychology, 26,* 332–346.

Simonson, J., & Apter, S. (1969). *Therapist disclosure in psychotherapy.* Paper presented at the meeting of the Eastern Psychological Association, Philadelphia, PA.

Simonson, N., & Bahr, S. (1974). Self-disclosure by the professional and paraprofessional therapist. *Journal of Consulting and Clinical Psychology, 42,* 359–363.

Slack, C. W. (1960). Experimenter-subject psychotherapy: A new method of introducing intensive office treatment for unreachable cases. *Mental Hygiene, 44,* 238–256.

Snyder, M. (1987). *Public appearances and private realities: The psychology of self-monitoring.* New York: W. H. Freeman.

Snyder, M., Berscheid, E., & Glick, P. (1985). Focusing on the exterior and the interior: Two investigations of the initiation of personal relationships. *Journal of Personality and Social Psychology, 48,* 1427–1439.

Snyder, M., Berscheid, E., & Matwychuk, A. (1988). Orientations toward personnel selection: Differential reliance on appearance and personality. *Journal of Personality and Social Psychology, 54,* 972–979.

Snyder, M., & Smith, D. (1986). Personality and friendship: The friendship worlds of self-monitoring. In V. J. Derlega & B. A. Winstead (Eds.), *Friendship and social interaction* (pp. 63–80). New York: Springer-Verlag.

Spinks, S. H., & Birchler, G. R. (1982). Behavioral-systems marital therapy: Dealing with resistance. *Family Process, 21,* 169–185.

Streltzer, N. E., & Koch, G. V. (1968). Influence of emotional role-playing on smoking habits and attitudes. *Psychological Reports, 22,* 817–820.

Strong, S. R., & Schmidt, L. D. (1970). Expertness and influence in counseling. *Journal of Counseling Psychology, 17,* 81–87.

Strupp, H. H. (1973). On the basic ingredients of psychotherapy. *Journal of Counseling and Clinical Psychology, 41,* 81–87.

Strupp, H. H., & Hadley, S. W. (1976). Contemporary views of negative effects in psychotherapy. *Archives of General Psychiatry, 33,* 1291.

Strupp, H. H., Hadley, S. W., & Gomes–Schwartz, B. (1977). *Psychotherapy for better or worse.* New York: Jason Aronson.

Truax, C. B., & Carkhuff, R. R. (1967). *Toward effective counseling and psychotherapy.* Chicago: Aldine.

Wachtel, P. L. (1980). What should we say to our patients?: On the wording of therapists' comments. *Psychotherapy: Theory, Research and Practice, 17,* 183–188.

Walsh, W. G. (1971). *The effects of conformity pressure and modeling on the attraction of hospitalized patients toward an interviewer.* Unpublished doctoral dissertation, Syracuse University, Syracuse, NY.

Willis, T. A. (1982). *Basic processes in helping relationships.* New York: Academic Press.

Wolberg, L. R. (1967). *The technique of psychotherapy* (2nd ed.). New York: Grune & Stratton.

3
Modeling Methods
Ted L. Rosenthal
Bruce D. Steffek

All around us, observing how others think, act, or express emotions steers the conduct of the people who observe. Movie stars, television and sports figures, leaders in business and government, and other celebrities—both admired and feared—can influence what people do, and the fashions in clothing or hairstyles, patterns of speech, and even food preferences. The processes by which information guides an observer (often without messages conveyed through language), so that conduct is narrowed from "random" trial-and-error toward an intended response, are collectively termed *modeling*. By intended response, we mean that much of the practice takes place covertly, through information-processing, decision-making, and evaluative events *in advance* of visible or audible overt performance. The observer need not attempt to climb high up a lofty tower until after some acrophobic distress has been removed at lower and safer altitudes. Nor does the novice canoe enthusiast attempt to run rapids until after grasping the rudiments of canoe navigation on dry land, and practicing the skills of paddling, avoiding snags, and judging the force of an eddy, in calm waters far removed from the target swift currents and cataracts. Thus, younger children may choose baseball over some other sport because an admired elder sibling stars on the high school team. The neophyte may gain interest in the game, learn its rules, learn much of how to catch, throw, hold a bat and swing, and even position fingers to pitch a curve ball, *before* ever engaging in overt baseball acts, from watching and listening to elder sib and teammates perform. Unfortunately, observation before direct practice can also spur interest in crack or illegal drugs, how to abuse them, and where to find them.

Human use of modeling cues long preceded study of modeling processes. Pictures of animals in lifelike poses, for instance in photos from Neanderthal caves such as Altimira and Lascaux, suggest that the beasts' pattern of movement and stance guided the hand of the cave artist. This was no "innate" skill, since the pictures range from marginal to likelike, and the suggestions of three-dimensional perspective seem to have evolved over time, as later artists improved their craft from exposure to the precedents left them by earlier mentors. Among the first mentions of modeling within recorded thought was Aristotle's definition of dramatic tragedy in terms of *imitation* of life events rather than narration about them. Aristotle appears to have meant imitation (*mimeses*) to signify showing or demonstrating the scenes on stage, not just relating them as in Homer's epic poetry. Unfortunately, at times modeling has been confused with imitation as exact and slavish copying, rather than learning by example. We mean modeling in a far broader sense to encompass a range of information from specific motor acts and illustrations of acceptable social conduct, to very abstract strategies such as metatheories about which alternative strategies to apply when confronted by an obstacle—be it narrow bridges or crowded freeways for agoraphobics, or old "user friends" who offer chemicals to drug abusers. Let us foreshadow the hierarchical nature of the information that modeling can transmit by an example: Suppose that your job is to find and rescue the aging King who has gotten lost in a labyrinth. Due to early Alzheimer's disease, the King cannot aid you directly. And a raging minotaur, confined to part of the labyrinth, can destroy you or the King if you bumble into the danger zone. What kind of help would you prefer? To have a model *tell* you where to turn right, or left, or keep straight ahead at choice points, in order to find and save the King? To have a model *show* you, on a small-scale replica of the maze, how and where to move at those choice points? To have the model code the route into a symbolic chain of acts:

RRRSLLRRRSSLLRRRSSSLLRRRSLLRRRSSLLRRRSSSLLRRRSLLR
RRSSLLRRRSSSLLRRRSLL

to summarize the sequence of right turns (*R*), straight ahead (*S*) choices, and left turns (*L*)? Or to give you as a summary rule the very abstract principle: Always 3 rights; then 1 *S* and 2 *L*; the next time 2 *S* and 2 *L*; the next time 3 *S* and 2 *L*; then back to 1 *S* and 2 *L*. Or, 3 R; 1,2,3,1,2,3. . .S; 2L? Especially if half the kingdom and the hand in marriage of the beautiful prince or princess were the reward, most of us would choose the last (strategic) modeling option to map our safe entry and exit to rescue the lost monarch from the maze. All other options, from narrated and performed motor choices, to a long chain of elements coded as *R, S,* or *L*, would severely tax one's capacity to remember. In contrast, the abstract rule only requires memory of *RRR*, then 1 *S* then 2 then 3 *S* going in, followed by *LL* to reach the King safely. Then, one can reverse the *L* turns to rights, the *R* turns to lefts, and the sequence of straights to descending order; that is, *SSS* then *SS* then *S* and repeat, in order to escape. Granted, the strategy is complex enough, but it also suggests further cognitive aids (Rosenthal & Downs, 1985). For instance, a pegboard marked $RRR\ S_1\ S_2\ S_3\ LL$ for the way in, and $RR\ S_3\ S_2\ S_1\ LLL$ for the way out would be a simple mnemonic device to tell the correct path. Would you prefer the long sequence of elements RRRSLLRRRSSLLRRR etc. to track on a pegboard? Why not?

Note that the preceding example called attention to two separable but intermeshing aspects of modeling: first, how the clues to the safe route were organized or structured and sequenced as overt guidance operations or stimulus events. Second, how the alternative stimulus formats would affect observers' ease of processing the options in terms of extracting (covert coding) and retaining (covert storage and retrieval) the information. With this preamble, we may now provide a definition as follows: "A model is any stimulus array so organized that an observer can extract and act upon the main information conveyed by environmental events without first needing to perform overtly" (Rosenthal & Bandura, 1978). In the maze example, would you need first to walk inside to make use of the $RRR\ S_1\ S_2\ S_3\ LL$ guidance principle?

Despite its antiquity and a brief flurry of interest early in the twentieth century, modeling was largely neglected by science until the work of Albert Bandura. In part, the naive behaviorism that followed John B. Watson resisted "mentalistic" views that one could really learn without doing. In part, the overt practice bias of the Hullian school led to experiments so narrow in their scope that a false conclusion arose, that modeling was a weak way to alter the behavior of patients, students, or other trainees. Bandura revived the topic by showing that a host of knowledge and action ensembles—not known to learners previously—could be acquired through observation and put into use without tedious overt practice (Bandura & Walters, 1963). Bandura also—and almost single-handedly—construed modeling as information that is cognitively processed via symbolic operations, rather than emphasizing imitative motor responses or simple acts (Bandura, 1969, especially chapter 9). Also, Bandura began the serious study of clinical modeling, to remove fears and to transmit useful adjustment skills. Recent writers on Pavlovian conditioning offer explanations much closer to Bandura's informational views than to the old stereotypes of UCS-UCR-CR chains joined by contiguous association without cognitive mediation (Rescorla, 1988).

Over 25 years have passed since Bandura's first book on social learning. By now, the pervasive role of modeling is somewhat commonplace because it is all around us in psychology, psychiatry, and related disciplines. Like Moliere's *Bourgeois Gentilhomme*, who was stunned to find he had been speaking prose all his life, so many modeling elements affect the behavioral sciences that one may neglect the forest due to a mind-boggling host of trees. Bandura's clinical work has had great conceptual impact. For instance, his self-efficacy theory of behavioral change, soon to be discussed, has altered the goals, measurement, and conception of progress in treatment. His innovations in therapeutic modeling have been tested and applied by his colleagues, his students, and their students. Yet routine use of modeling methods for treatment delivery could be expanded, and a goal of this chapter is to invite more modeling applications by clinicians in practice or in training. This goal is somewhat ironic given the power and versatility of modeling methods, which first aroused broad interest when they were shown clinically superior to competing techniques to teach autistic children (and adults) useful new coping, self-care, and social skills.

Perhaps reducing wider application of modeling options has been the reluctance of Bandura and his associates to present their approach as a school of therapy. Despite its own special emphases, its proponents regard it as one important variant of cognitive-behavioral thrusts, which are siblings or kissing-cousins (Rosenthal, 1982). Thus, Meichenbaum (1986, this book, third edition, chapter 9) recommends interventions involving a horde of modeling components, both concrete and strategic, as do Kanfer and Gaelick (1986, this book, third edition, chapter 8) for self-management methods. Credit for first pressing some variety of grape seems less critical than the quality of the vintages produced: Few if any current behavioral nostrums do not contain some modeling juices—whether as a dominant elixir or only to enhance an aggregate blending.

A Guide to Background and Related Readings

A fairly voluminous literature exists on modeling, and readers will find further mentions elsewhere in this volume. This is no way and no need to try to recapitulate all that work. What is needed is a "sketch map" to aid a reader in search of more depth or earlier references. The current status of social-cognitive theory is presented in detail by Bandura (1986) and summarized elsewhere (Rosenthal, 1984a). The most complete historical discussion of modeling, the research and procedures involving concept attainment, and the information-processing literature which underlies much of this work probably is offered by Rosenthal and Zimmerman (1978). Reviews of the older clinical research on modeling therapies appear in many sources (e.g., Bandura, 1969, 1971, 1977; Rosenthal, 1976, 1980; Rosenthal & Bandura, 1978; Rosenthal & Rosenthal, 1983, 1985). Except to illustrate a principle, technique, or issue under discussion, less mention is made of work that appeared before 1980, and more prominence is given to studies published subsequently. We seek to emphasize newer designs, novel applications, and promising domains—actual or potential—for clinical exploration and harvest.

PROSOCIAL MODELING

For applied contexts and goals, *prosocial* modeling falls into three spheres: preventative, therapeutic, and educative or pedagogical. Preventative thrusts attempt to promote more healthful practices or better care of oneself and loved ones. Therapy can remove dysfunctional conduct patterns, such as irrational fears and phobias and avoidant withdrawal, and also create, refine, or refresh useful skills such as interpersonal tact, better attitudes toward oneself, and greater candor, expressiveness, or self-assertion. Education may aim at clinicians and trainers or at the patient's spouse, parent, offspring, friend or employer, as well as at clients themselves. Thus, we may try to teach interaction partners how to respond constructively to persons who suffer from panic episodes or obsessional rituals. Often, major handicaps such as alcoholism spur group efforts to support and teach the loved ones of the sufferer (e.g., Al-Anon, Al-A-Teen and Al-A-Tot) as well as to help the alcoholics (via AA). When skill or knowledge is severely curtailed, as with retarded or autistic people, modeling has often proven the best guidance mode to initiate cognitive or social advances. Many people show no prominent symptoms or deficits but suffer greatly due to excessive inhibitions, constriction of options, or perfectionistic and self-driving attitudes. Modeling interventions can aid such clients by helping them to evolve and implement more permissive personal philosophies which invite more tolerant and commodious lifestyles. Before we address the preventive, therapeutic, and educative spheres, let us bring together in tabular form a number of terms and contrasting alternatives that often enter technical discussions of modeling methods. Readers should study the box with some care (as a preparatory example) before reading further. Review of the box may clarify procedures mentioned later on.

Preventive Thrusts

The clinical ideal is to intervene *before* deficiencies can lead to symptoms of frank pathology. Modeling programs to strengthen desirable behavior and attitudes hence become very promising directions. An ambitious and innovative study by Ozer and Bandura (in press) provides an extended example to illustrate some principles and techniques that can be applied. The goal was to assist women to deal effectively with the risk of sexual assault—which all feared and some 40% had suffered in the past. The danger had constricted diverse spheres of living. The women hesitated to enter settings where an assault might occur, such as using public transportation. It was not a phobia of physical assault but reluctance to take that chance. As a result, the women's range of cultural, educational, and social activities grew impoverished. They lacked a strong enough sense of ability (*self-efficacy*) to handle dangers that might arise from venturing out alone. Their limited confidence in handling (or perceived self-efficacy to cope with) the hazards of a possible assault led them to surrender diversions they would have liked to pursue.

The researchers designed and offered a community self-defense program and enrolled some 45 volunteers. The basic strategy was to teach self-defense skills through participant modeling so that the women would learn how to fend off an assailant and increase their confidence about coping with any attack attempted. It was essential for each woman to gain trust in her self-defense ability. If not, she might lack confidence (self-efficacy) to risk visiting settings where assaults could arise. To supply guidance in self-protection, an instructor modeled and clarified the elements to be learned. For meaningful practice, the women resisted onslaughts from two male model assailants (who wore protective outfits to prevent injury). The men attacked the women who, in turn, practiced their growing skills on their padded model adversaries. As each woman fought off an assault, the others were vicariously involved too, rooting for their fellow student and shouting guidance about which blows and maneuvers would best overcome what the model assailant had begun. Here is how the graduated steps leading to mastery of self-defense skills were organized:

> Initially, the component skills needed to escape a hold and to disable an assailant were modeled by the instructor. These component actions included eye strikes, biting, kicks, elbow, knee and palm strikes, and foot stomps. These types of disabling blows were directed at vital areas of the body such as the eyes, head, throat, knees, and groin. In most sexual assaults, women are thrown to the ground. Therefore, considerable attention was devoted to mastering safe ways of falling and striking assailants while pinned on the ground. The subjects performed the power blows and received corrective feedback until they had mastered them.
>
> The component skills were then integrated into self-defense sequences tailored for different circumstances of assault. These self-protective skills were developed in simulated attacks by male assistants wearing a heavily padded headpiece and specially designed protective gear. The assailants gradually increased the constraint and force of their assaults as subjects gained power and ability to defend themselves. Subjects were taught how to disable an assailant quickly when attacked from different positions—frontally, from behind, while lying down, thrown to ground, and pinned down. An assault sequence ended when the assailant signaled that the subject had delivered a knockout blow. Later in the series, the simulations required three knockout blows to provide experience on how to fight off a psychotic or drugged assailant with an impaired sense of reality. (Ozer & Bandura, in press)

It is not enough to acquire the skills to earn desired outcomes. People must also gain enough self-efficacy (confidence) that they can perform the needed acts despite stresses, dangers, moments of doubt, and can persevere in the face of setbacks. If one thinks, "I can only sail my boat in perfect weather, as long as there are *no* mishaps," one will not undertake ambitious sailing trips. In contrast, if one thinks, "I can sail my boat even if we hit rough weather—and if I hit a snag, I can get righted again and keep going," one's offshore undertakings will be more enterprising. Thus it was not enough just to empower the women with self-defense movement skills. They also were taught beliefs and tactics for nipping assaults in the bud; for example, they learned how to display a secure (versus fearful) appearance, how to fend off (versus submit to) the initial steps of intrusion by a potential assailant, and how to state firm and confident (versus timid or doubtful) warnings. Realistic precautions, the benefits of assertive (versus "worst case") self-statements, and other cognitive aids to support perseverence (versus surrender) were also supplied, often by demonstrating the conduct to be acquired, followed by a woman's overt and covert practice.

COMMON MODELING TERMS, PROCEDURES, AND DISTINCTIONS

1. Purely Observational (Nonperformance) Guidance

In overt, symbolic, and covert modeling, observers do *not* make actual motor (e.g., contacts with feared stimuli) or problem-solving (e.g., answering questions, stating principles, devising strategies or plans) responses during the teaching phase. This is called observational or vicarious acquisition. A typical session runs about 40–50 minutes, or 8 to 16 trials. For example, fearful clients first watch models approach easy tasks (stepladders, one caged garter snake). Tasks grow progressively harder (fire escapes, several serpents), ending with stringent items (lofty towers, many uncaged snakes), as in a hierarchy for systematic desensitization. Abstract concepts are also taught by showing a series of correct solutions. Observers attempt the task between sessions (or after a block of demonstrations) but usually not amidst teaching trials. Exceptions come with preschoolers and retardates, who may take turns with the model to keep their fragile attention on the task.

A. *Overt* model(s). One or more persons (or trained animals) illustrate the behavior to be learned or refined. The overt model may be a live tutor, recorded on film or videotape (or, mainly for aural responses, on audiotape).

B. *Symbolic* model(s). Animated cartoon or fantasy characters, schematics, narratives, or slides replace the overt tutor. For example, to teach student auto mechanics how to assemble and trouble-shoot the drive-train, the parts can be shown moving into or out of their proper arrangement. The steps needed to illustrate repairs can be repeated a number of times, either as a fixed program or a program that lets the learner control the amount of repetition.

A limiting case is a *target* model. Here, the desired product or work sample is arranged to help learners infer how to create similar correct responses from studying the sample. Examples include charts, diagrams, and such epitomes as correct place-settings, tactful letters, and completed jigsaw or crossword puzzles. Also among target models are illustrations that satisfy some governing rule—such as forceful phrasing to teach assertiveness, the winning move in a chess or a bridge game, or a list of antonyms and synonyms—even though the learner does not witness the actions or the reasoning that brought the target into being (see Rosenthal & Zimmerman, 1978).

C. *Covert* model(s). The tutor—whether a person, beast, cartoon character, or schematic diagram—is *imagined* rather than shown. Covert models may be oneself (called self-modeling) or others performing some behavior with increasing deftness. Various cues (e.g., specifying sensory images or inner reactions) can be supplied to support the scenario imagined. To remove fears, covert modeling by self blends into systematic desensitization in clinical structure and format. Depending on observer characteristics, some covert models will surpass others. For instance, to reduce fear in devout clients, visualizing Jesus or Mohammed as a helper will excel over secular tutors (see Rosenthal & Downs, 1985, for discussion).

2. Participant (Enactive) Guidance

This is a modeling version of guided practice. It involves actual practice—at least on some of the trials—by the observer(s) under naturalistic or quasi-naturalistic (e.g., role-playing, simulated settings) conditions. In the typical method, one or more teaching models demonstrate the desired behavior in graduated in vivo steps, starting with easier (short drives under light traffic conditions) and mounting to harder (driving jammed freeways at rush hour) tasks. Protective devices—also called response-induction aids—are often supplied to evoke early attempts from timid clients. For example, height phobics may wear safety lines; driving-fearful clients practice in dual-driver cars so that, if necessary, the tutor can take the wheel; these "crutches" are progressively withdrawn as confidence grows.

For most individual therapy, the model(s) demonstrate a step until the client feels ready to try it. The client keeps repeating the step (with reduced assistance) until able to perform it confidently, at which point the next-harder step is modeled, and so forth. Usually, group therapy is similar in format except that clients alternate taking turns performing the tasks—from easier to harder—after each step is demonstrated. Since progress moves at the client's pace, overly fear-arousing demands are not made on the enactive practice trials. Most often, the pace of group participant modeling is set at the level of the most fearful (or submissive, inhibited, or unskilled) group member.

Much the same tactics can be used—both individually and in groups—to teach problem solving, anger control, and relabeling of self-defeating attitudes (such as constricted self-expression or perfectionism).

3. Distinctions Found in All Forms of Modeling

A. *Single* (one tutor) versus *multiple* (a number of tutors) models. When multiple models are provided, they are best made diverse in such characteristics as age, gender, and appearance to suggest a broad spectrum of humanity.

B. *Coping* versus *mastery* models. A coping model starts out scared, or inept, or ignorant and progressively gains skill and confidence across repeated trials— much as do clients. A mastery model starts out confident, skillful, and knowledgeable thus demonstrating adept performance on all trials.

C. *Stylistic* modeling. It is not the purpose of conduct nor its products, but the style or manner of response, that is of main concern, as often found in social skills training. Thus, one may try to change the pace, or tempo, or intensity, or vividness, and so forth with which the client acts or speaks. Examples include slowing down anxious clients who "race through" speech and action (or speeding up dawdlers who tax partners' patience); showing shy folks to make eye contact and speak up loudly and forcefully; teaching inhibited learners to "let go" by introducing humor, colorful figures of speech, gestures to capture attention, and so forth when conversing with others or giving a talk.

Self-efficacy is not a global concept (confidence in general) but reflects perceived confidence to deal with *specific* aims. Thus, training was tested in several spheres: Efficacy for self-defense was measured on scales of perceived capacity to retaliate (e.g., with disabling blows) if assaulted. Efficacy to widen range of activities was measured on scales of perceived comfort to resume outdoor recreations and diversions (e.g., concerts, restaurants, and nightclubs) that take place after dark. Efficacy for interpersonal encounters was measured on scales of perceived capacity for assertive response if threatened or hassled in a wide range of social contexts (at work, on dates, in public transportation, at parties, etc.). Efficacy to control troublesome cognitions was measured by a scale of perceived capacity to stop ruminating about possible attacks. Finally, various ratings of thoughts about, vulnerability to, risk of facing, and fear concerning sexual assault were obtained. Behavioral responses to three simulated surprise attacks also assessed all subjects' tangible self-defense skills. As compared to a control phase before guidance, the modeling program created strong and highly significant gains in all the diverse spheres (just listed) of measured outcome (see Ozer & Bandura, in press).

Changing Perspective About Oneself

What created these changes in the women's self-efficacy? Put more broadly, what factors can raise or lower a person's perceived self-efficacy to accomplish some task? At base, we learn to deal with the world through four main sources: information based on actual experiences; information obtained vicariously from observing others' actions plus the consequences that result; information stemming from directions, encouragement, persuasion, and other sorts of social influence aimed at us; and information based on the physiological cues experienced as positive feedback (good, confident, calm, triumphant, cheer feelings) and negative feedback (stressful, worried, tense, discouraged, sad feelings). These feelings derive from the bodily states that follow our actions and the *anticipation* of performing some act before we engage in it.

Across all these cue domains, cognitive and judgmental processes alter the "raw" stimuli through interpretive events (Rosenthal, 1984a; Rosenthal & Zimmerman, 1978). For instance, we *infer* that a 6-foot high jump is very successful due to our customary yardsticks for making judgments, such as the norms, expectations, and evaluative criteria of our society. In a world of giants (or on a planet with weaker gravity), the same jump might count as a failure. We *infer* that the actress kissing the handsome prince has positive feelings. The movie screen will not tell us if the actor playing the prince needs a better deodorant or mouthwash. It often turns out that some of the "happiest" marriages we know end in divorce, and some of the "happiest" persons we know may attempt suicide. On the brighter side, a host of dire predictions—including nuclear war and the collapse of civilization due to pandemic AIDS—have not come to pass. These examples illustrate that inferences are imperfect.

Most of us face a barrage of social influences—from parents, teachers, friends and love partners, employers, the network and print media, advertisers, peers at church and at diverse clubs and organizations. Unless we are totally uncritical and also able to move near the speed of light, we literally cannot honor all those invitations and exhortations. We must be selective in accepting social persuasion: No lack of ulterior motives nor "con games" exist. Still, a trusted therapist who has helped us in the past may be an especially powerful source of influence in the future. Finally, no amount of reassurance will erase our sensations of terror, panic, or pain. We know while we endure them. The noxious sensations (and apprehensive thoughts that accompany them) are compelling danger cues we must grapple with. Reciprocally, the person who aspires to climb a mountain or win an Olympic medal and does so, who determines to confront a bully and does act courageously, who gets up the nerve to ask a winsome co-worker out and does get agreement for a date, will receive positive bodily feedback congruent with successful endeavor. One's confidence about similar efforts in the future may rise a notch. Such positive reactions may be especially vivid when a formerly fear-arousing challenge is performed with reasonable ease and security. The contrast that occurs when something formerly bad has been palpably transformed for the better may give special impact to one's progress. We have illustrated that the main channels to shift perspective about one's competence are enactive experience, observation, social influence, and physiological cues (Bandura, 1988), plus the judgments and inferences we assign to information however it reaches us. Let us now return to the women given the empowerment training to protect themselves from potential assault.

Among enactive elements that led to higher self-efficacy were the stepwise mastery experiences confirming the growth of self-protective skills. These began with movement components limited in scope, rose to more complex integration of ways to deliver various blows, and advanced to defensive strategies that would overcome various simulated assaults whose intensity gradually increased. Progressive mastery culminated with guided practice in counteracting surprise attacks that came when a woman was especially vulnerable—for example, prone or off balance. Note that the attacks closely simulated a range of naturalistic dangers, both in plain view and from ambush. Hence, a learner did not need to question her increasing skill. The evidence of her progressive mastery was verified by criterion-like work samples. Also, she could perceive greater capacity to control worrisome thoughts that otherwise might hamper her execution of the self-protective skills.

Among vicarious elements that raised self-efficacy were the instructor's demonstrations of what to do, what to avoid, and how to correct any errors provided during learning. Realistic facts were supplied about where, when, and how typical attacks occur, and ways to counter them. The assailants modeled convincing threats that were faithful examples of dangerous conditions. Each woman benefited from many trials spent watching and correcting her peers' self-defense tactics, as well as their feedback about her own efforts. Rarely in life do we receive such carefully designed and diversified preparation, from multiple models, to avert hazards or heartbreak. Most of us are not taught how to steer a car if a lurching vehicle suddenly looms ahead. Most of us are not taught what to expect—nor how to overcome the shock and loss—when a dearly loved parent, spouse, or child suddenly passes away. Often, we learn some crisis skills from our life experiences, but those are sporadic and happenstance, not systematically organized. (Systematic organization must be a powerful aid to learning or the brief duration of most psychotherapies could never overcome the years of dysfunctional behavior that clients often must revise.)

Among the elements of social persuasion were the caring and optimism of the instructor and the model assailants—who literally risked some injury to help the women gain skill—clearly implying that the mentors were convinced guidance would succeed. More obviously, each woman entered a social network of fellow-initiates: They mutually encouraged, supported, praised, and advised each other during the course of group training. Furthermore, social influence from diverse partners similar to oneself in goals and aspirations, who interact often as members of a cohesive group, will have much more impact than will influence from sources who are perceived as alien in needs or values, who are strangers, and who—unlike a total group—more readily may espouse deviant or idiosyncratic views.

Among the favorable physiological changes were reduced feelings of personal vulnerability and anxiety after training enhanced self-efficacy. Other evidence confirms that raising self-efficacy calms physiological distress. Thus, low self-efficacy to meet demands can activate secretion of stress-related catacholamines (Bandura, Taylor, Williams, Mefford, & Barchas, 1985) and reduce pain tolerance (Bandura, Taylor, Gauthier, & Gossard, 1987). In turn, increased self-efficacy appears to activate endogenous opioids (endorphins or encephalins) which have analgesic effects that reduce sensitivity to pain (Bandura, Cioffi, Taylor, & Brouillard, 1988).

If you wonder about the relative contributions of the enactive mastery versus nonenactive elements of the self-defense program, take time for a brief exercise: Reread the three foregoing paragraphs and ask yourself how you would feel if your own training to protect yourself from assault were limited to the vicarious and social persuasion facets of guidance. Do you think the self-efficacy changes— such as reduced personal vulnerability or anxiety—would have occurred without any firsthand evidence of growing skills to defend oneself? In fact, all psychotherapies—whatever techniques they comprise—must raise patients' self-efficacy if patients are to attempt, or persist at, activities they formerly avoided (e.g., contact with "contaminating" materials; long trips on which a panic attack might occur) or inhibited (e.g., allowing freer self-expression of feelings and desires; defending one's legitimate rights assertively). Clients who fear that some coping attempt will fail and bring distress (be it terror, embarrassment, or pain) may not persevere or even risk trying. Few of us are rash enough to begin a process that we view as akin to entering the lions' den wearing pork-chop underwear. Hence, psychotherapeutic approaches that are confined to the consulting room are liable to fail if they seek to promote behavior that is inhibited due to fearful perceptions and ruminations about facing the challenge.

Indeed, the jarring that occurs when a self-conception is switched from a prior, to some new equilibrium, has long captured human attention, as in the sharp transformations often found in fairy tales and myths. Some changes are for the better: Cinderella becomes a princess; the ugly duckling becomes a lovely swan. Some metamorphoses refute romantic assumptions: Oz, the "Great Wizard," proves much less powerful than expected. Other changes are downright calamities: The misshapen dwarf in Oscar Wilde's "The Birthday of the Infanta," who discovers his ugliness in a mirror, dies of a broken heart; when people look on Medusa, they turn to stone. Perhaps such changes are a fantasy means to express hopes and fears about drastic shifts in one's identity, status, or persona. Various psychotherapeutic viewpoints emphasize altering clients' self-images, self-percepts, and self-reactions for the better. The self-efficacy analysis suggests that a prime way to reach such goals would be for clinicians to leave their offices and assist the client to do better in naturalistic settings, thus to feel better and to witness one's own progress (i.e., participant modeling). That so much of clinical practice is restricted to office visits may tell more about the costs, convenience, or insurance liabilities for the health care system than about the power of the services delivered.

Abuse of Children

Not only women are high-risk targets for assault. Much evidence shows that both sexual and nonsexual abuse of children are frequent (see Emery, 1989). Increased public awareness has led to diverse preventive efforts, often located at school settings, and involving a mixture of guidance strategies. Among the goals has been teaching children to separate legitimate ("good touch") from illegitimate ("bad touch") intimate advances. For example, a physician or parent may need access to a child's crotch for treating an injury and monitoring hygiene. Few other adults have reason for similar contact. In one study, composite behavioral skill training helped more than presenting a teaching film to aid youngsters to learn about wrongful intimacies and how to resist them (Wurtele, Saslawsky, Miller, Marrs, & Britcher, 1986).

Ample research has found participant modeling considerably more powerful than purely observational guidance to change conduct patterns. This difference for overt actions does *not* necessarily hold to impart facts or principles that are relatively free of emotional burdens (Rosenthal & Bandura, 1978; Rosenthal & Zimmerman, 1978). The distinction hinges on acquisition versus performance. We may acquire the basic rudiments of many feats (bike riding, ice skating) or concepts (judging equal and unequal quantities)—and certainly the patterns of our native language—from observing social models. However, to perform with confidence and finesse, we must refine emerging skills by enactive practice. In *acquisition,* we learn the overall pattern or epitome of the new information. In *performance,* we learn to refine and apply those patterns to implement the knowledge, despite subtleties, complications, or emotional interference (Bandura, 1977).

The distinction was supported in another study to prevent abuse. Wurtele, Marrs, and Miller–Perrin (1987) compared participant modeling with the children rehearsing the element to be learned (e.g., being able to locate one's private parts; saying "No!" firmly and escaping from, or reporting, an adult molester) to pure observation. Kindergartners were matched on initial skill and assigned for group instruction to either the overt rehearsal or the observation-only condition. Training was just one 50-minute session. Enactive modeling not only supplied practice but assured that all learners had mastered each step before the next step was introduced. The pure observation group received the same information from the same tutor but *without* stepwise practice and pacing new guidance to ensure grasp of the previous material. There were two main dependent measures. An individually administered "What If" test contained situational vignettes to assess how well a child recognized illicit adult advances *and* knew how to repel them. On this measure, both modeling conditions showed gains from pretest, but the enactive method brought significantly greater progress. The second measure, also individually administered, was a questionaire testing the child's knowledge about (rather than skill to resist) sexual abuse. On this device, both groups improved from pretest with no differences between the participant and nonparticipant modeling formats. Likewise, the children enjoyed both programs, but neither version was more popular. Hence, this study started to open research on child molesting to comparative modeling emphases. Obviously, much more can be done: The duration and depth of teaching can be expanded. Teaching films—using cartoon or animal protagonists if more acceptable to the community—can be woven into the enactive modeling program to illustrate graphically what kinds of coaxing and caresses the child must fend off. The frightening ambiguities that may surround "telling on a grown up" might also be dispelled by demonstrations that depict how to report—to parent, police, or teacher—attempted molestation. Thus, parental cooperation can be sought to have at least one parent per child present during the simulations of how to report a transgression. In that way, the child can gain confidence that parents really want such embarrassing content disclosed rather than kept silent.

At times, a parent is the miscreant, and the abuse is nonsexual. All too often, neglect and mistreatment of children go undetected, unsubstantiated, and unmodified (Eckenrode, Powers, Doris, Munsch, & Bolger, 1988), and children's social and emotional development can suffer. Modeling methods have been tested to reduce social withdrawal by abused toddlers. In a recent study, maltreated preschoolers—selected for low rates of social interaction—were drawn into play by peer versus adult "friendly models." The peers were primed to initiate acts of sharing and play, as they had been taught to via role-playing. The adult confederates issued invitations to an isolate child to match the number offered by the peer models. Otherwise, the peer and adult modeling conditions were similar. A control group made trivial changes over time. The maltreated children given friendly peer models significantly increased several types of social responsiveness. In contrast, abused toddlers significantly *decreased* outgoing social behavior after contact with the new adult models. Thus, a background of maltreatment by adults seemed to impair youngsters' ability to relate to new adult models, even when generous and prepared to nurture the toddler (Fantuzzo et al., 1988). The earlier, abusive contacts made it harder for the children to benefit from adults who were kindly disposed. It might well require gradual and sustained familiarity—across multiple contacts—with nurturant adults to overcome the avoidant social handicaps, a topic worth more study. This unfortunate transfer by children to the new grown-ups suggests that the best prevention would be to alter the harmful child care practices of abusive parents. Such a trial was attempted with high-risk parents, under scrutiny by a child protective services agency. The agency got involved after public health nurses became concerned about a child's welfare during home visits. Nearly all parents were mothers (few male adults would take part), but none were under court order nor in the hands of the criminal justice system for unacceptable parenting. On average, the babies were only 24 months, and their mothers just 21 years old; nearly all homes received welfare funds. The therapists were graduate students with no personal experience in raising a child. They were trained and supervised by techniques that included modeling demonstrations of how to guide parents. One set of parents attended two 2-hour information groups per week for an average of 20 sessions. These information control subjects took part in informal discussions of health and family, nutrition, personal growth and maturity, and arts and crafts. The systematic training was briefer, averaging just 9 sessions. Training focused on providing child management skills and overcoming mothers' emotionality if their child was loud, demanding, or overly active. Instructions, demonstrations, and guided rehearsal were used to instill apt use of praise by the mothers. Later on they were taught to give clear demands, to handle concrete problems affecting their child, and to foster language skills by modeling speech sounds for their baby. Videotapes of parent-child interactions were played back for the mothers to judge and critique, as a way to spark their interest in improved child care. The systematic training was stepwise: Basic proficiencies were attained before more advanced elements were added. Thus, the systematic group reported fewer high-risk (potentially abusive) feelings and beliefs than the controls, and actually reached the normal range on a parental risk inventory. They also showed significantly reduced depression scores and fewer and milder complaints about behavior problems with their child. Further, social caseworkers rated the systematically trained mothers as managing better, and as at less risk to maltreat their child than were the controls. Although a "difficult," low socioeconomic (SES) target population, the systematic group expressed strong satisfaction with the guidance they had received (Wolfe, Edwards, Manion, & Koverola, 1988). Obviously, all the foregoing child abuse work is somewhat tentative. Sustained training, tighter matching of time durations, and other procedural safeguards, plus more overt behavioral evidence of robust progress, seem called for. Yet the data augur well: Collectively, they suggest that expanded efforts would prove fruitful, and that modeling applications can help ameliorate diverse kinds of abuse—and its consequences—in many ways.

A related thrust involved training in fire safety skills for children fearful of getting burned but poor at escaping from fires. The children were taught in small groups and took turns performing. A tutor demonstrated graded escape responses, telling how each was managed, and then a child enacted the step—with some correction of errors if needed—before the next task was modeled. Also, some children received extra elaboration: The child was asked how to respond correctly, told why to do so, and then was required to tell how correct response would help in safe escapes. The explanations and summaries were skipped for other children, and time was equalized with more safety facts. Both forms of guidance improved concrete escape responses as compared to untrained controls. However, only the elaborated practice group reduced fears of fire; they also better grasped the reasons for safe escape techniques (Jones, Ollendick, McLaughlin, & Williams, 1989). Similar research—with expanded guidance regimens—could promote safer practices when swimming, boating, skating, crossing streets, and for other situations where prevention spares more costly treatment.

Prevention and Behavioral Medicine

In principle, modeling applications for medicine overlap most spheres of treatment, many diagnostic activities, and nearly all information-provision efforts with patients—whether to educate them (e.g., about proper hygiene), to counsel them (e.g., about needed lifestyle changes), or to instruct them (e.g., about how to follow or alter some pharmacological regimen). As yet, multiple directions are under study, but most attempts reflect an early stage of technical sophistication. Many clinical trials involve small sample sizes, brief study durations, and mainly illustrate that modeling *can* play a useful role among a mélange of guidance components. Little is then done to clarify the processes or mechanisms of change, or to test alternative therapies for relative impact.

A first example studied children who could not swallow prescribed pills. Training was individual, using candies that ranged from very small to capsule sizes. An adult demonstrated how to place a candy at the rear of the tongue without bending the tongue, to sip water, tilt back the head, and then swallow. After the child earned a prize for swallowing two of the smallest candies, the entire process was repeated—the adult demonstrating and the child practicing—until the next prize was won with a larger candy, culminating in the child downing a capsule. In this way, five of six youngsters learned to swallow pills and could do so at a 3-month follow-up (Blount, Dahlquist, Baer, & Wuori, 1984).

Sometimes a study planned as treatment has very clear preventive relevance. Thus, a multicomponent program taught three closed head-injury patients problem-solving skills to mend cognitive deficits (in knowledge of community facilities, ways to handle emergencies, and the hazards of alcohol and drugs). The injuries had occurred several years earlier, and patients' IQs were close to average, but all displayed problem-solving lacks that blocked them from living independently. An array of problems—drawn from high-frequency events in their residential settings—was devised. Each item sketched a scenario (e.g., a friend takes a medicine but soon after breaks out in a bad rash), and then asked for a solution (e.g., how would one help the friend?). In a baseline phase, the patients took turns answering the items, and then both other peers were asked for alternative solutions. During group training, learners first received cards (later omitted) to clarify criteria for good answers. A tutor supplied feedback and guided modeling to help each subject reach acceptable solutions or, if the patient failed, the tutor demonstrated a correct sample solution. As sessions continued, performance requirements rose, in stepwise fashion, to reflect the learner's growing competence. A dollar was earned each session that a patient met the goal. After proficiency emerged, new generalization items tested the stability of progress. The results were quite encouraging. Correct answers rose from 28.5% in baseline to 92% after training; generalization 6 months later was nearly as high at 86%. The trainees surpassed a contrast group of fellow-patients, and ended up similar in problem-solving to normal staff members used for comparison (Foxx, Martella, & Marchand–Martella, 1989). It is of interest that the procedures followed for training seem reminiscent of methods first used with retardates and young children (see Rosenthal, 1979). Yet such guidance benefited adult victims of neurological trauma. Perhaps more *comparative* research on alternative tactics drawn from careful task analyses of the more common "troughs" of cognitive deficit from head trauma might suggest directions for further options to aid head injury patients.

Profound Deficits

Similar modeling techniques can help drastic cognitive handicaps as in autism and severe retardation, both congenital or traumatic in origin. The teaching strategy was pioneered by Lovaas (e.g., 1967) to expand symbolic skills in autistic children. The method divides the targeted response domain (talking; problem solving) into small, stepwise components and uses a combination of demonstrations by the trainer plus operant reward and chaining tactics (e.g., bites of food at mealtimes) to instate and refine competency. Further details are given elsewhere (e.g., Rosenthal, 1976, 1979). More recently, analogous cognitive retraining procedures have shown promise to maintain and restore symbolic skills in geriatric patents (see Baltes, 1988; Baltes & Lindenberger, 1988). Readers with special concerns about severe cognitive deficits should consult the papers mentioned earlier.

Especially when content is brand new (golf-swings for neophytes; language for infants; novel concepts with no roots in prior experience, such as tensor analysis for mathematical novices) or when a task strains the information-processing capacity of the learner (as with very retarded persons), a few points should be noted: Organizing stimuli into categories—rather than leaving cues discrete or randomly structured—is a basic feature of information processing by normal higher animals, even swamp sparrows (Nelson & Marler, 1989). In profound deficits, one must first create guidelines that group together, or separate, the teaching cues into categories. It is usually far more difficult to establish the rudiments and proper boundaries of new competence than to expand it from crude to fairly skillful levels. People think in terms of structured categories that are often organized around a few prototypes that epitomize the entire category. For example, hammer and screwdriver are prime instances of *tools,* roses of *flowers,* and doctor and lawyer of major *professions.* Hence, until such foundations are built, not much grasp of the task may be evident. The beginner keeps falling until some threshold is crossed, after which skiing or biking or skating continues largely upright. The autistic or severely retarded child may seem totally refractory to guidance until, "suddenly," the act or protoconcept begins to gel. The chronic psychotic or handicapped adult, who has been confined to custodial care at some poorly funded institution, may seem quite hopeless despite weeks of diligent training in which the core of the action or concept has been demonstrated for hundreds—or even thousands—of trials. At such times, the clinician may despair that the patient will even take the first steps and, even if taken, that the remaining distance demands too much teaching to be feasible.

In fact, if the first few members of some class of acts or knowledge can be set going, the remaining components (short of Olympic finesse) usually are added much more quickly. (It once took the senior author weeks of almost daily "growling lessons" during walks with an especially peaceful springer spaniel to get the dog to growl. After the first time he emulated the human model's growl, the dog began to growl spontaneously when appropriate.) However, due to the categorically and semantically organized nature of human cognition, discrete "bits" of an act or idea may seem senseless if taught as context-free elements. Generations of children never learned the piano because they practiced tedious scales in lieu of songs. Hence, teach naturalistic "chunks" whose pattern and value can be grasped quickly. Model skits, proverbs, and quips rather than ambiguous movements, piecemeal nonsense syllables, or unrelated vocabulary words to be learned by rote drill (Rosenthal & Downs, 1985). Even drudgery can be embedded in a more meaningful context such as a game-like format, a group "adventure," or can be tied to a familiar activity the observer enjoys and can perform. For instance, dessert, access to a toy or a music box, or any other relished treat could be put in a padlocked case with the correct response becoming the "magic wand" that unlocks the container for the trainee. Draw these morals: (1) *Persevere!* The course of radical new acquisition is downhill—not uphill—for tutor and learner.

(2) *Be alert!* Seek ways to hold attention and interest by "dressing" the task in a vivid, engaging context. (3) *Recenter to a social mode if solo efforts fail.* Dreary duties for one person may gain appeal if turned into a group project—witness fence painting in *Tom Sawyer* or the prevalence of husking bees to shuck corn before modern machinery.

Reducing Weight and Smoking

Obesity and tobacco use have proven stubborn problems. Despite repeated efforts to diet or quit smoking, relapse is painfully frequent. Pounds lost slowly by struggle can be regained with alarming speed and ease. Thus, maintenance programs (akin to Alcoholics Anonymous, Cocaine Anonymous, and Narcotics Anonymous to promote abstinence) may be crucial for food or tobacco "addicts" to continue in remission. In one careful study, a behavioral program was given to rather obese adults. Part of therapy for *all* clients covered aerobic exercises, as taught by therapist modeling and overt practice during sessions plus written directions. In addition, some clients received 26 biweekly lessons in personal problem solving from a clinician. Other clients faced the same biweekly contacts plus diverse forms of peer social support as a maintenance technique. A third group got biweekly contacts plus therapist-led exercise workouts at maintenance sessions. A final group was given it all: biweekly contacts, plus group social influence, plus exercise workouts. During the time of behavioral treatment, all groups lost about equal and substantial amounts of weight. After 6 months, all the with-maintenance groups surpassed the treatment-only controls in progress, and the contacts plus social influence plus aerobic workouts group lost more pounds than all others. However, by 12- and 18-month follow-ups, no discernible weight differences existed among groups given *any* kind of maintenance even though they all maintained weight loss far better than the treatment-only controls (Perri et al, 1988; also see Craighead and Blum, 1989).

Let us draw some parallels from the Ozer and Bandura (in press) empowerment study, to suggest other maintenance options that are open to empirical trials. It would be interesting to see if naturalistic group practice (e.g., at restaurants and clients' homes) in resisting caloric temptations, preparing and eating tasty, low-fat meals, and going to supermarkets as a group (or as pairs of "buddies") to monitor each others' purchases and to prompt detours around the cookie, candy, cheese, and cream counters would augment continued weight loss. A "recovering" sponsor (akin to AA tradition) who modeled gustatory restraint and who could promptly support a client when a craving struck might also be tested. Few obese people—nor those with other addictive problems—lack understanding of how to act in order to be abstinent. The real hazard is losing zeal amidst a protracted bout of resisting tempting cuisine. Perhaps cooperative efforts among the overweight might spur demand for a supermarket that sold most items at competitive prices but did not stock the fattening products of greatest concern (e.g., red meats, sweets, and snacks). Then, prototypes of rich edibles would not be present to undermine restraint. Computerized checkouts permit some amusing possibilities: "balloon-waisted" silhouettes of obese people; *danger* printed in red next to high-calorie items; a special checkout aisle for the diet conscious where a computer chides customers for taboo items, "Put it back before you buy it!" One might instead imagine a "social cost surcharge" taxing highly caloric foods in amounts beyond some set fraction of the total bill (analogous to taxes on alcohol and tobacco) as now technologically possible. Since the familiar excise taxes have not curbed drinking or smoking, a "calorie tax" would not aim to exile fattening foods from the grocery cart but to help society finance health programs.

Progress in ending smoking and preventing its relapse has also been discouraging. Several studies address a smoker's self-efficacy about giving up the habit. One promising option has been lowering the discomfort of cessation with mild doses of antidepressant medication, which can attenuate withdrawal symptoms (Edwards, Murphy, Downs, Ackerman, & Rosenthal, 1989), so that optimism rises about enduring quitting. Any interventions that raise confidence about getting and staying "clean" should improve outcomes, since people's self-efficacy about staying abstinent plays some mediating role in not smoking and is a powerful predictor of relapse (Condiotte & Lichtenstein, 1981). Thus, low confidence during follow-up among clients who stopped smoking strongly predicted later relapse and the concrete situations in which it took place (Baer, Holt, & Lichtenstein, 1986). Coping strategies to resist temptations decreased relapse, but exposure to companions who modeled smoking raised failure rates (Bliss, Garvey, Heinhold, & Hitchcock, 1989; Stevens & Hollis, 1989). Recent data on rural teenagers implicates modeling in the epidemiology of smoking. Positively valenced peers who smoked, plus little concern about the future, played divergent roles depending on gender and social subgroups. Some boys may have joined together *because* smoking and other "macho" conduct already begun may have drawn them to like-minded peers. In contrast, girls mainly smoked despite ample fear and may have used other harmful substances due to social pressures from admired companions (Mosbach & Leventhal, 1988). These results tell a cautionary tale: They highlight the power and complexity of social networks and sociopsychological factors in modulating problem behavior. Effective interventions to prevent youth from exploring and sharing addictive substances will need to penetrate more deeply the natural social environments and cohesive alliances of teenagers (see Morgan, Ashenberg, & Fisher, 1988). Naive media harangues to "Just say no!" and similar propaganda seem futile ways to allocate scarce resources in order to curb the use of tobacco and other chemicals of abuse.

Cancer

The word *cancer* strikes terror in many human breasts. However, the fear so aroused has failed to get women to examine their breasts regularly, although periodic breast self-examination (BSE) is a prime means to detect this frequent tumor in its early—and most treatable—stages. BSE is neither painful nor lengthy, but is quite boring; also, some women are embarrassed to scrutinize their breasts. Hence, much older research on ways to promote BSE proved discouraging (Rosenthal & Downs, 1985). One recent study, with a large college sample, compared three ways to promote BSE. A first component gave a lecture about breast cancer, the need for prompt detection, and how and why to execute BSE. A second component gave a demonstration of how to perform BSE using a foam rubber manikin. The last component was mailing or withholding monthly reminders (notes) to practice BSE. All combinations of components were tested for impact, but only the reminders raised self-reported BSE frequency; the demonstration did improve women's knowledge of the technique (Craun & Deffenbacher, 1987). In related work, hospital employees who attended a BSE program were followed up in two ways: Some only received biweekly prompts by mail. Beside those reminders, others also received biweekly visits at work from a researcher to spur them to perform a BSE and to offer verbal praise for so doing. A behavioral measure disclosed that personal contact follow-ups led to more BSE during the 6-month study, but compliance decreased over time in both conditions (Mayer et al., 1987). Perhaps no intervention can create better hygiene (whether BSE, exercise, or flossing teeth) *without* continuing efforts. (The law does not expect most drivers to keep their vehicles in safe shape *without* periodic inspections.) Yet the costs of health care and insurance to employers, and to society, comprise a large chunk of the Gross National Product. In an era of two-career families, one can envision some kind of health promotion arrangement at the worksite. The government, employers, and the insurance industry jointly might require regular exercise sessions (gratis, on released time) at which other relevant preventive checks (of BSE, flossing, weight loss) could be done. In exchange for those services and worker time, tax credits and lower insurance rates might compensate all parties by reducing health costs. Some corporation or institution needs to test, refine, and model such a mandatory system with its work force to show it can be cost-effective.

Demonstrations have helped to prepare patients for noxious but necessary procedures such as chemotherapy for cancer victims. The medicines induce nausea and vomiting, which often become anticipatory, generalize beyond what is inevitable, and greatly magnify emetic side-effects plus anxiety. Muscular relaxation and peaceful covert modeling before chemotherapy, and during the first few treatments, can reduce subsequent nausea and other symptoms as compared to control patients not prepared (e.g., Burish, Carey, Krozely, & Greco, 1987). A next study aimed to cut the costs of relaxation given by expert models. One set of chemotherapy patients was taught, as prior, by experienced clinicians. A second set observed nonprofessionals (who had taken a thorough course in teaching relaxation), a third group instead received audiotaped relaxation training, and a last, control group was not taught to relax. Only the patients trained by expert clinicians surpassed the controls in reducing anxiety, indices of autonomic arousal, and in better appetites after chemotherapy. The results seem to suggest that expert models are essential to lower emetic side-effects (Carey & Burish, 1987). Nonetheless, economy permits other options. Once the patient meets, and starts relaxation with, an expert clinician, the costs of subsequent contacts might be curtailed by showing videotapes of the same expert mentor conducting the more routine parts of training (e.g., with peer coping models). After the recorded sessions, there could be face-to-face contacts to let the clinician maintain personal rapport, answer patient questions, and so forth. Also, beyond relaxation training, guidance to generate coping cognitions (Meichenbaum, 1986) or to distract oneself from stressful covert scenarios and from focusing attention on negative cues (Rosenthal, 1980) could well be added to preparatory efforts and tested for yield. Thus, a videotaped coping model plus a movie to distract attention from body cues assisted the composure of patients undergoing hyperbaric oxygen therapy (Allen, Danforth, & Drabman, 1989). Likewise, there seems good reason to prepare spouses, parents, and other caretakers more adequately for the patient's potential distress and with ways to alleviate it. Far more could be done than is now customary to avert fear, helplessness, and painful surprises for the loved ones of people with cancer and other grave or terminal illnesses (see Johnson, Lauver, & Nail, 1989; Suls & Wan, 1989).

Surgery

Dating from the 1970s, a body of data exists showing that children facing diverse surgical and hospital procedures can profit from advance preparation through modeling. The general strategy is to depict—step by step—what will actually transpire from admission, while the child undergoes treatment, to eventual discharge (e.g., Melamed & Siegel, 1975). So long as modeled content is clear and reassuring, alternative formats have worked well. For instance, children facing oral surgery observed divergent modeling. Some watched an accurate scenario enacted by an animal puppet. Others either watched an accurate, or a somewhat inaccurate, scenario conveyed on film by a child actor. The modeling preparation was robust. All prepared conditions were judged as calmer than controls by parents, nurses, and raters both before and after surgery, but no noteworthy contrasts emerged among the modeling variations (Peterson, Schul-theis, Ridley–Johnson, Miller, & Tracy, 1984). These results may change with more drastic incisions or longer regimens. Hence, future research might target surgical techniques that especially trouble youngsters, and thereby strain hospital staff, to assess format differences that best curb emotional distress.

Adults who undergo major surgery also can benefit from careful preparation. Thus, a control group of male coronary artery bypass cases received the ordinary hospital orientation. Another group also saw a film depicting recovered cardiac patients recount their hospital experiences from admission to discharge. A last group received the orientation, saw the film, and then watched a program sketch the postoperative exercises (e.g., turning in bed, maintaining range of motion) that would occur in hospital. Both formally prepared groups reported less anxiety than the controls, were rated by nurses as less emotionally stressed than controls, and had a lower incidence of postoperative acute hypertension than controls, but the alternative preparations did not differ (Anderson, 1987). That both methods had a similar impact may stem from patients' main concerns being focused on surviving surgery (as depicted to each group by filmed peer models) rather than coping with postsurgery movements in the hospital. A more interesting design would be to compare preparatory modeling confined to inpatient procedures with broader guidance that also shows how recuperative cases can safely resume work, exercise, sex, and other normal activities as recovery progresses *after* discharge. Some combination of structured preparation (to allay the fears and misconceptions of most patients) *plus* individualized guidance tuned to idiosyncratic doubts and worries could surpass any routine set of messages.

Back and Musculo-Skeletal Problems

As people live longer, the chance of biomechanical injury and the need to consult a physiatrist or orthopedist keep growing; this makes behavioral techniques—modeling among them—germane. The pervasive complaint of back pain has led to some research efforts. In one, physical therapy groups (combining pain control, exercises, relaxation, and body mechanics) were compared to behavior therapy groups (discussion, role-playing, modeling, and rehearsing ways to abate pain). There were some advantages for each approach. The physical therapy improved bodily strength and motion and back-protection skills more than behavior therapy, which did reduce emotional distress slightly more. Yet both thrusts decreased pain complaints about equally (Heinrich, Cohen, Naliboff, Collins, & Bonebakker, 1985). Those data suggest combining the two spheres of guidance. Moreover, anyone who has tried to grasp motor sequences—for instance, how to perform stretching exercises—from printed material alone, even with diagrams, should be eager for videotapes to accompany the text and demonstrate how to enact the various movements. Likewise, modeling films to show caregivers how to massage a back patient seem an obviously useful and simple direction for study.

Modeling contrasts can assist assessment. Thus, videotaping back pain patients as they perform specific acts records pain at entry for judges to rate. Such overt motions covaried with self-report measures of discomfort. After inpatients were given pain management training (a composite of physical and behavior therapy techniques), later videotapes disclosed fewer signs of pain and reduced depression as movement improved (Romano et al., 1988). Perhaps the very acts that express pain can demonstrate what motions patients must change, as well as serving assessment functions. Preventive programs to foster movement hygiene and proper back care (e.g., for newly identified outpatients) using modeling films and related methods have scarcely been studied. Yet such options appear very promising directions for future work in primary and secondary prevention.

Recall that a person's level of self-efficacy to endure—or to persevere with—the events required by medical care can influence compliance, and hence, outcome (Bandura, 1990). By monitoring patients' self-efficacy to accomplish the concrete steps of preventive or treatment regimens, clinicians can assess the prospects that the person will tolerate, or comply with, therapy. When self-efficacy is low, one has early warning that further guidance is needed (Altmaier, Leary, Halpern, & Sellers, 1985; Hurley, 1987; McAuley, 1985).

Chemical Dependency

Apart from data that models can alter observers' consumption of alcohol, addiction is another sphere in which modeling options have been too little studied. There is evidence suggesting complex interactions between nature and nurture in alcohol abuse (see Akiskal, King, Rosenthal, Robinson, & Scott–Strauss, 1981; Rosenthal, Akiskal, Scott–Strauss, Rosenthal, & David, 1981). It is therefore refreshing to find a modeling study with a novel biobehavioral emphasis as was conducted by Chipperfield and Vogel–Sprott (1988). They studied the effects of a heavy- or light-drinking peer model on the alcohol consumed by college men who did versus did not come from a hereditary line with a history of problem drinking. When studied, the subjects did *not* differ in their imbibing habits. After observing a heavy-drinking model, the subjects with positive alcohol histories significantly increased their consumption (as measured by amount ingested and blood alcohol concentration) over what was drunk by peers shown a light-drinking model. Among students with negative family histories for alcohol, the pattern was similar but the difference between heavy- and light-drinking peer modeling was nonsignificant. Thus, modeling a large intake had stronger effects on those subjects from lineages where heavy alcohol use existed. These results illustrate how including biological markers may help clarify the impact of social modeling on more and less genetically disposed clients. Further diagnostic and therapeutic work on modeling factors in chemical dependency might emulate facets of this research strategy. For instance, the data are consistent with greater responsiveness by positive history subjects to demonstrations of both low and high drinking, which suggests social milieu tactics of special value to clients at hereditary risk for alcohol abuse, for example, early prevention support groups. Such directions seem well worth exploration.

Personal Tuning

Whatever risk factors must be reduced (or averted), probably no single strategy will suffice. Meaningful public health campaigns to promote apt self-regulation by the public will likely demand consistent messages and evolving reminders that stay fitted to the individual's needs and priorities (Rosenthal, 1984b; Rosenthal & Downs, 1985). Such a method for post-heart attack patients has been devised by De Busk (cited in Bandura, 1989) as a computer program. Depending on personal need, coronary patients can obtain guidance in dietary regimens to reduce weight or to lower cholesterol, modules for smoking cessation and stress reduction, and exercises to strengthen the heart. A single human coordinator can oversee the computer system to alter and maintain self-directed habit changes for many patients. The computer monitors their progress from data patients send the coordinator, who can make phone calls and offer personalized feedback and support. Periodically, the computer constructs a report for each client defining new subgoals to advance the next cycle of changes and depicting by graphs how much progress the person has attained. Thus far, reactions are favorable to De Busk's computerized risk-reduction program. Patients value its flexibility, which lets them control much of their own change toward recovery. More such research on self-steered, intensive, personalized, but economically feasible health-promotion options is badly needed.

Therapy Interventions

Removing and lowering maladaptive fears is the "classic" domain of therapeutic modeling. The more severe the fear, the longer it has been entrenched, and the more avoidant withdrawal away from meeting fear-laden cues it has spawned, the harder will be the clinical task. Otherwise, it seems to matter little whether specific monosymptomatic phobias (e.g., of heights or animals) or diverse performance anxieties (e.g., speaking in public, asserting oneself in social encounters) become the targets of change. In nearly all comparisons, participant modeling has been found more powerful than purely observational guidance, but both create viable gains (see Rosenthal and Bandura, 1978; Rosenthal, 1984a). Sometimes, one must facilitate participant modeling with verbal or physical (e.g., arm around shoulder or waist) encouragement, or with protective devices (safety lines and nets in treating height phobics; heavy gloves to convince snake phobics that a serpent cannot bite them) which are progressively removed as confidence mounts. It is often wise to supply cognitive aids that enhance the client's understanding of the treatment strategy.

Whether overt, symbolic, covert, or participant, the model(s) will start by first illustrating approach to the easy, low items of a task hierarchy while the clients observe. In nonperformance scenarios, after achieving successful approach, the model proceeds to the next-harder item, and so forth upwards through the task hierarchy, usually demonstrating some 8 to 16 trials per session. Actual performance efforts take place after treatment or between sessions *if* the client gains enough self-efficacy to attempt naturalistic approaches. In participant modeling, once an approach step is demonstrated, the client must perform it until successful and less fearful, before tackling the next task; it then is demonstrated and later attempted by the client, and so forth. At times, considerable clinical ingenuity is required to elicit approach from the anxious client. For instance, a youngster who is reluctant to emulate a model who peers down from a high, windy parapet may venture to attempt the task if allowed to use a video camera to record the vista that unrolls. In both nonperformance and participant modeling, clients with similar fears can often be treated in small groups *provided that* (1) no one is so fearful or (2) so iconoclastic that failure or panic becomes the dominant content. We will exemplify these principles in some detail, using research by Downs (née Davis) and colleagues (Davis et al., 1981).

The first study involved teenage girls who were screened to assure strong fear of spiders on a behavioral avoidance test. For individual treatment, half met live spiders, and the others faced toys which the girls were told to imagine as real. Participant modeling with live arachnids far surpassed using toys, and the live–toy contrast accounted for some 88% of the between-groups variance. Yet each treated group reduced fear significantly more than untreated controls. Within both live and toy conditions, some teenagers received a detailed rationale to explain how treatment worked, including a cartoon-like poster depicting the nature of participant modeling. Those adolescents significantly outperformed peers who were not given the rationale. Also, within each combination of conditions, the pacing of treatment was varied: One third of clients were treated *immediately* after intake for a block of 3 hours. A second group waited a week and then got a 3-hour block of *delayed* treatment. The remaining clients waited a week and then began *spaced,* 1-hour weekly sessions (3 hours total), as in conventional therapy scheduling. This pacing variation also led to significantly different gains in the order immediate > delayed > spaced. Eventually, the wait-list controls received a 3-hour block of group participant modeling with the rationale plus cartoon supplied. The girls took turns. One started, but all completed, each task before the next item was demonstrated and then attempted. Group fear reduction (at less cost per client) was as good as all but the strongest—live spider, with rationale, immediate pacing—combination of individual modeling conditions (Davis, Rosenthal, & Kelley, 1981). Thus, actual (real spider) versus facsimile (toy) stimulus, a clear rationale (Rosenthal & Downs, 1985), and rapid delivery of services (Rosenthal, 1980) all enhanced results, with group and individual modeling therapies proving comparable.

The institutional bathing regimen for the elderly in nursing homes was studied next. Baths for geriatric patients often bring grief to both residents and staff due to the whirlpool equipment. Since tub walls are high (at least 1 meter), patients cannot enter nor exit the tub alone. Usually, one straps the patient into a chair; a machine raises it high enough for feet to clear the tub. The chair is then lowered into water up to the patient's waist or chest for washing, and then lifted up and over the tub for the return journey. These baths are critical for personal hygiene and to relieve pain from geriatric ailments such as arthritis and bursitis, but many residents resist bathing. They show fear, may hurl insults at staff, or may struggle by flailing, kicking, and so forth. Therefore, the prospect of bath-time at a nursing home may trigger dread and acrimony for all concerned.

For assessment and therapy, the bathing routine was divided into 36 steps, some of which follow to illustrate the task hierarchy: #1 Patient leaves room for bathroom and #4 undresses (with or without help). Patient #5 enters lift chair, #6 lets straps be fastened and tolerates being lifted up, #8 from 0.15 to 0.30 m, #12 from 0.76 to 0.91 m, and #15 from 1.22 m to maximum height off floor. Patient tolerates #22 descent till foot is level with top of water, and then #25 immersion to midchest, enduring same #27 for 10–20 minutes until the sequence is reversed, the patient #34 is swung away from the tub, and #36 removed from the lift chair.

Group therapy was first tried with quartets of same-sexed elderly who were clad throughout all procedures. Some of the bath-resistant residents observed in groups while *filmed* peer coping models illustrated the steps of participant modeling, but treatment did not contain actual bathing. Matched peers instead took part in participant modeling. A tutor first described (e.g., "Now I will sit in the chair and put the strap on") and then demonstrated each step before asking residents to perform it, taking turns in Round Robin fashion. Both forms of therapy lasted a total of 4 hours. As expected, participant modeling reduced resistance to bathing much more than purely observational guidance. However, enactive group therapy had unforeseen drawbacks. One distressed man disrupted his group, limiting peer progress. Also, some kin were dismayed that a loved one was bathed with others, even of the same sex and not nude.

Therefore, the basic design was repeated with a larger sample of elderly women who were treated individually. The results were much as before, but without protests from residents or relatives. Filmed modeling decreased fears significantly below those of untreated controls. Participant modeling of equal duration was far more effective. Thus, filmed modeling allowed residents to be lifted some 0.3 m above the floor, that is, *below* the top of the tub, whereas participant modeling brought comfort at a height of over 1.0 meters, that is *above* the tub (Downs, Rosenthal, & Lichstein, 1988). Yet filmed modeling, the less costly method, aroused no complaints when given both in groups or individually, but did significantly reduce bath avoidance. Thus, one might study group filmed modeling (shown both to patients and kin) to pave the way for later participant group trials (see Downs, Rosenthal, & Lichstein, 1988). Also, more effort to involve relatives in the treatment process, to expand the scope of therapy to other geriatric problems (e.g., diminished socialization and recreational activities), and to improve the self-care and cognitive skills of aging persons (Baltes, 1988; Baltes & Lindenberger, 1988) all seem promising directions. Likewise, modeling could promote appropriate toileting (Burgio, Engel, McCormick, Hawkins, & Scheve, 1988), personal grooming, and social conduct for the elderly, as well as teaching caregivers.

Stress Abatement

A host of conditions—some known as diagnostic entities, and others "preclinical" warning signs and symptoms of biobehavioral duress—share in common that chronic stress has been draining and preoccupying the person. Much evidence confirms that prolonged stress can compromise immunocompetence and invite a myriad of psychiatric and somatic risks (Rosenthal & Rosenthal, 1985). Fortunately, stressful lifestyles seem responsive to many interventions that decrease the *cumulative* level of excessive demands burdening the person. Some sources of stress cannot be readily changed (e.g., intrinsic career or financial strains; death or major illness of a loved one). Nonetheless, if the therapist can help lower those stressors most amenable to change, the client may be able to accept whatever burdens remain (see Rosenthal & Rosenthal, 1985).

As an example, consider research with teachers who complained about negative physical (e.g., moistening lips and other "jittery" body movements; speech disfluencies) and emotional (e.g., tension and apprehension) reactions to the pressures of classroom duties. Two therapy conditions and a no-treatment control group were randomly formed. One strategy emphasized better understanding of stress and taught coping skills, including relaxation and rational restructuring of problems. The other intervention instead showed how to observe student behavior, identify problems therein, and structure incentives to encourage positive student conduct. Both treatments supplied live and videotaped models, role-playing, and task assignments to advance their respective goals. Each treated group surpassed the controls on symptom reduction as measured by self-reported distress, motor signs of anxiety shown in the classroom, and improved verbal reinforcement (more apt praise and less scolding) of students. Neither therapy was clearly better than the other (Sharp & Forman, 1985).

So often in clinical work, methods that seem distinctive prove roughly comparable to "skin the same cat." In the Sharp and Forman (1985) study, modeling advanced apparently divergent therapies, but both strategies diminished teacher stress. This may illustrate, (1) the principle that reducing some burdens makes the remainder more tolerable, or (2) that people generalize inferentially from a defined sphere—by reasoning, improved ability to detect trouble spots, and more self-efficacy about striving—to related spheres. Most likely, a combination of the two principles acts jointly. Note that principle elements of stress permeate and worsen many conditions, even when stress is not the main feature of the syndrome. The contributory and complicating role of stressful lifestyles is especially visible in the conditions marked by anxiety and phobic symptoms; these often require stress management as part of the total intervention (Rosenthal & Rosenthal, 1985).

Anxiety Disorders

Differences aside, in these cases apprehensive anticipation about dreaded events and self-referent brooding about one's own inability (or fragile ability) to control maladaptive reactions (e.g., fear and avoidance) worry the patient. Modeling methods have been most helpful with a number of anxiety disorders. Social phobia is a case in point.

Mattick and Peters (1988) studied participant modeling confined solely to avoidant *acts,* in contrast with also making maladaptive and catastrophic thoughts part of the treatment for social phobia. The subjects were adults in their thirties who greatly feared scrutiny by others. Hence, eating or drinking in company, signing one's name while watched, and entering public places were among the situations dreaded. None of these phobics lacked social *skills*. They knew what to do and say, but were inhibited by fears that constricted their lives markedly. Treatment took place in small groups for 12 total hours over an interval of 6 weeks. The pure approach group ignored cognitive strains and progressively visited more fearsome locales (similar to other participant modeling earlier described). The restructuring group was also helped to stop and recast their fearful thinking. They were taught to refute frightening assumptions (e.g., that experienced anxiety was patently visible to onlookers) and to revise their perceptions of how they looked to others and what was likely in social settings to more realistic expectations. Behavioral and self-report measures were obtained. Both treatments brought considerable progress, but results were clearly better when maladroit ruminations were part of therapy. Thus, at follow-up, the pure approach group finished some 60% of the avoidance task hierarchy, but the restructuring group finished over 80% of the hierarchy items. Likewise, 48% of the pure approach subjects remained avoidant in phobic situations, whereas only 14% of peers given the combined treatment were so hampered. The impact of negative self-referent thinking dominated a regression analysis: Fear of unfavorable reactions from other people was by far the most central mediator in social phobia.

In a sequel, the guided approach versus the cognitive restructuring components of participant modeling treatment were factorially compared. Outcome was better with cognitive restructuring included than when confined to tolerating graduated social situations. However, both versions of enactive modeling initially reduced social avoidance better than "pure" cognitive restructuring (which did have some minor advantages on rating measures). Over time, the pure approach group deteriorated a bit and the cognitive restructuring only group made some further gains. Hence, these "pure" groups differed little at follow-up. As before, the group combining participant approach trials with cognitive revisions was best, if less dramatically superior than in the prior study, but all treatments far surpassed wait-list controls. Once more, fear of negative evaluations from others was the main attitude-mediating social phobia (Mattick, Peters, & Clarke, 1989). Naturally, in clinical work we would take pains to resolve cognitive facets of the patient's woes as was done in the Ozer and Bandura empowerment research and the fear removal studies by Downs and colleagues, earlier discussed.

Perhaps efforts to separate cognitive from noncognitive elements of complex modeling (and other behavioral) therapies have reached sharply diminishing returns. Procedural advances may eventually permit more precise dissection of the symbolic and action facets of molar behavior. If so, such research would likely entail highly controlled laboratory methods and not occur as part of clinical trials. Instead, it seems wiser to study ways to strengthen useful existing techniques, rather than straining to untie the Gordian Knot. Sometimes, adding or deleting simple cues can bring large changes. For instance, switching from a secular to a sacred model (e.g., Jesus) can shift outcomes for devout patients (Rosenthal & Downs, 1985). Likewise, playing appealing music seems to aid in overcoming phobic responses (Eifert, Craill, Carey, & O'Conner, 1988). In contrast, efforts to sever the separate threads of interwoven treatment vectors have been unimpressive over the past decade.

Modeling methods can help panic disorder cases, and in the debilitating constriction of living imposed by agoraphobia. Among other antecedents, increased carbon dioxide, infusions of calcium lactate, and episodes of tachycardia can bring on panic attacks among predisposed patients. In one study, patients were taught to slow their heart rates by vagal innervation, slower abdominal breathing, and relaxation. The therapist demonstrated elements of guidance for patients to practice with favorable results: Thus, the symptoms of panic dropped 50% and frequency of attacks declined (Sartory & Olajide, 1988).

Agoraphobia is often incapacitating. It may restrict a patient's life to a tiny fraction of the activities and options otherwise possible. Even participant modeling trials that do help many agoraphobics typically bring little or no benefit to a substantial minority. Some treatment failures may occur because fearful people procrastinate, or "forget" to do assigned tasks, especially if they doubt ultimate success or fear the uncertainties that progress and a changed lifestyle would bring. Sometimes, social pressures weigh against gains, as when spouses encourage an agoraphobic's dependent adjustment pattern. Then, individualized graded approach may prove disappointing (e.g., Michelson et al., 1986). In studies on long-term follow-up of agoraphobia treated with and without spouse collaboration, advantages were found after 2 years for involving patients' partners in therapy (Barlow, Craske, Cerny & Klosko, 1989; Cerny, Barlow, Craske, & Himadi, 1987).

The merits of spouse participation and lower marital discord are shown in research by Arnow, Taylor, Agras, and Telch (1985). In order for an agoraphobic woman to take part, her spouse's involvement in treatment was required. All patients met DSM-III diagnostic criteria for agoraphobia with panic attacks. The women received some 12 hours of in vivo group participant modeling during a first week without their partners. The structuring and graduation of tasks to overcome agoraphobic avoidance is much like the hierarchies illustrated earlier with other fear problems. For example, patient(s) and therapist might begin in a familiar convenience store at an uncrowded time of day, and quickly buy some item near the entrance (i.e., close to the checkout counter). The tasks ascend to more shoppers present, more items obtained, and to purchases less accessible, for example, high up on shelves or at the back of the store. The hierarchy might then move to a large supermarket where the patient(s) must face deeper and longer entries into the store (a) for more items, (b) at busier times of day, and (c) with checkout lines of increasing length. Eventually, the patient would advance to other kinds of excursions, to more distant settings, and so forth.

After the first week of intensive group participant modeling, the patients and spouses met in small groups for 90 minutes weekly. The focus of sessions was implementing further home practice (personalized homework assignments) and removing any obstacles to compliance. This spouse practice phase continued for 3 weeks. Then patients were matched on amount of progress and, with their spouse, were assigned to couples' training, either in relaxation or in communication skills. The communications program spanned ways to formulate and clarify dyadic issues between partners and how to offer feedback constructively, and taught spouses some conflict resolution techniques.

The group participant modeling plus spouse-assisted homework practice created substantial symptom reduction, with wider mobility and range of activities, on both behavioral and self-report measures. The communications training raised positive and lowered hostile exchanges between partners. The women shown how to communicate also reported less fear and more solo excursions and made stronger behavioral approach gains than did matched peers instead given relaxation training with spouses. This differential pattern held after treatment and at follow-up 8 months later (Arnow et al., 1985).

The presence of living partners may confirm that loved ones really do encourage (rather than pay lip service to) positive changes and support patients' efforts to master homework tasks. Unlike the sample just discussed (where treatment *required* spouse involvement), some couples may disagree about the pros and cons of recovery. Not all partners value an independent mate, and may undercut or sabotage therapy aimed at raising patient autonomy. Hence, it is useful to assess *both* partners' attitudes about drastic progress early in planning treatment. Other group therapy data, from the depression area, also vouch for social cohesion and the ability to master demands as key determinants of therapy outcomes (Hoberman, Lewinsohn, & Tilson, 1988). It may prove essential to enlist crucial social partners, and to embed therapy in the patient's naturalistic home (or career or school or recreational milieu) if we are to achieve major stable gains in such stubborn syndromes as agoraphobic or obsessional avoidance. Similar points about the need to penetrate the real-life environments of severely handicapped patients were made over 20 years ago (e.g., Fairweather, Sanders, Maynard, & Cressler, 1969) but still have not been truly heeded.

The question arises if sheer proximity (exposure) to feared stimuli is the essential element in participant modeling, or whether guided mastery of a hierarchy of graded tasks is also critical. Obviously, any effective fear-removal technique must restore approach to (i.e., reduce avoidance of) the feared cues. However, overly abrupt or poorly dosed exposure need not quell fears; it might further sensitize a client to the phobic cues rather than neutralizing them (Rosenthal & Bandura, 1978). The facilitative role of restored mastery in improving self-efficacy and coping is elsewhere discussed in depth (Bandura, 1986). For an empirical test, some agoraphobics were exposed to feared tasks without therapist modeling or support. The therapist instead helped guided mastery clients perform hard tasks by giving encouragement and corrective feedback, as in usual participant modeling. For both groups, practice was held to just 1 hour. There were stronger anxiety reductions and self-efficacy gains for the guided mastery group. Furthermore, guided mastery brought added progress after a month's follow-up, unlike sheer stimulus exposure whose benefits declined across the same time interval (Williams & Zane, 1989).

Other Treatment Directions

In principle, virtually all groundless fears and their associated avoidance should be amenable to modeling treatments. Extensions to new arenas keep emerging. Here, we illustrate some of these opportunities with a pastiche of recent applications.

Eating disorders seem to have become epidemic among college-age women, whether spurred by contemporary stressors, merely reported more freely than in past years, or both. Many clinical efforts to remedy anorexia and bulimia have met limited success. More encouraging results were found with severe bulimics given a response-prevention plus guided task regimen. Before outpatient treatment, the women averaged 24 binge–purge episodes weekly. Most met criteria for some type of depressive diagnosis and disclosed that one parent or both suffered from maladjustment (mainly depression or alcohol abuse). Nearly half learned to purge from a friend or kin; others drew on models presented in media accounts of bulimia. During treatment sessions, the client ate some wholesome nondiet food to trigger moderate anxiety. Then, while waiting for her anxiety to decline, the therapist provided support, factual guidance, and fostered cognitive restructuring for false notions concerning calories, weight gain, and so forth. Once distress was lowered (usually within 45 minutes), the client was asked to eat the same food again *without* purging before the next session. Where indicated, a friend was recruited to monitor her in vivo practice. Most treated women made clinically noteworthy progress that persisted across a follow-up of over 60 weeks (Giles, Young, & Young, 1985). The foregoing method would allow for group or "buddy system" practice, joint eating to monitor each other's diet, help from natural interaction partners, teaching films, modeling by successful former clients, and a host of other variations that appear worth exploring. With college students, pairing obese with bulimic clients for mutual self-help (e.g., as part of an eating problems research project) offers potentialities, and a ready clinical population, for research.

Some serious diseases entail repeating noxious but necessary procedures. The traumatic effects of bone marrow aspirations and lumbar punctures for child cancer victims strain patients, parents, and hospital staff. A composite—largely modeling—approach was tested with youngsters (age range 3.5 through 7 years) selected for emotional distress and unruly behavior. Therapy was conducted before and during the bone marrow or puncture episode. The children learned a breathing exercise involving covert symbolic modeling, visualized a superhero (e.g., Wonderwoman) help them endure the discomfort, pretended to be a doctor who performed a bone marrow aspiration or lumbar puncture on a doll while a psychologist modeled coping responses for the doll, and then emulated the doll by breathing regularly and remaining calm. A filmed coping model who took events in stride was also shown. Finally, during the actual procedure, a parent coached the child to follow the foregoing guidance. This multiple thrust reduced distress among the small sample studied (Jay, Elliott, Ozolins, Olson, & Pruitt, 1985), results surely inviting more application and refinement.

Changing Misbehavior

Plentiful research, mainly with children, confirms that modeling can dispel aggressive conduct and the social retaliation it invites. Both unruly acts and poor self-control skills have been improved (Bandura, 1986). Such efforts are illustrated by a composite program that included modeling, role-playing, and corrective feedback. It helped very antisocial children reduce misbehavior and maintain progress at 1-year follow-up (Kazdin, Bass, Siegel, & Thomas, 1989). Unfortunately, too little work of this sort has been woven into the routine planning at settings that seek to rehabilitate delinquent or explosive persons. Most efforts remain limited to small samples and brief durations, as "demonstration projects" that often wither after researchers depart the institution.

For instance, inpatient adolescent boys at a psychiatric unit, selected for conduct problems, first watched a brief modeling film that depicted the "wrong way" to handle aggression. This orientation recruited boys for a voluntary 12-session program to control anger. Volunteers' responses to simulated annoyances were videotaped before and after training for rating by judges. Staff members also rated behavior on the ward that brought some disciplinary action. Then, anger control was taught by various modeling demonstrations and overt rehearsal methods. The youths learned to identify cues that trigger anger, to practice appropriate assertion in conflict situations, to edit their own incipient arousal, and to make plans to curtail it. They were shown other self-control options including relaxation. This anger-control program reduced violations and restrictions to one's room on the unit, reflecting fewer angry outbursts (Feindler, Ecton, Kingsley, & Dubey, 1986).

Another study emphasized the provision of problem-solving skills to conduct-disorder inpatient adolescents. Troublesome situations were selected by both staff and patients: for example, temper displays if a nursing tech wrongly accuses the adolescent of defacing bathroom walls. Problem solving was taught for thirteen 45-minute sessions via instructions, modeling demonstrations, practice by the youngsters, and then corrective feedback. Ample improvement in analyzing problems was found, with some transfer of the conciliatory cognitive strategies to conflicts arising in daily living (Tisdelle & St. Lawrence, 1988).

Naturally, efforts to change a wayward youngster will gain power if social partners and custodians—peers, parents, nursing staff, probation officers—are also taught to nurture desirable conduct. The reciprocal impact between guiding consumers and suppliers of services is not confined to unruly delinquents. The training of health professionals offers many cases in point. For example, women sometimes complain about overly rough or bumbling ministrations by fledgling gynecologists giving pelvic examinations. To rectify such protests, a two-pronged modeling strategy prepared medical students to conduct pelvic exams. A group of model patients were intensively trained to aid neophytes by sharing their reactions and providing feedback while a student performed the exam. Before examining the model patients, a videotape was played in small groups to convey the inner thoughts and emotions of a young woman before and during an exam given by a student. Stream-of-consciousness narration accompanied the events in order to externalize the covert reactions of both the model patient and the student doctor. Thus, a female voice expressed concerns about the appearance of her undergarments and possible body odor, as well as worries about the student (e.g., "He looks young—I hope he knows what he's doing"). The film reduced student worries about their next pelvic exams, as did guided practice with the model patients (R. Rosenthal et al., 1980). Teaching scenarios and simulations of these sorts have many applications for preparing trainees to care for, manage, or discipline clinical populations. We turn now to teaching efforts that can supplement or augment therapy, and at times comprise intervention.

Parent and Caregiver Education

The transition to prophylactic education is eased by starting with conduct-disordered children. Various directions have been explored to create prosocial changes. In one study, the problem child and mother met for nine weekly sessions with a therapist who demonstrated positive parent-child exchanges; these work samples were then role-played by mother and child with corrective feedback from the teacher. An alternative tactic supplied the same amount of training to groups of mothers but *without* participation by their youngsters. The parents observed both exemplary and faulty adult-child exchanges by means of a modeling tape; it was followed by group discussion to clarify the requisite parenting skills. As compared to wait controls, each trained condition benefited, both from less deviant conduct by children and from better parenting by mothers. There were *no* differences between the less-costly videotape training format and the live mother-child dyad format (Webster–Stratton, 1984).

A later experiment was broader in scope and enlisted fathers as well as mothers of children with conduct problems. Some parents received modeling videotapes plus therapist-led group discussion much as previously. Another variation skipped group discussion and feedback but supplied the same videotapes for self-administration by parents. The last training condition omitted the videotapes but maintained the same therapist-led group discussions. Home observations disclosed that the children of trained parents surpassed controls in improved behavior, with few outcome differences among the training methods. In terms of patient satisfaction, immediate advantages were found among mothers given all the treatment elements, which also led to more reports of child improvement than any other variation. However, after a year, group discussion alone caught up to the full treatment parents; both conditions reported more satisfaction than their videotapes-only counterparts (Webster–Stratton, 1989). It would be interesting to compare satisfaction if the videotapes method also allowed telephone access to a counselor who could answer questions, clarify ambiguities, and provide support at modest cost, similar to De Busk's treatment coordinator described earlier. Likewise, parent training might improve if spouses were conjointly treated for marital strains that difficult progeny often intensify and then exploit by playing one parent against the other (Jacobson, Holtzworth–Munroe, & Schmaling, 1989).

Efforts to help family caregivers of very refractory cases have met some success. Guidance in solving problems and coping with stress was fused with social support and heightened access to community resources. This omnibus training for 12 total hours was given to some—but withheld from other—relatives who care for schizophrenics. The trained kin claimed less anxiety and personal distress and improved management of home life, as compared to control caregivers (Abramowitz & Coursey, 1989). Family members who tend frail or impaired elderly relatives also can suffer strains from those continuing duties. Educational efforts have lightened such geriatric burdens. Thus, a comparison of alternative classes that respectively emphasized increasing pleasant respites versus improving problem-solving skills brought equal gains to caregivers. After 10 weekly 2-hour sessions, both classes showed less stress and depression plus enhanced morale (Lovett & Gallagher, 1988).

In related work, ministering relatives were taught new ways to handle handicapped senior citizens, with positive results. It seems ironic that caregivers' training largely was based on modeling, practice through role-playing, and corrective feedback; in contrast, they were taught to use operant reinforcement tactics with their elderly kin (Pinkston, Linsk, & Young, 1988). Yet evidence shows clearly that social feedback with correction is more efficient than purely incentive operations, even for the brain injured (e.g., Lewis, Nelson, Nelson, & Reusink, 1988). Also, strong data confirm that consistent agreement among mentors and messages promotes better grasp of the prototypes that comprise the foundations of new learning than is conveyed by more variable guidance (e.g., Zimmerman & Blom, 1983). Hence, if caregivers are guided via modeling, they might well learn modeling approaches to care for their elderly charges. Similar concerns arise from efforts to teach nursing staff to manage tough cases, for example, incontinent geriatric inpatients (Burgio et al., 1988). Despite the contributions of operant technology, much room for improvement remains. Modeling strategies, as earlier illustrated (Downs, Rosenthal, & Lichstein, 1988), can assist impaired oldsters and deserve further exploration in residential contexts.

The advantages of exemplary guidance were validated in cross-community research. The aim was to disseminate novel job-seeking skills at inpatient units that served substance abusers. Some settings were only sent printed material, both to introduce the job-finding program and to give detailed instructions about how to conduct it. Other settings received the same printed content but also were invited to send a delegate to a 2-day conference (all expenses paid) to assure further face-to-face diffusion of job-hunting knowledge for the representatives selected. The remaining units were given the printed material plus a 1-day on-site workshop in how to implement the job-seeking program; this means of dissemination was akin to participant modeling for the staffs visited at their units. The on-site guidance created significantly greater adoption (28.1%) of the jobs program than the conference option (19.4%), or just the printed information (3.7%). The units given either form of social guidance were more satisfied with the research program than were their counterparts only sent the printed messages (Sorensen et al., 1988). Parallel conclusions resulted from a field study testing ways to teach college-level content to grammar school children in their classrooms. Those who received modeling demonstrations learned more and enjoyed their lessons better than did peers given the same information but through a mainly lecture-like format (White & Rosenthal, 1974).

CONTRAINDICATIONS TO MODELING APPROACHES

Modeling is not a panacea. Sometimes, attempts are made that simply fail to work. Other times, technical errors can attenuate or nullify the value of guidance. A common example entails adding a weak or redundant element to an intervention that is already working pretty well. Thus, cumbersome written content failed to augment a parent training program that might have profited from videotaped demonstrations (Calvert & McMahon, 1987). Another problem arises when verbal narration is joined to exemplary modeling without careful pilot testing. Less can be more. Often the extra words will add no benefits (Weinstein, 1988). At times, the narration may even reduce acquisition or transfer: Neither the impact of verbal supplements, nor the knowledge to be gleaned from "easier" versus "harder" versions of a learning task, need be intuitively apparent until empirically assessed. Hence, it is often necessary to measure the trade-off between adding information relative to interference with attention or storage when devising modeling programs (see Rosenthal & Zimmerman, 1978 for a fuller discussion). There is no substitute for pilot work in order to tune some message to an audience of patients or trainees.

A practical guideline is that if a message in narrative form can be readily grasped and executed, demonstrations will add little and will not prove cost-efficient. Reciprocally, when information is not easily processed (or implemented) from oral or written instructions, demonstrations will enhance learning or performance. Thus, sometimes grade school children have parsed a concept from narration just as well as when the principle was exemplified. Yet, with other concepts that did not seem very hard to attain, college students were much aided when illustrations were provided (Rosenthal & Zimmerman, 1978).

There are no analytic yardsticks to specify in advance how much complexity will hamper narrative transmission. Let us epitomize the issues with two different rules. First: For every set of items presented to you, always pick the green item or object. Few if any readers will fail to follow the rule consistently. Nor will added illustrations enhance understanding. Now consider a second rule: Some words have the sound of letters of the alphabet, such as *be* and *bee* for the letter *B*. How many consecutive letters of the alphabet can you list by such English words (no proper nouns) that are two (e.g., *be*) or three (e.g., *bee*) letters in length?

Although most adults can grasp this concept fairly easily, many readers will be helped by the following model list that:

I = eye & aye	N = en
J = jay	O = owe
K = cay	P = pea
L = el & ell	Q = cue
M = em	R = are

A collegiate or unabridged dictionary should verify that we did not cheat in "unpacking" the letter/homonyn word rule. Ask and answer for yourself: How many consecutive letters would you have scored without the model list to help decipher the rule?

Note that all the contraindications to modeling mentioned so far only involve issues of cost-efficiency or clarity. Indeed, for all the clinical and educational applications thus far discussed, there are no obvious dangers. It is more a question of devising a modeling format that will capture a client's attention and transmit the intended message with reasonable fidelity. For very young or deficient learners, many repetitions using the simplest possible stimuli *that still capture attention* (versus boring or satiating the learner) may be essential. This sanguine view of potential hazards in using modeling techniques refers to the *prosocial* demonstrations and guidance dealt with thus far in this chapter.

Indeed, civic dangers loom larger for commercial television than for clinical modeling. Merchants selling viewing time have edited events to please sponsors and to exploit or lull an unwary public. Viewers accustomed to "news" have instead observed reality simulated or recreated to boost ratings and, hence, profits. Such media practices could reduce people's concern and ability to separate fact from fiction. Therapeutic modeling does present hazards when content shifts from prosocial to punitive.

Caution is required for aversive scenarios (or those that, by contrast, leave the client with a relative deficit or loss). Although none of the noxious modeling methods to be discussed next has, to date, brought noteworthy side-effects to clinical patients or research subjects, such aversive modeling is best considered an option for clinical research. Until further validated and studied, it should not be dispensed in the guise of routine or customary services.

MODELING NASTY EVENTS

We may regret the existence of violence and cruelty but cannot deny that they infringe on much of current living. Every day, the mass media flaunt highjackings, "wilding," and other wanton mayhem both factual and fictional. Too often, emphasis is put on the savage acts performed. Too rarely are the pain and lasting consequences for victims given enough attention. No simple relationship exists between enduring aggression and later engaging in deviant conduct that invites retaliation by the community. Yet research confirms that modeling influences can encourage negative emotions and hostile acts (Bandura, 1986; Heath, Bresolin, & Rinaldi, 1989). For instance, children who are neglected or abused show increased risk for delinquent, violent, and criminal behavior in the future (Widom, 1989). Consequently, it is no surprise that society and clinicians consider aversive sanctions to stop misconduct, despite ethical debates (Bernstein, 1989) and realistic doubts about the value of punishment procedures *unless* temporary suppression of unwanted behavior is exploited to teach new, effective, and positive behavior to replace it. The social control pressures at issue invite steep costs for the society and the wrongdoer. This is illustrated by some efforts to "tame" aggressive acts through irreversible surgery. Thus, a bilateral amygdalotomy was performed to curb intractable rage reactions, with evidence that the patient's autonomic reactivity was reduced after surgery (Lee et al., 1988). Still, one hopes the method will not become the norm for disposing of criminals in the 21st century. Compared to procedures so drastic and invasive, modeling techniques seem highly desirable and humane substitutes. In two main spheres, modeling noxious events holds out applied promise: to shift existing personal criteria or expectations; to inhibit or punish the observer in order to assess stress-reactivity or to disrupt maladaptive habit patterns.

Changing Customary Standards

Many circumstances alter our familiar assumptions and prototypes by exposing us to events remote from usual experience. In the context of an awesome disaster, a less severe calamity may be perceived as relatively minor, and much less dire than without the disaster setting one's frame of reference. As a bridge to prosocial modeling, it may be that the same demonstration or message will constitute positive modeling for one audience, but will shake the yardstick of judgment for another. For example, consider some anecdotes about a legless RAF pilot reported by the late actor, David Niven (1975, p. 39). The war hero, Group Captain Bader, was sent to motivate fellow casualties with similar losses as a positive coping model who had triumphed over adversity:

> He had come out to tour the hospitals and encourage hundreds of double amputees who were wondering what the future could possibly hold for them. He did untold good recounting to them his own story of bailing out over France, where he buckled

one of his artificial limbs. The German commandant of the prison camp was so impressed by Bader that it was agreed . . . one Spitfire could fly over the camp and drop him a new leg. When the leg arrived, Bader thanked the commandant, put it on, and that night escaped. At dawn he was recaptured, hobbling gamely along ten miles from camp. Thereafter both his legs were taken from him at night and locked up in the guardroom [i.e., till morning].

For the audience of double amputees, Bader was a hopeful model. What about an audience with less drastic injuries? Might they take Bader's example as a spur to reduce worry about, and pity for, themselves and their futures? Some evidence suggests that such contrast effects can and do occur. When White (1975) conducted a series of field studies feigning very extreme altruism as the dominant campus norm, college students shifted their opinions (with no real response costs) toward greater generosity about how much they should donate to help the disadvantaged. There were no boomerang effects away from the extremely charitable anchor standards.

However, in other work using *aversive* stimuli, results were different. When two noxious models were presented, contrast effects were found: It appeared that the worst events reduced how badly the other negative events were judged (Rosenthal, Rogers, & Durning, 1972). In essence, the most horrid alternatives drained the competing options of some of their negative impact if presented by themselves. Likewise, great good fortune (e.g., winning a lottery) can afterward spoil smaller rewards, just as exposure to the strains that characterized life in harder times has led observers to count more blessings than were perceived when judgments lacked any harsh comparison standards (see Rosenthal, 1980).

Data of these kinds prompted research to test whether unassertive college students would act with greater firmness if provided models more submissive than themselves. Matched for initial assertion, several conditions were studied. One group was exposed to an *extremely* submissive model who, on a date with an attractive partner, could not turn away an intruder. The intruder "cut in" and "captured" the date. The hapless model skulked off, embarrassed and miserable, but totally unable to confront the intruder. Other groups observed a model who was *somewhat more* or *no more* submissive than themselves, and the final group did not get any comparison modeling. Directly afterward, the client was asked to defy a feisty telephone adversary, who was actually a confederate trained to thwart assertive attempts by harassing the client through standardized obstructions. On various behavioral measures, students given the extremely submissive model far surpassed all other groups in assertive behavior (Hung, Rosenthal, & Kelley, 1980). These basic findings were later replicated (Hung, 1979). In both Hung's studies, the initial advantages of extremely submissive (strongest contrast) comparison models were not maintained when all clients were eventually given therapy to promote self-assertion. However, swift capitalization on the courage raised through contrast modeling (see Davis, Rosenthal, & Kelley, 1981) might stabilize enhanced assertiveness if prompt overt practice brought confirming experiences. Once forceful conduct was enacted safely, clients should increase self-efficacy about assertion in the future.

More generally, the research on contrast modeling suggests that encounters with others who are much worse off may serve a viable role in treatment development. What is called for is to bring the victim of negative self-perceptions into contact with people who are far more disadvantaged, under safe conditions. The client would then be aided to try more adaptive new responses that could be rewarded and expanded while minimizing hazards and failures.

It seems likely that learning about what others have overcome, and their mishaps en route (e.g., to achieve sobriety), is part of the benefits wrought by Alcoholics Anonymous (Alford, 1980) and the programs offered by similar support groups. In all, the extant evidence invites more study of comparison modeling as a way to change self-defeating assumptions and expectations. Providing anchors "worse off" than the client would not, of course, comprise all of treatment. It might help "prime the pump," by goading refractory cases to attempt the early steps of a behavior change plan faster than they would otherwise.

Also, it is interesting to conjecture about the potential role of contrast anchors for evaluating the behavioral effects of pharmacotherapy. If the lifestyle realities facing a patient stay constant, and response to well-studied contrast anchors shifts as the drug is absorbed or its dosage increased, the alteration in perceived contrast might act as a yardstick of drug efficacy. For example, imagine that some greatly depressing modeling scenarios are shown before and after the administration of a new thymoleptic. If the drug does reduce despair, the patient should perceive more relative advantage or well-being (greater contrast with the standard) as the chemical takes effect. Given normative assessment research, a reasonably nonintrusive and inobvious strategy to measure how psychoactive medications change phenomenology for the patient might be devised and calibrated. Moreover, the judgment responses could be made nonverbal, through selection of happier-to-sadder or mellow-to-angry stimuli graduated on a computer display, rather than relying on self-reports exclusively. It is odd that no standardized assembly of tasks as yet exists to weigh the subjective effects of pharmaceuticals. Differential contrast measures might be a useful part of such an enterprise.

Stressful Modeling

Let us first consider altering (rather than evoking) response to stressful cues. Suppose that a noxious event occurs. Even if the direction of qualitative reaction is toward distress, the quantitative degree of appropriate conduct often is unclear. Sometimes, exposure to a comparison model can lead people to question the magnitude of their own responses as too great or too weak. When Hamlet (Act 3, Scene 1) watches an actor pretend grief over the plight of the long-deceased Queen Hecuba, he berates himself for his timid stance, as compared to the model's:

What's Hecuba to him, or he to Hecuba, that he should weep for her? What would he do, had he the motive and the cue for passion that I have? He would drown the stage with tears and cleave the general ear with horrid speech, make mad the guilty and appall the free, confound the ignorant, and amaze indeed the very faculties of eyes and ears. Yet I, a dull and muddy-mettled rascal, peak like John-a-dreams, unpregnant of my cause, and can say nothing.

Likewise, sometimes a model's precedents can help calibrate the intensity with which punishing cues will be perceived and dealt with. The influence of models' demeanor to modulate the strength of observers' affective reactions to pain stimuli has been confirmed by Craig and his colleagues in a continuing research program. Much of the earlier work is summarized elsewhere (Craig, 1978). In a current experiment, undergraduate women were selected for initial tolerance to shock-induced pain. Some were then retested alone, and others in the company of a peer who was more, less, or equally resistant to the shocks. Divergent social partners shifted pain thresholds, but students who at first were very distressed raised their tolerance after habituation to repeated shock experiences, regardless of the modeling supplied (Prkachin & Craig, 1986).

There is evidence that both healthy and chronically ill persons coped with sickness as had their parents. If parents had avoided work when ill or in pain, their offspring were more likely to avoid duties than did the children of parents who had been more stoic when faced with adversity (Turkat & Noskin, 1983). Concurrent modeling can also shift tenacity. Subjects given noxious pressure to a finger kept working on tasks longer if exposed to a pain-tolerant model than to a model who quickly surrendered to discomfort (Turkat, Guise, & Carter, 1983).

Not too much has been done to exploit the clinical applications of stoic modeling (nor to promote freer self-expression by alexithymic patients). One would think that applications would abound for raising endurance to distress. Perhaps rehabilitation and chronic pain treatment services might choose the more stalwart or pain-resistant patients to serve as exemplary mentors for less steadfast peers. Particularly when a therapy (movement practice, graduated exercise regimens, anti-inflammatory medication) entails considerable delay before progress is evident, more advanced patients at several stages of recovery might be routinely involved. They could share their attainments over time with new and recent admissions. In some settings, a "senior" helping "junior" patient buddy-system could be evolved. Thus far, the focus has been on demonstrations that enhance or diminish reactions to overtly noxious stimuli. We next turn to the creation of stress by means of modeling.

Vicarious Arousal

Persistent emotional responses have been established by witnessing another person's distress. This emotionality can be achieved without observers having *any* firsthand contact with the noxious stimuli whose effects the model portrays. Through mediating processes, perceiving someone else's duress suffices to bring on nervous system reactivity akin to direct experience with aversive sensations. Most older research that verifies arousal elicited by modeling is discussed elsewhere (e.g., Rosenthal, 1976, 1979). Our present emphasis is to offer some guidelines for staging noxious modeling displays. For this purpose, we shall examine in some depth one of the first clear instances of vicariously created emotional arousal.

When a naive male subject reached the test room high up in the Stanford Medical Center, another male student (actually the confederate model) also arrived just before or after. The experimenter announced that, by random selection, the model had been assigned to the "pain emotion" condition and the subject to the control group. To assure that an impression of suffering was conveyed to observers, the model had been trained with a few real shocks. Those exemplars aided the model to grimace vividly and depict realistic arm-spasm when the pseudoshock occurred. The visual pain cues were enhanced by means of a pursuit rotor—a turntable with a target on which a stylus was to be placed—assigned to the model as a cover task. When a shock was "delivered," the loosely hinged stylus would leave the turntable and "whiplash" while the model's arm thrashed in pain. These arrangements transmitted a powerful image of shock-induced distress to the observer, who was positioned and instructed to maintain alert attention throughout.

In fact, after initial training before the study, the actual signal to the model was a CS buzzer. It sounded just prior to the ostensible shock, and soon afterward the model flexed his arm, "whiplashed" the stylus, and dropped it. These procedures effectively conveyed the perception of pain to subjects who saw the model's feigned distress. As measured by GSR (galvanic skin) responses, the observers' GSRs rose sharply from baseline (after adaptation)—both during probes amidst acquisition, and also in an extinction phase—when the CS buzzer was sounded and the observer was tested without witnessing the pain cues. The few students who did not manifest vicarious arousal reactions stated that, in essence, they strove actively to interfere with the noxious modeling routine. For instance, one man reported that "I finally just tried to think about the girl I slept with last night; it kept my mind off those damn shocks." Thus, once the buzzer became a cue portending the model's "suffering," the subjects' GSRs grew similar to the reactions expected if they themselves were to experience the impending shock (Bandura & Rosenthal, 1966). With undergraduate women, a similar modeling routine, but omitting the pursuit rotor, created heart rate increases in observers greater than those of peers who received actual shocks, or imagined being shocked (Rosenthal, Rosenthal, & Chang, 1977).

Concordant results have emerged in recent research using covert modeling scenarios to develop two new psychosocial stressors. One task requires the subject to rank order 10 items drawn from the Holmes and Rahe (1967) social readjustment rating scale. After items are ranked, the subject visualizes in turn the third-worst, second-worst, and then the most noxious event. The other task entails eight realistic, but unavoidable, everyday situations that might place a person under stress. The subject must read, and vividly ponder, each aversive vignette. Examples of some of the items comprising the new stressors are presented in the box.

HOLMES–RAHE VISUALIZATIONS (H–RV) TASK

Items to Rank-Order and Imagine

1. Jail term
2. Fired at work
3. Divorce
4. Death of close friend
5. Death of close family member
6. Personal injury
7. Illness of loved one
8. Death of spouse
9. Marital separation
10. Foreclosure of mortgage or loan

Alternate Items from Your Everyday Life Pressures (YELP) Scale

1. Your favorite star is coming to town for only one performance. Some other people are keen to go. They offer to pick up the tickets. You all plan to meet before the show. You are right on time, but the others aren't. You wait and wait. The show is sold out. There's no way to get in without the tickets. The others finally come very late. A lot of the show is over but they don't seem to care.

3. Very special loved ones plan and save for years to build a home in the country. The time comes to start. You promise to keep a photo record for them, from the ground breaking until the house is all done. Your loved ones are thrilled. For months you take scads of pictures to trace the growth of their home. At last it is finished. You turn in many rolls of film to be developed. Somehow they get lost. The people at the photo lab search and search but they can't find your pictures. They tell you they're very sorry but all they can do is give you new rolls for the lost film.

5. You see two teenagers knock a lady to the ground, snatch her purse, and run off. You go to help her and tell her you had a good look at the thieves. Later on they are caught and you must be a witness at the trial. You have to come to court on quite a few days because they keep postponing the case. Finally, the judge lets the thieves off with a slap on the wrist since they are underage and don't have police records.

7. You feel very close to a young lady relative. She was a wonderful, sweet, popular child. You have watched her grow into a lovely and gifted woman. She won a scholarship to a good college, where she is starting her third year and doing fine. Everyone in the family is proud of her. Then her parents contact you. They are heartbroken. She has gotten mixed up with a married man. He has a criminal record for dealing in drugs. She says she is going to drop out of college and run away with him. It looks like her whole life will be ruined. Her parents beg you to talk some sense into her. You go to see her and try your best, but get nowhere. She tells you she is pregnant and insists she won't leave the man she loves.

Adapted from Rosenthal et al., *Behavior Therapy* (1989).

In a set of comparative studies, both stressors were rated as nastier than a number of competing stimuli. Next, the psychosocial tasks were pitted against more familiar research stressors and fared well: On heart rate and EMG measures, the psychosocial tasks generally led to greater arousal than doing mental arithmetic problems under time pressure. The new stressors also proved not much weaker than, or comparable to, cold pressor (immersing a hand in ice water as long as possible) stimulation (Rosenthal et al., 1989). Hence, the data suggested that, in the future, such modeling options might serve a useful role for studying stress-reactivity and how responses to stress relate to symptomatic status in various illnesses.

In Pavlovian terms, the evidence reviewed has found that noxious modeling can serve as an effective UCS to engender emotional arousal. Can that vicariously conditional emotionality be used to disrupt undesirable habits for clinical purposes?

Vicarious Aversion Therapy

A number of efforts have sought to replace overt with vicarious punishment, or to reduce direct aversion trials by combining a few overt punishments to clients with multiple vicarious substitutes. A diversity of modeled stressors can inhibit troublesome behavior. For instance, an in vivo treatment for sexual exhibitionists required the patient to visit the clinic and expose himself while persons who knew him jeered at his perverse conduct. Some patients refused the social taunting experiences, and others were excluded due to risk of psychosis or medical complications. Instead, these exhibitionists observed videotapes of peers who did endure aversive taunting trials, and were also taught how to nullify tempting cognitive and affective cues to expose. In a case series followed up over considerable time, the aversive modeling tactics proved successful with the few patients studied (Wickramasekera, 1976). Replication of this work is invited.

Two controlled experiments with severe nail-biters have compared in vivo peripheral electric shocks with symbolic facsimiles. A single-session procedure delivered eight painful shocks to the wrists of some clients. Other clients instead imagined the shocks (via "covert sensitization"). The last group watched a trained peer model enact the aversion trials. All treatments reduced symptoms on behavioral measures of nail growth, and on self-reports about ease of resisting the habit, but there was no hint that overt surpassed modeled or imagined pain to suppress biting (Rosenthal, Rosenthal, & Chang, 1977).

A next aversion study administered punishments across four sessions in a group context. Some nail-biters covertly visualized shocks to themselves on every trial. Another group witnessed a model apparently receive shocks on every trial. The last, "Hotseat," condition combined a partial shock schedule with observation of peers, group cohesion, and stressful anticipation. Each client present was unforeseeably given one or a few shocks per session, and watched different peers shocked on the other trials in a randomized sequence. This unpredictable format consistently led to the strongest habit disruption. The purely vicarious shock clients showed the next-best outcome changes. In contrast, the imaginal aversion group only changed marginally, and no-treatment controls did not improve over baseline (Rosenthal et al., 1978).

Despite some logistical difficulties (scheduling, more complex apparatus demands), the "Hotseat" concept—which minimizes overt punishment, apart from the few prototypic jolts each client endures, and capitalizes instead on shared social modeling—seems worthy of further exploration. For example, multiple session group aversion therapy has been tested to stop cigarette smoking. The noxious stimuli are typically delivered to all clients on all trials (e.g., Walker & Franzini, 1985). Perhaps a "Round Robin" format, with the noxious sensations rotated among direct and vicarious cues might reduce the risks of attrition and physiological hazard without impairing the power of treatment.

Aversive modeling has also assisted problem children. Observing video-taped peers deal with sibling conflicts peaceably, or instead receiving a scolding and "time-out," plus watching mother role-play with dolls the "time-out" rules that similar infractions would bring the culprit, reduced in vivo aggression toward siblings at home (Olson & Roberts, 1987). Temper tantrums in public can be audiotaped and replayed later when deterrants are more readily supplied (e.g., Rolider & Van Houten, 1985). Thus, it may be that some combination of overtly noxious events plus self-modeling playback of former punishment episodes could lower the number of direct aversive transactions. There is evidence showing that *consistent* modeling and feedback, whether rewarding or punishing, steer children's conduct better than do "mixed messages" from adults (Acker & O'Leary, 1988; Zimmerman & Blom, 1983). Yet few institutions, if any, that care for conduct-disordered youths seem to devise or apply structured programs to "thin" punitive sanctions by vicarious substitutes.

Indeed, the beneficial potentialities of negative modeling more often appear accidental than rationally organized. People who have observed the painful costs of forgetting automobile restraints or safety seats for infants (e.g., in surgical and rehabilitation settings) are conscientious about using the devices. Not many physicians who treat cancer and other pulmonary diseases are tobacco smokers. Therapists who serve patients with chronic back pain often become more careful about their own body mechanics, and stop inviting preventable injuries (e.g., the consequences of lifting heavy loads). Such cautionary tales are legion, but little is typically done to harness negative modeling examples for prophylactic purposes, even in spheres where the prudent acts—as with donning seatbelts or checking the readiness of smoke alarms—need not overcome strong opposing habits. We anticipate that more use can and will be made of vicarious aversion tactics in the future.

WHAT NEXT?

It is fitting to close this chapter with a glimpse of new vistas. Historically, two practical obstacles limiting modeling procedures have been (1) the cost and technical complexity of devising and staging or representing the guidance scenarios for the audience of observers, and (2) it has been even less feasible to adjust generic scenarios to fit idiosyncratic needs and preferences, except by the covert cognitive refinements or embellishments that individual observers might bring to the theaters of their minds. Technology is now amidst a revolution that can overcome these barriers: With the explosive growth of computer graphics, people have vast new capacities to externalize their covert images. A myriad of insights and fantasies—scientific as well as artistic—can be depicted vividly as faithful representations and epitomes of the ideas that spawn them (e.g., Ward, 1989). In turn, computer simulations can then serve as models to steer new behavior—both conceptual and practical—as well as to correct former errors. In principle, neurosurgeons can perform trial "dry runs" of operations on a particular brain before the actual incision is made. Facsimile descents to alternative sites on the surface of Mars can precede human footfalls. Dental students can refine the elements of extractions and root canals before going into the mouths of live patients. Communities and their architectural planners, as well as prospective homeowners, can attain consensus before building projects are cast in stone or mortar. Dick and Jane can practice and polish their golf swings, public speaking, and social skills before entering the in vivo arenas. We envision an era of prodigious modeling applications.

SUMMARY

We sum up in verse to help you to rehearse that modeling spans both actions and plans. Observers can spurn overt practice yet learn. When the model first shows how activity goes (to steer efforts made later), skill gains are greater. Cast content in samples through diverse examples that start with the core thoughts before you add more thoughts. Whether concepts or coping, reduce early groping by gradual pacing rather than racing: Once the basics are had, then you can add illustrations more rare with boundaries less clear. For instance, with mammals, do *not* start with *camels*. *Dog* or *cat* heads the cast, but *vole* comes near last. The same holds for fears or you will cause tears: From low to high heights will minimize frights until height-phobic people can mount to the steeple. Hold back scary surprises till confidence rises that clients can master tough tasks given faster. Whatever you teach, help the client to reach enough skill and self-trust that composure won't bust if circumstance curdles with unforeseen hurdles. Trials of conquering mishaps will reduce risk of relapse.

When deficiencies lurk, demonstrations may work to create novel poise or revise inept ploys. Modeled guidance has use to prevent child abuse and to lower the fear of medical care. The deficits treated can be new or deep-seated, and bear on a wealth of problems for health. These include weight and smoking, plus tension-evoking and worrysome brooding over dangers intruding. Despite concrete restrictions for specific afflictions, there is much common ground among strategies sound: Support, praise, and coddle the fearful, but model with minimal ache the steps they must take. When casting your spell, try to show more than tell, lest the message lose vim and attention grow dim. After boredom starts irking, the mind ceases working, and you'll pay a steep cost, since much teaching gets lost. If ideas must be spoken, we offer this token: Keep words vivid and clear for observers to hear. Rhythm, humor, and rhyme are never a crime to capture attention from the learners we mention.

You will treat in the main to eliminate pain, to remove fear and worry and self-driving hurry, to foster relief and prevent needless grief. However, one faces some deviant cases where aversion is needed for laws to be heeded, or for habits unpolished that should be abolished because they cause harm and social alarm. In those sad conditions, reflective clinicians might try modeled events that are noxious portents of overt deterrents, such as painful shock currents. Vicarious stress may equal duress brought on by direct cues, so why not elect cues that punish quite plainly, and yet more humanely?

As research keeps on flowing, applications keep growing in modeling's range to help people change. And for all this bravura, thank Albert Bandura.

REFERENCES

Abramowitz, I. A., & Coursey, R. D. (1989). Impact of an educational support group on family participants who take care of their schizophrenic relatives. *Journal of Consulting and Clinical Psychology, 57,* 232–236.

Acker, M. M., & O'Leary, S. G. (1988). Effects of consistent and inconsistent feedback on inappropriate child behavior. *Behavior Therapy, 19,* 619–624.

Akiskal, H. S., King, D., Rosenthal, T. L., Robinson, D., & Scott–Strauss, A. (1981). Chronic depressions: Part I—Clinical and familial characteristics in 137 probands. *Journal of Affective Disorders, 3,* 297–315.

Alford, G. S. (1980). Alcoholics Anonymous: An empirical outcome study. *Addictive Behaviors, 5,* 359–370.

Allen, K. D., Danforth, J. S., & Drabman, R. S. (1989). Videotaped modeling and film distraction for fear reduction in adults undergoing hyperbaric oxygen therapy. *Journal of Consulting and Clinical Psychology, 57,* 554–558.

Altmaier, E. M., Leary, M. R., Halpern, S., & Sellers, J. E. (1985). Effects of stress innoculation and participant modeling on confidence and anxiety: Testing predictions of self-efficacy theory. *Journal of Social and Clinical Psychology, 3,* 500–505.

American Psychiatric Association. (1980). *Diagnostic and statistical manual of mental disorders* (3rd ed). Washington, DC: Author.

Anderson, E. A. (1987). Preoperative preparation for cardiac surgery facilitates recovery, reduces psychological distress, and reduces the incidence of acute postoperative hypertension. *Journal of Consulting and Clinical Psychology, 55,* 513–520.

Arnow, B. A., Taylor, C. B., Agras, W. S., & Telch, M. J. (1985). Enhancing agoraphobia treatment outcome by changing couple communication patterns. *Behavior Therapy, 16*, 452–467.

Baer, J. S., Holt, C. S., & Lichtenstein, E. (1986). Self-efficacy and smoking reexamined: Construct validity and clinical utility. *Journal of Consulting and Clinical Psychology, 54*, 846–852.

Baltes, M. M. (1988). The etiology and maintenance of dependency in the elderly: Three phases of operant research. *Behavior Therapy, 19*, 301–319.

Baltes, P. B., & Lindenberger, U. (1988). On the range of cognitive plasticity in old age as a function of experience: 15 years of intervention research. *Behavior Therapy, 19*, 283–300.

Bandura, A. (1969). *Principles of Behavior Modification*. New York: Holt, Rinehart & Winston.

Bandura, A. (Ed.). (1971). *Psychological Modeling—Conflicting Theories*. Chicago: Atherton/Aldine.

Bandura, A. (1977). *Social Learning Theory*. Englewood Cliffs, NJ: Prentice-Hall.

Bandura, A. (1986). *Social Foundations of Thought and Action: A Social Cognitive Theory*. Englewood Cliffs, NJ: Prentice-Hall.

Bandura, A. (1988). Self-efficacy conception of anxiety. *Anxiety Research, 1*, 77–98.

Bandura, A. (1989). Self-efficacy mechanism in psychobiologic relations. Invited address to the British Psychological Society, St. Andrews, Scotland, March, 1989.

Bandura, A. (1990). Psychological aspects of prognostic judgments. In R. W. Evans, D. S. Baskin, & F. M. Yatsu (Eds.), *Prognosis in Neurological Disease*. New York: Oxford University Press.

Bandura, A., Cioffi, D., Taylor, C. B., & Brouillard, M. E. (1988). Perceived self-efficacy in coping with cognitive stressors and opioid activiation. *Journal of Personality and Social Psychology, 55*, 479–488.

Bandura, A., & Rosenthal, T. L. (1966). Vicarious classical conditioning as a function of arousal level. *Journal of Personality and Social Psychology, 3*, 54–62.

Bandura, A., Taylor, C. B., Gauthier, J., & Gossard, D. (1987). Perceived self-efficacy and pain control: Opioid and nonopioid mechanisms. *Journal of Personality and Social Psychology, 53*, 563–571.

Bandura, A., Taylor, C. B., Williams, S. L., Mefford, I. N., & Barchas, J. D. (1985). Catecholamine secretion as a function of perceived coping self-efficacy. *Journal of Consulting and Clinical Psychology, 53*, 406–414.

Bandura, A., & Walters, R. (1963). *Social Learning and Personality Development*. New York: Holt, Rinehart & Winston.

Barlow, D. H., Craske, M. G., Cerny, J. A., & Klosko, J. S. (1989). Behavioral treatment of panic disorder. *Behavior Therapy, 20*, 261–282.

Bernstein, G. S. (1989). Social validity and the debate over use of aversive/intrusive procedures. *The Behavior Therapist, 12*, 123–125.

Bliss, R. E., Garvey, A. J., Heinold, J. W., & Hitchcock, J. L. (1989). The influence of situation and coping on relapse crisis outcomes after smoking cessation. *Journal of Consulting and Clinical Psychology, 57*, 443–449.

Blount, R. L., Dahlquist, L. M., Baer, R. A., & Wuori, D. (1984). A brief, effective method for teaching children to swallow pills. *Behavior Therapy, 15*, 381–387.

Burgio, L., Engel, B. T., McCormick, K., Hawkins, A., & Scheve, A. (1988). Behavioral treatment for urinary incontinence in elderly inpatients: Initial attempts to modify prompting and toileting procedures. *Behavior Therapy, 19*, 345–357.

Burish, T. G., Carey, M. P., Krozely, M. G., & Greco, F. A. (1987). Conditioned side effects induced by cancer chemotherapy: Prevention through behavioral treatment. *Journal of Consulting and Clinical Psychology, 55*, 42–48.

Calvert, S. C., & McMahon, R. J. (1987). The treatment acceptability of a behavioral parent training program and its components. *Behavior Therapy, 18,* 165–179.

Carey, M. P., & Burish, T. G. (1987). Providing relaxation training to cancer chemotherapy patients: A comparison of three delivery techniques. *Journal of Consulting and Clinical Psychology, 55,* 732–737.

Cerny, J. A., Barlow, D. H., Craske, M. G., & Himadi, W. G. (1987). Couples treatment of agoraphobia: A two-year follow up. *Behavior Therapy, 18,* 401–415.

Chipperfield, B., & Vogel–Sprott, M. (1988). Family history of problem drinking among young male social drinkers: Modeling effects on alcohol consumption. *Journal of Abnormal Psychology, 97,* 423–428.

Condiotte, M. M., & Lichtenstein, E. (1981). Self-efficacy and relapse in smoking cessation programs. *Journal of Consulting and Clinical Psychology, 49,* 648–658.

Craig, K. D. (1978). Social modeling influences on pain. In R. A. Sternbach (Ed.), *The Psychology of Pain.* New York: Raven Press.

Craighead, L. W., & Blum, M. D. (1989). Supervised exercise in behavioral treatment for moderate obesity. *Behavior Therapy, 20,* 49–59.

Craun, A. M., & Deffenbacher, J. L. (1987). The effects on information, behavioral rehearsal, and prompting on breast self-exams. *Journal of Behavioral Medicine, 10,* 351–365.

Davis, A. F., Rosenthal, T. L., & Kelley, J. E. (1981). Actual fear cues, prompt therapy, and rationale enhance participant modeling with adolescents. *Behavior Therapy, 12,* 536–542.

Downs, A. F. D., Rosenthal, T. L., & Lichstein, K. L. (1988). Modeling therapies reduce avoidance of bath-time by the institutionalized elderly. *Behavior Therapy, 19,* 359–368.

Eckenrode, J., Powers, J., Doris, J., Munsch, J., & Bolger, N. (1988). Substantiation of child abuse and neglect reports. *Journal of Consulting and Clinical Psychology, 56,* 9–16.

Edwards, B., Manion, I., & Koverola, C. (1988). Early intervention for parents at risk of child abuse and neglect: A preliminary investigation. *Journal of Consulting and Clinical Psychology, 56,* 40–47.

Edwards, N. B., Murphy, J. K., Downs, A. D., Ackerman, B. J., & Rosenthal, T. L. (1989). Antidepressents as an adjunct to smoking cessation: A double-bind pilot study. *American Journal of Psychiatry, 146,* 373–376.

Eifert, G. H., Craill, L., Carey, E., & O'Conner, C. (1988). Affect modification through evaluative conditioning with music. *Behaviour Research and Therapy, 26,* 321–330.

Emery, R. E. (1989). Family violence. *American Psychologist, 44,* 321–328.

Fairweather, G. W., Sanders, D. H., Maynard, H., & Cressler, D. L. (1969). *Community Life for the Mentally Ill: An Alternative to Institutional Care.* Chicago: Aldine.

Fantuzzo, J. W., Jurecic, L., Stovall, A., Hightower, A. D., Goins, C., & Schachtel, D. (1988). Effects of adult and peer social initiations on the social behavior of withdrawn, maltreated preschool children. *Journal of Consulting and Clinical Psychology, 56,* 34–39.

Feindler, E. L., Ecton, R. B., Kingsley, D., & Dubey, D. R. (1986). Group anger-control training for institutionalized psychiatric male adolescents. *Behavior Therapy, 17,* 109–123.

Foxx, R. M., Martella, R. C., & Marchand–Martella, N. E. (1989). The acquisition, maintenance, and generalization of problem-solving skills by closed head-injured adults. *Behavior Therapy, 20,* 61–76.

Frisch, M. B., & Froberg, W. (1987). Social validation of assertion strategies for handling aggressive criticism: Evidence for consistency across situations. *Behavior Therapy, 18,* 181–191.

Giles, T. R., Young, R. R., & Young, D. E. (1985). Behavioral treatment of severe bulimia. *Behavior Therapy, 16,* 393–405.

Heath, L., Bresolin, L. B., & Rinaldi, R. C. (1989). Effects of media violence on children: A review of the literature. *Archives of General Psychiatry, 46,* 376–379.

Heinrich, R. L., Cohen, M. J., Naliboff, B. D., Collins, G. A., & Bonebakker, A. D. (1985). Comparing physical and behavior therapy for chronic low back pain on physical abilities, psychological distress, and patients' perceptions. *Journal of Behavioral Medicine, 8,* 61–78.

Hoberman, H. M., Lewinsohn, P. M., & Tilson, M. (1988). Group treatment of depression: Individual predictors of outcome. *Journal of Consulting and Clinical Psychology, 56,* 393–398.

Holmes, T. H., & Rahe, R. H. (1967). The social readjustment rating scale. *Journal of Psychosomatic Research, 11,* 213.

Hung, J. H. F. (1979). Harnessing of social comparison effects in assertion training. Unpublished doctoral dissertation, Memphis State University.

Hung, J. H. F., Rosenthal, T. L., & Kelley, J. E. (1980). Social comparison models spur immediate assertion: "So you think you're submissive?" *Cognitive Therapy and Research, 4,* 223–234.

Hurley, J. (1987). The relationship among negative attributions, conformity, and modeling behavior. *Journal of Clinical Psychology, 43,* 360–365.

Jacobson, N. S., Holtzworth–Munroe, A., & Schmaling, K. B. (1989). Marital therapy and spouse involvement in the treatment of depression, agoraphobia and alcoholism. *Journal of Consulting and Clinical Psychology, 57,* 5–10.

Jay, S. M., Elliott, C. H., Ozolins, M., Olson, R. A., & Pruitt, S. D. (1985). Behavioral management of children's distress during painful procedures. *Behaviour Research and Therapy, 23,* 513–520.

Johnson, J. E., Lauver, D. R., & Nail, L. M. (1989). Process of coping with radiation therapy. *Journal of Consulting and Clinical Psychology, 57,* 358–364.

Jones, R. T., Ollendick, T. H., McLaughlin, K. J., & Williams, C. E. (1989). Elaborative and behavioral rehearsal in the acquisition of fire emergency skills and the reduction of fear of fire. *Behavior Therapy, 20,* 93–101.

Kanfer, F. H., & Gaelick, L. (1986). Self-management methods. In F. H. Kanfer & A. P. Goldstein (Eds.), *Helping People Change* (3rd ed., pp. 283–345). Elmsford, NY: Pergamon Press.

Kazdin, A. E., Bass, D., Siegel, T., & Thomas, C. (1989). Cognitive-behavioral therapy and relationship therapy in the treatment of children referred for antisocial behavior. *Journal of Consulting and Clinical Psychology, 57,* 522–535.

Lee, G. P., Arena, J. G., Meador, K. J., Smith, J. R., Loring, D. W., & Flanigin, H. F. (1988). Changes in autonomic responsiveness following bilateral amygdalotomy in humans. *Neuropsychiatry, Neuropsychology, and Behavioral Neurology, 1,* 119–129.

Lewis, F. D., Nelson, J., Nelson, C., & Reusink, P. (1988). Effects of three feedback contingencies on the socially inappropriate talk of a brain-injured adult. *Behavior Therapy, 19,* 203–211.

Lovaas, O. I. (1967). A behavior therapy approach to the treatment of childhood schizophrenia. In J. P. Hill (Ed.), *Minnesota Symposia on Child Psychology* (Vol. 1, pp. 108–159). Minneapolis: University of Minnesota Press.

Lovett, S., & Gallagher, D. (1988). Psychoeducational interventions for family caregivers: Preliminary efficacy data. *Behavior Therapy, 19,* 321–330.

Mattick, R. P., & Peters, L. (1988). Treatment of severe social phobia: Effects of guided exposure with and without cognitive restructuring. *Journal of Consulting and Clinical Psychology, 56,* 251–260.

Mattick, R. P., Peters, L., & Clarke, J. C. (1989). Exposure and cognitive restructuring for social phobia: A controlled study. *Behavior Therapy, 20,* 3–23.

Mayer, J. A., Dubbert, P. M., Scott, R. R., Dawson, B. L., Ekstrand, M. L., & Fondren, T. G. (1987). Breast self-examination: The effects of personalized prompts on practice frequency. *Behavior Therapy, 18,* 135–146.

McAuley, E. (1985). Modeling and self-efficacy: A test of Bandura's model. *Journal of Sport Psychology, 7,* 283–295.

Meichenbaum, D. (1986). Cognitive-behavior modification. In F. H. Kanfer & A. P. Goldstein (Eds.), *Helping People Change* (3rd ed., pp. 346–380). New York: Pergamon Press.

Melamed, B. G., & Siegel, L. J. (1975). Reduction of anxiety in children facing hospitalization and surgery by use of filmed modeling. *Journal of Consulting and Clinical Psychology, 43,* 511–521.

Michelson, L., Mavissakalian, M., Marchione, K., Dancu, C., & Greenwald, M. (1986). The role of self-directed in vivo exposure in cognitive, behavioral, and psychophysiological treatments of agoraphobia. *Behavior Therapy, 17,* 91–108.

Morgan, G. D., Ashenberg, Z. S., & Fisher, E. B., Jr. (1988). Abstinence from smoking and the social environment. *Journal of Consulting and Clinical Psychology, 56,* 298–301.

Mosbach, P., & Leventhal, H. (1988). Peer group identification and smoking: Implications for intervention. *Journal of Abnormal Psychology, 97,* 238–245.

Nelson, D. A., & Marler, P. (1989). Categorical perception of a natural stimulus continuum: Birdsong. *Science, 244,* 976–978.

Niven, D. (1975). *Bring on the Empty Horses.* New York: Dell.

Olson, R. L., & Roberts, M. W. (1987). Alternative treatments for sibling aggression. *Behavior Therapy, 18,* 243–250.

Ozer, E. M., & Bandura, A. (in press). Mechanisms governing empowerment effects: A self-efficacy analysis. *Journal of Personality and Social Psychology.*

Perri, M. G., McAllister, D. A., Gange, J. J., Jordan, R. C., McAdoo, W. G., & Nezu, A. M. (1988). Effects of four maintenance programs on the long-term management of obesity. *Journal of Consulting and Clinical Psychology, 56,* 529–534.

Peterson, L., Schultheis, K., Ridley–Johnson, R., Miller, D. J., & Tracy, K. (1984). Comparison of three modeling procedures on the presurgical and postsurgical reactions of children. *Behavior Therapy, 15,* 197–203.

Pinkston, E. M., Linsk, N. L., & Young, R. N. (1988). Home-based behavioral family treatment of the impaired elderly. *Behavior Therapy, 19,* 331–344.

Prkachin, K. M., & Craig, K. D. (1986). Social transmission of natural variations in pain behavior. *Behaviour Research and Therapy, 24,* 581–585.

Rescorla, R. A. (1988). Pavlovian conditioning: It's not what you think it is. *American Psychologist, 43,* 151–160.

Rolider, A., & Van Houton, R. (1985). Suppressing tantrum behavior in public places through the use of delayed punishment mediated by audio recordings. *Behavior Therapy, 16,* 181–194.

Romano, J. M., Syrjala, K. L., Levy, R. L., Turner, J. A., Evans, P., & Keefe, F. J. (1988). Overt pain behaviors: Relationship to patient functioning and treatment outcome. *Behavior Therapy, 19,* 191–201.

Rosenthal, R. H., Ling, F. W., Wheeler, L., Rosenthal, T. L., & Buxton, B. H. (1980). Use of a videotape "coping model" for teaching pelvic examinations. *Journal of the Tennessee Medical Association, 73,* 635–637.

Rosenthal, T. L. (1976). Modeling therapies. In M. Hersen, R. M. Eisler, & P. M. Miller (Eds.), *Progress in Behavior Modification* (Vol. 2, pp. 53–97). New York: Academic Press.

Rosenthal, T. L. (1979). Applying a cognitive behavioral view to clinical and social problems. In G. J. Whitehurst & B. J. Zimmerman (Eds.), *The Functions of Language and Cognition* (pp. 265–293). New York: Academic Press.

Rosenthal, T. L. (1980). Social cueing processes. In M. Hersen, R. M. Eisler, & P. M. Miller (Eds.), *Progress in Behavior Modification* (Vol. 10, pp. 111–146). New York: Academic Press.

Rosenthal, T. L. (1982). Social learning theory. In C. M. Franks & G. T. Wilson (Eds.), *Handbook of Behavior Therapy* (pp. 339–363). New York: Guilford Press.

Rosenthal, T. L. (1984a). Cognitive social learning theory. In N. S. Endler (Ed.), *Personality and the Behavior Disorders* (rev. ed., pp. 113–145). New York: John Wiley & Sons.

Rosenthal, T. L. (1984b). Some organizing hints for communicating applied information. In B. J. Gholson & T. L. Rosenthal (Eds.), *Applications of Cognitive Developmental Theory* (pp. 149–172). New York: Academic Press.

Rosenthal, T. L., Akiskal, H. S., Scott–Strauss, A., Rosenthal, R. H., & David, M. (1981). Familial and developmental factors in characterogical depressions. *Journal of Affective Disorders, 3,* 183–192.

Rosenthal, T. L., & Bandura, A. (1978). Psychological modeling: Theory and practice. In S. L. Garfield & A. E. Bergin (Eds.), *Handbook of Psychotherapy and Behavior Change* (2nd ed., pp. 621–658). New York: John Wiley & Sons.

Rosenthal, T. L., & Downs, A. (1985). Cognitive aids in teaching and treating. *Advances in Behaviour Research and Therapy, 7,* 1–53.

Rosenthal, T. L., Linehan, K. S., Kelley, J. E., Rosenthal, R. H., Theobald, D. E., & Davis, A. F. (1978). Group aversion by imaginal, vicarious and shared recipient-observer shocks. *Behaviour Research and Therapy, 16,* 421–427.

Rosenthal, T. L., Montgomery, L. M., Shadish, W. R., Jr., Edwards, N. B., Hutcherson, H. W., Follette, W. C., & Lichstein, K. L. (1989). Two new, brief, practical stressor tasks for research purposes. *Behavior Therapy, 20,* 545–562.

Rosenthal, T. L., Rogers, C., & Durning, K. (1972). Sequences of extreme belief-incongruent versus neutral information in social perception. *Australian Journal of Psychology, 24,* 267–273.

Rosenthal, T. L., & Rosenthal, R. H. (1983). Stress: Causes, measurement and management. In K. Craig & R. J. McMahon (Eds.), *Advances in Clinical Behavior Therapy* (pp. 3–26). New York: Brunner/Mazel.

Rosenthal, T. L., & Rosenthal, R. H. (1985). Clinical stress management. In D. Barlow (Ed.), *Clinical Handbook of Psychological Disorders* (pp. 195–205). New York: Guilford Press.

Rosenthal, T. L., Rosenthal, R. H., & Chang, A. F. (1977). Vicarious, direct and imaginal aversion in habit control: Outcomes, heart rates, and subjective perceptions. *Cognitive Therapy and Research, 1,* 143–159.

Rosenthal, T. L., & Zimmerman, B. J. (1978). *Social Learning and Cognition.* New York: Academic Press.

Sartory, G., & Olajide, D. (1988). Vagal innervation techniques in the treatment of panic disorder. *Behaviour Research and Therapy, 26,* 431–434.

Sharp, J. J., & Forman, S. G. (1985). A comparison of two approaches to anxiety management for teachers. *Behavior Therapy, 16,* 370–383.

Sorensen, J. L., Hall, S. M., Loeb, P., Allen, T., Glaser, E. M., & Greenberg, P. D. (1988). Dissemination of a job seekers' workshop to drug treatment programs. *Behavior Therapy, 19,* 143–155.

Stevens, V. J., & Hollis, J. F. (1989). Preventing smoking relapse, using an individually tailored skills-training technique. *Journal of Consulting and Clinical Psychology, 57,* 420–424.

Suls, J., & Wan, C. K. (1989). Effects of sensory and procedural information on coping with stressful medical procedures and pain: A meta-analysis. *Journal of Consulting and Clinical Psychology, 57,* 372–379.

Tisdelle, D. A., & St. Lawrence, J. S. (1988). Adolescent interpersonal problem-solving skill training: Social validation and generalization. *Behavior Therapy, 19,* 171–182.

Turkat, I. D., Guise, B. J., & Carter, K. M. (1983). The effects of vicarious experience on pain termination and work avoidance: A replication. *Behaviour Research and Therapy, 21,* 491–493.

Turkat, I. D., & Noskin, D. E. (1983). Vicarious and operant experiences in the etiology of illness behavior: A replication with healthy individuals. *Behaviour Research and Therapy, 21,* 169–172.

Walker, W. B., & Franzini, L. R. (1985). Low-risk aversive group treatments, physiological feedback, and booster sessions for smoking cessation. *Behavior Therapy, 16,* 263–274.

Ward, F. (1989). Images for the computer age. *National Geographic, 175,* 718–751.

Webster–Stratton, C. (1984). Randomized trial of two parent-training programs for families with conduct-disordered children. *Journal of Consulting and Clinical Psychology, 52,* 666–678.

Webster–Stratton, C. (1989). Systematic comparison of consumer satisfaction of three cost-effective parent training programs for conduct problem children. *Behavior Therapy, 20, 103–115.*

Weinstein, M. (1988). Preparation of children for psychotherapy through videotaped modeling. *Journal of Clinical Child Psychology, 17,* 131–136.

White, G. M. (1975). Contextual determinants of opinion judgments: Field experimental probes of judgmental relativity boundary conditions. *Journal of Personality and Social Psychology, 32,* 1047–1054.

White, G. M., & Rosenthal, T. L. (1974). Demonstration and lecture in information transmissions: A field experiment. *Journal of Experimental Education, 43,* 90–96.

Wickramasekera, I. (1976). Aversive behavior rehearsal for sexual exhibitionism. *Behavior Therapy, 7,* 167–176.

Widom, C. S. (1989). The cycle of violence. *Science, 244,* 160–166.

Williams, S. L., & Zane, G. (1989) Guided mastery and stimulus exposure treatments for severe performance anxiety in agoraphobics. *Behaviour Research and Therapy, 27,* 237–245.

Wolfe, D. A., Edwards, B., Manion, I., & Koverola, C. (1988). Early intervention for parents at risk of child abuse and neglect: A preliminary investigation. *Journal of Consulting and Clinical Psychology, 56,* 40–47.

Wurtele, S. K., Marrs, S. R., & Miller–Perrin, C. L. (1987). Practice makes perfect? The role of participant modeling in sexual abuse prevention programs. *Journal of Consulting and Clinical Psychology, 55,* 599–602.

Wurtele, S. K., Saslawsky, D. A., Miller, C. L., Marrs, S. R., & Britcher, J. X. (1986). Teaching personal safety skills for potential prevention of sexual abuse: A comparison of treatments. *Journal of Consulting and Clinical Psychology, 54,* 588–692.

Zimmerman, B. J., & Blom, D. E. (1983). Toward an empirical test of the role of cognitive conflict in learning. *Developmental Review, 3,* 18–38.

4

Operant Methods

Carol J. Nemeroff
Paul Karoly

This chapter deals with an approach to behavior change that derives from the learning theory tradition within general psychology. Most often associated with the ideas and procedures of B. F. Skinner, the perspective to be elaborated emphasizes freely emitted, overt (observable) actions and the immediate environmental forces that ostensibly "control" these actions. The determinants of behavior are generally thought to consist of (a) signals (or cues) that inform the person (or animal) that a particular response is or is not likely to pay off (in the form of a *reward*; and (b) the pattern of rewards or punishers that are linked to the omission of the response. Skinner's (1938) term *operant conditioning* highlights the fact that organisms are active in their interchanges with the world (they *operate* on the environment) and that the frequency or probability of various operant responses is conditional on the presence of environmental signals (cues) and response-contingent events (the prompt delivery of rewards or removal of punishments). Thus, the operant behavior therapist is most concerned with the "controlling cues and consequences" of human action. This deceptively simple scenario forms the basis for a science of behavior management which is highly precise and clearly amenable to empirical confirmation/disconfirmation. Although operant conditioning principles were initially investigated in controlled, laboratory settings, the last 35 years have witnessed an exciting expansion of investigative focus into everyday life and its vicissitudes by practitioners who call themselves *applied behavior analysts*. In general, applied behavior analysts seek to mount interventions that are: *applied, behavioral, analytic, technological, conceptual, effective,* and *capable of generalized outcomes* (Baer, Wolf, & Risley, 1987).

First, an *applied* intervention is one that addresses important social problems, including but not limited to the clinically disturbing behavior of individuals. Thus, a child who steals or drinks excessive amounts of alcohol might be a target of an operant change program. But so too might a group or a community of persons whose actions constitute a problem for society at large. Consequently, advocates of applied behavior analysis might attempt to decrease highway littering or eliminate the sale and use of illicit drugs in the inner city.

In the context of clinical application, being *behavioral* means adhering to a set of operational principles in pursuit of the general objectives of prediction or control of instrumental action. Among the principles are: (a) a focus on behavior rather than on thought or emotion; (b) a focus on single behaviors observed across periods of time rather than on multiple behaviors observed or measured in a single session; (c) the use of direct observation by trained observers as a means of assessing the frequency of adaptive or maladaptive behavior; (d) the attempt to contextualize behaviors in terms of the antecedent events which trigger them and the consequent events that reinforce them; and (e) a disavowal of interference, particularly about possible causes "inside the head" of the child or adult whose behavior is the subject of analysis.

Applied behavior analysts are *analytic* and *conceptual* when they demonstrate their capacity to bring about specific changes in behavior and when they do so in ways that are conceptually consistent with their working principles. The *technology* of applied behavior analysis—the *operant methods* referred to in the title of this chapter—is represented by the explicit procedures for behavior modification which are themselves amenable to careful specification and analysis. These procedures, when fully articulated, are capable of being flexibly applied so as to be compatible with the requirements of local situations. In this way, no two operant programs for toilet training are going to match in all their particulars, because the learning capacities of children (their backgrounds, their preferences for rewards, etc.) will differ, and these differences must be taken into account (Dumas, 1989).

To be *effective* is, naturally, the central aspiration of all treatment regimens. Yet operant practitioners seek to establish the multiple objectives of insuring that change methods are correctly applied, that, when applied, the methods lead to alterations in problem behavior(s), and that any behavior changes so instigated eventuate in improvements in the person's (or group's) social "survival potential."

Finally, Baer, Wolf, and Risley (1987) assert that the field of applied behavior analysis is committed to facilitating behavioral changes that extend into the client's foreseeable future and that, in addition to being durable, are capable of being applied in novel situations (the twin goals of *maintenance* and *generalization*).

THE NATURE AND MULTIPLE FUNCTIONS OF BEHAVIORAL ASSESSMENT

Although we shall be concerned mainly with detailing methods for effectively altering maladaptive behavior, we would be remiss if we failed to point out that the determination of which change technology to employ is heavily dependent on the prior selection of the so-called *target* behavior (the response presumably in need of alteration). At a superficial level, clients may present themselves for treatment (or be brought to the attention of the applied behavior analyst) because they seem to be either doing too much of something that is undesirable (e.g., smoking, eating, missing school, fighting with siblings, littering the highways, physically abusing a child, etc.) or doing too little of something healthful or necessary (e.g., studying, speaking up for their rights, conserving water, socializing after the death of a spouse, etc.). Within a behavioral framework, even intrapsychic or experiential disorders can be viewed as either doing too much or too little of something (e.g., schizophrenia involves *too much* bizarre talk, while depression implies *too little* engagement of pleasurable environmental opportunities). Yet, while textbooks make the nature of so-called behavioral excesses or behavioral deficits appear obvious, in the real world of clinical application the process of defining a target is rarely a cut-and-dried, ethically neutral decision.

As learning-based approaches to psychopathology have matured, so too have ideas concerning the nature of appropriate target behaviors. Earlier, choices were often made on the basis of an action's ready observability, ease of assessment, the availability of a change program, or other considerations which placed convenience ahead of conceptualization (Mash, 1985). In addition, when defining the *problem space* for the selection of a change-worthy behavior, early behaviorists tended to place restrictive boundaries on the field—often ignoring the forest (the larger context of the patient's life) for the trees (the immediately obvious behavioral excess or deficiency). Therefore, in addition to taking into account what the client (or the client's family) represents as "the problem" and what the behavioral assessor can confirm via his or her clinical observations, a systematic analysis would also include attention to such considerations as the seriousness of the behavior in terms of current life functioning; the likelihood that a change will be maintained, will promote growth, and/or be supported by significant others; consistency of the change within the client's overall life plan; and the impact of changing behavior X on the rest of the client's behavioral repertoire (e.g., Kanfer, 1985; Kanfer & Schefft, 1988). Having systematically determined that an individual is engaging in an excessive amount of activity that can serve as a change target (e.g., that a child's aggressive behavior is getting him in serious trouble with peers and teachers) or is engaging in too little of a needed activity (e.g., too little homework completed), the behavioral assessor is next required to define the target objectively, clearly, and as completely as possible and then attempt to fix it within a network of controlling stimuli (antecedent events that serve to cue its occurrence or omission) and reinforcing (supportive) events (those consequences that routinely follow the behavior).

This so-called *functional assessment* is accomplished by means of varied methods for (a) counting and recording behavior, (b) actually sampling the behavior and its determinants in context, and (c) insuring that the obtained observation records are reliable (Kazdin, 1989). Typically, the problem behavior is observed for a sufficiently long period, prior to the introduction of any change program, to determine its operant or *baseline* rate of occurrence. Information concerning the baserate of problem behavior and its determinants is useful in further sharpening the *descriptive analysis* and in *intervention strategy selection*. That is, the applied behavior analyst can confirm that the most reasonable target has indeed been chosen and can decide whether to try to manipulate antecedent or consequent events in order to bring about a clinically meaningful change in the target. The data collected during baseline observation can also serve as the cornerstone of one's *treatment program evaluation* (i.e., if one is seeking either to increase deficient behavior or decrease excessive behavior, the baseline performance rate serves as the standard of comparison).

Although the application of the procedures discussed in this chapter may be viewed as following from a fairly value-free interpretation of basic theoretical principles, specification of the target behavior is clearly a value-laden decision. Parents often seek treatment for their child to reduce the child's noncompliant behavior (that is, to increase the child's obedience). Most behavior therapists would consider such a treatment goal to be potentially inappropriate without close examination of other aspects of the situation. For example, the parents could be making unreasonable demands given the child's level of prior knowledge and experience or developmental stage, or they may be inappropriately intolerant of or insensitive to the child's own needs. Thorough, thoughtful evaluation of behavior in its total context is always called for. For further discussion on target selection and behavioral assessment issues and procedures, the reader may consult Ciminero, Calhoun, and Adams (1986), Hersen and Bellack (1988), Kanfer and Schefft (1988), and Mash and Terdal (1988).

Four phenomena are basic to operant learning: acquisition of a response habit (learning of the relation between a response and its consequences); extinction of a response habit (learning that the response–consequence relation no longer holds); discrimination (learning to distinguish between stimuli that signal that consequences will or will not follow a particular behavior and/or to distinguish between responses that will/will not result in particular consequences); and generalization (the tendency to engage in learned responses in situations other than the original learning situation). Each of these will be examined in turn as we detail ways of increasing response likelihood, decreasing response likelihood, bringing responses under stimulus control, and building generalization and maintenance.

INCREASING RESPONSE LIKELIHOOD
Positive Reinforcement (Reward)

Assume that preliminary considerations have been addressed in the intake session: The target behavior has been carefully defined, baseline data on the frequency and context of its occurrence have been gathered, and an increase in behavior frequency has been agreed on by the therapist and client as the treatment goal. The most obvious way to accomplish this goal is to apply positive reinforcement each time the target behavior occurs. E. L. Thorndike and B. F. Skinner thoroughly documented that behaviors that are followed by favorable consequences are likely to be repeated. By definition, a reinforcement is any consequence that tends to increase the probability of the response that preceded it. The term *positive reinforcement* refers to adding or applying something to increase the probability of the behavior. Examples would be giving food to a hungry pigeon who has pecked an appropriate key, or a dessert to a child who has eaten all of his dinner. The things that will serve as positive reinforcers can differ from person to person, and must be empirically described—if John does not like chocolate, rewarding him with it for good behavior is unlikely to be effective.

There are two conceptually distinct types of reinforcer: primary reinforcers, and secondary reinforcers. Primary reinforcers are defined as those which are innately, biologically important, satisfying basic needs of the organism, such as food, water, or avoidance of pain. Secondary (or conditioned) reinforcers are things which initially were neutral to the organism but which have, through association with primary reinforcers, acquired reinforcing properties and thus the capacity to influence the probability of behaviors. Examples of secondary reinforcers include money, social approval, tokens in a token economy, or watching one's favorite night-time soap opera after completing a homework assignment.

In practice, it can be difficult to identify what will serve as a reinforcer for a given individual, especially if one is trying to use secondary reinforcers. A conceptual approach of particular utility in such situations is Premack's (1959) view of "response as reinforcement." Premack posits that one behavior can itself reinforce another behavior if the former is the "preferred activity," that is, the stronger of the two responses. Strength of response can be estimated by the amount of time that the individual freely spends engaging in the behavior. By discovering the activities in which the client voluntarily and habitually engages during his or her free time, the therapist can identify potentially powerful reinforcers in those behaviors which occur with the greatest frequency. Assuming that those behaviors are not themselves undesirable or problematic if engaged in even more (e.g., listening to music), the opportunity to engage in the more frequent behavior can be made contingent on the exhibition of the low-frequency (but desirable) target behavior. For example, Favell (1977) cited the use of a client who regularly took a shower before going to bed. The behavioral goal was to increase the amount of time the client spent studying. The opportunity to take a shower was therefore made contingent on time spent studying, thereby effectively increasing study time. Watching a favorite television show, talking on the phone with friends, shopping for clothes, and calling up a soap-opera hotline have all been effectively used toward the same behavioral goal by students of the first author in a class exercise.

It is important to note that no reinforcer, no matter how potent for a given individual, will be effective in all circumstances. Even a chocolate "addict" will be unlikely to find chocolate reinforcing if it is offered just after consuming a 5-pound box of miniatures. Secondary reinforcers can also lose their power depending on circumstances: A $5 incentive will be unimpressive to a person who has just won a large lottery. It is therefore important to have a variety of reinforcers available for dispensation, whenever possible. Positive reinforcement was used by Pfiffner, Rosen, and O'Leary (1985) to manage the behavior of eight second- and third-grade children with behavior problems. An individualized reward system was used, such that children received songtime, special recess activities, permission to read comic books, play musical instruments, write stories, draw, or have their work posted on a "superstar" board all contingent on both appropriate behavior and complete academic work. In addition, deserving students selected one reward from a daily menu which included having a positive note sent home, helping the teacher with various tasks, and so on. Results indicated that children's rates of on-task behavior were high and stable and that academic productivity improved, demonstrating that an "all-positive approach to classroom management" is indeed feasible.

Positive reinforcement has also been used to increase healthy food choices in preschoolers. Following general nutrition training, Stark, Collins, Osnes, and Stokes (1986) implemented a color code classification system for snack foods, and contingent rewards for selecting healthy ones. Children responded to the program by modifying their food choices.

Positive reinforcement is not always intentionally given. Indeed, it is often discovered to be maintaining *un*desirable behaviors. For example, Baltes (1988) conducted a series of studies analyzing *dependency behavior* in the elderly (defined as helplessness or powerless, e.g., inability to carry out self-care behaviors). She found that both institutionalized elderly people and those living in their own homes were likely to receive a great deal of social attention and an "immediately supportive social environment" for dependent behaviors, while independent behaviors were "rarely followed by observable responses from the social environment." The author points out that, "in a world where social contact is rare . . . " (and thus no doubt highly valued), "such a behavior sequence should have great implications" (p. 307). This pattern was in direct contrast to what was observed with institutionalized children, for whom constructively engaged (competent) behaviors were most likely to elicit attention and support.

A different kind of situation involving behavior inadvertently positively reinforced is discussed by Klonoff and Biglan (1987). They describe a case of anxiety believed to be associated with hypoglycemia. They note that the usual instructions given by doctors to hypoglycemic patients (to eat when they experience anxiety, since it can be a symptom of a plunge in blood sugar) may actually reward (positively reinforce) the anxiety. They conclude that it may be necessary to instruct some patients to avoid eating anything contingent on the occurrence of anxiety-like symptoms, to relax prior to any ingestion, and to eat on a fixed schedule, so that anxiety symptoms are not inadvertently rewarded by food.

Negative Reinforcement (Escape from Unpleasantness)

In contrast to positive reinforcement, where something is *added* to the situation when a desired behavior occurs, negative reinforcement involves the *removal* of something following a desired response, to increase the probability of that behavior. Obviously, this situation is likely to be experienced as reinforcing only if what was removed was unpleasant. Negative reinforcers are generally aversive, such that the individual is motivated to exhibit a desired (target) behavior in order to "turn off," avoid, or escape from the unpleasant condition. Examples would be the individual who pays his bills because it will terminate continual harrassment by bill collectors, the person who learns to do stretching exercises to remove ongoing stiffness and pain in his neck and legs, or the person who finally learns to put the cap back on the toothpaste tube after each use to avoid nagging by her spouse.

Negative reinforcement, like positive reinforcement, need not always be intentional. For example, Carr and Newsom (1985) have identified negative reinforcement as the driving force behind "demand-related tantrums." These investigators observed developmentally disabled children during a series of sessions in which instructional demands were systematically varied. Tantrums occurred at a very high rate when demands were being made of the children and dropped almost to zero when no demands were being made. Since demands usually decreased in the face of the children's tantrums, the tantrum behavior was serving as an escape response. By introducing strongly preferred reinforcers into the demand situation, so that by remaining in the situation children could gain access to them, the "escape from aversiveness" function of the tantrums was reduced and hence the frequency of tantrum behavior.

It is important to note that negative reinforcement is *not* the same as punishment. With negative reinforcement, an ongoing aversive stimulus is removed or terminated following the desired behavior in order to *increase* the probability of the response, while with punishment, an aversive stimulus is added or *applied* following an undesired behavior in order to *decrease* its probability of occurrence. Punishment and other means of decreasing probability of behaviors will be discussed in depth later.

Schedules of Reinforcement and Their Consequences

In order to "build in" a desired target behavior most effectively, it seems self-evident that consistency of application should be the rule. That is, a behavior should be reinforced each time it occurs, and as soon as possible following its occurrence, in order for learning to be maximized. Reinforcing a behavior every time it occurs is called continuous reinforcement, and it is indeed the most rapid way to build in a response. However, there is a major problem with this approach to (or schedule of) reinforcement: Outside of the clinical or experimental setting, few behaviors actually are (or even can be) reinforced every time they occur. Recognizing that in the real world reinforcement rarely occurs on a continuous basis, Skinner and his colleagues (e.g., Ferster & Skinner, 1957) devoted a great deal of attention to the investigation of "reinforcement schedules," that is, the precise specification of the effects on behavior of the contingencies determining reinforcement after emission of responses: how quickly, how regularly, after how many discrete responses, or after how much elapsed time, reinforcement is applied.

There are four simple schedules of noncontinuous or partial reinforcement: fixed interval, variable interval, fixed ratio, and variable ratio. Each schedule gives rise to a distinctive pattern of responding. The interval schedules require the passage of time before the possibility of reinforcement will again be available to the responding organism. Fixed interval schedules employ a set time period—for example, the first pecking response a pigeon makes after 5 minutes has elapsed since the last reward will then be rewarded. Behavior acquired on a fixed interval schedule of reinforcement shows a characteristic temporal pattern, with responding dropping off immediately after reinforcement has been delivered (since the organism knows no more is forthcoming for a while), and increasing as the end of the reinforcement-free interval nears, because the organism knows the next response may soon be rewarded. The study habits of most college students with prescheduled exams illustrates the effect on behavior of such a reinforcement schedule.

In variable interval schedules the time periods vary around an average value, with some being quite short and others longer. The timing interval begins from the moment the last reinforcer is delivered. Variable interval schedules are associated with more constant rates of responding across the intervals, since the organism never knows for sure when a response might result in reinforcement. Teachers sometimes resort to "pop quizzes" for exactly this reason.

With ratio schedules, reinforcement is dependent on the *number* of responses emitted rather than on a time interval. Fixed ratio schedules, in which reinforcement occurs only after a fixed number of responses has occurred, tend to produce high and stable rates of responding, since the more one emits the desired behavior, the more reward one earns. If the ratio of responses required for reward is fairly high, a pause will generally develop following reinforcement—essentially, the organism is resting prior to launching the next major effort. The piecework system employed in some industries is an example of a fixed ratio reinforcement schedule.

With variable ratio schedules, the response-to-reinforcement ratio varies around an average value. Variable ratio schedules produce high, almost constant rates of responding; since there is no way the organism can know which of its responses will bring reward (whether the next, the 10th, or the 100th), the pause following reinforcement is eliminated. Slot machines employ variable ratio reinforcement schedules.

Effects noted by Agras and Werne (1977) illustrate one reason why it is important to be mindful of effects of various schedules of reinforcement in setting up a behavioral contract or contingency program. In using positive reinforcement for weight gain in anorexic patients, fixed interval schedules for delivery of reinforcing consequences generally vary from 1 to 7 days (Bemis, 1987). The advantage of the longer interval schedules (e.g., weekly reinforcement) is that they acknowledge the less-than-perfect relationship between food intake and weight gain, thereby neither rewarding nor penalizing patients for fluctuations in metabolic changes and fluid redistribution that are beyond their control. However, Agras and Werne point out that schedules with periods longer than daily reinforcement can actually encourage anorexics to concentrate their eating in the last few days of the interval and may result in a pattern of alternating restriction and uncontrolled eating—which is characteristic of bulimia.

Another reason partial reinforcement schedules are of interest in clinical application is that they enhance maintenance or resilience of treatment gains by more closely mirroring the usual experience in the real world. The partial reinforcement effect and the reason for it will be discussed later.

Building in New Behaviors: Shaping

When the target behavior already exists in the client's repertoire, it is a very straightforward matter to set up a behavioral program in which you wait until the target response is emitted and then immediately reinforce it, in order to get its frequency to increase. But what if that response is not ever made in the first place? That is, what if it does not currently exist in the behavioral repertoire? An organism can learn even very unusual responses if its behavior is suitably "shaped" by the method of "successive approximations." Shaping involves initially reinforcing an existing behavior that is different from, but similar to, the target behavior. The criterion for reinforcement then changes throughout training, so as to select and reinforce only those behaviors that are increasingly similar to the desired target behavior.

Shaping is most clearly described using a simple animal example. An experimenter wants a rat to learn to press a lever which he has placed so high on the wall that the rat must stand up on its hind legs to reach it. Left to itself, the animal will probably not make this response. The experimenter would begin by first reinforcing the animal whenever it walked into the general area where the lever is located. Soon it will be hovering regularly in the neighborhood of the lever. At that point, the experimenter might reinforce it only when it faces the lever; then, when it is doing that regularly, only for stretching its body upward; then only for touching the lever with its paws; and so on until he finally reinforces it only when it actually depresses the lever.

Lovaas (1977) has been using this technique for many years to establish verbal and social behavior in autistic children. In this approach, the therapist initially reinforces any vowel-like sound that happens to be emitted by the child. (A physical prompt, such as manual positioning of the child's lips, is sometimes used to let the natural release of air produce a particular vocalization, which is then immediately reinforced.) Once the child is reliably making sounds, the criterion is shifted: The therapist can reinforce a vocalization only if it occurs within 5 seconds after a verbal prompt. When the child is reliably responding to verbal prompts, the therapist can try to elicit imitation, only reinforcing accurate matching, and so on.

DECREASING RESPONSE LIKELIHOOD

Response-Contingent Aversive Stimulation (Punishment)

Using *punishment,* the probability of an undesirable target behavior is decreased by providing negative consequences contingent on its emission. A punisher is an aversive stimulus such as a spank on the rear for a child or an electric chock for a laboratory rat. In general, organisms will learn whatever they must to minimize such occurrences.

Obviously, the aversive stimulus is intended to be perceived by the client as painful, unpleasant, or noxious. However, it is important to recognize that just as different things are reinforcing to different people, events that appear to one person to be punishing may be reinforcing to another. Yelling at a child at home or in class when he misbehaves may have a paradoxical effect and *increase* the frequency of his acting out, if the yelling is the only kind of attention he is getting. Thus punishment, like reinforcement, is correctly defined *only* in terms of its effects on behavior. A punishment by definition *decreases* the probability of the particular behavior on which it is contingent. Just as for reinforcers, punishing stimuli may be either primary (innately aversive to the organism) or secondary (conditioned).

Response-contingent aversive stimulation (RCAS) has provoked a great deal of ethical and legal debate, and for good reason. Punishment has some serious practical limitations. First, punishment procedures seem only temporarily to suppress responding, rather than permanently removing it. This implies that when punishment is discontinued or is avoidable, the punished behavior may reappear. Indeed, Myers (1986) cites Skinner as stating that what punishment often teaches is simply how to avoid punishment. Second, punishing stimuli can create fear, so that the person administering it and the situation in which it is administered can themselves become classically conditioned aversive stimuli. Third, especially when physical punishment is used to control aggressive behavior, it may in fact serve to demonstrate or model the use of violence as a way of coping with problems. Thus, while the behavior may be suppressed in the presence of the punisher, it may actually *increase* elsewhere. Finally, punishment procedures are relatively uninformative in that they only indicate to the recipient what *not* to do (and sometimes the substitute behavior that emerges is as problematic as the behavior being treated). For all of these reasons, RCAS is generally proposed as a treatment strategy of last resort. It is mainly when behaviors involve immediate physical danger to the client or to others in the environment, or when misbehavior cannot be controlled in other ways, that RCAS might be considered the treatment of choice.

Along these lines, Spreat, Lipinski, Dickerson, Nass, and Dorsey (1989) showed vignettes describing a client, problem behaviors, and an RCAS program using electric shock to 94 mental retardation professionals, and asked them to judge the acceptability of the method. The use of response-contingent electric shock was rated as more appropriate if the behavior was serious, frequent, and had failed to respond to less intrusive interventions.

RCAS is most commonly used in the suppression of self-injurious behavior and in situations "where the use of a relatively small pain in the present can prevent a relatively large pain in the future" (Lovaas & Newsome, 1976). A prototypical example is a study by Rojahn, McGonigle, Curcio, and Dixon (1987) where water mist and aromatic ammonia were used to suppress pica in a severely retarded, autistic adolescent. Pica refers to the persistent eating of inappropriate (nonnutritive) substances. Depending on what is ingested, the practice may be life threatening. The authors compared the efficacy of room temperature water mist, sprayed into the client's face from a distance of 15 cm contingently on attempting to eat an inappropriate substance, with the efficacy of crushing a capsule containing aromatic ammonia directly under the client's nose and holding it there for 3 seconds. The water mist was clearly more effective—possibly because the client seemed initially to find the ammonia stimulating rather than aversive. Water mist maintained almost complete suppression of pica behavior over 3 months of follow-up.

Although self-injurious behavior is reported to occur more often in combination with mental retardation and psychosis, Altman, Haavik, and Higgins (1983) reported on the effective use of RCAS (Tabasco sauce) in eliminating persistent and severe finger biting in an infant with spina bifida (and diminished pain sensitivity) who was intellectually normal. Other places where self-injurious behaviors are not uncommonly found are in eating-disordered and borderline personality disordered individuals. However, given the tendency of these types of client to engage in power struggles with staff, it is wise to proceed with caution in applying aversive controls to their behavior.

When RCAS must be used, it is, like the other procedures described next which are used to weaken a behavior, most effective when used in combination with procedures designed to strengthen *alternate* behaviors. Simply removing behaviors is likely to leave a void; thus it is exceedingly helpful to work simultaneously to strengthen other positive behaviors, that is, to give individuals an idea of what *to do* to gain rewards, putting them more in control of getting what they want from others and from life.

Negative Punishments (Reinforcer Withdrawal): Response Cost and Time-Out

In the same way that reinforcement may consist either of adding something positive (reward) or removing something unpleasant (escape), one can *decrease* behavioral tendencies either by adding something aversive *or* by removing something that is rewarding.

Response cost (RC) is a form of punishment in which previously acquired reinforcers are forfeited contingent on the emission of an undesired response. For example, taking the car keys away from an adolescent who drives recklessly would be described as response cost. Obviously, the client must possess reinforcers that can be contingently and ethically removed in order for this technique to be implemented. Speeding tickets, fines for overdue library books, the practice of docking pay for lateness or absence, and the loss of privileges commonly used in inpatient psychiatric settings and in prisons are all common examples of response costs.

In a classic example of the therapeutic use of response cost, Boudin (1972) treated a female graduate student who had been using amphetamines for 3 years prior to treatment. Having resorted to lying and stealing in order to obtain drugs, she was panic-stricken at the idea that she had become an addict. The treatment plan included, among other things, a response cost arrangement in which the client established a joint bank account with her therapist that included all of her capital ($500). She signed ten $50 checks which needed only the therapist's signature to be valid. It was agreed that each episode of drug use or suspected drug use would result in the loss of one check. (In addition the therapist told the client, who was black, that forfeited checks would be sent to the Ku Klux Klan, adding a distinct element of RCAS to the contingency.) The RC contingency needed to be used only once during the 3-month contract.

Response cost in the form of loss of free time has been used to decrease the off-task behaviors of boys with attention deficit disorder with hyperactivity (Rapport, Murphy, & Bailey, 1982). A within-subject design ($N = 2$) suggested that response cost procedures were superior to methylphenidate (Ritalin) in promoting the desired behavior change. As with other aversive techniques, however, it is well to be cautious in the use of RC. Hogan and Johnson (1985) explored the effects of eliminating the response cost component of a token economy program being used to control the behavior of emotionally disturbed adolescents. The research was carried out in a community-based treatment and special education program. On eliminating the response cost procedure and keeping only positive components of the program, the authors found that morale improved and so did clients' behaviors. The authors point out that, although response cost may be effective in inducing behavioral conformity, "it undoubtedly stimulates the development of negative attitudes toward those administering it. Anyone who has ever had to pay a traffic fine or parking ticket could testify to this" (p. 88).

Another technique based in "negative" punishment is time-out (TO). Time-out refers to time out from reinforcement, that is, to a specified period of time during which no reinforcement is administered or available. Typically, the individual whose behavior is being managed is sent to an isolated corner of a room, or to another small room, which is removed both from the "scene of the crime" and from any and all rewards that may have been reinforcing inappropriate activities. Time-out procedures can be very effective in producing rapid decreases in problem behaviors and are particularly well suited for use in situations where it is difficult to identify and/or control the exact reinforcers maintaining undesirable responses. It also works well in group or institutional settings, such as classrooms or hospital wards, where it is generally easier to deal with a disruptive individual by removing him or her from the group rather than trying to apply specific contingency management in the context of the group as a whole.

For the time-out technique to be effective, it must be used consistently and following each and every occurrence of the problem behavior. It is also important to determine that all reinforcements are truly absent from the time-out situation. Sending a child to a basement which is equipped with a television, musical instruments, and toys is likely to be ineffective in reducing target behaviors. Many recommend using a chair facing a corner, especially for very young children (e.g., Eyberg & Robinson, 1982). In addition to providing a response cost, time-out may well decrease the individual's general level of stimulation and so aid him or her in regaining self-control.

It is important not to get carried away in applying time-outs. Fairly brief time-out periods, 1 to 5 minutes, have been shown to be as effective with young children as 20- to 30-minute periods (Patterson & White, 1969) and have the advantage of seeming less punitive and traumatic. In most time-out programs, a brief explanation or "signal" is given immediately following the problem behavior and before the client is placed in time-out (for example, "You hit your brother so now you'll have to sit in the chair. Stay in the chair until I tell you you may get up"). Usually the time-out period is ended when both the predetermined time period has elapsed *and* the individual is relatively quiet, so as to avoid serendipitously reinforcing crying, tantrums, and so on with the termination of the time out (Hobbs, Forehand, & Murrary, 1978). It can be helpful to set a clock and place it in full view of the child, to diminish bargaining or whining behaviors. A common way of using time-out is to add a contingent delay for inappropriate behaviors while in time-out. Thus, if a child whines or gets out of the chair while in a 2-minute time-out period, one might reset the clock for an additional 15–30 seconds. There are, however, liabilities associated with the use of contingent delay. First, very resistant individuals may end up remaining in TO for durations well beyond what is necessary for effectiveness. Second, the more time spent in time-out, the less opportunities there are for engaging in appropriate, reinforcing behaviors.

Mace, Page, Ivancic, and O'Brien (1986) compared the effectiveness of brief time-out, with and without contingent delay, on three young children with severe behavior disorders, and concluded that delay and no-delay conditions were equally effective in reducing the frequency of the target behaviors.

Olson and Roberts (1987) reported on the use of time-out social skills training, or a combination of procedures in the treatment of 18 clinic-referred aggressive pairs of siblings and their mothers. Training procedures consisted of observing videotaped models reacting to conflict situations, plus verbal rehearsals and role-playing. Parents were then trained to administer either time-out, or additional social skills-oriented discussion, or a combination, at home. Time-out training was more effective than social skills training, and the combination appeared to be no more effective than time-out alone.

The TO procedure has at times been misapplied, and misrepresented, with some institutions claiming use of the technique to justify extreme and unethical practices, such as isolation and extreme deprivation, under the guise of therapy. For this reason modified time-out procedures have been proposed in which reinforcement, particularly social reinforcement, is temporarily stopped but the subject is not physically removed from the situation (nonexclusionary time-out). Foxx and Shapiro (1978) first described the advantages and disadvantages of such a procedure. Foxx, Foxx, Jones, and Kiely (1980) reported on the use of this technique in the reduction of episodes of intransigent aggressive behavior in an institutionalized, psychotic-like, mentally retarded adult male. The nonexclusionary time-out procedure was used as part of a treatment package which also included reinforcement for appropriate behavior and relaxation training. Time-out involved elimination of all social interaction with the subject for 24 hours following an aggressive episode. However, he was not physically removed from the regular environment. Several measures indicated a substantial reduction in aggressive behavior.

Extinction: Decreasing Behavior by Reinforcer Cessation

In actuality, most undesirable behavior persists because it is maintained by external reinforcement of one sort or another, whether or not the reinforcement process is recognized as such by those implementing it. One example is the aforementioned differential reinforcement of dependent versus independent behaviors of elderly people. Another common example is that of parents who unwittingly condition their child into whining or crying by attempting to comfort and console their children contingently on the whining. This is not to say that there is anything wrong with responding to a child's needs; however, if the comfort occurs regularly following whining, and is relatively unavailable otherwise, this strategy will almost certainly increase the probability of whining in the future. Meanwhile, since comforting the child tends to stop the whining on an immediate, short-term basis, the parents are being positively reinforced for this strategy and are more likely to continue to use it.

Given that undesirable behaviors are generally being maintained by "hidden" or unintentional reinforcers, an obvious way to decrease the likelihood of their occurrence is to remove the reinforcement completely. The technique of extinction involves terminating reinforcement for the target behavior.

Ayllon and Michael (1959) provided one of the first demonstrations of the efficacy of extinction in the treatment of psychotic talk by hospitalized patients. Prior to implementing the extinction program, ward nurses systematically observed patient behavior, recording the frequency of problem behavior and the kind and frequency of naturally occurring reinforcement. It became clear that much of the undesirable behavior was being maintained by contingent attention of the nursing staff. Subsequently, the nurses, who served as the agents of change (or behavioral engineers) were instructed to "ignore the behavior and act deaf and blind whenever it occurs." The goal for a delusional patient named Helen was extinction of her psychotic talk. After the nurses were instructed to use extinction (plus reinforcement of appropriate talk), the sick talk, which initially comprised approximately 90% of her total conversation, dropped steadily to a low of less than a 25% relative frequency by the 10th week. The delusional talk had persisted for 3 years previously. The reader is referred to Ayllon and Azrin (1968) for further illustrations of extinction with hospitalized patients, to O'Leary and O'Leary (1977) for examples of classroom applications, to Harris and Ersner–Hershfield (1978) for discussion of applications to severely disturbed and mentally retarded populations, and to Melamed and Siegel (1980) for applications to medical problems.

In a recent application, Lewis, Nelson, Nelson, and Reusink (1988) compared the effects of contingent attention and interest, systematic ignoring (extinction), and correction on the inappropriate talk of a brain-injured 21-year-old male. Inappropriate talk was defined as any unintelligible, foolish, or absurd statement not fitting the context of the conversation. Predictably, contingent attention and interest resulted in the behavior increasing, while both ignoring (extinction) and correction ("You're talking nonsense; people won't understand you; start again and tell me something that makes sense") resulted in decreases. Correction was, however, more effective than extinction.

Unlike externally reinforced behaviors, some behaviors such as head banging appear to be self-stimulating (self-reinforcing) and, as such, tend to undercut the therapist's success in eliminating their reinforcing components. Standard extinction procedures are generally not effective in eliminating this type of activity (Rincover, 1978) since they remove external but not intrinsic reinforcement for the behavior. However, Rincover and his colleagues (Rincover, 1978; Rincover, Cook, Peoples, & Packard, 1979) have demonstrated that, when the particular sensory feature reinforcing a particular behavior can be identified, for example, the sound of a spinning plate, it may be possible to use specific sensory extinction to effectively eliminate the behavior in question (e.g., block the child from experiencing the sound).

It would be reasonable to assume that a response that has been extinguished has been unlearned. In fact, this is not the case, as evidenced by a phenomenon known as reconditioning: A conditioned response that has been extinguished can be resurrected with relative ease by presenting further reinforced trials. Typically, reconditioning requires few reinforced trials to bring the response back to its former strength, suggesting that the response was not abolished by extinction so much as simply suppressed or masked. Thus, 2 months of work at not responding to a child's bedtime tantrums resulting at last in blessed peace in the evenings might be at least temporarily undone through a few well-meaning episodes by a visiting relative or baby sitter. Similarly, in the foregoing example of Helen and her psychotic talk, Ayllon and Michael note that the psychotic talk later reappeared at a higher frequency than originally; it was eventually found that Helen was obtaining "bootleg" reinforcement from individuals not familiar with the extinction program.

It is particularly important to be aware of two phenomena which occur in extinction training. The first is the extinction burst. When reinforcement is withheld in the early stages of the extinction process, the behavior is likely to actually increase in frequency or intensity, getting worse before it gets better. In essence the organism, whether adult, child, or pigeon, does not yet "believe" that reinforcement is not eventually forthcoming, figuring that a bit of additional effort will bring on the desired reinforcement, albeit a bit late. Thus, a good way to train a child into having particularly excruciating tantrums is to start out by ignoring the screams but, as they get louder, eventually to give in. The child learns that perserverence pays off in the end. It is especially important to keep the extinction burst in mind when considering extinction procedures for problem behaviors that are physically harmful or extremely destructive.

The second phenomenon is the partial reinforcement effect mentioned briefly in the foregoing discussion of schedules of reinforcement. The rate at which a behavior is extinguished has been shown to be a function of the reinforcement schedule maintaining it. Behaviors learned or maintained under partial reinforcement schedules (sometimes the parent ignores the tantrum, sometimes comforts or bribes the child) are generally far more resistant to extinction than those that have been continuously reinforced. The differential resilience of behaviors acquired on continuous versus partial schedules of reinforcement inspired Neisworth, Hunt, Gallop, and Madle (1985) to attempt an innovative approach to diminishing problematic behavior, one which they called *reinforcer displacement*. They hypothesized that it might be possible to shift the control of a behavior from some historic and inaccessible partial schedule to a clinically imposed continuous one, by positively reinforcing a target behavior on a continuous schedule, then suddenly discontinuing reinforcement. Ideally, the behavior should undergo rapid extinction. They applied this method to self-stimulatory behavior in two severely retarded 19-year-old males, one of whom engaged in handflapping, against wall, light switch, venetian blinds, and so on, and the other of whom exhibited repetitive finger flicking on his chair. Initially, both boys were reinforced for their behavior on a continuous schedule, with applesauce, pretzel bits, and fruit juice. Then, reinforcement was abruptly stopped. Both clients showed major decreases in the targeted behaviors. However, only the client who underwent an extinction burst maintained treatment gains at a 2-week follow-up. The authors hypothesize that, used in combination with other techniques, reinforcer displacement might prove useful in the treatment of resilient behaviors. (Obviously, such an approach could not be used for behaviors that constituted any danger to client or others.)

It is easy to confuse extinction with negative punishment, reinforcer withdrawal, or omission techniques like time-out or response cost, since all involve absence of reinforcement. The distinction is that, in omission techniques, good things that are otherwise present and available to the individual are withheld or removed contingently on undesirable behaviors, as a punishment. In extinction, reinforcement that previously occurred contingently on the behavior and which maintained it is no longer provided.

Decreasing Response Likelihood: Alternatives to Punishment and Extinction

Satiation: Making the Reinforcer Nonreinforcing

Extinction involves explicitly withholding reinforcement of an undesirable behavior. There are, however, ways of removing reinforcement without actually withholding it. Recall that one of the difficulties in implementing positive reinforcement programs is that reinforcers may lose their reinforcing properties at times (for example, a turkey sandwich sounds far less tempting several hours after Thanksgiving dinner than several hours before it). The principle underlying the loss of reinforcing properties is called satiation, and it can be used to advantage to decrease problem behaviors.

The technique involves providing the client with an overabundance of activities (response satiation) or of reinforcing commodities (stimulus satiation), to a point where they cease to be pleasant for the client. In a classic study, Ayllon (1963) decreased the extreme towel-hoarding behavior of a psychiatric inpatient by instructing the ward staff to give the patient as many towels as she wanted, completely noncontingently, rather than trying to block her efforts at acquiring them. After she had accumulated approximately 635 towels in her room, the woman voluntarily removed all of them, and permanently discontinued the behavior. In accordance with the law of supply and demand, the towels had ceased to be a valuable commodity to her (the "market glut" having destroyed her worth).

The satiation approach to the treatment of cigarette smoking is based on the same principle—that too much of a good thing is not good any more. The technique requires that smokers engage in continuous smoking and experience the effects of it until it becomes intolerable to them. The most common technique is rapid smoking (RS). As implemented by Schmale, Lichtenstein, and Harris (1972), RS resulted in abstinence rates at 6 months on the order of 60%. Unfortunately, there are physical risks associated with the rapid smoking procedure. While one could screen out those people who fall into high-risk categories, they are exactly the people most in need of treatment. In response to this problem, Walker and Franzini (1985) developed a low-risk procedure which they call taste satiation (TS). The technique involves having clients take smoke into their mouth, and hold it for 30 seconds while focusing on the unpleasant sensations in the mouth and throat. Following the exhale, they then inhale the next breath into their lungs, where they hold the smoke for 20 seconds, again focusing on aversive sensations. Mouth and lung inhales are alternated, and only five lung inhales are permitted per cigarette. A 5-minute break is given following each cigarette, and four cigarettes are smoked per session. To assess whether the taste satiation technique is doing anything beyond simply having smokers focus on the normal negative sensations associated with smoking, Walker and Franzini compared the efficacy of TS with focused smoking (FS). Taste satiation was indeed more effective than FS. Note that depending on the particular nature of the effects, certain so-called satiation procedures may in fact be drawing on true punishment, for example, if continuous smoking makes one ill rather than just tired of or satiated with the sensation.

Satiation is infrequently used, perhaps because of several difficulties that tend to be associated with it. First, it cannot be used in situations where it is not possible to identify and manipulate the reinforcing stimulus. Second, sometimes even when the reinforcer can be identified and manipulated, the potentially harmful effects of the reinforcer make it impractical and/or unethical. For example, the use of satiation to decrease self-injurious behavior seems ill advised, as does its application to the eating of sweets by a diabetic patient. Finally, social reinforcement may well not be subject to the effects of satiation (at least, not at the levels at which it is feasible to provide it).

Differential Reinforcement of Other (or of Incompatible) Behavior (DRI/DRO)

Differential reinforcement of incompatible (DRI) but appropriate behavior is often used in combination with extinction procedures. The key to its use is in identifying a behavior that is truly incompatible with the problem behavior. The basic principle is that one cannot do two incompatible things at once. Ideally, in addition to depending on the impossibility of doing two incompatible things at once, the therapist draws on the likelihood that reinforcement of the appropriate behavior will potentiate the effects of nonreinforcement of the inappropriate behavior. For example, Allen, Hart, Buell, Harris, and Wolf (1964) described a 4-year-old girl who spent minimal time interacting with other children in the nursery school setting but who elicited almost constant adult attention. By making adult attention contingent on her interaction with other children, and concurrently ignoring her during periods of social isolation or during attempts to elicit adult attention only, the treatment team successfully increased her appropriate social behavior. The particularly excellent thing about this technique is that it essentially involves providing the individual with alternative, more effective ways of getting the rewards he or she wants while undoing the problematic strategies for achieving them.

Azrin, Besalel, Jamner, & Caputo (1988) used an interruption procedure with simultaneous use of interruption to reduce head-banging behavior in mentally retarded clients. The technique was as follows: A trainer would stay behind the seated client while he or she engaged in an activity. If the client attempted the self-injurious behavior, the trainer blocked the movement of the offending arm or fist, reprimanded him or her, then held the hands for 2 minutes. At the end of this period, the client's hands were released and he or she was redirected to the task. Differential reinforcement of the incompatible task was implemented as the client displayed progressively longer periods without engaging in the target self-injurious behavior.

Along similar lines, Underwood, Figueroa, Thyer, and Nzeocha (1989) used a combination of interruption and DRI in the treatment of self-injurious behavior in two mentally retarded and autistic boys. Interruption plus DRI proved highly effective for one client, but not for the other. In accounting for the failure with the second client, the authors note that he had frequently been able to escape from the restraint imposed by trainers and seemed to enjoy doing so, thus making the interruption procedure positively reinforcing. In fact, then, he was not receiving differential reinforcement for incompatible behavior—rather, he was receiving reinforcement across the board. This illustrates, once again, the individual nature of reinforcement and punishment.

A slightly different approach involves reinforcing the client for exhibiting any behavior at all other than the problem behavior, during a specified period of time. This technique is referred to as differential reinforcement of other behavior (DRO). The underlying principle is that there is only so much time available in which to behave, and by definition, the more one is doing of certain things, the less one must do of other things. Most of the clinical reports of DRO refer to applications in the reduction of self-injurious behavior (Favell, McGimsey, & Jones, 1978; Repp & Deitz, 1974; Spiegler, 1983; Weiker & Harmon, 1975).

Overcorrection, Positive Practice, and Habit Reversal

A set of closely related alternative techniques for reducing unwanted behavior involves overcorrection. Overcorrection is composed of two components: restitution and positive practice. Restitution requires that, if behavior has led to environmental disruption, the person responsible for that disruption must repair or restore the setting to a state *better* than it was before the disruption (hence *over*correction). For example, if a person has thrown a tray of food on the floor, restitution might call for him to mop up not only the area of the floor that he dirtied, but perhaps to clean the whole room. Positive practice, originally proposed by Azrin and his colleagues (e.g., Azrin & Nunn, 1973; Azrin & Powers, 1975; Foxx & Azrin, 1972) as a means of reducing unwanted maladaptive behavior, involves repeated practice of adaptive behaviors. (Habit reversal is another term for the same procedure.) An example of positive practice would be for the aggressor in the aforementioned scenario to be required to practice setting the table, or serving dinner trays to his peers in an appropriate manner. Overcorrection is particularly appropriate for behaviors that occur at high rates, when there are few alternative behaviors available to reinforce and few effective reinforcers to remove contingent on inappropriate responding. When the behavior to be decreased does *not* cause environmental disruption, the restitution component is not called for and positive practice should be used alone.

Overcorrection has been used to improve oral reading and spelling among mentally retarded children (Singh, 1987; Singh & Singh, 1986; Stewart & Singh, 1986). A typical overcorrection approach involves having the teacher correct a child's error, then having the child repeat the correct pronunciation or spelling five times. Positive practice overcorrection has been demonstrated to be more effective than standard drills in increasing oral reading proficiency (Singh & Singh, 1986).

Habit reversal has been shown to be useful in the treatment of nail biting (Azrin, Nunn, & Frantz, 1980), neurodermatitis (Rosenbaum & Ayllon, 1981), and head banging (Gibbs & Luyben, 1985; Strauss, Rubinoff, & Atkeson, 1983). More recently it has been used in the treatment of muscle tics, in studies aimed at elucidating exactly how and why the procedure works. In their initial description of the technique of habit reversal, Azrin and Nunn (1973) stated that the competing response to be used should be "opposite or incompatible to that of the tic behavior or nervous habit" (p. 623). However, Miltenberger and Fuqua (1985) questioned whether the effects of habit reversal were due to the strengthening effect of the competing response procedure, or to the contingency of the alternative response on the response to be reversed. They compared the effects of a response-contingent competing response procedure with one requiring the noncontingent practice of a competing response, and found that noncontingent competing response practice was ineffective in reducing the target behaviors. That a contingency was necessary for outcomes to occur suggested to them that the effectiveness of the habit reversal technique may be based in a punishment process rather than a muscle strengthening process. (The superiority of positive practice overcorrection over drill in oral reading training documented by Singh & Singh is suggestive of the same.) In a follow-up study, Sharenow, Fuqua, and Miltenberger (1989) tested whether the topography of the competing response actually need to be similar to the response to be decreased and found that even dissimilar competing responses were in fact effective, if applied contingently, lending further credence to the conceptualization of habit reversal as a punishment procedure.

BRINGING RESPONSES UNDER STIMULUS CONTROL

Discrimination: Distinguishing When Behavior Will Result in Reinforcement

It is obviously simplistic to try to help a client change a behavior without some consideration of the situational and contextual factors involved. While an instrumental behavior is not elicited by external stimuli the way a classically conditioned response is, this does not mean that such stimuli have no effect; they exert considerable control over behavior by serving as discriminative stimuli. Few behaviors are appropriate in every situation. Discriminative stimuli tell us when which consequences may be expected given a particular response. Suppose a rat is trained to press a bar to obtain some rat chow. When a green light is on, pressing the bar will pay off. But when a red light is on, the response will be of no avail; no food pellets are delivered. In such circumstances, the green light will become a positive discriminative stimulus, the red light a negative one. That is, the rat will learn to bar press in the presence of the green light, and not to bar press in the presence of the red light. The light signals a particular relationship between a behavior and reinforcement—for example, "if you respond now, you'll be reinforced." The ringing of a doorbell is a discriminative stimulus; it does not compel a response, but rather serves as a cue that reinforcement (or punishment) is likely to occur if the response of opening the door is made. The essence of operant psychology, the three-term contingency, involves an antecedent cue or discriminative stimulus, followed by an operant response (the target), followed by the contingent consequences (reward or punishment):

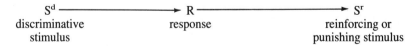

$$S^d \longrightarrow R \longrightarrow S^r$$

discriminative stimulus · · · · · · · · · · response · · · · · · · · · · reinforcing or punishing stimulus

Maladaptive behavior is often the result of responding to an inappropriate stimulus, or failing to respond to a stimulus, such that otherwise reasonable behavior is emitted at inappropriate times or places or is not emitted when it should have been.

The process of manipulating the antecedent conditions that set the stage for reinforced or reinforceable responding is the process of bringing a response under *stimulus control*. It is often easier, cheaper, faster, or more efficient to program (build in) antecedent stimuli for appropriate behavior than to alter actual situational contingencies of reward or punishment. That is, it is easier to learn discriminative stimulus "cues" which will encourage or discourage a particular response rather than actually to change the naturally occurring reinforcement or punishments that follow the behavior in the real world. An example is a typical component of many weight reduction programs: One can instruct a client to eat only in the kitchen and/or at particular times of day and not elsewhere or at other times. Eventually, the kitchen at mealtimes becomes a discriminative cue for eating and other places and times become discriminative cues for not eating. Clearly this technique is easier to implement than would be administering electric shock following episodes of snacking. Likewise, encouraging students to set aside a regular place for studying can help them to concentrate better, since the place becomes a cue for the behavior.

Stimulus control may employ the provision of cues for appropriate behavior, weakening of cues for inappropriate behavior, or both. Nolan (1968) reported on the use of stimulus control procedures in the reduction and eventual elimination of smoking behavior. In this case report, the client was first instructed to smoke only while seated in one particular chair. The chair faced a corner and other behaviors, such as reading, talking with family member, and so on were prohibited while the client was seated in it. In a second phase of treatment the chair was removed to the client's basement. This effectively reduced the range of cues that preceded smoking (and limited the external reinforcement for the undesirable behavior).

Prompting

Another application of discriminative stimulus training is the technique known as prompting. Prompting is widely used in combination with reinforcement techniques; in early stages of treatment, its purpose is essentially to get the behavior to occur enough for the reinforcement contingencies to strengthen it. The purpose of the prompt is to cue that behavior that will elicit reinforcement. Prompts are verbal, physical, or environmental cues used to direct the learner's attention to the required behavior. A prompt must initially be effective in provoking the response every time it is presented so that, at the beginning of treatment, a very conspicuous prompt might be necessary.

Prompting has been used to a multitude of innovative ends in recent years. For example, White, Mathews, and Fawcett (1989) used prompting to train people confined to wheelchairs to do wheelchair push-ups, an effective way of avoiding painful and dangerous pressures sores. Two 11-year-old children with spina bifida were given instruction about the nature of pressure sores and how and why to do wheelchair push-ups. Each client was then provided with a programmable watch which emitted a beep every half-hour. On hearing the beep, the child was required to do a wheelchair push-up for at least 3 seconds. If no push-up was done, a pressure-sensitive air bladder under the seat would trigger an aversive 6-second alarm. Both clients showed substantially increased rates of regular wheelchair push-ups.

In another application of the prompting procedure, Burgio, Engel, McCormick, Hawkins, and Scheve (1988) attempted to treat urinary incontinence in elderly institutionalized patients. A schedule of prompting and toileting every 2 hours was instituted for four clients. They were approached by staff, prompted to toilet, and were taken to the bathroom unless protesting that they did not need it. Dry pants were praised, while wet pants elicited corrective feedback such as the statement "Hold it and let us know if you need assistance." Results showed a mean increase in dryness from 30% of "pants checks" initially, to 62% during the treatment phase. For two clients, prompting was eventually "thinned" to a once every 4 hours schedule, and for a third, to once every 3 hours. (No improvements were noted, however, in self-initiated, independent toileting.)

In other recent applications, prompts in the form of signs, and human prompters, have been used to promote parents' use of safety belts found in shopping carts for young children (Ferrari & Baldwin, 1989) as well as the use of safety belts in automobiles (Williams, Thyer, Bailey, & Harrison, 1989).

In a properly applied intervention, the prompt should be gradually "faded" and finally eliminated so that at the conclusion of training the target response should occur reliably without prompting. It is important to note that, although prompts are faded out, contingent reinforcement should continue. If responding ceases during fading, an earlier prompt can be reinvoked until the response is reestablished. Fading can then proceed at a slower pace, in more gradual steps.

Chaining

Operant methods are most usually used in situations where the target behaviors are relatively simple, discrete stimulus-response units. However, through the management of discriminative stimuli in a process known as chaining, it is possible to develop and manage exceedingly complex forms of behavior. Chaining is called for when the behavior to be learned is composed of several different elements that must be performed sequentially. Complex motor skills like pole vaulting or serving a tennis ball are generally learned in this way, and the technique has been used to develop tooth brushing and even social skills.

In chaining, each component behavior of the chain acts as both a cue (discriminative stimulus) for the next behavior in the sequence and as a reinforcer for the preceding behavior. By means of this technique, animals have been trained to perform incredibly complex response chains. For example, "Priscilla, the Fastidious Pig" was trained to do an advertisement for a particular brand of farm feed. She learned to turn on a radio, eat breakfast at a kitchen table, pick up dirty clothes and drop them in a hamper, vacuum the floor, and finally push a shopping cart down an aisle where she selected the sponsor's feed in preference to Brand X (Breland & Breland, 1951).

Chaining can proceed in either a forward or a backward direction; that is, the first behavior is to be conditioned through positive reinforcement can be either the first behavior in the chain or the last behavior in the chain. However, backward chaining is often considered to be more effective since it avoids the risk of extinction occurring to the components already built in as one is working on the next piece in the chain.

MAINTENANCE OF GAINS AND GENERALIZATION OF NEW LEARNING BEYOND THE THERAPEUTIC SITUATION

The term *generalization* has been used broadly to mean that behavior change carries over (transfers or generalizes) to conditions other than those included in training. The extension of behavior change over time is generally called *response maintenance* (or *resistance to extinction*), while the extension of behavioral changes to new situations and settings is termed *transfer of training*. Both are particularly important to behavioral treatment programs, and both are difficult to ensure.

Essentially, in contrast to discrimination, where an organism learns to distinguish between situations where behavior will or will not be reinforced, generalization involves the organism's responding to a new stimulus or situation in more or less the same way as to a familiar one. For example, unless previously trained to discriminate, a pigeon trained to peck at a key illuminated with a particular color light, say yellow, will also peck another key illuminated with a similar color light, say orange-yellow (although, since it is not an identical stimulus, the response is likely to be smaller in magnitude or slightly different in form). Generalization from one stimulus to another, and from one response situation to another, is one of the keys to maintaining therapeutic gains outside the clinical situation (i.e., in the real world) since a major difficulty in applying operant techniques is that, when the program ends, discriminative stimuli and reinforcement contingencies change, and all too often, behavior patterns will as well. In order to increase the durability of treatment gains, a number of strategies may be used.

One approach depends on bringing responses under the control of discriminative cues or reinforcers that have been selected based on their actual existence and likelihood of occurrence in the client's everyday life. In this way continuity between clinical training and the real world is built in, and a minimal "stretch" is required to generalize responses. This may be referred to as bringing behavior under the control of natural contingencies.

A second approach is to gradually phase out the need for prompts and reinforcement contingencies used to build and strengthen behavior (a method known as fading). Once the target behavior is occurring regularly in response to prompts, one can begin to fade out the prompts, using more and more subtle or minimal ones more and more sporadically, until finally no prompts are used at all. A similar principle underlies the thinning of reinforcement. A child trained to do homework in exchange for monetary rewards may first receive reinforcement daily, then every second day, then weekly, and so on until finally, in the ideal world, the improvement in grades and increased self-esteem that comes with the increased studying will serve to maintain the behavior in the absence of any artificial rewards.

In fading, cues are gradually becoming less and less prominent so that the client is gradually weaned from dependence on external stimuli and comes to rely more on internal (or naturally occurring external) ones. In thinning, the same is happening, and in addition, one is effectively taking a relatively continuous schedule of reinforcement and switching over to a partial (intermittent) one, thus capitalizing on the partial reinforcement effect. In both of these cases, it is particularly helpful if one can ensure that the behavior being trained will come to elicit *natural* reinforcers in the real world—money, competence, approval, and so on—and to set up the schedules of cueing and reinforcement such that control over behavior gradually shifts from the artificially provided (treatment-centered) cues/rewards to the naturally occurring ones in the real world.

Among the most effective ways to ensure maintenance of treatment gains is to use a broad-based sample of situations for training. In this way, the therapist sets up training so that the client learns a generalized response rather than a specific behavior for a specific situation. Day and Horner (1989) clearly demonstrated this in a study comparing the relative efficacy of two approaches to teaching profoundly mentally retarded clients liquid pouring. In one condition, clients received general case instruction guidelines, with a full set of eight teaching examples of pouring liquid from a pitcher into a receptacle. Receptacles varied in size and shape, and examples ranged from very easy to fairly difficult. In the second condition, clients were taught only the three easiest of the examples from the full set. Results clearly indicated that only after training with the full set of general case examples did the learners become competent with nontrained generalization probe tasks. Furthermore, the set of easy examples resulted in learners making topographically predictable errors when tested on generalization tasks.

Horner, Eberhard, and Sheehan (1986) have suggested basic guidelines for establishing generalization: First, specify the set of stimulus situations across which the behavior is desired to generalize. Second, define the range of relevant dimensions across which they vary. Third, define the range of response variations required across the various stimulus situations. Fourth, select and teach examples that sample the full range of stimulus situations and responses.

Finally, one can increase the likelihood of maintenance by making use of social support (e.g., peer facilitators, training of family members, etc.) and, when applicable, teaching self-management techniques.

RECOMMENDATIONS FOR IMPLEMENTING
SPECIFIC TECHNIQUES

Having described the basic terms and principles underlying operant methods, and having equipped the beginning applied behavior analyst with a full arsenal of concepts, we turn now to a step-by-step description of how to implement selected techniques properly.

Positive Reinforcement

1. Select reinforcers. Do not expect that what is a reward for one person will necessarily be a reward for another. Identify reinforcers by observing their functional effects on behavior. If using the Premack principle (using a relatively high-probability behavior to reinforce a lower-probability behavior), identify activity reinforcers through systematic observation of the individual in a variety of settings.
2. When delivering reinforcement, rewards should be administered immediately, contingently (i.e., both occurring when behavior occurs, and *not* occurring when behavior does not occur) and consistently to maximize effectiveness.
3. Use a variety of different reinforcers to minimize the loss of potency due to satiation.
4. Reinforce behavior often while bringing it to optimal frequency (e.g., continuous schedule of reinforcement), then thin out reinforcement gradually (e.g., shift to partial reinforcement) to minimize loss of potency of the reinforcer and to increase durability of effects.
5. Use social reinforcement whenever feasible to permit the developing behavior to be maintained in the real world. If necessary, develop social reinforcer effectiveness by fading the use of primary reinforcers.

Negative Reinforcement

1. When using the termination of an aversive stimulus to reward a behavior, termination should occur immediately, contingently, and consistently following the target behavior.
2. The time between trials must not be too brief. The aversive stimulus should be off long enough that the relief is enjoyable, otherwise it cannot serve as an effective reward.
3. If, over time, the individual is not making reliable responses, interrupt training and try to determine if unknown contingencies outside of therapy are interfering with the program or if the aversive consequences are indeed functionally aversive.
4. In avoidance conditioning, an individual learns to make a response in order to avoid a noxious stimulus. In this paradigm, two events are connected—the aversive stimulus itself, and the cue to the onset of the aversive stimulus (there must be such a cue for avoidance to be possible; if no signal precedes aversive stimulus, the organism can only wait for it to occur, then m

escape response rather than avoid it altogether). Individuals who learn to remove themselves reliably from a situation containing the cue to the onset of the aversive stimulus also undergo extinction of the relation between the cue and the aversive event that follows it, since each time they avoid the aversive stimulus, the cue is followed by no consequences. To prevent avoidance from starting to weaken as a result of these unintentional extinction trials, it is advisable to pair the cue and the aversive stimulus on an intermittent basis with decreasing frequency.

Shaping

1. Observe the individual whose behavior repertoire is considered deficient. What responses occur at a high frequency? Identify the antecedent and consequent environmental stimuli associated with these high-frequency behaviors. Note the variability in topography (form, force, or duration) of the available responses. Based on these observations, decide whether the desired response can be differentiated out of existing behaviors, and if so, what a first approximation to the end goal should be.

2. Establish the criterion for the first approximation. As Blackwood (1971) puts it: "In setting the criterion, we are dividing the responses into two classes; responses most like those we want and responses least like those we want. Notice here that the criterion must be set low or all responding will be extinguished" (p. 6).

3. Arrange the situational context for maximum likelihood of response emission. If the desired response involves other people or stimuli, arrange to have them present during shaping.

4. Differentially reinforce variants of ongoing behavior that meet the criterion for approximations of the desired response, while withdrawing reinforcement from variants that are incompatible with the desired goal. If repeated reinforcement fails to reliably establish a response, the criterion might need to be lowered.

5. Observe shifts in the direction of the goal behavior and shift the criterion accordingly. For example, when a child is reliably turning to look at the sound of his name within 10 seconds of being called, the criterion may be shifted to require a response within 5 seconds.

6. The use of verbal or gestural cues or instructions is recommended at all stages of the shaping process, even though they may not at first reliably elicit the behavior being shaped. The cues to be used by the shaper can initially be determined from baseline observations of the child's behavior. For example, if a child routinely looks in the direction of a novel sound, one can make an unusual noise, then call the child's name, then reinforce him or her for looking. In this way, the looking response will eventually come to be controlled by the sound of the name being called.

Response-Contingent Aversive Stimulation (Punishment)

When positive control and nonphysical forms of punishment are ineffective in changing behavior, the use of response-contingent aversive stimulation works best if used in accordance with the following guidelines:

1. Use it in conjunction with positive reinforcement of appropriate behavior.
2. Deliver RCAS as soon as possible after the target behavior. Use a continuous schedule until the response is suppressed or eliminated.
3. The duration of RCAS need not be very long. With moderate electric shocks, a duration of 0.1 second has proven effective. Check the materials used to deliver the punishment often for safety (see Butterfield, 1975). Aversive stimuli which are effective but not unduly harsh should be sought. For example, hand slapping, shaking, even tickling can suppress behaviors in youngsters. (Recall the use of water mist in the suppression of pica.) All methods should be applied with care and caution. Extended periods of RCAS should be avoided, and all those involved in its administration should be on guard for negative side-effects.
4. The client should be informed of the nature of the RCAS contingency.
5. To promote appropriate maintenance and generalization of effects, different individuals should be involved in the delivery of RCAS, including, where called for, those persons with whom the client will have contact outside of therapy. Use fading techniques to bring punished responses under discriminative control (e.g., use a warning cue prior to delivering punishment; in time it may be enough to stop the target behavior). Do not apply positive reinforcers in close proximity to the delivery of RCAS to avoid the risk of creating approach-avoidance conflicts.
6. The individual who delivers RCAS should do so only if he or she is in agreement with the clinical decision that dictates its use.

Negative Punishment: Response Cost

1. As with any aversive technique, response-cost procedures should be used in conjunction with positive reinforcement for appropriate and incompatible behaviors.
2. In establishing an RC system, the first step is to choose effective and appropriate reinforcers to be lost. Begin by determining if the reinforcers to be lost are actually valued in the sense that the client will work to earn them. Arrange the program so that items lost or forfeited cannot be easily or rapidly replaced. Be sure to arrange the overall earnings-cost program so that "fines" are realistic, not bankrupting the individual for a single infraction nor making too little a dent in his or her savings to be noticed. For individuals who have not earned them, it may be necessary to supply reinforcers noncontingently at first so that RC procedures can be applied.
3. Institute fines as soon as possible after a misbehavior.

4. By pairing RC with verbal criticism, it becomes possible to fade out the tangible punishment contingency and bring behavior under verbal control.

Negative Punishment: Time-Out

1. Again, as with any aversive procedures, time-out should be used in conjunction with positive reinforcement of desirable behaviors.
2. Arrange the time-out area to be free of attractive or distracting activities. If possible, monitor the individual's behavior while in TO. The individual who can make a game out of TO will not benefit from it. The TO area should be small but well ventilated. A chair facing into a remote corner is suitable for young children. If feasible, arrange the area where appropriate behavior is desired to be as attractive as possible, with many reinforcing activities and objects immediately available for appropriate behavior in order to maximize the contrast between time-out and time-in. Absence of effects for TO are often attributable to the relatively low magnitude of payoff for correct responding.
3. Long durations of TO are undesirable because the individual is removed from opportunities to carry out and learn adaptive responses. It is advisable to begin with short durations of TO first, and work up to longer durations if necessary, rather than the reverse. Most successful programs with children employ TO durations of between 5 and 20 minutes, and for very young children, periods as short as 1 to 5 minutes may be effective. In keeping with these duration guidelines, distance and travel time to the TO area should also be short.
4. Try not to reinforce any behaviors (either with positive attention or with a display of anger or disappointment) while going to or returning from the TO area. Similarly, never use TO if the situation from which the individual is being removed is an unpleasant one, to avoid turning TO into an escape or avoidance opportunity and thus increasing rather than decreasing the frequency of the behavior on which it is contingent.
5. Use verbal and/or nonverbal signals before initiating TO. The chain of behaviors leading up to the TO signal should include a "stop cue" which, if noticed, can come to suppress the disruptive behavior at lower magnitudes and without necessitating going through with the TO.

Differential Reinforcement of Incompatible/Other Responses

1. When the target undesirable behavior occurs at high rates, it may be necessary to begin by prompting the other or incompatible response. Begin by employing brief time intervals for initial reinforcement of the desirable response to permit the learner to earn sufficient reward for its emission. If using DRI, try to select an incompatible response that is already in the client's behavioral repertoire and which is likely to be maintained in the natural environment. Be sure to avoid reinforcing other behaviors that themselves are likely to become problematic to the client in the long run.

2. Use DRO schedules consistently to eliminate the undesirable behavior in as many contexts as it is likely to occur.
3. Avoid sole use of these procedures if the response to be eliminated is life threatening and must be rapidly suppressed. (See Sulzer–Azaroff & Mayer, 1977, for further discussion of these and other methods.)

Overcorrection, Positive Practice, or Habit Reversal

1. Overcorrection is particularly useful in dealing with behavior that infringes on the rights of others. (cf. Spiegler, 1983, pp. 155–156).
2. These procedures should be applied as quickly as possible after the target undesirable behavior.
3. Try to insure that the restitution and positive practice components focus on actions that will be beneficial to the client, rather than merely unpleasant and/or embarrassing.
4. Use these procedures only with clients capable of understanding them or of cooperating with their intended educational function.
5. As always, use them together with positive reinforcement of appropriate behaviors.
6. Be alert for changes in other inappropriate but nontargeted behaviors, during and following training periods.

NEW APPLICATIONS AND EXTENSIONS

As the illustrations of the basic principles in the preceding sections may reflect, the majority of behavior modification programs have traditionally been carried out in institutional settings for the mentally retarded, the chronically mentally ill, or emotionally disturbed youth, as well as in regular classroom or home situations. Recently, a wide range of new situations and problems have become part of the domain of applicability of behavior modification. We will sample four major innovative current applications of behavioral technology: behavioral medicine, gerontology, neuropsychology, and community/ecological psychology.

Behavioral Medicine

Behavioral medicine can be described as the application of behavioral science principles and methods to the prevention, assessment, and treatment of physical health problems. Behavioral interventions have been used to promote preventative practices (e.g., using combined approaches including stimulus control, reinforcement contingencies, satiation, and cognitive techniques to achieve cessation of smoking; see Glasgow & Lichtenstein, 1987, for a review of approaches and long-term results; also more recently using instructions, feedback, and reinforcement to train women to self-examine for early symptoms of breast cancer and men to self-examine for symptoms of testicular cancer (Friman, Finney, Glassock, Weigel, & Christopherson, 1986; Hall et al., 1980). Behavioral techniques have also been applied to the ever-present problem of getting patients to adhere to medical treatment regimens (compliance) (e.g., reinforcement and instruction to increase compliance with special diet, exercise, and medication regimens among patients with various conditions including coronary disease, hypertension, diabetes and renal disorders; Dubbert, Rappaport, & Martin, 1987; Epstein et al., 1981; Russo & Varni, 1982; Stuart, 1982).

Cognitive behavioral approaches are currently the treatment of choice for the eating disorders, both anorexia nervosa and bulimia. For anorexia, the basic approach consists of isolating patients from reinforcers (material or social) which are then delivered contingently on specified amounts of calories ingested or weight gained. It is currently the most effective way of producing short-term weight gain. Although this approach fares less well in the long run, with significant relapse rates and nonaddressing of other symptomatology, even short-term success is of considerable importance in a life-threatening disorder where the population to be treated frequently does not acknowledge a problem and is highly resistant to treatment. Although the emerging concensus is that a single-modality treatment approach is inadequate to handle anorexia, operant techniques will no doubt continue to be a core part of any multi-modal treatment package. (See Bemis, 1987; Garfinkel & Garner, 1982; and Halmi, 1985 for reviews of this literature.) A caveat to be particularly aware of when dealing with this population is that, in implementing treatment programs, one should avoid as much as possible engaging in power struggles and making patients "feel tricked into relinquishing control over their bodies and their lives" (Bruch, 1978, p. 652).

The degree to which behavioral medicine has become a major focus of interest for applied behavior analysts is illustrated by the fact that an entire recent issue of *Behavior Modification* (Vol. 11, July 1987) was devoted to the topic (see Russo & Budd, 1987 and Williamson, 1987 for an overview of the role, possibilities, and limitations of behavior therapy as applied to behavioral medicine).

Behavioral Gerontology

A second domain in which operant techniques are gaining popularity involves geriatric problems and populations. We have already discussed the use of behavioral analysis in identifying the conditions giving rise to dependency among the elderly, and the use of prompting and toileting to manage urinary incontinence in the institutionalized elderly. If widely applied, treatment for urinary incontinence could save millions of dollars in diaper and laundry costs alone (Burgio & Burgio, 1986). Yet, as Burgio and Burgio point out, "elderly persons are (still) under-represented in research and clinical applied behavior analysis, in spite of data suggesting that behavior problems are quite prevalent in both community dwelling and institutionalized elderly" (p. 321). Behavioral gerontology is the study of how environmental antecedents and consequents interact with the aging process to give rise to behavior problems. Behavior problems are commonly cited as the major causes of stress among caregivers and are major determinants of decisions to institutionalize.

Two general strategies are suggested by gerontologists: teaching self-management skills to elderly persons (as, for example, in Whitehead, Burgio, & Engel's 1985 study using self-directed scheduled toileting and biofeedback to reduce fecal incontinence in 17 elderly patients); and the training of caregivers, as, for example, the work of Pinkston and colleagues who teach behavioral principles and skills to family members to help them manage problems as they occur (e.g., Pinkston & Linsk, 1984). Similarly, Baltes and Barton (1977), Burgio, Burgio, Engel, and Tice (1986), and others have trained institutional staff in behavioral principles to decrease dependency behaviors and to increase self-care and mobility. While one must be sensitive to the special needs of an elderly population, adapting procedures to take into account physiological changes and decline in health, the evidence suggests that behavioral principles and techniques can effectively be applied to this population (see Burgio & Burgio, 1986 and Carstensen, 1988 for further discussion).

Treatment of Neurologically Impaired Individuals

Recently there have been attempts to provide a perspective on the interface between neuropsychology and behavior therapy (e.g., Gouvier, 1987; Horton & Miller, 1985). While neuronal cell bodies do not regenerate after destruction, the term *recovery of function* refers to return to improved or near-normal status following injury to the nervous system. While there may be some degree of structural or neurophysiological recovery and while pharmacological agents may aid in facilitating recovery of function, a fast-growing area involves behavioral approaches to rehabilitation of the neurologically impaired.

The behavioral mechanisms can be divided into two types: (a) reorganization of the brain via specific, intensive, retraining experiences; and (b) behavioral strategy change, whereby different internal and external cues are employed to encourage adequate performance by calling on alternate preexisting (and spared) behavioral skills. It is possible to train an intact brain region in one cerebral hemisphere to take over for a damaged region in another hemisphere; to get a more elementary neurologic system to compensate for a higher cortical area of the brain; or to get a higher center to serve when a lower structure is impaired. These approaches (originally described by Luria) focus on using existing strengths to compensate. A somewhat different approach taken by Diller and colleagues (e.g., Diller & Gordon, 1981) focuses on cognitive retraining of deficits.

In a broad review of the research on the use of behavior therapy with brain-damaged individuals, Horton and Miller (1985) conclude that there are substantial data indicating that behavior therapy methods are effective with

brain-damaged individuals for problems ranging from uncooperative and negativistic behavior, to resisting physical therapy, to memory and attentional deficits,
aphasia, and alexia (inability to speak and read, respectively) and motor problems.
Furthermore, Prigatano (1985) and others have begun to investigate the efficacy of
treatments for the emotional and self-awareness aspects of neurological deficits,
reporting that although full recovery is unlikely, the degree of gain may be
sufficient to have significant impact on a patient's quality of life and capacity
for independence. As advances result in more and more individuals surviving
strokes, head injuries, and the like, this field of application will no doubt continue
to grow.

Community/Ecological Applications

The final domain of current application of behavioral techniques can loosely be
termed *public safety and public issues*. Techniques have been applied to various
areas of safety to prevent injury and death. For example, numerous studies have
focused on increasing the use of seat belts. Rudd and Geller (1985) devised a
cost-effective incentive program which was implemented by the campus police of
a large university. For each of three 3-week intervention periods, campus police
officers recorded license plate numbers of vehicles with drivers wearing a shoulder
belt. From these numbers, 10 raffle winners were drawn who received gift
certificates donated by community merchants. Faculty and staff increased belt
usage substantially; students did so less, perhaps because of irregular schedules on
campus and thus less exposure to the program. Furthermore, community opinions
of police improved over the course of the program.

In a similar vein, Sowers–Hoag, Thyer, and Bailey (1987) increased belt use
among children who attended an after-school day care program. Information was
provided to the children about seat belt use, and assertiveness training and
role-playing were employed to help children ask where to find and how to fasten
seat belts. In addition, children practiced fastening various types of seat belts. A
reward system was also used such that children who had used seat belts were
eligible for a lottery the next day. Seat belt use was assessed daily as parents picked
up their children in the parking lot. Seat belt use increased dramatically, and gains
were maintained 3 months after completion of the program.

Behavioral programs have also been used in industry to promote safety practices on the part of employees. For example, Fox, Hopkins, and Anger (1987)
used an incentive program at two open-pit mines in the form of trading stamps
(tokens) to decrease job-related injuries, days lost from work, and medical/
insurance and equipment damage costs from accidents. Trading stamps were
provided at the end of each month to workers who had avoided injury and the need
for medical care due to accidents. Bonuses were provided to all members of a
group (all those working under a given supervisor) if no one in that group had been
injured, as well as to employees whose suggestions for improving safety were

adopted. Stamps were lost contingently on missing work for injury or causing an accident. The stamps were redeemable for hundreds of items. Both number of accidents among workers and monetary costs to the company were dramatically reduced.

A FINAL WORD

We have briefly outlined and illustrated the fundamental change principles that derive from an operant learning view of behavior and its determinants. Rather than summarize what we have said, we end with a few words of caution and of encouragement.

On an encouraging note, we believe that, in the years ahead, the principles and practices of applied behavior analysis will continue to find a place in the clinician's armamentarium. Furthermore, growth will occur both through the recombination of basic concepts and the integration of operant and nonoperant (social, developmental, cognitive, etc.) perspectives.

We find, however, that a strain of old-fashioned positivism, operationalism, and reductionism is still quite dominant among many behavioral investigators—to the point that only one level of analysis (the act) is considered appropriate and only environmental forces are viewed as potentially causal. The limitations engendered by such a strict (radical behavioral) approach are beginning to be appreciated by many clinicians who once saw the learning perspective as the antidote to "mentalism," but who now recognize that careful analyses, beyond the level of instrumental performance, can and should be employed if a complete picture of the adaptive process is desired. Fortunately, the reader will find, among the other chapters in this volume, the conceptual and practical raw material for just such an integrative or systematic approach—an approach wherein operant methods will surely occupy a central role.

REFERENCES

Agras, W. S., & Werne, J. (1977). Behavior modification in anorexia nervosa. In R. A. Vigersky (Ed.), *Anorexia nervosa*. New York: Raven Press.

Allen, K. E., Hart, B., Buell, J. S., Harris, F. R., & Wolf, M. M. (1964). Effects of social reinforcement on isolate behavior of a nursery school child. *Child Development, 35,* 511–518.

Altman, K., Haavik, S., & Higgins, S. (1983). Modifying the self-injurious behavior of an infant with Spina Bifida and diminished pain sensitivity. *Journal of Behavior Therapy and Experimental Psychiatry, 14,* 165–168.

Ayllon, T. (1963). Intensive treatment of psychotic behavior by stimulus satiation and food reinforcement. *Behaviour Research and Therapy, 1,* 53–62.

Ayllon, T., & Azrin, N. H. (1968). *The token economy: A motivational system for therapy and rehabilitation*. New York: Appleton-Century-Crofts.

Ayllon, T., & Michael, J. (1959). The psychiatric nurse as a behavioral engineer. *Journal of the Experimental Analysis of Behavior, 2,* 323–334.

Azrin, N. H., Besalel, V. A., Jamner, J. P., & Caputo, J. N. (1988). Comparative study of behavioral methods of treating self-injury. *Behavioral Residential Treatment, 3,* 119–152.

Azrin, N. H., & Nunn, R. (1973). Habit reversal: A method of eliminating nervous habits and tics. *Behaviour Research and Therapy, 11,* 619–628.

Azrin, N. H., Nunn, R., & Frantz, S. E. (1980). Habit reversal vs. negative practice treatment of nailbiting. *Behaviour Research and Therapy, 18,* 281–285.

Azrin, N. H., & Powers, M. A. (1975). Eliminating classroom disturbances of emotionally disturbed children by positive practice procedures. *Behavior Therapy, 6,* 525–534.

Baer, D. M., Wolf, M. M., & Risley, T. R. (1987). Some still-current dimensions of applied behavior analysis. *Journal of Applied Behavior Analysis, 20,* 313–327.

Baltes, M. M. (1988). The etiology and maintenance of dependency in the elderly: Three phases of operant research. *Behavior Therapy, 19,* 301–319.

Baltes, M. M., & Barton, E. M. (1977). New approaches toward aging: A case for the operant model. *Educational Gerontology: An International Quarterly, 2,* 383–405.

Bemis, K. M. (1987). The present status of operant conditioning for the treatment of anorexia nervosa. *Behavior Modification, 11,* 432–463.

Blackwood, R. O. (1971). *Operant control of behavior.* Akron, OH: Exordium Press.

Boudin, H. M. (1972). Contingency contracting as a therapeutic tool in the deceleration of amphetamine use. *Behavior Therapy, 3,* 604–608.

Breland, K., & Breland, M. (1951). A field of applied animal psychology. *American Psychologist, 6,* 202–204.

Bruch, H. (1978). Dangers of behavior modification in treatment of anorexia nervosa. In J. P. Brady & H. K. H. Brodie (Eds.), *Controversy in psychiatry* (pp. 645–654). Philadelphia: W. B. Saunders.

Burgio, L. D., & Burgio, K. L. (1986). Behavioral gerontology: Application of behavioral methods to the problems of older adults. *Journal of Applied Behavior Analysis, 19,* 321–328.

Burgio, L. D., Burgio, K. L., Engel, B. T., & Tice, L. M. (1986). Increasing distance and independence of ambulation in elderly nursing home residents. *Journal of Applied Behavior Analysis, 19,* 357–366.

Burgio, L., Engel, B. T., McCormick, K., Hawkins, A., & Scheve, A. (1988). Behavioral treatment for urinary incontinence in elderly inpatients: Initial attempts to modify prompting and toileting procedures. *Behavior Therapy, 19,* 345–357.

Butterfield, W. H. (1975). Electric shock safety factors when used for the aversive conditioning of humans. *Behavior Therapy, 6,* 98–110.

Carr, E. G., & Newsom, C. (1985). Demand-related tantrums. Conceptualizations and treatment. *Behavior Modification, 9,* 403–426.

Carstensen, L. L. (1988). The emerging field of behavioral gerontology. *Behavior Therapy, 19,* 259–281.

Ciminero, A. R., Calhoun, K. S., & Adams, H. E. (Eds.). (1986). *Handbook of behavioral assessment* (2nd ed.). New York: John Wiley & Sons.

Day, H. M., & Horner, R. H. (1989). Building response classes: A comparison of two procedures for teaching generalized pouring to learners with severe disabilities. *Journal of Applied Behavior Analysis, 22,* 223–229.

Diller, L., & Gordon, W. A. (1981). Intervention for cognitive deficits in brain-injured adults. *Journal of Consulting and Clinical Psychology, 49,* 822–834.

Dubbert, P. M., Rappaport, N. B., & Martin, J. E. (1987). Exercise in cardiovascular disease. *Behavior Modification, 11,* 329–347.

Dumas, J. E. (1989). Let's not forget the context in behavioral assessment. *Behavioral Assessment, 11,* 231–247.

Epstein, L. H., Beck, S., Figueroa, J., Farkas, G., Kazdin, A. E., Daneman, D., & Becker, D. (1981). The effects of targeting improvements in urine glucose on metabolic control in children with insulin-dependent diabetes. *Journal of Applied Behavior Analysis, 14*, 365–375.

Eyberg, S. M., & Robinson, E. A. (1982). Parent-child interaction training: Effects on family functioning. *Journal of Clinical Child Psychology, 11*, 130–137.

Favell, J. E. (1977). *The power of positive reinforcement*. Springfield, IL: Charles C Thomas.

Favell, J. E., McGimsey, J. F., & Jones, M. L. (1978). The use of physical restraints in the treatment of self-injury and as positive reinforcement. *Journal of Applied Behavior Analysis, 11*, 225–241.

Ferrari, J. R., & Baldwin, C. H. (1989). From cars to carts. Increasing safety belt usage in shopping carts. *Behavior Modification, 13*, 51–64.

Ferster, C. B., & Skinner, B. F. (1957). *Schedules of reinforcement*. New York: Appleton-Century-Crofts.

Fox, D. K., Hopkins, B. L., & Anger, W. K. (1987). The long-term effects of a token economy on safety performance in open-pit mining. *Journal of Applied Behavior Analysis, 20*, 215–224.

Foxx, C., Foxx, R. M., Jones, J. R., & Kiely, D. (1980). Twenty-four hour social isolation. *Behavior Modification, 4*, 130–144.

Foxx, R. M., & Azrin, N. H. (1972). Restitution: A method of eliminating aggressive-disruptive behavior of retarded and brain-damaged patients. *Behaviour Research and Therapy, 10*, 15–27.

Foxx, R. M., & Shapiro, S. T. (1978). The time out ribbon: A non-exclusionary timeout procedure. *Journal of Applied Behavior Analysis, 11*, 125–136.

Friman, P. C., Finney, J. W., Glassock, S. T., Weigel, J. W., & Christopherson, E. G. (1986). Testicular self-examination: Validation of a training strategy for early cancer detection. *Journal of Applied Behavior Analysis, 19*, 87–92.

Garfinkel, P. E., & Garner, D. M. (1982). *Anorexia nervosa: A multidimensional perspective*. New York: Brunner/Mazel.

Gibbs, J. W., & Luyben, P. D. (1985). Treatment of self-injurious behavior. Contingent versus noncontingent positive practice overcorrection. *Behavior Modification, 9*, 3–21.

Glasgow, R. E., & Lichtenstein, E. (1987). Long-term effects of behavioral smoking cessation interventions. *Behavior Therapy, 18*, 297–324.

Gouvier, W. D. (1987). Assessment and treatment of cognitive deficits in brain-damaged individuals. *Behavior Modification, 11*, 312–328.

Hall, D. C., Adams, C. K., Stein, G. H., Stephenson, H. S., Goldstein, M. K., & Pennypacker H. S. (1980). Improved detection of human breast lesions following experimental training. *Cancer, 46*, 408–414.

Halmi, K. A. (1985). Behavioral management for anorexia nervosa. In D. M. Garner & P. E. Garfinkel (Eds.), *Handbook of psychotherapy for anorexia nervosa and bulimia*. New York: Guilford Press.

Harris, S. L., & Ersner–Hershfield, R. (1978). Behavioral suppression of seriously disruptive behavior in psychotic and retarded patients: A review of punishment and its alternatives. *Psychological Bulletin, 85*, 1352–1375.

Hersen, M., & Bellack, A. S. (Eds.). (1988). *Behavioral assessment: A practical handbook* (3rd ed.). Elmsford, NY: Pergamon Press.

Hobbs, S. A., Forehand, R., & Murray, R. (1978). Effects of various durations of time-out on the noncompliant behavior of children. *Behavior Therapy, 9*, 652–656.

Hogan, W. A., & Johnson, D. P. (1985). Elimination of response cost in a token economy program and improvement in behavior of emotionally disturbed youth. *Behavior Therapy, 16,* 87–98.

Horner, R. H., Eberhard, J. M., & Sheehan, M. R. (1986). Teaching generalized table bussing: The importance of negative teaching examples. *Behavior Modification, 10,* 457–471.

Horton, A. M., & Miller, W. G. (1985). Neuropsychology and behavior therapy. *Progress in Behavior Modification, 19,* 1–55.

Kanfer, F. H. (1985). Target selection for clinical change programs. *Behavioral Assessment, 7,* 7–20.

Kanfer, F. H., & Schefft, B. K. (1988). *Guiding the process of therapeutic change.* Champaign, IL: Research Press.

Kazdin, A. E. (1989). *Behavior modification in applied settings* (4th ed.). Pacific Grove, CA: Brooks/Cole.

Klonoff, E. A., & Biglan, A. (1987). "Hypoglycemic" anxiety. The role of reinforcement in psychophysiological disorders. *Behavior Modification, 11,* 102–113.

Lewis, F. D., Nelson, J., Nelson, C., & Reusink, P. (1988). Effects of three feedback contingencies on the socially inappropriate talk of a brain-injured adult. *Behavior Therapy, 19,* 203–211.

Lovaas, O. I. (1977). *The autistic child.* New York: Lexington.

Lovaas, O. I., & Newsome, C. (1976). Behavior modification with psychotic children. In H. Leitenberg (Ed.), *Handbook of behavior modification and behavior therapy* (pp. 303–360). Englewood Cliffs, NJ: Prentice-Hall.

Mace, F. C., Page, T. J., Ivancic, M. T., & O'Brien, S. (1986). Effectiveness of brief time-out with and without contingent delay: A comparative analysis. *Journal of Applied Behavior Analysis, 19,* 79–86.

Mash, E. J. (1985). Some comments on target selection in behavior therapy. *Behavioral Assessment, 7,* 63–78.

Mash, E. J., & Terdal, L. G. (Eds.). (1988). *Behavioral assessment of childhood disorders* (2nd ed.). New York: Guilford Press.

Melamed, B. G., & Siegel, L. J. (1980). *Behavioral medicine: Practical applications in health care.* New York: Springer.

Miltenberger, R. G., & Fuqua, R. W. (1985). A comparison of three treatment procedures for nervous habits. *Journal of Behaviour Treatment and Experimental Psychiatry, 16,* 196–200.

Myers, D. G. (1986). *Psychology.* New York: Worth.

Neisworth, J. R., Hunt, F. M., Gallop, H. R., & Madle, R. A. (1985). Reinforcer displacement. A preliminary study of the clinical application of the CRF/EXT effect. *Behavior Modification, 9,* 103–115.

Nolan, J. D. (1968). Self-control procedures in the modification of smoking behavior. *Journal of Consulting and Clinical Psychology, 32,* 92–93.

O'Leary, K. D., & O'Leary, S. G. (Eds.). (1977). *Classroom management.* Elmsford, NY: Pergamon Press.

Olson, R. L., & Roberts, M. W. (1987). Alternative treatments for sibling aggression. *Behavior Therapy, 18,* 243–250.

Patterson, G. R., & White, G. D. (1969). It's a small world. The application of "time out" from positive reinforcement. *Oregon Psychological Association Newsletter (Supplement), 15,* 2.

Pfiffner, L. J., Rosen, L. A., & O'Leary, S. G. (1985). The efficacy of an all-positive approach to classroom management. *Journal of Applied Behavior Analysis, 18,* 257–261.

Pinkston, E., & Linsk, N. (1984). Behavioral family intervention with the impaired elderly. *The Gerontologist, 24,* 576–583.

Premack, D. (1959). Toward empirical behavior laws: I. Positive reinforcement. *Psychological Review, 66,* 219–233.

Prigatano, G. (1985). *Neuropsychological rehabilitation after brain injury.* Baltimore: Johns Hopkins University Press.

Rapport, M., Murphy, H. A., & Bailey, J. (1982). Ritalin vs. response cost in the control of hyperactive children. *Journal of Applied Behavior Analysis, 15,* 205–216.

Repp, A. C., & Deitz, S. M. (1974). Reducing aggressive and self-injurious behavior of institutionalized retarded children through reinforcement of other behavior. *Journal of Applied Behavior Analysis, 7,* 313–325.

Rincover, A. (1978). Sensory extinction: A procedure for eliminating self-stimulatory behavior in autistic children. *Journal of Abnormal Child Psychology, 6,* 299–310.

Rincover, A., Cook, R., Peoples, A., & Packard, D. (1979). Sensory extinction and sensory reinforcement principles for programming multiple adaptive behavior change. *Journal of Applied Behavior Analysis, 12,* 221–233.

Rojahn, J., McGonigle, J. J., Curcio, C., & Dixon, M. J. (1987). Suppression of Pica by water mist and aromatic ammonia. A comparative analysis. *Behavior Modification, 11,* 65–74.

Rosenbaum, M., & Ayllon, T. (1981). Treating bruxism with the habit reversal technique. *Behavior Research and Therapy, 19,* 87–96.

Rudd, J. R., & Geller, E. S. (1985). A University-based incentive program to increase safety belt use: Toward cost-effective institutionalization. *Journal of Applied Behavior Analysis, 18,* 215–226.

Russo, D. C., & Budd, K. S. (1987). Limitations of operant practice in the study of disease. *Behavior Modification, 11,* 264–285.

Russo, D. C., & Varni, J. W. (Eds.). (1982). *Behavior pediatrics: Research and practice.* New York: Plenum Press.

Schmale, D., Lichtenstein, R., & Harris, D. (1972). Successful treatment of habitual smokers with warm smoky air and rapid smoking. *Journal of Consulting and Clinical Psychology, 38,* 105–111.

Sharenow, E. L., Fuqua, R. W., & Miltenberger, R. G. (1989). The treatment of muscle tics with dissimilar competing response practice. *Journal of Applied Behavior Analysis, 22,* 35–42.

Singh, N. N. (1987). Overcorrection of oral reading errors. A comparison of individual- and group-training formats. *Behavior Modification, 11,* 165–181.

Singh, N. N., & Singh, J. (1986). Increasing oral reading proficiency. A comparative analysis of drill and positive practice overcorrection procedures. *Behavior Modification, 10,* 115–130.

Skinner, B. F. (1938). *The behavior of organisms: An experimental analysis.* New York: Appleton-Century-Crofts.

Sowers–Hoag, K. M., Thyer, B. A., & Bailey, J. S. (1987). Promoting automobile safety belt use by young children. *Journal of Applied Behavior Analysis, 20,* 133–138.

Spiegler, M. D. (1983). *Contemporary behavioral therapy.* Palo Alto, CA: Mayfield.

Spreat, S., Lipinski, D., Dickerson, R., Nass, R., & Dorsey, M. (1989). The acceptability of electric shock programs. *Behavior Modification, 13,* 245–256.

Stark, L. J., Collins, F. L., Osnes, P. G., & Stokes, R. F. (1986). Using reinforcement and cueing to increase healthy snack food choices in preschoolers. *Journal of Applied Behavior Analysis, 19,* 367–379.

Stewart, C. A., & Singh, N. N. (1986). Overcorrection of spelling deficits in moderately mentally retarded children. *Behavior Modification, 10,* 355–365.

Strauss, C., Rubinoff, A., & Atkeson, B. (1983). Elimination of nocturnal head banging in a normal 7-year-old girl using overcorrection plus rewards. *Journal of Behavior Therapy and Experimental Psychiatry, 14,* 269–273.

Stuart, R. B. (Ed.). (1982). *Adherence, compliance, and generalization in behavioral medicine*. New York: Brunner/Mazel.

Sulzer–Azaroff, B., & Mayer, G. R. (1977). *Applying behavior analysis procedures with children and youth*. New York: Holt, Rinehart & Winston.

Underwood, L. A., Figueroa, R. G., Thyer, B. A., & Nzeocha, A. (1989). Interruption and DRI in the treatment of self-injurious behavior among mentally retarded and autistic self-restrainers. *Behavior Modification, 13*, 471–481.

Walker, W. B., & Franzini, L. R. (1985). Low-risk aversive group treatments, physiological feedback, and booster sessions for smoking cessation. *Behavior Therapy, 16*, 263–274.

Weiker, R. G., & Harmon, R. E. (1975). The use of omission training to reduce self-injurious behavior in a retarded child. *Behavior Therapy, 6*, 261–268.

White, G. W., Mathews, R. M., & Fawcett, S. T. (1989). Reducing risk of pressure sores: Effects of watch prompts and alarm avoidance on wheelchair push-ups. *Journal of Applied Behavior Analysis, 22*, 287–295.

Whitehead, W. E., Burgio, K. L., & Engel, B. T. (1985). Biofeedback treatment of fecal incontinence in geriatric patients. *Journal of the American Geriatrics Society, 33*, 320–324.

Williams, M., Thyer, B. A., Bailey, J. S., & Harrison, D. F. (1989). Promoting safety belt use with traffic signs and prompters. *Journal of Applied Behavior Analysis, 22*, 71–76.

Williamson, D. A. (1987). Recent advances in behavioral medicine. *Behavior Modification, 11*, 259–263.

5
Fear Reduction Methods
Richard J. Morris

Much of the effort of psychotherapists is directed toward helping people overcome their fears of situations, other people, animals, and objects. Fear is a very strong emotion and is associated with many signs of anxiety, for example, pallor, rapid pulse rate and a "pounding heart," very tense muscles, perspiring in a room of average temperature and humidity, "butterflies" in the stomach, irritability, feelings of panic and/or self-statements regarding the need to leave a situation, inability to concentrate, dizziness, and headaches. These reactions can be placed in three categories. *Motoric reactions* involve avoidance of the feared stimulus, object, or event or at least a very cautious and prudent approach toward the stimulus. *Cognitive reactions* involve unpleasant subjective feelings or cognitions associated with the feared stimulus, including feelings or cognitions of muscular tenseness ("I'm tense"), panic ("I have to get out of here or I will collapse!"), irritability ("I don't like it here and I wish I hadn't agreed to come"), and losing control ("What if something happens to me . . . can I be sure that someone will know or that someone will find me?"). *Physiological reactions* involve rapid breathing, pallor, increased heart rate, pupillary dilation, and a desire to urinate (e.g., Marks, 1969; Morris & Kratochwill, 1983, 1990).

When someone experiences fear in a situation where there is no obvious external danger, the fear is irrational and is called a phobia. Table 5.1 lists a number of common phobias that people experience. When a person begins to avoid a nondangerous feared situation—even though she or he realizes that such behavior is foolish or irrational—the fear becomes a phobic reaction. In differentiating between a fear and a phobia, Marks (1969, p. 3) suggested that a phobia is a subcategory of fear that

1. is out of proportion to demands of the situation,
2. cannot be explained or reasoned away,
3. is beyond voluntary control, and
4. leads to avoidance of the feared situation.

To these criteria, Miller, Barrett, and Hampe (1974) added that a phobia "persists over an extended period of time . . . is unadaptive . . . [and in the case of children] is not age or stage specific" (p. 90).

Phobic reactions are among the most common forms of maladaptive behaviors in people. They occur in children, adolescents, and adults. Some phobias, because of their high incidence, are considered normal in children, whereas others are viewed as normal in adults. For example, fear of dogs and other animals, the dark, ghosts, strangers, and being alone are among the more common childhood phobias; fear of heights, public speaking, spiders and other bugs, and snakes frequently occur in adults. Some irrational fears are transitory whereas others persist over a long time.

When fears become intolerable, professional help is often sought. Over the past 75 years, various procedures have been used in the treatment of fears. Psychoanalysis, Adlerian therapy, client-centered therapy, and other forms of verbal therapy have been utilized, as well as drugs, hypnosis, electroconvulsive shock treatment, and certain forms of brain surgery (e.g., leucotomy). In general, these methods have been found to be only moderately successful.

Some therapy procedures, however, have been found to be much more effective. These procedures are based on the learning theory positions of, for example, Skinner (1938, 1953), Pavlov (1927), Hull (1943), Mowrer (1950), and Bandura (1969, 1977; Bandura & Walters, 1963). Though the specifics of each therapy method differ, they do share certain general underlying assumptions: (a) phobias and the avoidance reactions that accompany them are learned by the

Table 5.1. Selected Phobias that People Experience

TECHNICAL NAME	FEAR
Acrophobia	Heights
Agoraphobia	Open places
Aichmophobia	Sharp and pointed objects
Aquaphobia	Going into water
Claustrophobia	Enclosed places
Mikrophobia	Germs
Menophobia	Being alone
Nyctophobia	Darkness
Ochlophobia	Crowds
Pyrophobia	Fires
Thanatophobia	Death
Xenophobia	Strangers
Zoophobia	Animals

individual, (b) phobias do not occur as a result of innate factors, and (c) phobias are not the result of an underlying psychic or psychological disturbance (see, for example, Morris & Kratochwill, 1983).

An alternative learning theory view on the etiology of fears has been developed by Seligman (1971). He does not completely agree with each of these assumptions. Seligman has incorporated the notion of *biological preparedness* into his theory and states that people, for example, are "prepared" to develop particular fears based on the biological and evolutionary significance of certain stimuli and situations that are tied to their struggle for survival. The present chapter will discuss two therapy procedures that have been found to be effective in the treatment of phobic reactions and fears: systematic desensitization and flooding-related therapies. Variations of these methods will also be discussed. Each method will be described in detail, and case examples will be presented that demonstrate its use. The discussion will focus primarily on fear reduction methods with adults. For a thorough discussion of fear reduction methods with children and adolescents, the reader is referred to King, Hamilton, and Ollendick (1988), Morris and Kratochwill (1983, 1985, 1990); Morris, Kratochwill, & Aldridge (1988), Morris, Kratochwill, and Dobson, (1986), and Ramirez, Kratochwill, and Morris (1987).

SYSTEMATIC DESENSITIZATION

Systematic desensitization was developed in the early 1950s by Joseph Wolpe (e.g., Wolpe, 1958, 1962). The basic assumption of this technique is that a fear response (for example, a fear response to heights) is learned or conditioned and can be inhibited by substituting an activity that is antagonistic to the fear response. The response that is most typically inhibited by this treatment process is anxiety, and the response frequently substituted for the anxiety is relaxation and calmness. For example, if a salesman has a fear of being in high-rise office buildings and taking an elevator higher than the third floor, we would help him inhibit the anxiety in this situation by teaching him to relax and feel calm. Thus we would desensitize the person or countercondition his fear of heights.

Desensitization is accomplished by exposing an individual, in small, graduated steps, to the feared situation while the person is performing the activity that is antagonistic to anxiety. The gradual exposure to the fear stimulus can take place either in the person's fantasy, where she or he is asked to imagine being in various fear-related situations, or it can occur in real life (i.e., in vivo). Wolpe termed the principle that underlies the desensitization process *reciprocal inhibition*. He described this principle in the following way: "If a response inhibitory to anxiety can be made to occur in the presence of anxiety-evoking stimuli, it will weaken the connection between these stimuli and the anxiety responses" (Wolpe, 1958, p. 562).

The Initial Interview

Before initiating the desensitization procedure, or any of the other fear reduction methods discussed in this chapter, the therapist must first identify the client's fear or phobia and the circumstances under which the fear occurs. This is not an easy assignment. The interview must be conducted within a therapeutic atmosphere of respect for the client, sensitivity to and understanding of the client's difficulties, and genuine concern for the client's overall well-being. The therapist has to probe thoroughly into the client's life history to make sure both therapist and client have a clear understanding of all aspects of the client's fear and of those factors that have contributed (and continue to contribute) to the fear or phobia.

The goal of the interview, however, is not to identify the causal factor or factors that is responsible for the client's fear or phobia. Therapists who use the fear reduction methods discussed in this chapter generally accept the premise that people's learning histories are very complex, and to assume that a time-limited retrospective account of one's past will uncover the factor(s) that caused a fear or phobia is a fruitless endeavor. The best that an interview can be expected to accomplish is to provide the therapist with a comprehensive picture of who the client is, what kind of environment the client comes from, how the client came to be what she or he is today, and what the circumstances were that led to the initial occurrence of the fear or phobia. The interview will also help the therapist support or refute various hypotheses about the client's problem, specify the goals of therapy, determine which fear reduction method is most appropriate for the client, and assess whether the treatment objectives can be accomplished within the limitations set by the client and her or his life situation (Kanfer & Grimm, 1977). It is therefore likely that the initial interview will last over a number of sessions. Though there is neither a standardized approach nor a standard set of questions used in the initial interview, most therapists explore the following topic areas with clients.

Identification of the Target Behavior

This topic area involves not only helping the client identify what is specifically troubling him or her but also trying to determine the types of situations and circumstances in which the fear or phobia occurs. In addition, the therapist asks how long the client has had the fear, whether it has gotten better or worse with the passage of time, and the types of situations in which it seems to be better or worse than "usual." It is also desirable to ask the client about his or her thoughts and feelings concerning the fear.

General Background Information

Discussion of this topic centers on the date and place of the client's birth, number and age of siblings, where the client stands in the family birth order, and a retrospective account of the types of interactions the client had with siblings, parents, and significant other persons to whom the client was exposed while growing up. Inquiry is made into which of the children was favored in the family, as well as how the client viewed the manner in which she or he was treated by each of the parents relative to the other children. The therapist should also discuss other items regarding the parents such as who did the disciplining in the family, how the client was punished for misbehavior during childhood and adolescence, and which characteristics in each parent were liked and which disliked the most by the client. It is also important to know the manner in which parents interacted with each other and to determine what type of role models the parents provided for the client. For example, did they generally like one another; did they fight, and, if so, was it usually in front of the children and was the fighting verbal or physical; did they ever talk about divorce or separation; and, did one parent try to use one or all of the children against the other parent?

For many clients, a favorite aunt, uncle, grandparent, neighbor, or friend may have been as important as—or even more important than—their parents during childhood. These significant others should also be discussed to determine the unique contribution(s) of such people in the client's life.

One additional aspect of the individual's background information involves the fears that were experienced during childhood. The therapist should not only determine the particular childhood fears but also when they occurred, when (and if) they ended, and whether any of them continued into the adult years.

School and Job Information

For this category, inquiry should be made into the client's likes and dislikes in elementary school, high school, and college; the best and least liked subjects, what the client did after school, the client's extracurricular activities, and so forth. Moreover, the therapist should discuss the client's friendships in and out of school, for instance, whether the client had any close friends and if these friendships were maintained over the years.

The client's work experience should also be brought into this discussion, with the therapist asking how far the client went in school and, if appropriate, why he or she did not continue. Particular attention should be paid to the client's work history, likes and dislikes about a job, ability to advance, and consistency of the present job with the client's goals and desires.

Dating and Marriage Information

The therapist explores the client's dating pattern during the teenage and adult years. In addition, the client's sexual experiences before and after marriage are discussed. If appropriate, difficulties in the marriage are discussed, relationships with in-laws and children are explored, and the environment in which the client lives is looked at. Because these are very sensitive topics for some people, they should be explored within a nonjudgmental framework that demonstrates understanding and acceptance of the client.

A summary of a suggested guide for the initial interview is presented in Table 5.2. As the reader has no doubt already determined, the information gained in the initial interview is quite extensive. Some therapists use tape recorders to record this information, whereas others take notes on the client's answers. Still others ask their clients to fill out a standard background information packet that contains many of the same types of questions as those outlined in Table 5.2.

An excerpt from part of the first session of an initial interview with a recently divorced woman, 35 years of age, illustrates the manner in which an interview is

Table 5.2. Suggested Guide for the Conduct of the Initial Interview

A. *What is the problem behavior? . . . What seems to be troubling you?*
  1. How long have you had this difficulty?
  2. When does this fear or thought usually come into your mind? When does this problem seem to occur the most? In what types of situations or circumstances does the problem occur? Are there any reasons you can think of for its occurrence?
  3. Has the problem been the same all along—or has it gotten better or worse?
      (a) is there any situation that you can associate with it getting better or worse?
B. *General Background*
  1. When born? Where?
  2. How many brothers and sisters do you have?
      (a) Where are you in the birth order?
      (b) How much older is your eldest or youngest same-sex sibling?
      (c) How did (do) you get along with him (her)?
  3. Parents—are they still alive? When did each die?
C. *Father*
  1. What kind of person was (is) he—especially during your childhood?
  2. Was he interested in you? Were you interested in what he had to say?
  3. Did he ever punish you?
  4. Did he play favorites with the children? How did you feel about this?
D. *Mother*
  Same questions asked about the father
E. *Parents*
  1. Did they like each other? Did they like you?
  2. Did they behave toward you as though they liked you?
  3. Did they get along together?
      (a) Fight much? . . . Divorce threats? etc.
      (b) Did they fight in front of children or in privacy?
F. *Significant others*
  1. Were there any other adults who played an important part in your life?
  2. Describe what they were like and how they played an important role in your life.
G. *Fears during childhood*
  1. Any particular fears?
  2. When did they occur?
  3. Do you still have some of these? When did they stop?
H. *School*
  1. Like school?
  2. Best liked subjects? Least liked subjects?
  3. Sports—Did you participate in them or watch them?
      (a) How were you in them?

4. Friends
   (a) Did you make any friends at school (college)?
   (b) Any close ones?
   (c) Do you maintain any of those friendships today?
   (d) Anyone at school (college) that you were afraid of? Was the person the same sex as you? Were you afraid of any teachers? Why?
   (e) How far did you go in school? Why did you stop your education?
5. What did you do after you stopped school?

I. Job
   1. What kind of work do you do?
   2. Do you like your job? What do you like the best/least about your job?
   3. Any thoughts about quitting?
   4. What other types of jobs have you had? Why did you leave them?
   5. If client is a homemaker, ask: How do you like being a homemaker?
      What do you specifically like about it?
      Was it your choice to be a homemaker?
      Would you like to be doing something else? What?

J. Sex
   1. At what age did you begin to have any kind of sexual feelings?
      (a) If client has problem in answering, ask: Well, roughly, were you 10, 15, 20 . . . more or less?
      (b) or go to the following: Before 10? . . . Before 15? . . . Before 20? . . .
   2. In what kind of situation did you have your first sexual feelings? For example, was it out with boys? . . . (girls?) . . . At a movie house? Or what?
   3. At this stage, did you date several boys (girls) or just one at a time?
      (a) Did you go to parties?
      (b) What was the pattern of your dating? . . . Always movies? . . . Dinners?
   4. When did you especially become interested in anybody?
   5. Was there anyone else whom you became interested in?
   6. When did you become really serious? (implying steady dating, become engaged, etc.) Or, have you ever become serious with anyone?
      (a) What did you like about him (her)?
   7. Have you ever petted (made out) with anyone? Did you ever masturbate? Any feelings of guilt or fear about doing (not doing) either of these?
   8. Have you ever had intercourse? Have you ever wanted to? What stopped you?
   9. (If married, ask: Did you ever have intercourse before you were married?)

K. Marriage
   1. When did you meet your husband (wife)?
      (a) What did you like about him (her)?
   2. When did you feel that you were ready to marry him (her)?
   3. Was he (she) interested in marrying you?
   4. Since (or while) you were married, did you ever become interested in other men (women)?
   5. Is (was) your marriage satisfying? What about it makes it satisfying? What about it doesn't make it satisfying? In what way would you like to change your marriage?
   6. If divorced and remarried, how about with your second husband (wife)? Is this marriage satisfying?
      (a) How is he (she) different from your first husband (wife)?
      (b) How soon after the divorce did you remarry?
      (c) Was he (she) married before?

L. Sex and Marriage
   1. How is the sexual side of your marriage (dating)? How about the sexual side of your second marriage?
   2. Do you have orgasms?
      (a) How often?

(continued)

Table 5.2. *(Continued)*

---

3. Are you happy with your marriage (the person you are dating)?
   (a) Any complaints?
4. Do the two of you fight with each other? That is, are there arguments?
   (a) What do you usually fight about?
   (b) How long do they usually last?
   (c) How are your fights usually resolved?
5. Any plans for marriage (thoughts of divorce)?

M. *Children*
   1. How many children do you have? (Do you plan to have children? How many?)
   2. Do you like all of your children? Any favorites?
      (a) Are they all well?
   3. How old is each?
   4. Were they each planned?

N. *Environment*
   1. Do you like where you are now living?
   2. Anything that you are not satisfied with?
   3. What's your religion?
      (a) Is it important to you? In what way?
      (b) How religious are you? . . . not at all, mildly, moderately, or extremely?
      (c) Do you spend a lot of time in church activities?

---

conducted. (Throughout this chapter the case transcripts, case descriptions, and hierarchies have been changed slightly to protect the anonymity of the clients involved.)

Therapist: What is the difficulty that you are having?

Client: I can't fly in airplanes or go up in elevators . . . at least not higher than the third floor, though I am still nervous even then.

Therapist: Let's talk about the airplane difficulty first. What about flying makes you feel uncomfortable?

Client: Well, watching a plane take off is fearful, though as a child I did take lessons in flying and was not afraid. (Pause) It's the feelings of being suspended in air and immobile, and of being trapped and feeling that I can't get out.

Therapist: When do you remember this fear beginning?

Client: It started about 10 years ago. My husband had to fly as part of his job with his company, and I would go with him on a number of occasions. Then the fear began getting worse as I would fly more, and about five years ago I began having difficulty looking down [out the window]. Now I can't look down at all or even out the window—even if I got up enough nerve to fly in a plane.

Therapist: Can you think of any situation regarding flying that doesn't make you feel uneasy?

Client: Yes (laughs), if I don't think about it, it doesn't bother me.

Therapist: Let's be a little more specific. If we could rate your level of fear about airplanes on a 10-point scale, what about flying would be most anxiety provoking to you; that is, a 10 for you?

Client: Flying over the ocean.

Therapist: What would be a zero?

Client: Being at the airport to pick someone up.

Therapist: What would be a five?

Client: The plane taking off.

Therapist: So, your fear is related to all aspects of you actually flying in a plane. What about seeing a plane on television or in a movie, for example, seeing one in the air?

Client: That bothers me, too . . . especially watching a movie of a plane which was filmed from another plane, and especially when the plane banks.

Therapist: What number would this be on the rating scale?

Client: A five or six.

Therapist: Are there any reasons that you can think of, or ideas that you might have, concerning the development of your fear?

Client: Not really, except that around the time my nervousness began my husband was seeing another woman, and sometime during that period the fear developed. . . . I guess I was feeling very threatened that we would break up.

Therapist: What was your relationship with your husband like during this time?

Client: Very poor . . . a lot of fighting and yelling.

Therapist: Any talk of divorce at that time?

Client: No, not really. I guess we both knew that the marriage was shaky, but that we would stay together at least until the children got older.

Therapist: And what about your fear of elevators? When did it begin?

Client: (Pause) I think it goes back almost 20 years ago. I remember being in a tall building in Chicago . . . don't remember why . . . and getting a feeling of fright in an express elevator. But I guess you can say I became really scared about five years ago. And, it became very bad three years ago, right after I took an express elevator to the 20th floor of the Acme building and threw up as I came out, after feeling so nervous and nauseous while going up.

Therapist: Is there anything about riding in an elevator or about elevators in general that doesn't make you feel uncomfortable?

Client: Walking past an elevator with someone and knowing that I don't have to go in.

Therapist: What about going past it, and you're by yourself?

Client: It bothers me a bit. It's at the point now where just walking by one by myself makes me feel uncomfortable.

Therapist: How much—using for a moment our 10-point rating scale?

Client: About one.

Therapist: What would be zero?

Client: Walking past it with someone and knowing I don't have to take it.

Therapist: What would be a 10?

Client: (Laughs and then pauses) Being stuck in the elevator and alone by myself.

Therapist: Any thoughts about what events contributed to this fear?

Client: None. I can't figure it out, unless it's related to my airplane fear. But I don't know how.

Therapist: Let's hold on that for a bit and talk a little more about your background. Where were you born and in what year?

Client: In Chicago . . .

At the end of the first or second session, the therapist often gives the client some questionnaires to fill out at home for the next session. They are used to help the therapist gain additional information about the client which was or could have been missed during the initial interview. Two of the most popular questionnaires appear in the chapter appendix and are briefly discussed next.

Fear Survey Schedule. This five-point rating scale asks the client to rate the amount of fear or discomfort caused by each of the things and events listed in the questionnaire from *Not at All* to *Very much.*

The Willoughby Questionnaire. This questionnaire also uses a five-point rating scale. It contains questions about how the client reacts in various situations. The client must respond with one of the following answers: *Never/Not at All, Somewhat/Sometimes, About as Often as Not, Usually/A Good Deal.*

In addition, it is a good idea for the therapist to ask the client to write out a paragraph or two about his or her fears or phobias, describing each of them, any reasons why the client feels they occur, and any thoughts about them. An example of this type of write-up follows, written by a 42-year-old male who was the vice-president of a large corporation.

> For as long as I can remember, I have been aware and concerned about other people and their estimation of me or how they thought I was doing and whether they liked me. The other part of this has to do with my perception that everyone that I know (my boss, my wife and children, my colleagues, and the people who work for me) expects me to succeed in every aspect of my work. This makes me very nervous and scared that I won't live up to their estimation and expectations of me—and that they are constantly making judgments on what I am doing.
>
> Now I know that I'm not good at everything that I do (in spite of what others think), so I try to avoid as much personal and social contact with people as I can—going to as few company functions as is possible and not going to parties with friends if I can avoid it.
>
> This is all very frustrating to me. Objectively, I know I do well. I make a very good living and have been promoted in my company many times, and have a great deal of responsibility for the manufacturing of our products. But, I am so damned concerned about what others are thinking and saying about me that I go out of my way to be Mr. Nice Guy to make sure that they say good things about me. I don't want to be worried all the time about how I am doing with people at work, with my wife and with my children, and with friends. I want to stop being concerned with how people judge me.
>
> Maybe my mother and father started it all when I was young with always drilling me about doing better in school—even when I got B's—about watching how I act and what I say to people. I don't know.

The information gained from the interview, personal statement, and questionnaires should provide the therapist with a thorough analysis and understanding of (a) the client's life situation, (b) the circumstances and situations under which the client's fear or phobia occurs, and (c) the relative intensity in various situations of the feelings associated with the feared situation. The general assumption is that a person's fear or phobia is learned and that it can be unlearned by applying procedures based on theories of learning (Morris & Kratochwill, 1983).

The therapist must remember, however, that in an interview the client is also assessing the therapist. The client is concerned with whether the therapist understands the nature of his or her problem, whether the therapist is concerned with his or her welfare, whether he or she feels comfortable talking with the therapist, and so forth. The interview, therefore, should not be so mechanical and matter-of-fact that the client as a person is disregarded. The therapist should take care that the amount of detailed information gained from the interview not be obtained at the expense of the client's comfort. This is where the therapeutic relationship and rapport with the client are important. The therapist might even want to anticipate some of the client's concerns by informing him or her that some of their discussions will involve detailed questioning, explaining that details provide the therapist with a thorough understanding of his or her problem, which is necessary for successful therapy (Goldfried & Davison, 1976).

Specific questions are asked, and extensive discussion occurs in the interview because the goal of therapy is very specific, namely, the reduction of the person's fear or phobia. Because of this, it is important to learn as much about the nature of the problem and the circumstances under which it occurs as is reasonably possible. No attempt is made in therapy to reorganize the client's personality, nor is there any general goal of helping the client achieve a higher level of emotional and psychological functioning. The only goal is to reduce the client's fear or phobic reaction, using a procedure best suited for the client, to a point where she or he can carry on daily activities without being bothered by the fear.

If the therapist believes it is possible that the client is suffering from a physical disorder that could be causing the problem or that could interfere with treatment, he or she should refer the client to a physician for a thorough physical examination before proceeding further.

The Desensitization Procedure

After obtaining all of the relevant information about the client, the therapist then decides on the treatment procedure and discusses with the client what will take place next. If systematic desensitization is used, the therapist briefly explains the rationale behind the treatment procedure and describes the various stages in the treatment process. For example, the therapist might say the following:

> The emotional reactions that you experience are a result of your previous experiences with people and situations; these reactions oftentimes lead to feelings of anxiety or tenseness which are really inappropriate. Since perceptions of situations occur within ourselves, it is possible to work with your reactions right here in the office by having you . . . [imagine] or visualize those situations. (Paul, 1966, p. 116)

The therapist would then mention that a technique called systematic desensitization is going to be used with the client, and that it consists of two primary stages.

> The first stage consists of relaxation training where I am going to teach you how to become more relaxed than you have probably felt in a very long time. Once you have learned to relax, we will then use this relaxed state to counter the anxiety and tenseness that you feel whenever you are in the feared situation(s). We will do this by having you imagine—while you are still very relaxed—a series of progressively more tension-provoking scenes which you and I will develop . . . and which are directly related to your fear. We will thus counter-condition your fear or desensitize your tenseness to the feared situation(s).

This procedure has been found to be very effective in the treatment of many types of fears, and we have used it successfully in the past with people who have fears like yours. We will start the procedure by first teaching you how to become more relaxed and then asking you to practice the procedure at home. Do your have any questions? (Adapted from Paul, 1966)

Before proceeding further, the therapist should answer any questions that the client has about the procedure or his or her expectations regarding treatment.

Throughout this initial period, as well as during the remainder of therapy, the therapist should make sure that she or he has established a good relationship with the client. The therapist should behave in a way that conveys warmth and acceptance of the client. Many writers (e.g., Goldfried & Davison, 1976; Morris & Magrath, 1983; Wilson & Evans, 1977) have suggested that desensitization procedures should be conducted within the context of a sound therapist-client relationship. In fact, therapist warmth was found by Morris and Suckerman (1974a, 1974b) and Ryan and Moses (1979) to be a significant factor in the outcome of systematic desensitization. (The reader is referred to chapter 2 of this volume by Goldstein and Higginbotham for a detailed discussion concerning methods of enhancing the therapeutic relationship in psychotherapy.)

There are essentially three steps in the use of systematic desensitization: (a) relaxation training, (b) development of the anxiety hierarchy, and (c) systematic desensitization proper. Because therapists differ from one another in regard to some of the details of systematic desensitization, what is described here is the manner in which the present author conducts this therapy.

Relaxation Training

The therapist begins desensitization by training the client to relax. This training should take place in a quiet, softly lighted room located in a building where there is a negligible amount of outside noise (where possible, the therapist should use the same room as the one in which the initial interview took place). Besides comfortable office furniture, the therapist should have either a couch or a recliner chair in the room, so that relaxation will be facilitated by having the client lie down.

The first step in the procedure is to have the client lean back in the chair or lie down on the couch and close his or her eyes. The therapist then says the following:

I am going to teach you how to become very relaxed. In doing this I am going to ask you to tense up and relax opposing sets of muscles—proceeding through a series of these. That is, I am going to ask you to tense up and relax different sets of muscles so that there is a cumulative effect of relaxation over your whole body. (Pause) Okay, now, I would like you to . . .

The relaxation steps presented in Table 5.3 are then initiated. These steps represent a modified version of a technique developed by Jacobson (1938) for inducing deep muscular relaxation. The procedure should be presented in a very quiet, soft, and pleasant tone of voice. Each step should take about 10 seconds, with a 10- to 15-second pause between each. The whole procedure should take 20 to 25 minutes.

Before initiating the relaxation procedure, it is often helpful, as a precaution, to ask the client if any physical problem exists that might interfere with the tensing and relaxing of various muscles. If the client mentions a problem area, the therapist should omit this muscle group from the procedure and not request the client to tense this set of muscles strongly.

During the first relaxation training session, it is often helpful for the therapist to practice the relaxation procedure with the client, so that the client can observe (whenever necessary) how to perform a particular step. It is also advisable for the therapist to pace the presentation of each step to the client's ease of performing the steps.

Table 5.3. An Introduction to the Relaxation Training Steps of Systematic Desensitization

Steps in Relaxation

1. Take a deep breath and hold it (for about 10 seconds). Hold it. Okay, let it out.
2. Raise both of your hands about half way above the couch (or, arms of the chair), and breathe normally. Now, drop your hands to the couch (or, down).
3. Now hold your arms out and make a tight fist. Really tight. Feel the tension in your hands. I am going to count to three and when I say "three," I want you to drop your hands. One . . . Two . . . Three.
4. Raise your arms again, and bend your fingers back the other way (toward your body). Now drop your hands and relax.
5. Raise your arms. Now drop them and relax.
6. Now raise your arms again, but this time "flap" your hands around. Okay, relax again.
7. Raise your arms again. Now, relax.
8. Raise your arms above the couch (chair) again and tense your biceps until they shake. Breathe normally, and keep your hands loose. Relax your hands. (Notice how you have a warm feeling of relaxation.)
9. Now hold your arms out to your side and tense your biceps. Make sure that you breathe normally. Relax your arms.
10. Now arch your shoulders back. Hold it. Make sure that your arms are relaxed. Now relax.
11. Hunch your shoulders forward. Hold it, and make sure that you breathe normally and keep your arms relaxed. Okay, relax. (Notice the feeling of relief from tensing and relaxing your muscles.)
12. Now turn your head to the right and tense your neck. Relax and bring your head back again to its natural position.
13. Turn your head to the left and tense your neck. Relax and bring your head back again to its natural position.
14. Now bend your head back slightly toward the chair. Hold it. Okay, now bring your head back slowly to its natural position.*
15. This time bring your head down almost to your chest. Hold it. Now relax and let your head come back to its natural resting position.*
16. Now open your mouth as much as possible. A little wider, okay, relax. (Mouth must be partly open at end.)
17. Now tense your lips by closing your mouth. OK, relax. (Notice the feeling of relaxation.)
18. Put your tongue at the roof of your mouth. Press hard. (Pause) Relax and allow your tongue to come to a comfortable position in your mouth.
19. Now put your tongue at the bottom of your mouth. Press down hard. Relax and let your tongue come to a comfortable position in your mouth.
20. Now just lie (sit) there and relax. Try not to think of anything.
21. To control self-verbalization, I want you to go through the motions of singing a high note—Not aloud! Okay, start singing to yourself. Hold that note, and now relax.
22. Now sing a medium note and make your vocal cords tense again. Relax.

(continued)

Table 5.3. *(Continued)*

23. Now sing a low note and make your vocal cords tense again. Relax. (Your vocal apparatus should be relaxed now. Relax your mouth.)
24. Now, close your eyes. Squeeze them tight and breathe naturally. Notice the tension. Now relax. (Notice how the pain goes away when you relax.)
25. Now let your eyes relax and keep your mouth open slightly.
26. Open your eyes as much as possible. Hold it. Now, relax your eyes.
27. Now wrinkle your forehead as much as possible. Hold it. Okay, relax.
28. Now take a deep breath and hold it. Relax.
29. Now exhale. Breathe all the air out . . . all of it out. Relax. (Notice the wondrous feeling of breathing again.)
30. Imagine that there are weights pulling on all your muscles making them flaccid and relaxed . . . pulling your arms and body into the couch.
31. Pull your stomach muscles together. Tighter. Okay. Relax.
32. Now extend your muscles as if you were a prize fighter. Make your stomach hard. Relax. (You are becoming more and more relaxed.)
33. Now tense your buttocks. Tighter. Hold it. Now, relax.
34. Now search the upper part of your body and relax any part that is tense. First the facial muscles. (Pause . . . 3–5 sec.) Then the vocal muscles. (Pause . . . 3–5 sec.) The neck region. (Pause . . . 3–5 sec.) Your shoulders . . . relax any part that is tense. (Pause) Now the arms and fingers. Relax these. Becoming very relaxed.
35. Maintaining this relaxation, raise both of your legs (to about a 45° angle). Now relax. (Notice that this further relaxes you.)
36. Now bend your feet back so that your toes point toward your face. Relax your mouth. Bend them hard. Relax.
37. Bend your feet the other way . . . away from your body. Not far. Notice the tension. Okay, relax.
38. Relax. (Pause) Now curl your toes together—as hard as you can. Tighter. Okay, relax. (Quiet . . . silence for about 30 seconds.)
39. This completes the formal relaxation procedure. Now explore your body from your feet up. Make sure that every muscle is relaxed. (Say slowly)—first your toes, . . . your feet, . . . your legs, . . . buttocks, . . . stomach, . . . shoulder, . . . neck, . . . eyes, . . . and finally your forehead—all should be relaxed now. (Quiet—silence for about 10 seconds.) Just lie there and feel very relaxed, noticing the warmness of the relaxation. (Pause) I would like you to stay this way for about 1 more minute, and then I am going to count to five. When I reach five, I want you to open your eyes feeling very calm and refreshed. (Quiet—silence for about 1 minute.) Okay, when I count to five, I want you to open your eyes feeling very calm and refreshed. One . . . feeling very calm; Two . . . very calm, very refreshed; Three . . . very refreshed; Four . . . and, Five.

Note: Adapted in part from Jacobson (1938), Rimm (1967, personal communication), and Wolpe and Lazarus (1966).
* The client should not be encouraged to bend his or her neck either all the way back or forward.

It is not uncommon for clients to feel uncomfortable during the first relaxation session and not to achieve a very deep relaxation level. But over a few sessions, the client will become more comfortable and will be able to practice the relaxation at home alone, preferably twice a day for 10 to 15 minutes. To enhance the client's practice at home, some therapists record the relaxation procedure on cassette tapes and have the client play the tape while practicing each day. Others give the client an outline of the muscle groups to be relaxed. Both could be done. The most important goal is to teach the client how to relax by himself or herself with a fair degree of ease.

In most cases, relaxation training will last for about two or three sessions and will usually overlap with part of the initial interview. Throughout this training, it is a good idea to repeat such phrases as "Breathe normally," "Smooth, even breathing," "Keep your (particular muscle group) relaxed," "Just let your body relax . . . and become more and more relaxed."

It is also helpful throughout relaxation training to point out to the client the changes she or he will be experiencing in bodily sensations. For example, the therapist might say: "Notice the warm, soft feeling of relaxation"; "Notice how your (particular muscle group) now feel . . . they are warm, heavy, and relaxed"; "Notice how relaxed your (particular muscle group) feel in contrast to when you were tensing them"; "Notice how you are becoming more and more relaxed—feeling relaxation throughout your whole body."

For various reasons, a few clients have difficulty relaxing with this procedure (see, for example, Deffenbacher & Suinn, 1988). No matter how motivated they are, they just find it difficult to respond. They have learned over the years not to relax, to be tense, and it might take time for them to change. For example, some have difficulty closing their eyes for longer than a few seconds, some feel uneasy when they lie back in a recliner chair or on a couch while someone is watching them. A few have even reported being afraid to relax. In an attempt to deal with this problem effectively, some writers (e.g., Brady, 1966, 1972; Friedman, 1966) have recommended the use of drugs like Brevital (sodium methahexital) to help their clients relax during relaxation training and desensitization. Others have suggested the use of hypnosis or carbon dioxide-oxygen (e.g., Wolpe, 1982; Wolpe & Lazurus, 1966), a shaping procedure (Morris, 1973), or biofeedback-assisted relaxation (e.g., Deffenbacher & Suinn, 1988; Javel & Denholtz, 1975; Reeves & Maelica, 1975). A modified version of relaxation training, called *applied relaxation training,* has also been used in the treatment of people having generalized anxiety difficulties or experiencing panic attack (e.g., Öst, 1987, 1988).

Development of the Anxiety Hierarchy

On completion of the initial interview and during the relaxation training phase, the therapist begins planning an anxiety hierarchy with the client for each of the identified fears. This hierarchy is based on the fear that the therapist and client have agreed on as requiring change and that the therapist has consented to treat and the client has agreed to work on. The therapist should not impose treatment on a client for a fear that the client has not agreed is in need of being reduced.

At the end of the first relaxation training session (assuming the initial interview has now been completed), the client is given ten 3 in. × 5 in. index cards and asked to come to the next session with the cards filled out, each containing a description of a situation that produces a certain level of anxiety. Specifically, the client is asked to identify on the cards those situations that are related to the fear and that produce increasingly more anxiety and tension. The client is asked to divide up the fear on a 0 to 100 scale and assign an anxiety-provoking situation to every 10th value (100 representing the most anxiety-provoking situation). Examples of some initial anxiety hierarchies are listed in Table 5.4.

The exact nature of a hierarchy varies, depending on the client's particular fear and perception of the various situations. For example, someone who has a fear of being criticized might describe a number of very different situations when this fear

Table 5.4. Samples of Initial Anxiety Hierarchies

Fear of being alone
10. Being with a group of people at the lab either at night or during the day.
20. Being alone in a room with another female.
30. Thinking about the possibility of being alone in my house during the day.
40. Walking in class early in the morning when there are few people outside.
50. Actually alone in my bedroom at home and it's daylight.
60. Driving a car alone at night and feeling a man is following me.
70. Walking alone on a city street downtown at night with a girlfriend.
80. Being alone in a house with a young child for whom I am babysitting.
90. Thinking about being alone at night a few hours before I will actually be alone.
100. Sitting alone in the living room of my house at night with the doors closed.

Fear of driving in high places
10. Entering a ramp garage on ground level.
20. Going up to third level of the garage from the second level.
30. Riding with a friend in a car and approach the bridge over the Chicago River on Michigan Avenue.
40. Driving a car with a friend and begin to approach the bridge over the Chicago River.
50. Driving my car over the Chicago River bridge.
60. Driving a friend and crossing the bridge over the Mississippi River near Moline.
70. Driving my car on the bridge over the Mississippi River near Moline.
80. Driving my car with a friend on a hilly road in Wisconsin.
90. Driving my car with a friend on a hilly road in Wisconsin going halfway up a fairly steep hill.
100. Driving my car with a friend up to the top of a fairly steep hill. We get to the top and get out of the car and look around at the valley below . . . then go into a restaurant nearby—and later drive back down the hill.

Fear of flying in airplanes
10. Watching a movie of a plane moving up and down and banking.
20. Sitting in a private plane—on the ground with the motor idling.
30. Sitting in a private plane on the ground and the pilot begins to taxi down the runway.
40. Sitting in a private plane on the ground, taxiing, and the pilot revs the engine.
50. Planning a trip with a friend on a commercial jet and it's three months before the trip.
60. One month before the trip by jet.
70. Three weeks before the trip by jet.
80. Three days before the trip by jet.
90. In a private plane at take-off.
100. In a commercial jet over land.

Fear of leaving the house
10. Going out the front door to my car to go to the store.
20. Getting in the car and starting it up.
30. In the car and pulling out of the driveway.
40. On the street and pulling away from my house.
50. Two blocks from my house on way to the store.
60. Arrive at the store and park.
70. Enter the store.
80. Get a shopping cart and begin looking for items on my list.
90. Have all the items and go to check-out counter.
100. Have all the items and have to wait in a long slow line to go through check-out.

occurs, each differing in the level of fear that it arouses. Someone else might have a very specific fear, where the descriptions of the increasing anxiety-provoking situations differ on a spatio-temporal dimension. This was the case of the woman in Table 5.4 who had a fear of leaving her house. The hierarchy can also vary in terms of the number of people present in a particular situation (e.g., an elevator), the perceived attitudes of others toward the client, and combination of some of these dimensions (see the fear of flying hierarchy in Table 5.4).

When the client returns with the prepared hierarchy, the therapist goes through it with him or her and adds intermediary items where it seems appropriate. The final hierarchy should represent a slow and smooth gradient of anxiety-provoking situations, each of which the client can easily imagine. Most hierarchies contain 20 to 25 items. It is not unusual, however, for those hierarchies that represent a very specific fear (e.g., driving on the highway at night, driving onto suspension bridges, and fear of spiders) to contain fewer items, whereas those representing a more complex fear (e.g., fear of being alone, fear of evaluation, and fear of open spaces) contain more items. In Table 5.5 we have listed an example of a final hierarchy.

The therapist should also determine what the client considers a relaxing scene, one that would be a zero (0) on the hierarchy. This is often called the *control scene*. The scene should be unrelated to the client's fear(s) and totally satisfying and comforting. Some common "zero-level" scenes are the following:

> Walking through the forest on a nice sunny day with my wife (husband).
> Lying on the beach by the ocean on a sunny, warm day.
> Lying in bed and reading an interesting novel.
> Sitting in a lounge chair in my backyard on a beautiful spring day.
> Lying on the couch and watching a good movie on TV.

Hierarchy development usually occupies at least part of two or three sessions, though less time can be spent with those cases that involve a single phobia.

Systematic Desensitization Proper

Desensitization proper usually begins about three or four sessions after the completion of the initial interview. By this time, the client has had the opportunity to practice relaxation at home as well as in the therapist's office and has been able to construct the anxiety hierarchy. If the client has developed a number of hierarchies, the therapist should first work on the one that is most distressing and troublesome to the client. If time allows, the therapist can also work on other hierarchies during the hour but probably should not expose the client to more than three different hierarchies in a given session.

The first desensitization session starts with having the client spend about 3 to 5 minutes relaxing himself or herself on the couch or in the recliner chair. During this time, the therapist suggests to the client that he or she is becoming increasingly more relaxed and is achieving a deeper and deeper level of relaxation. The therapist might add the following comments during this phase:

Table 5.5. Sample of Final Hierarchy

Elevators

*1. At my (therapist's) office and seeing the elevator as you walk down the stairs.
2. Pushing button to summon elevator at my office (on second floor)
3. Elevator comes to second floor . . . doors open . . . and you go inside and down to first floor.
*4. In the new elevator with others at the Acme building below the fourth floor—going down.
5. You enter the elevator at my office, the doors close, and there is a slight pause before it begins going down.
6. Alone in the elevator in my office building going up from the first to the third floor.
*7. In a new elevator alone at the Acme building, going up between the first and fourth floors.
*8. In the new elevator with others at the Acme building going down between the 15th and 4th floors (15-story building)
9. In the elevator at my office going down. As the elevator reaches the first floor there is a slight pause before the doors open.
*10. In a new elevator with others at the Acme building and going up between the 4th and 15th floors.
11. In the elevator alone at the Acme building, going up between the 4th and 15th floors, and as you reach the 12th floor to get out there is a momentary pause before the doors open.
*12. You're on the fifth floor of the Marshall building (a very familiar old building to the client) and you enter the elevator alone, push the button, and its starts to go down to the first floor.
13. As you are going down in the elevator you begin hearing a few noises from the elevator machinery.
*14. You enter the Marshall building and walk up to the elevator, step inside, and press the button to go up to the fifth floor.
*15. You enter the elevator alone in the Ajax building (30 floors) and you take it up to the 10th floor.
16. . . . to the 15th floor.
17. . . . to the 20th floor.
*18. You enter the elevator alone in the Thomas building (50 floors) and you take it to the 20th floor.
19. . . . to the 30th floor.
20. You are in the elevator alone in my office building and press the button to go up to the fifth floor, and it doesn't stop until the seventh floor.
21. You are in the elevator alone at the Marshall building, going down to the first floor, and it stops between the second and first floors. You press the first floor button again and the elevator goes to the first floor.
*22. You are in an elevator alone in the Thomas building going up to the 45th floor and it gets stuck between the 20th and 21st floors—and then starts up a while later after you have pressed the alarm button.

* Original items that client developed

Your whole body is becoming heavier . . . all your muscles are relaxing more and more. Your arms are becoming very relaxed. (Pause) Your shoulders. (Pause) And your eyes . . . very relaxed. Your forehead . . . very relaxed . . . noticing that as you become more relaxed you're feeling more and more calm. (Pause) Very relaxed . . . relaxing any part of your face that feels the least bit tense. (Pause) Now, back down to your neck . . . your shoulders . . . your chest . . . your buttocks . . . your thighs . . . your legs . . . your feet . . . very, very relaxed. (Pause) Feeling very at ease and very comfortable.

The client is also asked by the therapist to indicate, by raising his or her right index finger, when he or she has achieved a very relaxing and comfortable state.

After the client signals, the therapist asks him or her to visualize a number of scenes from the hierarchy that the two of them developed over the past few sessions. The therapist asks the client to imagine each scene as clearly and vividly as possible—"as if you are really there"—while still maintaining a very relaxed state. If the client feels the least bit of anxiety or tension when he or she imagines a particular scene, the client is told to signal immediately with the right finger.

At this point, the therapist asks the client to indicate with an index finger if she or he is still feeling very calm and relaxed. If the client signals, the therapist presents the control scene. If the client does not signal, the therapist reviews with the client the earlier relaxation sequence until she or he no longer signals feeling tense.

The control scene is presented for approximately 15 seconds. The therapist then proceeds with the desensitization procedure. Here is an example of a desensitization session with a test-phobic individual.

> Now stop imagining that scene and give all your attention once again to relaxing. . . . Now imagine that you are home studying in the evening. It is the 20th of May, exactly a month before your examination. [Pause of 5 seconds] Now stop imagining the scene. [Pause of 10–15 seconds] Stop imagining the scene and just think of your muscles. Let go, and enjoy your state of calm. [Pause of 15 seconds] Now imagine again that you are studying at home a month before your examination. [Pause of 10–15 seconds] Stop the scene and think of nothing but your own body. [Pause of 15 seconds] (Wolpe, 1969, p. 126. Material in brackets added by present author)

Each hierarchy scene is presented three to four times with a maximum exposure time of 5 seconds for the first presentation and a gradual increase up to 10 seconds for subsequent presentations. The hierarchy items are presented first, in ascending order starting with the lowest feared item first, with relaxation periods between each scene varying from 10 to 15 seconds. In most cases, three to four different scenes are presented per session. This means that a particular desensitization session will last between 15 and 20 minutes. The remainder of the hour can be devoted to discussing issues related to the client's fear (e.g., what occurred during the week regarding the fear), to the desensitization of another fear hierarchy, or to working on some other problem/issue with the client.

After the last scene is presented for a particular session, and if the decision is not to go onto another hierarchy, the therapist usually asks the client to relax for a short period of time. The therapist then starts the ending phase of the session by saying the following:

> Just relax . . . feeling very comfortable and at ease. I would like you to stay this way until I count to five. When I reach five, I want you to open your eyes feeling very calm and refreshed. (Pause) One . . . feeling very calm; two . . . very calm, very refreshed; three . . . very refreshed; four . . . ; and, five.

The same general format is followed for all subsequent desensitization sessions. The scenes should not be presented in a rapid manner; rather, they should be presented in a conversational manner that conveys both understanding and concern for the client. The therapist should repeatedly present a particular scene until the client has experienced three consecutive successes with that scene (i.e., three consecutive presentations in which no anxiety was reported). If the client signals anxiety with a particular scene, imagination of the scene should be stopped and the client should be encouraged to relax and to imagine the relaxation (or control) scene. The previously failed scene is then presented again. If the client again signals anxiety, then the previous relaxation sequence is reintroduced. If the client does not signal anxiety, then she or he is encouraged to continue imagining the scene until the 10-second period is over. The scene is then introduced again until three consecutive successes are experienced.

If the client has two consecutive failures on a particular scene, the therapist should go back to the previous successfully passed scene and work back up again. If failure persists, the previously passed scene should be presented again, so that the client ends the session with a positive experience. The ending phase of the procedure should then begin. The problems associated with the difficult scene should be discussed with the client and modifications made either in the scene or in other aspects of the desensitization procedure.

Even if a client does not signal anxiety, it is often helpful during the conduct of desensitization (especially during the first few sessions) to determine if the client was disturbed by a particular scene, whether the client was able to imagine the scene fully, and if the client continues to feel very relaxed. To do this, the therapist states between scene presentations, "If you were not the least bit disturbed by that particular scene ("If your were able to imagine that scene very clearly," or "If you continue to feel very relaxed") do nothing; otherwise raise your right index finger." If the client raises his or her finger, the therapist then takes appropriate action, which might entail going through additional relaxation-enhancing suggestions or presenting either the problematic scene or the control scene again and suggesting that the client imagine it in detail. If, after reintroducing a particular scene, the client indicates again that she or he was disturbed by it or could not vividly imagine it, the session is stopped, using the aforementioned ending phase. The therapist then explores in detail the difficulty the client is having and makes any modifications necessary in the hierarchy or relaxation procedure.

A second useful procedure involves assessing the client's overall level of relaxation before, during, and after a particular desensitization session. This usually takes place after desensitization has been completed for the day. The client is asked to rate his or her relaxation level on a 10-point scale, where 0 is *Extremely Relaxed* and 10 is *Not At All Relaxed*. This approach not only gives the therapist information regarding the client's relative change in relaxation level from pretreatment to posttreatment across sessions, but also provides feedback to the client regarding his or her own progress.

Additional Considerations. Throughout desensitization proper, the client should be watched for signs of fatigue. In this regard, it may be helpful to ask the client whether she or he feels too many scenes (or hierarchies) are being presented at each session. It is also advisable to be sensitive to any discomfort the client is showing during either relaxation training or desensitization proper. Some of the ways clients express discomfort while lying on the couch or sitting back in a recliner are the following: moving their bodies around as if to find a comfortable position; crossing and uncrossing their legs; moving their eyelids rapidly; moving their fingers in a rhythmic or nonrhythmic manner; yawning excessively; or making unsolicited verbalizations while their eyes are closed.

Occasionally, as in the following example, discomfort can be unrelated to the client's fear.

> Mrs. Farber was well into her fifth desensitization session, progressing slowly but steadily up her hierarchy concerned with a fear of being alone in her house. She fluttered her eyelids sporadically, but did not indicate any anxiety about the scenes being presented. During subsequent relaxation-enhancing instructions, she began crossing her legs and shifting her body around. Just as the therapist was about to inquire about her relaxation level, she opened her eyes, sat up in the recliner chair, and said, "You'll have to excuse me. I had a lot to drink today and must go to the washroom. I forgot to go before I came here."

At other times, as in the next example, deep relaxation might set the occasion for very tense clients to begin thinking about their problem.

> Mr. Martin had difficulty learning how to relax. Several sessions passed with him unable to achieve a relaxation level lower than 4 on the 10-point self-report relaxation rating scale. In the fourth session, a relaxation enhancing technique was used. He became very relaxed, more relaxed than on previous occasions, and seemed to be pleased with his success. Within a few minutes, he began moving his head from one side to the other, and tears began falling down his cheeks. He then started crying and said that this was the first time he has ever "let . . . [himself] really think about" the difficulties he has had with his impotence "and all the turmoil it has caused in my life."

Similar events can also contribute to a client's repeated failure of an item in a session. In the following example, the particular hierarchy item did not produce the signaled anxiety; rather, the anxiety was triggered by a telephone call that day from an old friend of the client.

> Mrs. Carol was progressing steadily through her agoraphobia hierarchy over the first eight desensitization sessions. During the ninth session, an item was presented concerned with driving by herself nine miles to the therapist's office. As soon as the item was presented, she signaled anxiety and repeated this action until the session was stopped. Upon inquiring about her repeated signaling, she began crying and said she had received a telephone call that day from an old college friend with whom she was very close but had not seen for 10 years. The friend had an unexpected 3-hour layover at the airport and decided to call Mrs. Carol and ask her to come out to see her (a distance of 20 miles). Mrs. Carol wanted to go very, very much but was afraid to

take a chance and declined, but she did talk to her friend on the telephone for a long time. She felt terrible and angry at herself for having such a "stupid problem."

Another reason for repeated failure of a hierarchy item could be the psychological distance between the last passed item and the next failed one. Two examples of this situation are the following:

> *Item passed.* Flying in the plane after leveling off at 30,000 feet and not hearing any change in the sound of the engines. (Item 60 on the hierarchy)
> *Item failed.* Feeling the tilt of the plane as it is banking, and not hearing any change in the sound of the engines. (65 on the hierarchy)
> *Item passed.* Planning a trip on an airplane with a close friend to the Bahama Islands 9 months before the trip. (20 on the hierarchy)
> *Item failed.* Reviewing plans of airplane trip to the Bahamas with close friend 1 month before the trip. (25 on the hierarchy)

In the first example, the client and the therapist decided on an intermediary scene that described a change in the noise of the airplane engines that the client could hear just before she felt the plane banking. A temporal dimension, on the other hand, was inserted between the two scenes in the second example. Specifically, three additional scenes were developed: 6 months before the planned trip, 4 months before, and 2 months before. In both cases these additions to the respective hierarchies facilitated successful passage of the heretofore failed items.

Just as some clients signal repeated difficulty with one or more hierarchy scenes, others never signal anxiety about particular scenes. In some cases, this is good because it suggests that the hierarchy represents a smooth, even gradation of the client's fear. In other cases, this means that the client feels reluctant to signal that anxiety is indeed being experienced. To reduce the possibility of the client's not signaling anxiety when, in fact, she or he should, it is a good idea for the therapist to mention at various times throughout the session: "Remember to signal whenever you feel the slightest amount of anxiety." The therapist should also make every effort to convey neither dissatisfaction with a client's signaling of anxiety nor satisfaction that a client did not signal anxiety at all during a particular session. In both instances, the client might begin to feel that the therapist does not really want any signaling of anxiety.

It is also important for the therapist to end each desensitization session with a positive experience for the client (i.e., ending on a hierarchy item that was passed successfully). Moreover, the therapist should leave sufficient time at the end of the session (as well as before the session begins) to discuss any issues or concerns that the client has or to discuss how things went during the week.

Most desensitization sessions last from 30 minutes to 1 hour depending on the number of different hierarchies presented. Some researchers, however, have reported successfully treating a phobia by conducting a *massed desensitization* session that lasted 90 minutes (Wolpin & Pearsall, 1965), whereas others (e.g., Deffenbacher & Suinn, 1988; Richardson & Suinn, 1973) have reported success after a 3-hour massed session or other concentrated period of time when there is not a great deal of time available to help the client reduce his or her fear responses. In most cases, however, the spacing of desensitization sessions varies from once a week to twice a week, though Wolpe (1982) reported that some clients have received two or more sessions per day.

Finally, during the initial stages of systematic desensitization, the client is encouraged to avoid the temptation of entering the actual feared situation. Because this could be an unrealistic request for some clients, they are asked to try to avoid the feared situation at "full throttle." As desensitization progresses, however, they are encouraged to enter aspects of the feared situation that correspond to lower hierarchy items that have been passed successfully and for which they now feel little, if any, tension or anxiety.

Variations of Systematic Desensitization

Various alternatives to systematic desensitization have been proposed by researchers. In *in vivo desensitization* (e.g., Kipper, 1980; Levine & Wolpe, 1980; Schneider, 1982; Sherman, 1972; Southworth & Kirsch, 1988), the client is exposed to the items on the hierarchy in the real situation rather than through imagination. Relaxation training is not used as the counterconditioned response to the situation. Instead, those feelings of comfort, security, and trust that the client has developed for the therapist (that have emerged from the therapeutic relationship) are used as the counterconditioning agent. The therapist goes into real-life situations with the client and urges him or her to go through each item on the hierarchy gradually. An example of this procedure is the following:

> Mr. Kay is a very successful salesman in a large metropolitan area. But he is extremely afraid of elevators. Lately his fear has become so intense that he has avoided attending meetings that occur on a level higher than the fourth floor. *In vivo* desensitization entailed having Mr. Kay and the therapist approach various elevators throughout the city, ride up and down in them, and purposely get stuck in them, following a hierarchy sequence developed earlier with the therapist. Mr. Kay was also encouraged to go up in elevators, etc., on his own while the therapist waited for him at various floors.

A similar technique called *contact desensitization* (e.g., Morris & Kratochwill, 1983; Ritter, 1968, 1969a, 1969b) is used with both children and adults. This technique also involves a graded hierarchy but adds to it modeling, touch, information/feedback, and a practice component in addition to the therapist's interpersonal relationship with the client. The procedure is outlined in the next example from Bandura (1969):

> In the application of this method to the elimination of snake phobia, at each step the experimenter himself performed fearless behavior and gradually led subjects into touching, stroking and then holding the snake's body with first gloves and then bare hands while he held the snake securely by the head and tail. If a subject was unable

to touch the snake after ample demonstration, she was asked to place her hand on the experimenter's and to move her hand down gradually until it touched the snake's body. After subjects no longer felt any apprehension about touching the snake under these secure conditions, anxieties about contact with the snake's head area and entwining tail were extinguished. The experimenter again performed the tasks fearlessly and then he and the subject performed the responses jointly; as subjects became less fearful the experimenter gradually reduced his participation and control over the snake until subjects were able to hold the snake in their laps without assistance, to let the snake loose in the room and retrieve it, and to let it crawl freely over their bodies. Progress through the graded approach tasks was paced according to the subjects' apprehensiveness. When they reported being able to perform one activity with little or no fear, they were eased into a more difficult interaction. (p. 185, reprinted with permission)

A third variation is very similar to desensitization proper, but involves the use of an audiotape recorder, videotape recorder, and/or computer. It is called *automated desensitization* (e.g., Biglan, Villwock, & Wick, 1979; Migler & Wolpe, 1967; Thomas, Rapp, & Gentles, 1979). In this procedure, the client goes through the desensitization process by listening to or viewing a series of tape-recorded scene presentations or reading a series of hierarchy items displayed on the computer screen, prepared by the therapist with the client's assistance. Developed by Lang (Wolpe, 1969) and later used by Migler and Wolpe (1967) and others (e.g., Chandler, Burck, Sampson, & Wray, 1988), this procedure allows the client to pace himself or herself in the desensitization process and to become desensitized at home. Although a few writers (e.g., Deffenbacher & Suinn, 1988) have raised some questions about when this procedure should be used, it does appear to be useful when an individual therapist or a group procedure are not immediately available to a client.

A variation of the automated procedure is called *self-directed desensitization* (Baker, Cohen, & Sauders, 1973; Krop & Krause, 1976; Rosen, 1976; Rosen, Glasgow, & Barrera, 1976). In this procedure, clients use instructional materials typically provided them by the therapist and conduct the treatment at their own pace. In some cases the therapist continues to function as a consultant, whereas at other times the therapist sees the client only once for the initial structuring of treatment. The major difference between this procedure and automated desensitization is that with the latter method the client uses electronic equipment to present the treatment package to himself or herself. An interesting fading procedure that makes use of both automated and self-directed methods of fear reduction has been discussed by Öst (1978a). He reports that this procedure is as effective as live desensitization (Öst, 1978b).

The one issue that seems to transcend each of these self-directed types of desensitization procedures is related to the notions of client compliance and follow through (e.g., Deffenbacher & Suinn, 1988). That is, will some clients avoid completing their self-desensitization treatment because of the fear and related anxiety that is aroused by exposing themselves to the anxiety hierarchy? If the therapist believes that this might be the case for a particular client, then a different desensitization procedure should be implemented.

Another variation is *self-control desensitization* (Deffenbacher & Michaels, 1981; Deffenbacher, Michaels, Michaels, & Daly, 1980; Goldried, 1971). In this approach, the desensitization procedure is construed as training the client in coping skills; that is, desensitization treatment is viewed as teaching the client to cope with anxiety. Clients are told, for example, to apply relaxation training whenever they become aware of an increase in their feelings of anxiety and tension. They are also encouraged, during the desensitization proper phase, to continue imagining a scene that produces anxiety and to "relax away" the anxiety and/or imagine themselves becoming fearful and then seeing themselves coping with the anxiety and tenseness that they feel. This variation is based on the view that clients will not always be in a position where they can readily leave a fearful and anxiety-arousing situation, that they must learn to cope with the situation on their own. Rehearsal for this possibility, therefore, should take place in the therapist's office. In this regard, it is not important for the anxiety hierarchy to be theme oriented as in standard systematic desensitization (Goldfried & Goldfried, 1977). The hierarchy need only be composed of situations arousing increasing amounts of anxiety, independent of theme. The following rationale for clients has been suggested by Goldfried:

> There are various situations where, on the basis of your past experience, you have learned to react by becoming tense (anxious, nervous, fearful). What I plan to do is help you to learn how to cope with these situations more successfully, so that they do not make you as upset. This will be done by taking note of a number of those situations which upset you to varying degrees, and then having you learn to cope with the less stressful situations before moving on to the more difficult ones. Part of the treatment involves learning how to relax, so that in situations where you feel yourself getting nervous you will be better able to eliminate this tenseness. Learning to relax is much like learning any other skill. When a person learns to drive, he initially has difficulty in coordinating everything, and often finds himself very much aware of what he is doing. With more and more practice, however, the procedures involved in driving become easier and more automatic. You may find the same thing occurring to you when you try to relax in those situations where you feel yourself starting to become tense. You will find that as you persist, however, it will become easier and easier. (1971, p. 231)

A fourth variation is called *group desensitization* (see, for example, Deffenbacher & Kemper, 1974a,b; Snyder & Deffenbacher, 1977). This procedure involves the same basic phases as individual systematic desensitization, but the phases are adapted for group administration. Typically, this procedure takes approximately three sessions longer than individual systematic desensitization—assuming the same fear is being treated (Deffenbacher & Suinn, 1988). Groups of five to nine persons are usually treated in this procedure, with each group member having the same fear. Relaxation training is conducted on a group basis, with members of the group reclining on patio chaise lounges or on foam rubber mats on the floor. Hierarchy construction occurs in one of three ways: (a) the therapist and group members develop the hierarchy items together, and then the group rank orders the items; (b) the therapist brings to the group a potential set of hierarchy items—like the ones presented in Table 5.6—and the group determines which ones are appropriate and/or need modification and what ranking should be assigned to each; or (c) the therapist works with each client individually to develop his or her own unique hierarchy for the specific fear, with the understanding that during the desensitization proper phase each client will focus their imagining on those items in their particular hierarchy.

Table 5.6. Possible Items for a Test Anxiety Hierarchy

You hear about a friend who has a test soon.

On the first day of class, the teacher announces the number of tests she will be giving during the first grade period.

Your teacher announces that there will be a test in one week.

It's a couple of days before the test and you still have a lot to study. You know that you will be able to prepare adequately for the exam only if you work steadily and efficiently.

You start studying for the test.

You are studying and wondering how you will remember everything for the test.

It's the night before the exam and you're reviewing everything.

You get ready for your class and it's a few minutes before you have to leave for school.

You're at school and you walk to your class where you have to take the test, and you're thinking about the test.

You enter the classroom where the exam is given.

You take your seat and wait for the teacher to come to you with the test.

Others around you are talking about the material being covered on the test, and you're trying to answer their questions to yourself.

You see the teacher handing out the exams, and you watch others get their copy of the test.

You get your copy of the exam and look it over.

You see a lot of questions you think you should know, but you can't remember the answers to them.

You start the test and wonder how well you are doing compared with the others in your class.

You get to your class expecting a routine discussion or lecture and the teacher passes out a surprise quiz.

You come to an ambiguous question. You think you know the answer, but the question can be interpreted in more than one way.

While answering an essay question, you realize that what you are writing is incorrect and that you will have to cross out what you have written and begin again.

The teacher has just told the class that only half the time remains for you to complete the exam. You have completed less than half of the test and realize that you will have to work more rapidly in order to finish the exam.

You see others finish the test and hand in their papers, and you aren't finished yet.

There are two minutes remaining in the test. If you work very quickly, you will be able to answer all the questions.

You didn't answer the questions the same way they did.

Note: Adapted in part from *A comparison of self-control desensitization with systematic desensitization in the reduction of test anxiety* by L. Martinez, 1978. Unpublished dissertation, Syracuse University.

The desensitization proper phase is conducted in a slightly different fashion than in individual systematic desensitization, and the typical treatment session may last as long as 75 minutes. In the group approach, this phase is geared to the slowest progressing person in the group. For example, if one person in a group of text-anxious college students is reporting anxiety over the imagination of a particular hierarchy item, the other people in the group would be told to continue relaxing or, in some cases, to imagine their control scene. The therapist would then go through repeated presentations of the particular hierarchy item and/or previously passed hierarchy items until the person successfully imagined the difficult scene without reporting anxiety. A variation of group systematic desensitization, called *group vicarious desensitization* (e.g., Altmaier & Woodward, 1981), has clients observe videotapes of people undergoing systematic desensitization for the same fear as that reported by the clients.

FLOODING-RELATED THERAPIES

Like systematic desensitization, flooding methods use the imaginal presentation of anxiety-provoking material. But, unlike the desensitization methods, flooding-related therapies from the very beginning have the client imagine a fearful and threatening scene of high intensity for a prolonged period of time, without any previous relaxation training. The purpose of flooding methods, therefore, is to produce a frightening imaginal experience in the client of such magnitude that the experience will actually result in a reduction in his or her fear phobia rather than a heightening of it. Two major types of flooding therapy have been discussed in the literature: *implosive therapy* and *flooding*. These two methods have many common characteristics.

Implosive Therapy

Developed by psychologist Thomas G. Stampfl (Stampfl, 1961, 1970; Stampfl & Levis, 1967), this method utilizes principles from both learning theory and psychodynamic theory (e.g., Sigmund Freud's psychoanalytic theory). Though Stampfl maintains that fears and their associated anxiety are learned, he does not assume that such fears can most effectively be reduced by using a countercondi- tioning approach. Rather, he believes that a person can best unlearn a fear by using a procedure based on an *extinction model*. Here, extinction refers to the gradual reduction in the occurrence of an anxiety response, as a result of the continuous presentation of the fear-producing stimulus in the absence of the reinforcement that perpetuates the fear. In therapy, this extinction process is accomplished by having the therapist "represent, reinstate, or symbolically reproduce the stimuli (cues) to which the anxiety response has been conditioned . . ." without present- ing the concomitant reinforcement that maintains the response (Stampfl & Levis, 1967, p. 499). (In this statement, Stampfl and Levis are using the term *reinforce- ment* in the classical conditioning sense of the word, that is, the procedure of following a conditioned stimulus [CS] with an unconditioned stimulus [UCS].)

Development of the Avoidance Serial Cue Hierarchy

From information gathered during the initial interview, the therapist develops hypotheses as to what are the important cues involved in the client's fear or phobia. Many of these cues are situational events in the client's life and can be readily identified. For example, in the case of people who have a fear of heights, situational events could be the sight of high-rise office and/or apartment buildings, winding roads in the mountains, airplanes, bridges, and so forth.

The remaining cues are formulated by the therapist and are based on psychodynamic theory and on the therapist's knowledge of common reactions by clients with similar problems. They are derived from the client's statements in the initial interview and from the client's nonverbal behavior, and they represent those psychodynamic areas that the therapist believes are relevant to the client's fear. These cues are usually related to themes of aggression and hostility, oral and anal activity, sexual activity, punishment, rejection, bodily injury, loss of impulse control, and guilt. For example, Stampfl and Levis (1967) described four of the hypothesized dynamic cues in the following manner:

> *Aggression.* Scenes presented in this area usually center around the expression of anger, hostility, and aggression by the patient toward parental, sibling, spouse, or other significant figures in his life. Various degrees of bodily injury are described including complete body mutilation and death of the victim.
> *Punishment.* The patient is instructed to visualize himself as the recipient of the anger, hostility, and aggression of the various significant individuals in his life. The punishment inflicted in the scene is frequently a result of the patient's engaging in some forbidden act.
> *Sexual material.* In this area a wide variety of hypothesized cues related to sex are presented. For example, primal and Oedipal scenes and scenes of castration, fellatio, and homosexuality are presented.
> *Loss of control.* Scenes are presented where the patient is encouraged to imagine himself losing impulse control to such an extent that he acts out avoided sexual or aggressive impulses. These scenes usually are followed by scenes where the individual is directed to visualize himself hospitalized for the rest of his life in a back ward of a mental hospital as a result of his loss of impulse control. This area is tapped primarily with patients who express fear of "becoming insane" or concern about being hopeless and incurable. (p. 501, reprinted with permission)

Those cues that are lowest on the hierarchy are assumed to be situations and events that the client can associate with his or her fear or phobia. The highest cues are those internal dynamic cues that the therapist believes are closely associated with the client's basic psychological problem. The particular dynamic themes emphasized in the hierarchy depend on the client's problem and the information obtained in the initial interview.

The hierarchy scenes are developed by the therapist after the initial interview is completed. They are not developed jointly by the client and the therapist, as in systematic desensitization. Overall, the hierarchy is quite different from the one developed in systematic desensitization. For example, the Avoidance Serial Cue Hierarchy contains only items that are thought to be capable of producing a maximum level of anxiety in the client. This is not the case with the desensitization hierarchy. The latter hierarchy is developed for a different reason, namely, to proceed gradually up the hierarchy in order to minimize the possibility that the client will experience any anxiety. The Avoidance Serial Cue Hierarchy starts with items that produce anxiety in the person and proceeds from external stimuli that evoke anxiety to hypothesized internal stimuli that also produce a maximum level of anxiety. An example of this type of hierarchy concerned with a fear of enclosed spaces is described by Stampfl (1970):

> [The client] is instructed to imagine that he is slowly suffocating to death. . . . [The therapist supplies many details about suffocation and then, based on information obtained in the interview, might present] scenes involving wrongdoing, with a parental figure supervising confinement to the closed space as a punishment. The parental figure might beat and scold the patient while he suffocates. Early traumatic incidents that appear to be related to the phobia may also be introduced, as represented in teasing sequences by being covered and held under blankets. If the patient appears to have been involved in a typical Oedipal situation in childhood, the therapist may suggest scenes that include sexual interaction with a mother figure followed by apprehension by a father figure, who places the patient in a closed space and castrates him. . . . The cues related to bodily injury are vividly described. (pp. 199–200, reprinted with permission)

Implosive Therapy Proper

After the hierarchy has been planned, the therapist describes implosive therapy to the client. This usually occurs at the beginning of the third session. It involves telling the client that a number of scenes will be presented to him or her, and that he or she is to sit back in the recliner chair and make every effort to lose himself or herself in that part of the scene that is being imagined. In addition, the client is told to "live" the scenes with genuine emotion and feeling. The goal then is "to produce in the absence of physical pain, as good an approximation as possible, the sights, sound, and tactual experiences originally present in the primary" situation in which the fear was learned (Stampfl & Levis, 1968, p. 33).

The client is neither asked to accept the accuracy of what he or she is imagining nor to agree that the scenes are representative of his or her fear. The scenes are then described by the therapist and are elaborated on in vivid detail. The more dramatic the presentation of the scenes, the easier it is for the client to participate fully in the experience. Then, as Stampfl and Levis (1967) state:

> An attempt is made by the therapist to attain a maximal level of anxiety evocation from the patient. When a high level of anxiety is achieved, the patient is held on this level until some sign of spontaneous reduction in the anxiety-inducing value of the cues appears. . . . the process is repeated, and again, at the first sign of spontaneous reduction of fear, new variations are introduced to elicit an intense anxiety response. This procedure is repeated until a significant diminution in anxiety has resulted. (p. 500)

One way of determining if the scenes are producing anxiety in the client is to observe if the client is flushing, sweating, grimacing, moving his or her head from side to side, or exhibiting increased motoric activity in the chair. The implosive procedure is maintained for about 30 to 40 minutes. After a scene has been presented a few times and the client is observed to experience anxiety to this scene, she or he is given the opportunity to present the scene to herself or himself through imagination and is encouraged to act out fully participation in the scene. The therapist continues to monitor the presence of anxiety and aids the client by suggesting that she or he imagine the scene vividly. Sometimes during treatment the client mentions to the therapist a few additional situations or events that produce fear. These should be noted by the therapist and included in the next implosive therapy session.

The session ends after 50 to 60 minutes and after the client has demonstrated a diminution in his or her anxiety response to the implosive scene. The client is then told to practice imagining the implosive scenes at home about once a day until the next session. This practice not only extends treatment outside the therapist's office and therefore aids in the generalization of the treatment effects, but it also helps the client realize that he or she can effectively deal with his or her fear or phobia by using the implosive therapy procedure. In fact, it "is hoped that at the termination of treatment the patient will be able to handle new anxiety-provoking situations without the therapist's help" (Stampfl & Levis, 1967, p. 500).

The following excerpt from a therapy session of a snake-phobic woman demonstrates how implosive therapy has been used. The reader will notice that external stimuli associated with the fear are first introduced into the imagined scene.

> Close your eyes again. Picture the snake out in front of you, now make yourself pick it up. Reach down, pick it up, put it in your lap, feel it wiggling around in your lap, leave your hand on it, put your hand out and feel it wiggling around. Kind of explore its body with your fingers and hand. You don't like to do it, make yourself do it. Make yourself do it. Really grab onto the snake. Squeeze it a little bit, feel it. (Hogan, 1969, p. 1979)

In the next excerpt, the client's level of anxiety is increased by including material in the imagined scene that is based on hypothesized internal stimuli that are contributing to the fear.

> Okay, now put your finger out towards the snake and feel his head coming up. Now, it is in your lap, and it is coming up. Its head [is] towards your finger and it is starting to bite at your finger. Let it, let it bite at your finger. Let the snake kind of gnaw at your finger. Feel it gnawing, look at the blood dripping off your finger. Feel it in your stomach and the pain going up your arm. Try to picture your bleeding finger. And the teeth of the snake are stuck right in your finger, right down to the bone. (Hogan, 1969, p. 180)

In the next excerpt, the psychodynamic interpretation of the fear or phobia is presented.

> *Therapist:* I want you to picture yourself getting ready to get into your bed and there in your bed are thousands of snakes. Can you see them there crawling around in your

bed? I want you to lay down with them. Get down with them. Feel yourself moving around with the snakes and they are crawling all over you. And you are moving and turning in bed and they are touching you. Feel them crawling on you, touching you, slimy and slithering. Feel yourself turn over in your bed, and they are under you and on you and around you, and touching your face and in your hair. And they are crawling across your face. Can you feel them touch you? Describe the feeling.

    Subject: Kind of cold.

    Therapist: Feel, you are now cold and clammy like a snake and they are touching you with their cold, clammy, wet, slimy, drippy, cold bodies that are wiggling and touching your skin and feel them. Uhhh how can you feel them touch you? They are touching you. Can you feel them touch you? Move around so you can get greater contact. Move your body like that woman in the Sealy [mattress] ad and feel them touch you, uhh, wiggly and slimy, they are crawling on you, on your face. Uhhh! (Hogan, 1969, p. 181)

Flooding

The major difference between flooding and implosive therapy is in the type of scenes to which clients are exposed. Instead of exposing clients to horrifying scenes to imagine, in which certain aversive consequences occur (e.g., eating flesh, castrating people, death), scenes are described in which the feared external stimuli are presented for an extended period of time (e.g., Chambless, Foa, Groves, & Goldstein, 1982; Chaplin & Levine, 1981; Fairbank & Keane, 1982). For example, compare the previous implosive therapy excerpt with the following scene from an imaginal flooding procedure:

> Imagine that you are going out of the front door of this house. You walk through the front garden and then you are in the street. You turn left and walk in the shopping center where you have to go and buy something. Imagine it as well as you can: the houses you walk past, the cars that rush past you. You are walking there alone and you are going in the direction of the railway crossing. The bars are down and you have to wait. A group of people is standing there waiting and they look at you. You find it very disturbing, this waiting, and you hop a bit from one leg to the other. At last the bars are going up, you walk on, and arrive in the shopping center. It is fuller there, there are more and more people. You begin to feel rather bad now. You become dizzy. You feel it in your legs. But nevertheless walk on, because there is no where you can go there on the street, you cannot flee inside anywhere. Now you have to cross the street. There is a string of cars and you run between them. On the other side of the street there are still more people. Now you are feeling completely dizzy. Your legs are heavy. But there you are walking in the middle of the pavement and there is no where you can go. You begin to panic and you think, "I want to go away," "I want to go home," but you cannot go home. You hold onto a gate for a while, but you can't manage anymore. You are sweating terribly, you take another couple of steps and then you fall. You fall there in the middle of the street. People come and stand all around you and are wondering what has happened. And there you lie, in the middle of the street. (Emmelkamp, 1982, p. 61)

Thus, psychodynamic cues and/or interpretations are not used in the formulation of the flooding scenes; rather, the therapist uses only the external cues and vividly describes the scenes for the client to imagine. Scenes are presented for about the same period of time as in implosive therapy, with some research suggesting that continuous exposure of a flooding scene is superior to interrupted exposure (e.g., Chaplin & Levine, 1981; Stern & Marks, 1973).

A variation of the flooding procedure is called *in vivo flooding* (e.g., Emmelkamp, 1982; Emmelkamp, Brilman, Kuiper, & Mersch, 1986; Emmelkamp & Wessels, 1975; Marshall, Gauthier, Christie, Currie, & Gordon, 1977). In this procedure, the client is exposed in real life to the flooding procedure involving the actual feared situation, event, or object. For example, Yule, Sacks, and Hersov (1974) placed an 11-year-old boy with a noise phobia (i.e., the noise associated with the bursting of balloons) in a small room filled with 50 balloons. The therapist began popping some of the balloons, and the child did the same thing. In the next session, the child was surrounded by 100 to 150 balloons and encouraged to pop them, with prompting by the therapist. After two sessions there were no signs of balloon phobia, and at a 25-month follow-up period there was no indication of any recurrence of the phobia.

Emmelkamp (1982) and others (e.g., Stern & Marks, 1973) have suggested that this real-life flooding approach is far more effective than the imaginal flooding procedure. In vivo flooding, however, could be too terrifying for some clients. Some researchers (e.g., Marshall et al., 1977) have therefore suggested adding a brief real-life exposure component to an imaginal flooding procedure following the end of each treatment session.

A second variation of flooding is called *self-directed in vivo flooding* (see, for example, Emmelkamp, 1982; Ghosh, Marks, & Carr, 1988; Mattick & Peters, 1988; Mavissakalian & Michelson, 1983, 1986; Michelson, Marchionne, Marchionne, Testa, & Mavissakalian, 1988). With this method, the client is encouraged to enter actual phobic situations on his or her own, and to remain in these situations until his or her anxiety or discomfort decreases to a fairly comfortable level. The particular conditions, however, under which this or the other in vivo procedure should be used, or with which types of phobias, have not been specified in the literature.

Limitation of Flooding-Related Therapies

With regard to implosive therapy, Stampfl and Levis (1967) state that "the more accurate the hypothesized cues and the more realistically they are presented the greater the extinction effect . . . will be" (p. 499). This statement suggests that the therapist should be quite knowledgeable in psychodynamic theory, especially psychoanalytic theory. If the therapist is not, she or he should probably refrain from using the approach. Furthermore, some writers (Marshall et al., 1977; Redd, Porterfield, & Anderson, 1979) have suggested that imaginal exposure to horrifying situations might, under certain conditions, strengthen a client's fear. Other writers (e.g., Emmelkamp, 1982) have concluded that the inclusion of horrifying situations during imaginal flooding does not enhance the effectiveness of the method and that imaginal flooding with pleasant scenes could be more effective, "at least with respect to anxiety reduction" (Emmelkamp, 1982, p. 67). Even though the flooding-related therapies appear to be effective in reducing fears and phobias in people, it appears that this method should be used with caution. The therapist should be familiar with identifying anxiety cues with a client who might have a very negative experience with the anxiety-provoking scenes presented.

SUMMARY

The two methods discussed in this chapter have been widely used in the reduction of fears and phobias in adults. Each of these fear reduction methods has in common the exposure of the client to the feared situation, event, or object. The exposure can be either imaginal or in vivo, or it can be either graduated along a hierarchy or involve the immediate presentation of the noxious aspects of the fear or phobia. No definitive statement can be made at this time regarding which of the latter exposure methods when combined is more effective than any of the other combined exposure methods for the vast array of fears and phobias that people experience, even though the outcome of some research comparing these different exposure methods has been published (see, for example, Bernstein & Kleinknecht, 1982; Biran & Wilson, 1981; Cullington, Butler, Hibbert, & Gelder, 1984; Emmelkamp, 1982; Howard, Murphy, & Clarke, 1983; Mavissakalian & Barlow, 1981; Shaw, 1979; Williams, Dooseman, & Kleifield, 1984). Thus, a major question still exists regarding the treatment of fears and phobias, namely, which fear reduction method should be used, under what conditions, and for which type of fear? This question cannot be answered easily at this time.

Without a doubt, the most heavily researched fear reduction method is systematic desensitization and its variants. It has been shown in many studies to be very effective in reducing various types of fears. The prime limitation of systematic desensitization treatment, however, is that it is extremely time consuming to conduct, especially when the client has a large number of fears needing reduction. Flooding methods have also been found to be effective in reducing fears and phobias. A flooding approach could be used for those clients who can tolerate being exposed initially to some of the major noxious aspects of their fears or phobias, either imaginably or in real life. This, however, raises an interesting ethical question. Given that we cannot state at the present time which fear reduction method is the treatment of choice for a particular fear or phobia, and given that flooding methods expose clients initially to noxious aspects of their fears, whereas desensitization methods use a graduated exposure approach, should a client have a choice in determining which fear reduction method will be used on him or her? Again, this is not an easy question to answer.

Because of the active clinical research that has been conducted over the last 2 decades in the area of fear reduction methods, we find that some very promising treatment methods have emerged. The next series of steps should be the detailing of the conditions under which each method is effective and for which types of fears and phobias. In addition, based on the findings of Öst (1989), more empirical work is needed on developing methods for maintaining over time the positive fear reduction results that clients have experienced in therapy.

REFERENCES

Altmaier, E. M., & Woodward, M. (1981). Group vicarious desensitization of test anxiety. *Journal of Counseling Psychology, 28,* 467–469.

Baker, B. L., Cohen, D. C., & Saunders, J. T. (1973). Self-directed desensitization for actrophobics. *Behavior Research and Therapy, 11,* 79–89.

Bandura, A. (1969). *Principles of behavior modification.* New York: Holt, Rinehart & Winston.

Bandura, A. (1977). *Social learning theory.* Englewood Cliffs, NJ: Prentice-Hall.

Bandura, A., & Walters, R. H. (1963). *Social learning and personality development.* New York: Holt, Rinehart & Winston.

Bernstein, D. A., & Kleinknecht, R. A. (1982). Multiple approaches to the reduction of dental fear. *Journal of Behavior Therapy and Experimental Psychiatry, 13,* 287–292.

Biglan, A., Villwock, C., & Wick, S. (1979). The feasibility of a computer controlled program for the treatment of test anxiety. *Journal of Behavior Therapy and Experimental Psychiatry, 10,* 47–49.

Biran, M., & Wilson, G. T. (1981). Treatment of phobic disorders using cognitive and exposure methods: A self-efficacy analysis. *Journal of Consulting and Clinical Psychology, 49,* 886–899.

Brady, J. P. (1966). Brevital-relaxation treatment of rigidity. *Behaviour Research and Therapy, 4,* 71–77.

Brady, J. P. (1972). Systematic desensitization. In W. S. Agras (Ed.), *Behavior modification: Principles and clinical applications* (pp. 127–150). Boston: Little, Brown.

Chambless, D. L., Foa, E. B., Groves, G. A., & Goldstein, A. J. (1982). Exposure and communication training in the treatment of agoraphobia. *Behaviour Research and Therapy, 20,* 219–231.

Chandler, G. M., Burck, H., Sampson, J. P., & Wray, R. (1988). The effectiveness of a generic computer program for systematic desensitization. *Computers in Human Behavior, 4,* 339–346.

Chaplin, E. W., & Levine, B. A. (1981). The effects of total exposure duration and interrupted versus continuous exposure in flooding therapy. *Behavior Therapy, 12,* 360–368.

Cullington, A., Butler, G., Hibbert, G., & Gelder, M. (1984). Problem-solving: Not a treatment for agoraphobia. *Behavior Therapy, 15,* 280–286.

Deffenbacher, J. L., & Kemper, C. C. (1974a). Counseling test-anxious sixth graders. *Elementary Guidance and Counseling, 7,* 22–29.

Deffenbacher, J. L., & Kemper, C. C. (1974b). Systematic desensitization of test anxiety in junion high students. *School Counselor, 22,* 216–222.

Deffenbacher, J. L., & Michaels, A. C. (1981). Anxiety management training and self-control desensitization—15 months later. *Journal of Counseling Psychology, 28,* 459–462.

Deffenbacher, J. L., Michaels, A. C., Michaels, T., & Daley, P. C. (1980). Comparison of anxiety management training and self-control desensitization. *Journal of Counseling Psychology, 27,* 232–239.

Deffenbacher, J. L., & Suinn, R. M. (1988). Systematic desensitization and the reduction of anxiety. *The Counseling Psychologist, 16,* 9–30.

Emmelkamp, P. M. G. (1982). *Phobic and obsessive-compulsive disorders*. New York: Plenum Press.

Emmelkamp, P. M. G., Brilman, E., Kuiper, H., & Mersch, P. P. (1986). The treatment of agoraphobia: A comparison of self-instruction training, rational emotive therapy and exposure *in vivo*. *Behavior Modification, 10,* 37–53.

Emmelkamp, P. M. G., & Wessels, H. (1975). Flooding in imagination vs. flooding in vivo: A comparison with agoraphobics. *Behaviour Research and Therapy, 13,* 7–15.

Fairbank, J. A., & Keane, T. M. (1982). Flooding for combat-related stress disorders: Assessment of anxiety reduction across traumatic memories. *Behavior Therapy, 13,* 499–510.

Friedman, D. E. (1966). A new technique for the systematic desensitization of phobic symptoms. *Behaviour Research and Therapy, 4,* 139–140.

Ghosh, A., Marks, I. M., & Carr, A. C. (1988). Therapist contact and outcome of self-exposure treatment of phobias: A controlled study. *British Journal of Psychiatry, 152,* 234–238.

Goldfried, M. R. (1971). Systematic desensitization as training in self-control. *Journal of Consulting and Clinical Psychology, 37,* 228–234.

Goldfried, M. R., & Davison, G. (1976). *Clinical behavior therapy*. New York: Holt, Rinehart & Winston.

Goldfried, M. R., & Goldfried, A. P. (1977). Importance of hierarchy content in the self-control of anxiety. *Journal of Consulting and Clinical Psychology, 45,* 124–134.

Hogan, R. A. (1969). Implosively oriented behavior modification: Therapy considerations. *Behaviour Research and Therapy, 1,* 177–184.

Howard, W. A., Murphy, S. M., & Clark, J. C. (1983). The nature and treatment of fear of flying: A controlled investigation. *Behavior Therapy, 14,* 557–567.

Hull, C. L. (1943). *Principles of behavior*. New York: Appleton-Century-Crofts.

Jacobson, E. (1938). *Progressive relaxation*. Chicago: University of Chicago Press.

Javel, A. F., & Denholtz, M. S. (1975). Audible GSR feedback and systematic desensitization: A case report. *Behavior Therapy, 6,* 251–254.

Kanfer, F. H., & Grimm, L. G. (1977). Behavioral analysis: Selecting target behaviors in the interview. *Behavior Modification, 1,* 7–28.

King, N. J., Hamilton, D. I., & Ollendick, T. H. (1988). *Children's phobias: A behavioural perspective*. New York: John Wiley & Sons.

Kipper, D. A. (1980). In vivo desensitization of nyctophobia: Two case reports. *Psychotherapy: Theory, Research, and Practice, 17,* 24–29.

Krop, H., & Krause, S. (1976). The elimination of a shark phobia by self-administered systematic desensitization: A case study. *Journal of Behavior Therapy and Experimental Psychiatry, 7,* 293–294.

Levine, B., & Wolpe, J. (1980). In vivo desensitization of a severe driving phobia through radio contact. *Journal of Behavior Therapy and Experimental Psychiatry, 11,* 281–282.

Marks, I. M. (1969). *Fears and Phobias*. New York: Academic Press.

Marshall, W. L., Gauthier, J., Christie, M. M., Currie, D. W., & Gordon, A. (1977). Flooding therapy effectiveness, stimulus characteristics, and the value of brief *in vivo* exposure. *Behaviour Research and Therapy, 15,* 79–87.

Mattick, R. R., & Peters, L. (1988). Treatment of severe social phobia: Effects of guided exposure with and without cognitive restructuring. *Journal of Consulting and Clinical Psychology, 56,* 251–260.

Mavissakalian, M., & Barlow, D. H. (Eds.). (1981). *Phobia: Psychological and pharmacological treatment*. New York: Guilford Press.

Mavissakalian, M., & Michelson, L. (1983). Self-directed *in vivo* exposure practice in behavioral and pharmacological treatments of agoraphobia. *Behavior Therapy, 14,* 506–519.

Mavissakalian, M., & Michelson, L. (1986). Phobia: Relative and combined effectiveness of therapist-assisted *in vivo* exposure and imipramine. *Journal of Clinical Psychiatry, 47*, 117–122.

Michelson, L., Marchionne, K., Marchionne, N., Testa, S., & Mavissakalian, M. (1988). Cognitive correlates and outcome of cognitive, behavioral and physiological treatments of agoraphobia. *Psychological Reports, 63*, 999–1004.

Migler, B., & Wolpe, J. (1967). Automated self-desensitization. A case report. *Behaviour Research and Therapy, 5*, 133–135.

Morganstern, K. P. (1973). Implosive therapy and flooding procedures: A critical review. *Psychological Bulletin, 79*, 318–334.

Morris, R. J. (1973). Shaping relaxation in the unrelated client. *Journal of Behavior Therapy and Experimental Psychiatry, 4*, 343–353.

Morris, R. J., & Kratochwill, T. R. (1983). *Treating children's fears and phobias. A behavioral approach*. Elmsford, NY: Pergamon Press.

Morris, R. J., & Kratochwill, T. R. (in press). Childhood fears and phobias. In R. J. Morris & T. R. Kratochwill (Eds.), *The practice of child therapy* (2nd Ed.). Elmsford, NY: Pergamon Press.

Morris, R. J., & Kratochwill, T. R. (1985). Behavioral treatment of children's fears and phobias: A review. *School Psychology Review, 14*, 84–93.

Morris, R. J., Kratochwill, T. R., & Aldridge, K. (1988). Fears and phobias. In J. C. Witt, S. N. Elliott, & F. M. Gresham (Eds.), *Handbook of behavior therapy in education* (pp. 679–718). New York: Plenum Press.

Morris, R. J., Kratochwill, T. R., & Dodson, C. L. (1986). Fears and phobias in adolescence. In R. L. Fedman & A. Stiffman (Eds.), *Advances in adolescent mental health* (Vol. 1, Part A, pp. 63–118). Los Angeles: JAI Press.

Morris, R. J., & Magrath, K. H. (1983). The therapeutic relationships in behavior therapy. In M. Lambert (Ed.), *The therapeutic relationship in systems of psychotherapy*. Homewood, IL: Dorsey Press.

Morris, R. J., & Suckerman, K. R. (1974a). Automated systematic desensitization: The importance of therapist warmth. *Journal of Consulting and Clinical Psychology, 42*, 244–250.

Morris, R. J., & Suckerman, K. R. (1974b). The importance of the therapeutic relationship in systematic desensitization. *Journal of Consulting and Clinical Psychology, 42*, 148.

Mowrer, O. H. (1950). *Learning theory and personality dynamics*. New York: Roland Press.

Öst, L. G. (1978a). Fading: A new technique in the treatment of phobias. *Behaviour Research and Therapy, 16*, 213–216.

Öst, L. G. (1978b). Fading vs. systematic desensitization in the treatment of snake and spider phobias. *Behaviour Research and Therapy, 16*, 379–390.

Öst, L. G. (1987). Applied relaxation: Description of a coping-technique and review of controlled studies. *Behaviour Research and Therapy, 25*, 397–409.

Öst, L. G. (1988). Applied relaxation vs. progressive relaxation in the treatment of panic disorder. *Behaviour Research and Therapy, 26*, 13–22.

Öst, L. G. (1989). A maintenance program for behavioral treatment of anxiety disorders. *Behaviour Research and Therapy, 27*, 123–130.

Paul, G. L. (1966). *Insight in psychotherapy*. Palo Alto, CA: Stanford University Press.

Pavlov, I. P. (1927). *Conditioned reflexes*. London: Oxford University Press.

Ramirez, S. Z., Kratochwill, T. R., & Morris, R. J. (1987). Cognitive behavioral treatment of childhood anxiety disorders. In M. Ascher & L. Michelson (Eds.), *Cognitive behavior therapy* (pp. 75–103). New York: Guilford Press.

Redd, W. J., Porterfield, A. L., & Anderson, B. L. (1979). *Behavior modification*. New York: Random House.

Reeves, J. L., & Maelica, W. L. (1975). Biofeedback: Assisted cue-controlled relaxation for the treatment of flight phobias. *Journal of Behavior Therapy and Experimental Psychiatry, 6,* 105–109.

Richardson, F. C., & Suinn, R. M. (1973). A comparison of traditional systematic desensitization, accelerated massed desensitization, and anxiety management training in the treatment of mathematics anxiety. *Behavior Therapy, 4,* 212–218.

Ritter, B. (1968). The group desensitization of children's snake phobias using vicarious and contact desensitization procedures. *Behaviour Research and Therapy, 6,* 1–6.

Ritter, B. (1969a). Treatment of acrophobia with contact desensitization. *Behaviour Research and Therapy, 7,* 41–45.

Ritter, B. (1969b). The use of contact desensitization, demonstration-plus participation and demonstration-alone in the treatment of acrophobia. *Behaviour Research and Therapy, 7,* 157–164.

Rosen, G. (1976). *Don't be afraid: A program for overcoming your fears and phobias.* Englewood Cliffs, NJ: Prentice-Hall.

Rosen, G., Glasgow, R. E., & Barrera, M., Jr. (1976). A controlled study to assess the clinical efficacy of totally self-administered systematic desensitization. *Journal of Consulting and Clinical Psychology, 44,* 208–217.

Ryan, V., & Moses, J. (1979). Therapist warmth and status in the systematic desensitization of test anxiety. *Psychotherapy: Theory, Research, and Practice, 16,* 178–184.

Schneider, J. W. (1982). Lens-assisted *in vivo* desensitization to heights. *Journal of Behavior Therapy and Experimental Psychiatry, 13,* 333–336.

Seligman, M. E. P. (1971). Phobias and preparedness. *Behavior Therapy, 2,* 307–320.

Shaw, P. (1979). A comparison of three behavior therapies in the treatment of social phobia. *British Journal of Psychiatry, 134,* 620–623.

Sherman, A. R. (1972). A comparison of three behavior therapies in the treatment of social phobia. *British Journal of Psychiatry, 134,* 620–623.

Skinner, B. F. (1938). *The behavior of organisms.* New York: Appleton-Century.

Skinner, B. F. (1953). *Science and human behavior.* New York: Macmillan.

Snyder, A. L., & Deffenbacher, J. L. (1977). Comparison of relaxation as self-control and systematic desensitization in the treatment of test anxiety. *Journal of Consulting and Clinical Psychology, 45,* 1201–1203.

Southworth, S., & Kirsch, I. (1988). The role of expectancy in exposure-generated fear reduction in agoraphobia. *Behaviour Research and Therapy, 26,* 113–120.

Stampfl, T. G. (1961). *Implosive therapy: A learning theory derived psychodynamic therapeutic technique.* Paper presented at the University of Illinois, Champaign-Urbana, IL.

Stampfl, T. G. (1970). Implosive therapy: An emphasis on covert stimulation. In D. J. Levis (Ed.), *Learning approaches to therapeutic behavior change* (pp. 182–204). Chicago: Aldine.

Stampfl, T. G., Levis, D. J. (1967). Essentials of implosive therapy: A learning-based psychodynamic behavioral therapy. *Journal of Abnormal Psychology, 72,* 496–503.

Stampfl, T. G., & Levis, D. J. (1968). Implosive therapy: A behavioral therapy? *Behaviour Research and Therapy, 6,* 31–36.

Stern, R., & Marks, I. (1973). Brief and prolonged flooding. *Archives of General Psychiatry, 28,* 270–276.

Thomas, M. R., Rapp, M. S., & Gentles, W. M. (1979). An inexpensive automated desensitization procedure for clinical application. *Journal of Behavior Therapy and Experimental Psychiatry, 10,* 317–321.

Williams, S. L., Dooseman, G., & Kleifield, E. (1984). Comparative effectiveness of guided mastery and exposure treatments for intractable phobias. *Journal of Consulting and Clinical Psychology, 52,* 505–518.

Wilson, G. T., & Evans, I. M. (1977). The therapist-client relationship in behavior therapy. In A. S. Gurman & A. M. Razdin (Eds.), *Effective psychotherapy: A handbook of research* (pp. 544–565). Elmsford, NY: Pergamon Press.

Wolpe, J. (1958). *Reciprocal inhibition therapy*. Stanford, CA: Stanford University Press.

Wolpe, J. (1962). The experimental foundations of some new psychotherapeutic methods. In A. J. Bachrach (Ed.), *Experimental foundations of clinical psychology* (pp. 554–575). New York: Basic Books.

Wolpe, J. (1969). *The practice of behavior therapy*. Elmsford, NY: Pergamon Press.

Wolpe, J. (1982). *The practice of behavior therapy* (3rd ed.). Elmsford, NY: Pergamon Press.

Wolpe, J., & Lazarus, A. A. (1966). *Behavior therapy techniques*. Elmsford, NY: Pergamon Press.

Wolpin, M., & Pearsall, L. (1965). Rapid deconditioning of a fear of snakes. *Behaviour Research and Therapy, 3,* 107–111.

Yule, W., Sacks, B., & Hersov, L. (1974). Successful flooding treatment of a noise phobia in an 11 year old. *Journal of Behavior Therapy and Experimental Psychiatry, 5,* 209–211.

APPENDIX 1

Fear Survey Schedule

The items in this questionnaire refer to things and experiences that may cause fear or other unpleasant feelings. Write the number of each item in the column that describes how much you are disturbed by it nowadays.

	NOT AT ALL	A LITTLE	A FAIR AMOUNT	MUCH	VERY MUCH
1. Open wounds					
2. Dating					
3. Being alone					
4. Being in a strange place					
5. Loud noises					
6. Dead people					
7. Speaking in public					
8. Crossing streets					
9. People who seem insane					
10. Falling					
11. Automobiles					
12. Being teased					
13. Dentists					
14. Thunder					
15. Sirens					
16. Failure					
17. Entering a room where other people are already seated					
18. High places on land					
19. Looking down from high buildings					
20. Worms					
21. Imaginary creatures					

	NOT AT ALL	A LITTLE	A FAIR AMOUNT	MUCH	VERY MUCH
22. Strangers					
23. Receiving injections					
24. Bats					
25. Journeys by train					
26. Journeys by bus					
27. Journeys by car					
28. Feeling angry					
29. People in authority					
30. Flying insects					
31. Seeing other people injected					
32. Sudden noises					
33. Cockroaches					
34. Crowds					
35. Large open spaces					
36. Cats					
37. One person bullying another					
38. Tough looking people					
39. Birds					
40. Sight of deep water					
41. Being watched working					
42. Dead animals					
43. Weapons					
44. Dirt					
45. Crawling insects					
46. Sight of fighting					
47. Ugly people					
48. Fire					
49. Sick people					
50. Dogs					
51. Being criticized					
52. Walking on dark streets alone					
53. Being in an elevator					
54. Witnessing surgical operations					
55. Angry people					
56. Mice					
57. Blood					
(a) Human					
(b) Animal					
58. Parting from friends					
59. Enclosed places					
60. Prospect of a surgical operation					
61. Feeling rejected by others					
62. Airplanes					
63. Medical odors					
64. Feeling disapproved of					
65. Harmless snakes					
66. Cemeteries					
67. Being ignored					
68. Darkness					
69. Premature heart beats (missing a beat)					
70. Nude men (a) Nude women (b)					

(*continued*)

	NOT AT ALL	A LITTLE	A FAIR AMOUNT	MUCH	VERY MUCH
71. Lightning					
72. Doctors					
73. People with deformities					
74. Making mistakes					
75. Looking foolish					
76. Losing control					
77. Fainting					
78. Becoming nauseous					
79. Spiders (harmless)					
80. Being in charge or responsible for making decisions					
81. Sight of knives or sharp objects					
82. Becoming mentally ill					
83. Being with a member of the opposite sex					
84. Taking written tests					
85. Being touched by others					
86. Feeling different from others					
87. A lull in conversation					
88. Laboratory rats					
89. Taking any type of test					
90. Public speaking (speaking in front of groups)					
91. Looking down from high places					

Note: Adapted from *The practice of behavior therapy* (2nd ed., pp.283–286) by J. Wolpe, 1973, Elmsford: Pergamon Press. Copyright 1973 by Pergamon Press, Inc. Used with permission.

APPENDIX 2

Revised Willoughby Questionnaire for Self-Administration

Instructions. The questions in this schedule are intended to indicate various emotional personality traits. It is not a test in any sense because there are no right and wrong answers to any of the questions. After each question you will find a row of numbers whose meaning is given below. All you have to do is draw a ring around the number that describes you best.

0 means "No," "never," "not at all," etc

1 means "Somewhat," "sometimes," "a little," etc.

2 means "About as often as not," "an average amount," etc.

3 means "usually," "a good deal," "rather often," etc.

4 means "Practically always," "entirely," etc.

1. Do you get anxious if you have to speak or perform in any way in front of a group of strangers? — 0 1 2 3 4

2. Do you worry if you make a fool of yourself, or feel you have been made to look foolish? — 0 1 2 3 4

3. Are you afraid of falling when you are on a high place from which there is no real danger of falling—for example, looking down from a balcony on the tenth floor? — 0 1 2 3 4
4. Are you easily hurt by what other people do or say to you? — 0 1 2 3 4
5. Do you keep in the background on social occasions? — 0 1 2 3 4
6. Do you have changes of mood that you cannot explain? — 0 1 2 3 4
7. Do you feel uncomfortable when you meet new people? — 0 1 2 3 4
8. Do you daydream frequently, i.e. indulge in fantasies not involving concrete situations? — 0 1 2 3 4
9. Do you get discouraged easily, e.g. by failure or criticism? — 0 1 2 3 4
10. Do you say things in haste and then regret them? — 0 1 2 3 4
11. Are you ever disturbed by the mere presence of other people? — 0 1 2 3 4
12. Do you cry easily? — 0 1 2 3 4
13. Does it bother you to have people watch you work when you do it well? — 0 1 2 3 4
14. Does criticism hurt you badly? — 0 1 2 3 4
15. Do you cross the street to avoid meeting someone? — 0 1 2 3 4
16. At a reception or tea do you go out of your way to avoid meeting the important person present? — 0 1 2 3 4
17. Do you often feel just miserable? — 0 1 2 3 4
18. Do you hesitate to volunteer in a discussion or debate with a group of people whom you know more or less? — 0 1 2 3 4
19. Do you have a sense of isolation, either when alone or among people? — 0 1 2 3 4
20. Are you self-conscious before ''superiors'' (teachers, employers, authorities)? — 0 1 2 3 4
21. Do you lack confidence in your general ability to do things and to cope with situations? — 0 1 2 3 4
22. Are you self-conscious about your appearance even when you are well dressed and groomed? — 0 1 2 3 4
23. Are you scared at the sight of blood, injuries, and destruction even though there is no danger to you? — 0 1 2 3 4
24. Do you feel that other people are better than you? — 0 1 2 3 4
25. Is it hard for you to make up your mind? — 0 1 2 3 4

Note: From *The practice of behavior therapy* (3rd ed.) (pp. 339–340) by J. Wolpe, 1982, Elmsford: Pergamon Press. Copyright 1982 by Pergamon Press, Inc. Used with permission.

6
Aversion Methods

Jack Sandler
Holly Villareal Steele

The use of unpleasant or aversive stimuli to change behavior is as old as the history of humankind. In their conventional form, such "punishment" practices are typically designed to terminate or reduce undesirable behavior. An infinite number of examples are available from our daily experiences: Parents spank children for aggressive behavior, teachers require unruly students to remain after school, judges fine traffic violators, and so on. The general principle underlying each of these examples is that such aversive experiences serve to deter the future occurrences of the problem behavior. Borrowing from this principle, similar techniques and procedures have also been reported in the clinical literature. These procedures are variously termed aversive therapy, punishment procedures, reduction programs, and so on and are here grouped together under the term *aversion therapy* to designate their use in treatment settings, that is, to accomplish clinically useful objectives.

Both the popular and the clinical uses of aversive procedures to change behavior have been the subject of considerable controversy. The issues raised by the critics are quite complex, and a comprehensive analysis of the various arguments is beyond the scope of the present review. Suffice it to say that aversive procedures have been questioned on ethical, theoretical, and practical grounds. Recently, several position papers have clearly articulated the antiaversive argument. In 1981, for example, the executive board of the Association for Persons with Severe Handicaps called for a termination of the use of aversive procedures. Subsequently, the Association published a historical review and critique which questioned the effectiveness and ethics of such efforts (Guess, Helmstetter, Turnbull,

& Knowlton, 1987) followed by an epilogue (Laski, 1987) essentially reaffirming the initial resolution. Similarly, the American Association of Mental Deficiency urged the immediate elimination of "inhuman forms of aversion therapy techniques" (Berkowitz, 1987, p. 1118). On the other side of the debate, a number of authorities have argued with equal vigor for the use of aversive procedures within scientific and ethical guidelines (Baer, 1970; Johnston, 1972; Solomon, 1964). Related to this position is a report issued by a task force of the Association for Behavior Analysis (VanHouten et al., 1988). Although the report sidesteps a clear endorsement of aversive procedures, the general thrust of this position argues that "an individual is entitled to effective and scientifically validated treatment" (Van Houten et al., 1988, p. 383) and that the failure to provide such treatment is equally unacceptable.

This latter position defends the clinical use of aversive procedures on the same grounds that unpleasant and even painful events are often also involved in medical and dental treatment. Thus, as is true in medical treatment, the decision to use aversive procedures should be made on the basis of the risk-to-benefit ratio where the pain and discomfort associated with surgery is justified in terms of the greater long-term health benefits to be realized by the patient. Within this context, ethical guidelines governing the use of aversive procedures to change problem behavior have slowly emerged that also offer the behavioral practitioner a general frame of reference for determining the risk-to-benefit ratio. These guidelines can be summarized as follows.

1. Minimally intrusive and low-risk forms of intervention should always be considered before resorting to more intrusive, higher risk procedures. Thus, nonaversive procedures are generally favored over aversive procedures and (as detailed later in this chapter) aversive procedures themselves can be ordered from the least intrusive to the most intrusive.
2. The severity of the problem condition in terms of its physical and psychological impact should be taken into account. In this context, less serious problem behaviors would rarely, if ever, be treated aversively, but severe problem behaviors representing a clear threat to the individual's health and psychological welfare would be regarded as immediate targets for aversion therapy.

In actual practice, the guidelines suggest, for example, that mild nuisance behavior should be dealt with by nonaversive methods (as described in other chapters) or, at most, by mild forms of aversive procedures; whereas severe self-injurious behavior as in head banging, eye gouging, hair pulling, and so on (behaviors often observed in, but not restricted to, severely mentally retarded or emotionally disturbed individuals) would represent immediate targets for aversion therapy, especially if less intrusive techniques had already been unsuccessful. Within this framework, the decision to use aversion therapy can be made on the basis of scientific evidence rather than on the basis of preconceived biases (Baer, 1970). No doubt, the controversy over the use of intrusive procedures will continue. For the present, however, it seems quite evident that not every practioner will ascribe to the extreme position which advocates the immediate elimination of any type of aversive or intrusive procedure in any and all circumstances. On the contrary, the literature demonstrating their efficacy continues to grow at a rapid rate even while the search for noncontroversial procedures continues. It is to this literature that we now turn our attention.

GENERAL DESCRIPTION

At the practical level, a description of aversive procedures appears to be relatively straightforward and uncomplicated. For the most part, such arrangements involve an undesirable and/or maladaptive behavior on the part of the patient or client and the presentation of an unpleasant stimulus in close time relationship with the behavior. Almost all examples of aversive procedures reflect these characteristics, whether the purpose is to terminate a commonplace problem behavior, as in the case of a parent who spanks a child for playing with matches, or whether the purpose is to produce a clinical outcome, as in the case of administering shock to the fingertips of a child molester while he is handling children's clothing.

If terminating or disrupting undesirable behavior were the only question to be considered, we could simply detail the circumstances under which such effects can be optimized and treat all problem behaviors in this fashion. Unfortunately, the use of aversive procedures is much more complex than would seem to be true on the basis of casual observation. First, as we have seen, deciding when to use aversive procedures is no simple matter, and secondly, even when this decision is relatively clear-cut, there are many additional issues that must be taken into account including the durability of the therapeutic effects, the risk of undesirable side-effects, and the general impact of such treatment on overall psychosocial adjustment.

It is only relatively recently that a clearer understanding of the complexity of aversive procedures has begun to emerge, primarily as a result of laboratory studies with animals and clinical applications with actual cases. A framework for understanding these issues can be formulated by reviewing briefly the two major theories that have attempted to explain the effects of aversive stimuli on behavior. Although there are areas of overlap between the two theories, they involve different assumptions, rely on different experimental procedures, and generate different treatment practices. Most of the aversion therapy reports in the literature reflect either one or the other of these theoretical biases, although in actual practice the difference between the two is often blurred.

The first of these two theories emerged out of Pavlov's well-known research on conditioned responses in dogs. In this model, a previously neutral stimulus such as a buzzer or light is presented in close temporal contiguity with an unconditioned stimulus, that is, a stimulus that naturally elicits a reflex reaction such as a tap of the knee eliciting the patellar reflex. Similarly, when an organism is exposed to an aversive stimulus, certain physiological reflexes are elicited (rapid heart rate, increased perspiration, etc.) that are typically regarded as correlates of the fear response.

Extraneous stimuli that are also present at the time acquire the power to evoke the same or a similar reaction. In this fashion, the fear response to a painful event is "conditioned" to these previously neutral stimuli. Although this is by necessity an oversimplification of the conditioned fear hypothesis, the principle underlying Pavlov's work has been invoked to explain both the manner in which certain maladaptive behaviors such as phobias are acquired and the manner in which undesirable behaviors can be changed in treatment programs. For example, if an alcoholic is required to drink liquor while exposed to a painful stimulus, after a sufficient number of such "trials," the fear response elicited by the painful stimulus will become conditioned to the liquor. Subsequently, the sight, taste, and smell of liquor will elicit the physiological reactions associated with the painful stimuli, and the patient will be repelled by such substances. In fact, procedures of this type have been employed in a variety of problem conditions with varying degrees of success.

The second theory emphasizes the consequences of behavior to explain the effects of aversive stimuli on behavior (Skinner, 1953) rather than on the association between stimuli that precede a response. In this operant theory (see chapter 4 for a more detailed description of operant conditioning) virtually all behaviors, abnormal and normal, are considered to be influenced heavily by the consequences of the behavior. Thus, behaviors are acquired and/or maintained because they are rewarded (positive reinforcement), or because they terminate or postpone unpleasant events (negative reinforcement). Conversely, responses that are followed by unpleasant events (punishment) or by no consequences (extinction) decline in frequency. In the example of the alcoholic just noted, shock administered "contingent" on the drinking response (e.g., just as the patient reaches for the drink) will suppress the drinking rate. The effectiveness and/or durability of the suppression effect depends on a number of variables. Some of these variables are associated with the aversive event (e.g., the intensity and the frequency of the unpleasant stimulus); some of the variables are associated with the history of the response targeted for change (e.g., duration of the response, magnitude of reinforcing events). In operant conditioning procedures, "naturally" occurring response-consequence relationships are favored over Pavlovian discrete trial procedures.

These descriptions are based largely on laboratory procedures. Applied situations may reflect a considerable departure from these examples such that attributing clinical outcomes to either one of these explanations is precluded. Thus, in actual practice, Pavlovian procedures can inadvertently be combined with operant procedures, and vice versa. Consequently, the reasons for any observed changes in client behavior cannot be determined completely. In the example of the alcoholic, a Pavlovian procedure might dictate pairing shock on each trial independent of the patient's behavior. In the actual arrangement, however, the shock might not be administered if the patient declines to make the relevant response (e.g., to drink the liquor), thereby introducing operant effects (i.e., a response-consequence relationship). Similarly, the circumstances surrounding an operant training procedure can be interpreted within the context of Pavlovian theory. Thus, punishment might be administered contingent on the drinking response in a *free operant* procedure, but the systematic programming of the relevant events could involve a discrete-trials procedure as in Pavlovian conditioning.

Although the aversion therapy literature continues to expand at a rapid rate, many questions remain unanswered. A great deal of the clinical work, for example, is reported in the form of uncontrolled case studies, or involves a combination of treatment procedures in uncontrolled ways, or fails to provide follow-up information. Although these problems are often the result of practical and ethical constraints, they make analysis of treatment efficacy difficult. Nevertheless, some tentative observations can be made, especially where a treatment outcome has been heavily replicated.

In reviewing this literature, an operant framework will be used, for the most part, because this theoretical position has the clearest relevance to clinical phenomena, the majority of the studies reported in the areas of aversion therapy were formulated in this context, and the general methodology employed has been at least satisfactory.

MAXIMIZING THE EFFECTS OF AVERSION THERAPY

Once the decision to use aversion therapy has been made, it is the therapist's responsibility to apply the chosen technique in the most effective manner possible; that is, his or her efforts should include all of the ethical and scientific safeguards that are part of any therapeutic procedure. Ideally, then, the procedure should be designed to eliminate the problem condition permanently, as quickly as possible, and without undesirable residual effects.

As indicated, in operant terms, there are two major sets of variables to take into account in this connection: those variables associated with the aversive events, and those that relate to the problem behavior. An excellent description of the former is available in Azrin and Holz's (1966) summary.

First and foremost, at least at the beginning of treatment, the aversive event should be completely coincident with the problem behavior. That is, it should be administered each time the response occurs, and it should not be administered in the absence of the response. This rationale stems from research that indicates that response reduction occurs most rapidly when the aversive stimulus immediately follows the response.

In many instances this principle can be easily applied without fear of error because of the specific characteristics of the response. A pronounced facial tic, for example, is usually easily identified (i.e., has discrete and relatively invariant characteristics) and is of brief duration. With such a problem behavior, it is a relatively easy task to insure that the aversive event will be paired with each response and that it will never be presented under other circumstances.

A slightly more complex situation is encountered with head banging, which can actually encompass a variety of responses with different topographies and durations. Thus, the head banger can involve different muscle groups from time to time; he or she may move the head forward, backward, or from side to side or strike with different intensity. Furthermore, the head banging response also involves components of normal head movement that might be misinterpreted as precursors to the head banging. In actual practice, such subtle variations could result in the delivery of stimulation when unwarranted or in failure to deliver such stimulation when appropriate.

Even greater difficulties are presented by the aversive treatment of alcoholism, which involves elaborate response chains that are subject to considerable variation from time to time and place to place.

One way to resolve these problems is to circumscribe the variability of the behavior, for example, in head banging, by applying a mechanical device that enables only a forward thrust of the head, thus increasing the reliability of treatment. The disadvantage of this approach is that the treatment regime becomes somewhat artificial because it differs from the natural circumstances under which the response occurs. This problem is dealt with in detail later on.

A second recommendation for maximizing treatment effects is to continue treatment until the problem behavior is no longer evident, thus enhancing the durability of the effect. This might appear to be so obvious as to require no elaboration. The fact of the matter, however, strongly suggests that aversion therapy is frequently ineffective precisely because the clinician has failed to continue treatment beyond some limited time range. How long therapy should be maintained can only be answered empirically; that is, it could be terminated after some reasonable length of time has elapsed (2 weeks, 6 months), during which time the response has not occurred under nonclinical circumstances. A good criterion (and one that, unfortunately, is rarely employed) is the appearance of adaptive behavior under circumstances in which the problem behavior had previously occurred.

A third recommendation is to employ a stimulus or an event that is in fact aversive (in the sense that it would ordinarily be avoided) and not merely a stimulus that is alleged to be aversive on the basis of some prior consideration. Again, the obvious requires explanation. Many ostensibly aversive stimuli can lose their noxious qualities with repeated occurrences. Under special circumstances, they can even acquire reinforcing properties, thereby producing an effect that is directly opposite to the goal of aversion therapy. For example, there are numerous instances in the clinical literature referring to individuals who continually expose themselves to normally painful stimuli. Such masochistic behavior has been the subject of considerable interest in clinical psychology (Sandler; 1964). In general, most socially offensive stimuli such as threats, ridicule, insults, and menacing gestures are characterized by such limitations, but even physically painful stimuli can on occasion become reinforcing. It is probably for this reason that a number of aversion therapists have advocated the use of electric shock. The advantages of shock have been described on numerous occasions and require little elaboration (Azrin & Holz, 1966). Suffice it to say that electric shock can be considered an almost universal aversive stimulus when used appropriately. Paradoxically, shock can actually serve to minimize the criticisms associated with conventional physical punishment such as paddling, beating, or slapping.

More recently, the search for equally effective nonphysical aversive events has produced several new techniques, some of which represent extensions of traditional fines and penalties. Again, however, the efficacy of these techniques depends on the extent to which the critical variables can be appropriately applied.

With regard to the variables governing the targeted behavior in question, several suggestions are readily available. First, the events that reinforce or maintain the behavior should be eliminated or administered only for adaptive responses. Second, in general, treatment efficacy is enhanced by dealing with responses of short history rather than those of long history (thus, the longer or more chronic the problem behavior, the more resistant to change). In general then, aversion therapy is most effective when dealing with a problem behavior of relatively short history, when the circumstances (consequences) that maintain the behavior can be made available only contingent on adaptive behavior, when a genuinely aversive event is administered on each occurrence of the response (at least during the initial stages of treatment), and all of these circumstances are continued until there is good evidence that a durable effect has been achieved.

There are, of course, many other aspects of aversion therapy procedures that enhance their effectiveness, especially when they are combined with other techniques, as described in a later section. To paraphrase Johnston (1972), the successful use of aversion therapy cannot be reduced to a concise summary of principles; the basic principles must be expanded in application to a variety of procedural details, the importance of any one of which will vary with each situation. Ignoring any of these variables will not doom necessarily any particular therapeutic endeavor; rather the probability of maximal effectiveness is increased to the extent that such factors are carefully considered in the therapeutic attempt (Johnston, 1972).

PROCEDURES AND TECHNIQUES
Pavlovian Procedures

Although many examples of aversion therapy formulated with the Pavlovian model have been reported, as indicated earlier they are subject to a variety of criticisms (Feldman, 1966; Franks, 1963; Kushner & Sandler 1966; Rachman, 1965).

We have already mentioned the major difficulty in this connection, that is, applying the Pavlovian model to problem behaviors that have pronounced operant components. In addition, Franks (1963) has argued that some Pavlovian procedures (especially those used in the treatment of alcoholism) might not be as durable as those generated by means of operant conditioning procedures. For these reasons, the current review is restricted to several examples that have been interpreted within the Pavlovian conditioning paradigm.

One of the most extensive bodies of literature based on Pavlovian aversive methods has been reported by investigators concerned with alcoholism. Of these, Lemere and Voegtlin (1950) presented the most extensive and systematic series of observations. In their procedure, patients are administered emetine or apomorphine (unconditioned stimuli), which frequently elicit nausea and vomiting within 30 minutes. Shortly before vomiting occurs, the patient is instructed to drink his or her preferred alcoholic beverage. This procedure is repeated several times each day for 10 days. Occasional "booster" sessions are administered after the patient is discharged. Voegtlin (1947) reported that about half of the patients treated in this fashion remained abstinent for at least 2 years.

The Pavlovian rationale is evident in this procedure. Ostensibly, after a sufficient number of trial pairings with emetine, the taste, sight, and smell of liquor should elicit nausea and vomiting. A similar rationale is offered in the treatment of alcoholism with antabuse, a drug that causes a violent physiological reaction when mixed with alcohol. Obviously, the validity of the rationale depends on how closely these procedures approximate the Pavlovian paradigm. In fact, it would appear that such techniques involve considerable departure from classical conditioning procedure (Franks, 1963). Moreover, if a patient responds very quickly or very slowly (and this is hard to determine with certainty), the alcohol can be delivered too early or even after the patient experiences nausea, representing a further departure from the Pavlovian paradigm.

More recently, Wiens and Menustik (1983) summarized the effectiveness of a similar aversive Pavlovian conditioning program for 312 alcoholics who were treated during a 12-month period at the Raleigh Hills Hospital in Portland, Oregon. Of the 278 patients who completed the entire program and were available for follow-up, 190 patients (63%) were still abstinent for 12 months subsequent to their discharge from the hospital. The inpatient phase of the Wiens and Menustik treatment program typically lasts 14 days, with an intervening day between each of five aversion conditioning sessions. Despite the apparent Pavlovian emphasis, it is interesting to note that the procedure is described as one in which "the approach response to alcohol is punished immediately by an aversive reaction, and the patient is expected to transfer the resulting avoidance of alcohol from the clinical situation to all other occasions when he or she has the opportunity or desire to drink" (Wiens & Menustik, 1983, p. 1090).

Aversive Pavlovian procedures have also been reported in treatment programs for sexual deviancy, drug addiction, compulsive gambling, cigarette smoking, kleptomania, and other problem behaviors. For example, Laws, Meyer, and Holman (1978) reported a successful outcome using an olfactory aversion procedure with an institutionalized sexually sadistic 29-year-old male. Sexual arousal (as measured by a penile plethysmograph) to sadistic stimuli was reduced to near-zero levels by the end of treatment. In virtually all of the aforementioned procedures, however, the investigators failed to control for operant conditioning effects. For this reason, such procedures are reviewed in the next section.

Operant Procedures

The second major category of aversion therapy techniques generally reflects the characteristics of the operant model. The rationale here stems from the assumption that behavior that results in unpleasant consequences will decrease in frequency. Although there are important exceptions to this rule, the assumption has been well documented in both laboratory and applied circumstances.

As we have seen, there are a number of conditions that must be taken into account, perhaps the most important of which is the close temporal relationship between the response and the aversive event (the contingency). For this reason, operant conditioners frequently describe such arrangements as examples of *response-produced aversive stimulation,* even when the noxious event is administered by an external agent.

This requirement can be implemented properly in the laboratory situation where the appropriate procedural controls are available. In clinical practice, however, limitations arise that frequently require some departure from the laboratory procedures. The degree of departure depends on a variety of circumstances, the most important of which is the nature of the problem condition. For example, if therapy is designed to reduce the frequency of a writer's cramp, then the real-life circumstances in which such behavior occurs can reasonably be represented in the clinic, enabling the use of a contingency with the same or a similar response. The situation changes quite drastically, however, in the case of other problem conditions. For example, it is difficult (but not impossible) to create a reasonable approximation of the real-life circumstances related to excessive drinking, and even greater problems are encountered with certain sexual deviations and aggressive behavior. Consequently, practitioners have devised a number of methods designed to circumvent this problem. Although such techniques are by now almost standard practice, it must be acknowledged that these procedures involve (perhaps, at best) problem-related events rather than the actual problem behaviors themselves. That is not to imply that such techniques are therefore ineffective; on the contrary, many of these efforts have resulted in important therapeutic effects. The reasons for the success, however, remain to be identified, because these procedures involve processes beyond those specified by a strict response-consequence model.

This section describes a number of aversive procedures that have been used in therapeutic circumstances. They vary in degree of intrusiveness from those generally considered to be relatively mild (for example, time-out) to maximally intrusive procedures (shock).

Time-out from Positive Reinforcement

Over the last few years, increasing attention has been focused on an aversive technique that has been termed *time-out from positive reinforcement* (TO). This procedure assumes that a decrease in frequency can be effected if the opportunity to obtain positive reinforcement is denied the individual on the basis of some target behavior, for example, separating a child from the opportunity to receive peer reinforcement contingent on show-off behavior.

There are two major TO procedures: (a) removing the reinforcer from the individual, and (b) removing the individual from the reinforcing system. In most instances, the choice is made on the basis of practical considerations. In the first case, the major changes involve the removal of reinforcement, with little change in the individual's status. A commonplace example is turning off the TV set as a result of an argument between children over a program preference. This makes the reinforcement inaccessible for a while. Or, a clinical example would be turning away from a child during a rewarding activity when the child began to engage in a temper tantrum. Thus, the adult's potential reinforcing stimuli are temporarily removed. In the second case, the major changes usually involve the physical removal of the individual from the potentially available reinforcers. The teacher who isolates an aggressive child from the reinforcing effects of peer attention exemplifies a commonplace use of TO.

TO can be applied successfully with individuals of differing ages, personal characteristics, and problem conditions. Several examples are given in a later section of this chapter. In each case, the successful use of the technique depends on (a) identifying the positive reinforcement, and (b) insuring that the interruption of positive reinforcement is immediately and precisely contingent on the target behavior. In other words, before considering the use of TO, the practitioner must specifically isolate the positive reinforcement and develop a procedure that insures the response-contingent nature of the arrangement. When these rules are neglected in actual practice, the effectiveness of TO is reduced. The teacher who removes an aggressive child from a class activity that the child dislikes is not fulfilling the requirements of TO. Moreover, if the child is sent to the office and becomes the target of individual attention on the part of the guidance counselor or principal, the undesirable behavior could increase rather than decrease in frequency. Similarly, the parent who sends a misbehaving child to a room in which there are games, a TV, and toys has not deprived the child of positive reinforcement and has therefore failed to maximize TO.

Some question has also been raised regarding the duration of TO. That is, once the undesirable response-reinforcement relationship has been determined, how long should the individual remain in TO? Although there is no simple rule of thumb, the duration should be established on the basis of combining practical and behavioral criteria. If a child is placed in TO, for example, in general she or he should remain there until she or he has lost several reinforcement opportunities and the undesirable behavior has stopped. In actual practice, it is probably best to limit TO to 10 to 15 minutes (although occasionally longer durations are required initially) and then to reduce gradually the duration, thus more clearly defining the response-consequence relationship.

In some cases, the difference between TO and an extinction procedure (see chapter 4 for a detailed discussion) is obscure. For example, the popular current practice of turning away from a child during a temper tantrum is frequently regarded as an attempt to extinguish such behavior, but it can also be regarded as time-out, primarily depending on whether or not the reinforcement is completely withdrawn, as in extinction, or is merely withheld, as in TO. Obviously, in actual practice, it is difficult to distinguish between such arrangements.

In any event, the TO technique makes available to the clinician concerned with reducing the frequency of undesirable behavior an important addition to the more conventional aversive methods. When used as just described, there are many clinical problems amenable to such treatment.

Response Cost

A second aversive procedure that has received increasing attention has been termed response cost (Weiner, 1962). These aversion arrangements are analogous to the conventional penalty technique in which an individual is fined for undesirable behavior. The major difference between the two is in terms of the systematic nature of response cost. Thus, driving illegally may occasionally result in a fine under the assumption that the loss of money will serve as a deterrent to such future behavior. These efforts, however, frequently do not produce the desired outcome or are effective for only a limited duration.

Response cost, on the other hand, requires a clear explication of the relationship between each undesirable response and the appropriately assigned penalty. When these requirements are maximized, the effectiveness of response cost as a deterrent is maximized. Perhaps for this reason, the clinical application of response cost has usually involved a loss of rewards earned for appropriate behavior.

For example, hospitalized patients might be operating under a token economy in which several different dimensions of constructive behavior earn tokens exchangeable for tangible rewards or privileges. Additional rules could be involved in which behavioral infractions resulted in the loss of tokens. Such combined reward, response cost arrangements are usually very effective in generating desirable changes in constructive behavior.

On the other hand, if the ratio between amount earned and amount lost results in an overall deficit, the incentive of working for reinforcement decreases and the system can break down. It is important, then, for the practitioner to monitor continuously the effects of response cost in relation to earnings and to adjust the values of each accordingly.

Feedback

Several behavior modification techniques include the monitoring of behavior for the purpose of recording the frequency of a response. The monitoring procedure can take a variety of forms, which range from a patient observing her or his own heart rate on an oscilloscope to the mere act of making a mark on a sheet of paper, as in the case of an individual recording the number of cigarettes smoked.

Under such circumstances, and independent of any formal treatment, the mere act of alerting the individual to the response occurrence can influence the rate of the response (see discussion of self-monitoring in chapter 8). Such effects have been termed *feedback* because they essentially provide information not ordinarily available to the person that a particular response has occurred. With certain problem conditions, feedback can result in a decrease in the frequency of a response. Although the causes of these effects are not well understood, the changes produced can have implications for aversion therapy.

Thus, a number of investigators have suggested procedures designed to enhance the effectiveness of feedback in reducing the frequency of a response. There are several examples in the behavior modification literature that demonstrate that self-charting has resulted in a reduction in the frequency of smoking, drinking, overeating, or arguing. In these cases, it would appear that merely bringing attention to the high incidence of the behavior in question was sufficient to effect a constructive change. The client who suddenly realizes she or he is smoking three packs per day, rather than the two initially reported, must make an adjustment to this new information.

In still other situations, the effectiveness of feedback can be enhanced if it is systematically presented in connection with an appropriate change in behavior. Several investigators, for example, have found that stuttering rates can be suppressed if each dysfluency is immediately followed by delayed auditory feedback (Siegel, 1970). In these cases, because delayed auditory feedback is regarded as aversive by most individuals, the procedure seems to be analogous to the punishment paradigm described in greater detail later in this chapter.

There are still many questions that remain to be answered about the effectiveness of feedback techniques. Their major role in the treatment would seem to be largely in terms of generating initial changes, but these changes are probably transitory unless feedback is used with other techniques.

Overcorrection

Another procedure in the list of operant aversive techniques has been termed *overcorrection*. Foxx and Azrin (1973) identified two components of the overcorrection procedure: (a) restitutional overcorrection, and (b) positive practice. The first component requires the individual to "overcorrect" the effects of inappropriate behavior (e.g., retrieve a book thrown in anger as well as straightening up other objects in the room). The second component requires the individual to practice the "correct" behavior that is incompatible with the inappropriate behavior. Overcorrection can be used to accomplish several objectives, including the suppression of undesirable behavior, and for this reason is often considered a punishment procedure.

Despite its relative recency, the overcorrection procedure has achieved rapid popularity, judging by the increasing number of such reports in the applied operant literature (Foxx & Azrin, 1973). The reasons for this enthusiasm are due, no doubt, to the advantages offered by overcorrection. For one, it represents a viable alternative to more intrusive approaches. For another, it can be applied to a wide variety of problem behaviors from the commonplace (e.g., rude table manners) to the most severe (e.g., head banging). A third advantage involves the educative function and the opportunity to reward constructive changes offered by the positive practice component. Finally, overcorrection skills are easily acquired by behavior change agents.

As we will see in the following review, overcorrection has been used successfully to change a wide range of problem behaviors.

Physically Aversive Stimuli

By far the bulk of the operant aversion therapy literature involves the use of stimuli that are physically unpleasant or even painful. In these techniques, the noxious event occurs in a response-produced or response-correlated arrangement. A wide variety of stimuli have been employed for this purpose, most of which would ordinarily elicit the withdrawal response (for example, water spraying, visual screening, foul odors, uncomfortable sounds, and painful stimuli such as slaps, hair pulls, and electric shock applied to an area of the limbs). Sometimes these stimuli have been paired with explicit conditioned stimuli such as shouts, reprimands, and disapproving gestures and facial expressions.

Although the search for low-risk physically aversive stimuli continues, the vast majority of these efforts have employed shock, because it complies with the requirements for maximizing the effects of aversion therapy as described earlier. In addition, the intensity and duration of shock can be adjusted in light of treatment requirements. For these reasons, the current review is largely restricted to shock techniques.

The usual procedure in the employment of shock involves the following sequence of events before initiating treatment:

1. an analysis of the history of the problem condition clearly documenting the ineffectiveness of less severe procedures;
2. an analysis of the problem condition in terms of how often it occurs, when it occurs, where it occurs, and any other relevant circumstances; and

3. involvement of qualified professionals familiar with shock procedures and the ethical guidelines that obtain under such circumstances.

A number of shock delivery devices are commercially available for use in aversion therapy, the most practical of which are battery operated, portable instruments. The responsible practitioner should insure that the device incorporates appropriate safeguards as well as those features that will facilitate a successful outcome. Thus the device should be purchased from a reputable vendor with a complete description of its safety features. The electrode unit (typically attached to a limb) should be small, comfortable, and unobtrusive, thereby minimizing interference with normal routine.

The shock control unit should provide easily identified controls and offer a variety of shock intensities and durations, with the lowest ranges below detectable thresholds. Prior to the use of the device with a client, the clinician should self-administer the shock, starting at the lowest level and gradually increasing the intensity up to the point of discomfort.

The initial treatment session should be conducted in accord with the information obtained from the prior analysis. For example, with a child who displays a high rate of head banging, the child should be moved to a quiet, isolated room and restraints removed. An observably safe intensity level and duration (e.g., 0.05 sec) of shock is applied to the limb each time the response occurs. In addition, a high density of tangible reinforcers should be provided in the absence of the head banging response. The initial session should usually last about 30 minutes, after which the child is returned to the prevailing routine. This is repeated each day until the behavior no longer occurs during the treatment session. These effects are generally observed within three to four sessions. As aversive control over the behavior is acquired, additionally relevant circumstances are generally incorporated into the procedure for the purpose of generalizing the effects over a wider range of circumstances. In the typical case, by the fourth or fifth session, merely strapping on the electrodes is sufficient to control the behavior. Once the effect has generalized over all the relevant circumstances, the electrode routine is gradually faded so that the ultimate control over the behavior falls completely under the positive contingencies and the shock procedure can be abandoned. Occasional "booster" sessions might be required if the problem condition recurs.

Considerable research with shock, both in the laboratory and in clinical situations, has been conducted, providing good descriptions of the manner in which the effectiveness of shock can be maximized.

In order to achieve the optimal aversion therapy effect, initially the shock should be delivered at a safe, but very unpleasant intensity (rather than gradually increased), relatively briefly (0.5 sec, for example), and coincident with the onset of each target response (Azrin & Holz, 1966). Appropriate levels of shock intensity are typically described in equipment manuals provided by the manufacturer. At some later stage in treatment, a shift to a variable schedule of shock delivery (see chapter 4 on operant conditioning) might be considered in order to enhance the durability of the suppression effect.

The variety of problem conditions that have been treated via such procedures ranges across a wide behavioral spectrum, from relatively commonplace responses, such as cigarette smoking, to broad dimensions of complex pathological behaviors, such as child molesting and disturbing obsessions. A review of several clinical investigations and case studies is presented in the section entitled "Practical Applications."

Combining Aversion Therapy with Other Techniques

This section is concerned with the manner in which the techniques just described can be used with additional procedures to maximize treatment effectiveness. Although they are usually a part of any behavior change program (and as such they are also described in other chapters), the emphasis here is on their use in conjunction with aversion therapy.

There are two reasons for including such practices. *First,* practically speaking, as we have seen, any attempt to apply a laboratory procedure to clinical situations usually results in some departure from the use of the technique under "pure" circumstances. *Second,* there is increasing evidence that the effects of aversion therapy can be enhanced if the practitioner systematically includes other learning techniques. That is, a more rapid and longer lasting reduction of the undesirable behavior can be achieved under such circumstances than would be true if time-out, response cost, and other techniques were used alone.

Including Response Alternatives

Several studies have shown that a change in target behavior can be expedited if an alternative response is available to the patient. In some cases, the therapist can explicitly encourage such "new" learning, and if this technique is combined with a procedure designed to eliminate an undesirable response, positive treatment results can be maximized. Although such procedures have been variously termed *counterconditioning, differential reinforcement of omitted behavior* (DRO), or *reinforcement of incompatible behavior* (DRI), they share the practice of concurrently manipulating more than one response dimension in a treatment program. Thus, a counterconditioning program might involve shock contingent on an undesirable response such as aggressive behavior and, at the same time, provide positive reinforcement for an adaptive alternative response, for example, cooperative behavior.

Although it can be assumed that some new response will emerge in every aversive procedure, the response alternative technique requires that the alternative response be identified prior to treatment. For this reason, we distinguish between those programs that formally and explicitly incorporate a response alternative and those procedures in which this process might have occurred but was not planned for. Obviously, the clinician interested in such techniques must acquire an in-depth understanding of general learning principles that include the full range of other techniques in addition to aversive conditioning.

The advantages of the response alternative procedure are numerous: It can be used with all of the aforementioned techniques; it enhances the treatment process, thereby reducing the number of aversive experiences required to modify behavior; it enhances the durability of the effect; and, perhaps most important of all, it offers an adaptive alternative to the individual that might generalize outside the clinic arena. The common practice of substituting candy for cigarettes reflects some of the features of the response alternative technique.

Fading

As we have seen, constructive changes that occur in one situation do not necessarily generalize to other situations. The child who is trained to cooperate in the classroom may continue to be aggressive at home or on the playground. Such "limited" change effects are particularly characteristic of attempts to treat certain problem conditions such as alcohol abuse. It is not unusual, for example, for patients in a hospital treatment program to show a reduction in alcoholic behavior while in the hospital, only to relapse soon after return to the environment in which the original drinking behavior occurred. The problem can be construed as an example of different reactions to different circumstances.

Obviously, then, the most effective treatment is that which accomplishes the greatest generality of change, and the fading technique offers distinct advantages in this connection (also described in conjunction with operant methods in chapter 4).

Essentially, fading involves a gradual change in the treatment situation such that either (a) reduction in undesirable behavior is maintained in the presence of new (and preferably more "relevant") circumstances, or (b) new circumstances are introduced to enhance changes in behavior. Such techniques have been used informally for many years.

A growing practice in penology, for example, involves a gradual series of *discharge experiences,* in which a prisoner is first placed on a work-release program for limited duration while readjusting to the requirements of normal life. The prisoner might also at first see his or her parole officer perhaps several times a week. If successful, he or she could be advanced to a halfway house, and the number of parole visits would be reduced. In this fashion, the transition from prison life to normal life is gradually effected under the assumption that constructive changes in behavior are better maintained in the process.

Similarly, improving psychiatric hospital patients are first allowed several weekend passes at home, and, if no problems arise, advance to a month's "trial visit." This can subsequently be extended, depending on the patient's adjustment outside the hospital.

The difference between these practices and a systematic fading technique involves the greater degree of detail and rigor in the latter case. An ideal fading technique would provide for a gradual exposure to the patient's real-life physical and social stimuli, so that all of the natural events relevant to the problem behavior are ultimately reflected in the treatment situation.

The closer the fading technique approaches the ideal, the greater the generality of treatment effects. One growing practice in the modification of children's behavior involves first instructing parents in the treatment skills and then gradually increasing their share of responsibility for treatment. Similarly, in aversion therapy, parents are instructed in the use of a shock procedure to be applied in the home situation. In this fashion, the fading technique incorporates those individuals and those situations that ultimately determine the durability of any constructive changes that first occurred in the treatment setting.

Schedules

Another technique that in some respects resembles fading involves changes in the schedule of the relevant events. It was mentioned earlier that treatment is initially most effective if the aversive event is applied to each instance of the undesirable response, because this results in the most rapid reduction of behavior. Greater durability of the desired reduction, however, can probably be achieved if the schedule of aversive events is unpredictable, that is, every third or fourth response on the average. The frequency of aversive stimulation can be further gradually reduced if desired, although at some stage the practitioner will obviously be dealing with events that occur only infrequently.

Use of Significant Others

Where possible and appropriate, individuals who bear an important relationship to the patient can be incorporated into the treatment program. The rationale here again is similar to that underlying the use of fading, that is, enhancing the durability of the change. Some instruction is obviously necessary, including specifically designating a time-out area, a response cost system, and even the use of response-contingent shock. We will see later where this has been attempted and, depending on the degree of instruction and preparation, the results have been most impressive. For example, self-injurious behavior in disturbed children is very effectively controlled when parents are instructed to use the treatment technique in the home environment.

Self-Control

Finally, and perhaps most important, considerable attention has increasingly been focused on the use of techniques designed to make the patient responsible for change (see chapter 8 on self-management). The rationale here scarcely requires any explanation, although this is a development representing, in many respects, a radical departure from some conventional treatment practices that covertly, if not overtly, place the major responsibility for change on the therapist.

Techniques of this sort were first initiated in conjunction with problem behaviors that were difficult to analyze because they can occur both publicly and privately; for example, smoking, obsessions, or compulsions. More recently, self-control techniques have been employed with a wider range of problem behaviors, including aggression, family arguments, and temper tantrums. Essentially, the procedure requires instructing the patient in a variety of techniques designed to alter one or more of the following: (a) typical undesirable reactions to particular occasions, (b) the sequence of responses constituting the aggregate response (breaking up the chain), and (c) the consequences of the undesirable behavior. Thus, an analysis of the relevant components of an undesirable behavior might reveal that it occurs under certain identifiable circumstances; that it is comprised of several discrete responses; and that it produces certain reinforcing events. Cigarette smoking, for example, usually occurs at regular intervals and in typical stimulus situations. This would provide a picture of the frequency of the smoking behavior. The chain for one smoker might be characterized by removing the package from the shirt pocket, withdrawing a cigarette with the right hand, tapping it on a hard surface, inserting it in the mouth, lighting it, taking several deep drags, keeping it dangling from the lips, alternating between deep drags and knocking off the ashes, and smoking it down rapidly to a short butt before extinguishing the cigarette. This would provide a picture of the topography of the response. Finally, an attempt might be made to analyze the response-reinforcement relationship.

With this information, the patient can be instructed in self-control techniques that enhance the aversion therapy effects. For example, the patient might be instructed to avoid some of the circumstances in which smoking occurs with high frequency, or he or she might be instructed to change some of the components of the chain, such as holding the cigarette in the left hand, placing the cigarette in an ashtray between drags, smoking less rapidly, and so forth. Finally, the patient might also be instructed in the self-administration of aversive events, which could range anywhere from accumulating all the butts and inhaling the stale aroma and placing a picture of a diseased lung in the pack, to self-imposing fines, denying privileges, and delivering shock.

Kanfer and Grimm (1980) offered a learning theory analysis of the issues related to self-control processes. Among other things, they suggested the manner in which seven relevant phases can be employed to enhance clinical objectives. They pointed out the necessity for increasing client motivation, for example, through contractual negotiation of treatment objectives between the client and the therapist; for monitoring progress; and for programming generalization of the effects. There are probably additional procedures that should be considered along with these. In practice, there is sufficient overlap between the techniques such that the distinctions between them are often blurred. For the most part, the practitioner need not be concerned with the theoretical purity of the technique. Again, what is probably more important is that as many as possible should be employed in a systematic fashion, thereby optimizing the chances of a successful outcome.

In brief, the information advanced in the preceding sections suggests several important steps that the therapist must take in any program using aversion methods. First, the therapist should provide evidence that the event to be employed is indeed aversive, that it be applied on a response-contingent basis, and that it be maintained long enough to suppress the behavior for as long as possible.

Furthermore, durable changes can be insured if an alternative (adaptive) response is available; if ordinary, real-life circumstances are represented in the treatment setting; and if self-control techniques are integrated into the treatment program.

PRACTICAL APPLICATIONS

Until now, the discussion has focused on general principles and guidelines. Representative applications from the operant aversion therapy literature will be described in the present section.

An arbitrary distinction is offered between (a) those problem conditions that are relatively circumscribed and easily defined and, (b) problem behaviors that are more complex in their response dimensions and less accessible to a public analysis.

There is some reason to believe that, at least with our present state of knowledge, greater success has been realized with problems in the first category. This conclusion must be qualified by the fact that successful treatment is determined not only by the complexity of the problem condition but also by the precision and rigor of the treatment technique. Where possible, examples contrasting each major aversion therapy technique within a problem condition are described.

Discrete or Easily Defined Problem Conditions

Self-Injurious Behavior

One of the problem behaviors frequently encountered in extreme forms of pathology is various forms of self-injurious behavior (SIB). Although many other problem conditions such as smoking, alcoholism, and gambling reflect similar characteristics, the SIB label is usually reserved for those behaviors that, if left unchecked, would shortly threaten the biological welfare of the individual. Thus, they require immediate intervention including physical restraint. Unfortunately, most of these interventions are temporary and ineffective.

In the clinical literature, the term SIB usually implies the involvement of the voluntary motor-response system as manifested by head banging, self-mutilation, pulling one's hair out, and so on. The present review also includes examples possibly involving involuntary (or autonomic) processes.

Head Banging, Self-Biting, and Similar Problem Behaviors. By far the most extensive application of aversion therapy with discrete problem conditions has involved the use of painful shock, contingent on head banging and self-mutilation in children. There are now a sufficient number of observations that confirm the effectiveness of such procedures, especially when compared with nonaversive techniques, in terms of rapid suppression of the behavior. Furthermore, when additional measures are incorporated into the procedure (for example, treatment administered by parents of SIB children in the home), the suppressive effects generalize, enabling the emergence of other more productive responses.

The earliest strong evidence of the efficacy of aversion therapy in such cases is provided by Lovaas and Simmons (1969). In this study, three severely mentally retarded children displaying extreme forms of SIB (thereby requiring long periods of time in physical restraints) were exposed to response-contingent shock. In each case, SIB was effectively and completely suppressed in the treatment setting after only a few shocks. The same treatment was also successfully applied by other individuals in other situations to maximize the generality of the effects.

Similar results have been reported by a number of other investigators. Tate and Baroff (1966) administered response shock to a blind 9-year-old boy who employed a wide assortment of SIB (head banging, face slapping, self-kicking, etc.). During 24 minutes prior to the treatment condition, 120 instances of SIB were recorded. For the next 90 minutes, a half-second shock was administered for each SIB, and only five SIB responses occurred. The child was also praised for non-SIB. As the treatment progressed, the child was moved from restraints for increasing time intervals (fading). The rate of SIB continued to decline, and no such responses were observed for 20 consecutive days. Interestingly enough, an increase in prosocial behavior emerged during this time.

These efforts have been followed by a host of similar procedures with highly successful outcomes. Corte, Wolf, and Locke (1971) almost immediately and completely reduced SIB (including self-slapping, eye poking, hair pulling, and scratching the skin) in four mentally retarded adolescents with response-contingent shock, after an extinction procedure and a DRO procedure proved ineffective. Again, the treatment had to be applied outside the first treatment setting to enhance generalization.

These early efforts were followed by a number of equally successful similar studies (Merbaum, 1973; Scholander, 1972). In each of these cases severe, high-rate forms of self-injurious behaviors were reduced to virtually zero rates almost immediately following the beginning of treatment and, at least in the one case reporting follow-up information, the effects were maintained for as long as 1 year posttreatment.

As suggested earlier, the search for effective but less intrusive procedures continues. One such possibility has been advanced by Lutzker (1978). In this case, self-injurious behavior (head and face slapping with hands and fists) in a 20-year-old mentally retarded client was treated by "facial screening" for 30-minute periods over 30 consecutive days. After each instance of SIB, the trainer would hold a large, loosely tied bib over the client's face and in back of the head until the SIB had stopped for 3 seconds. The problem behavior decreased to zero levels within five sessions after the facial screening procedure was implemented.

Rapoff, Altman, and Christopherson (1980) examined the effectiveness of several alternative procedures including DRO, overcorrection, lemon juice, and aromatic ammonia on severe, high-rate self-injurious behavior (self-poking of the facial area) in a profoundly mentally retarded, nonambulatory 5-year-old boy. "Lemon juice therapy" involved squirting 5 cc of lemon juice into the child's mouth contingent on the poking response; the ammonia procedure involved placing an ammonia capsule under the child's nose for 3 seconds immediately following the target response. Of the various procedures attempted, the ammonia treatment proved to be the most effective reducing, the SIB response to zero rates in the treatment setting and at home. Several problems in the use of ammonia, however, have been reported by Jones and Andersen (1981). Given the questionable status of this technique, they recommend against the clinical use of ammonia at the present time.

An excellent example of combining several treatment procedures in a systematic approach was provided by Wesolowski and Zawlocki (1982). The subjects in this study were two 6-year-old identical twin girls diagnosed as totally blind and profoundly mentally retarded. Both subjects frequently pushed their fingers up into their eye sockets, causing tissue damage around their eyes. The first attempt to reduce this behavior involved time-out from auditory stimuli. This was administered by placing soundproof earmuffs over the subjects' ears for 2 minutes following each eye-gouging response. This technique reduced the response rate to zero levels within 12 sessions, but the effect was not maintained. This was then followed by five training sessions combining both auditory time-out and response interruption, that is, holding the subjects' hands down in their laps for 2 seconds. Again, responding quickly decelerated, and the effect was maintained for about 2 months. The third and last procedure involved auditory time-out plus a reward of 20 cc of apple juice contingent on a 2-minute interval in which the SIB response did not occur (DRO procedure). Response rates declined to zero within 2 weeks after this procedure was instituted. Follow-up observations 1 year later revealed that eye gouging was no longer a matter of concern for either subject.

Further evidence of the efficacy of aversive techniques with SIB was reported by Dorsey, Iwata, Ong, and McSween (1980), who reduced the rate of mouthing, hand biting, and head banging in nine profoundly retarded individuals using a water mist punishment procedure. Gross, Wright, and Drabman (1980) success-fully treated finger gnawing behavior in a 5-year-old boy by administering a lemon juice punisher. Finally, Romanczyk, Colletti, and Plotkin (1980) treated SIB, agression, and screaming in a 13-year-old retarded male with a response-contingent thigh slap. Supression of the problem behaviors was rapid and complete with the effect generalizing to the residential setting.

Another problem condition that is related to SIB and is also frequently observed in mentally retarded and emotionally disturbed individuals is excessive self-stimulation and stereotypic behavior. These terms encompass a wide variety of repetitive, idiosyncratic activities that can involve such responses as hand movements (e.g., finger flipping), lip "strumming," continuous rubbing of a part of the body, nonfunctional vocalizations, and jumping or hopping. Such high-frequency inappropriate responses sometimes "blend" with self-injurious behavior and are obviously incompatible with adaptive behaviors. Consequently, they represent a prominent target for behavior change procedures. Here again, aversive approaches have proved to be particularly effective. McGonigle, Duncan, Cordisco, and Barrett (1982), for example, used a visual screening procedure to suppress a variety of stereotypic responses in four moderately retarded children. After analysis of the frequency of the responses, the visual screening procedure was implemented. This involved placing one hand over the child's eyes for a minimum of 5 seconds, contingent on the inappropriate behavior. Treatment was continued until self-stimulatory behavior was either substantially reduced or eliminated from each child's repertoire. In all four cases, follow-up data (at least 6 months after treatment) revealed no evidence of stereotyped behavior in any of the four children.

Epstein, Doke, Sajwaj, Sorrell, and Rimmer (1974) used an overcorrection procedure to treat self-stimulatory behavior in two children who revealed a wide range of dysfunctional behaviors. After earlier efforts to control the self-stimulatory behavior by means of time-out or instruction had failed, a series of overcorrection procedures was administered during daily 30-minute training sessions. When a target response was emitted, the child was instructed or physically guided to engage in a 2.5-minute series of physical exercises. The results revealed a drastic reduction to near-zero rates of stereotyped behavior in both children within five sessions of the treatment program. Furthermore, one of the children showed a spontaneous and concurrent increase in appropriate play behavior that was correlated with the treatment procedure.

More recently, Cavalier and Ferreti (1980) reduced the rate of stereotype behavior and collateral SIB in a profoundly retarded 5-year-old girl to zero levels on the first day of treatment, which involved a mild slap (punishment) plus DRO. Again, this effect partially generalized across trainers, settings, and time.

Trichotillimania. Another type of SIB which has frequently been observed in normal individuals as well as special populations is excessive hair pulling. In its most severe form, such behavior is characterized by high rates resulting in bare spots on the scalp. This condition has been termed *trichotillimania,* reflecting its "compulsive" qualities. Three recent studies have been reported in which trichotillimania was treated by aversion therapy. In one case (Crawford, 1988), a 29-year-old female with a 16-year history of severe hair pulling was administered response-contingent shock. The treatment reduced the problem behavior to a zero level almost immediately, an effect that was still maintained at a 6-month follow-up. The remaining two studies are similar in that a collateral behavior, treated aversively, also resulted in significant reductions in the target behavior. In one case (Altman, Grohns, & Friman, 1982) a 3-year-old girl who engaged in high rates of hair pulling when thumb sucking was punished by applying an aversive-tasting substance to the thumb, which resulted in a significant reduction of both behaviors. Similar results were obtained when the same procedures were applied to two other children, ages 2 and 5 (Friman & Hove, 1987).

This survey represents only a small sample of the wide variety of aversion therapy applications with SIB and self-stimulatory behavior. Suffice it to say that, in this area, aversion therapy has been highly successful not only in rapidly reducing the frequency of undesirable behavior but also in establishing long-term constructive changes. We have also seen that some of the reservations regarding the use of shock procedures are not supported by the evidence. On the contrary, it would appear that, once control over the SIB is established, the path is clear for the development of other more adaptive responses.

Self-Induced Vomiting

Perhaps as a result of the growing confidence in aversion therapy with SIB, several clinicians have attempted to use similar procedures with other serious problem conditions that have been traditionally resistant to treatment.

One potentially dangerous but fortunately rare problem behavior involves self-induced vomiting. This is a condition characterized by the absence of physiological determinants as well as resistance to drug therapy, thus suggesting the influence of psychological factors. In extreme cases, such conditions can result in a severe loss of weight, retarded development, and even loss of life. For these reasons, immediate intervention is frequently required, and three studies report the successful cure of excessive nonorganically determined vomiting behavior.

Luckey, Watson, and Musick (1968) employed a response-contingent shock procedure with a chronic 6-year-old mentally retarded vomiter, after standard medical treatment had failed to produce any improvement. The child was observed throughout the day, and a 1-second uncomfortable shock was administered whenever vomiting or its precursors occurred. By the fifth day, the treatment was reduced to 2 hours at each meal. Further reductions were introduced at later stages as the frequency of the behavior decreased.

Except for a minor relapse several days after the treatment was initiated, no evidence of vomiting was observed on the last 9 days of the treatment. Again, this marked reduction in maladaptive behavior was accompanied by improvement in a variety of prosocial and self-care dimensions.

Lang and Melamed (1969) employed a similar procedure with a 9-month-old chronic vomiter whose life was threatened by continuation of the behavior. In this case, the vomiting act was preceded by sucking behavior and accompanied by vigorous throat movements. The aversion therapy procedure involved a 1-second shock administered as soon as vomiting occurred and continued until the response was terminated. The vomiting response was substantially reduced after two brief sessions, and, by the third session, only one or two responses occurred. These changes were accompanied by a substantial weight gain and increased alertness and responsiveness to the environment. After approximately 3 weeks, the child was discharged from the hospital and was continuing to do well 1 year after treatment.

Kohlenberg (1970) reported similar success in treating excessive vomiting in a 21-year-old severely mentally retarded female. In this case, shock was administered contingent on the presence of stomach tensions that served as the precursor to the vomiting response.

Finally, Marholin, Luiselli, Robinson, and Lott (1980) showed that a taste aversion (lemon juice, Tabasco sauce, etc.) procedure could successfully reduce ruminative vomiting in two profoundly retarded youngsters. In both of these cases, the problem behavior was of a long-standing and life-threatening nature. Complete cessation of the vomiting responses occurred 40 days after the treatment program was initiated. Follow-ups conducted 1½ to 2½ months later revealed no evidence of relapse.

Another problem behavior that is related to ruminative vomiting sometimes occurs in certain eating disorders, particularly anorexia nervosa and bulimia. Anorexia nervosa is a condition most often observed as severe reduction in food intake, sometimes serious enough to warrant hospitalization. Bulimia is characterized by the binge–purge syndrome, typically superimposed over an anorexic pattern. Here, reduction in food intake alternates with periodic excessive eating episodes (binge eating) followed by self-induced vomiting (purging). This form of vomiting is clearly different from the ruminative vomiting behavior described earlier inasmuch as the latter typically occurs after each meal and does not reflect the more "voluntary" quality of the purging response. A number of behavioral treatments emphasizing the reacquisition of more normal dietary patterns have been successful with eating disorders. In such cases, the vomiting component of bulimia is treated "indirectly" rather than as a specific change objective, as in aversion therapy. Thus, as the more normal eating pattern emerges, the desire to engage in the binge–purge sequence spontaneously declines, although, conceivably, this component of the bulimia could also be treated adjunctively by aversive procedures.

Seizures

As in the case of vomiting, seizures are generally considered to be the result of some physiological dysfunction. However, some investigators have argued that such conditions might also be induced or influenced by external factors. In any event, if left unchecked, the frequency and severity of seizures can constitute a serious threat to the individual, and a report by Wright (1973) suggested that at least some forms of seizure-related events can be suppressed by aversion therapy, resulting in a decrease in seizure activity.

Wright worked with a 5-year-old mentally retarded boy who induced his own seizures by moving his hand back and forth before his eyes and blinking while looking at a light source. Observation and EEG recordings confirmed the correlation between these events and seizure episodes. They further revealed the occurrence of several hundred self-induced seizures per day.

Consequently, shock was delivered contingent on each hand-eye response in five 1-hour sessions extending over a 3-day period. All responses were suppressed by the third session. However, 5 months later the child was again inducing as many as 400 seizures per day by blinking. Shock was then administered contingent on the blinking response, resulting in a substantial reduction of seizures by the fourth session. A 7-month follow-up revealed a 90% decrease from the pretreatment frequency of hand-eye responses.

Enuresis

Several examples of aversion therapy have also been employed for the purpose of reducing nocturnal bed wetting (enuresis). Tough, Hawkins, McArthur, and Ravenswaay (1971) found that a cold bath contingent on bed wetting, plus praise for bladder control (DRO), completely eliminated the enuresis problem in a mentally retarded 8-year-old boy but was less effective for his younger brother.

Atthowe (1972) found that a combination of aversive events could reduce enuresis in even severely disabled elderly patients. Chronically enuretic patients (who otherwise participated in a token reward program) were moved to a generally aversive environment: crowded ward, lights turned on for 10 minutes four times each night, and patients escorted to the bathroom for 10 minutes. These procedures were maintained for 2 months, after which continence was rewarded (DRO), whereas incontinence resulted in loss of reward (response cost). By the eighth month of the program, all of the patients were continent, including several who were severely neurologically disabled, an effect that was maintained almost 4 years after the study was initiated.

By far the largest number of successful attempts to treat enuresis have used a variety of the Mowrer alert system, in which bed wetting results in a signal that arouses the individual. After a number of such experiences, most children begin to wake up prior to wetting the bed and are then encouraged to urinate appropriately.

When the apparatus was first described by Mowrer (Mowrer & Mowrer, 1938), he invoked a Pavlovian model to explain the effectiveness of the technique. Thus, the distended bladder served as a conditioned stimulus (CS), which was paired with the unconditioned stimulus (UCS, the alerting stimulus). By means of Pavlovian conditioning, the CS alone would result in arousal and, subsequently, voiding. More recently, Jones (1960) has suggested that the technique relies on an operant aversion therapy model.

Sneezing

Kushner (1970) has shown that excessive sneezing can also be controlled by means of aversion therapy. This case involved a 17-year-old girl who had been vigorously and rapidly sneezing (approximately one response per 40 seconds) for 6 months with no relief. Extensive medical examinations had failed to isolate the cause of this condition, and a variety of treatment techniques had not produced any substantial improvement.

During treatment, a microphone was placed around her neck that was connected to a voice key and a shock source. Each sneeze activated the voice key and automatically delivered a shock to the fingertips (response-contingent shock). Following an adjustment of the shock procedure, in which the electrodes were taped to her arm, thereby insuring better contact, the patient stopped sneezing after 4 hours of treatment. There was no evidence of a relapse during a 13-month follow-up period.

Functional ("Hysterical") Paralysis

In an unpublished study conducted at the Veteran's Administration Hospital in Miami, Florida, a modified aversion therapy program was employed for the purpose of treating a functional paralysis. The patient was a middle-aged male whose complaint was a loss of feeling and impaired locomotion in the lower half of the left leg, causing him to be confined to a wheelchair. Extensive neurological examination ruled out the possibility of any organic dysfunction. The aversion therapy procedure was conducted as follows: Electrodes were placed on the patient's leg and on two fingertips. He was then informed that a mild shock would be administered to his leg, followed in 5 seconds by a stronger shock to his fingers. If he felt the leg shock he was to press a switch that he held in his hand. No further instructions were provided, although each switch response enabled the patient to avoid the shock to the fingers.

This procedure was presented for three trials in the first session, during which time no avoidance responses occurred. The second session was interrupted after the first trial because the patient became nauseated. In the third session, the patient emitted two switch-press responses and verbally indicated that feeling had returned to his leg, whereupon the electrodes were removed and the patient walked back to the ward. He was discharged several days later without complication. Although the results in this case were successful, the procedure employed represents a departure from the typical response-contingent paradigm and seems to be more similar to the anticipatory avoidance procedure described more fully later.

Writer's Cramp

Two studies have appeared that report attempts to treat various forms of writer's cramp by means of aversion therapy. This form of motor impairment is usually characterized by muscular contractions or spasms and prevents the individual from continuing tasks that require the use of hand fatigue or emotional problems. Sufferers of writer's cramp are frequently capable of performing other tasks even though such tasks involve the operation of the same or similar hand muscles.

Liversedge and Sylvester (1955) identified 39 cases of writer's cramp as a function of either hand tremors or muscular spasms; each of these conditions was separately treated with a different apparatus. The tremor patients were required to insert a metal stylus into a series of progressively smaller holes in a metal chassis. Deviations (striking the side of the hole) resulted in shock. The contraction response was treated by delivering shock to the patient whenever excessive thumb pressure (as measured by a gauge) was applied to a pen. Normal writing was regained after 3 to 6 weeks of treatment in 24 patients. These improvements were maintained for up to 4½ years.

Kushner and Sandler (1966) used a similar procedure for treating a hand contraction response in a 42-year-old male teletype operator. The patient was required to operate a typewriter in the clinic, and pretreatment observation revealed a high frequency of rapid spasmodic contractions of the right hand, resulting in errors at the keyboard. The patient was then seen for twelve 30-minute sessions, with shock delivered contingent on each contraction response. The electrodes were removed during the next three sessions, and no contractions were observed. Shortly thereafter, however, the contraction response recurred, and his performance remained erratic and gradually declined through the 46th session. Consequently, the number of weekly sessions was increased. No contractions were observed by the 61st session, and the patient was then switched to a teletype machine. Almost immediately, he was functioning effectively, even when the electrodes were removed.

Stuttering

The behavior modification literature reveals a long and continued interest in the use of aversive techniques for improving the speech of stutterers. Numerous response-contingent events have reduced the frequency of stuttering, including delayed auditory feedback, response cost arrangements, time-out arrangements, and electric shock. Because only a brief overview of these efforts is provided in the present account, the interested reader is referred to Siegel's comprehensive review (Siegel, 1970). In each of the studies described, stuttering is defined in terms of the frequency of speech dysfluencies (repetitions, interjections, prolongations, interruptions, etc.).

Adams and Popelka (1971) employed a time-out technique with eight young adult stutterers. Essentially, the procedure imposed a nonspeaking period contingent on each dysfluency, under the assumption that the opportunity to speak was positively reinforcing. Although the dysfluency rate decreased during the TO condition, it seems apparent that the results are subject to alternative explanations.

Kazdin (1973) compared the relative effectiveness of response cost, loud response-contingent sound, and feedback on the suppression of dysfluent speech in 40 mentally retarded patients. In the response cost procedure, tokens that could be exchanged for tangible rewards were removed on the occurrence of dysfluencies. In the second condition, a loud noise was presented contingent on each dysfluency; and in the feedback condition, each dysfluency was marked by a light being turned on. The results indicated that both response cost and aversive stimulation procedures reduced dysfluencies, but response cost was more effective in every respect including generalization of treatment effects during a posttest.

Delayed auditory feedback (DAF) has also been studied in this connection because such events seem to involve aversive properties. Typically, the DAF procedure involves a brief delay of the dysfluency and is then transmitted through the client's earphones during a speech task. This requires the individual to reduce her or his verbal rate while simultaneously speaking and listening for dysfluencies. Goldiamond (1965) has shown that such treatment produces fluent and rapid speech. Soderberg (1968) obtained similar results with 11 student stutters, and, in addition, observed that these effects generalized beyond the experimental condition.

Daly and Frick (1970) employed a shock procedure with 36 adult male stutterers. Stuttering expectations and actual stuttering responses were treated independently in some patients and simultaneously in others. The results indicated that shocking stuttering expectancies did not reduce the frequency of stuttering responses, but shocking both responses simultaneously did produce a constructive change. Furthermore, these effects were maintained during a 20-minute posttest period.

More recently, Newman (1987) has questioned such procedures on the grounds that they result in undesirable alternative behaviors. In his study, 10 normal adult males were required to speak spontaneously for 15 minutes. During the experimental phase of the procedure, each dysfluency (verbal repetition) was followed by informing the subject, "You repeated." This procedure resulted in a reduction of speech rate. Concurrently, however, the subjects also displayed avoidance behaviors that were characteristic of stuttering. Newman (1987) suggested that those procedures focusing exclusively on the reduction of stuttering may actually facilitate the rate of collateral stuttering responses.

Complex Problem Conditions

General Compulsions

As noted, there is an extensive literature describing attempts to deal with chronic, compulsive-type problems via aversion therapy. Perhaps it is natural for behavior therapists to turn in this direction, because most conventional treatment efforts in this area have not been very successful. The literature is replete with examples of treated alcohol abusers who have fallen off the wagon, dieters who eat more after treatment than before, cigarette smokers who quit during treatment only to smoke again at higher rates after discharge, and so on.

One of the problems encountered with some of these conditions (especially the first of the following three) is that they are directly promoted and reinforced in certain (sometimes many) circumstances. Drinking and smoking are for the most part socially acceptable and, in fact, abstinence can even result in social disapproval. Eating, of course, is a biological necessity, and the rewards are built into the response. It is only when these behaviors occur at excessive frequency or under inappropriate circumstances that they represent problems. The current review is not an attempt to survey the entire range of studies in this area but is rather a sampling of representative efforts.

Alcoholism. The history of the aversive treatment of alcoholism surprisingly stretches back to the Roman era. It is only within recent years, however, that these techniques have achieved an advanced level of sophistication. Starting in the early and middle 1960s, behavior therapists began to employ aversive controls under carefully planned conditions. As indicated, many of the early studies clearly reflected a Pavlovian methodology, but the more recent investigations are more congruent with operant procedures. Furthermore, they are characterized by attempts to find alternatives to shock, and, in some cases, the objectives are to establish controlled (moderate, socially appropriate) drinking rather than complete abstinence. A study by Blake (1965) is perhaps representative of the earlier aversion therapy efforts involving operant techniques. In this procedure, electric shock was presented at the same time the patient complied with instructions to sip his drink. The shock was increased until the patient spat out the drink, thus terminating the shock (escape behavior). In addition, the shock was presented only 50% of the time in a random manner. When this treatment was combined with relaxation training, Blake found that approximately 50% of the 37 patients in the program remained abstinent 1 year after follow-up.

In a similar procedure, Vogler, Lunde, Johnson, and Martin (1970) served liquor to alcoholic patients in a simulated bar arrangement. Each drinking response was accompanied by a shock, which was maintained until the patient spat out the drink. Although, again, it is difficult to isolate the punishment effects (the shock for drinking) from the escape effects (the cessation of shock contingent on spitting the drink out), these investigators did include several control conditions and also provided for "booster" treatments after discharge. The results indicated that abstinence was engendered by the treatment.

The Vogler technique, in which treatment was conducted in a naturalistic setting, represents an important development and is being used with increasing frequency. Wards have been converted so that they reflect many of the characteristics of settings in which the drinking response actually occurs. Obviously, the effects produced under these conditions stand a better chance of generalizing to the patient's real-life situation than would seem to be true when more artificial circumstances are used.

More recently, Cannon, Baker, and Wehl (1981) reported the results of an aversion procedure that involved either emetic aversion or shock aversion embedded in a broad-spectrum approach to treatment. The subjects were male chronic alcoholics who were already participating in a multifaceted program that consisted of psychotherapy, vocational rehabilitation, alcohol education, and other elements. Their findings suggested that the taste aversion approach (emetic procedure) was more effective than the shock aversion procedure, although neither of the approaches produced significant changes 1 year after treatment was terminated. Subsequently, Cannon, Baker, Gino, and Nathan (1986) administered a chemical aversion procedure to 60 alcoholics and found that the greater the aversive reaction during treatment, the longer the duration of abstinence. Wiens, Menustic, Miller, and Schmitz (1982–1983) have shown that chemical aversion therapy procedures may also be effective with older (age 65+ years) alcoholics.

More recently, Kishore and Dutt (1986) treated 60 alcoholics with a shock aversion procedure or shock aversion plus psychotherapy. About one half of each group were abstinent by the end of treatment, and 80% of this number remained abstinent 6 months after treatment.

Despite the numerous claims of success, however, aversion therapy for alcoholism remains a controversial issue with many investigators continuing to question the efficacy of such procedures. Ewing (1984), for example, reported the results of a study in which 32 male and 13 female alcoholic patients received relevant "imagery-related" shock or sham shock. The subjects were then contacted 13 to 40 months posttreatment with no differences demonstrated between the two groups in terms of several adjustment dimensions. However, subjects who had originally scored higher on a paper and pencil test in terms of being more calm, self-reliant, and disciplined did the best posttreatment regardless of the treatment group to which they had been assigned.

Additional questions have been raised regarding the relative efficacy of shock aversion versus chemical aversion. Cannon and Baker (1981), for example, compared the effects of emetic aversion conditioning to shock aversion conditioning and a no-treatment group. Beneficial changes were obtained in only the emotive aversion group. Thus, both Cannon (1982) and Nathan (1985) argue in favor of chemical aversion over electrical aversion in the treatment of alcoholism. Finally, Fehl, Revusky and Mellor (1980) have raised the question of which drug to use in chemical aversion therapy with their report which favors lithium over more standard nausea-producing substances. Wilson (1987) has brought the whole issue full circle by questioning the claims that have been made regarding their efficacy as well as their cost-effectiveness.

Cigarette Smoking. Almost from the beginning of aversion procedures in the 1960s, many therapists have revealed a strong interest in the use of such methods for cigarette smoking. By now, the number of suggested techniques that incorporate some form of aversive control probably runs into thousands. Unfortunately, this burgeoning development has not been accompanied by a comparable effort in providing evidence to support the efficacy of the various techniques, especially in terms of preventing relapse (Hunt & Matarazzo, 1973). With this concern

over poor methodology and limited long-term effects in mind, let us consider
several aversion therapy procedures that have been used in this area.

An early study by Gendreau and Dodwell (1968) is representative. These
investigators applied an "increasing shock-escape response" technique to reduce
the frequency of cigarette smoking. Patients received shock as soon as they
complied with instructions to light up a cigarette. Shock intensity was gradually
increased until the patient extinguished the cigarette. Differences in smoking rates
between treated and nontreated smokers were observed both at the end of treatment
and 2 years later.

By the late 1960s, a whole series of studies was reported that involved
techniques and equipment designed to enhance the effects of shock aversion
therapy with smokers. Perhaps the most sophisticated of these involves a portable
shock apparatus that automatically administers shock at some point during the
cigarette smoking period. The assumption that seems to underlie such efforts is
that if the patient complies with the instructions he or she will receive response
shock contingent on each smoking response, and in every smoking situation. This
will result in a satisfactory treatment outcome. Although the assumption is a
reasonable one, appropriate well-controlled designs have not been exercised in
these studies, and the assumption remains to be verified. The limitation of these
procedures is that they rely completely on the cooperation and reliability of the
individual patient.

In one of the best controlled studies in this area, Dericco, Brigham, and
Garlington (1977) assessed the effectiveness of three aversive treatment programs:
satiation, cognitive control, and response-contingent shock. The subjects were 24
volunteers varying in age, socioeconomic background, and smoking rates. In the
satiation procedure, subjects were instructed to smoke continuously for 30
minutes. In the cognitive control procedure, the subjects reclined in a lounger and
heard two recorded messages, one of which associated pleasant images with
continuous smoking. The subjects were also instructed to imagine the pleasant
scene before smoking and the unpleasant scene after smoking. In the contingent
shock procedure, 25 painful shocks were administered to the subjects' forearms at
various (unpredictable) times throughout the smoking sequence. The subjects
were contacted 6 months after the treatment was terminated in order to assess the
long-term comparative effects of the three procedures. The results clearly
demonstrated the superiority of the shock procedure. Though the bewildering
assortment of aversive treatment programs that have been applied to cigarette
smoking demonstrates only limited success, the Dericco et al. study does suggest
that if a response shock procedure is employed that involves frequent, intense, and
extended shock, success rates increase and relapse rates are reduced. The Dericco
et al. study also represents the more recent focus in this area, that is, the
development of aversive procedures that not only result in immediate reduction in
cigarette smoking but which also produce long-term abstinence. Another promising approach in this connection has been termed the *rapid smoking/blown smoky
air* procedure (Lichtenstein & Rodriguez, 1977). This procedure combines two

aversive conditions: (a) continuous, rapid smoking concentrated over a short time period until the subject can no longer tolerate lighting up another cigarette; while (b) simultaneously, and for the same time period, exposing the subject to a high density of cigarette smoke directed at the face. Lichtenstein and Rodriguez reported a 34% abstinence rate for subjects 2 to 6 years after they had undergone the treatment procedure.

The "rapid smoking" or "fast smoking" technique has been used in a number of variations with varying effects. Lichstein and Stalgaitis (1980), for example, instructed six couples to smoke each time they observed their spouse smoking. This treatment resulted in a 60% plus reduction in smoking rates, which was maintained at a 6-month follow-up. Danaher, Jeffery, Zimmerman, and Nelson (1980) enhanced the rapid smoking effect by providing subjects with audiotaped instructions to be practiced at home. Hall, Rugg, Tunstall, and Jones (1984) found that a skills training procedure also enhanced the fast-smoking effect especially for light smokers. Tiffany, Martin, and Baker (1986) analyzed the effects of three different rapid-smoking procedures together with counseling on smoking rate and found that at 6 months posttreatment the full-scale rapid-smoking (i.e., rapid smoking/blown smoky air procedure) group produced the best outcome.

Another recent development reflects the use of alternative aversive therapy procedures in the treatment of smoking behavior. Murray and Hobbs (1981) prescribed a self-reward and self-punishment (monetary fines) contingent on daily smoking performance procedure which was moderately effective in reducing smoking rate in a majority of their subjects for as long as 6 months posttreatment in a single subject design. If the subject failed to reduce his smoking rate in stages, he was required to contribute to an undesirable charity (changing criterion design).

Lando and McGovern (1982) have suggested that abstinence rates can be further enhanced by combining such aversive approaches with several long-term, broad-spectrum forms of intervention including contracts, booster sessions, and group support. Indeed, their results reveal better than 40% abstinence rates for 12 to 36 months following treatment termination.

The more recent studies in this area have used a combination of techniques in addition to aversion therapy in order to further reduce relapse rates, as suggested by Lando and McGovern (1982). Such more individualized treatment programs, plus developments in the self-control literature, offer a cautious note of optimism for dealing with one of our more resistant problem behaviors.

Overeating. As with cigarette smoking, prematurely applied aversive treatment methods are widely used for the treatment of obesity, resulting in the emergence of questionable practices and undocumented claims of effectiveness. Again, because of the lack of rigorous studies, only several examples from the aversion therapy literature are presented.

Perhaps the earliest example of a response-contingent shock procedure with two overweight women is described by Meyer and Crisp (1964). Temptation food (food for which the patient had most craving as distinguished from food on a prescribed diet) was displayed for increasing periods of time, and the patients received shock for approach responses. The shock contingency was gradually faded while weight changes were constantly monitored. Any increase in weight resulted in a return to the treatment regime. Although the results for one patient were highly satisfactory (a weight reduction of about 75 lb during 6 months, which was maintained almost 2 years after discharge), no durable constructive change was observed in the second patient.

As is true in the treatment of cigarette smoking, popularized versions of aversion therapy for overeating have found expression in numerous commercial weight control programs. In some of these cases, aversive stimuli such as foul odors and even shock have been administered contingent on the excessive eating response. A number of authors, however, have criticized such approaches because of their poor long-term effects (Brightwell & Sloan, 1977).

More promising approaches involving a combination of treatment procedures, however, might produce longer lasting effects. Rodriguez and Sandler (1981), for example, used a variation of the response cost technique to enhance gradual and consistent reductions in weight. In this case, volunteer subjects were required to deposit 10 valuable items, which were only returned to them if they met an individually designed eating standard. Gradual change objectives of specific eating patterns were formulated on a week-by-week basis, and, if the subject failed to meet the agreed-on objective, the valuable for that week was donated to an undesired organization. All of the subjects in the treatment group showed a gradual and systematic weight loss during the 10-week treatment program that continued over a 6-month follow-up period. Thus, it appeared that the changes in eating patterns induced by the treatment program continued to be used by the subjects even in the absence of formal treatment procedures.

Other Compulsive Conditions

Other investigators have reported the successful treatment of gambling (Baker & Miller, 1968), shoplifting (Kellam, 1969), and idiosyncratic rituals. Barrett, Staub, and Sisson (1983), for example, used visual screening to suppress two ritualistic behaviors in a developmentally disabled 4½-year-old boy. Both of these responses involved heavy preoccupation with shoes, which dominated his daily routine and interfered with the acquisition of adaptive skills. The visual screening procedure used was essentially similar to that of McGonigle et al. (1982) described earlier. Each time the response occurred, the therapist verbalized the inappropriate behavior and placed one hand over the child's eyes for a minimum of 30 seconds while holding the back of the child's head with the other hand. The procedure was first implemented during free-play activities and later in a classroom setting. The results revealed an almost immediate decrease in the ritualistic behavior in the treatment settings. This effect generalized and was maintained in the home setting for at least 12 months after formal treatment was discontinued.

Matson, Coleman, Dilorenzo, and Vucelik (1981) have also reported the successful reduction of stealing behavior in five emotionally disturbed children through the use of overcorrection. Although the characteristic of the target behavior in this study might not satisfy the clinical definition of kleptomania (compulsive and habitual stealing), the procedures might also be useful in extreme cases. In the present study, the stealing behavior was part of a general pattern of inappropriate behavior with children who were inpatients in a psychiatric facility. Each child resided in an individual room, and a daily inventory of his possessions was made enabling the staff to determine the frequency of stolen items. Restitution and overcorrection were administered each time a stolen item was discovered, which consisted of requiring the child to return the stolen item, apologize, and to do cleanup at work time. Moreover, the cleanup activity was cumulative; that is, two stolen items resulted in 10 minutes of punishment, four items in 20 minutes, and so on. Although the children initially differed considerably in the frequency of pretreatment stealing behavior (e.g., from 4 stolen items per day to 40 items per day), dramatic reductions occurred in each case within 5 days of the start of the overcorrection procedure. Two- and 4-month follow-up inquiries revealed zero instances of the problem behavior in the home. In a case involving a 56-year-old woman with a 14-year history of shoplifting (kleptomania), Glover (1985) used covert sensitization to good effect. Aversive imagery involving nausea and vomiting were paired with shoplifting impulses with the subject reporting only one instance of shoplifting behavior at a 19-month follow-up.

Covert Problem Conditions

Another interesting development that has emerged over the last several years involves the use of aversion therapy in the treatment of covert problem conditions. In such cases, the patient's verbal complaint is usually regarded as the external concomitant of disturbing thoughts frequently involving sexual or aggressive ideations. Despite this commonly accepted assumption, the following review suggests that such conditions are also amenable to aversion therapy.

Kushner and Sandler (1966) used a shock procedure for treating suicidal thoughts in a 48-year-old male. These obsessions were characterized by persistent, daily ruminations focusing on six different suicidal images. The patient was instructed to imagine a particular scene and received shock on a signal that the image was clear. Fifteen to 20 such trials were presented in each session, and, after the 12th session, the patient reported that only one image was still present. Treatment was temporarily discontinued after three more sessions because of a death in the family but reinstated after his return. (No suicidal ruminations occurred during this time.) Treatment was terminated after five more sessions and a total of 350 trials. A 3-month follow-up revealed no recurrence of the former problem.

Bucher and Fabricatore (1970) employed a self-shock procedure in an attempt to reduce the frequency of hallucinations in a 47-year-old hospitalized patient diagnosed as a paranoid schizophrenic. The hallucinations were described as frequent, obscene, and critical voices that occurred from four to seven times per day and lasted for as long as 20 minutes.

The patient was supplied with a portable shock device and instructed to administer shock to himself at the onset of the hallucinations. This resulted in an apparent immediate and virtually complete cessation of hallucinatory episodes during 20 days, after which the shock device was abruptly removed, and the patient was unfortunately discharged without his consent. He was returned to the hospital 2 weeks later, the voices apparently having "returned."

Haynes and Geddy (1973) showed that hallucinations could also be suppressed by means of a time-out procedure. The patient was a 45-year-old hospitalized female diagnosed as schizophrenic. She showed a high incidence of loud and incomprehensible verbal behavior that was considered to be evidence of hallucinations. During treatment, each hallucinatory episode resulted in a staff member informing the patient that she had to go to the TO room because she was talking to herself, then leading the patient to the TO room, closing the door, and opening the door 10 minutes later. Two treatment periods were separated by a nontreatment interval, to observe the effects of discontinuing treatment. The results indicated that the hallucinatory behavior decreased by about one half during the two TO procedures. Even more pronounced changes were produced in a second patient displaying similar problems.

Response-contingent "white noise" was used to treat auditory hallucinations with three adult female schizophrenic patients by Fonagy and Slade (1982). Marked reductions in hallucinations were reported for two of the patients and a moderate reduction in the third. In addition, a general reduction in hallucinations was also reported outside the treatment setting.

Sexual Deviation

An extensive variety of aversion therapy techniques has been employed for the purpose of modifying deviant sexual behavior. The work in this area has been particularly singled out for criticisms as described in the introduction to this chapter. Once again, many of these criticisms do not appear to be warranted in the sense that a large number of previously at-risk individuals have achieved a more satisfactory level of sexual adjustment as a consequence of such treatment. Nevertheless, the concern for better controlled observations is genuine, and one can only hope that this will be resolved by future research.

As was true in the case of alcoholism, many of the earlier aversive procedures were formulated in the context of the Pavlovian model, although it shortly became apparent that operant processes (frequently uncontrolled) intruded into the procedures. The major value of this earlier work is more of a heuristic and historic nature than of a contribution of hard knowledge to theory and practice. Moreover, the initiative displayed by these investigators in attacking complex problems via previously suspect methods, thereby challenging many prevailing myths, should not pass unmentioned.

One of the first attempts to apply an operant aversion therapy procedure with sexual deviations is reported by Blakemore, Thorpe, Barker, Conway, and Lavin (1963). Prior to this study, most efforts used nausea-producing drugs to produce a conditioned aversion in the presence of stimuli related to the deviant practices. The particular problem condition treated in the Blakemore study was a long-standing tranvestism. A variety of transvestite activities, usually culminating in masturbation, was reported by the patient. Marital and legal imperatives served as the impetus for his seeking assistance.

The treatment was conducted in a private room of a hospital which housed a full-length mirror and an electric grid floor. The patient's "favorite outfit" of female clothing was placed on the chair. The procedure involved a series of trials in which the patient was instructed to start dressing in the female clothes. At some point during a trial, he received a signal to start undressing. The signal was either a buzzer or a shock to the feet. These were randomly presented and occurred at varying time intervals while all the female clothes were being removed. Following a 1-minute rest, the procedure was repeated for a total of five trials in each treatment session. A total of 400 trials was administered over 6 treatment days. Because no transvestite behavior was reported 6 months after treatment, the procedure was evidently successful.

A more clearly operant procedure was reported in the treatment of pedophilia (i.e., child molesting) that was so serious that the patient was being considered for brain surgery (Bancroft et al., 1966). The procedure attempted to simulate the natural conditions in which the pedophilia-related behaviors occurred. Pictures of young girls were presented to the patient, and, when a penile reaction occurred (as measured by the penile plethysmograph), a painful shock was administered to the arm. Shocks were continued until there was a reduction in the response. Each trial lasted 10 minutes, with no shock administered in the absence of a criterion response. Six to eight trials were administered each day over a period of 8 weeks for a total of 200 shock trials. In addition, on every fourth trial, the shock apparatus was disconnected, and the patient saw photographs of adult women while being encouraged to engage in normal sexual fantasies.

A more successful outcome using a similar procedure for a client with a similar problem condition has been reported by Josiassen, Fantuzzo, and Rosen (1980). In this case, the patient was a 37-year-old single male with a long history of pedophiliac activities. Significant reductions in arousal to deviant stimuli in the treatment setting generalized to the patient's natural environment. Training in appropriate heterosexual skills further facilitated the treatment outcome. By the 18th week of treatment, the patient reported virtually no instances of pedophiliac arousal.

Perhaps the most convincing evidence for the efficacy of aversion therapy with child molesters was provided by Quinsey, Chaplin, and Carrington (1980). Eighteen inpatient residents with well-defined child-molester histories served as the subjects in this clinical study. Treatment involved 10 sessions of biofeedback plus an aversion therapy component in which sexual arousal to inappropriate stimuli (slides of children) was accompanied by shock. Almost all of the subjects showed considerable improvement in terms of their prior inappropriate sexual age preferences. The durability of these effects was also impressive. Thirty child molesters, previously treated in the same manner, were followed for an average of 29 months. Only six of these subjects subsequent to treatment committed child-molesting offenses.

Covert aversive procedures continue to be used with varying degrees of success in the treatment of fetishism. Moreover, one now finds combinations of covert sensitization with other aversive techniques (Rangaswamy, 1987) as well as with strategies designed to enhance self-control (Haydn–Smith, Marks, Buchaya, & Repper, 1987) or to assist in the acquisition of appropriate sexual behaviors (Josiassen et al., 1980). These efforts underscore Lester's argument (Lester, 1982) that aversive treatment by itself will seldom be successful unless the therapist replaces the deviant sexual behavior with normal sexual behavior. Card's study (1982) using biofeedback suggests that most sexual deviants can learn to suppress inappropriate sexual stimuli, increase their arousal to positive stimuli, and transfer sexual facilitation to in vivo situations, thereby enhancing self-control, bringing us closer to an optimal treatment program.

One last study is included in this review because of its recency, superior design, and general interest. Earls and Castonguay (1989) evaluated the effect of an olfactory aversion procedure on a 17-year-old male with a history of sexual aggression against both male and female children. Sexual preference was measured by penile tumescence responses to 20 photographs depicting males and females of various ages, as well as six audiotaped descriptions of violent and nonviolent interactions between a male adult and a female child or a male child. In addition, audiotaped episodes were constructed to simulate the client's own sexual experiences encompassing nonviolent sex with a male and a female child, violent sex with a male and a female child, and mutually consenting sex with a female of an appropriate age. During the treatment phase, the client was instructed to listen to whichever tape was presented and to inhale from a 6-ounce bottle of ammonia crystals as soon as he experienced arousal to the inappropriate tapes, but not to the appropriate tapes. The treatment phase was organized in terms of a multiple baseline in order to examine the effects of treatment in a systematic sequence. Two to four treatment sessions were employed each week, interspersed with one assessment session (hearing the tape without the use of the ammonia technique) for a total of 20 treatment sessions. In sum, the client self-administered the aversive stimulus 86 times in connection with the "boy" audiotapes and 95 times for the "girl" tapes. Follow-ups were conducted 1 week and 1 year after the treatment phase. Pretreatment measures revealed maximum penile responding to all stimulus categories. Pairing the aversive odor with arousal to deviant sexual stimuli clearly reduced the response to near-zero rates by the end of the treatment phases. Furthermore, these effects were largely maintained during the follow-up assessment. Despite the constructive changes, the authors correctly caution that the relationship between such laboratory derived outcomes, even when impressive and dramatic, and subsequent sexual behavior in the natural environment still remains to be determined. Again, the critical issue that remains is the maintenance and generalization of effects.

Generalized Asocial Behaviors

The last problem condition to be considered represents a category that encompasses a wide variey of socially deviant acts, from mild forms of nuisance and asocial behaviors to dangerous acts of aggression directed at objects and other people. The literature in this area is quite extensive, and only a brief overview is presented here.

This is by now a series of studies indicating the effectiveness of time-out for reducing a wide assortment of aggressive, asocial, negativistic behaviors. In addition, these studies have been conducted with a wide range of individuals in a diversity of institutional and natural settings. Bostow and Bailey (1969), for example, reduced severe disruptive and aggressive behaviors (loud abusive vocalizations, attacks on others) in two mentally retarded female adults by making brief TO contingent on such responses. White, Nielsen, and Johnson (1972) extended these observations to 20 mentally retarded children. Ramp, Ulrich, and Dulaney (1971) reduced out-of-seat behaviors and inappropriate talking in a classroom situation, and Wahler (1969) demonstrated that similar techniques could be employed in the home environment through parental instruction. Tyler and Brown (1967) found that aggressive asocial behavior (throwing objects, physical assault, etc.) in 15 adolescent males could be similarly treated.

Aggressive behavior has also been effectively reduced by means of response cost. Winkler (1970), for example, suppressed episodes of violence and loud noise in chronic psychiatric patients by removing tokens contingent on such responses. Kazdin (1972) provided a review of the relevant literature in which he described the variety of problem behaviors successfully treated by response cost (smoking, overeating, stuttering, psychotic talk); the durability of such procedures in terms of long-range effects; and several aspects of response cost procedures that could enhance their efficacy.

Finally, response-contingent shock has also been employed, especially when the problem behaviors are highly dangerous. In this fashion, Bucher and King (1971) suppressed the rate of highly destructive acts in an 11-year-old psychotic boy in the treatment setting and at home when the treatment was continued by the child's parent. Royer, Flynn, and Osadca (1971) also used a shock procedure to reduce the frequency of fire setting in a severely regressed disorganized psychiatric patient. In this case, shock correlated with arson-related words had no effect on the patient's actual behavior. Subsequently, the patient was required to rehearse a series of fire-setting activities, with shock administered on a response-contingent basis. This procedure resulted in a marked reduction of the problem behavior and a complete absence of such acts during a 4-year follow-up assessment.

Several more recent studies provide additional evidence of the efficacy of aversive procedures in the treatment of aggressive behavior. Again, these studies run the gamut of aversive techniques. Gross, Berler, and Drabman (1982) reduced aggressive classroom behavior to near-zero rates in a 4-year-old retarded male by dispensing a water mist to the face as a punishment for the maladaptive behavior; and Doke, Wolery, and Sumberc (1983) achieved similar results in a 7-year-old by administering ammonia contingent on a variety of antisocial behaviors. The constructive changes in the child's behavior were still evident at a 14-month follow-up. Dick and Jackson (1983) trained the parents of a retarded child to administer lemon juice and overcorrection on a variety of her aggressive responses. The treatment eliminated all of her problem behaviors with significantly reduced rates still evident as long as 18 months posttreatment. Finally, Foxx McMorrow, Bittle, and Bechtel (1986) offer one additional example of the use of electric shock with aggressive behavior. The client was a 20-year-old deaf, institutionalized male with a long history of noncompliance and severe, frequent aggression directed at both other clients and staff. A variety of interventions (including drugs and physical restraints) had been attempted with essentially no change in his behavior. Following a 30-day period in which rates for the problem behaviors were recorded (hair pulling, zero to three times per day, aggressive episodes 1 to 11 times per day, and property destruction less than two times per day), a response-contingent shock procedure was initiated. Shock was administered by a direct stimulator to the back of the client's upper arm. All three problem behaviors were reduced to near-zero rates within 3 days. Subsequently, the same treatment program was implemented in the client's living unit and at school. As maintenance of the reduced rates emerged under these conditions, the treatment procedure was transferred to the client's teacher, parents, and ultimately, direct-care staff. By the 28th day of treatment, there were no further instances of the problem behaviors in any of the client's settings. Furthermore, these effects were maintained for over a year of follow-up observations. As suggested earlier, this study indicates that shock procedures, when properly implemented, extend the variety of aversive techniques for serious problem behaviors that do not respond to less intrusive alternatives. Equally important, the Foxx et al. study (1986) offers a precise, detailed rationale, description of procedures, and overview of the ethical imperative that are relevant to such circumstances.

SUMMARY

During the last 20 years, considerable progress has been made in the development of effective aversively based procedures for changing maladaptive behavior in terms of expanding the range of problem behaviors treated and of enhancing the durability of the effects beyond simply reducing target behaviors during intervention. Perhaps most important, several well-controlled, large studies have been reported that provide good support for the efficacy of such approaches. A number of studies have systematically combined aversive procedures with other forms of intervention, and one recent study (Charlop, Burgio, Iwata, & Ivancic, 1988) varied several combinations of punishers. These recent efforts should offer additional insights into the enhancement of treatment effectiveness. The search for alternative minimally intrusive techniques is also reflected in the recent literature. Finally, further refinement of ethical and practical guidelines continues to be a focus of attention.

As a consequence of these developments, at least in many quarters and in spite of the continuing controversies, aversion therapy is rapidly achieving the status of respectability in the total range of services to be considered by professionals concerned with behavior change objectives. Moreover, many of the earlier criticisms that have been raised regarding the use of such procedures have not been confirmed. That is not to say, however, that all of the issues and questions have been resolved. On the contrary, future work might be directed at comparing the relative effectiveness of different aversive procedures, at relating treatment outcome measures and relapse with specific patient characteristics, and at expanding the variety of problem behaviors that are amenable to aversion therapy.

REFERENCES

Adams, M. R., & Popelka, G. (1971). The influence of "time out" on stutterers and their dysfluency. *Behavior Therapy, 2*, 334–339.

Altman, K., Grahns, C., & Friman, P. (1982). Treatment of unobserved trichotillimania by attention-reflection and punishment of an apparent covariant. *Journal of Behavior Therapy and Experimental Psychiatry, 13*(4), 337–340.

Atthowe, J. M., Jr. (1972). Controlling nocturnal enuresis in severely disabled and chronic patients. *Behavior Therapy, 3*, 232–239.

Azrin, N. H., & Holz, W. C. (1966). Punishment. In W. K. Honig (Ed.), *Operant behavior: Areas of research and application*. New York: Appleton-Century-Crofts.

Baer, D. M. (1970). A case for the selective reinforcement of punishment. In C. Neuringer & J. L. Michael (Eds.), *Behavior modification in clinical psychology*. New York: Appleton-Century-Crofts.

Baker, J. C., & Miller, M. E. (1968). Aversion therapy for compulsive gambling. *Journal of Nervous and Mental Disorders, 146*, 285–302.

Barrett, R. P., Staub, R. W., & Sisson, L. A. (1983). Treatment of compulsive rituals with visual screening: A case study with long-term follow-up. *Journal of Behavior Therapy and Experimental Psychiatry, 14*, 55–59.

Belles, D., & Bradlyn, A. S. (1987). The use of the changing criterion design in achieving controlled smoking in a heavy smoker: A controlled case study. *Journal of Behavior Therapy and Experimental Psychiatry, 18*(1), 77–82.

Berkowitz, A. J. (1987). The AAMD position statement on aversive therapy. *Mental Retardation, 25*, 118.

Bernstein, G. S. (1989). Social validity and the debate over use of aversive/intrusive procedures. *Behavior Therapist, 12*(6), 123–125.

Blake, B. G. (1965). The application of behavior therapy to the treatment of alcoholism. *Behaviour Research and Therapy, 3*, 75–85.

Blakemore, C. B., Thorpe, J. B., Barker, J. C., Conway, C. G., & Lavin, N. I. (1963). The application of faradic aversion conditioning in a case of transvestism. *Behaviour Research and Therapy, 1*, 29–34.

Bostow, D. E., & Bailey, J. B. (1969). Modification of severe disruptive and aggressive behavior using brief time-out and reinforcement procedures. *Journal of Applied Behavior Analysis, 2*, 31–38.

Brightwell, L. R., & Sloan, L. L. (1977). Long-term results of behavior therapy for obesity. *Behavior Therapy, 8*, 899–905.

Bucher, B., & Fabricatore, J. (1970). Use of patient-administered shock to suppress hallucinations. *Behavior Therapy, 1*, 382–385.

Bucher, B., & King, L. W. (1971). Generalization of punishment effects in the deviant behavior of a psychotic child. *Behavior Therapy, 2*, 68–77.

Cannon, D. (1982). Alcohol aversion therapy in the 80's. *Bulletin of the Society of Psychologists in Substance Abuse, 1*(2), 34–36.

Cannon, D. S., & Baker, T. B. (1981). Emetic and electric shock alcohol aversion therapy: Assessment of conditioning. *Journal of Consulting and Clinical Psychology, 49*(1), 20–33.

Cannon, D. S., Baker, T. B., Gino, A., & Nathan, P. E. (1986). Alcohol-aversion therapy: Relation between strength of aversion and abstinence. *Journal of Consulting and Clinical Psychology, 54*(6), 825–830.

Cannon, D. S., Baker, T. B., & Wehl, C. K. (1981). Emetic and electric shock alcohol aversion therapy: Six and twelve month follow-up. *Journal of Consulting and Clinical Psychology, 49*, 360–368.

Card, R. D. (1982). Biofeedback in the treatment of sexual deviation. *American Journal of Clinical Biofeedback, 5*(1), 31–42.

Cavalier, A. R., & Ferretti, R. P. (1980). Stereotyped behaviour, alternative behaviour and collateral effects: A comparison of four intervention procedures. *Journal of Mental Deficiency Research, 24*(3), 219–230.

Charlop, M. H., Burgio, L. D., Iwata, B. A., & Ivancic, M. T. (1988). Stimulus variation as a means of enhancing punishment effects. *Journal of Applied Behavior Analysis, 21*(1), 89–95.

Corte, H. E., Wolf, M. M., & Locke, B. J. (1971). A comparison of procedures for eliminating self-injurious behavior of retarded adolescents. *Journal of Applied Behavior Analysis, 4*, 201–215.

Crawford, D. A. (1988). Aversion therapy in the treatment of trichotillomania: A case study. *Behavioural Psychotherapy, 16*(1), 57–63.

Daly, D. A., & Frick, J. V. (1970). The effects of punishing stuttering expectations and stuttering utterances: A comparative study. *Behavior Therapy, 1*, 228–239.

Danaher, B. G., Jeffery, R. W., Zimmerman, R., & Nelson, E. (1980). Aversive smoking using printed instructions and audiotape adjuncts. *Addictive Behaviors, 5*(4), 353–358.

Dericco, D. A., Brigham, T. A., & Garlington, W. K. (1977). Development and evaluation of treatment paradigms for the suppression of smoking behavior. *Journal of Applied Behavior Analysis, 10*, 173–181.

Dick, D. M., & Jackson, H. J. (1983). Symposium on behavior modification treatments III: The parent-administered treatment of the inappropriate behaviours of a retarded infant. *British Journal of Mental Subnormality, 29*(57, part 2), 81–86.

Doke, L. A., Wolery, M., & Sumberc, C. (1983). Treating chronic aggression: Effects and side effects of response-contingent ammonia spirits. *Behavior Modification, 7*(4), 531–556.

Dorsey, M. F., Iwata, B. A., Ong, P., & McSween, T. E. (1980). Treatment of self-injurious behavior using a water mist: Initial response suppression and generalization. *Journal of Applied Behavior Analysis, 13*(2), 343–353.

Durand, V. M. (1987). "Look homeward angel": A call to return to our (functional) roots. *Behavior Analyst, 10*(2), 299–302.

Earls, C. M., & Castonguay, L. G. (1989). The evaluation of olfactory aversion for a bisexual pedophile with a single-case multiple baseline design. *Behavior Therapy, 20*, 137–146.

Epstein, L. H., Doke, L. A., Sajwaj, T. E., Sorrell, S., & Rimmer, B. (1974). Generality and side effects of overcorrection. *Journal of Applied Behavior Analysis, 7*, 385–390.

Ewing, J. A. (1984). Electric aversion and individualized imagery therapy in alcoholism: A controlled experiment. *Alcohol, 1*(2), 101–104.

Fehl, R. W., Revusky, S., & Mellor, C. S. (1980). Drugs employed in the treatment of alcoholism: Rat data suggest they are unnecessarily severe. *Behaviour Research and Therapy, 18*(2), 71–78.

Feldman, M. P. (1966). Aversion therapy for sexual deviation: A critical review. *Psychological Bulletin, 65*, 65–79.

Fonagy, P., & Slade, P. (1982). Punishment vs. negative reinforcement in the aversive conditioning of auditory hallucinations. *Behaviour Research and Therapy, 20*(5), 483–492.

Foxx, R. M., & Azrin, N. H. (1973). The elimination of autistic self-stimulatory behavior by overcorrection. *Journal of Applied Behavior Analysis, 6*, 1–14.

Foxx, R. M., McMorrow, M. J., Bittle, R. G., & Bechtel, D. R. (1986). The successful treatment of a dually-diagnosed deaf man's aggression with a program that included contingent electric shock. *Behavior Therapy, 17*(2), 170–186.

Franks, C. M. (1963). Behavior therapy: The principles of conditioning and the treatment of the alcoholic. *Quarterly Journal of Studies on Alcohol, 24*, 511–529.

Friman, P. C., & Hove, G. (1987). Apparent covariation between child habit disorders: Effects of successful treatment for thumb sucking on untargeted chronic hair pulling. *Journal of Applied Behavior Analysis, 20*(4), 421–425.

Gardner, W. I. (1989). But in the meantime: A client perspective on the debate over the use of aversive/intrusive therapy procedures. *Behavior Therapist, 12*(8), 179–181.

Gendreau, P. E., & Dodwell, P. C. (1968). An aversive treatment for addicted cigarette smokers: Preliminary report. *Canadian Psychologist, 9*, 28–34.

Glover, J. H. (1985). A case of kleptomania treated by covert sensitization. *British Journal of Clinical Psychology, 24*(3), 213–214.

Goldiamond, I. (1965). Stuttering and fluency and manipulative operant response classes. In L. Drasner & L. P. Ullman (Eds.), *Research in Behavior Modification*. New York: Holt, Rinehart & Winston.

Griffith, R. G., & Spreat, S. (1989). Aversive behavior modification procedures and the use of professional judgement. *Behavior Therapist, 12*(7), 143–146.

Gross, A. M., Berler, E. S., & Drabman, R. S. (1982). Reduction of aggressive behavior in a retarded boy using a water squirt. *Journal of Behavior Therapy and Experimental Psychiatry, 13*(1), 95–98.

Gross, A. M., Wright, B., & Drabman, R. S. (1980). The empirical selection of a punisher for a retarded child's self-injurious behavior: A case study. *Child Behavior Therapy, 2*(3), 59–65.

Guess, D., Helmstetter, E., Turnbull, H. R., & Knowlton, S. (1987). Use of aversive procedures with persons who are disabled: An historical review and critical analysis. *Monograph of the Association for Persons with Severe Handicaps, 2*(10), 1–18.

Hall, S. M., Rugg, D., Tunstall, C., & Jones, R. T. (1984). Preventing relapse to cigarette smoking by behavioral skill training. *Journal of Consulting and Clinical Psychology, 52*(3), 372–382.

Haydn–Smith, P., Marks, I., Buchaya, H., & Repper, D. (1987). Behavioural treatment of life-threatening masochistic asphyxiation: A case study. *British Journal of Psychiatry, 150,* 518–519.

Haynes, S. M., & Geddy, P. (1973). Suppression of psychotic hallucinations through time-out. *Behavior Therapy, 4,* 123–127.

Hunt, W. A., & Matarazzo, J. D. (1973). Three years later: Recent developments in the experimental modification of smoking behavior. *Journal of Abnormal Psychology, 81,* 107–114.

Johnston, J. M. (1972). Punishment of human behavior. *American Psychologist, 27,* 1033–1054.

Jones, H. G. (1960). The behavioral treatment of enuresis nocturna. In H. J. Eysenck (Ed.), *Behavior therapy and the neuroses.* Oxford: Pergamon Press.

Jones, M., & Andersen, M. (1981). Problems involved in the use of ammonia in the treatment of self injurious behavior. *Australian Journal of Developmental Disabilities, 7*(1), 27–31.

Josiassen, R. C., Fantuzzo, J., & Rosen, A. C. (1980). Treatment of pedophilia using multistage aversion therapy and social skills training. *Journal of Behavior Therapy and Experimental Psychiatry, 11,* 55–61.

Kanfer, F. H., & Grimm, L. G. (1980). Managing clinical change: A process model of therapy. *Behavior Modification, 4,* 419–444.

Kazdin, A. E. (1972). Response cost: The removal of conditioned reinforcement for therapeutic change. *Behavior Therapy, 3,* 533–546.

Kazdin, A. E. (1973). The effect of response cost and aversive stimulation in suppressing punished and non-punished speech dysfluencies. *Behavior Therapy, 4,* 73–82.

Kellam, A. P. (1969). Shoplifting treated by aversion to a film. *Behaviour Research and Therapy, 7,* 125–127.

Kishore, R., & Dutt, K. (1986). Electrically induced aversion therapy in alcoholics. *Indian Journal of Clinical Psychology, 13*(1), 39–43.

Kohlenberg, R. J. (1970). The punishment of persistent vomiting: A case study. *Journal of Applied Behavior Analysis, 3,* 241–245.

Kunjukrishnan, R., Pawlak, A., & Varan, L. R. (1988). The clinical and forensic psychiatric issue of retifism. *Canadian Journal of Psychiatry, 33*(9), 819–825.

Kushner, M. (1970). Faradic aversive controls in clinical practice. In C. Neuringer & J. L. Michael (Eds.), *Behavior Modification in clinical psychology.* New York: Appleton-Century-Crofts.

Kushner, M., & Sandler, J. (1966). Aversion therapy and the concept of punishment. *Behaviour Research and Therapy, 4,* 179–186.

Lando, H. A., & McGovern, P. G. (1982) Three year data on a behavioral treatment for smoking: A follow-up note. *Addictive Behaviors, 7,* 177–181.

Lang, P. J., & Melamed, P. G. (1969). Case report: Avoidance conditioning therapy of an infant with chronic ruminative vomiting. *Journal of Abnormal Psychology, 74,* 1–8.

Lasky, V. (1987). Epilogue. *Monograph of the Association for Persons with Severe Handicaps, 2,*(10).

Laws, D. R., Meyer, J., & Holmen, M. L. (1978). Reduction of sadistic arousal by olfactory aversion: A case study. *Behaviour Research and Therapy, 16,* 281–285.

Lebow, M. D., Gelfand, S., & Dobson, W. R. (1970). Aversive conditioning of a phenothiazine-induced respiratory stridor. *Behavior Therapy, 1,* 222–227.

Lemere, R., & Voegtlin, W. L. (1950). An evaluation of aversion treatment of alcoholism. *Quarterly Journal of Studies on Alcohol, 11,* 199–204.

Lester, D. (1982). The treatment of exhibitionists. *Corrective and Social Psychiatry and Journal of Behavior Technology, Methods, and Therapy, 28*(3), 94–98.

Lichstein, K. L., & Stalgaitis, S. J. (1980). Treatment of cigarette smoking couples by reciprocal aversion. *Behavior Therapy, 11*(1), 104–108.

Lichtenstein, E., & Rodriguez, M. R. P. (1977). Long-term effects of rapid smoking treatment for dependent smokers. *Addictive Behaviors, 2,* 109–112.

Liversedge, L. A., & Sylvester, J. D. (1955). Conditioning techniques in the treatment of writer's cramp. *Lancet, 2,* 1147–1149.

Lovaas, O. I., & Favell, J. E. (1987). Protection for clients undergoing aversive/restrictive interventions. Special issue: New developments in the treatment of a person exhibiting autism and severe behavior disorders. *Education and Treatment of Children, 10*(4), 311–325.

Lovaas, O. I., & Simmons, J. Q. (1969). Manipulation of self-destruction in three retarded children. *Journal of Applied Behavior Analysis, 2,* 143–157.

Luckey, R. E., Watson, C. M., & Musick, J. K. (1968). Aversive conditioning as a means of inhibiting vomiting and rumination. *American Journal of Mental Deficiency, 73,* 139–142.

Luiselli, M. K. (1984). Application of immobilization time-out in management programming with developmentally disabled children. *Child and Family Behavior Therapy, 6,* 1–15.

Lutzker, J. L. (1978) Reducing self-injurious behavior by facial screening. *American Journal of Mental Deficiency, 82,* 510–513.

Marholin, D., Luiselli, M. K., Robinson, M., & Lott, I. T. (1980). Response contingent taste aversion in treating chronic ruminative vomiting of institutionalized profoundly retarded children. *Journal of Mental Deficiency Research, 24,* 47–56.

Matson, J. L., Coleman, D., Dilorenzo, T. M., & Vucelik, I. (1981). Eliminating stealing in developmentally disabled children. *Child Behavior Therapy, 3,* 57–66.

McConaghy, N., Armstrong, M. S., & Blaszczynski, A. (1981). Controlled comparison of aversive therapy and covert sensitization in compulsive homosexuality. *Behaviour Research and Therapy, 19,* 425–467.

McGonigle, J. J., Duncan, D., Cordisco, L., & Barrett, R. P. (1982). Visual screening: An alternative method for reducing stereotypic behaviors. *Journal of Applied Behavior Analysis, 15,* 461–467.

Merbaum, M. (1973). The modification of self-destructive behavior by a mother-therapist using aversive stimulation. *Behavior Therapy, 4,* 442–447.

Meyer, V., & Crisp, A. (1964). Aversion therapy in two cases of obesity. *Behaviour Research and Therapy, 2,* 143–147.

Miltenberger, R. G., Lennox, D. B., & Erfanian, N. (1989). Acceptability of alternative treatments for persons with mental retardation: Ratings from institutional and community-based staff. *American Journal on Mental Deficiency, 93*(4), 388–395.

Mowrer, O. H., & Mowrer, W. M. (1938). Enuresis. A method for its study and treatment. *American Journal of Orthopsychiatry, 8,* 436–459.

Murray, R. G., & Hobbs, S. A. (1981). Effects of self-reinforcement and self-punishment in smoking reduction: Implications for broad-spectrum behavioral approaches. *Addictive Behaviors, 6*(1), 63–67.

Nathan, P. E. (1985). Aversion therapy in the treatment of alcoholism: Success and failure. *Annals of the New York Academy of Sciences, 443,* 357–364.

Newman, L. E. (1987). The effects of punishment of repetitions and the acquisition of "stutter-like" behaviors in normal speakers. *Journal of Fluency Disorders, 12*(1), 51–62.

Newmann, M., & Gaomi, B. (1975). Preferred food as the reinforcing agent in a case of anorexia nervosa. *Journal of Behavior Therapy and Experimental Psychiatry, 6,* 331–333.

Quinsey, V. L., Chaplin, T. C., & Carrigon, W. F. (1980). Biofeedback and signaled punishment in the modification of inappropriate sexual age preferences. *Behavior Therapy, 11,* 567–576.

Rachman, S. (1965). Aversion therapy: Chemical or electrical? *Behaviour Research and Therapy, 2,* 289–300.

Ramp, E., Ulrich, R., & Dulaney, S. (1971). Delayed timeout as a procedure for reducing disruptive classroom behavior: A case study. *Journal of Applied Behavior Analysis, 4,* 235–239.

Rangaswamy, K. (1987). Treatment of voyeurism by behavior therapy. *Child Psychiatry Quarterly, 20*(3–4), 73–76.

Rapoff, M. A., Altman, K., & Christopherson, E. R. (1980). Suppression of self-injurious behavior: Determining the least restrictive alternative. *Journal of Mental Deficiency Research, 24,* 37–46.

Rodriguez, L., & Sandler, J. (1981). The treatment of adult obesity through direct manipulation of specific eating behaviors. *Journal of Behavior Therapy and Experimental Psychiatry, 12,* 159–162.

Romanczyk, R. G., Colletti, G., & Plotkin, R. (1980). Punishment of self-injurious behavior: Issues of behavior analysis, generalization, and the right to treatment. *Child Behavior Therapy, 2*(1), 37–54.

Royer, F. L., Flynn, W. F., & Osadca, B. S. (1971). Case history: Aversion therapy for fire-setting by a deteriorated schizophrenic. *Behavior Therapy, 3,* 229–232.

Sandler, J. (1964). Masochism: An empirical analysis. *Psychological Bulletin, 62,* 197–204.

Scholander, T. (1972). Treatment of an unusual case of compulsive behavior by aversive stimulation. *Behavior Therapy, 3,* 290–293.

Siegel, G. M. (1970). Punishment, stuttering, and disfluency. *Journal of Speech and Hearing Research, 13,* 677–714.

Skinner, B. F. (1953). *Sciences and human behavior.* New York: Macmillan.

Soderberg, G. A. (1968). Delayed auditory feedback and stuttering. *Journal of Speech and Hearing Disorders, 33,* 260–267.

Solomon, R. L. (1964). Punishment. *American Psychologist, 19,* 239–253.

Tate, B. G., & Baroff, G. S. (1966). Aversive control of self-injurious behavior in a psychotic boy. *Behavior Therapy, 4,* 281–287.

Tiffany, S. T., Martin, E. M., & Baker, T. B. (1986). Treatments for cigarette smoking: An evaluation of the contributions of aversion and counseling procedures. *Behaviour Research and Therapy, 24*(4), 437–452.

Tough, J. H., Hawkins, R. P., McArthur, M. M., & Ravenswaay, S. V. (1971). Modification of neurotic behavior by punishment: A new use for an old device. *Behavior Therapy, 2,* 567–574.

Turkington, C. (1986). Aversives: Report faulting institute refuels debate on its use. *APA Monitor, 18,* 24–25.

Tyler, V. O., Jr., & Brown, G. D. (1967). The use of swift, brief isolation as a group control device for institutionalized delinquents. *Behaviour Research and Therapy, 5,* 1–9.

VanHouten, R., Axelrod, S., Bailey, J. S., Favell, J. E., Foxx, R. M., Iwata, B. A., & Lovaas, O. I. (1988). The right to effective behavioral treatment. *Journal of Applied Behavior Analysis, 21*(4), 381–384.

Voegtlin, W. L. (1947). Conditioned reflex therapy of chronic alcoholism. Ten years' experience with the method. *Rocky Mountain Medical Journal, 44,* 807–812.

Vogler, R. E., Lunde, S. E., Johnson, G. R., & Martin, P. L. (1970). Electrical aversion conditioning with chronic alcoholics. *Journal of Consulting and Clinical Psychology, 34,* 302–307.

Wahler, R. G. (1969). Oppositional children: A quest for parental reinforcement control. *Journal of Applied Behavior Analysis, 2,* 159–170.

Weiner, H. (1962). Some effects of response cost upon human operant behavior. *Journal of the Experimental Analysis of Behavior, 5,* 201–208.

Wesolowski, M. D., & Zawlocki, R. J. (1982). The differential effects of procedures to eliminate an injurious self-stimulatory behavior (Digito-Ocular Sign) in blind retarded twins. *Behavior Therapy, 13,* 334–345.

White, G. D., Nielsen, G., & Johnson, S. M. (1972). Timeout duration and the suppression of deviant behavior in children. *Journal of Applied Behavior Analysis, 5,* 111–120.

Wiens, A. N., & Menustik, C. E. (1983). Treatment outcome and patient characteristics in an aversion therapy program for alcoholism. *American Psychologist, 38,* 1089–1096.

Wiens, A. N., Menustik, C. E., Miller, S. I., & Schmitz, R. E. (1982–83). Medical-behavioral treatment of the older alcoholic patient. *American Journal of Drug and Alcohol Abuse, 3*(4), 461–475.

Wilson, G. T. (1987). Chemical aversion conditioning as a treatment for alcoholism: A re-analysis. *Behaviour Research and Therapy, 25*(6), 503–516.

Winkler, R. C. (1970). Management of chronic psychiatric patients by a token reinforcement system. *Journal of Applied Behavior Analysis, 3,* 47–55.

Wright, L. (1973). Aversive conditioning of self-induced seizures. *Behavior Therapy, 4,* 712–713.

7
Cognitive Change Methods
David A. F. Haaga
Gerald C. Davison

The cognitive trend in behavior therapy has become increasingly prominent in the past 15 years, but its roots extend further back (e.g., Bandura, 1969; Beck, 1964; Davison, 1966; Ellis, 1962; Kelly, 1955; London, 1964; Rotter, 1954). Diverse cognitive-behavioral approaches can be discriminated, but all share the assumption that emotions and behavior are primarily a function of how events are construed. Clinical improvement, in turn, depends critically on changes in thinking. In brief, "we tell ourselves stories in order to live" (Didion, 1979, p. 11), and this chapter describes some of the stories cognitive-behavioral therapists encourage clients to tell themselves.

We shall outline the essentials of cognitive change methods. Such textbook descriptions of techniques and how they are sequenced can unintentionally convey the misleading impression that therapy always proceeds smoothly and is inevitably goal directed. Realistically, one often backslides, stumbles, guesses, and errs, but one also moves forward with a client unexpectedly quickly, enjoys breakthroughs, and the like. Therapists also listen with what Reik long ago called "the third ear" and use their own reactions as clues to what could be going on with the client. Above all, therapists are fallible problem solvers, and their positive movement with clients is rarely as unidirectional as might appear from chapters such as this one.

On the basis of prominence, empirical support, and nonoverlap with other chapters in this volume, we selected for presentation three systems of cognitive behavior therapy (CBT): Rational-Emotive Therapy (RET; Ellis, 1962), Cognitive Therapy (CT; Beck, 1964), and Problem Solving Therapy (PST; D'Zurilla &

Goldfried, 1971). With respect to each system, we discuss first its theory of psychopathology; that is, according to this approach how does cognition contribute to initiating or maintaining psychological distress? Next, we provide an overview of treatment procedures, a summary of the empirical status of both the psychopathology theory and the therapy, and a discussion of conceptual issues especially relevant to that system of therapy. In a final section we discuss some practical and conceptual issues facing CBT as a whole.

Our focus is on individual treatment of adult outpatients with primary nonpsychotic DSM-III-R Axis I syndromes (American Psychiatric Association, 1987). Excluded are CBT methods for group therapy (e.g., Covi, Roth, & Lipman, 1982) or for the treatment of children (e.g., Braswell & Kendall, 1987), couples (e.g., Epstein & Baucom, 1989), inpatients (e.g., Miller, Norman, Keitner, Bishop, & Dow, 1989), or personality disorders (e.g., Freeman & Leaf, 1989).

RATIONAL-EMOTIVE THERAPY
Theory of Psychopathology

The essence of RET's "ABC" theory of psychopathology is that activating events (A) do not directly cause emotional or behavioral consequences (C). Instead, beliefs (B) about these events are the most important causes of feelings and actions. In particular, irrational beliefs (IBs) lead to dysfunctional overt behaviors and emotional responses. Beliefs are considered irrational if they are unlikely to find empirical support in a person's environment and if they do not promote survival and enjoyment. Specific IBs number in the hundreds (Ellis, 1976), but all are considered derivations of a few basic ones (Ellis & Bernard, 1985): (a) "I must do extremely well and win approval, or else I rate as a rotten person." (b) "Others must treat me considerately and kindly in precisely the way I want them to treat me; if they don't, society and the universe should severely blame, damn, and punish them for their inconsiderateness." (c) "Conditions under which I live must be arranged so that I get practically all that I want comfortably, quickly, and easily, and get virtually nothing that I don't want."

Some common forms of irrational thinking (Walen, DiGiuseppe, & Wessler, 1980) which transcend specific content include:

1. *awfulizing:* concluding that an inconvenient situation is awful and unmanageable;
2. *musturbating:* believing that some unfortunate situation should not or must not exist, or that a highly desired situation must exist. This style of thinking is considered harmful in that it can lead to secondary emotional problems. For instance, one might feel depressed by the loss of an important relationship (primary problem) but then add on anger (in this instance a secondary problem) by believing that this negative situation *must* not exist, that the person should not have left; and

3. *evaluations of human worth:* global judgments of the overall worth of a person, typically oneself. These global ratings of worth are viewed as counterproductive (Ellis, 1977) because they engender self-criticism when one performs poorly; anxiety over possible future self-criticism even when one performs well. Moreover, such ratings are seen as illogical because there is no objective unidimensional scale for measuring human worth. RET thus differs with the widespread notion that psychological health is associated with high self-esteem. Instead, "self-esteeming" per se is considered unhealthy, whereas self-acceptance (including evaluating one's specific behaviors but not overall worth) is healthy (Boyd & Grieger, 1986).

Therapeutic Procedures

RET tends to be highly active and directive, with the therapist doing a large share of the talking during early sessions (Ellis, 1984). Its essential goals are to (a) persuade the client that a rational-emotive analysis of problems is useful, (b) identify the most important irrational beliefs underlying the presenting complaint, (c) show the client how to dispute these IBs, and (d) generalize this learning to the point that the client can serve as his or her own RET therapist in the future, disputing IBs relating to new problems.

It is important to clarify early what the client can expect, for the process of RET conflicts with some common expectations for psychotherapy (e.g., that one will express feelings for much of the session, that childhood events will be reviewed in detail to understand the causes of current problems).

To begin teaching the model, the therapist needs a brief working description of A (the most pressing event associated with distress) as perceived by the client. Next, one determines Cs, the emotional and behavioral difficulties that the client sees as caused by the A. Not all negative emotions are deemed in need of modification. RET acknowledges that negative emotions can be appropriate (e.g., transient sadness after a loss). They might even be adaptive in that they motivate corrective action to solve practical problems. Moreover, Cs themselves are not disputed. They are considered natural outcomes of the clients' irrational beliefs, which are the appropriate therapeutic targets. Indeed, if a client sounds especially self-critical *about* Cs, being ashamed of overreacting emotionally for instance, a priority would be to dispute the IBs mediating this secondary problem (perhaps, "I should not become highly anxious").

The next phase of RET involves determining the beliefs lying between the A and the Cs. This task is less straightforward than it might appear. Clients sometimes respond to questions about beliefs with statements about emotions ("I was thinking that I was upset"). To elicit thoughts rather than emotions, Walen et al. (1980) suggest such questions as "What were you telling yourself when . . .?" and "Were you aware of any thoughts in your head when . . .?"

First responses often consist of rational beliefs. For instance, if a man were upset about losing a satisfying job he had held for several years, he might describe his belief about it as, "I was telling myself that it would probably be difficult to find another job as good as that one." According to RET, though, this belief is rational and would lead to moderate disappointment, not the kind of emotional state that has brought him into therapy. To determine beliefs mediating more extreme and debilitating emotions, it is necessary to probe further and see if he actually believed something more like, "It's unlikely that I'll get as good a job as I had before, and that's awful. I'm a total jerk for having lost it. I can't stand it."

Once the apparently critical IBs have been identified, the core of RET, disputation, begins. Walen et al. (1980) outlined a sequence of disputation beginning with attempting to persuade the client of the advantages of substituting rational for irrational beliefs. Negative consequences of adhering to IBs are usually readily accessible, not the least of which is the emotional distress that has brought the client to therapy. Substitute rational beliefs are suggested, and the client is invited to imagine how she or he might feel if these were truly believed.

Once there is agreement that learning rational thinking would be helpful, the therapist begins to dispute specific IBs. Often this begins with questioning the evidence in support of the beliefs. As many IBs (e.g., I must do extremely well, or I rate as a rotten person) do not express truth claims, the question "What is the evidence that . . . ?" is often rhetorical (Becker & Rosenfeld, 1976, found that 16% of Ellis's statements in initial psychotherapy sessions, as coded from transcripts, were rhetorical questions. Such questions can seem strange to some clients, but they are useful in that they may disrupt habitual thinking styles and provide "distance" from upsetting thoughts. It might become clear, for instance, that the client usually believes IBs just because they often occur, or because emotional reactions suggest them (e.g., "I'm not standing it, so I can't stand it"). The very question "What's the evidence?" introduces the idea of questioning one's own beliefs, an uncommon practice among nontherapy participants. (If handled poorly, this line of questioning can alienate clients. The artistry involved in adapting one's style to particular clients (or at least of learning to recognize and to refer elsewhere types of clients with whom one does not work effectively) is an important nontechnological factor in cognitive change methods.)

If there *is* evidence that the client's situation is especially difficult, and a negative appraisal is warranted, it is still possible to "decatastrophize" the situation by examining worst-case scenarios. That is, one can explore the question "What is the worst that could happen, and how catastrophic would that really be?"

If the client's mood is improved by this type of questioning, it is important to assess her or his conclusion about IBs and the utility of RET disputation. Ideally, the conclusion would be that beliefs might contribute to emotional problems and that these beliefs are questionable and perhaps modifiable. If instead the client inferred that "I'm irrational, and my therapist belittled me," then this thought itself would become a therapeutic focus.

Regardless of how well in-session disputation proceeds, it is unlikely to suffice for lasting belief change. IBs are often longstanding, subjectively convincing, and in some cases culturally reinforced. Indeed, Ellis (1976) posits that irrational thinking could be a universal, biologically based tendency. Given the apparent tenacity of IBs, then, much effort by both client and therapist is likely to be necessary in order to generalize and maintain initial cognitive shifts. Ellis has therefore promoted a highly forceful, confrontative therapeutic style, noting as a common error that "therapists are too namby-pamby, or unforceful in encouraging RET clients to surrender their irrational thinking" (Ellis, 1983, p. 168).

Homework assignments between sessions are frequently used in RET to help clients assimilate new learning. These might include reading popular works on RET (e.g., Ellis & Harper, 1975), listening to audiotapes of sessions, and self-monitoring attempts to use disputation in vivo. RET also utilizes behavioral assignments, often beginning by asking clients to experiment with new behaviors in the very situations they find *most* distressing. Because Ellis (1986) contends that more gradual approaches (e.g., systematic desensitization; Wolpe, 1958) inadvertently reinforce the belief that one cannot tolerate much discomfort, RET advocates taking greater risks. "Shame-attacking" exercises, for example, ask socially inhibited clients to do something outrageous in public to learn that no catastrophic consequences ensue.

It is important in RET to balance this principle of forceful intervention with the goal of not making rationality yet another "must" in the client's life. A client who applies perfectionistic standards to the learning of RET skills ought to be assisted in disputing these beliefs. Such standards are both counterproductive, leading to discouragement about the rate of therapeutic progress, and unrealistic, for clients' improvement is often nonlinear.

Procedural Variant: Systematic Rational Restructuring

As noted earlier, RET eschews excessive therapist warmth and often entails exerting considerable pressure on clients to acknowledge their irrational thinking. This style could induce reactance from many clients (Goldfried & Davison, 1976), possibly leading them to drop out of treatment (see Young's comments in Ellis, Young, & Lockwood, 1987). Systematic rational restructuring (SRR; Goldfried, Decenteceo, & Weinberg, 1974) offers an alternative model for implementation of rational-emotive principles, featuring a less confrontative style.

SRR requires first creating a hierarchy of upsetting situations (analogous to the technique employed in systematic desensitization; see chapter 5, this volume). Instead of muscle relaxation to reduce emotional arousal while imagining the scene, SRR teaches the use of rational self-statements. Unlike in RET, it is assumed that rational restructuring works best by beginning with easy situations and progressing gradually to the situations about which the client finds it most difficult to think rationally.

Rational self-statements developed in trying to cope with a scene from the hierarchy are evaluated both in terms of accuracy of perceptions (of A, the activating event) and appropriateness of inferences based on that perception (derivatives of B). For example, consider a client who reacts with extreme anxiety if her husband speaks to her in a grouchy manner. SRR (as in Beck's cognitive therapy, described later) would encourage considering alternative explanations (e.g., he might not be specifically angry at her, but rather preoccupied with something having little to do with her). By considering that a less ominous perception of A might be plausible, the client could be able to reduce her anxiety. However, as in RET, one can go beyond this point and assume the worst, that is, that her husband in fact is quite angry at her. The goal then would be to decatastrophize this situation by changing B, the client's beliefs about A (maybe an overly demanding standard about the acceptability of marital conflict).

Empirical Status

Many studies have found positive correlations between irrational beliefs and negative affects such as anxiety (e.g., Deffenbacher, Zwemer, Whisman, Hill, & Sloan, 1986) and depression (e.g., Vestre, 1984) (for a review, see Smith & Allred, 1986). However, these findings provide only limited support for rational-emotive theory because the construct validity of the IB measures used in most studies is doubtful. Convergent and discriminant validity studies suggest that the most commonly used IB scales could as easily be said to measure negative affectivity (Watson & Clark, 1984) or trait anxiety as IBs (Smith, 1989). To be sure, even if research never strongly supported RET psychopathology postulates, the therapy could be useful. That is, clients might benefit from acting *as if* IBs are part of the problem.

A recent review of treatment outcome studies (Haaga & Davison, 1989a) concluded that SRR has shown its best results in the treatment of test anxiety and social anxiety, perhaps exceeding the effectiveness of imaginal exposure to feared stimuli alone (e.g., Goldfried, Linehan, & Smith, 1978). SRR also improves assertiveness, though no more so than standard behavioral skill training programs (e.g., Linehan, Goldfried, & Goldfried, 1979). SRR appears less useful than in vivo exposure treatments for simple phobias (e.g., Biran & Wilson, 1981) and in general seems to have a greater effect on self-report than on behavioral or psychophysiological indices of anxiety.

Promising results suggest a role for RET in the treatment of depression (e.g., McKnight, Nelson, Hayes, & Jarrett, 1984), anger (e.g., Conoley, Conoley, McConnell, & Kimzey, 1983), and especially social phobia. For example, RET-based rational restructuring significantly enhanced the effects of behavioral exposure for social phobics; these effects were correlated, as expected, with reductions in fear of negative evaluation by other people (Mattick, Peters, & Clarke, 1989).

On the other hand, RET seems inferior to exposure treatment for agoraphobia (e.g., Emmelkamp, Brilman, Kuiper, & Mersch, 1986) and does not seem to add to the effectiveness of standard behavioral treatments for unassertiveness (e.g., Hammen, Jacobs, Mayol, & Cochran, 1980).

In a number of other areas, methodological difficulties preclude drawing strong conclusions about the effects of RET or SRR. Moreover, outcome research has unfortunately contributed little to showing *how* RET works when it works. Some of RET's most distinctive postulates about clinical change (e.g., that RET improves long-term outcome by disrupting self-criticism about having symptoms; that a forceful style is especially useful in dislodging irrational beliefs) remain untested (Haaga & Davison, 1989b). Besides the difficulties noted earlier in measuring IBs, some problems in conducting definitive research on RET stem from the difficulty of operationally defining the treatment. Most outcome researchers restrict RET to the procedures we have described, emphasizing especially rational disputation. Ellis (1980), on the other hand, calls such procedures "preferential" (or "specialized"; Dryden & Ellis, 1988) RET, while subsuming the whole of cognitive behavior therapy within "general" RET.

In other words, Ellis contends that teaching patients forcefully to dispute their own IBs is the first, preferred goal of RET. However, if this is not successful, then more palliative approaches such as the use of coping self-statements, relaxation training, and the like would be initiated, and this would still be considered RET. The research goal of specifying and distinguishing treatments so as to study their unique effects may therefore not do justice to the full flexibility of RET, as suggested by Ellis's (1989) contention that "in virtually no instance do the studies that Haaga and Davison . . . [review] . . . utilize this kind of 'real' RET" (p. 230). On the other hand, adequately testing "real" or "general" RET might have to await further theoretical developments designed to specify more clearly the conditions under which one would select one or another of the vast array of techniques Ellis views as RET.

Conceptual Issues Specific to RET

Conceptual definition of the central RET construct, "rationality," is difficult (Cohen, 1981; Haaga & Davison, 1989b). Definitions based on the consequences of beliefs (e.g., "rational thoughts are . . . thoughts that help people live longer and happier"; Ellis & Bernard, 1986, p. 7) are circular. Definitions based on the use of objective, rigorous information processing would eliminate much of the thinking of nondistressed people (Taylor & Brown, 1988). Acknowledging these difficulties, Ellis and Dryden (1987) concluded that "rationality is not defined in any absolute sense" (p. 4). (Since the completion of this chapter, Rorer [1989a; 1989b] has outlined the philosophical basis and empirical implications of a reformulation of RET theory, which addresses problems in prior definitions of rationality. He hypothesized two categories of IBs: "(1) grandiose beliefs that the world or someone or something in it should be different than it, she, or he is, because one wants it to be, and (2) beliefs that evaluations are factual rather than definitional" [Rorer, 1989a, p. 484].)

The issue of therapeutic style also remains critical in RET. RET style has long been noted as highly forceful, which we saw earlier was part of the motivation for the development of SRR as an alternative system of treatment. Garfield's (1989) analysis, however, raised the possibility that the confrontative style advocated in RET is balanced by other, less-articulated tactics to communicate that the RET therapist is engaged, cares about helping, believes that the client can make significant progress, and truly understands what is wrong.

Forcefulness is often intertwined with notions about the proper timing of disputations and the role of assessment in RET, but this connection may be unnecessary. There is no intrinsic link between using dramatic, vivid language, on one hand, and jumping in quickly with presumptions about what clients' IBs must be, whether or not they are aware of them. Bernard (1981) argued that private thoughts, difficult to verbalize during initial ABC assessments, could be highly influential. They are less likely to come to light if RET practitioners begin disputation too quickly. This is a delicate issue, calling for tradeoffs between (a) socializing the client into the treatment model and rationalizing it is plausible and effective, and (b) not intervening before one has sufficiently elaborated the client's phenomenology so as to formulate an adequate plan for the case.

To be sure, it remains an open empirical question whether case formulations improve treatment efficacy (Nelson, 1988), and if so whether they need to be validated (or merely hypothesized) before targeted interventions proceed (Turkat, 1988).

Besides these possible limitations, RET shows distinct conceptual strengths. First, it might be especially adept at inducing in clients the dialectical process of (a) working hard on attempts to change while (b) accepting current reality (Linehan, 1987). RET shares with humanistic therapies an emphasis on accepting oneself as a fallible human being and taking responsibility for one's life. On the other hand, RET shares with behavioral therapies an active, directive mode of intervention designed to facilitate rapid movement in therapy. Contrast, for example, systematic desensitization, which strongly emphasizes the need for change and may underplay acceptance skills, or client-centered therapy, which prioritizes acceptance and may underplay instigation of change.

Second, the RET model of psychological health, while partly a claim about what exists (e.g., nondistressed people tend to show rational beliefs and take risks), is also prescriptive (according to RET, it would be *preferable* if more people were long-range hedonists, primarily individualistic, and ethically relativistic—foregoing irrational demands that other people behave in a particular fashion). One can take issue with these values and can prefer communitarian values to RET's individualism (e.g., Wachtel, 1983). Still, it is clearly to Ellis's credit that RET's values are explicit, more so than in most other therapies (Woolfolk & Sass, 1989).

COGNITIVE THERAPY

We turn now to Beck's (1964) cognitive therapy (CT). As will become obvious, the name *cognitive therapy* is somewhat misleading, as behavioral techniques figure prominently, but we will retain consistency with the literature by calling the treatment CT. CT has been applied to numerous psychological disorders (Freeman, Simon, Beutler, & Arkowitz, 1989); we will illustrate it by considering in detail CT for major depression (its original application), adding briefer accounts of CT for panic disorder and bulimia nervosa.

Depression

Theory of Psychopathology

Beck's model of depression acknowledges the importance of biological, emotional, and behavioral features (e.g., Beck, 1987) but primarily emphasizes aberrant cognitive factors associated with depression. These can be described at several levels: cognitive events, cognitive processes, and cognitive structures (Marzillier, 1980; see Table 7.1).

Cognitive events are "thoughts and images occurring in the stream of consciousness" (Marzillier, 1980, p. 252). The cognitive events emphasized in CT are negative "automatic thoughts" (ATs). They are considered "automatic" because they appear to come on involuntarily and are not easily dismissed by the client. Beck sees the ATs of depressed people as centering on themes of loss. Descriptively they reveal a "cognitive triad" (Self, Environment, Future). Depressed people have negative views of themselves, believing that they are losers who lack the attributes necessary to attain contentment. They see the environment as presenting insurmountable obstacles preventing them from gaining satisfaction. Finally, they see the future as holding little hope of improvement in their situations.

Cognitive processes "transform and process environmental stimuli" (Marzillier, 1980, p. 252) and include attention, abstraction, and encoding of information. CT holds that cognitive processes in depression are biased, which could account for the extreme negativity shown by depressed people (e.g., thinking that things will *never* get better), even when more positive constructions would also be plausible.

Table 7.1. A Taxonomy of Cognitions Applied to Cognitive Therapy

MARZILLIER (1980) SCHEME	CORRESPONDING BECKIAN CATEGORY	EXAMPLE
1. Cognitive event	Automatic thought	"I'm a lousy parent. How terrible!"
2. Cognitive process	Biased information processing	Selective abstraction; for example, "I lost my temper yesterday and yelled at my kids. On the basis of this one incident, I conclude I am no good as a parent."
3. Cognitive structure	Dysfunctional beliefs	"I must always be competent in every area of life."

These cognitive biases have often been labeled *distortions* (e.g., Beck, 1976), but *bias* appears to be a more appropriate term. *Bias* refers to "a tendency to make judgments in a systematic and consistent manner . . . (e.g., a tendency to draw negative conclusions about oneself . . .)" (Alloy & Abramson, 1988, p. 227), whereas a distortion is a "judgment or conclusion that disagrees or is inconsistent with some commonly accepted measure of objective reality" (Alloy & Abramson, 1988, p. 226). The concept of bias is more broadly applicable to the cognitions of interest in CT, for in many relevant situations (e.g., evaluating a client's outlook on the future) there is no accepted measure of objective reality to which the cognition can be compared.

Different types of cognitive bias have been identified, including the following:

1. *Selective abstraction:* Forming conclusions based on an isolated detail of an event, ignoring other evidence. For instance, someone might give a largely successful party but then conclude on the basis of one apparently bored guest that it was a failure.
2. *Overgeneralization:* Holding extreme ideas based on particular events and applying them to dissimilar settings. A student might have difficulty in math and then conclude that he or she will do very poorly in all courses.
3. *Dichotomous thinking:* Thinking in all-or-none terms, categorizing experiences and people only in one of two extremes, with no middle ground. For example, someone might think of herself as only lovable and good, or totally unlovable and bad, vacillating between these extremes based on recent feedback.

Finally, *cognitive structures* are general, stable cognitive characteristics, the principles governing interpretation of events. CT posits the existence of stable, negative beliefs (or "schemas") that render people vulnerable to becoming depressed (Kovacs & Beck, 1978).

The term *schema* has been used in multiple ways in CT theory and research (Haaga, Dyck, & Ernst, 1990; Segal, 1988). Beck uses it to describe tacit beliefs or attitudes, exemplifying the "stored beliefs" sense of cognitive structure (Ingram & Kendall, 1986). Other clinical researchers define *schema* as a cognitive structure, such as an interconnected network of elements in memory (e.g., Segal, Hood, Shaw, & Higgins, 1988). This usage reflects the "cognitive architecture" sense of cognitive structure (Ingram & Kendall, 1986) and is more consistent with the meaning of *schema* in cognitive and social/personality psychology. Therefore, to avoid confusion we refer to the cognitive vulnerability to depression in CT theory as dysfunctional "beliefs" rather than "schemas."

Under favorable conditions, these dysfunctional beliefs remain latent. If the beliefs are activated by negative events, though, biased processing and negative automatic thoughts will follow, along with sadness, loss of energy, and other depressive symptoms.

The dysfunctional (tacit) belief construct is similar to the RET notion of irrational beliefs. These beliefs are probably learned early in life and can be thought of as rules for making sense of one's environment. An example would be, "In order to be happy, I have to be successful in whatever I undertake" (Beck, Rush, Shaw, & Emery, 1979, p. 246). A significant failure experience could activate this belief and initiate a depressive episode for this person, whereas the same experience might not be as depressing for someone lacking the same cognitive vulnerability.

Therapeutic Procedure

CT for depression is described as a 15–25 session program, though in practice (as with each of the therapies depicted in this chapter) the length of treatment can vary considerably depending on client and therapist goals and styles. Often depressed clients are seen twice a week for the first month or so and then weekly.

Session structure in CT is distinctive in several ways. For example, CT therapists try to obtain feedback from the client at regular intervals about his or her conclusions from the discussion (checking on whether the point is getting across) as well as any reactions to the therapist or the therapy. This practice illustrates CT's emphasis on *collaboration* between therapist and client and also models the empiricist habit of seeking evidence (i.e., the therapist does not *assume* what the client's reaction is but rather investigates the issue).

Moreover, CT advocates setting an agenda of topics for each session in the first few minutes. Although this might suggest a businesslike, somewhat sterile interaction with the client (Meagher, 1982), it can be rationalized as an attempt to demonstrate an important skill (focusing and setting priorities) and as a way to make maximal use of the client's time, which is of course money. Agenda setting also provides a concrete framework in which to act out a gradual shift of responsibility for therapy from clinician to client. In early sessions the therapist might state several points to be discussed in the session and ask if the client has anything to add. Over time one would switch by degrees to a point at which the client is entirely responsible for the agenda.

For agenda setting, the suggestions of Kanfer and Schefft (1987) about wording therapist statements to promote an appropriate set are useful (their "self-management therapy" is quite similar to CT in this respect). "The clinician does not begin sessions by using such common and familiar phrases as 'How are things going?' or 'How are you feeling?' These phrases tend to elicit well-learned, repetitive and stereotypic responses" (Kanfer & Schefft, 1987, p. 15). More apt would be something like "What would you like to focus on today?" Analogous questions (e.g., "What did you find most important in what we covered today?") are useful for eliciting summaries.

In terms of content, it is valuable in the first interview to address a client's expectations for therapy. For example, some depressed clients mistakenly (according to CT) believe that they must first feel better before they can become active. Indeed, most lay people as well as health professionals probably believe this, sometimes invoking the notion that it is important always to act in a manner that is true to one's feelings. However, the typical sequence of techniques in CT requires acting contrary to this assumption by becoming active right away.

The initial interview also affords an opportunity to begin teaching the CT rationale for depression and its treatment. Therapy can be presented as an experiment with an approach that works for many people but might not prove optimal for this one (Piasecki & Hollon, 1987). This framing may reduce the perceived demand for long-term commitment while still conveying optimism and an attitude of willingness to experiment.

Some CT practitioners begin socialization before the first session by asking clients to read introductory materials such as Burns (1980) or Beck and Greenberg (1974). This procedure has not been experimentally evaluated in CT but would seem useful based on other studies of pretherapy role induction procedures (e.g., Hoehn–Saric et al., 1964).

The client's own cognitions are often useful in teaching the model. If, say, a client felt discouraged before coming to the first session, one might ask what thoughts accompanied this feeling. This material could help in illustrating the impact of thoughts on feelings, the negativistic thoughts typical of depression, and the different feelings that might have emerged given other thoughts about the same event (e.g., "I'm looking forward to getting help").

Behavioral techniques. Beck et al. (1979) suggested that behavioral techniques are especially important early in therapy with depressed clients. The depressive cycle of (a) reduced activity level, (b) sense of personal incompetence, (c) hopelessness, (d) increasing immobility, (e) lack of reinforcement, and (f) lower mood must be disrupted in order to show the client that therapy can work.

The use of behavioral techniques in CT differs somewhat, though, from their use in an orthodox behavioral treatment (e.g., Lewinsohn, 1974). Increased activity with potential for positive reinforcement is not considered an end in itself, but rather a means toward achieving a cognitive shift. The results of behavioral interventions constitute evidence indicating that pessimism might have contributed to the client's decreased activity level and that a more optimistic viewpoint might be warranted.

It is not taken for granted, though, that cognitive change will follow behavioral change. Therapists need to assess how clients interpret changes and to emphasize exactly how results of behavioral experiments contrast with their predictions. Such predictions should be recorded in advance, so that they cannot be "adjusted" later, as in post hoc elevation of the standard for a success. Because they are intended as data-gathering exercises, it is best if behavioral assignments are specifically devised to yield data relevant to the client's cognitions. This is distinct from a practice of prescribing generic pleasant events regardless of the client. Common behavioral procedures in CT include:

1. *Activity scheduling:* Particularly with extremely inactive depressed clients, the therapist helps draw up a detailed, even hour-by-hour, plan of what the client will do, starting with easy tasks (e.g., get out of bed, make a simple breakfast, read the newspaper, return a phone call, go to a movie). This sort of procedure should be presented as a "no-lose" diagnostic study of the effects of activity level on mood. If engaging in activities improves mood, fine. If not, then that is useful feedback on the activities. There might have been too few "wants" and too many "should" activities on the list (Marlatt, 1985). Or perhaps the client carried out activities normally considered pleasant but discounted them as unimportant achievements, or felt guilty about engaging in them at the expense of other obligations. These interfering cognitions would become grist for the mill in subsequent sessions.

2. *Mastery and pleasure tasks:* As noted, depressed clients can sometimes do a lot but derive neither enjoyment nor a sense of competence from their actions. They might be ruminating on negative thoughts while performing tasks ("I'm not doing as well as I should"), or they might believe they do not deserve to do things for the sake of their own enjoyment. Such clients need assistance in seeing that their strategy is self-defeating, that engaging in pleasant, mood-elevating events would enhance their capacity for all activities, including the ones to which they believe they "should" devote themselves.

   Besides monitoring activities, the client is encouraged to self-monitor (e.g., on 0–15 scale) the degree of pleasure and sense of mastery or competence associated with each. Use of a continuous rating scale is intended to instill the habit of recognizing partial successes (or "small wins;" Weick, 1984) as opposed to dichotomizing experiences as either "success" or "failure."

   Monitoring the results of these exercises should counteract selective abstraction. If asked to summarize over a few days or a week, a depressed person might conclude, if something bad happened that morning, that no progress had occurred since the previous therapy session. A detailed record might reveal, however, at least a few experiences of pleasure or mastery. Piasecki and Hollon (1987) suggest making this emphasis explicit. They present self-monitoring assignments with the rationale that one does not want to rely on memory, given that depression can influence memory processes.

3. *Task assignments:* This category refers to goal-oriented activities. Consider a client who was dysphoric because he believed he was stuck in a dissatisfying job. He could be encouraged to break down the goal of achieving job satisfaction into manageable chunks, beginning with easier assignments (call for an appointment with a career counselor, update resume). If the client completes the assignment, the therapist will want to call attention to this success and its implications. Success should be explicitly credited to the client's skill and effort, thus helping to sell the client the idea that it is possible to carry on CT on a self-directed basis in the future. Finally, follow-up assignments are planned to build on initial successes.

It is sometimes useful to employ imagery rehearsal in advance of task assignments. The client goes through the task in imagination, trying to foresee any obstacles that might prevent its completion. Therapist and client can together devise ways around each barrier. Then the client imagines going through the assignment successfully, including coping with all obstacles.

In this early, largely behavioral, phase of CT much of the effort and enthusiasm may need to come from the therapist. CT is often contrasted with other approaches by virtue of its collaborative nature, but it would be unrealistic to expect to be met halfway by a very depressed client in the first weeks of treatment on the issue of the value and meaning of behavioral assignments.

Cognitive techniques. The key therapeutic goals of the cognitive phase of CT for depression are to identify maladaptive automatic thoughts, evaluate and (usually) modify these thoughts, uncover dysfunctional beliefs, and modify beliefs.

Identifying negative automatic thoughts. The thoughts targeted in CT are "ideation that interferes with the ability to cope with life experiences, unnecessarily disrupts internal harmony, and produces inappropriate or excessive emotional reactions that are painful" (Beck, 1976, p. 235). Beck argues that the therapist's notion of which thoughts are maladaptive should not be imposed on the client, but rather discovered in collaboration with the client. Still, the identification of a thought as maladaptive is highly subjective, and clients are often easily influenced on this point. Clinician judgment in this regard may be influenced by factors (e.g., whether the client is seen individually or in couples therapy) that are, strictly speaking, irrelevant. This is not to derogate the *ideal* of collaborating with the client in planning cognitive interventions, only to highlight the difficulty of realizing this ideal, for therapists cannot help but influence their clients (Davison, 1976; London, 1986).

The first technical goal in identifying maladaptive cognitions is to train the client to self-monitor negative automatic thoughts (ATs). These can be defined as verbal thoughts or images that seem to come without effort and are associated with feeling upset. ATs in principle are easily brought into awareness if the client is encouraged to tune into them. A pragmatic definition some clients find useful is that ATs are whatever they would answer to the question, "What is going through your mind right now?"

Piasecki and Hollon (1987) suggested several ways to facilitate assessment of ATs: (a) Ask for them when there is an abrupt mood shift in the session; (b) use evocative role-plays of difficult situations from the client's life; (c) engage in a "think-aloud" process to demonstrate one's own ATs; and (d) do not insist that the thought must have *preceded* an emotional reaction, though the theory suggests that it does.

Once the client understands ATs, a useful homework assignment is to record (e.g., on a Daily Record of Dysfunctional Thoughts (DRDT); Beck et al., 1979) an activating event, the accompanying emotion (rated on 0–100 scale of intensity, again fostering the habit of thinking in continua rather than dichotomies), and the ATs. These thoughts should be recorded as soon as possible. A common difficulty is the sometimes artificial differentiation between thoughts and emotions (e.g., "I can't stand it" vs. "I'm so upset!"). They need to be differentiated, though, in order to proceed with questioning the thoughts (as in RET, the fact that a client was, say, angry is not questioned). Finally, the client rates degree of belief in the AT on a scale of 0 to 100%. This assessment itself serves as a possible intervention (cf. Davison, 1969) by providing the client with a more sanguine conception of problems, such as, "My emotions seem to be related to my thoughts, maybe even caused by them. Since I can control my thoughts a lot of the time, maybe I can gain some control over my emotions." Most people have not habitually rated the *degree* of belief in their own thoughts nor viewed them as hypotheses to be evaluated.

Evaluating and modifying automatic thoughts. In-session reviews of self-monitored ATs are used to teach several techniques for evaluating them and thereby uncovering cognitive biases.

1. *What's the evidence?* The first line of questioning usually concerns the evidence for and against a thought. For example, suppose the situation were that one was alone on the weekend, and the AT associated with feeling sad about it was "Nobody ever wants to be with me." Unlike in RET, a CT therapist would not immediately challenge the belief underlying this thought (e.g., "I must be approved of by others"). To do so would be to forego an opportunity to modify a possibly biased perception of the activating event or stressor. First, evidence would be elicited. How have the last 10 people you invited out responded? In the last year, has anybody ever invited you to lunch?

   A careful review of evidence pro and con sometimes decreases the degree of belief in a negative thought. However, it is also common for the depressed person to be able to cite substantial evidence for the negative thought. Research on the social relationships and skills of depressed people confirms that at times their behavior is aversive and evokes negative reactions from others (Coyne, 1976; Krantz, 1985). Moreover, depressed individuals can be expected to exaggerate the significance of the evidence favoring negative views. Depression is associated with easier access to memories congruent with a depressed mood (Blaney, 1986), and people form predictions mainly on the basis of easily accessed past events (Kahneman, Slovic, & Tversky, 1982), not a balanced consideration of evidence.

2. *Is there any other way to look at it?* Supposing the evidence appears sound, a second line of questioning explores alternative conceptualizations of the data. In other words, is there any other interpretation that is at least as plausible as the one endorsed by the client? The techniques of reattribution therapy (Forster-ling, 1980, 1988) can be brought to bear in generating possible benign explanations for the event. In particular, explanations that suggest that change

It is more realistic to expect to budge old entrenched beliefs, then gradually replace them, with some setbacks, rather than to expect the client to be overcome suddenly with relief at the truth of the rational response.

3. Try it on for size (cf. Davison, in Brady et al., 1980): It is not necessary that the client consider the rational response more plausible than the AT. It is enough that she or he be willing to consider it, to try it on for size, to retain an open mind and experiment with this new perspective in daily life and assess its utility. (Abelson's [1986] theory of beliefs and belief change is consistent with this metaphor of the would-be cognition changer as a salesperson. In his view, the ultimate goal is for the target of persuasion to "possess" rather than merely "borrow" a belief. Many CT operations are consistent with Abelson's hypotheses about how best to induce possession [e.g., becoming aware of the value of a belief, elaborating and explaining the belief, and suffering for it—therapy is not easy for the client, either].)

A second difficulty in rational responding is that some clients develop the habit of responding to ATs perfunctorily (Hollon & Beck, 1979), often by simply negating them ("It's not true") or practicing positive (wishful) thinking (e.g., "Somebody will call next weekend"). The problem with these responses is that they tend not to promote constructive action, do not reinforce CT skills, and are unlikely to be convincing for long to anyone who thought the AT in the first place. They are like positive mood-induction statements (e.g., Velten, 1968), which have only a brief mood-elevating effect (Clark, 1983), presumably because they are not based on any new experience or reevaluation of prior experience and therefore are not strongly believed (Coyne, 1982).

A legal metaphor is sometimes useful in explaining this point to clients. If a lawyer presented an interpretation (the AT) of the facts of a case (the activating event), and the opposing lawyer (rational responder) offered as a rebuttal "That is not true," impartial jurors would be unlikely to find the rebuttal persuasive. In the same vein, it is unrealistic for the client to expect to convince herself or himself with such an "argument."

Third, a slight variation on the perfunctory rational responder is the client who uses self-directed thought-stopping ("Don't think that!"). For such clients, reference can be made to the paradoxical (enhancing) effects of thought suppression (Wegner, Schneider, Carter, & White, 1987), the typically low clinical efficacy of thought stopping (Mahoney & Arnkoff, 1978), and (in all likelihood) the limited success with which they have used this technique in the past.

Finally, some self-critical clients use the rational response essentially to insult themselves ("That's ridiculous"; "That's stupid"). These responses seem not only useless (for the same reasons as for negation statements) but perhaps even counterproductive. They create "secondary problems" (see RET section)—feeling bad about thinking wrongly and therefore feeling even worse. One way to explain the dysutility of such responses is to invoke Mahoney and Gabriel's (1987) concept of a "relationship" or "interaction" with *oneself* as an important factor in personal development. The insulting rational response interferes with fostering a positive, constructive relationship with oneself.

Identifying tacit beliefs. Increases in behavioral activity and modification of specific negative ATs do not guarantee lasting improvement, according to CT theory. It is also necessary to alter the core dysfunctional beliefs underlying negative ATs. Assessment of beliefs can be difficult. Although some psychometric measures are available (e.g., the Dysfunctional Attitude Scale; Weissman & Beck, 1978), the main tool for identifying core beliefs is the clinician's inference (Safran, Vallis, Segal, & Shaw, 1986).

One can start by looking for common themes in ATs. For example, if a client reported ATs such as "She is angry with me", "I should not have offended him", and "Wonder what they'll think of me?", one could hypothesize a theme of overconcern with social evaluation, possibly indicating a belief such as "I must please everyone." The data (ATs) do not compel this interpretation, nor this the client necessarily aware of harboring this belief. It would be presented to the client as a hypothesis, not a fact to which they will be pressured to agree. Indeed, checking out hypotheses about beliefs may reveal idiosyncratic meanings; the same negative thought will not mean the same to everyone (Huber & Altmaier, 1983).

This illustrates a clear difference in preferred therapeutic style between CT and RET. Beck et al. (1979) advocate that therapists not be overly didactic and forceful. Extensive use of Socratic questioning, rather than lectures, is believed to model for clients a questioning, nondogmatic approach to life.

It is possible to garner theoretical and analogue empirical support for one or another of these styles. Cognitive therapists cite research indicating that enduring attitude change accompanied by behavior change consistent with the new attitudes requires extensive processing of relevant evidence by the subject (e.g., the "central route" to persuasion in the Elaboration Likelihood Model; Petty & Cacioppo, 1986). Ellis, by contrast, postulates a need for forceful intervention to overcome biological predispositions to irrationality. Evidence on such microissues of style is too weak, though, to account for strongly held opinions. It seems likely that therapist personality also affects the selection of a fitting style for interventions (Barlow, Hayes, & Nelson, 1984).

Other ways of generating hypotheses about basic beliefs, culled from Beck et al. (1979), Piasecki and Hollon (1987), and Safran et al. (1986), include:

1. *Methods focusing on the content of cognitions:*
   (a) Tie ATs to underlying beliefs via the "downward arrow" technique (Burns, 1980), which consists of asking recursively "What would be upsetting to you about that?" with respect to each thought in turn until a seemingly critical belief has been reached.
   (b) Attend to global words the client uses. If many people or actions are labelled "failures," for instance, tacit beliefs might concern achievement more than affiliative themes.

(c) Inquire about the client's explanations of negative ATs, occasional positive moods, or the well-being of others. For example, someone who feels better after receiving a compliment, ascribes the happiness of others to their social support systems, and explains negative ATs by citing criticism from others might hold basic beliefs about the necessity of social approval.

(d) Pay particular attention to self-referent thinking, for beliefs about the self may be especially likely to be of central importance.

2. *Methods focusing on the form of cognitions:*

(a) Determine the most typical cognitive bias evident in the client's ATs. If it is overgeneralization, for example, basic beliefs might also be in the form of sweeping generalizations.

(b) Note the ATs whose exploration is associated with intense emotion, as these are especially likely to relate to core beliefs.

A useful approach to this ongoing assessment process is to bear in mind the essentially phenomenological nature of CT. Ask yourself how *this* client could come to think *x, y,* and *z,* not *a, b,* and *c.* Rather than reacting to each cognition as it comes and trying to shoot it down, one is building a developmental model of the case and testing it via interventions (Persons, 1989).

Modifying dysfunctional beliefs. Once basic beliefs are identified, methods for evaluating and modifying them are often the same as those used with ATs (e.g., considering the utility of holding the belief). Also, it is sometimes useful simply to trace the origins of the beliefs (e.g., in early experiences, parental rules, peer values). This process can help clients understand how they could have developed these notions without being crazy. Also, as in psychoanalysis, they can begin to see their childhood notions as in some ways arbitrary and as ill-suited to adult circumstances.

Early origins of tacit beliefs may not, however, be frozen in time (Wachtel, 1977) but rather might still be reinforced in the client's present environment. An agoraphobic client, for example, concluded that she had learned some of her fear-related beliefs from her mother. This connection did not lead only to retrieval and reevaluation of childhood events, though. Her mother was *still* thinking aloud about catastrophic possibilities inherent in ambiguous situations. It was important for this client's progress that she learn to ask her mother not to share these potentially contagious frightening thoughts with her.

Finally, if the beliefs are shoulds and musts as described by RET, response prevention can be a powerful antidote. That is, what would happen if the client were not to do what "must" be done? For instance, a man might have assumed that he must defer to his wife in all situations in order to get along and be loved. The therapist might suggest that he try the experiment of forcing himself not to defer, to assert his opinions calmly at the next sign of conflict. The client should be asked for a prediction of the outcome of this experiment (to concretize the implications of later results). If the incident does not result in disaster (and the therapist needs to assess this likelihood in advance), this datum can be used to suggest the overly restrictive nature of the initial belief.

CT for depression is an optimistic treatment. The therapist has to maintain a problem-solving, antidepressant outlook (these negative thoughts are likely to be at least somewhat biased, and there may be another way to look at it, or there may be a way to change the situation, or the interpretations may be accurate but not as devastating as first feared, and so on), rather than giving in and joining the client's hopelessness if things do not go smoothly. This style makes sense in light of CT's origins as a treatment of depression and in light of Beck's research on the association of hopelessness with suicidal ideation and behavior (e.g., Beck, Steer, Kovacs, & Garrison, 1985). The motto of the therapy could be described as "A positive is a positive; a negative is a chance to gather information and practice the techniques." Insofar as this orientation can be passed on to clients, they should become relatively hardy people who can help themselves when, as is altogether likely (Belsher & Costello, 1988), they become at least mildly depressed again.

Empirical Status

Theory. The empirical status of CT theory of depression is quite controversial; research on it has been summarized as offering little support for the theory (Coyne & Gotlib, 1983), as fairly promising (Segal & Shaw, 1986), and as so conceptually and methodologically flawed as to prohibit any conclusions about the validity of the theory (Abramson, Alloy, & Metalsky, 1988). A middle-ground summary might be that the description of cognitive events typical of depression is essentially accurate. The hypothesis that dysfunctional beliefs are stable, preexisting vulnerability factors in reactive depression has to date received little support (Barnett & Gotlib, 1988). More definitive conclusions might be premature, though, as researchers are still developing improved methods of testing some of the more subtle aspects of CT as a causal theory (e.g., that dysfunctional beliefs are latent except under appropriately stressful conditions; Miranda & Persons, 1988).

Therapy. Efficacy. Cognitive therapy for nonpsychotic, nonbipolar outpatients with major depression has the most substantial empirical support of the cognitive-behavioral approaches. Studies have confirmed the efficacy of the entire treatment package (e.g., Rush, Beck, Kovacs, & Hollon, 1977) as well as the hypothesis that both cognitive and behavioral components contribute to its effectiveness (e.g., Wilson, Goldin, & Charbonneau–Powis, 1983). A quantitative review concluded that CT achieves greater short-term symptom relief than wait-list controls, pharmacotherapies, behavioral treatments, or a heterogeneous set of "other psychotherapies" (Dobson, 1989). The findings of the NIMH Treatment of Depression Collaborative Research Program (TDCRP; Elkin, Parloff, Hadley, & Autry, 1985) will add considerable information regarding CT. Initial efficacy results suggest a general equivalence of short-term symptom relief among CT, interpersonal therapy (Klerman, Weissman, Rounsaville, & Chevron, 1984), and imipramine with clinical management (Elkin et al., 1989).

Qualitative reviews (e.g., Hollon & Najavits, 1988) of earlier studies suggest that combining tricyclic antidepressants with CT usually shows a statistically nonsignificant advantage over CT in acute response (e.g., Hollon et al., 1989). CT apparently leads to greater maintenance of improvement than does pharmacotherapy alone (Blackburn, Eunson, & Bishop, 1986; Evans et al., 1989; Simons, Murphy, Levine, & Wetzel, 1986).

Prediction of response to CT. Simons, Lustman, Wetzel, and Murphy (1985) found that CT is especially beneficial, in contrast to pharmacotherapy, for subjects initially scoring high on learned resourcefulness (Rosenbaum, 1980). This result can be interpreted as an indication that agreeing with the rationale of CT (you can control your thinking, help yourself, etc.) improves response. Also consistent with this interpretation is a post hoc analysis of CT outcome by Fennell and Teasdale (1987). About one half of their CT group responded very quickly (within 2 weeks), seemingly on the basis of being presented with the model and agreeing that it fit them (cf. Davison, 1969). These subjects did not differ from less responsive clients on pretreatment depression but did score especially high on "depression about depression" (Teasdale, 1985) (i.e., negative reactions to aspects of depression experience itself).

Contrary to some clinical lore, endogeneity is not a contraindication for CT (Hollon & Najavits, 1988), nor is being of only average intelligence (Haaga, DeRubeis, Stewart, & Beck, 1989). Although further research is needed, severe marital discord may contraindicate individual CT. Social learning-based marital therapy might address the depression in one spouse as well as does individual CT, and the relationship problems better than individual CT (O'Leary & Beach, 1990).

Mechanisms of action. CT and pharmacotherapy both alter negative automatic thoughts in successfully treated subjects (Simons, Garfield, & Murphy, 1984), though this does not rule out the possibility that cognitive change is a causal mediating mechanism in CT (Hollon, DeRubeis, & Evans, 1987). Attributional style is a promising candidate for such a cognitive mediator. Improvement in depressive attributional style occurs in successful CT but not in unsuccessful CT nor in pharmacotherapy (DeRubeis et al., 1989) and is positively correlated with the degree of relief from depressive symptoms during CT (Seligman et al., 1988).

Finally, a fine-grained analysis of CT for depression (DeRubeis & Feeley, 1989) revealed an interesting temporal pattern of effects. Therapist behavior in the second session involving concrete activities (e.g., devising homework assignments, examining evidence for and against ATs) predicted favorable subsequent response. The quality of the helping alliance between therapist and client (Morgan, Luborsky, Crits–Christoph, Curtis, & Solomon, 1982), on the other hand, appeared to be more a consequence of symptom relief than a prior cause of it.

We now describe the adaptation of CT to panic disorder and bulimia nervosa. Given that many of the principles are the same as in CT for depression, we highlight mainly unique aspects.

Panic Disorder

CT hypothesizes that anxious people selectively attend to, and efficiently process, stimuli related to danger (Beck, Emery, & Greenberg, 1985). As a result of this selective attention, perceptions of threat and vulnerability are exaggerated. Deploying attention mainly to signs of danger decreases one's focus on task-relevant features. Therefore, besides exaggerated perceptions of threat, anxious clients may underestimate their coping resources. Finally, at a less accessible level, anxious clients may believe that "To be secure I must anticipate and prepare for all possible dangers" or "I must be in control at all times" (note again the similarity to irrational beliefs posited in RET).

This cognitive perspective on anxiety has been applied in particular to a cognitive conceptualization of panic attacks ("discrete periods of intense fear or discomfort, with at least four characteristic associated symptoms"; American Psychiatric Association, 1987, p. 235), which hypothesizes the following sequence of events (Clark, 1986a):

1. A stimulus, usually internal (e.g., an image) but sometimes external (e.g., being in a place one has panicked before) is perceived as dangerous.
2. The person becomes apprehensive, which is accompanied by
3. Anxiety-related bodily sensations.
4. If these sensations are interpreted as signals of impending catastrophe (e.g., mental or physical breakdown), anxiety and apprehension increase.
5. A vicious cycle is now set into motion, sometimes fueled by hyperventilation, culminating in
6. Intense fear, loss of capacity to check one's perceptions against reality (Beck, 1988), and a panic attack.

The sensations starting this process need not stem from anxiety. They can be entirely innocuous (e.g., the residue of caffeine intake or exercise), as long as the person misinterprets them as signaling imminent catastrophe. Once a single panic attack has occurred, the person may become hypervigilant to any changes in body sensations, contributing to the fear of subsequent attacks and agoraphobic avoidance behavior that are characteristic of panic disorder.

The essential goals of treatment are (a) to change the patient's misinterpretation of sensations, replacing it with a more benign explanation of their meaning (cf. Goldfried & Davison, 1976), (b) to encourage behavioral exposure to previously avoided situations and to feared sensations themselves (Rapee, 1987), and (c) to teach more appropriate methods of breathing and other skills for coping with panic.

CT begins by eliciting a specific description of a typical panic attack, including situational antecedents and the sequence of sensations and thoughts, as well as the client's current perception of how dangerous the panic attack was. If the client now sees his or her sensations as less dangerous than during the panic attack itself, one can use this variation to support the idea that cognitions during an attack may be inaccurate.

The most effective reattribution technique is believed to be intentional recreation of feared sensations in the session (cf. Davison, 1966). For example, many clients respond with attenuated panic-like reactions to "overbreathing," breathing rapidly and deeply for a period of two minutes. If the sensations are similar to those in a panic attack, it is possible to explore the benign explanation that hyperventilation, rather than a heart attack (or whatever is the client's fear), could account for them.

Treatment of panic disorder, like treatment of bulimia nervosa, particularly calls for collaboration with physicians. It is wise to request that the client obtain M.D. clearance before trying overbreathing or any other techniques oriented toward replicating physical symptoms. Moreover, M.D. evaluation can be useful in assessing the possible contributory role of physical disorders that present with anxiety-like symptoms (Barlow, 1988, pp. 368–372).

In addition to reattribution, the client is taught controlled breathing (breathing slowly, shallowly, and regularly through the nose only), to be initiated early in any subsequent panic attacks. This behavioral technique again serves cognitive goals. If successful, it should be used as evidence against the catastrophic misinterpretation (e.g., if you were really having a heart attack, does it seem plausible that controlling your breathing would have warded it off?).

Overbreathing might not do much for someone whose panic symptoms are not similar to those of hyperventilation. Other means of symptom replication need to be devised for such people (e.g., Clark, 1986b). The goal, regardless of method, is to correct the misinterpretation of symptoms and derive a new "symptom equation." "If the initial equation reads, 'Heart racing = heart attack,' the new equation might read, 'Heart racing = normal, harmless reaction of the body to perception of danger, related to hyperventilation' " (Beck & Greenberg, 1988, p. 574). To reinforce in-session work, clients are encouraged to perform experiments such as overbreathing at home.

The major behavioral component of CT for panic overlaps standard behavioral exposure treatment of agoraphobic avoidance (e.g., Barlow & Waddell, 1985). Exposure assignments can be used to encourage an experimental attitude toward treatment, for instance by asking "What will you learn if you try to face your fear, and what will you learn if you don't?" (Beck et al., 1985). Beck et al. (1985) suggest a rationale for approach behaviors based on choice (electing to expand one's freedom of movement), not control (overpowering fears). This is thought to facilitate full, functional exposure, rather than subtle cognitive avoidance (cf.

Weitzman, 1967) during behavioral exposure by a client trying to maintain control.

The necessity of exposure must be underscored for clients. They usually are not argued out of their fears in the office; to get better, they need to experience the anxiety elicited by what they find fearsome. Most people will have had some prior experience of getting over fears in this fashion, which can be used in persuading them to undertake exposure assignments.

One cognitive technique we have found extremely helpful to clients as an adjunct for exposure assignments is to use the mnemonic AWARE (Beck et al., 1985). Clients are reminded to:

- Accept your feelings (it is natural to be anxious when you perceive threat. This is an opportunity to catch the thoughts and images associated with anxiety).
- Watch what's going on around you (stay involved in the situation rather than retreating into self-absorption. Notice that anxiety peaks and then declines rather than remaining high indefinitely).
- Act normal. (Act as if you are not anxious.)
- Repeat the foregoing routine as many times as needed.
- Expect the best.

CT for panic also incorporates self-monitoring of stressful life events and ATs that might contribute to general anxiety. Moreover, additional coping skills such as relaxation and distraction techniques are sometimes utilized. The most complete solution, though, requires that the client learn that panic symptoms do not signify imminent doom and that *even if,* for instance, one lost control and acted foolish during a panic attack, that would not be catastrophic or life threatening (cf. RET shame-attacking exercises).

Empirical Status

The cognitive model of panic has been criticized on the grounds of conceptual imprecision (Seligman, 1988). Nevertheless, it is at least consistent with descriptive research on cognitions of panickers (Chambless, 1988). The general idea that cognitive factors contribute to panic is supported by an experiment showing that subjects with panic disorder were significantly less likely to panic in response to the challenge of inhaling carbon dioxide-enriched air if they *believed* (nonveridically) that they had control over the source of the gas (Sanderson, Rapee, & Barlow, 1989). This parallels a long line of research on the emotional consequences of nonveridical perceived control over aversive stimulation (e.g., Geer, Davison, & Gatchel, 1970).

As far as treatment is concerned, an uncontrolled study of CT reported complete remission of panic attacks for all 17 subjects through 1-year follow-up (Sokol, Beck, Greenberg, Wright, & Berchick, 1989). CT appears more effective than supportive therapy (Beck, 1988) and more specific to panic (as opposed to general anxiety) than relaxation training alone (Barlow, Craske, Cerny, & Klosko, 1989). It may be more likely than alprazolam, a common pharmacotherapy for panic, to yield complete remission of panic (Klosko, Barlow, Tassinari, & Cerny, 1990).

Although these results are very encouraging, there are several reasons not to be complacent about the efficacy of CT for panic or about our understanding of its effects. First, elimination of panic attacks, while important, does not render clients nonanxious (Barlow et al., 1989). Second, there is no information yet on whether CT reduces the frequency of panic attacks among people with other anxiety disorders or with major depression. These clients' panic attacks appear to differ in some respects (e.g., less likely to involve fear of dying or going crazy) from those of people with panic disorder (Barlow et al., 1985; Sanderson, Rapee, & Barlow, 1987). Third, it is not clear that CT exceeds the effectiveness of standard behavior therapy for agoraphobia (Clark, 1988), though preliminary evidence suggests that it may reduce dropout from exposure programs (Clum, 1989). Finally, there is no evidence that CT works via cognitive mechanisms such as reattribution of feared sensations to benign causes (Teasdale, 1988).

Bulimia Nervosa

Bulimia nervosa is characterized by "recurrent episodes of binge eating," "a feeling of lack of control over eating behavior during the eating binges" (American Psychiatric Association, 1987, p. 68), attempts to counteract the effects of binge eating (e.g., self-induced vomiting), and chronic excessive concern about body weight and shape. CT for bulimia nervosa targets intrapersonal vulnerabilities (e.g., poor self-esteem, underdeveloped skills for coping with negative affect) and societal forces (e.g., cultural pressure to be thin) that increase the probability of severe dieting (Garner & Rosen, in press), which is in turn viewed as a proximal cause of bulimia (Polivy & Herman, 1985).

Initial assessment includes evaluation of weight, eating patterns, and attitudes toward weight and body shape, as well as more general aspects of functioning. Both questionnaire (e.g., Eating Disorder Inventory; Garner, Olmstead, & Polivy, 1983) and interview (e.g., Eating Disorder Examination; Cooper & Fairburn, 1987) measures are available for this assessment. It is important to understand the possible sequelae of disturbed eating patterns so as not to be misled during this phase. Many symptoms of psychological maladjustment may improve considerably if eating behavior is normalized (Garner, 1987). Thus, the noneating symptoms need not always be central treatment foci.

Garner and Rosen (in press) advocate working concurrently on disordered eating behaviors per se and on restructuring of ATs and underlying beliefs. To provide material for in-session work, clients self-monitor food intake (type and quantity), binge episodes, laxative abuse, vomiting, other weight loss behaviors, and feelings and thoughts about eating. The ATs listed (e.g., consumption of a forbidden food will lead to enormous weight gain) are tested in behavioral experiments, just as in CT for depression.

A problem in this behavioral component of CT for bulimia is that some clients' fears of gaining weight if they return to normal eating are realistic. Their pretreatment weight may have been unrealistically low for their body shape as a result of extreme dieting. When this outcome seems likely, "it is often helpful to propose initially gaining a small amount of weight as part of an 'experiment' with recovery" (Garner & Rosen, in press). This might prove more acceptable to clients than having to make a permanent commitment to a higher weight.

Goals for the cognitive restructuring component of CT for bulimia nervosa include:

1. Reattribution of food preoccupation, urges to binge, and emotional distress as symptoms secondary to dieting and weight suppression. This challenges the client's belief that she or he can recover psychologically while still eating abnormally.
2. Challenging cultural values associating thinness with personal control, attractiveness, and virtue.
3. Challenging the belief that dependence is unacceptable, that one must always be in control.
4. Supporting self-acceptance, rather than self-esteem based on dichotomous thinking (I rate well if I can control my weight and shape).
5. Questioning the evidence for putative advantages of having an eating disorder (e.g., caretaking from others, which usually becomes resentment later).

Tactics for achieving these cognitive goals parallel closely the methods of CT for depression. The special demands of treating bulimia nervosa include the need to understand the biology of weight regulation (e.g., the possibility that body weight is regulated to a "set point" [e.g., Nisbett, 1972] so that severe dieting amounts to putting oneself in conflict with one's own physiology) and the many serious physiological complications of binging and purging (Woods & Brief, 1988). Moreover, many attitudes supporting disordered eating are congruent with current cultural values and are especially rigidly held. (This observation brings to mind the limits of individual therapy and the frequent utility of taking a broader, community/institutional perspective on psychological phenomena [Rappaport, 1977; see also chapter 12, this volume].) They may therefore require a more zealous, more didactic approach to CT than do the socially disapproved cognitions common in depression or anxiety.

Empirical Status

Cognitive-behavioral treatment of bulimia nervosa has shown promising evidence of effectiveness. It appears roughly equal to antidepressant medication but with more evidence of long-term maintenance (Leitenberg & Rosen, 1988). One well-designed experiment found that 59% of CBT subjects were abstinent from purging 6 months after treatment; CBT also reduced depressive symptoms and dysfunctional attitudes about eating (Agras, Schneider, Arnow, Raeburn, & Telch, 1989). These results exceeded the effectiveness of wait-list control, self-monitoring coupled with nondirective therapy, and even CBT plus exposure to binging and response prevention.

It is not clear, though, that verbal cognitive restructuring is an essential element of CBT for bulimia nervosa. By itself it appears insufficient (Wilson, Rossiter, Kleifield, & Lindholm, 1986). Agras et al. (1989) compared their findings to other results and concluded that "self-monitoring of food intake, binge eating, and purging; instructions to eat three balanced meals each day combined with nutritional information; and exposure to feared foods may be the core procedures of cognitive-behavioral therapy" (p. 220). Outcome studies with bulimia nervosa thus underscore again the importance of enactive methods in CBT and the relative insufficiency of verbal methods alone (Hollen & Beck, 1986).

Conceptual Issues Specific to CT

Perhaps the most controversial issue in CT is the hypothesis that psychopathology is associated with various forms of cognitive distortion (see page 249). This central assumption is relevant to CT conceptualizations of all disorders, though the particulars of the hypothesized cognitive distortions vary. Most of the empirical work addressing this issue concerns depression.

Experiments have suggested that depression may actually be associated with *more* realistic perceptions (Alloy & Abramson, 1979). Some reviewers find the evidence of depressive realism compelling (Alloy & Abramson, 1988). Others are more skeptical (Ackermann & DeRubeis, 1989; Dobson & Franche, 1989), citing the difficulty of conducting ecologically valid research yet still having an objective standard against which to evaluate accuracy of cognitions. Also, the research in question has frequently used students screened on self-report depressive symptom measures as "depressed" subject groups. The latter practice can be misleading, in that there may be a curvilinear relationship between accuracy and level of depressive symptoms. That is, mild dysphoria may be associated with realism, clinical depression with negative distortions, and nondepression with positive distortions (Ruehlman, West, & Pasahow, 1985).

The safest conclusion emerging from this body of research is that rigorously realistic thinking in all situations is *not* the hallmark of nondistressed people (Taylor & Brown, 1988). As Gagnon and Davison (1976) put it, "to stay 'sane' you commonly have to doctor the books" (p. 534). Both distressed and nondistressed people probably use schematic knowledge representations and processing heuristics that sometimes lead to inaccuracies (Kahneman et al., 1982; Nisbett & Ross, 1980). The primary distinction between groups may be the *content* of cognitive biases rather than the existence of bias per se (Dykman, Abramson,

Alloy, & Hartlage, 1989; Evans & Hollon, 1988). An implication for treatment is that emphases on constructive action (What can I do about it?) and divergent thinking (Is there any other way to look at it?) may be more critical to the efficacy of CT than the elimination of misperceptions (What is the evidence?)

PROBLEM-SOLVING THERAPY

Experimental psychologists have long been interested in how people solve problems; indeed, their purview has extended to infrahuman species as well (Kohler, 1925). In this section we describe the use of problem-solving methods in psychotherapy. Several models for applying problem-solving techniques to problems in living have been developed, including Interpersonal Cognitive Problem Solving (e.g., Spivack, Platt, & Shure, 1976) and problem-solving methods included in self-management therapy (see chapter 8, this volume). We will present the problem-solving approach initiated by D'Zurilla and Goldfried (1971).

In Problem-Solving Therapy (PST; D'Zurilla, 1986; D'Zurilla & Goldfried, 1971), problems are defined as situations in which "no effective response alternative is immediately available to the individual confronted with the situation" (D'Zurilla & Goldfried, 1971, p. 108). Problem solving, in turn, is "a behavioral process, whether overt or cognitive in nature, which (a) makes available a variety of potentially effective response alternatives for dealing with the problematic situation and (b) increases the probability of selecting the most effective response from among these various alternatives" (D'Zurilla & Goldfried, 1971, p. 108). The process is completed when the situation is no longer problematic, assuming that side-effects are reasonably favorable.

PST teaches a general framework to use in solving diverse current and future problems, as opposed to trying to alleviate only pressing current concerns. A potential strength is that generalization of clinical improvement should be enhanced. A potential obstacle is that PST may conflict with clients' expectations of expert assistance in rapidly solving specific problems (Goldfried, 1980).

Stages

PST prescribes solving problems by working in a logical sequence of stages, though one may need to go back and forth at times in a less orderly manner (D'Zurilla & Nezu, 1982). The stages are (a) problem orientation, (b) problem definition and formulation, (c) generation of alternatives, (d) decision making, and (e) solution implementation and verification. The problem orientation stage is mainly motivational, whereas the remaining stages describe specific skills necessary for problem solving (D'Zurilla, in press). The Social Problem-Solving Inventory (D'Zurilla & Nezu, in press) could be useful for identifying strengths and weaknesses at each stage.

Problem Orientation

The goal of this stage is to foster in the client a constructive "set" or attitude toward problem solving. Specifically, this set would include (a) ability to identify problems (e.g., situations in which one feels frustrated), (b) acceptance of problems as normal, potentially changeable, and challenging (rather than inherently threatening), (c) belief that the PST framework is an apt way to deal with problems, (d) high self-efficacy expectations (Bandura, 1977) for executing the steps of the model, and (e) a habit of stopping and thinking, but then acting to try to solve a problem. This contrasts with either a habit of taking action impulsively or a habit of becoming hopeless and giving up when confronted with problems.

Problem Definition and Formulation

Most problems clients face are difficult to formulate in concrete terms, but effective problem solving requires clear formulations. If problems are defined vaguely, for instance, evaluation of the likely utility of alternative solutions will be difficult. Useful steps in Problem Definition and Formulation include (a) gathering all available information pertinent to the problem in specific terms, (b) separating facts from questionable assumptions, (c) breaking down the problem (what specifically makes it a problem? In what way is the current situation frustrating or less than what the client desires?), and (d) specifying realistic goals. If goals are too high, the client will never be satisfied with the outcome of the problem-solving process.

Generation of Alternatives

Once there is a suitable formulation, client and therapist try to develop a range of potentially effective, specific solutions. Principles guiding this work include:

1. *Defer judgment.* Good solutions are apt to be found if people are initially uncritical in brainstorming alternatives. Many clients require constant reminders of this principle. Depressed clients especially tend to generate one alternative and then immediately shoot it down as unworkable.
2. *Quantity breeds quality.* Good solutions will more likely arise if numerous possibilities are considered.
3. *Strategies before tactics.* First generate strategies (general directions one might take), then tactics (specific ways to implement the strategies). Strategies are regarded favorably if they appear likely to resolve the problem, while tactics are evaluated in terms of how well they implement the strategies.

   This distinction is subtle but important. Some clients fixate on tactics while losing sight of overall goals and strategies. For instance, a client who settled on as a *goal* "I want to leave my wife" focused on devising optimal tactics for achieving this goal (e.g., stay elsewhere briefly while requesting that she move out) but would never follow through. Progress could only be made by backing up, letting go of the previously certain tactic, and reconsidering goals (be in a loving relationship with someone) and strategies (give current marriage, which was not entirely hopeless, another chance). This work eventually led to selecting new tactics, including marital therapy.

Decision Making

The utility of a strategy or tactic is estimated by its likely consequences if carried out properly and by the likelihood that the client will implement it properly. A decision balance matrix (Janis & Mann, 1982) can help organize thinking at this stage. The matrix calls attention to both positive and negative, short- and long-term, probable consequences, for the client and for others, of either choosing or not choosing the alternative.

Solution Implementation and Verification

This final stage takes the problem solver into the world of action. Elements include (a) *performance* (client tries to execute the selected tactic), (b) *observation* (record the results of the performance, monitor the situation, behavior, and consequences), and (c) *evaluation* (compare results to goals. If the fit is satisfactory, administer self-rewards, and move on to other problems.)

If the outcome was not satisfactory, client and therapist diagnose the setback. If an inappropriate solution was chosen (i.e., actual consequences did not match expected consequences), they return to generating alternatives. If the goal now appears to have been unrealistic, they return to problem definition and formulation. If the solution was in principle suitable, but the client could not execute it, skill training would precede another try.

PST is a prescriptive, not descriptive, model of problem solving. For clients who are not used to approaching personal problems so systematically, it may be necessary at first to be highly didactic, perhaps thinking aloud while demonstrating the use of the model. Gradually, though, the client should see the techniques as effective and can take over direction of PST, with the therapist becoming more of a consultant.

Empirical Status

Depression is associated with generating fewer alternative solutions to problems, selecting poor solutions, and perceiving one's own problem-solving ability as poor (Nezu, 1987). Problem-solving effectiveness, on the other hand, may help to buffer people against the impact of stress. Effective problem solvers reporting high recent stress levels were less depressed than were ineffective problem solvers who had experienced high stress (Nezu, Perri, Nezu, & Mahoney, 1987).

Process research supports the utility of the PST stages (e.g., Cormier, Otani, & Cormier, 1986; D'Zurilla & Nezu, 1980; Nezu & D'Zurilla, 1979, 1981a, b), though there is no research on solution implementation and verification. However, such laboratory studies cannot capture idiographic aspects of PST (e.g., whether a seemingly effective solution is within the subject's range of competence and consistent with his or her ethics).

Outcome studies have shown PST to improve coping competencies and reduce drinking behavior among alcohol abusers (Chaney, O'Leary, & Marlatt, 1978). Also, depressed subjects responded better (through 6-month follow-up) to PST than to (a) problem-focused discussion without systematic PST training or (b) no treatment (Nezu, 1986). Reduction of depressive symptoms was accompanied by increases in self-reported problem-solving effectiveness. A dismantling study indicated that problem orientation training contributes to the efficacy of PST (Nezu & Perri, 1989). There are no data on which clients are most likely to benefit from PST (Nezu, Nezu, & Perri, 1989).

Not all PST postulates have been supported by clinical research. For instance, converging evidence has called into question the "quantity breeds quality" principle (Lakey, 1988). After generation-of-alternatives training, alcohol abusers could think of more alternatives, but their overall problem-solving effectiveness did not increase (Kelly, Scott, Prue, & Rychtarik, 1985). Likewise, the number of solutions subjects generated in response to problems did not predict dysphoria 2 months later. Indeed, generating a high proportion of irrelevant solutions predicted *increased* dysphoria (Wierzbicki, 1984).

Conceptual Issues Specific to PST

This section questions (a) whether PST offers the best prescriptions for how to solve problems in living, and (b) whether PST could have unintended negative consequences if applied inflexibly. First, Kanfer and Busemeyer (1982) contended that PST is suited mainly for "static" decision-making situations, in which a decision is to be made once and for all, and circumstances are more or less constant while you decide (e.g., whether or not to have surgery). Many clinical problems are instead dynamic. The client's goals change, and environmental consequences of behaviors can change as well.

In dynamic problem-solving models, evaluation is not reserved for the final stage; feedback is gathered at all stages. Each step may have unpredictable consequences. In turn, these consequences will influence the goals chosen for later stages. The problem solver tests hypotheses about actions that might lead closer to goal states, which are themselves always open to reevaluation. The dynamic model implies, therefore, a series of small decisions about how to move closer to satisfactory states, not one large decision about how to achieve a goal. For specific methods for reaching these decisions, see Kanfer and Busemeyer (1982).

Second, PST appears to endorse an extremely calculating approach to daily life, involving a rather dogged procedure of generating and evaluating alternative solutions and carefully monitoring the results. It might be wiser to suggest instead that life is replete with problems, but only a subset of them merit cranking up the full-blown PST apparatus to arrive at a solution. Leibenstein (1980) described *calculatedness* as a variable, an aspect of rationality but not identical to it. When stakes are relatively low, it is rational to expend less effort at calculating the utilities of possible solutions. Calculating is effortful for most people, and as such it makes sense to be selective in applying this skill. To a degree this might be achieved by using shortcuts in PST. For example, a rough preliminary screening in the decision-making stage could be used to weed out alternatives that are too risky or beyond the subject's competence. Similarly, combining generation of alternatives and decision making as one step could help in rapidly determining a reasonable solution even if not the best one (D'Zurilla, in press).

A more radical variation on PST would emphasize mainly the initial, orientation stage, elaborating the remaining stages only for especially refractory problems. For most problems, the problem solver's *attitude* may be more significant than the particular meta-cognitive methodology used. Pirsig (1974) suggested that the most important tool for any problem solver is "gumption." One way to maintain gumption in the face of difficult problems is to remain open to the possibility that solutions could lie outside the entire rational, PST framework. It may be necessary to let go of the model and simply take a step back and immerse oneself in observing the situation and not trying so hard to get unstuck right away by implementing solutions.

PST and the less rigorous attitude-based approach could perhaps be reconciled by invoking Prochaska's (1984) concept of multiple stages of change. Initial behavior change and early maintenance might be facilitated by adherence to somewhat obsessive approaches (cf. Kirschenbaum, 1987), whereas in the long run adaptive functioning is probably associated with a less calculating, more spontaneous approach to the majority of problems faced in daily life.

Related to the concern about possibly excessive demands for calculatedness, PST seems to advocate a very high degree of perceived control over events (Goldfried, 1980). One should stop and think but then act. If an attempted solution fails, reevaluate and try again. Life is full of problems best viewed as challenges. Underestimating control over situations can indeed perpetuate problems and distress. However, the PST attitude could also lead to some frustration and fruitless struggles to change the unchangeable. This determination to exert control could be an aspect of the Type A behavior pattern (Friedman & Rosenman, 1959), at least some components of which appear to confer elevated risk for coronary heart disease (Booth–Kewley & Friedman, 1987).

To be sure, this concern applies mainly to the excessive, inflexible application of certain PST methods. If problem solving is interpreted as a specific coping response (i.e., taking active steps to alter the problematic situation) within a more general framework of options for coping (Lazarus & Folkman, 1984; Tobin, Holroyd, Reynolds, & Wigal, 1989), then problem solving is indeed best reserved for situations that afford control and can be counterproductive if applied more widely. D'Zurilla (in press) contends, though, that PST is more versatile than this limiting perspective would suggest. "Solutions" selected by the problem solver need not feature attempts to control or master the environment but could also include emotion-focused attempts to manage one's own reaction to an unchanged situation. Specifically, "When the situation is appraised as changeable or controllable, then problem-focused goals would be emphasized. . . . However, if the problematic situation is appraised as *un*changeable or *un*controllable then emotion-focused goals would be emphasized. These goals can also be changed at different points. . . . For example, if the person initially attempts to find a problem-focused solution for a particular problematic situation, only to discover later that nothing works, he or she then has the option to switch to an emotion-focused goal" (D'Zurilla, in press).

GENERAL ISSUES IN COGNITIVE CHANGE METHODS

This final section concerns matters relevant to all forms of CBT, including (a) questions about the mechanisms of cognitive change, (b) tactics for achieving pragmatic aims such as increasing therapeutic compliance, (c) extensions of CBT therapy techniques such as the development of systematic methods for assessing cognitions, and (d) conceptual issues such as the possibility that strong negative emotions can be adaptive.

Mechanisms

Cognitive Restructuring or Replacement

The CBT systems described in this chapter rely most heavily on restructuring clients' beliefs about themselves and their problems; coping techniques are incorporated but generally viewed as secondary. It should be noted that other cognitive-behavioral approaches, especially Meichenbaum's (1986) self-instructional training, place a greater emphasis on the coping aspects of CBT, in particular the importance of learning specific self-statements to guide oneself through stressful situations. Meichenbaum's methods have enjoyed wide application in the treatment of children (for a review of empirical studies, see Dush, Hirt, & Schroeder, 1989) and a variety of stress-related conditions in adults (Meichenbaum, 1985).

Few studies have directly compared the efficacy of attempting to replace negative self-statements with coping self-statements to that of attempting to alter the beliefs alleged to underlie negative self-statements. One well-designed study found essentially no differences between the methods in reducing test anxiety (Arnkoff, 1986).

Therapist Behavior as an Independent Variable

The organization of our chapter, indeed the entire volume, reflects our assumption that the theory and specific techniques one utilizes in trying to help people change make a difference in the effectiveness of that effort. Empirical evidence that cognitive and behavioral methods are often highly effective has emerged in reviews of the treatment of specific disorders (e.g., Dobson, 1989) as well as a more general range of conditions (e.g., Shapiro & Shapiro, 1982). Nevertheless, it should also be acknowledged that individual *therapists* vary quite considerably in the outcomes they obtain even when using putatively the "same" treatment with equivalent samples of clients (Lambert, 1989). For example, a comparison of supportive-expressive psychotherapy with cognitive therapy for opiate-dependent patients found that success was associated with the "purity" of treatment (i.e., the extent to which the therapist behaved according to the theory-defined specifications of the therapy being delivered rather than mixing in elements of the other therapy) (Luborsky, McLellan, Woody, O'Brien, & Auerbach, 1985). This would support an hypothesis that therapist differences in success stem from differential adherence to theory-specified techniques. Alternatively, therapist differences in the *style* of intervening, especially verbal stylistics, may render some especially well suited to structured, directive treatments such as cognitive-behavioral therapies (Stiles, Shapiro, & Firth–Cozens, 1989). There may be, in effect, therapist-by-treatment interaction effects in determining treatment outcome; just as certain *clients* may be particularly responsive to CBT, so too certain *therapists* may be especially effective using these procedures rather than others.

Pragmatics

Cognitive Aids

The therapies described in this chapter make good use of "cognitive aids" (Rosenthal & Downs, 1985). Even an appropriate, exquisitely reasonable technique can help only if the client understands and remembers it. Writing down between-session assignments (e.g., Beck et al.'s [1979] Daily Record of Dysfunctional Thoughts, which contains its own instructions) seems to promote their completion (Dox, Tisdelle, & Culbert, 1988). Other aspects of cognitive change methods consistent with research on promoting the retention and use of new information (Rosenthal & Downs, 1985) include (a) having the client intermittently summarize important points in a session, (b) giving advance materials on the rationale for treatment, (c) citing research and novel theoretical developments in support of the therapy, and (d) using acronyms for key concepts. If clients are not making progress in therapy, and particularly if their verbal behavior seems to reflect lack of understanding of the treatment approach (e.g., they cannot accurately explain a CT conceptualization of their depression), it may be helpful to increase the use of cognitive aids relating to the major aspects of the therapy.

Compliance

Making interventions understandable, however, does not guarantee compliance, on which CBT relies to a great extent. Wood and Jacobson (1985) analyzed efforts to promote homework compliance as including stimulus control and response control strategies.

Stimulus control strategies attempt to prevent noncompliance. Tactics could include:

1. explicating the rationale for an assignment;
2. emphasizing its importance (e.g., by citing the positive correlation between homework completion and clinical improvement in CT; Persons, Burns, & Perloff, 1988);
3. eliciting a commitment to complete the assignment;
4. writing down the assignment;
5. starting with small assignments (Shelton & Levy, 1981);
6. negotiating the details of the assignment in collaboration with the client (Biglan & Campbell, 1981; e.g., given that the therapist considers it very important for the client to practice taking the risk of communicating feelings openly, the client can be given control over the details of when and with whom this experiment will take place);
7. verifying the client's understanding of assignments;
8. anticipating and disputing possible reasons not to comply (e.g., lack of time, failure to see the point);
9. relabelling the assignment—some clients react badly to the term *homework* (possibly because of aversive memories of school) but respond better to something like "self-help exercise" (C. Haaga, personal communication); and
10. allowing clients to call after performing an assignment (Goldfried, 1982). This procedure enhances accountability and allows the therapist to provide immediate reinforcement for compliance.

Making oneself available for telephone consultation adds significantly to the therapist's burden and may at times be impractical. However, though we know of no systematic research on this issue, it seems that one helpful between-session telephone consultation, usually early in treatment, can significantly bolster the client's sense that the therapist cares about his or her suffering. Indeed, Mahoney (1986) has hypothesized that all therapeutic techniques work primarily by communicating implicit messages about the therapist, the client, and the problems. In the long run, of course, progress would be indicated by the client's learning to use therapeutic techniques on her or his own.

Response control strategies address noncompliance after the fact; the most important is always to review homework in the next session. If completed, homework is reinforced with attention and praise and is used as material for in-session work. If not, one needs to diagnose and treat the obstacles that interfered with compliance. This practice communicates the message (which in CBT is often true) that homework is vital to therapy, that noncompliance is not satisfactory. Moreover, reviewing homework assignments provides the therapist with feedback on how well the client is applying CBT skills in vivo. By the same token, compliance will probably be reduced if the therapist neglects to check on homework; the message conveyed would be that between-session assignments are not that important after all.

Extensions

Cognitive Assessment

Skillful practice of CBT requires means of assessing the cognitions targeted for therapeutic intervention; consequently, cognitive assessment has become an active research area. Recent reviews of this research are available (Clark, 1988; Parks & Hollon, 1988; Segal & Shaw, 1988), so we will highlight only a few points.

The methods most easily applied in clinical practice are questionnaire, "endorsement" methods. Choice among these would depend on the client, the diagnosis, the type of therapy, and the level of analysis. For instance, in RET it is important to assess irrational beliefs. As noted, the most common IB measures may lack discriminant validity (Smith, 1989), but newer scales could help remedy this problem (e.g., Malouff & Schutte, 1986). In CT for depression, a fairly comprehensive cognitive assessment battery might include the Dysfunctional Attitude Scale (Weissman & Beck, 1978) for tacit beliefs, the Cognitive Bias Questionnaire (Krantz & Hammen, 1979) for cognitive biases, and the Automatic Thoughts Questionnaire (Hollon & Kendall, 1980), Cognitions Checklist (Beck, Brown, Steer, Eidelson, & Riskind, 1987), or Cognitive Triad Inventory (Beckham, Leber, Watkins, Boyer, & Cook, 1986) for cognitive events. The DAS could be especially useful near the end of treatment, as elevated DAS scores after depression has remitted may predict relapse (Simons et al., 1986). Endorsement measures with some supportive validity data are also available for measuring cognitions associated with anxiety (Kendall & Hollon, 1989) and specific anxiety problems such as social anxiety (Glass, Merluzzi, Biever, & Larsen, 1982) and agoraphobia (Chambless, Caputo, Bright, & Gallagher, 1984).

Many of these inventories assess the *frequency* with which a client experiences particular cognitions. At times it is important to examine other properties of cognitions as well. First, it may be valuable to know whether clients report certain cognitions *spontaneously* (Davison, Robins, & Johnson, 1983; Haaga, 1989; Weiner, 1985) rather than only at the direction of a questionnaire or interview probing for such thoughts. Open-ended assessment methods such as thought listing (Cacioppo & Petty, 1981) and articulated thoughts during simulated situations (Davison et al., 1983) can serve this purpose.

Second, open-ended measures may complement endorsement procedures by revealing the *sequencing* of cognitions. For example, a client might continue to have many negative thoughts after treatment but show a greater ability to cope with them and respond to them (as is taught in CT) rather than follow them with long chains of increasingly negative cognitions (Glass & Arnkoff, 1982; Notarious, 1981). This important topic has not yet received the extensive empirical attention it merits (Fichten, Amsel, & Robillard, 1988).

Third, it can be useful to assess the *strength* of a client's belief in a particular thought, a dimension included in most assessments of perceived self-efficacy (e.g., Colletti, Supnick, & Payne, 1985). Segal and Shaw (1988) hypothesized, for instance, that holding a few dysfunctional attitudes in an extreme, rigid manner might create as great a vulnerability to depression as endorsing a high number of dysfunctional attitudes.

Fourth, it could be important in selecting interventions to assess the *meaning* of cognitions to a client, rather than assuming that a given self-statement means the same thing to everyone. Arnkoff and Glass (1982) suggest, for example, that "I'm going to fail" could be a depressotypic negative prediction (I'm going to fail, as usual, and there's nothing I can do about it) or a self-motivating thought (I'm going to fail unless I get to work). These nuances of meaning can often be reconstructed in clinical interviews.

Fifth, clinicians should assess positive cognitions to supplement the usual focus on the negative (Ingram & Wisnicki, 1988). The States of Mind (SOM) model (Schwartz & Garamoni, 1986, 1989) implicates the SOM ratio (positive thoughts divided by [positive + negative]) as a proximal determinant of psychological well-being. Optimal functioning is said to be associated with a "positive dialogue" ("positively balanced but realistically cautious"; Schwartz & Michelson, 1987, p. 557) SOM ratio of approximately 0.62, mild psychopathology with an even split between negative and positive (the "internal dialogue of conflict," Schwartz & Gottman, 1976), and more severe pathology with an overbalance of negative thoughts. (Combining the possible curvilinear relationship between level of depression and realistic perceptions, on one hand, with the hypothesis that mild psychopathology is associated with an SOM ratio of about 0.5, on the other, yields an answer to a timeless philosophical question. "Reality" turns out to be about one half positive, one half negative.) Successfully treated agoraphobics (Schwartz & Michelson, 1987) slightly overshot the optimum balance to a borderline "positive monologue" SOM, which might provide a temporary buffer against distress.

This "overshooting" effect seems analogous to our speculative reconciliation of the obsessive PST framework with a problem-solving approach more like that of nondistressed people. In both cases it appears that the road to well-being passes through an atypical (in PST, "hypercalculating," in this case, "hyperpositive") state even farther away from the previous dysfunctional state than is normal functioning.

Finally, especially late in treatment when the client may no longer be dysphoric, inventory methods may fail to activate cognitions the client will experience in stressful situations (Haaga, 1989; Riskind & Rholes, 1984). Imagery procedures, simulation of provocative situations, or deliberate induction of negative mood (Miranda & Persons, 1988) might be needed for evaluation of lingering cognitive vulnerabilities.

Relapse Prevention

Possibly the best-established finding in CBT regarding relapse is that internal attribution of treatment gains predicts maintenance of change (e.g., Davison, Tsujimoto, & Glaros, 1973; for a review, see Brehm & Smith, 1986). This phenomenon might explain the higher rate of relapse after pharmacotherapy for depression than CT, as pharmacotherapy clients may ascribe their improvement externally to the medication rather than to their own efforts and skills. This principle suggests that it is important not only in *fact* to give clients increasing responsibility throughout therapy, but also to monitor whether they take credit for this rather than attributing all benefits to the therapist or other external factors.

A corollary to the message "You largely caused your improvement" is "You are largely accountable for keeping it up." If indeed CBT works by teaching such skills as how to respond to negative thoughts, then it stands to reason that practice of the skills would have to continue, on a self-directed basis if not with the therapist (the literature on addictive behaviors does not provide grounds for enthusiasm about the general utility of "booster sessions"; Brownell, Marlatt, Lichtenstein, & Wilson, 1986). Öst (1989) suggests giving clients the analogy of therapy as driver education. If someone learned enough to qualify for a license (termination) but then did not drive for several years, performance would surely deteriorate.

Besides internal attributions for improvement and continued practice of techniques, maintenance might be enhanced during therapy by targeting the area of functioning with which the client initially has greatest difficulty (e.g., situations with which they cope poorly or response channels that are especially aberrant). Although initial symptom relief might be achieved by utilizing client strengths (e.g., social skills therapy for depressed people already relatively skilled socially; Rude, 1986), long-term maintenance seems to require also targeting the greatest weaknesses. This hypothesis is consistent with the psychotherapy process model of Kanfer and Schefft (1987) as well as some empirical results. For instance, matching the modality of intervention to agoraphobic clients' most dysfunctional response class (psychophysiological, behavioral, cognitive) showed beneficial effects mainly at a follow-up assessment, rather than posttreatment (Michelson, 1986).

Conceptual Boundary Issues

Reconceptualizing Relapse

As a counterpoint to our discussion of relapse *prevention,* an alternate viewpoint suggests that the reemergence of problems is a normal and common occurrence. This perspective criticizes the surgery-like model of psychotherapy as fixing the client and rendering him or her permanently well, offering instead a "general practice" model of psychological services (Cummings & VandenBos, 1981; Jacobson, 1989). This perspective attempts to destigmatize the need for occasional "checkup" sessions. The goal would be to assist clients through stressful times and teach them something to increase the likelihood of responding constructively and courageously (which might include future, perhaps briefer, courses of treatment) to recurring challenges to adaptive functioning. Contrary to the imagery of cure, life is replete with difficulties and challenges; it is not "living happily ever after."

Reappraising the Adaptive Significance of Negative Emotion

CBT has been criticized for overemphasizing elimination of intense negative emotions (Mahoney, 1980). The possibility that strong negative emotions can be functional has been elaborated by several theorists (Greenberg & Safran, 1989; Guidano, 1987; Mahoney, 1988; Mahoney, Lyddon, & Alford, 1989). "From a developmental perspective, emotions serve as primitive and powerful 'knowing processes' " (Mahoney et al., 1989, p. 81). Experiencing negative emotions not readily handled with rational coping strategies can set the stage for growth:

> If the individual's attempts to cope . . . are unsuccessful . . . [t]he typical scenario then entails cycles or waves of emotional, cognitive, and behavioral disorder. . . . A successful resolution of this dilemma requires the emergence of higher-order knowing structures that are capable of accommodating the challenges associated with the ongoing crisis. As this transformational reorganization evolves—and it often involves substantial time, experience, and distress—the individual emerges as more differentiated and developed. A new and more complex level of emotional equilibrium is established and maintained until the next lifespan episode of disorder. (Mahoney et al., 1989, p. 82)

Greenberg and Safran likewise describe a number of ways in which emotional experience can be utilized effectively in cognitive behavior therapies, bringing them closer to humanistic therapies: "The goal of therapy is not to get rid of feelings but to help clients become aware of their meaning and to become more responsive to the action tendencies toward which feelings prompt them." (Greenberg & Safran, 1989, p. 21). The culprit in this account is "blocking or avoidance of potentially adaptive emotions and the information associated with them" (Greenberg & Safran, 1989, p. 23). Interestingly, this view is consistent not only with principles of experiential therapies but also with research on behavioral procedures for anxiety reduction. Exposure seems to work most efficiently for clients who achieve "effective" exposure (including heightened anxiety) when confronting feared stimuli (Foa & Kozak, 1986), consistent with decades of animal research on avoidance learning (for more elaboration of the role of affect in therapy, see chapter 9, this volume).

Personality and Its Disorders

Cognitive behavior therapies have traditionally paid little attention to personality theory (Ziegler, 1989), but this deficiency has begun to be corrected. Beck

(1983), for instance, postulated two overarching personality modes: sociotropy—valuing "positive interchange with others, focusing on acceptance, intimacy, support and guidance" (Beck, Epstein, & Harrison, 1983, p. 3)—and autonomy—valuing "independent functioning, mobility, choice, achievement, and integrity of one's domain" (Beck et al., 1983, p. 3). These are general ways of life, subsuming more specific beliefs (e.g., a sociotropic person might be likely to believe "My value depends on what others think of me," and "I cannot be happy without a good love relationship"). This aspect of Beck's model suggests that people with a given personality will be especially vulnerable to "matching" negative events. For instance, sociotropic people would be more likely to become depressed by personal rejections, autonomous people by failures (e.g., a loss of a job). Research on this scheme is in its infancy and has shown conflicting, inconsistent results (Haaga, Dyck, & Ernst, 1990). Refinements in the assessment of these personality dimensions may be necessary in order to make further progress in testing the validity of Beck's hypotheses (Robins, Block, & Peselow, 1989).

In evaluating clients' personality styles it is important not to overlook the potential *advantages* of a sociotropic orientation; being close to others and valuing intimacy and support can enhance well-being and otherwise lend meaning to life. It is only when these values are held to an extreme, rigid degree and are not matched by the actual conditions of one's life that depression would be expected to result. Indeed, it could be fruitful to think of investment in *both* affiliative and achievement domains as particularly advantageous. Linville's (1985, 1987) research suggests that having a complex (i.e., multiple self-construals, well-separated—e.g., recreational hiker, father, worker) view of oneself can provide a buffer against stress and negative emotions. Likewise, research suggests that participating in paid employment has a generally positive effect on women's physical and emotional health (Repetti, Matthews, & Waldron, 1989). This type of effect is difficult to discern if we derive our notions about personality mainly from clinical experience. That is, we might overlook the point that valuing an aspect of experience creates not only *vulnerability* to disappointments and losses in that domain but also *opportunity* for enhancing satisfaction and personal development.

At the more extreme end of personality variations are personality disorders (American Psychiatric Association, 1987), chronic maladaptive patterns of relating to others. This is an extremely important issue, as about one half of depressed outpatients meet criteria for a personality disorder (Shea, Glass, Pilkonis, Watkins, & Docherty, 1987), and one half of those with an Axis II diagnosis qualify for more than one (Morey, 1988). Personality disordered clients seem to derive less benefit from structured short-term treatments than do others (e.g., Pilkonis & Frank, 1988; Thompson, Gallagher, & Czirr, 1988; Turner, 1987).

Adapting CBT to the needs of Axis II clients might require longer periods of treatment (e.g., Turner, 1989; Young & Swift, 1988). A theoretical basis for adaptation could be worked out via Prochaska's (1984) stages of change model (Lazarus, 1989). Personality disordered clients might be "precontemplators" on the issues (blind spots, recurring patterns of ineffective behavior) that therapists view as critical to their problems. In contrast, they might be "actioners" regarding the anxiety, depressive symptoms, and so forth that brought them into treatment. Therapists in such cases must skillfully blend the use of techniques aimed at resolving the problem the consumer defines with attempts to raise consciousness on the issues the therapist sees as most significant.

At the same time, it is important not to assume that more is always better when it comes to planning the length of treatment. Most people will not (and probably could not afford to) attend psychotherapy for long. The median number of sessions is about six to eight (Garfield, 1986). Unless they are participating in a brief-therapy outcome trial, most therapists would probably consider this median client to have prematurely terminated treatment. The behavior could reflect, though, an intuitive wisdom on the part of clients as to the dose of psychotherapy necessary to achieve some substantial benefit (Howard, Kopta, Krause, & Orlinsky, 1986). Sometimes simplistic procedures can be quite useful; a little relaxation training, a rationale for how thoughts could affect emotions and how to gain distance from dysfunctional thoughts, along with reinforcement for carrying out the difficult early stages of change, may go a long way.

SUMMARY

In this chapter we have described the theoretical bases, clinical procedures, and empirical status of rational-emotive therapy, cognitive therapy, and problem-solving therapy and have reviewed some of the practical and theoretical issues facing the field of cognitive behavior therapy. RET contends that irrational beliefs lead to dysfunctional emotion and behavior and that these beliefs can be altered only through the use of forceful methods of disputation. This approach seems to be highly beneficial for clients who are overly concerned about being criticized by others (as in social phobia), but many of RET's distinctive hypotheses about how people change remain to be rigorously evaluated empirically.

CT also addresses the issue of dysfunctional (tacit) beliefs underlying emotional distress but first aims to help clients learn to test the validity of the readily accessible thoughts from which these tacit beliefs are inferred. Extensive evidence supports the efficacy of CT for depression, and research has begun to document its effectiveness in treating panic disorder and bulimia nervosa as well.

PST teaches clients an elaborate, multistage procedure for planning, implementing, and evaluating solutions to personal problems. Although we questioned some of the particulars of this approach and its underlying assumptions, flexible application of PST principles may provide a highly versatile means of improving unsatisfactory situations. Research has already indicated that PST can be very useful in the treatment of depression, for instance.

Thus, the cognitive trend in behavior therapy has yielded considerable evidence of clinical utility. In the coming years we look forward to (a) the completion of further research on the subject of which clients fare especially well in CBT, as well as what types of therapists employ CBT methods to good effect; (b) progress in answering the large question of *how* cognitive-behavioral procedures help people achieve important changes in their lives; and (c) further exploration of what we have described above as "conceptual boundary issues," which may bolster the role played by cognitive behavior therapists in the ongoing trend toward integration of diverse approaches to psychotherapy (e.g., Beitman, Goldfried, & Norcross, 1989).

REFERENCES

Abelson, R. P. (1986). Beliefs are like possessions. *Journal for the Theory of Social Behaviour, 16,* 223–250.

Abramson, L. Y., Alloy, L. B., & Metalsky, G. I. (1988). The cognitive diathesis-stress theories of depression: Toward an adequate evaluation of the theories' validities. In L. B. Alloy (Ed.), *Cognitive processes in depression* (pp. 3–30). New York: Guilford Press.

Ackermann, R., & DeRubeis, R. J. (1989). *Is depressive realism real? A critical analysis.* Manuscript submitted for publication.

Agras, W. S., Schneider, J. A., Arnow, B., Raeburn, S. D., & Telch, C. F. (1989). Cognitive-behavioral and response-prevention treatments for bulimia nervosa. *Journal of Consulting and Clinical Psychology, 57,* 215–221.

Alloy, L. B., & Abramson, L. Y. (1979). Judgment of contingency in depressed and nondepressed students: Sadder but wiser? *Journal of Experimental Psychology: General, 108,* 441–485.

Alloy, L. B., & Abramson, L. Y. (1988). Depressive realism: Four theoretical perspectives. In L. B. Alloy (Ed.), *Cognitive processes in depression* (pp. 223–265). New York: Guilford Press.

American Psychiatric Association. (1987). *Diagnostic and statistical manual of mental disorders, third edition, revised (DSM-III-R).* Washington, DC: Author.

Arnkoff, D. B. (1986). A comparison of the coping and restructuring components of cognitive restructuring. *Cognitive Therapy and Research, 10,* 147–158.

Arnkoff, D. B., & Glass, C. R. (1982). Clinical cognitive constructs: Examination, evaluation, and elaboration. *Advances in Cognitive-Behavioral Research and Therapy, 1,* 1–34.

Bandura, A. (1969). *Principles of behavior modification.* New York: Holt, Rinehart & Winston.

Bandura, A. (1977). Self-efficacy: Toward a unifying theory of behavioral change. *Psychological Review, 84,* 191–215.

Barlow, D. H. (1988). *Anxiety and its disorders: The nature and treatment of anxiety and panic.* New York: Guilford Press.

Barlow, D. H., Craske, M. G., Cerny, J. A., & Klosko, J. S. (1989). Behavioral treatment of panic disorder. *Behavior Therapy, 20,* 261–282.

Barlow, D. H., Hayes, S. C., & Nelson, R. O. (1984). *The scientist practitioner: Research and accountability in clinical and educational settings.* Elmsford, NY: Pergamon Press.

Barlow, D. H., Vermilyea, J., Blanchard, E., Vermilyea, B., DiNardo, P. A., & Cerny, J. (1985). The phenomenon of panic. *Journal of Abnormal Psychology, 94,* 320–328.

Barlow, D. H., & Waddell, M. T. (1985). Agoraphobia. In D. H. Barlow (Ed.), *Clinical handbook of psychological disorders: A step-by-step treatment manual* (pp. 1–68). New York: Guilford Press.

Barnett, P. A., & Gotlib, I. H. (1988). Psychosocial functioning and depression: Distinguishing among antecedents, concomitants, and consequences. *Psychological Bulletin, 104,* 97–126.

Beck, A. T. (1964). Thinking and depression: II. Theory and therapy. *Archives of General Psychiatry, 10,* 561–571.

Beck, A. T. (1976). *Cognitive therapy and the emotional disorders.* New York: International Universities Press.

Beck, A. T. (1983). Cognitive therapy of depression: New perspectives. In P. Clayton (Ed.), *Treatment of depression: Old controversies and new approaches* (pp. 265–290). New York: Raven Press.

Beck, A. T. (1987). Cognitive models of depression. *Journal of Cognitive Psychotherapy: An International Quarterly, 1,* 5–37.

Beck, A. T. (1988). Cognitive approaches to panic disorder: Theory and therapy. In S. Rachman & J. D. Maser (Eds.), *Panic: Psychological perspectives* (pp. 91–109). Hillsdale, NJ: Lawrence Erlbaum Associates.

Beck, A. T., Brown, G., Steer, R. A., Eidelson, J. I., & Riskind, J. H. (1987). Differentiating anxiety and depression: A test of the cognitive content-specificity hypothesis. *Journal of Abnormal Psychology, 96,* 179–183.

Beck, A. T., Emery, G., & Greenberg, R. L. (1985). *Anxiety disorders and phobias: A cognitive perspective.* New York: Basic Books.

Beck, A. T., Epstein, N., & Harrison, R. (1983). Cognitions, attitudes and personality dimensions in depression. *British Journal of Cognitive Psychotherapy, 1,* 1–16.

Beck, A. T., & Greenberg, R. L. (1974). *Coping with depression.* New York: Institute for Rational Living.

Beck, A. T., & Greenberg, R. L. (1988). Cognitive therapy of panic disorder. In A. J. Frances & R. E. Hales (Eds.), *American Psychiatric Press Review of Psychiatry* (Vol. 7, pp. 571–583). Washington, DC: American Psychiatric Association.

Beck, A. T., Rush, A. J., Shaw, B. F., & Emery, G. (1979). *Cognitive therapy of depression.* New York: Guilford Press.

Beck, A. T., Steer, R. A., Kovacs, M., & Garrison, B. E. (1985). Hopelessness and eventual suicide: A ten-year prospective study of patients hospitalized with suicidal ideation. *American Journal of Psychiatry, 142,* 559–563.

Becker, I. M., & Rosenfeld, J. G. (1976). Rational-emotive therapy: A study of initial treatment sessions of Albert Ellis. *Journal of Clinical Psychology, 32,* 872–876.

Beckham, E. E., Leber, W. R., Watkins, J. T., Boyer, J. L., & Cook, J. B. (1986). Development of an instrument to measure Beck's cognitive triad: The Cognitive Triad Inventory. *Journal of Consulting and Clinical Psychology, 54,* 566–567.

Beitman, B. D., Goldfried, M. R., & Norcross, J. C. (1989). The movement toward integrating the psychotherapies: An overview. *American Journal of Psychiatry, 146,* 138–147.

Belsher, G., & Costello, C. G. (1988). Relapse after recovery from unipolar depression: A critical review. *Psychological Bulletin, 104,* 84–96.

Bernard, M. E. (1981). Private thought in rational emotive psychotherapy. *Cognitive Therapy and Research, 5,* 125–142.

Biglan, A., & Campbell, D. R. (1981). Depression. In J. L. Shelton, R. L. Levy et al.

(Eds.), *Behavioral assignments and treatment compliance: A handbook of clinical strategies* (pp. 111–146). Champaign, IL: Research Press.

Biran, M., & Wilson, G. T. (1981). Treatment of phobic disorders using cognitive and exposure methods: A self-efficacy analysis. *Journal of Consulting and Clinical Psychology, 49*, 886–899.

Blackburn, I. M., Eunson, K. M., & Bishop, S. (1986). A two-year naturalistic follow-up of depressed patients treated with cognitive therapy, pharmacotherapy and a combination of both. *Journal of Affective Disorders, 10*, 67–75.

Blaney, P. H. (1986). Affect and memory: A review. *Psychological Bulletin, 99*, 229–246.

Booth–Kewley, S., & Friedman, H. S. (1987). Psychological predictors of heart disease: A quantitative review. *Psychological Bulletin, 101*, 343–362.

Boyd, J., & Grieger, R. M. (1986). Self-acceptance problems. In A. Ellis & R. M. Grieger (Eds.), *Handbook of rational-emotive therapy* (Vol. 2, pp. 146–161). New York: Springer.

Brady, J. P., Davison, G. C., Dewald, P. A., Egan, G., Fadiman, J., Frank, J. D., Gill, M. M., Hoffman, I., Kempler, W., Lazarus, A. A., Raimy, V., Rotter, J. B., & Strupp, H. H. (1980). Some views on effective principles of psychotherapy. *Cognitive Therapy and Research, 4*, 271–306.

Braswell, L., & Kendall, P. C. (1987). Treating impulsive children via cognitive-behavioral therapy. In N. S. Jacobson (Ed.), *Psychotherapists in clinical practice: Cognitive and behavioral perspectives* (pp. 153–189). New York: Guilford Press.

Brehm, S. S., & Smith, T. W. (1986). Social psychological approaches to psychotherapy and behavior change. In S. L. Garfield & A. E. Bergin (Eds.), *Handbook of psychotherapy and behavior change* (3rd ed., pp. 69–115). New York: John Wiley & Sons.

Brownell, K. D., Marlatt, G. A., Lichtenstein, E., & Wilson, G. T. (1986). Understanding and preventing relapse. *American Psychologist, 41*, 765–782.

Burns, D. D. (1980). *Feeling good: The new mood therapy*. New York: William Morrow.

Cacioppo. J. T., & Petty, R. E. (1981). Social psychological procedures for cognitive response assessment: The thought-listing technique. In T. V. Merluzzi, C. R. Glass, & M. Genest (Eds.), *Cognitive assessment* (pp. 309–342). New York: Guilford Press.

Chambless, D. L. (1988). Cognitive mechanisms in panic disorder. In S. Rachman & J. D. Maser (Eds.), *Panic: Psychological perspectives* (pp. 205–217). Hillsdale, NJ: Lawrence Erlbaum Associates.

Chambless, D. L., Caputo, G. C., Bright, P., & Gallagher, R. (1984). Assessment of fear in agoraphobics: The body sensations questionnaire and the agoraphobic cognition questionnaire. *Journal of Consulting and Clinical Psychology, 52*, 1090–1097.

Chaney, E. F., O'Leary, M. R., & Marlatt, G. A. (1978). Skill training with alcoholics. *Journal of Consulting and Clinical Psychology, 46*, 1092–1104.

Clark, D. A. (1988). The validity of measures of cognition: A review of the literature. *Cognitive Therapy and Research, 12*, 1–20.

Clark, D. M. (1983). On the induction of depressed mood in the laboratory: Evaluation and comparison of the Velten and musical procedures. *Advances in Behaviour Research and Therapy, 5*, 27–49.

Clark, D. M. (1986a). A cognitive approach to panic. *Behaviour Research and Therapy, 24*, 461–470.

Clark, D. M. (1986b). Cognitive therapy for anxiety. *Behavioural Psychotherapy, 14*, 283–294.

Clark, D. M. (1988). A cognitive model of panic attacks. In S. Rachman & J. D. Maser (Eds.), *Panic: Psychological perspectives* (pp. 71–89). Hillsdale, NJ: Lawrence Erlbaum Associates.

Clum, G. A. (1989). Psychological interventions vs drugs in the treatment of panic. *Behavior Therapy, 20,* 429–457.

Cohen, L. J. (1981). Can human irrationality be experimentally demonstrated? *Behavioral and Brain Sciences, 14,* 317–370.

Colletti, G., Supnick, J. A., & Payne, T. J. (1985). The smoking self-efficacy questionnaire (SSEQ): Preliminary scale development and validation. *Behavioral Assessment, 7,* 249–260.

Conoley, C. W., Conoley, J. C., McConnell, J. A., & Kimzey, C. E. (1983). The effect of the ABC's of rational emotive therapy and the empty-chair technique of gestalt therapy on anger reduction. *Psychotherapy: Theory, Research and Practice, 20,* 112–117.

Cooper, Z., & Fairburn, C. G. (1987). The Eating Disorder Examination: A semistructured interview for the assessment of the specific psychopathology of eating disorders. *International Journal of Eating Disorders, 6,* 1–8.

Cormier, W., Otani, A., & Cormier, L. S. (1986). The effects of problem-solving training on two problem-solving tasks. *Cognitive Therapy and Research, 10,* 95–108.

Covi, L., Roth, D., & Lipman, R. S. (1982). Cognitive group psychotherapy of depression: The close-ended group. *American Journal of Psychotherapy, 36,* 459–469.

Cox, D. J., Tisdelle, D. A., & Culbert, J. P. (1988). Increasing adherence to behavioral homework assignments. *Journal of Behavioral Medicine, 11,* 519–522.

Coyne, J. C. (1976). Depression and the response of others. *Journal of Abnormal Psychology, 85,* 186–193.

Coyne, J. C. (1982). A critique of cognitions as causal entities with special reference to depression. *Cognitive Therapy and Research, 6,* 3–13.

Coyne, J. C., & Gotlib, I. H. (1983). The role of cognition in depression: A critical appraisal. *Psychological Bulletin, 94,* 472–505.

Cummings, N. A., & VandenBos, G. R. (1981). The general practice of psychology. *International Review of Applied Psychology, 30,* 355–375.

Davison, G. C. (1966). Differential relaxation and cognitive restructuring in therapy with a "paranoid schizophrenic" or "paranoid state." *Proceedings of the 74th Annual Convention of the American Psychological Association.* Washington, DC: American Psychological Association.

Davison, G. C. (1969). Appraisal of behavior modification techniques with adults in institutional settings. In C. M. Franks (Ed.), *Behavior therapy: Appraisal and status* (pp. 220–278). New York: McGraw-Hill.

Davison, G. C. (1976). Homosexuality: The ethical challenge. *Journal of Consulting and Clinical Psychology, 44,* 157–162.

Davison, G. C., Robins, C., & Johnson, M. K. (1983). Articulated thoughts during simulated situations: A paradigm for studying cognition in emotion and behavior. *Cognitive Therapy and Research, 7,* 17–40.

Davison, G. C., Tsujimoto, R. N., & Glaros, A. G. (1973). Attribution and the maintenance of behavior change in falling asleep. *Journal of Abnormal Psychology, 82,* 124–133.

Deffenbacher, J. L., Zwemer, W. A., Whisman, M. A., Hill, R. A., & Sloan, R. D. (1986). Irrational beliefs and anxiety. *Cognitive Therapy and Research, 10,* 281–292.

DeRubeis, R. J., & Feeley, M. (1989). *Determinants of change in cognitive therapy for depression.* Manuscript submitted for publication.

DeRubeis, R. J., Hollon, S. D., Evans, M. D., Garvey, M. J., Grove, W. M., & Tuason, V. B. (1989). *Active components and mediating mechanisms in cognitive therapy, pharmacotherapy, and combined cognitive-pharmacotherapy for depression.* Manuscript submitted for publication.

Didion, J. (1979). *The white album.* New York: Pocket Books.

Dobson, K. S. (1989). A meta-analysis of the efficacy of cognitive therapy for depression. *Journal of Consulting and Clinical Psychology, 57,* 414–419.

Dobson, K., & Franche, R. (1989). A conceptual and empirical review of the depressive realism hypothesis. *Canadian Journal of Behavioural Science, 21,* 419–433.

Dryden, W., & Ellis, A. (1988). Rational-emotive therapy. In K. S. Dobson (Ed.), *Handbook of cognitive-behavioral therapies* (pp. 214–272). New York: Guilford Press.

Dush, D. M., Hirt, M. L., & Schroeder, H. E. (1989). Self-statement modification in the treatment of child behavior disorders: A meta-analysis. *Psychological Bulletin, 106,* 97–106.

Dykman, B. M., Abramson, L. Y., Alloy, L. B., & Hartlage, S. (1989). Processing of ambiguous and unambiguous feedback by depressed and nondepressed college students: Schematic biases and their implications for depressive realism. *Journal of Personality and Social Psychology, 56,* 431–445.

D'Zurilla, T. J. (1986). *Problem-solving therapy: A social competence approach to clinical intervention.* New York: Springer.

D'Zurilla, T. J. (in press). Problem-solving training for effective stress management and prevention. *Journal of Cognitive Psychotherapy: An International Quarterly.*

D'Zurilla, T. J., & Goldfried, M. R. (1971). Problem solving and behavior modification. *Journal of Abnormal Psychology, 78,* 107–126.

D'Zurilla, T. J., & Nezu, A. (1980). A study of the generation-of-alternatives process in social problem solving. *Cognitive Therapy and Research, 4,* 67–72.

D'Zurilla, T. J., & Nezu, A. (1982). Social problem solving in adults. *Advances in Cognitive-behavioral Research and Therapy, 1,* 201–274.

D'Zurilla, T. J., & Nezu, A. M. (in press). Development and preliminary evaluation of the Social Problem-Solving Inventory (SPSI). *Psychological Assessment: A Journal of Consulting and Clinical Psychology.*

Elkin, I., Parloff, M. B., Hadley, S. W., & Autry, J. H. (1985). NIMH Treatment of Depression Collaborative Research Program. *Archives of General Psychiatry, 42,* 305–316.

Elkin, I., Shea, M. T., Watkins, J. T., Imber, S. D., Sotsky, S. M., Collins, J. F., Glass, D. R., Pilkonis, P. A., Leber, W. R., Docherty, J. P., Fiester, S. J., & Parloff, M. B. (1989). National Institute of Mental Health Treatment of Depression Collaborative Research Program: General effectiveness of treatments. *Archives of General Psychiatry, 46,* 971–982.

Ellis, A. (1962). *Reason and emotion in psychotherapy.* New York: Lyle Stuart.

Ellis, A. (1976). The biological basis of human irrationality. *Journal of Individual Psychology, 32,* 145–168.

Ellis, A. (1977). Psychotherapy and the value of a human being. In A. Ellis & R. Grieger (Eds.), *Handbook of rational-emotive therapy* (Vol. 1, pp. 99–112). New York: Springer.

Ellis, A. (1980). Rational-emotive therapy and cognitive behavior therapy: Similarities and differences. *Cognitive Therapy and Research, 4,* 325–340.

Ellis, A. (1983). Failures in rational-emotive therapy. In E. Foa & P. M. G. Emmelkamp (Eds.), *Failures in behavior therapy* (pp. 159–171). New York: John Wiley & Sons.

Ellis, A. (1984). Rational-emotive therapy. In R. J. Corsini (Ed.), *Current psychotherapies* (3rd ed., pp. 196–238). Itasca, IL: F. E. Peacock.

Ellis, A. (1986). Discomfort anxiety: A new cognitive behavioral construct. In A. Ellis & R. M. Grieger (Eds.), *Handbook of rational-emotive therapy* (Vol. 2, pp. 246–274). New York: Springer.

Ellis, A. (1989). Comments on my critics. In M. E. Bernard & R. DiGiuseppe (Eds.), *Inside rational-emotive therapy: A critical appraisal of the theory and therapy of Albert Ellis* (pp. 199–233). San Diego, CA: Academic Press.

Ellis, A., & Bernard, M. E. (1985). What is rational-emotive therapy (RET)? In A. Ellis & M. E. Bernard (Eds.), *Clinical applications of rational-emotive therapy* (pp. 1–30). New York: Plenum Press.

Ellis, A., & Bernard, M. E. (1986). What is rational-emotive therapy? In A. Ellis & R. M. Grieger (Eds.), *Handbook of rational-emotive therapy* (Vol. 2, pp. 3–30). New York: Springer.

Ellis, A., & Dryden, W. (1987). *The practice of rational-emotive therapy (RET)*. New York: Springer.

Ellis, A., & Harper, R. A. (1975). *A new guide to rational living*. Englewood Cliffs, NJ: Prentice-Hall.

Ellis, A., Young, J., & Lockwood, G. (1987). Cognitive therapy and rational-emotive therapy: A dialogue. *Journal of Cognitive Psychotherapy: An International Quarterly, 1*, 205–255.

Emmelkamp, P. M. G., Brilman, E., Kuiper, H., & Mersch, P. (1986). The treatment of agoraphobia: A comparison of self-instructional training, rational-emotive therapy, and exposure in vivo. *Behavior Modification, 10*, 37–53.

Epstein, N., & Baucom, D. H. (1989). Cognitive-behavioral marital therapy. In A. Freeman, K. M. Simon, L. E. Beutler, & H. Arkowitz (Eds.), *Comprehensive handbook of cognitive therapy* (pp. 491–513). New York: Plenum Press.

Evans, M. D., & Hollon, S. D. (1988). Patterns of personal and causal inference: Implications for the cognitive therapy of depression. In L. B. Alloy (Ed.), *Cognitive processes in depression* (pp. 344–377). New York: Guilford Press.

Evans, M. D., Hollon, S. D., DeRubeis, R. J., Piasecki, J. M., Garvey, M. J., Grove, W. M., & Tuason, V. B. (1989). *Differential relapse following cognitive therapy, pharmacotherapy, and combined cognitive-pharmacotherapy for depression: II. A two-year follow-up of the CPT project*. Manuscript submitted for publication.

Fennell, M. J. V., & Teasdale, J. D. (1987). Cognitive therapy for depression: Individual differences and the process of change. *Cognitive Therapy and Research, 11*, 253–271.

Fichten, C. S., Amsel, R., & Robillard, K. (1988). Issues in cognitive assessment: Task difficulty, reactivity of measurement, thought listing versus inventory approaches, and sequences versus frequency counts. *Behavioral Assessment, 10*, 399–425.

Foa, E. B., & Kozak, M. J. (1986). Emotional processing of fear: Exposure to corrective information. *Psychological Bulletin, 99*, 20–35.

Forsterling, F. (1980). Attributional aspects of cognitive behavior modification: A theoretical approach and suggestions for technique. *Cognitive Therapy and Research, 4*, 27–37.

Forsterling, F. (1988). *Attribution theory in clinical psychology*. Chichester, England: John Wiley & Sons.

Freeman, A., & Leaf, R. C. (1989). Cognitive therapy applied to personality disorders. In A. Freeman, K. M. Simon, L. E. Beutler, & H. Arkowitz (Eds.), *Comprehensive handbook of cognitive therapy* (pp. 403–433). New York: Plenum Press.

Freeman, A., Simon, K. M., Beutler, L. E., & Arkowitz, H. (Eds.). (1989). *Comprehensive handbook of cognitive therapy*. New York: Plenum Press.

Friedman, M., & Rosenman, R. (1959). Association of specific overt behavior pattern with blood and cardiovascular findings. *Journal of the American Medical Association, 169*, 1286–1296.

Gagnon, J. H., & Davison, G. C. (1976). Asylums, the token economy, and the metrics of mental life. *Behavior Therapy, 7*, 528–534.

Garfield, S. L. (1986). Research on client variables in psychotherapy. In S. L. Garfield & A. E. Bergin (Eds.), *Handbook of psychotherapy and behavior change* (3rd ed., pp. 213–256). New York: John Wiley & Sons.

Garfield, S. L. (1989). The client-therapist relationship in rational-emotive therapy. In M. E. Bernard & R. DiGiuseppe (Eds.), *Inside rational-emotive therapy: A critical appraisal of the theory and therapy of Albert Ellis* (pp. 113–134). San Diego, CA: Academic Press.

Garner, D. M. (1987). Psychotherapy outcome research with bulimia nervosa. *Psychotherapy and Psychosomatics, 48,* 129–140.

Garner, D. M., Olmsted, M. P., & Polivy, J. (1983). Development and validation of a multidimensional eating disorder inventory for anorexia nervosa and bulimia. *International Journal of Eating Disorders, 2,* 15–34.

Garner, D. M., & Rosen, L. W. (in press). Cognitive-behavioral treatment for anorexia nervosa and bulimia nervosa. In A. S. Bellack, M. Hersen, & A. E. Kazdin (Eds.), *International Handbook of Behavior Modification and Therapy* (2nd ed.). New York: Plenum Press.

Geer, J. H., Davison, G. C., & Gatchel, R. J. (1970). Reduction of stress in humans through nonveridical perceived control of aversive stimulation. *Journal of Personality and Social Psychology, 16,* 731–738.

Glass, C. R., & Arnkoff, D. B. (1982). Think cognitively: Selected issues in cognitive assessment and therapy. *Advances in Cognitive-Behavioral Research and Therapy, 1,* 35–71.

Glass, C. R., Merluzzi, T. V., Biever, J. L., & Larsen, K. H. (1982). Cognitive assessment of social anxiety: Development and validation of a self-statement questionnaire. *Cognitive Therapy and Research, 6,* 37–55.

Goldfried, M. R. (1980). Psychotherapy as coping skills training. In M. J. Mahoney (Ed.), *Psychotherapy process: Current issues and future directions* (pp. 89–119). New York: Plenum Press.

Goldfried, M. R. (1982). Resistance and clinical behavior therapy. In P. L. Wachtel (Ed.), *Resistance: Psychodynamic and behavioral approaches* (pp. 95–113). New York: Plenum Press.

Goldfried, M. R., & Davison, G. C. (1976). *Clinical behavior therapy.* New York: Holt, Rinehart & Winston.

Goldfried, M. R., Decenteceo, E. T., & Weinberg, L. (1974). Systematic rational restructuring as a self-control technique. *Behavior Therapy, 5,* 247–254.

Goldfried, M. R., Linehan, M. M., & Smith, J. L. (1978). Reduction of test anxiety through cognitive restructuring. *Journal of Consulting and Clinical Psychology, 46,* 32–39.

Greenberg, L. S., & Safran, J. D. (1989). Emotion in psychotherapy. *American Psychologist, 44,* 19–29.

Guidano, V. F. (1987). *Complexities of the self: A developmental approach to psychopathology and therapy.* New York: Guilford Press.

Haaga, D. A. F. (1989). Articulated thoughts and endorsement procedures for cognitive assessment in the prediction of smoking relapse. *Psychological Assessment: A Journal of Consulting and Clinical Psychology, 1,* 112–117.

Haaga, D. A. F., & Davison, G. C. (1989a). Outcome studies of rational-emotive therapy. In M. E. Bernard & R. DiGiuseppe (Eds.), *Inside rational-emotive therapy: A critical appraisal of the theory and therapy of Albert Ellis* (pp. 155–197). San Diego, CA: Academic Press.

Haaga, D. A. F., & Davison, G. C. (1989b). Slow progress in rational-emotive therapy outcome research: Etiology and treatment. *Cognitive Therapy and Research, 13,* 493–508.

Haaga, D. A. F., DeRubeis, R. J., Stewart, B. L., & Beck, A. T. (1989). *Relationship of intelligence with cognitive therapy outcome.* Paper presented at the 23rd annual convention of the Association for Advancement of Behavior Therapy, Washington, DC, November 1989.

Haaga, D. A. F., Dyck, M. J., & Ernst, D. (1990). *Empirical status of cognitive theory of depression*. Manuscript submitted for publication.

Hammen, C. L., Jacobs, M., Mayol, A., & Cochran, S. D. (1980). Dysfunctional cognitions and the effectiveness of skills and cognitive-behavioral assertion training. *Journal of Consulting and Clinical Psychology, 48,* 685–695.

Hersen, M., Bellack, A. S., Himmelhoch, J. M., & Thase, M. E. (1984). Effects of social skill training, amitriptyline, and psychotherapy in unipolar depressed women. *Behavior Therapy, 15,* 21–40.

Hoehn–Saric, R., Frank, J. D., Imber, S. D., Nash, E. H., Stone, A. R., & Battle, C. C. (1964). Systematic preparation of patients for psychotherapy: 1. Effects on therapy behavior and outcome. *Journal of Psychiatric Research, 2,* 267–281.

Hollon, S. D., & Beck, A. T. (1979). Cognitive therapy of depression. In P. C. Kendall & S. D. Hollon (Eds.), *Cognitive-behavioral interventions: Theory, research, and procedures* (pp. 153–203). New York: Academic Press.

Hollon, S. D., & Beck, A. T. (1986). Cognitive and cognitive-behavioral therapies. In S. L. Garfield & A. E. Bergin (Eds.), *Handbook of psychotherapy and behavior change* (3rd ed., pp. 443–482). New York: John Wiley & Sons.

Hollon, S. D., DeRubeis, R. J., & Evans, M. D. (1987). Causal mediation of change in treatment for depression: Discriminating between nonspecificity and noncausality. *Psychological Bulletin, 102,* 139–149.

Hollon, S. D., DeRubeis, R. J., Evans, M. D., Wiemer, M. J., Garvey, M. J., Grove, W. M., & Tuason, V. B. (1989). *Cognitive therapy, pharmacotherapy and combined cognitive-pharmacotherapy in the treatment of depression: I. Differential outcome in the CPT project*. Manuscript submitted for publication.

Hollon, S. D., & Kendall, P. C. (1980). Cognitive self-statements in depression: Development of an automatic thoughts questionnaire. *Cognitive Therapy and Research, 4,* 383–396.

Hollon, S. D., & Najavits, L. (1988). Review of empirical studies of cognitive therapy. In A. J. Frances & R. E. Hales (Eds.), *American Psychiatric Press Review of Psychiatry* (Vol. 7, pp. 643–666). Washington, DC: American Psychiatric Press.

Howard, K. I., Kopta, S. M., Krause, M. S., & Orlinsky, D. E. (1986). The dose-effective relationship in psychotherapy. *American Psychologist, 41,* 159–164.

Huber, J. W., & Altmaier, E. M. (1983). An investigation of the self-statements of phobic and nonphobic individuals. *Cognitive Therapy and Research, 7,* 355–362.

Ingram, R. E., & Kendall, P. C. (1986). Cognitive clinical psychology: Implications of an information processing perspective. In R. E. Ingram (Ed.), *Information processing approaches to clinical psychology* (pp. 3–21). Orlando, FL: Academic Press.

Ingram, R. E., & Wisnicki, K. S. (1988). Assessment of positive automatic cognition. *Journal of Consulting and Clinical Psychology, 56,* 898–902.

Jacobson, N. S. (1989). The maintenance of treatment gains following social learning-based marital therapy. *Behavior Therapy, 20,* 325–336.

Janis, I. L., & Mann, L. (1982). A theoretical framework for decision counseling. In I. L. Janis (Ed.), *Counseling on personal decisions: Theory and research on short-term helping relationships* (pp. 47–72). New Haven: Yale University Press.

Kahneman, D., Slovic, P., & Tversky, A. (1982). *Judgment under uncertainty: Heuristics and biases*. Cambridge: Cambridge University Press.

Kanfer, F. H., & Busemeyer, J. R. (1982). The use of problem solving and decision making in behavior therapy. *Clinical Psychology Review, 2,* 239–266.

Kanfer, F. H., & Schefft, B. K. (1987). Self-management therapy in clinical practice. In

N. S. Jacobson (Ed.), *Psychotherapists in clinical practice: Cognitive and behavioral perspectives* (pp. 10–77). New York: Guilford Press.

Kelly, G. A. (1955). *The psychology of personal constructs.* New York: W. W. Norton.

Kelly, M. L., Scott, W. O. M., Prue, D. M., & Rychtarik, R. G. (1985). A component analysis of problem-solving skills training. *Cognitive Therapy and Research, 9,* 429–441.

Kendall, P. C., & Hollon, S. D. (1989). Anxious self-talk: Development of the Anxious Self-Statements Questionnaire (ASSQ). *Cognitive Therapy and Research, 13,* 81–93.

Kirschenbaum, D. (1987). Self-regulatory failure: A review with clinical implications. *Clinical Psychology Review, 7,* 77–104.

Klerman, G. L., Weissman, M. M., Rounsaville, B. J., & Chevron, E. S. (1984). *Interpersonal psychotherapy of depression.* New York: Basic Books.

Klosko, J. S., Barlow, D. H., Tassinari, R., & Cerny, J. A. (1990) A comparison of alprazolam and behavior therapy in treatment of panic disorder. *Journal of Consulting and Clinical Psychology, 58,* 77–84.

Kohler, W. (1925). *The mentality of apes.* New York: W. W. Norton, Liveright.

Kovacs, M., & Beck, A. T. (1978). Maladaptive cognitive structures in depression. *American Journal of Psychiatry, 135,* 525–533.

Krantz, S. E. (1985). When depressive cognitions reflect negative realities. *Cognitive Therapy and Research, 9,* 595–610.

Krantz, S., & Hammen, C. L. (1979). Assessment of cognitive bias in depression. *Journal of Abnormal Psychology, 88,* 611–619.

Lakey, B. (1988). Self-esteem, control beliefs, and cognitive problem-solving skill as risk factors in the development of subsequent dysphoria. *Cognitive Therapy and Research, 12,* 409–420.

Lambert, M. J. (1989). The individual therapist's contribution to psychotherapy process and outcome. *Clinical Psychology Review, 9,* 469–485.

Lazarus, A. A. (1989). The practice of rational-emotive therapy. In M. E. Bernard & R. DiGiuseppe (Eds.), *Inside rational-emotive therapy: A critical appraisal of the theory and therapy of Albert Ellis* (pp. 95–112). San Diego, CA: Academic Press.

Lazarus, R. S., & Folkman, S. (1984). *Stress, appraisal, and coping.* New York: Springer.

Leibenstein, H. (1980). *Beyond economic man: A new foundation for microeconomics.* Cambridge, MA: Harvard University Press.

Leitenberg, H., & Rosen, J. C. (1988). Cognitive-behavioral treatment of bulimia nervosa. In M. Hersen, R. M., Eisler, & P. M. Miller (Eds.), *Progress in Behavior Modification* (Vol. 23, pp. 11–35). Newbury Park, CA: Sage Publications.

Lewinsohn, P. M. (1974). A behavioral approach to depression. In R. J. Friedman & M. M. Katz (Eds.), *The psychology of depression: Contemporary theory and research* (pp. 157–178). New York: Winston-Wiley.

Linehan, M. M. (1987). Dialectical behavior therapy: A cognitive-behavioral approach to parasuicide. *Journal of Personality Disorders, 1,* 328–33.

Linehan, M. M., Goldfried, M. R., & Goldfried, A. P. (1979). Assertion therapy: Skill training or cognitive restructuring. *Behavior Therapy, 10,* 372–388.

Linville, P. W. (1985). Self-complexity and affective extremity: Don't put all your eggs in one cognitive basket. *Social Cognition, 3,* 94–110.

Linville, P. W. (1987). Self-complexity as a cognitive buffer against stress-related illness and depression. *Journal of Personality and Social Psychology, 52,* 663–676.

London, P. (1964). *The modest and morals of psychotherapy.* New York: Holt, Rinehart & Winston.

London, P. (1986). *The modes and morals of psychotherapy* (2nd ed.). New York: Hemisphere.

Luborsky, L., McLellan, A. T., Woody, G. E., O'Brien, C. P., & Auerbach, A. (1985). Therapist success and its determinants. *Archives of General Psychiatry, 42,* 602–611.

Mahoney, M. J. (1980). Psychotherapy and the structure of personal revolutions. In M. J. Mahoney (Ed.), *Psychotherapy process: Current issues and future directions* (pp. 157–180). New York: Plenum Press.

Mahoney, M. J. (1986). The tyranny of technique. *Counseling and Values, 30,* 169–174.

Mahoney, M. J. (1988). The cognitive sciences and psychotherapy: Patterns in a developing relationship. In K. S. Dobson (Ed.), *Handbook of cognitive-behavioral therapies* (pp. 357–386). New York: Guilford Press.

Mahoney, M. J., & Arnkoff, D. B. (1978). Cognitive and self-control therapies. In S. L. Garfield & A. E. Bergin (Eds.), *Handbook of psychotherapy and behavior change* (2nd ed., pp. 689–722). New York: John Wiley & Sons.

Mahoney, M. J., & Gabriel, T. J. (1987). Psychotherapy and cognitive sciences: An evolving alliance. *Journal of Cognitive Psychotherapy: An International Quarterly, 1,* 39–59.

Mahoney, M. J., Lyddon, W. J., & Alford, D. J. (1989). An evaluation of the rational-emotive therapy of psychotherapy. In M. E. Bernard & R. DiGiuseppe (Eds.), *Inside rational-emotive therapy: A critical appraisal of the theory and therapy of Albert Ellis* (pp. 69–94). San Diego, CA: Academic Press.

Malouff, J., & Schutte, N. (1986). Development and validation of a measure of irrational belief. *Journal of Consulting and Clinical Psychology, 54,* 860–862.

Marlatt, G. A. (1985). Lifestyle modification. In G. A. Marlatt & J. R. Gordon (Eds.), *Relapse prevention: Maintenance strategies in the treatment of addictive behaviors* (pp. 280–348). New York: Guilford Press.

Marzillier, J. S. (1980). Cognitive therapy and behavioural practice. *Behaviour Research and Therapy, 18,* 249–258.

Mattick, R. P., Peters, L., & Clarke, J. C. (1989). Exposure and cognitive restructuring for social phobia: A controlled study. *Behavior Therapy, 20,* 3–23.

McKnight, D. L., Nelson, R. O., Hayes, S. C., & Jarrett, R. B. (1984). Importance of treating individually assessed response classes in the amelioration of depression. *Behavior Therapy, 15,* 315–335.

Meagher, R. B., Jr. (1982). Cognitive behavior therapy in health psychology. In T. Millon, C. Green, & R. Meagher (Eds.), *Handbook of clinical health psychology* (pp. 499–520). New York: Plenum Press.

Meichenbaum, D. (1985). *Stress inoculation training.* Elmsford, NY: Pergamon Press.

Meichenbaum, D. (1986). Cognitive-behavior modification. In F. H. Kanfer & A. P. Goldstein (Eds.), *Helping people change: A textbook of methods* (3rd ed., pp. 346–380). Elmsford, NY: Pergamon Press.

Michelson, L. (1986). Treatment consonance and response profiles in agoraphobia: The role of individual differences in cognitive, behavioral, and physiological treatments. *Behaviour Research and Therapy, 24,* 263–275.

Miller, I. W., Norman, W.H., Keitner, G. I., Bishop, S. B., & Dow, M. G. (1989). Cognitive behavioral treatment of depressed inpatients. *Behavior Therapy, 20,* 25–47.

Miranda, J., & Persons, J. B. (1988). Dysfunctional attitudes are mood-state dependent. *Journal of Abnormal Psychology, 97,* 76–79.

Morey, L. C. (1988). Personality disorders in DSM-III and DSM-III-R: Convergence, coverage, and internal consistency. *American Journal of Psychiatry, 145,* 573–577.

Morgan, R., Luborsky, L., Crits–Christoph, P., Curtis, H., & Solomon, J. (1982). Predicting the outcomes of psychotherapy by the Penn helping alliance rating method. *Archives of General Psychiatry, 39,* 397–402.

Nelson, R. O. (1988). Relationships between assessment and treatment within a behavioral perspective. *Journal of Psychopathology and Behavioral Assessment, 10,* 155–170.

Nezu, A. M. (1986). Efficacy of a social problem-solving therapy approach for unipolar depression. *Journal of Consulting and Clinical Psychology, 54,* 196–202.

Nezu, A. M. (1987). A problem-solving formulation of depression: A literature review and proposal of a pluralistic model. *Clinical Psychology Review, 7,* 121–144.

Nezu, A., & D'Zurilla, T. J. (1979). An experimental evaluation of the decision-making process in social problem-solving. *Cognitive therapy and Research, 3,* 269–277.

Nezu, A., & D'Zurilla, T. J. (1981a). Effects of problem definition and formulation on decision making in the social problem-solving process. *Behavior Therapy, 12,* 100–106.

Nezu, A., & D'Zurilla, T. J. (1981b). Effects of problem definition and formulation on the generation of alternatives in the social problem-solving process. *Cognitive Therapy and Research, 5,* 265–271.

Nezu, A. M., Nezu, C. M., & Perri, M. G. (1989). *Problem-solving therapy for depression: Theory, research, and clinical guidelines.* New York: John Wiley & Sons.

Nezu, A. M., & Perri, M. G. (1989). Social problem-solving therapy for unipolar depression: An initial dismantling investigation. *Journal of Consulting and Clinical Psychology, 57,* 408–413.

Nezu, A. M., Perri, M. G., Nezu, C. M., & Mahoney, D. (1987). *Social problem solving as a moderator of stressful events among clinically depressed individuals.* Paper presented at the annual convention of the Association for Advancement of Behavior Therapy, Boston, November 1987.

Nisbett, R. E. (1972). Hunger, obesity, and the ventromedial hypothalamus. *Psychological Review, 79,* 433–453.

Nisbett, R. E., & Ross, L. (1980). *Human inference: Strategies and shortcomings of social judgment.* Englewood Cliffs, NJ: Prentice-Hall.

Notarius, C. T. (1981). Assessing sequential dependency in cognitive performance data. In T. V. Merluzzi, C. R. Glass, & M. Genest (Eds.), *Cognitive assessment* (pp. 343–357). New York: Guilford Press.

O'Leary, K. D., & Beach, S. R. H. (1990). Marital therapy: A viable treatment for depression and marital discord. *American Journal of Psychiatry, 147,* 183–186.

Öst, L. G. (1989). A maintenance program for behavioral treatment of anxiety disorders. *Behaviour Research and Therapy, 27,* 123–130.

Parks, C. W., Jr., & Hollon, S. D. (1988). Cognitive assessment. In A. S. Bellack & M. Hersen (Eds.), *Behavioral assessment: A practical handbook* (pp. 161–212). Elmsford, NY: Pergamon Press.

Persons, J. B. (1989). *Cognitive therapy in practice: A case formulation approach.* New York: W. W. Norton.

Persons, J. B., Burns, D. D., & Perloff, J. M. (1988). Predictors of dropout and outcome in cognitive therapy for depression in a private practice setting. *Cognitive Therapy and Research, 12,* 557–575.

Petty, R. E., & Cacioppo, J. T. (1986). The elaboration likelihood model of persuasion. *Advances in Experimental Social Psychology, 19,* 123–205.

Piasecki, J., & Hollon, S. D. (1987). Cognitive therapy for depression: Unexplicated schemata and scripts. In N. S. Jacobson (Ed.), *Psychotherapists in clinical practice: Cognitive and behavioral perspectives* (pp. 121–152). New York: Guilford Press.

Pilkonis, P. A., & Frank, E. (1988). Personality pathology in recurrent depression: Nature, prevalence, and relationship to treatment response. *American Journal of Psychiatry, 145,* 435–441.

Pirsig, R. M. (1974). *Zen and the art of motorcycle maintenance: An inquiry into values.* New York: William Morrow.

Polivy, J., & Herman, C. P. (1985). Dieting and binging: A causal analysis. *American Psychologist, 40,* 193–201.

Prochaska, J. O. (1984). *Systems of psychotherapy: A transtheoretical analysis*. Homewood, IL: Dorsey Press.

Rapee, R. (1987). The psychological treatment of panic attacks: Theoretical conceptualization and review of evidence. *Clinical Psychology Review, 7*, 427–438.

Rappaport, J. (1977). *Community psychology: Values, research, and action*. New York: Holt, Rinehart & Winston.

Repetti, R. L., Matthews, K. A., & Waldron, I. (1989). Employment and women's health: Effects of paid employment on women's mental and physical health. *American Psychologist, 44*, 1394–1401.

Riskind, J. H., & Rholes, W. S. (1984). Cognitive accessibility and the capacity of cognitions to predict future depression: A theoretical note. *Cognitive Therapy and Research, 8*, 1–12.

Robins, C. J., Block, P., & Peselow, E. D. (1989). Relations of sociotropic and autonomous personality characteristics to specific symptoms in depressed patients. *Journal of Abnormal Psychology, 98*, 86–88.

Rorer, L. G. (1989a). Rational-emotive theory: I. An integrated psychological and philosophical basis. *Cognitive Therapy and Research, 13*, 475–492.

Rorer, L. G. (1989b). Rational-emotive theory: II. Explication and evaluation. *Cognitive Therapy and Research, 13*, 531–548.

Rosenbaum, M. (1980). A schedule for assessing self-control behaviors: Preliminary findings. *Behavior Therapy, 11*, 109–121.

Rosenthal, T. L., & Downs, A. (1985). Cognitive aids in teaching and treating. *Advances in Behaviour Research and Therapy, 7*, 1–53.

Rotter, J. B. (1954). *Social learning and clinical psychology*. Englewood Cliffs, NJ: Prentice-Hall.

Rude, S. S. (1986). Relative benefits of assertion or cognitive self-control treatment for depression as a function of proficiency in each domain. *Journal of Consulting and Clinical Psychology, 54*, 390–394.

Ruehlman, L. S., West, S. G., & Pasahow, R. J. (1985). Depression and evaluative schemata. *Journal of Personality, 53*, 46–92.

Rush, A. J., Beck, A. T., Kovacs, M., & Hollon, S. D. (1977). Comparative efficacy of cognitive therapy and pharmacotherapy in the treatment of depressed outpatients. *Cognitive Therapy and Research, 1*, 17–37.

Safran, J. D., Vallis, T. M., Segal, Z. V., & Shaw, B. F. (1986). Assessment of core cognitive processes in cognitive therapy. *Cognitive Therapy and Research, 10*, 509–526.

Sanderson, W. C., Rapee, R. M., & Barlow, D. H. (1987). *The phenomena of panic across the DSM-III-Revised anxiety disorder categories*. Paper presented at the annual convention of the Association for Advancement of Behavior Therapy, Boston, November 1987.

Sanderson, W. C., Rapee, R. M., & Barlow, D. H. (1989). The influence of an illusion of control on panic attacks induced via inhalation of 5.5% carbon dioxide-enriched air. *Archives of General Psychiatry, 46*, 157–162.

Schwartz, R. M., & Garamoni, G. L. (1986). A structural model of positive and negative states of mind: Asymmetry in the internal dialogue. *Advances in Cognitive-Behavioral Research and Therapy, 5*, 1–62.

Schwartz, R. M., & Garamoni, G. L. (1989). Cognitive balance and psychopathology: Evaluation of an information processing model of positive and negative states of mind. *Clinical Psychology Review, 9*, 271–294.

Schwartz, R. M., & Gottman, J. (1976). Toward a task analysis of assertive behavior. *Journal of Consulting and Clinical Psychology, 44*, 910–920.

Schwartz, R. M., & Michelson, L. (1987). States-of-mind model: Cognitive balance in the treatment of agoraphobia. *Journal of Consulting and Clinical Psychology, 55*, 557–565.

Segal, Z. V. (1988). Appraisal of the self-schema construct in cognitive models of depression. *Psychological Bulletin, 103*, 147–162.

Segal, Z. V., Hood, J. E., Shaw, B. F., & Higgins, E. T. (1988). A structural analysis of the self-schema construct in major depression. *Cognitive Therapy and Research, 12*, 471–485.

Segal, Z. V., & Shaw, B. F. (1986). Cognition in depression: A reappraisal of Coyne and Gotlib's critique. *Cognitive Therapy and Research, 10*, 671–693.

Segal, Z. V., & Shaw, B. F. (1988). Cognitive assessment: Issues and methods. In K. S. Dobson (Ed.), *Handbook of cognitive-behavioral therapies* (pp. 39–81). New York: Guilford Press.

Seligman, M. E. P. (1988). Competing theories of panic. In S. Rachman & J. D. Maser (Eds.), *Panic: Psychological perspectives* (pp. 321–329). Hillsdale, NJ: Lawrence Erlbaum Associates.

Seligman, M. E. P., Castellon, C., Cacciola, J., Schulman, P., Luborsky, L., Ollove, M., & Downing, R. (1988). Explanatory style change during cognitive therapy for unipolar depression. *Journal of Abnormal Psychology, 97*, 13–18.

Shapiro, D. A., & Shapiro, D. (1982). Meta-analysis of comparative therapy outcome studies: A replication and refinement. *Psychological Bulletin, 92*, 581–604.

Shea, M. T., Glass, D. R., Pilkonis, P. A., Watkins, J., & Docherty, J. P. (1987). Frequency and implications of personality disorders in a sample of depressed outpatients. *Journal of Personality Disorders, 1*, 27–42.

Shelton, J. L., Levy, R. L., and contributors (1981). *Behavioral assignments and treatment compliance: A handbook of clinical strategies*. Champaign, IL: Research Press.

Simons, A. D., Garfield, S. L., & Murphy, G. E. (1984). The process of change in cognitive therapy and pharmacotherapy: Changes in mood and cognition. *Archives of General Psychiatry, 41*, 45–51.

Simons, A. D., Lustman, P. J., Wetzel, R. D., & Murphy, G. E. (1985). Predicting response to cognitive therapy of depression: The role of learned resourcefulness. *Cognitive Therapy and Research, 9*, 79–89.

Simons, A. D., Murphy, G. E., Levine, J. E., & Wetzel, R. D. (1986) Cognitive therapy and pharmacotherapy for depression: Sustained improvement over one year. *Archives of General Psychiatry, 43*, 43–48.

Smith, T. W. (1989). Assessment in rational-emotive therapy: Empirical access to the ABCD model. In M. E. Bernard & R. DiGiuseppe (Eds.), *Inside rational-emotive therapy: A critical appraisal of the theory and therapy of Albert Ellis* (pp. 135–153). San Diego, CA: Academic Press.

Smith, T. W., & Allred, K. D. (1986). Rationality revisited: A reassessment of the empirical support for the rational-emotive model. *Advances in Cognitive-Behavioral Research and Therapy, 5*, 63–87.

Sokol, L., Beck, A. T., Greenberg, R. L., Wright, F. D., & Berchick, R. J. (1989). Cognitive therapy of panic disorder: A nonpharmacological alternative. *Journal of Nervous and Mental Disease, 177*, 711–716.

Spivack, G., Platt, J. J., & Shure, M. B. (1976). *The problem-solving approach to adjustment*. San Francisco: Jossey-Bass.

Stiles, W. B., Shapiro, D. A., & Firth–Cozens, J. A. (1989). Therapist differences in the use of verbal response mode forms and intents. *Psychotherapy, 26*, 314–322.

Taylor, S. E., & Brown, J. D. (1988). Illusion and well-being: A social psychological perspective on mental health. *Psychological Bulletin, 103*, 193–210.

Teasdale, J. D. (1985). Psychological treatments for depression: How do they work? *Behaviour Research and Therapy, 23*, 157–165.

Teasdale, J. D. (1988). Cognitive models and treatments for panic: A critical evaluation. In S. Rachman & J. D. Maser (Eds.), *Panic: Psychological perspectives* (pp. 189–203). Hillsdale, NJ: Lawrence Erlbaum Associates.

Thompson, L. W., Gallagher, D., & Czirr, R. (1988). Personality disorder and outcome in the treatment of late-life depression. *Journal of Geriatric Psychiatry, 21,* 133–153.

Tobin, D. L., Holroyd, K. A., Reynolds, R. V., & Wigal, J. K. (1989). The hierarchical factor structure of the Coping Strategies Inventory. *Cognitive Therapy and Research, 13,* 343–361.

Turkat, I. D. (1988). Issues in the relationship between assessment and treatment. *Journal of Psychopathology and Behavioral Assessment, 10,* 185–197.

Turner, R. M. (1987). The effects of personality disorder diagnosis on the outcome of social anxiety symptom reduction. *Journal of Personality Disorders, 1,* 136–143.

Turner, R. M. (1989). Case study evaluations of a bio-cognitive-behavioral approach for the treatment of borderline personality disorder. *Behavior Therapy, 20,* 477–489.

Velten, E. (1968). A laboratory task for induction of mood states. *Behaviour Research and Therapy, 6,* 473–482.

Vestre, N. D. (1984). Irrational beliefs and self-reported depressed mood. *Journal of Abnormal Psychology, 93,* 239–241.

Wachtel, P. L. (1977). *Psychoanalysis and behavior therapy.* New York: Basic Books.

Wachtel, P. L. (1983). *The poverty of affluence: A psychological portrait of the American way of life.* New York: Free Press.

Walen, S. R., DiGiuseppe, R., & Wessler, R. L. (1980). *A practitioner's guide to rational-emotive therapy.* New York: Oxford University Press.

Watson, D., & Clark, L. A. (1984). Negative affectivity: The disposition to experience aversive emotional states. *Psychological Bulletin, 96,* 465–490.

Wegner, D. M., Schneider, D. J., Carter, S. R., III, & White, T. L. (1987). Paradoxical effects of thought suppression. *Journal of Personality and Social Psychology, 53,* 5–13.

Weick, K. E. (1984). Small wins: Redefining the scale of social problems. *American Psychologist, 39,* 40–49.

Weiner, B. (1985). "Spontaneous" causal thinking. *Psychological Bulletin, 97,* 74–84.

Weissman, A. N., & Beck, A. T. (1978). *Development and validation of the Dysfunctional Attitude Scale: A preliminary investigation.* Paper presented at the annual meeting of the American Educational Research Association, Toronto, Canada.

Weitzman, B. (1967). Behavior therapy and psychotherapy. *Psychological Bulletin, 74,* 300–317.

Wierzbicki, M. (1984). Social skills deficits and subsequent depressed mood in students. *Personality and Social Psychology Bulletin, 10,* 605–610.

Wilson, G. T., Rossiter, E., Kleifield, E. I., & Lindholm, L. (1986). Cognitive-behavioral treatment of bulimia nervosa: A controlled evaluation. *Behaviour Research and Therapy, 24,* 277–288.

Wilson, P. H., Goldin, J. C., & Charbonneau–Powis, M. (1983). Comparative efficacy of behavioral and cognitive treatments for depression. *Cognitive Therapy and Research, 7,* 111–124.

Wilson, T. D., & Linville, P. W. (1982). Improving the academic performance of college freshmen: Attribution therapy revisited. *Journal of Personality and Social Psychology, 42,* 367–376.

Wolpe, J. (1958). *Psychotherapy by reciprocal inhibition.* Stanford, CA: Stanford University Press.

Wood, L. F., & Jacobson, N. S. (1985). Marital distress. In D. H. Barlow (Ed.), *Clinical handbook of psychological disorders: A step-by-step treatment manual* (pp. 344–416). New York: Guilford Press.

Woods, S. C., & Brief, D. J. (1988). Physiological factors. In D. M. Donovan & G. A. Marlatt (Eds.), *Assessment of addictive behaviors* (pp. 296–322). New York: Guilford Press.

Woolfolk, R. L., & Sass, L. A. (1989). Philosophical foundations of rational-emotive therapy. In M. E. Bernard & R. DiGiuseppe (Eds.), *Inside rational-emotive therapy: A critical appraisal of the theory and therapy of Albert Ellis* (pp. 9–26). San Diego, CA: Academic Press.

Young, J., & Swift, W. (1988). Schema-focused cognitive therapy for personality disorders: Part I. *International Cognitive Therapy Newsletter, 4*(1), 5, 13–14.

Ziegler, D. J. (1989). A critique of rational-emotive theory of personality. In M. E. Bernard & R. DiGiuseppe (Eds.), *Inside rational-emotive therapy: A critical appraisal of the theory and therapy of Albert Ellis* (pp. 27–45). San Diego, CA: Academic Press.

8

Self-Management Methods

Frederick H. Kanfer
Lisa Gaelick–Buys

The traditional concepts underlying the activities of mental health workers imply an *administrative* model of treatment. This model presumes that clients seek assistance in an earnest effort to change their current problem situations. The helper administers a treatment to which the client submits and which eventuates in improvement in the client's life conditions. The model assigns a caretaking function to the clinician and a relatively passive, accepting, and trusting role to the client.

In some conceptual models, for example, those that rely heavily on the modification of the environment as a means of bringing about change (chapters 4, 6, and 10), the client's participation in the helping process is limited. In other approaches that rely heavily on changing cognitive behaviors (chapters 7 and 9) there is a basic presumption that the client is highly motivated to accept responsibility for changes. The view of the client either as a passive recipient, be it of drugs, conditioning treatments, or cognitive reorganizations, or as a person who is eager to change often runs into difficulty because of the paradox of the many clients who seek help on the one hand but resist external control on the other hand. The position of most professionals in the mental health field is that they can assist clients toward effective, *independent* functioning only by helping them to help themselves (Kanfer & Schefft, 1988; Seltzer, 1986).

Self-management therapy is based on a *participant* model which emphasizes the importance of the client's responsibility. Instead of offering a protective treatment environment, it encourages rehabilitative experiences in which the client accepts increasing responsibilities for his or her own behavior, for dealing with the environment, and for planning the future. The therapeutic environment is a transitory support system that prepares the client to handle social and personal demands more effectively. Self-management techniques are prescriptive methods that place much of the burden of engaging in the change process on the client. Nevertheless, they regard the therapist's role as crucial in providing the most favorable conditions for change. They also share the common features of most therapies; among them: the helper's optimistic orientation and compassionate understanding, the client's expectations of improvement, and the creation of opportunities for new (corrective) experiences (Frank, 1982; Goldfried, 1982; Stiles, Shapiro, & Elliott, 1986). The self-management framework presented in this chapter rests on the following rationale:

1. Many behaviors are not easily accessible for observation by anyone but the client. For example, some intimate behaviors, distressing thoughts, or emotional reactions can lead to client discomfort even though other people do not notice their occurrence. Participation of the client as a cooperative observer, reporter, and change agent is essential in these cases.
2. Changing behavior is difficult and often unpleasant. Many clients seek assistance, but often they are motivated not so much to change as to alleviate current discomforts or threats, preferably without altering their behavior or lifestyles. The client's acceptance of the goals and procedures of therapy is a basic motivational requirement. Therefore, the change process is conducted within a negotiation model that stresses the need for joint decisions on method parameters and on goals.
3. The utility of a change program lies not just in removing situation-specific problems or symptoms. What is learned in therapy should include a set of generalizable coping strategies and an ability to assess situations and anticipate behavioral outcomes, to aid the client in avoiding or handling future problems more effectively than in the past.

The acceptance of responsibility in treatment requires that the client develop a strong motivation to change. Therefore, the early phase of self-management therapy is designed to help the client accept the necessity for change and to develop clear objectives for treatment (Kanfer & Grimm, 1980). Modeling and learning to analyze problems and to work toward their resolution help the client practice toward more effective cognitive and interpersonal actions. By altering the social and physical environment, the client can alleviate the difficulty of changing and ease the maintenance of new behavior patterns. As new behaviors are carried out by the individual in the absence of the therapist, the helper fades into a role of diminishing importance. In this sense, the goal of the treatment process is its termination. The helper follows a "principle of least intervention," providing only as much assistance as is needed to enable the client to resume control over his or her life.

Self-management methods may aim at three outcomes: (1) to help the client acquire more effective interpersonal, cognitive, and emotional behaviors; (2) to alter the client's perceptions and evaluative attitudes of problematic situations; and (3) to either change a stress-inducing or hostile environment or learn to cope with it by accepting that it is inevitable. While most efforts have focused on changing rather than learning to accept problem situations, realistic appraisal sometimes also requires that clients learn to cope by adopting new attitudes toward situations that cannot be altered (Rothbaum, Weisz, & Snyder, 1982). Therapeutic techniques are temporary devices that facilitate the learning process, but do not necessarily become part of the person's everyday repertoire. In learning to use a typewriter, auxiliary charts and self-instructions that guide a finger to the correct key are critical in the learning process. But the accomplished typist uses none of these assists. Similarly, such techniques as self-observation, contingent self-rewards, problem solving, or contracts serve the function of facilitating change. As the person settles into a new and more satisfying behavior pattern, there is a decreasing need for their use. However, they are available on future occasions when the client faces difficulties.

Earlier behavior therapists have tended to disregard the client's thoughts and fantasies in planning therapy programs. Indeed, when strict control of behaviors is exercised by well-established rules, as in some institutions, in military organizations, and in cases where the individual is totally dependent on the social or physical environment, arrangements of environmental contingencies can be consistently applied, yielding extensive behavior change. In such environments, the person's self-regulatory processes contribute little to the shaping of behavior. A small child who is totally dependent for satisfaction of his physical needs on a few adults can easily be taught to change his behavior by simple rearrangement of reinforcement contingencies.

In our everyday experience, environmental controls are much less stringent, often contradictory, and frequently resented. Children are often rewarded or punished for the same behavior on different occasions and sometimes even in similar situations by different people. Verbal instructions, adult models in the family, and television screens frequently demonstrate the negative consequences but often also the benefits of aggressive behavior. Similarly, sexual behaviors, alcohol consumption, or smoking are under the control of conflicting social and physical consequences. A still larger group of behaviors, often called *neurotic*, include many interpersonal strategies for controlling other persons or for reducing the anxiety and discomfort of conflicting self-reactions. These behaviors are often determined by combinations of conflicting consequences. In these cases a person's thinking, fantasies, and other covert reactions can exert a significant influence in modifying the relationships between environmental inputs and the behavioral output that they aim to regulate.

The framework outlined in this chapter views behavior as the product of three sources of control: the immediate environment, the person's biological system, and the cues originating from the person's repertoire of cognitive and self-directive variables. These three spheres of influence interact, and it is their joint effect at a particular point in time that ultimately shapes behavior. Although the influence of a single factor can never be reduced to zero, its relative importance shifts across time and changing environments. For example, eating behavior is sometimes primarily under the control of the biological system. At other times, environmental variables such as the smell of fresh bread or the sight of other people eating are more important. Training in self-regulation can reduce the effect of temporary fluctuations in biological and environmental variables on a person's behavior, thereby freeing the individual to pursue self-imposed goals with some consistency across time and situations. However, such control breaks down when the strength of variables originating in the environment or in the person's biological system is substantially increased.

The methods described in this chapter provide a general structure for behavioral interview therapy. The procedures can be used in most cases but are supplemented for the individual client with other, problem-specific methods. Specific complaints, such as anxiety, depression, sexual dysfunction, or phobias, are attacked with programs designed specifically for these problems. But the general context of the change process is created by combining problem-specific techniques with the present methods.

A THEORETICAL FRAMEWORK OF SELF-REGULATION

To understand the general framework from which various self-management techniques have been derived, it is helpful to consider some of the psychological processes that occur in self-regulation (Kanfer, 1987; Karoly & Kanfer, 1982). Social-learning theory assumes that many everyday behaviors consist of chains of responses that have been previously built up so that a response is automatically cued by completion of the immediately preceding response. For example, typing, driving a car, and preparing breakfast are associated with well-learned repertoires stored in long-term memory. Their proper execution does not require continuous decision making about how to proceed. These well-learned sequences are related to the *automatic* mode of cognitive processing, which has been extensively studied by cognitive psychologists (Fisk & Schneider, 1984; Posner & Snyder, 1975; Schneider & Shiffrin, 1977).

Once established, automatic processes do not require attention, can be carried out in parallel with other activities, and are difficult to change. However, in some situations well-learned repertoires are not available, or previously learned repertoires are no longer effective. When new behaviors need to be learned, when choices need to be made, when goals are achieved or blocked, or when habitual response sequences are interrupted or ineffective, self-regulation processes are called into play. A qualitatively different mode of cognitive functioning called *controlled processing* marks the onset of self-regulation. Controlled processing demands focused attention and continuous decision making among alternative responses. When learning to drive, for example, a person must devote attention to each acceleration, turn, and gear shift: Overall performance is slow and deliberate. This is in sharp contrast with the expert driver, who not only engages in effortless driving behavior but is also able to carry on a conversation at the same time. Automatic processes are efficient because they ease the execution of many familiar behaviors without drawing on attentional resources. However, the effort involved in controlled processing is offset by the advantage of freedom from rigid, habitual behavior patterns. The individual has greater flexibility in selecting response alternatives, in developing novel responses, and in executing thoughtful, deliberate plans. Many maladaptive behaviors are associated with well-learned repertoires that are executed in an automatic fashion. The helper's task often involves assisting the individual to "deautomatize" troublesome behavior patterns, making them accessible to the self-regulation process, and to then "reautomatize" newly learned and more adaptive behavior chains.

Once initiated, the self-regulation process is characterized by three distinct stages (Kanfer, 1970b, 1971). To illustrate these, consider a social drinker who had never given much thought to his alcohol consumption, until his wife verbalized her intention to divorce him unless he stopped drinking. This event could startle the man, prompting him to attend more closely to his drinking behavior. This first stage is called the *self-monitoring stage* and involves deliberately attending to one's own behavior. For example, the social drinker might monitor the number of drinks he consumes each day or his behavior while drinking. On the basis of past experience, the drinker has built up expectations about acceptable drinking behavior. These might be called *performance criteria or standards,* the rules by which a person judges his or her own behavior. These rules are influenced by social values and personal experience.

The second stage of self-regulation consists of a comparison between the information obtained from self-monitoring and the person's standards for the given behavior. We have called this the *self-evaluation stage.* It involves a comparison between what one is doing and what one ought to be doing. Self-evaluation based on inappropriate or insufficient self-monitoring or on a vague and unrealistic standard interferes with effective self-regulatory behavior, because the comparison does not yield an effective guide for corrective action. For example, the social drinker might not detect a discrepancy if his standards for acceptable alcohol consumption were excessive or if he failed to monitor his behavior accurately.

The third stage in the self-regulation process is called *self-reinforcement.* During this stage, the person reacts cognitively and emotionally to the results of the self-evaluation. These reactions have both feedback effects, affecting the strength of the preceding behavior, and they have *feedforward* effects, influencing the client's expectations and behavior on future occasions.

In the case of the social drinker, if he determines that he drinks no more than others (his standards for desired performance are met), he may congratulate himself for having been correct in his judgment, continue to drink as before, and dismiss his wife's criticism as unjustified. Meeting standards can also have feedforward effects. The person may decide to change his standard to drink only three drinks per day instead of five, thereby creating a new discrepancy and setting the self-regulatory process in motion again. In addition, meeting a behavioral standard can lead to reevaluation of performance in related areas. For example, the social drinker who is successful in reducing alcohol intake may develop goals about reducing time spent in bars, or smoking, a behavior often closely linked to alcohol consumption. Failure to reach a standard similarly activates both negative reactions to the present behavior and changes in future goal setting, self-efficacy, or investment of increased effort on later occasions. Thus, both positive and negative self-generated feedback, together with individual personality differences and ecological variables, regulate future behaviors.

Kanfer and Hagerman (1981) have emphasized the importance of attributional processes at two stages of the model. First, to begin self-regulation the person must be engaged (or contemplate engagement) in goal-directed behavior. He or she must also view the requisite behavior as being under his or her control. It would make little sense, for example, to *self*-regulate the offensive behavior of a supervisor. However, aspects of one's own reactions to the supervisor could be under one's control and therefore within the purview of self-regulatory efforts. The behavior is also evaluated with respect to its relevance to the individual's short- and long-term goals. Trivial behaviors do not become the focus of self-regulatory activity. Secondly, in evaluating the causes of success or failure to reach the aspired criterion, the person can attribute the cause of a discrepancy to some aspect of self or to some external factor. Internal attributions create more arousal and stronger motivation for change, but they can also interfere with the change effort if they implicate global, negative, and unalterable characteristics of the person.

A sketch of the working model of self-regulation is given in Figure 8.1. This model has been derived from laboratory research, and it has been useful in developing clinical techniques for problems ranging from depression (Rehm & Kaslow, 1984) and addictive behaviors (Kanfer, 1986) to subassertive behavior (Schefft & Kanfer, 1987) and study skills (Greiner & Karoly, 1976). The model shows particular promise in the areas of health psychology and behavioral medicine (Holroyd & Creer, 1986; Karoly, in press). It has been applied for treatment of diabetic patients (Wing, Epstein, Nowalk, & Lamparski, 1986), cardiac patients (Lehr, 1986), hemodialytic patients (Kirschenbaum, Sherman, & Penrod, 1987), among many others. Although the model has been very useful and continuously tested and refined, we do not suggest that it represents the actual and universal presence of discrete psychological processes. In fact, it is quite likely that the total sequence of criteria setting, self-observation, evaluation, reinforce-

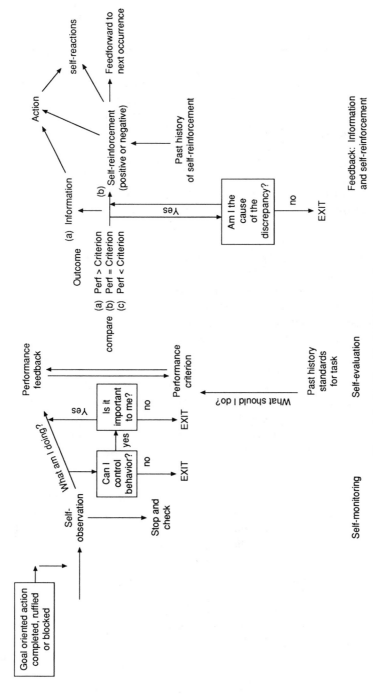

Figure 8.1. Working Model of Self-Regulation

ment, and planning of new actions proceeds rather quickly. Nevertheless, the model provides a framework for understanding the processes by which an individual organizes his or her own behavior and for pinpointing specific deficits that underlie self-regulation failures.

Rosenbaum has developed a scale to measure resourcefulness as a repertoire for effective self-control (1980, 1988) and has demonstrated differences in coping with various stressors associated with differences in resourcefulness repertoires (Rosenbaum & Palmon, 1984; Rosenbaum & Rolnick, 1983). In clinical situations, numerous methods have been used to increase the effectiveness of behavior at each stage of the self-regulation process. We describe these methods in the following sections.

The self-regulation model describes events at a time when self-directed action is needed. But the precursors to self-directed action begin much earlier. First, a vague reaction to a currently unsatisfactory situation orients the person to a new goal (Heckhausen & Kuhl, 1985). The person begins to think about a more desirable state of affairs, and motivation for attaining this state begins to build. As the goal is formulated more clearly, the person begins to examine, usually by imagery or thoughts, some possible strategies and pathways toward the desired goal. We have called this process *anticipatory self-regulation* (SR; Kanfer, 1987) because it involves similar processes as in the actual behavioral episode. For example, as an aggressive person imagines a new assertive repertoire, she would monitor her own imagined behavior and feelings and evaluate these against both social and personal standards for appropriate behavior. She might also imagine the consequences of the new behavior, in terms of her own reactions and those of others. Anticipatory SR is useful because it can sensitize clients to what they might encounter. People can prepare and improve various repertoires, eliminate alternatives on the basis of logical reasoning, and obtain information about their attitudes when imagining the event, as this may yield emotional responses of which such people have previously not been aware. A series of studies by Johnson and Raye (Johnson & Raye, 1981; Johnson Raye, Wang, & Taylor, 1979) has shown that imagined events often are remembered as actual happenings. These memories could enhance people's belief in their ability to carry out the actual behavior. Imagining scenarios has been shown to facilitate new behaviors (Anderson, 1983; Cervone, 1989). For example, Sherman and Anderson (1987) have applied this approach by asking incoming clients to imagine and explain why they would remain in therapy for at least four sessions. In comparison to the control group, significantly lower dropout rates were obtained for clients who imagined and explained their staying in therapy than for clients who were simply given equivalent information. Anticipatory self-regulation is useful to invoke specific emotions or moods that can help mobilize a person for action (Taylor & Schneider, 1989). For example, the feelings of pride and confidence resulting from imagining successful assertive behavior can help to energize actions that transform the imaginary scene into reality. These "thought experiments" (Kuhn, 1977) can shape realistic goals, reduce anxiety, enhance motivation, deepen commitment to act toward the goal, and increase readiness to act. However, a critical difference between anticipatory and corrective SR is that the former involves an imagined situation, which may or may not approximate reality. Since critical feedback from actual persons and situations is missing, anticipatory SR may be biased by the person's erroneous beliefs and expectations. In addition, anticipatory SR cannot help the person to attain high proficiency in a motor skill where practice is necessary (thinking of playing tennis is insufficient to attain mastery) and is also not efficient when moment-to-moment actions depend on the feedback from another person, such as in lovemaking.

Heckhausen and Gollwitzer (1987) have sharply separated this *predecisional* or motivational stage from the subsequent postdecisional or *volitional* stage. Once a decision has been made to work toward a certain goal, the person shifts attention from the earlier predominantly cognitive-evaluative activity to the task of translating the decision into action. During this stage, the client needs to confront reality. He or she must enact strategies, monitor and (if necessary) correct the behavior, develop rules to facilitate generalization, and finally continue the new behavior to maintain the desired goal state. For example, a person who is unhappy and whose social interactions are limited by timid and submissive behavior may vaguely develop an intention to change. He may imagine how his life would be enriched if he felt he was masterful and confident. At some point, the decision to do something about his timidity would be firmed by his positive imagery, and he would commit to a program for changing. In the postdecisional stage, anxiety reduction techniques, small graduated tasks to act more assertively, and social support may be utilized to bring about the behavioral change. Finally, in good therapeutic practice future problematic situations would also be anticipated to prevent relapse (e.g., Marlatt & Gordon 1985).

It should be clear that motivation may vary in each stage. For example, while a person may be willing to imagine new situations and talk about them in the predecisional stage, she may not be motivated to invest the time and effort needed to practice the new behavior or to protect it from decay after therapy is completed. Intentions can also be employed to elicit social approval or to reduce guilt over maladaptive behavior. When an alcoholic protests that he will stop drinking, or a gambler, after a large loss at the casino, says "I'll quit for good," it may be guilt reduction or social approval that strengthens the verbal response rather than a firm commitment to action. In fact, behavior is more likely to change if social consequences are contingent on execution, rather than on verbalized intentions (Kanfer, Cox, Greiner, & Karoly, 1974).

Commitment to change does not guarantee successful execution of new behaviors. The behavioral enactment is especially difficult when temporary environmental, social, or biological events undermine the commitment. For example, a cigarette smoker might have made a firm decision to quit after a night of heavy smoking, the urging of his friends, the challenge to willpower, and a hacking cough. However, later in the day, when alone and experiencing the physiological effects of nicotine withdrawal, the smoker might abandon his commitment. Similarly, clients with psychosomatic complaints, phobias, or other symptoms may have difficulties during the postdecisional stages, when plans need to be translated into action, because of intrusion of other factors or conflict with other goals that make the change process more difficult. Numerous techniques, such as distraction, repeated self-instructions, attention to the nonconsummatory aspects of tempting stimuli, and focusing on the ongoing activity, are among the techniques that protect a firm commitment and increase the likelihood of carrying out the necessary action (Kuhl & Beckmann, 1985; Halisch & Kuhl, 1987). Many of these techniques, including stimulus control, anxiety management, and self-reinforcement, are discussed in the remainder of this chapter. Cognitive strategies (noted also in chapter 7) and contingency arrangements can be employed to enhance motivation to make a firm decision and to carry out the actions required at each stage of the self-management process.

The term *self-regulation* applies to a general case in which a person's attentional resources and energies are allotted to the attainment of a single goal. For example, while bicycling or solving a math problem, all other concerns may be temporarily disregarded. But during therapy sessions, and particularly over a long period of time, several conflicting goals may rise and fall, draining attention and energies away from a therapeutic effort or even opposing it. When a motivation underlying the behavior to be changed is conflictual, we speak of the task of self-direction as *self-control*. In clinical problems, this case of self-regulation is most frequently encountered, and it is the one to which self-management methods are most often applied.

Self-Control as a Special Case of Self-Management

In common speech, such terms as *self-control, willpower,* and *self-discipline* are used interchangeably. Such behavioral dispositions have been considered to be personality traits resulting from the person's biological constitution or from past experiences with controlling actions and impulses. The view advocated in this chapter reserves the term *self-control* for a person's actions in a specific situation, rather than a personality trait. Our definition of self-control requires that (a) the behavior in question has nearly equal positive and aversive consequences; (b) prior to the occurrence of the behavior, that is, earlier in the chain leading up to it, a controlling response be introduced that alters the probability of the response to be controlled; (c) at the time of execution, the controlling response be initiated by self-generated cues and not under the direct control of the social or physical environment. Thus, when a person exercises self-control we talk about the fact that, in the absence of immediate external control, he or she engages in the behavior (the controlling response) that originally had a lower probability than that of a more tempting behavior (the controlled response) in such a way that the controlled response is less likely to occur (Kanfer, 1971; Thoreson & Mahoney, 1974).

Self-control skills are acquired in early training, and their success relates to the ultimate consequences supplied by the social environment. But at the moment of initiating the response, the person is not under direct environmental control. However, the likelihood that a person will begin a self-control program can be influenced by the environment. Feedback from the environment often underscores a discrepancy between behavior and standards, setting the self-regulation process in motion. For example, the decision to start a weight control program can be heavily influenced by (a) information from a physician that excessive weight is affecting one's health, (b) aftereffects of overeating during a holiday period, (c) inability to fit into most of one's clothing, (d) the decision of a friend to diet, and/or (e) criticism from a partner or spouse.

There are two types of self-control situations, differing in their time span and in the nature of their response requirements (Kanfer, 1977). In *decisional self-control*, a person is faced with a single choice in which a tempting goal-object or an escape from an aversive situation is given up in favor of an alternative that has greater ultimate (but usually delayed) utility. Acting on a decision terminates the conflict. Checking into a substance abuse center, passing up dessert when the waiter offers it, and deciding to board an airplane or a roller coaster that one fears are examples of this type of self-control. Once the choice has been made, it cannot be reversed. The shorter the time available for the decision, the smaller the influence of fluctuating considerations and variations in the attractiveness of the available reward. In contrast, resistance to temptation or tolerance of an aversive situation over a prolonged interval constitutes a *protracted self-control* situation. Concentrating on one's studies while a noisy party is in progress in an adjacent apartment, controlling aggressive behavior while caring for an obstinate, uncooperative child, or continuing to jog as fatigue increases are examples of this continuing self-control problem. In some situations the conflict between the two alternatives can continue over a very long time.

The decisional self-control situation is easier to handle than the protracted self-control situation. For example, it is easier to turn down an invitation to go to a tavern than to sit in a tavern all evening and refrain from drinking alcohol. Techniques to master both types of situations are necessary in a complete program. However, in the beginning it is easier to help the client master decisional self-control situations and to avoid prolonged exposure to temptation. An individual might be instructed to avoid friends who smoke during the first few days of a smoking cessation program. During this time, alternate patterns of behavior can be attached to the cues that previously elicited smoking behavior. When the individual later interacts with friends who smoke, his or her new repertoire will decrease the probability of reaching for a cigarette. Because self-control is easier in the decisional situation, the individual will be more likely to succeed in change efforts. This early success can bolster client motivation and perceived control over the problem behavior.

Although behavior change can be made easier through a carefully developed program, the self-control situation still requires considerable effort by the client.

For many clients, the main obstacle is to overcome the immediate rewards or negative reinforcements associated with the problem behavior. A sexual exhibitionist, for example, could find himself in a tempting situation that promises sexual fulfillment from carrying out the act. Although the prospect of apprehension by the police might make him anxious, this outcome is distant and uncertain. The therapist can help to alter the balance by making the aversive consequences more salient to the client, perhaps by discussing these consequences in therapy or by exposing the individual to environments or people related to the undesirable outcomes. It is particularly important to introduce variables that produce or increase the conflict in cases in which a client has been referred for treatment by another person or an agency, such as the court, for a problem that the client does not recognize. An increase in the client's concern over the problem behavior might be needed before he or she can accept the treatment program.

Training in self-management requires strong early support from the helper, with the client gradually relying more and more on newly learned skills. These include skills in (a) self-monitoring, (b) establishment of specific rules of conduct by contracts with oneself or others, (c) seeking support from the environment for fulfillment, (d) self-evaluation, and (e) generating strong reinforcing consequences for engaging in behaviors that achieve the goals of self-control. If an individual thoroughly enjoys an activity, even though it has long-range aversive consequences, no conflict is created and the question of self-control does not apply. For example, the person who indulged in heavy smoking prior to knowledge of the aversive consequences, or who fully recognizes the dangers but is unwilling to sacrifice immediate pleasure for a longer life, is not engaging in behavior that falls within the self-control analysis. Similarly, the person who had at one time engaged in excessive eating but who, over many years, has acquired new eating habits and rarely finds himself torn between dieting and indulging is not exercising self-control when he eats in moderation. We speak of self-control only when the person initiates some behavior that attempts, successfully or not, to alter a highly probable but undesirable behavior chain.

Persons who successfully cope with their difficulties do not seek help. Inquiry among persons who have achieved control over conflicting behaviors on their own suggests an overlap between the techniques that have evolved from self-control research and the many methods that people use spontaneously and successfully (DiClemente & Prochaska, 1982; Prochaska & DiClemente, 1982). Delaying an undesirable act, engaging in competing cognitive or motor behaviors, setting up challenges for oneself, rehearsing the positive consequences of self-control, and contingent self-praise or self-criticism are widely used. But there are differences between those who are successful and those who are unsuccessful with naturally occurring self-control. Successful self-controllers differ from their unsuccessful peers in using more techniques for a longer period of time, in rating themselves as more committed to personal change, in generating more plans and schedules to facilitate change, and in using the methods more frequently and consistently

(Baer, Foreyt, & Wright, 1977; Heffernan & Richards, 1981; Perri, Richards, & Schultheis, 1977). Further, the specific techniques used by successful self-controllers vary according to the particular problem. Clients often have the required skills or can easily learn them. Most frequently, what is needed is the encouragement of deliberate and systematic use of various methods and the development of positive expectations for their utility.

Training can help a client to cope with self-control conflicts in later situations, even though some elements have changed. The generalization effect has been noted in the clinic, but its demonstration in controlled research has been relatively weak (Richards & Perri, 1977; Turkewitz, O'Leary, & Ironsmith, 1975). Recent concern with maintenance of the benefits of behavior change programs is resulting in growing efforts to build preparation for posttreatment maintenance into the intervention strategy (Goldstein & Kanfer, 1979; Karoly & Steffen, 1980).

Marlatt and his co-workers (Marlatt & Gordon, 1985) have emphasized the importance of preparing clients *during* treatment for posttherapy crises in order to arm them for successfully avoiding or handling relapses. Essentially, their program—designed originally for addictive disorders—suggests the need for examining situations in which an individual is particularly vulnerable to relapse, preparing clients to cope with such events and reducing the abstinence violation effect (AVE). The AVE refers to the common conclusion by clients, when having a recurrence of symptoms or urges to engage in maladaptive behaviors, that their treatment has not been effective. In addictive behaviors the consequence often is a return to previously established abuses of alcohol or drugs; in neurotic clients the setback often results in a reappearance of the full syndrome. In an analysis of the factors that result in self-regulatory failure, Kirschenbaum (1987) proposes a strategy for maintenance of change in which clients are prepared to sustain self-regulated behavior past therapeutic sessions through continued self-monitoring and sensitivity to situations in which they may be vulnerable. He advocates continued awareness of the need to regulate one's environment, thoughts, and actions, to improve coping skills and to "compulsively" continue self-controlling behaviors that have been acquired in therapy. Other therapists suggest "booster sessions" after treatment termination. These sessions help clients to recognize that a newly acquired but fragile behavior needs nurturance before it blends into the natural life sequence.

The Functional Analysis and Selection of Target Behaviors

Behaviorally oriented clinicians have always emphasized the importance of the functional analysis in the design of change programs. We have expanded the traditional S-O-R-K-C framework (Kanfer & Phillips, 1970) to encompass the network of interrelated biological, cognitive, and environmental events in which the problem behavior is embedded. A detailed knowledge of this network often .

leads to the realization that the problem behavior can be influenced through multiple pathways and that the target of a change program need not be equivalent to the behavior one ultimately wishes to affect. It is often possible to identify a response that covaries with the problem behavior but is easier for the client to control. For example, glucose metabolism is related to the activity of the autonomic system, leading to the hypothesis that behavioral interventions that reduce autonomic activity would be useful in the management of diabetes. Relaxation procedures have proven effective in reducing insulin requirements and might also have desirable effects on other areas of the diabetic's life, such as reducing blood pressure and increasing subjective well-being (Surwit, Feingloss, & Scovern, 1983).

A number of issues should be considered when selecting a target behavior and planning a change program, such as client acceptance of the program, its ease of execution and likelihood of success, and the secondary effects of the program (Kanfer, 1985). In a self-control program, the target behavior must be primarily under the client's control, and the client must believe in his or her ability to exert such control (either before or as a result of early treatment sessions). Maladaptive behavior that functions as an escape response from an aversive emotional state is not a good choice for an initial target behavior. Instead, interventions should target on responses that are easier for the client to control such as those occurring very early in the chain of events leading up to the maladaptive behavior. For example, a change program for a child abuser should target on the initial feelings of irritation with, rather than on the final aggressive behavior toward, the child.

One never changes an isolated behavior: Change in one area of the client's life always introduces secondary changes that affect the functioning of the entire life system. The success or failure of a change program can depend on whether these secondary effects support the initial treatment goals. For example, drug withdrawal programs often involve avoidance of environmental cues associated with drug use, to reduce the automatic execution of consummatory responses. These cues can also function to elicit physiological responses that increase craving for the drug. Thus, avoidance of drug-related environments is an excellent intervention, as it impacts on both the psychological and physiological systems in ways that support treatment goals.

Unfortunately, the secondary effects of change often interfere with the client's efforts. For example, drastic reductions in calorie intake can lead to decreases in metabolic activity, with the paradoxical effect that weight loss becomes more difficult (Rodin, 1982). Similarly, the alcoholic who successfully avoids a favorite bar might find that his social network is substantially diminished. Careful assessment allows the therapist to anticipate these secondary effects and to help the client avoid them or develop coping strategies to ameliorate their impact.

A continuing assessment of relevant system parameters is often necessary, as the impact of an intervention may be delayed or changed over time (Kanfer & Busemeyer, 1982). For example, in the weeks following cessation of smoking, reduced metabolic activity and an increased preference for sweets can cause weight gain, despite earnest efforts by the client to avoid this undesirable outcome (Rodin, 1987). Such weight gain could have a demoralizing effect, perhaps causing a return to smoking, unless the client is prepared for this possibility and preventive measures are taken, such as increasing metabolic rate through aerobic exercise. Change introduces further change, and it is critical to the success of the program that these secondary changes support the initial goals. The fact that change has multiple effects is not necessarily disadvantageous. But it has important consequences for the maintenance of new behaviors, as maladaptive habits are often woven into many facets of the client's life, and changing a set of behaviors can require widespread change in the individual's lifestyle.

The Role of Perceived Control in Self-Management Methods

In addition to the practical advantages of involving a client in the change program, there are indications from different areas of research that a person's actions are influenced by beliefs about the causes of the behavior. When people believe that they have responsibility for some action, that a successful outcome is due to personal competence, that the behavior is voluntary and not controlled by external threats or rewards, they tend to learn more easily, to be more highly motivated, and to report more positive feelings than when operating under perceived external pressures (Deci & Ryan, 1987). Perceived control also reduces problems of resistance and reactance in therapy and enhances maintenance of treatment gains.

Perceived control is a broad construct, encompassing at least three dimensions that are relevant to change in the therapeutic context: (a) perceived choice over target behavior selection and program development (decisional control), (b) perceived control over program execution (self-efficacy), and (c) perceived control over program outcomes. For example, decisional control in a treatment program for a phobia can be established by allowing the client to participate in the choice of specific intervention techniques. If the use of self-directed desensitization is negotiated and agreed on, the client actively shares in planning the details of the relaxation procedure, the nature and ordering of the items in the anxiety hierarchy, and the time and frequency of at-home practice sessions. Self-efficacy requires the client to have confidence in his or her ability to execute the desensitization program. Perceived outcome control means that the client believes that its execution will yield the desired effect.

Before using techniques to enhance perceptions of control, the therapist should evaluate the actual constraints operating in the client's life and the appropriateness of the treatment for the client's problem. For example, if a client's weight problem is due to an endocrine disorder, then an exercise regimen will not lead to weight loss, regardless of how strongly the client believes in the effectiveness of this treatment. Similarly, self-efficacy beliefs will soon be undermined if a client lacks critical skills. For example, in overcoming test anxiety, the belief in one's ability must be supplemented with study skills and preparation time. Bolstering client perceptions of control when they in fact lack such control can lead to failure, eroding self-esteem and creating doubts about the very possibility of change. The client's actual control over the problem behavior should be ascertained early. If deficits are noted, needed skills must be taught or the change program be modified accordingly.

Available research suggests that perceived control serves to reduce anxiety (Stotland & Blumenthal, 1964), increase tolerance of painful stimuli (Averill, 1973; Kanfer & Seidner, 1973; Langer, Janis, & Wolfer, 1975), and enhance task performance and persistence (Brigham & Stoerzinger, 1976; Liem, 1975). For example, Kanfer and Grimm (1978) asked college students to complete a reading task and found that perceived choice significantly facilitated performance and effort. Similarly, when residents in a home for the aged were given greater choice in their daily routines, they showed a significant improvement in alertness, active participation, and self-rated well-being (Langer & Rodin, 1976; Rodin & Langer, 1977). In most programs, there are many parameters that permit opportunities for choice. Even with standardized programs, the client can be given choices about how the treatment will be tailored to the details of day-to-day life. The perception of decisional control can also be enhanced by the therapist's interpersonal behavior with the client. The client's preferences, opinions, and goals should always be considered. Negotiation and cooperation rather than didactic and authoritarian prescription is the hallmark of the approach.

Another important dimension of perceived control concerns the client's feelings of self-efficacy, or the confidence in his or her ability to execute the change program. Self-efficacy is often low at the beginning of therapy because people typically seek help only after repeatedly failing to solve problems on their own. Because low self-efficacy interferes with the initiation and maintenance of new behavior repertoires (Bandura, 1977), enhancing client confidence should be an early intervention target. Self-efficacy has been extensively studied and has been found to relate to successful behavior change in reducing smoking (Prochaska, DiClemente, Velicer, Ginpil, & Norcross, 1985), depression (Stanley & Maddux, 1986), athletic performance (Wuertele, 1986), and assertiveness (Lee, 1983). Bandura (1977) identified four sources of information that influence self-efficacy beliefs: past performance accomplishments, watching the behavior of others, exposure to verbal persuasion efforts, and emotional arousal related to task performance. Past performance is the most heavily weighted information source, suggesting that successful execution has the greatest impact on self-efficacy beliefs. Therapeutic tasks should therefore be designed to guarantee success by insuring that task demands not exceed the client's capacities at the time. Self-efficacy can also be strengthened by adequately preparing the client for execution of the change program. For example, role-plays and prehearsal can provide a feeling of success before the task is executed in natural settings. Another way to enhance self-efficacy involves helping the client prepare alternate plans of action in case the original plan cannot be executed or is unsuccessful. A more flexible plan of action and a backup alternative make the client feel more confident about his or her chances for success.

Clients often hold stable beliefs about their inability to execute certain behaviors, and success experience can be easily forgotten or discounted against the weightier evidence of past failure. The therapist can help the client to process success experiences cognitively in ways that maximize their impact on self-efficacy beliefs (Goldfried & Robins, 1982). For example, clients should be encouraged to evaluate success against past behavior in similar situations. Comparisons with other people or with ultimate goals provide less satisfying anchor points for assessing change. The client should also be encouraged to attribute success to stable, internal qualities. This can be done by focusing discussion on the ways in which the client's behavior directly led to success. Research suggests that participants and observers differ in their attributions of the cause of a behavior, with observers emphasizing qualities of the person more than qualities of the environment (Jones & Nisbett, 1971). Therefore, causal reattribution of success and failure experiences as originating in self and environment, respectively, can lead to a more objective view of behavior and increased self-efficacy (Försterling, 1988). Change in self-efficacy beliefs requires readjustment in stable cognitive representations, and these changes often lag behind objective measures of behavioral accomplishments. The helper can reduce this lag by initiating frequent discussions of past success, perhaps using objective indexes of improvement such as graphs or self-monitoring records for emphasis.

Decisional control is also important in establishing *intrinsic motivation,* or the belief that one is behaving in a certain way because one really wants to do so (Deci & Ryan, 1985). Research suggests that intrinsic motivation facilitates the learning process: Subjects who are internally motivated generally select harder tasks, are more creative, produce performance of higher quality, and are subsequently more interested in working at the task than subjects working for external rewards on the same problem (Condry, 1977). External rewards encourage individuals to view their behavior as purely instrumental for obtaining rewards. They are also less likely to maintain the behavior once the external contingency is no longer in effect. However, this does not mean that external rewards have no place in the treatment program. When employed with care, external rewards can be very useful in the initial stages of the change program, when the client requires additional incentives to initiate new behaviors. The negative effects of external rewards can be minimized if the client retains decisional control over the change program and if the reward conveys information about the client's competence. Rewards can also be more effective if their content is related to the task, such as rewarding weight loss with a new dress instead of with money. Of course, the crucial transition to integrating new behavior into the person's repertoire (internalization) requires that the newly developed skills eventually be maintained and reinforced by the client.

In our society in which autonomy, independence, and individuality are strongly emphasized, the client who requires the assistance of a helper to resolve psychological difficulties is presented with a dilemma. On the one hand, the client often actively seeks professional assistance, recognizing his or her inability to cope and the need to comply with the helper's prescriptions and programs. On the other hand, turning over control over one's life decisions to another person elicits opposition and is not in the client's best long-term interests. Sufficient evidence has been accumulated in the literature on reactance (Brehm, 1966) and clinical discussions of resistance and countercontrol phenomena (Anderson & Stewart, 1983; Davison, 1973; Ellis, 1985; Wachtel, 1982) to suggest that a therapist's assumption of full control and responsibility for the change program can hamper progress. In fact, compliance with a therapeutic regimen is often remarkably poor even with patients whose survival depends on execution of a doctor-prescribed program (DiMatteo & DiNicola, 1982; Meichenbaum & Turk, 1987). Taken together, the research findings suggest that an optimal treatment program provides clients with extensive opportunities to participate in the selection of treatment procedures and to attribute the cause of behavior change to themselves. Such a course of treatment does not free the helper from responsibility to assist the client and guide him or her toward proper choices, nor does it relegate the helper to a nondirective role. It speaks for a judicious balance between client and helper participation in such a way that the client never perceives the helper as imposing objectives or strategies.

Clients and therapists may hold beliefs and expectations about the helping process that undermine the adoption of a self-management perspective. Clients might see themselves in a passive and subordinate role, viewing the therapist as the powerful expert who will "cure" them. Other clients might enter treatment with skeptical attitudes toward psychotherapy or with visions of lying on a couch and free-associating. Helpers might also hold beliefs about clients and the helping process that interfere with progress. Wills (1978) found that helpers adopt a frame of reference that is biased toward pathology. In comparison with control groups of lay persons, therapists overattributed dependency and helplessness to other people, even if the rated target behavior was depicted as normal. Therapists who hold these beliefs about those they assist might deliver mixed messages, endorsing responsibility at a verbal level but reinforcing dependency through subtle, nonverbal behaviors.

The acceptance of responsibility in treatment is frequently related to the very problem for which the client seeks help. We have observed at least five patterns that suggest sources of reluctance on the part of the client to assume responsibility. Self-management treatment requires that these sources of reluctance be dealt with, before other programs can be initiated. These sources are:

1. Clients who have developed life-long habitual dependency patterns are skillful in eliciting caretaking behaviors, maintaining passivity, avoiding decision

making, and maneuvering others to take responsibility. Consequently, they tend to reject the therapist's invitation to participate actively in the change process. For example, Baltes (1978) found that residents in a nursing home were quite effective in exerting control over their environment through passive behaviors. They were reluctant to participate, even though increased activity was associated with positive consequences. In such cases, alterations of interpersonal patterns in small steps and by gradual increases from a very low level of responsible behavior might represent the focus of treatment during early sessions.

2. Clients who have maintained a fairly consistent and rigid pattern of behavior and who have suffered from the consequences of their psychological difficulties for a long time might be afraid to give up their known, though distressing, state for a new and possibly worse one. These clients are afraid of risks and of the unknown involved in changing. Therapeutic attention must first be focused on reducing the aversiveness to change before a specific program can be undertaken.

3. Clients who have previously learned that their own actions have no strong influence on the eventual outcomes of events often show both an unwillingness and an inability to commit themselves to change or to engage in therapeutic tasks. Such learned incompetency due to past experiences of helplessness requires involvement in tasks of increasing difficulty that permit clients to alter their self-perception and increase control over their environments.

4. Clients may be genuinely interested in change but lack the skills for initiating it. Deficits in decision making, planning, or interpersonal skills might have blocked previous efforts to change maladaptive behavior. For these clients, training in the missing skills and practical exercises in gradually changing their life patterns are indicated.

5. Clients who present themselves for treatment because they engage in socially unacceptable behaviors that provide strong satisfaction, such as addictions or antisocial activities, or clients who are supported by a partner, friend, or agency for maintaining the current ineffective behavior (a conflict between desiring change and maintaining some element of the status quo) can be reluctant to assume responsibility for change. For such clients, clarification of objectives and discussion of benefits associated with change are probably required before a change process is undertaken.

METHODS FOR THERAPEUTIC CHANGE
Creating the Context for Change

The model of self-regulation and self-control has led to the development of various treatment techniques. The methods are most easily applied when the client is deeply concerned about a problem, can anticipate some improvement by its resolution, and is firmly committed to complying with every step of the therapeutic program. In reality, such ideal clients for whom the employment of an effective therapeutic procedure is all that is necessary are relatively rare. Factors such as resistance, reactance, countercontrol, and intrusive counterproductive influences in a person's everyday life can undermine techniques that may be highly effective under more favorable conditions. For these reasons, close attention is paid to motivational variables throughout self-management therapy, but particularly during the early phases of treatment. When a client expects the tasks to be difficult, perceives the goals not to be very attractive, and is constantly bombarded by countervailing influences from the social environment, he or she is likely not to return.

Unlike many therapies, self-management approaches do not consider motivation as a fixed characteristic of the client. Rather, the burden is on the therapist to help the client develop treatment goals and maintain sufficient motivation to complete the various tasks. Further, motivation is not viewed as a unitary construct. In answering the question "motivation for what," the client's current concerns and momentary objectives as well as the distant goals of the program must be considered. An effective working relationship and a clear definition of the roles of the client and the therapist can contribute much to the client's commitment and to a positive outcome (Kanfer & Schefft, 1988; Lambert, 1983; Sweet, 1984). The client must come to view the therapist as someone who understands and accepts his or her life goals, has the knowledge and experience to help, and is acting professionally in the relationship. Clients are expected to participate actively, to carry out exercises associated with the program, to take responsibility for initiating and maintaining therapeutic actions, and to share the development of therapeutic goals. Helpers assist them with professional skills, techniques, support, tolerance, information, and feedback about both the development of treatment goals and the progress toward them. Clients, particularly those who have never been in therapy before, need to understand and accept these roles, as conveyed by direct statements or the therapist's demeanor in sessions. This structure of the therapeutic relationship, for example, means that a helper does not respond directly to client's requests for advice about changing a job or selecting a friend. Rather, the therapist would work with the client until the elements of the decision are labeled, and the outcomes of each alternative are clearly stated in terms of their effects on the client and on other people. The choice is then made by the client. This role structure is quite different from those advocated explicitly by some other schools of therapy and implicitly by the cultural stereotypes of therapy.

Although clients enter treatment with the presumed and often expressed desire to change, there are many factors that motivate a person to seek treatment. The decision to seek treatment may be influenced by the client's desire to change the behavior of a partner, reduce guilt over some maladaptive behavior, elicit social approval from the community for seeking assistance, or to obtain reassurance that his or her behavior is normal and that the client is not going crazy. For example, an abusive husband's decision to seek help may be occasioned by his need to reduce his own guilt or his efforts to appease a wife who threatens divorce. An agoraphobic may consult yet another therapist in search of confirmation of his firm belief that his illness is attributable to genetic or biological factors and nothing can be done. The decision to seek help cannot be taken as evidence of a firm commitment toward change. The problems are even more critical for clients who have been referred for treatment by a physician, a court, or a partner for a problem that the clients themselves do not recognize.

During initial sessions the main task may consist in establishing the therapeutic relationship and converting a vague intention for change into a clear and deeply committed decision. In addition to use of information and modeling, clients are asked to engage in cognitive exercises in which they imagine specifically how their daily routine would change and what life would be like if treatment goals were attained. In this stage of anticipatory self-regulation, problem-solving activity, role-play, and tasks that make the therapeutic goals more attractive are often used. Goal and value clarification techniques help the client specify particular goals and increase motivation for achieving them. The goal and value clarification procedure is designed to help the client shift perspectives from current concerns to long-term goals. For example, motivation to work on controlling obsessional behaviors, phobic reactions, or aggressive behaviors is enhanced when such efforts are linked with the achievement of personal or vocational ambitions, desired relationships, or opportunities to participate in activities and pleasures that were out of reach because of the current symptoms. Some questions that are useful for these exercises are found in both popular and technical books (e.g., Koberg & Bagnall, 1976; Lakein, 1973; Meichenbaum & Turk, 1987; Stock, 1987).

After the client establishes major goals, the focus of treatment shifts to consideration of subgoals and specific change strategies. For example, after making a firm decision on improving a client's self-confidence and ability to enter satisfying relationships, a dysphoria that stands in the way would be attacked by setting up such subgoals as monitoring and increasing activity level, decreasing self-critical thoughts, practicing assertive behaviors, and enhancing sensory awareness of pleasurable experiences. The subgoals can be tackled sequentially, beginning with one that has the lowest cost and difficulty level and the highest incentive value for the client. On the basis of professional knowledge and a functional analysis of the problem behavior, the therapist can guide this process and suggest specific techniques. Alternate routes for goal attainment, and the benefits and obstacles associated with each of these routes, are examined jointly in a spirit of negotiation between client and therapist.

Once a firm commitment has been made, the program becomes more heavily action oriented. There are many specific techniques that can insure that the person does not recycle to reevaluating his or her commitment and that the firm decision is protected from alternatives at this stage (Cervone, 1989; Heckhausen & Gollwitzer, 1987). For example, clients can be encouraged to seek opportunities to execute planned behaviors in their everyday life, attend to factors that improve performance, boost self-confidence and familiarity with new behaviors, and anticipate how to cope with obstacles that may be encountered.

In this section we have suggested that systematic attention needs to be paid to the development of goals and maintenance of their attractiveness throughout therapy. Although developing a therapeutic alliance and utilization of various cognitive and behavioral techniques in sessions are important to lay the ground work, continuous client efforts to apply the newly gained knowledge and skills in everyday life are essential. The development of goals and channeling motivations toward them is not only a cognitive enterprise. Feelings, moods, and emotions also affect client activities, either to support or interfere with goal-directed actions. The role of emotions has not been treated systematically in behavioral approaches until recently. They were viewed as undesirable states that needed to be controlled, eliminated, or suppressed. More recent analyses of the effects of moods and emotional states have suggested that emotions can be motivating. This new view of emotions (e.g., Frijda, 1986; Greenberg & Safran, 1987) stresses that emotional states and moods predispose individuals to action toward specified goals. They influence information processing, willingness to cooperate and to take risks, as well as selective recall of past events (Isen, 1984; Mackie & Worth, 1989; Schwarz, in press; among others). Some of these implications for therapeutic strategies are discussed in chapter 9. Considering the recency of the application of this research area to clinical procedures, we state here only that the reader should be aware that both positive and negative moods and emotions may be useful instruments for behavior change even though they may be obstacles at other times. A reexamination of such well-established techniques as catharsis, systematic desensitization, or deliberate arousal of emotions by confrontation may lead to a better understanding of the processes and mechanisms involved and therefore to a broader application of these techniques.

Self-management methods rely heavily on tasks and assignments to serve the dual purpose of enhancing client motivation and structuring the change program. In the next section, some general comments are made on the use of homework assignments that play a pivotal role in most treatment programs.

Tasks and Assignments

Assignment of particular tasks has long been used as an adjunct therapeutic technique (e.g., Herzberg, 1945; Shelton, 1979; Shelton & Levy, 1981). However, in a self-management program, this feature takes on a central role. The assignment of tasks that are graded in difficulty gives meaning to the helper's description of self-management methods as procedures that require clients to take responsibility for changing their behavior. Tasks stress the importance of changing behaviors outside the helping relationship and help the client perceive the continuity between treatment sessions and daily life experiences. In addition, homework assignments yield information about the client's skills and the feasibility of tentative treatment objectives.

Homework assignments can also increase commitment to change. Ideally, treatment objectives represent current concerns, or short- and long-term goals that the individual is actively striving to obtain (Klinger, Barta, & Maxeiner, 1979). Current concerns serve to heighten attention to goal-relevant cues, to increase the utilization of skills, and to motivate fantasies and thoughts related to goal attainment. Increasing a current concern can sensitize individuals to search their own repertoire and the environment for ways of achieving their goal and to channel thoughts and fantasies to the same end. For example, when a client complains of loneliness, increased frequency of social interactions can be a therapeutic objective. Assignments can help to increase her sensitivity to opportunities for establishing social contacts. The client might be asked to observe others, to obtain information about where social activities take place, or to initiate brief social contacts. A task for a client looking for work might involve asking friends for information about jobs, searching newspapers, imagining himself in the position of other persons at work, and asking himself while shopping for services or goods what opportunities for work there might be for him. Assignments can intensify the client's involvement in the change process by creating specific incentives in addition to the benefits derived from their therapeutic aspects (e.g., practice of skills, reduction of anxiety, and collection of information).

Homework assignments are often presented as tentative (and safe) efforts to acquire new behavioral repertoires. They provide opportunities to experience new life patterns, in the guise of tryouts for which there are no aversive consequences. It is important that the client participate in planning the particular forms that the assigned behavior takes. Goals should be realistic, to minimize the possibility of failure.

There are four steps to follow whenever a client is asked to complete a task or assignment: (a) information, (b) anticipatory practice or *prehearsal,* (c) execution in natural settings, and (d) review. Inclusion of all four steps increases the probability of success and maximizes the learning potential of the experience. During the information stage, the requirements of the assignment are clarified. This could involve didactic instruction about a particular technique or discussion of how the technique can be tailored to fit the client's daily routine.

Prehearsal is an application of anticipatory self-regulation to a specific situation. During prehearsal, the client imagines and practices the assigned task within the safety of the therapy environment. Prehearsal provides opportunities for the helper to model various behaviors, to clarify the details of the situation and the behavior to be executed, and to extinguish some of the anxiety associated with them. Role-plays are commonly used during prehearsal. They can involve scenarios of interpersonal situations or rehearsals of what the client will later think, fantasize, or say to himself or herself. By varying the details in a series of role-plays, the client can be taught to approach the task in a flexible fashion, increasing the ability to execute the task in the face of changing external factors. The helper initially provides guidance and structure for the role-play in the session and for preparing the behavior associated with the assigned task. As the client shows increased competence, the helper reduces participation, except to maintain encouragement and reinforcement.

After a task has been executed in a natural setting, it should be reviewed in detail during the following therapy session. Memories of task execution are likely to be experiential or *episodic* (Tulving, 1972). Such memories are tied to a specific spatial and temporal context, are difficult to retrieve, and are usually discounted if they are inconsistent with other knowledge. As clients discuss their experiences, they begin to form semantic memories representing basic knowledge about themselves. Semantic memories are easier to recall and are therefore more likely to influence thoughts and behaviors on future occasions. Semantic memories are formed slowly, and can require the successful execution and discussion of many similar tasks before they are established and integrated with other knowledge. In reviewing a task, the helper should also promote the client's sense of self-efficacy, according to the aforementioned guidelines. When the client reports progress or defines some difficulty in a situation, the task is modified accordingly. The helper must be careful to offer encouragement and reinforcement only for those accomplishments that can be attributed to the client's execution of the previously planned behavior and not for success or failure that has been caused by the behaviors of others. When a shy client approaches another person, he or she has accomplished the therapeutic task, whether the person accepts or rejects the client's overture.

When the client is fearful about some component of a situation, the task could emphasize a contrived purpose in order to bring about initial emission of the behavior. For example, a client with fears of social interaction can be given a highly specific task that would help her overcome the initial fear. With an extremely withdrawn client, we have used such contrived tasks as going to a drugstore for a cup of coffee and specifically recording the number and types of interactions of people sitting at the counter for a 15-minute period. A shy and insecure young woman was asked to attend a social gathering for the specific purpose of obtaining information about the occupational background and current jobs of several guests. In these cases, the tasks served several purposes. First, they provided an opportunity for execution of behaviors that had been a problem in the past. At times this helps to dispel the client's expectations that something terrible will occur. Second, the client's self-observation and discussion with the helper give the client greater efficiency and comfort in the newly acquired role. Clients can also be asked to say what they thought their impact was on the behavior of others and to discuss their feelings during the interactions witnessed (Kopel & Arkowitz, 1975). These new experiences permit individuals to reevaluate their perceptions of self and of their skills. They also make possible the utilization of problem-solving skills in the interview sessions and ultimately in the client's daily life.

As the change program progresses, the client should be given increasing responsibility in the planning and execution of tasks. The assignment of tasks is faded as the end of therapy approaches. During training, helpers often complain that in the initial interviews they cannot think of a proper task for the client, but even a first interview offers the opportunity for numerous assignments. Whenever clients are not clear about some aspect of the problem or express uncertainty about their ability to carry out some behavior, or whenever they indicate that they have thought of but never tried a particular behavior strategy, the helper has themes for possible assignments. The tasks should be relatively simple at first; for example, to list desirable outcomes of some relationship, to observe how the client responds to other people's anger, or to respond positively to a partner. In a first interview, these assignments serve the dual purpose of providing information relevant to treatment and structuring therapy as a situation that requires the client's active participation.

Contracts

A therapeutic contract is a written statement that outlines specific actions that the client has agreed to execute and establishes consequences for fulfillment and nonfulfillment of the agreement. Contracts can be used to (a) help the client initiate specific actions, (b) establish clear-cut criteria for achievement, and (c) provide a mechanism for clarifying the consequences of engaging in the behavior. Contracting provides both the helper and the client with a record of what has been agreed on and an opportunity to evaluate progress by comparison against the terms of the agreement. It also provides the client with a set of rules that govern the change process and with practice in the process of clearly defining goals and instrumental acts to reach them. Negotiating the contract requires a careful review of the behavioral requirements and can be embedded within the information and prehearsal stages of the model. Finally, the explicit and public nature of the contract enhances the client's commitment to execute the intended behaviors.

Contracts can be unilateral, when clients obligate themselves to a change program without expecting specific contributions from another person, or they can be bilateral. Bilateral contracts, commonly used in marriage counseling, in families, or between teacher and child, specify obligations and mutual reinforcements for each of the parties. Contracts can also be made by an individual with himself or herself, with the helper, with others when the helper serves as a monitor and negotiator, or with a group such as a classroom or family.

There are seven elements that should be considered in every behavioral contract. Each of these elements should be spelled out in detail, arrived at by negotiation, and accepted fully by the client. Good contracts should have short-range goals and should be written. The behaviors required in the contract should be rehearsed prior to execution, and all efforts should be made to avoid a contract that might be difficult or impossible for the person to attain. The seven elements in the contract provide that:

1. A clear and detailed description of the required instrumental behavior be stated.
2. Some criterion be set for the time or frequency limitations constituting the goal of the contract.
3. The contract specifies positive consequences, contingent on fulfillment of the criterion.
4. Provisions be made for some aversive consequences, contingent on nonfulfillment of the contract within a specified time or with a specified frequency.
5. A bonus clause indicates the additional positive reinforcements obtainable if the person exceeds the minimal demands of the contract.
6. The contract specifies the means by which the behavior is observed, measured, and recorded: A procedure is stated for informing the client of his or her achievements over the duration of the contract.
7. The timing for delivery of reinforcement contingencies be arranged to follow the response as quickly as possible.

Clinical examples of successful behavioral contracting, combined with other self-management techniques, come from the treatment of almost all psychological dysfunctions. Contracts can reduce clients' fears that they will never overcome their problems by requiring only small behavior changes at first and by providing a framework within which other self-management techniques could be carried out. Reports of successful contract use are available in cases of addictive behaviors (Bigelow, Sticker, Leibson, & Griffiths, 1976), weight control (Jeffrey, Gerber, Rosenthal, & Lindquist, 1983), excessive smoking (Spring, Sipich, Trimble, & Goeckner, 1978), as well as marital discord (Jacobson, 1977) and other problem behaviors. A review of the literature on contracting is found in Kirschenbaum and Flanery (1983).

Behavioral contracts can be enhanced if they are associated with public commitment to either a friend, a spouse, or a group of co-workers. However, caution must be exercised in the use of public commitment, because the client might set the criterion for the contracted behavior higher than he or she can reasonably achieve, in order to impress others. Furthermore, the client's difficulties in fulfilling the contract might lead him or her to avoid a person who knows of the commitment or to engage in actions that might even endanger the relationship with someone who is party to the client's unfulfilled contract. For example, in marital therapy, there has been a decline in use of contingency contracts in which behaviors of each partner are employed to create positive control over the other's actions. Instead, general directives to each partner with many alternatives toward a similar goal, independent of the partner's acts, have been preferred (Jacobson, 1983).

Self-Monitoring

Self-monitoring (SM) was initially proposed as an operation that parallels the measurement of behavior in situations where a client is under the continuous observation of a therapist or an experimenter. However, later research indicated that the accuracy of SM, when compared with independent measures of the same behavior, varies widely across different situations (Kazdin, 1974). The schedule on which the behavior is monitored, competition from concurrent responses, awareness that SM is independently assessed by an observer, the valence of the target behavior, reinforcement for accurate SM, and the nature of the instructions are among the variables that affect SM accuracy (Kanfer, 1970a; McFall, 1977; Nelson, 1977). There are restrictions on the use of SM when precise, numerical data about a target behavior are required. However, if certain conditions are met, SM data can still be used to provide estimates of behavior or to monitor relative change in behavior over time.

SM also serves a number of functions that do not require absolute accuracy in recording. SM can be used to obtain qualitative information that is relevant to the functional analysis and treatment planning. For example, clients might be asked to monitor the antecedents and consequences of a target behavior or to record their emotional states while engaging in the behavior. SM can also increase client motivation for change. Baseline data, collected before treatment implementation, can provide an incentive for future change. Later in the program, the achievement of a criterion can be graphically displayed and can provide a visual guide for the administration of reinforcement, by the therapist and by the client. For example, various common self-indulgences, such as buying a luxury item, engaging in pleasurable activity, or taking a brief rest, can be tied directly to the achievement of a change in the target behavior.

Another important feature of SM is that it can be incompatible with continuation of an undesirable behavior. For example, in a case of the author's, a husband and wife with severe marital problems were asked to monitor hostile and aggressive thoughts toward each other. The monitoring task included making a tape recording of any interactions that threatened to develop into a fight. The couple reported reduced frequency of fighting and explained laughingly that on several occasions the tape recorder was not handy. The clients then jointly set up the recorder. By that time, the hostile interpersonal interaction had been interrupted, and the couple could no longer remember what they were going to fight about.

In some instances, self-monitoring assignments alone have produced favorable changes in the target behavior and clinicians have utilized SM as a therapeutic technique in its own right. Studies with obese patients (Romanczyk, 1974), with smokers motivated to stop (Abrams & Wilson, 1979), with school children (Broden, Hall, & Mitts, 1971), with students having study problems (Johnson & White, 1971; Richards, 1975), with agoraphobics (Emmelkamp, 1974), and with retarded adults (Nelson, Lipinski, & Black, 1976) have reported reductions in undesirable behaviors. However, other investigators (e.g., Mahoney, Moura, & Wade, 1973) have failed to reproduce these findings. The processes underlying SM reactivity appear to be complex and to reflect the operation of many variables. The valence and importance of the behavior, the level of task mastery, the availability of performance feedback, and the delay between response execution and the SM activity all influence the extent to which the SM task is reactive (Fremouw & Brown, 1980; Kirschenbaum & Tomarken, 1982; Komaki & Dore, 1978). Also, these variables do not function in a simple fashion. For example, monitoring successful execution produces favorable change if the response is poorly mastered, but it interferes with performance if the response is well mastered.

The conditions inducing reactivity can be better understood in the context of the self-regulation model. According to the model, changes in the target behavior can result when the SM task triggers the self-regulation process. The critical role of increased self-attention is supported by research in which instructions to increase self-awareness produced reactive effects similar to those obtained from instructions to self-monitor (Kirschenbaum & Tomarken, 1982). The self-regulation model also explains the finding that favorable behavior change can result when another person monitors the target behavior (Hayes & Nelson, 1983). External monitoring is effective if obtrusive feedback is given to the person, thereby disrupting ongoing automatic processes. Finally, consider the data on the differential impact of self-monitoring on well-mastered versus poorly mastered tasks. Well-mastered tasks are already automatized. Interventions disrupt the smooth progression of the behavior sequence. Poorly mastered tasks, on the other hand, require close attention to behavior and would benefit from the additional attention to it. The self-regulation model integrates many seemingly disparate findings on SM reactivity and can provide a guide for helpers who wish to maximize these effects.

The mere mechanics of SM do not lead to favorable behavior change unless other conditions of self-regulation are met. For example, change does not occur if the person lacks standards for a given behavior or if there is no discrepancy between these standards and the monitored behavior. Further, reactivity is influenced by the causal attributions the person makes about the behavior and by the importance he or she assigns to the behavior (e.g., see Ewart, 1978). A frequent observation concerns the temporary nature of the change associated with SM tasks. Over time, the execution of the SM task can become increasingly automatic and might no longer trigger self-regulatory processes. To maintain the effectiveness of SM interventions, therapists should modify the SM task from time to time.

A critical feature of SM is the specific behavior selected for monitoring and the temporal relationship between the behavior and the monitoring. Investigators have reported the use of SM for ruminating thoughts, for urges to engage in a problematic behavior, for simple motor behaviors, for pain episodes, and for complex social behaviors. SM can be carried out prior to the execution of the undesirable behavior, immediately following it, or at a much later time. In choosing among these alternatives, the therapist should carefully consider the functions the SM task is intended to serve. The need for accuracy suggests a simple monitoring task, executed immediately after the target behavior has occurred. Assignments designed to provide information about the target behavior might involve more detailed observations of environmental antecedents and consequences. To maximize the reactive effects of SM, the task should require high attention to one's actions and the disruption of ongoing activity. For example, daily monitoring of body weight might be an accurate measure of weight loss, but instructions to count mouthfuls swallowed produce greater behavior change (Green, 1978). In general, summary recording of the target behavior after several hours or at the end of the day introduces a long delay and weakens any reactive effects of SM.

SM tasks that emphasize the negative effects of a target behavior can also increase reactivity (Hayes & Nelson, 1983). For example, one might monitor excess food intake with packages of lard representing body fat, or record cigarettes smoked with a metric based on the smoking habits of the average lung cancer patient. Premonitoring, or monitoring the urge to engage in a maladaptive behavior, is a promising intervention for addictive behaviors (Fremouw & Brown, 1980). Urges that occur early in the chain of events leading to the consummatory response are easier to control than later events in the chain. Another possibility, which has proven successful in reducing smoking behavior, involves monitoring conquered urges, or instances where an incompatible behavior is executed in response to an urge to engage in undesirable action (O'Banion, Armstrong, & Ellis, 1980). The conquered urge can also elicit feelings of self-satisfaction, introducing a reinforcement component to this technique.

Establishing SM in Individual Adult Programs

In introducing SM to the client, the therapist begins by discussing its general nature and by giving examples of its utility in the therapeutic program. Together with the client, the helper should clearly specify the class of behaviors to be observed and should discuss examples to illustrate the limits of this class. A good rule is to use frequency counts for behaviors that are clearly separable, such as smoking a cigarette or making a specific positive self-statement, and to use time intervals for behaviors that are continuous. For example, duration of studying or of obsessive ruminations is clocked by recording the time started and stopped. If the target behavior is very frequent or extends over a long period of time, it is possible to use a time-sampling technique. This method requires that the person make self-observations only during previously specified time intervals. To insure adequate sampling of the behavior, the helper can develop a program, best based on randomization of all periods during which the behavior occurs, and ask for SM during specified periods only. For persons who interact with others during much of their working day as part of their occupation, the occurrence of particular responses such as aggressive or subassertive behaviors can be sampled by randomly selecting half-hour periods during each of a number of days for observation. If the goal of SM is to foster behavior change, selection of time periods would invoke consideration of the intervals in which change most easily occurs.

Next, the helper should discuss with the client the recording method. Care must be taken to select a recording instrument that is always available where and when the behavior is likely to occur. When the therapist wishes to maximize accuracy, the recording instrument should be simple, unobtrusive, and convenient. Complex monitoring procedures, such as written accounts of thoughts or emotional reactions, can be involved when emphasis is placed on the reactive effects of SM.

Finally, the therapist should role-play and rehearse the entire self-monitoring sequence with the client. It is advisable to provide clients with record sheets or to have them purchase the recording devices so that they can rehearse the actual procedure with the instruments at hand. The therapist should also demonstrate the graphing of a set of frequency recordings or time intervals for visual inspection. Self-monitoring assignments should be reviewed during the interviews following the session in which they were assigned. At this time, problems with implementation can be discussed, and the task can be modified.

Variations of SM include the use of the graph for display, either as a reminder to the client or for social recognition and support in a small group. The graph serves as a concise summary of improvement over the course of therapy, and it is often helpful to review the graph when motivation flags. It is sometimes beneficial to make the graph available to others. For example, SM data have been displayed by institutionalized clients at their bedside, by family members in an accessible part of the home, or by children in classrooms. Social reinforcement for progress can add to the effectiveness of this technique. However, great care must be taken to insure that the record not emphasize the client's deficiencies, violate confidentiality, or embarrass the client.

There are modifications of SM techniques that require more elaborate equipment. For example, audiotape and videotape playback have been used as a means by which clients can observe their own behavior. Later, these self-observations serve as a base for attempts to improve the actions. This type of self-observation is generally an integral part of a more complex intervention program. It often involves participation of group members and helpers who initiate a self-correcting process by helping the client to discriminate and pinpoint particular problematic aspects of his or her interaction behavior. More desirable behaviors are then modelled and reinforced. Although originating from a different perspective, biofeedback techniques also function as useful SM techniques. Clients are helped to recognize variations in physiological activities by means of visual or auditory displays of their heart rates, electrical skin resistance, brain waves, or other physiological outputs.

In summary, SM is a useful component of a total self-management program. It does not always provide a sufficiently reliable assessment technique, but it can serve as an important program component and motivating device. When SM is employed as an agent of behavior change, it is important to add additional techniques, such as contracting, self-reinforcement, and stimulus control and to insure that the self-evaluative and self-reinforcement stages of the self-regulation process occur.

Modification of the Environment

The client whose problems are suitable for treatment by self-management techniques has probably made repeated previous attempts to alter his or her behavior. Failure might have been due to lack of environmental support, lack of knowledge of specific behavior change methods, or lack of sufficient incentives for trying to change. The techniques described in the following two sections require only a minimal self-initiated step by the client, namely to trigger a change in the environment in such a way that subsequent behaviors naturally follow (decision self-control). For example, the alcoholic who calls a fellow AA member to accompany her on a walk through the park is programming environmental conditions that will reduce the need for generating self-controlling responses to compete with the urge for a quick trip to the liquor store.

Stimulus control procedures set up conditions that make it either impossible or unfavorable for the undesirable behavior to occur. They include such extremes as physical prevention of the undesired behavior, which could include voluntary confinement in an institution, locking oneself in a room, or turning car keys over to a friend. In each case, some undesirable behavior is avoided simply by the fact that the individual has relinquished control over the behavior to an external agent. The effects of such control are usually only temporary. In addition, the client frequently develops avoidance or hostility toward the agent to whom he or she has given control. At the other extreme, stimulus control methods include training of self-generated verbal responses without changing the physical environment. For example, repeated self-instructions that emphasize long-range aversive conse-quences of the behavior, statements about the positive aspects of tolerating an unpleasant situation or resisting a temptation, self-rewarding statements about one's willpower, or similar verbal cues can serve as stimuli that exert powerful control over subsequent action.

In the following section we consider stimulus control techniques that involve manipulations of the physical environment, rearrangement of the social en-vironment, and self-generation of controlling stimuli and controlling responses. The techniques to be covered in a later section on covert conditioning overlap with stimulus control methods, because training a person to generate stimuli in fantasy or imagination represents an example of altering controlling stimuli. However, unlike alteration of external physical stimuli or reprogramming of the social environment, covert conditioning methods require continued activity by clients in rearranging their own behavior and in reorganizing their habitual ways of thinking.

Stimulus control techniques can be separated according to their function in (a) altering the physical environment so that execution of the undesirable response is impossible, (b) altering the social environment so that opportunities for execution are heavily controlled by other persons, (c) changing discriminative stimulus functions so that the target behavior is specifically restricted to particular environments or the presence of distinctive cues, or (d) altering the physical condition of the person so that changes in the target behavior are produced. As with most self-control techniques, these methods can reduce the problem behavior, but their effects are substantially increased if a new behavioral repertoire is built up at the same time. This dual approach is especially important when the target behavior is suppressed or eliminated only through temporary rearrangement of the environment.

Environmental Stimulus Control

Numerous clinical reports have described the use of alteration of physical or social environments to prevent a response. For example, cigarette cases or refrigerators have been equipped with time locks that make access impossible except at preset intervals. Persons on weight reduction programs have been advised to keep only as much food in the house as can be consumed in a short time, thus eliminating late evening snacking. The ancient use of chastity belts (and other confining garments) represents a use of stimulus control to make sexual contact difficult by altering accessibility. In everyday life, most persons use this technique incidentally. Mothers put mittens on small children to reduce thumb sucking, students find isolated areas for study, some persons do not carry credit cards, others play loud music or flee from houses that hold past memories, all in order to control undesired behaviors or fantasies.

For most people, the presence of other persons is a strong determinant of behavior. By selecting the appropriate person or social environment, clients can relieve themselves of much of the burden of generating their own controlling responses. For example, in a smoking-cessation program, an individual might give his cigarettes to a friend who has agreed to help. Smoking becomes more difficult as the person must endure inconvenience and embarrassment before obtaining a cigarette. A more subtle use of the social environment to control smoking might involve deliberate interactions with adamant nonsmokers. In this case, social control over behavior operates indirectly, mediated by knowledge of the attitudes and typical reactions of others to smoking. Similarly, socializing with calorie counters or exercise buffs can facilitate certain behaviors without the costs of relinquishing control to another person. In these social environments, aversive affective and self-evaluative reactions provide a strong deterrent to the execution of certain behaviors.

Stimulus Narrowing

This technique involves strengthening the association between a behavior and a specific setting; that is, the behavior is put under S^d control. Undesirable behavior can be reduced by gradually decreasing the range of stimulus conditions in which the behavior occurs. For example, overweight clients are requested to eat only in the dining room, at a table with a particular color tablecloth, or in the presence of other family members (Ferster, Nurnberger, & Levitt, 1962; Stuart & Davis, 1972). Over a period of time, the numerous cues previously associated with eating gradually lose control over the response. The relationship between a desirable behavior and a certain set of stimulus conditions can be strengthened by decreasing the range of other behaviors that occur in that setting. For example, insomniacs can be taught to restrict the bedroom environment to sleeping (and sexual behavior) and to avoid sleep-incompatible behaviors such as worrying, watching TV, eating, or reading (Bootzin & Nicassio, 1978; Nicassio & Buchanan, 1981). Similarly, study habits have been improved by setting up specific environments in which no other activities take place. In establishing S^d control, the client is asked to leave the study area when daydreaming or engaging in other activities. Among the most powerful and convenient S^ds are clocks and watches. Specific time intervals have been employed as cues for engaging in assertive behaviors, smoking, daydreaming, worrying, skin picking, or nail biting. A program for chronic worriers requires that clients postpone all worry behavior until a preset "worry period," occurring at the same time and place every day (Borkovec, Wilkinson, Folensbee, & Lerman, 1983). The treatment package involves other components, such as monitoring worry behavior and substituting present-oriented thoughts, but its essence involves stimulus control techniques. The association between worrying and a myriad of environmental and internal stimuli is reduced, and the behavior is restricted to a limited interval.

When a target behavior is to be reduced, stimulus control techniques are frequently combined with increasing response cost. For example, in addition to requiring that the behavior occur only in a certain place or at a given time, one can gradually increase other demands so that execution of the behavior becomes more and more cumbersome. Ultimately, the ritual is sufficiently aversive that the effort outweighs the anticipated consequences of the target behavior. For example, in establishing control over smoking, clients might deliberately place the pack in a distant place, remove matches from the usual location, remove all ashtrays, and, finally, restrict smoking to a specified "smoking chair." Clients who have been helped to arrange these procedures have reported that the undesirable behavior dropped out "because it was just too much trouble to go through all that."

Another use of stimulus narrowing focuses on the association between a target behavior and certain bodily cues. Before using this approach, it is essential to teach the client to recognize somatic stimuli through self-monitoring procedures and through emphasis on the characteristic events surrounding or preceding certain physiological states. Clients can be taught to eat only when hungry, to respond to anxiety with relaxation, or to recognize sexual arousal and make appropriate responses. Other procedures operate to reduce somatic cues that trigger maladaptive behavior. For example, low-calorie, high-bulk foods can reduce cues for eating; for an alcoholic the intake of nonalcoholic fluids prior to a party can control internal thirst cues. Finally, the client's interpretation of bodily cues can be altered, reducing the association between these cues and maladaptive behavior. For example, relabeling social anxiety as a normal fear of strangers can reduce negative self-statements and lead to more adaptive behavior in new settings.

The methods just described help the client recognize and regulate environmental and somatic variables that control behavior. Stimulus control techniques have also been used to help the client change the nature of self-generated verbal cues. In contrast with the preceding methods, the control of self-generated stimuli is relatively tenuous, because the individual can easily remove self-instructions, imagined sequences, or thoughts. In altering external controlling stimuli, the individual need only initiate a change of events, exercising decisional self-control. The remaining sequence is determined by the natural environment or by the behavior of others. In the case of self-produced controlling stimuli, the individual must often maintain the cues over time and in the presence of an environment that encourages and supports the problem behavior. We deal with these methods for protracted self-control in a later section of this chapter.

Changing Self-Generated Behavioral Consequences

Feelings of satisfaction or dissatisfaction with one's behavior allow individuals to maintain many everyday behaviors in the absence of immediate external consequences. However, these naturally occurring reactions are not always effective in regulating behavior. For some people, low rates of positive self-reinforcement limit the achievement of goals. Other clients believe that self-reinforcement is undesirable or immodest; they are highly self-critical or show excessive standards for achievement, so that positive self-reinforcement rarely occurs. In addition, some behaviors are associated with strong emotional or environmental consequences that oppose and overpower self-reactions. In these cases, it is often helpful to use self-administered reinforcement techniques to establish stronger incentives for desirable behavior. These procedures involve the introduction of additional reinforcing stimuli, which the individual administers to himself or herself only when previously established contingencies are met. The use of this technique requires that the target behavior, performance criteria, reinforcing stimuli, and contingency relationships be clearly specified. This clarification offers opportunities to correct problematic components of the self-regulation process and also facilitates the disruption of automatic processes by encouraging the individual to pay closer attention to his or her behavior.

Positive self-reinforcement, or self-reward (SR), is most commonly used in self-management programs and has been the focus of most research. Other types of self-administered reinforcement have been used, paralleling the various forms of external reinforcement contingencies. These procedures are summarized in

Table 8.1. Aversive self-reinforcement could follow a response, delivered in the form of self-criticism, self-punishment, or withholding of positive self-reinforcement. For example, a person can deny herself a night at the movies if she fails to complete preparation for the next day's work. Withholding of a positive SR after previous continued administration and self-imposed extinction have also been used in self-management programs. Finally, a person can present himself with an aversive stimulus that is removed or terminated only when the self-prescribed escape or avoidance response is carried out. Although the self-administered reinforcement techniques overlap the externally administered techniques, there is controversy over whether they share a common underlying mechanism (e.g., Castro, Perez, Albanchez, & de Leon, 1983; Nelson, Hayes, Spong, Jarret, & McKnight, 1983). However, few theorists would argue with the general conclusion that these techniques serve a motivational function.

Positive self-administered reinforcement encompasses two different operations: (a) approaching or consuming a material reinforcer that is freely available in the person's environment (for example, when a person rewards herself for hard work with a cup of coffee, she is applying a self-administered material consequence); or (b) delivery of contingent verbal-symbolic self-reinforcement such as self-praise for a completed task. The first procedure involves the administration of external reinforcement by the client. External reinforcers are used in two ways: (a) self-presentation of a new reinforcer that is outside the everyday life of the client such as a small luxury item or attendance at a special event; and (b) initial denial of some pleasant everyday experience and administration of it only as a contingent reinforcer for a desired behavior (Thoreson & Mahoney, 1974). For example, making an enjoyable phone call, going to a movie, or having a cup of coffee might be initially postponed, and carried out only as a reward for the accomplishment of a prescribed task. This requires that the person initially deny himself or herself the experience, introducing the conflict elements of a self-control situation. The client can postpone easily available rewards more effectively if very small delays are introduced at first and the behavioral requirements for the reward are only gradually increased.

Table 8.1. Some Combinations of Self-Reinforcement

QUALITY OF CONSEQUENCE	CONSEQUENCE OPERATION	
	GIVE	TAKE AWAY
Positive	Positive Self-Reinforcement (a) self-administered (b) verbal-symbolic	Covert Extinction self-imposed time-out (temporary)
Aversive	Self-Punishment (a) self-administered (b) verbal-symbolic	Negative Self-Reinforcement (a) self-administered (b) verbal-symbolic

Verbal-symbolic SRs consist of such verbal statements as "I did well," "That was good," or other self-statements by which the individual clearly labels his or her own satisfactions with the achievement. These procedures help clients acknowledge that they have successfully negotiated a given task and also give them permission to feel satisfied and proud. Deliberate programming of such verbal-symbolic self-rewards can be carried out by first asking the person to say these positive statements aloud in sessions and by later making them contingent on a specified event.

Several studies have reported that the addition of SR improves behavior change programs (Bellack, Schwartz, & Rozensky, 1974; Mahoney et al., 1973; Rehm & Kornblith, 1979; Tressler & Tucker, 1980). There have been reports of effective use of self-reinforcement to improve study skills, enhance weight reduction, increasing dating skills and assertive behavior, and raise activity levels in depressed patients. Although training the administration of SR contingencies is more difficult than exposure of a client to external consequences, SR procedures have the advantage that the individual can eventually apply them independently of the helper and can also use the same procedures for problems that are not related to the central complaint. Laboratory research with children and adults has demonstrated that self-reinforcing operations show the two characteristic properties of reinforcing stimuli: They alter the probability of occurrence of the response that precedes them, and they motivate new learning (Bandura & Perloff, 1967; Kanfer & Duerfeldt, 1967; Montgomery & Parton, 1970). In comparisons with the administration of the same reinforcement by another person, positive SR has been shown to be generally equal, if not slightly superior, in effectiveness (Johnson & Martin, 1973; Lovitt & Curtiss, 1969). The literature on the self-reinforcement concept, most of it carried out with positive SR, has also demonstrated that self-reinforcement is not always independent of the environment (Jones, Nelson, & Kazdin, 1977). Although SR operations make it possible for a client to be temporarily independent, ultimate positive consequences from the environment would seem to be necessary to maintain the newly developed behavior in the long run.

Establishing SR in Individual Adult Programs

As we have suggested, the goal of the helper is to start a behavior change program that is carried out by the client and to achieve changes that are maintained without continuing therapist reinforcement. Most programs of this type incorporate SR as a treatment component, either to bolster naturally occurring self-reactions or to correct deficits in the individual's self-regulatory processes. The nature of the program often depends on which of these goals is given stronger emphasis. For example, the self-administration of valued material rewards might be effective in creating incentives for behavior, whereas positive self-statements might be more useful in helping a highly self-critical client. A thorough functional analysis is necessary to pinpoint the nature of the problem and to guide construction of the treatment plan. The following steps summarize the usual procedures in aiding an individual toward effective use of positive SR.

1. Selection of Appropriate Reinforcers. Although some questionnaires can aid in the preliminary selection of reinforcers, it is desirable to discuss and negotiate individual reinforcers in interviews with the client. Asking the client about his or her current practices of self-reward, both symbolic and material; inquiring about luxury items that the client would like to acquire; and obtaining verbal statements that would express self-satisfaction frequently yield suggestions for appropriate SRs. What is often most effective is a rearrangement of behavioral contingencies for self-rewards that the person normally administers noncontingently or only in conjunction with behaviors other than the problem responses. Novel material SRs can be added as a special incentive for a prolonged program. The list of material reinforcers, enjoyable activities, and positive self-statements is compiled on the basis of the client's current behaviors. For example, acquisition of inexpensive luxury items that the client has wanted but never obtained might include the purchase of a paperback book, a small item of jewelry, clothing accessories, or cosmetics. Among activities, the individual's preference might be to take a trip to a museum, go to a rock concert, go away for a weekend vacation, or spend time at hobbies.

Verbal-symbolic reinforcers include positive self-statements that are employed in self-praise; reaffirmation of one's adequacy, self-worth or competence; congratulating oneself on physical appearance, physical strength, social attractiveness, interpersonal skill, or any other appropriate content. It is crucial that the selected reinforcers be acceptable to the client as something he or she wants, could easily acquire or do, and would feel good about. If a complex and long-range program is designed, several reinforcing stimuli should be equated for approximate value, so that they can be interchanged. This prevents satiation with a single item or statement. In a long-term program, a series of small reinforcers should also be exchangeable for one larger reinforcer at infrequent intervals. A person who has accumulated a predetermined number of symbolic SRs because he has shown improvement in the target response might work toward a larger material reinforcer such as purchase of a luxury item, contingent on achievement of a desired goal within a fixed time period. The list of exchangeable reinforcers, therefore, should contain both small items obtained from the person's current activities and larger items that are just outside the range of daily enjoyments.

2. Definition of Specific Response-Reinforcement Contingencies. The client is encouraged to list variations within the target response class and to indicate the precise conditions and methods for delivery of SR. For example, if the person is on a weight control program, a verbal-symbolic reinforcer might be used for such target behaviors as rejecting offers of food, staying within the allotted daily caloric intake, or choosing an alternate low-calorie food. In addition, a larger SR, such as buying a new dress or wardrobe accessory, might be made contingent on achieving a predetermined weight loss within a specified time period.

In establishing the response-reinforcement contingency, care must be taken to select a good match. For example, it would obviously be foolish to choose a rich dessert as an SR for weight loss for an obese client. It has been pointed out (Seligman, 1970) that there are predispositions for some reinforcers to be more effective than others with particular behaviors. Whenever possible, the SR should be one that is essentially compatible with the target behavior. For example, the ex-smoker might select the purchase of new perfume or having teeth cleaned and polished, because such rewards emphasize the positive aspects of not smoking in terms of whiter teeth and increased sensitivity to smell.

After the appropriate contingencies are established, specific provisions should be made for the delivery and recording of SR. On occasion, high frequency of the desired behavior or involvement in a long-term program might require use of intermittent schedules of reinforcement. For instance, one client who had set small material SRs as his reward for improving his study habits decided to add both interest value and effectiveness to his SR schedule by setting up an intermittent reinforcement schedule. He accomplished this by using a deck of playing cards. He assigned SR values only to cards and values above 10. Prior to administering a material SR, he would shuffle and cut a deck of cards and reward himself only if a card of 10 or higher appeared.

3. Practice of Procedures. After selecting appropriate reinforcers and establishing reward contingencies, the helper should rehearse with the client several instances of occurrence of the target behavior and the self-reinforcing sequence. These role-playing sessions provide the client with a model and the initial experience in an activity in which he or she might feel uncomfortable. Of course, the helper's presence, encouragement, and approval not only strengthen the likelihood that the client will carry out the behavior, but might also eliminate the common misconception that such simple mechanics for self-management do not require effort, careful programming, or diligent practice.

4. Checking and Revising Procedures. The client should bring in records of the target behavior and contingent SRs for discussion with the helper and for necessary adjustments of the procedure. For example, if the target is a general increase in positive self-statements, it would be desirable to change their specific content rather frequently in order to extend the program over a wide range of the client's daily activities. The monitoring sessions can also be used to model administration of SRs under different conditions. This helps the client to develop a repertoire of appropriate verbal-symbolic SRs and permits the gradual decrease of material reinforcers. The ultimate goal is not to eliminate long-range luxury reinforcers completely but to make them sufficiently infrequent and to increase the desired performance to the point where it can be maintained by the client. The purpose of the program is to help the client use self-administered reinforcement to handle psychological difficulties that might arise after contacts with the helper have terminated.

Self-Generated Aversive Consequences

There are essentially two different types of self-generated aversive consequences that can be used in the control of behavior—self-punishment and negative self-reinforcement. These two sets of operations differ in that *self-punishment* is aimed at interrupting or decelerating a response, whereas *negative reinforcement* is aimed at increasing a response that serves to terminate or avoid an unpleasant stimulus. The former is illustrated by executing a boring chore as self-punishment for aggressive behavior. The negative SR paradigm is exemplified by lowering the temperature in one's home at 9 p.m. to promote an earlier bedtime. In this case, feeling cold is the unpleasant stimulus that is escaped by going to bed. Thus, aversive consequences can be used either to decrease the preceding response or to increase a new target behavior. In addition, just as for self-generated positive consequences, the aversive event can also consist of verbal-symbolic SRs such as self-criticism or self-deprecatory statements.

Self-punishment can also involve the removal of a positive stimulus following an undesirable behavior. For example, a person could leave a party as self-punishment for having acted foolishly. A more complex procedure involves levying a fine (removal of money, widely held to be a positive reinforcer) following a response that has been targeted for decrease. For example, in the control of smoking behaviors, some clinicians have requested that the client donate $1 to the most disliked political organization after smoking a cigarette. The use of withdrawal of a positive reinforcer has been infrequently reported. In a weight control program, Mahoney et al. (1973) found that this procedure was not very effective when used alone. There are some logical advantages to this technique, although there is limited evidence that it works. Because aversive stimuli are not used, the problems associated with techniques of self-administered punishment are avoided. At the same time, the consequences of persuading a person to give away or destroy a valued item as a contingency are not known. This technique has not been sufficiently explored to warrant wide clinical application.

Many clients have a long history of childhood experiences in which they discovered that one way to "have your cake and eat it too" was to carry out the undesired behavior and suffer punishment as well. Helpers who work with families are familiar with the problem of children who fail to respond to physical punishment. Frequently, the externally administered and eventually self-generated punishment response serves to alleviate guilt and anxiety associated with the behavior, clearing the way for repetition. Also, unusual individual histories in which punishment served as a positive reinforcer, or as an S^d for affect, leads some clients to use physical self-punishment excessively. For these reasons, both verbal-symbolic and physical methods of punishment should be used only when no alternative is possible.

Another example of self-administered punishment is the use of an aversive conditioned reinforcer in the thought-stopping technique (Cautela, 1969; Cautela

& Wisocki, 1977). In this procedure, the therapist asks the client to think aloud about ruminations or fantasies that are targeted for decrease. When the client is fully immersed in these thoughts, the clinician shouts "Stop!" loudly enough to evoke a startled reaction from the client. After several trials of the procedure, the client initiates the shout, first aloud and then in his or her imagination. Frequent practice is needed in addition to actual use of the procedure whenever the problem behavior occurs. This method has been reported to be helpful in the first stages of eliminating disturbing thoughts.

A similar technique has been suggested by Mahoney (1971). A client was instructed to wear a heavy rubber band around his wrist. On occurrence of ruminations that were the target for deceleration, the client snapped the rubber band to produce mild pain. Self-administered aversive consequences, much like other SRs, are effective not because of their capacity for producing pain but because they make the undesirable response clearly stand out from the total flow of behavior. They serve as cues for self-monitoring and self-correction, described earlier as essential ingredients of the self-regulation sequence.

Aversive SRs have been used in some weight control programs. For example, the client is instructed to place a large piece of lard or beef fat in the refrigerator as a continually present aversive stimulus representing his or her excess poundage. With successive weight losses, the client cuts away pieces of the lard, gradually removing the aversive stimulus.

When a response of high frequency is to be modified, *satiation,* or negative practice, has been suggested as a behavior change technique. This procedure consists of deliberate repetition of a behavior past the point of desire. For example, an excessive cigarette smoker might be instructed to light and smoke cigarettes continuously until he feels physically ill. A positive stimulus can lose its reinforcing properties with frequent repetition and acquire an aversive character. After a long smoking session, lighting a cigarette might actually become a cue for feeling ill or dizzy. The procedure is frequently used in conjunction with other aversive stimuli, such as confining the person in a small room where the increased smoke level itself becomes noxious, or in conjunction with relief responses (see discussion of the aversion-relief technique in chapter 6).

Covert Conditioning

Covert conditioning (Cautela & Kearney, 1986) is based on the rationale that covert operants, or coverants, can be treated much like operant responses, even though the exact nature of the coverant is difficult to ascertain because it is not publicly observable (Homme, 1965). The various paradigms of covert conditioning parallel those of operant conditioning except for the use of client imagery as stimuli, responses, or reinforcing events. We have differentiated these techniques from the use of spoken verbal cues because covert processes usually include verbal, symbolic, and imaginal representations that are produced by the client on instruction of the helper. The use of these techniques is justified by rather modest empirical data and some support for clinical utility (Kazdin, 1977). In this section we will illustrate the most widely used techniques, including covert sensitization, covert reinforcement, and covert modeling.

Covert Sensitization

This technique has been used to reduce undesirable behaviors, including addictive behaviors—for example, alcoholism (Miller & Dougher, 1984) and sexual deviations (Lamontagne & Lesage, 1986; Lanyon, 1986)—that are generally difficult to attack. The client is asked to imagine a scene that portrays the undesirable behavior and that currently offers some satisfaction. After the positive image is built up to high intensity, the client is requested to change abruptly to imagining a highly aversive event. Both physical and social aversive imagery are usually used and modified according to the client's personal history. Then the client is asked to imagine fleeing the problem situation and the aversive events associated with it. After the escape, the client visualizes relief and reduction of discomfort. Strong positive reinforcement by the helper, and eventually by the client, is offered for escaping or avoiding the situation, and verbal statements are used to summarize the implications of the experience. Thus, the maladaptive behavior is paired with aversive consequences, and escape from the total situation is rewarded by the relief experience. All of these events take place with guidance by the helper.

To illustrate the procedure, consider a case in which the target behavior is excessive alcohol consumption. The helper first explains the rationale of the technique and obtains detailed descriptions of the setting in which excessive drinking occurs and of positive and aversive consequences that are meaningful to the client. The client might be asked to imagine aloud a scene in which she is comfortably seated at her favorite bar. When the client appears to be immersed in the imagery, perhaps describing her enjoyment when raising a full glass to her lips, the helper introduces the aversive event. For instance, it can be suggested that the client suddenly gets sick and begins to vomit. The helper's description is detailed, and the client is asked to imagine, visualize, smell, and feel the aversive scene as vividly as possible. When the client appears to be experiencing aversive consequences, she is asked to imagine turning away in disgust from the bar and rushing out to get a breath of fresh air. As she does so, a previously established positive event is imagined. For example, an attractive person smiles at the client as she breathes fresh air and experiences pride because of the escape from her alcohol habit. Favorable summaries are offered that the client can use as a self-statement, such as "Why do I do silly things like drinking? It only makes me sick." Initially, client and therapist work through a number of different scenes in about 10 trials each. The scenes should be varied to encompass different settings and consequences, and some scenes might involve training in avoidance. For example, the alcoholic might imagine being offered a drink and responding, "No, I won't have any alcohol" and then sensing relief. After learning the procedure, the client is asked to present the scenes to herself aloud and to practice between sessions. Variations of the procedure have involved tape-recorded presentations of scenes that can be used with groups of people who share a similar problem.

Clinical experience suggests that careful preparation of the client is needed for successful use of the technique. If the client lacks skill in imagining the suggested scene, his or her ability can be built up by training in imagining and describing various events. The client must be motivated and the scenes must be varied sufficiently to provide generality of effect. It is also important that strong personal reinforcers be used. For instance, if the alcoholic in our example is socially oriented, vomiting could be portrayed as accidentally soiling an outraged, attractive person on the next bar stool. Nausea can be an especially effective aversive event for alcohol problems, as many drinkers have experienced an association between nausea and drinking. Although both in vivo and covert production of nausea have been used to treat alcohol problems, the covert procedure is easier to use and is associated with fewer side-effects (Elkins, 1980).

Covert sensitization provides a useful clinical tool because it requires no particular settings, can be carried out fairly unobstrusively by the client, and has been reported to be effective after only a few sessions. However, it is best used to suppress undesired behavior temporarily and should be combined with other techniques to build and maintain new behavioral repertoires. A limited body of research supports its effectiveness, although most studies have focused on the use of nausea imagery for alcohol problems (Elkins, 1980; Little & Curran, 1978). Treatment effects are mediated by the extent to which nausea is established as a conditioned response to alcohol cues, suggesting that vivid imagery involving descriptions of visual, olfactory, gustatory, and tactile sensations should be used. In contrast with the classical conditioning explanation of covert sensitization, some authors argue that the essential ingredient involves the disruption of the behavior chain that is caused by the introduction of the imagined aversive event (Foreyt & Hagan, 1973). According to this view, any event, positive or negative, would serve equally well in the effective use of this technique.

Covert Reinforcement

This method generally parallels the operations carried out in self-administered reinforcement. The client is trained to imagine a well-practiced scene that is experienced as happy or pleasant. A verbal cue, preferably a word that is the client's own expression of a positive feeling, can be attached to the positive imagery to help the client recall the scene. As with any reinforcing stimulus, the imagery is evoked contingent on the occurrence of a target response. The imagined scenes are first practiced with the helper, and eventually the client is instructed to deliver the reinforcement to himself or herself.

Covert negative reinforcement consists of practice in imagining an unpleasant situation that can later be used in place of other aversive reinforcers. In addition to the use of covert negative reinforcement for deceleration of a target response, it can be used as a noxious stimulus for escape conditioning. In this procedure, clients first imagine the rehearsed unpleasant scene. Subsequently, they imagine the response to be increased. For example, after imagining themselves experiencing a very distasteful situation, they visualize walking into a room full of people and feeling comfortable or calling up someone for a date. Covert negative reinforcement should be used judiciously, because aversive scenes can leave residual unpleasant feelings that could become associated with the behavior to be increased. For instance, a client who selects feeling anxious as an aversive event might not be able to terminate the imagery quickly. If the desirable escape response is one that had previously been associated with great anxiety, detrimental effects might follow.

The use of imagery in covert conditioning can include not only scenes that the person has actually experienced but also imagery about ideal situations, feared situations, or other fantasy constructions. In all of these procedures, care must be taken to rehearse the self-presented scenes in detail, to ascertain that the necessary elements are indeed self-presented. Despite rehearsal, however, some problems in dealing with imagery techniques remain. The helper has little control over the nature of the stimuli and responses that the client employs. The helper is therefore limited in his or her ability to insure that the client is following instructions or using adequate visualizations. These problems have made research on covert procedures quite difficult.

Covert Modeling

Cautela (1976), Kazdin (1979), Kazdin and Mascitelli (1982), and others have reported the use of imagined stimuli as substitutes for live or film models in the reduction of fearful behavior. The procedure combines covert methods with those of modeling techniques (see chapter 3). The client practices imagining the problematic situation in detail for a series of trials. Then, he or she is asked to imagine another person, the model, performing the desirable behavior, such as stroking a dog or entering a crowded room. The helper describes the model as initially hesitant and uncertain, but as gradually overcoming his or her fear and executing the behavior in a smooth and competent fashion. Research supports the use of covert modeling for reducing phobic behavior, acquiring social skills, and increasing assertiveness (e.g., Kazdin & Mascitelli, 1982). The use of imagined models who emit coping self-statements can increase the effectiveness of the technique (Tearman, Lahey, Thompson, & Hammer, 1982).

A variation of covert modeling has been described by Susskind (1970). In the idealized self-image technique, clients visualize their ideal selves as they competently perform the desired behavior. Clients are first helped to formulate an ideal self-image, by asking that they recall an incident or experience that yielded a strong feeling of accomplishment or satisfaction. They then imagine the desired behavior and gradually superimpose their idealized self-image on their current self-image, observing the gradual change in their actions. Thus, clients are requested to act, feel, and see themselves in ways that are consistent with their idealized self-image. The idealized self-image and other covert modeling methods bear some relationship to Kelly's fixed role therapy (Kelly, 1955).

OTHER SELF-MANAGEMENT METHODS

Self-management methods vary widely in the degree to which the client is responsible for learning and executing specific techniques. Some techniques are taught and practiced in therapy sessions, under the assumption that this experience will produce changes in the target behavior. Other techniques, the *self-directed* procedures, are discussed in session, but the burden is on the client to self-administer or implement the technique on his or her own. Benefit from these procedures is expected only to the extent that the client applies them to problem situations in daily life. For example, in self-directed desensitization, clients are instructed in the use of systematic desensitization and provided with a standard relaxation tape. They are then responsible for self-administering the treatment at home. The self-directed procedures allow a more economical use of therapy time and offer increased opportunities to enhance the client's perceptions of control and self-efficacy beliefs. As with any other technique, self-directed procedures should be used in conjunction with self-monitoring, self-reinforcement, and regular reports to the helper, who must maintain the client's progress by encouragement and support.

In addition to self-directed densensitization, several other self-directed procedures for anxiety control have emerged from the traditional desensitization paradigm (Rosenbaum & Merbaum, 1984). Many of these procedures, such as anxiety-management training and cue-controlled relaxation, aim to reduce anxiety whenever the client notes inner signs of tension, rather than in response to specific fear stimuli. It is critical that the client initiate the technique as soon as he or she detects the onset of anxiety, as these procedures are not effective once the feeling has progressed. In anxiety-management training (Suinn & Richardson, 1971), the client is taught to recognize physical signs of anxiety and to apply relaxation whenever these signs are perceived. After training in deep relaxation, specific cues for anxiety and relaxation are identified and rehearsed. Anxiety is then induced and quickly followed by imagining a happy or relaxed scene. Deep breathing serves as a cue for relaxation. While the client is relaxed, the anxiety cues are presented and terminated by a rapid shift to instructions for relaxation. These sequences can be taped with appropriate sounds or background music to accompany them. Cue-controlled relaxation is a similar technique, which involves the self-presentation of cue words for relaxation whenever anxiety reduction is desired. Training involves repeatedly pairing a deeply relaxed state with a cue word, such as *relax* or *peace*. The client then self-presents the cue word whenever he or she detects the initial signs of anxiety in daily life. The effectiveness of this technique has not been well demonstrated (Grimm, 1980), and research has yet to evaluate the classical conditioning rationale for treatment effects.

Time-management, problem-solving, and decision-making skills have also been incorporated into self-directed treatment packages. As with other self-directed techniques, the client is instructed in the basic principles of the method but is expected to implement the procedure alone, with support and reinforcement from the helper. For example, in time-management training (Lakein, 1973), the client is taught to prioritize goals and rearrange daily schedules so that important goals can be accomplished. The client then uses these principles in restructuring his or her daily routine. These techniques not only help the client to deal with circumscribed problems, but also provide general coping skills that can be used in various life situations.

Self-Help Resources

Self-help resources refer to instructional materials and support groups that are designed to facilitate or maintain behavior change without the direct involvement of a mental health professional. Recent growth in the self-help movement has led to increased availability of books, tapes, films, and other instructional devices (Gartner & Riessman, 1984). However, these programs vary widely in quality, and there is little empirical evidence for their effectiveness and validity (Glasgow & Rosen, 1978, 1979). In fact, self-help programs can have detrimental consequences (Rosen, 1982). Consumers can incorrectly diagnose their problems, select inappropriate methods, or fail to comply with key program requirements. However, under close guidance of a helper, carefully chosen self-help resources can be integrated into the total self-management program. It is a basic requirement that the helper be familiar with their content and that the materials and exercises be discussed in session. The utilization of self-help groups and other community resources is discussed in detail in chapter 10.

Self-help books, programs, and organizations represent resources that can supplement common therapeutic interventions beyond the limits of the typical 1-hour office session. These activities create a bridge to the client's daily activities. But other activities can also be integrated into a therapy program. For example, cultural, religious, educational, and recreational programs are not utilized fully in most behavior change programs. A client's involvement in a physical training program, a consciousness-raising groups, a church-based or synagogue-based social group, or an adult education class can provide excellent opportunities for personal growth, for improvement of behavioral repertoires, and for testing new skills in different settings. These resources have been much undervalued. It should be clear, however, that benefits do not occur simply through the client's participation in such activities. Careful joint planning, clear justification of the relationship of the prescribed activity to the main therapeutic objectives, and consideration of the client's abilities and limitations are essential in selecting the resources.

Limitations and Cautions

We have suggested that self-management techniques should not be used unless the client accepts the treatment goals as desirable and is motivated toward their achievement. Research evidence for the effectiveness of the programs described in this chapter, although still limited, is generally favorable (Kanfer & Schefft, 1988). The theoretical framework on which self-management techniques rest is tentative and incomplete. Some investigators have achieved success with certain methods, whereas others, drawing from the same theoretical assumptions but employing slightly different procedures, have been unable to achieve similar results. In part, the difficulty lies in the fact that self-management programs require the skillful combination of many elements in matching the program to the needs of each individual client, whereas research usually tests the effects of only one element at a time. Interactions between various components can produce effects that could not have been foreseen from research on the isolated elements.

The combining of individual elements into a program requires a thorough behavioral analysis of the problem before the program is undertaken, as well as a helper-client relationship that can promote the change process. Because behaviors that are targeted for self-management are often difficult to observe, the helper's reliance on the cooperation of the client is greater than it is in other behavior change methods. It is not infrequent that clients, because of their past history, are unwilling, ashamed, or afraid to describe target behaviors that are of greatest concern to them until they are sure that they can trust the helper. If the circumstances under which the client is referred for help are unfavorable for a trusting relationship, as when a client is referred by a court, pressured into treatment by others, or too disturbed to enter interpersonal relationships, self-management methods are not immediately applicable. Under these conditions, it is still possible to work toward creating an atmosphere in which prerequisites of self-management are met. However, the appropriate self-management methods can be introduced only after this prior goal is accomplished. Clients with low intellectual skills can be trained in some self-management methods, albeit at a slower pace and with simplified procedures (Litrownik, 1982). The use of methods based on our model of self-regulation has also been reported with psychotic clients (Breier & Strauss, 1983). The model described here is not appropriate for crisis intervention because of the immediate need for action by persons other than the client.

SUMMARY

In this chapter we have presented methods of behavior change based on the assumption that clients can alter their own behavior through the use of newly learned skills and rearrangements of their environment. A brief outline of the theoretical framework of self-regulation was presented, and it was pointed out that even in self-management clients require initial support and help from their environment. The importance of the client's perception as controlling the behavior change process was discussed. Self-control problems were defined as arising from situations in which a behavior is associated with positive consequences or avoidance of negative consequences in the short term, but ultimately leads to negative effects. Techniques for helping clients to cope with self-control problems were discussed.

Prior to the training of particular self-management techniques, favorable conditions for change must be created. Contracts, role-play, self-monitoring, and assignment of tasks aid to motivate the client toward change. Self-administered positive or aversive consequences, whether the material or verbal-symbolic, can provide additional incentives. Similarly, self-produced satiation and deprivation have been described as techniques in the service of behavior change. One group of change strategies has been classified under the term *stimulus control*. They involve rearrangement of the social and physical environment or the use of self-generated behaviors. A special case of rearrangement of self-generated reinforcing consequences, the covert conditioning techniques, involves the use of imaginal presentation of stimuli and behaviors.

The typical treatment plan incorporates multiple techniques that are tailored to the client's particular problem and life situation. However, most effective treatments include the following general sequence of steps (Kanfer & Grimm, 1980):

1. Establish a working relationship with the client including basic rapport-building and educating the client about the instigative model of therapy.
2. Create motivation for change through anticipatory self-regulation, goal and value clarification, self-monitoring, prehearsal, and discussion about possible positive outcomes.
3. Conduct a behavioral analysis that describes the network of biological, environmental, and psychological variables controlling the target behavior, and identify the optimal point of intervention.
4. Develop a plan for behavior change. Negotiate a contract with clear specification of the goals, the time allowed for the program, the consequences of achieving it, and the methods for producing change.
5. Introduce a self-reinforcement program that relies increasingly on the client's self-reactions, is sufficiently varied to avoid satiation, and is effective in changing the target behavior.

6. Prehearse the change strategy, providing information about the treatment and opportunities for modeling and role-play.
7. Ask the client to execute new behaviors in his or her natural environment, with discussion and correction of performance as needed. Include a system for recording qualitative and quantitative data documenting change.
8. Review progress, helping the client to solidify semantic memories of his or her experience. Discuss the nature of procedural effects, the means by which they are achieved, and situations to which they can be applied in the future.
9. Continue strong support for any activity in which the client assumes increasing responsibility for following the program accurately and extending it to other problematic behaviors.
10. Summarize what has been learned in the change process and prepare the client to transfer the new knowledge and skills to future situations.

REFERENCES

Abrams, D. B., & Wilson, G. T. (1979). Self-monitoring and reactivity in the modification of cigarette smoking. *Journal of Consulting and Clinical Psychology, 47,* 243–251.

Anderson, C. A. (1983). Imagination and expectation. The effects of imagining behavioral scripts on personal intentions. *Journal of Personality and Social Psychology, 45,* 293–305.

Anderson, C. M., & Stewart, S. (1983). *Mastering resistance: A practical guide to family therapy.* New York: Guilford Press.

Averill, J. H. (1973). Personal control over aversive stimuli and its relationship to stress. *Psychological Bulletin, 80,* 286–303.

Baer, P. E., Foreyt, J. P., & Wright. S. (1977). Self-directed termination of excessive cigarette use among untreated smokers. *Journal of Behavior Therapy and Experimental Psychiatry, 8,* 71–74.

Baltes, M. M. (1978). Environmental factors in dependency among nursing home residents: A social ecology analysis. In T. A. Wills (Ed.), *Basic processes in helping relationships* (pp. 405–425). New York: Academic Press.

Bandura, A. (1977). Self-efficacy: Toward a unifying theory of behavioral change. *Psychological Review, 84,* 191–215.

Bandura, A., & Perloff, B. (1967). Relative efficacy of self-monitoring and externally imposed reinforcement systems. *Journal of Personality and Social Psychology, 7,* 111–116.

Bellack, A. S., Schwartz, J., & Rozensky, R. H. (1974). The contribution of external control to self-control in a weight reduction program. *Journal of Behavior Therapy and Experimental Psychiatry, 5,* 245–249.

Bigelow, G., Sticker, O, Leibson, I., & Griffiths, R. (1976). Maintaining disulfram ingestion among outpatient alcoholics: A security deposit contingency contracting program. *Behaviour Research and Therapy, 14,* 378–380.

Bootzin, R. R., & Nicassio, P. (1978). Behavioral treatment for insomnia. In M. Hersen, R. Eisler, & P. Miller (Eds.), *Progress in behavior modification* (Vol. 6, pp. 1–45). New York: Academic Press.

Borkovec, T. D., Wilkinson, L., Folensbee, R., & Lerman, C. (1983). Stimulus control applications to the treatment of worry. *Behaviour Research and Therapy, 21,* 247–251.

Brehm, S. (1966). *The application of social psychology to clinical practice.* Washington, DC: Hemisphere.

Breier, A., & Strauss, J. S. (1983). Self-control in psychotic disorders. *Archives of General Psychiatry, 40,* 1141–1145.

Brigham, T. A., & Stoerzinger, A. (1976). An experimental analysis of children's preference for self-selected rewards. In T. A. Brigham, R. Hawkins, J. Scott, & T. F. McLaughlin (Eds.), *Behavior analysis in education: Self-control and reading.* Dubuque, IA: Wm. C. Brown, Kendall/Hunt.

Broden, B., Hall, R. V., & Mitts, B. (1971). The effect of self-recording on the classroom behavior of two eighth grade students. *Journal of Applied Behavior Analysis, 4,* 191–199.

Castro, L., Perez, G. C., Albanchez, D. B., & de Leon, E. P. (1983). Feedback properties of "self-reinforcement": Further evidence. *Behavior Therapy, 14,* 672–681.

Cautela, J. R. (1969, September). *The use of imagery in behavior modification.* Paper presented at the annual meeting of the Association for the Advancement of Behavior Therapy, Washington, DC.

Cautela, J. R. (1976). The present status of covert modeling. *Journal of Behavior Therapy and Experimental Psychiatry, 6,* 323–326.

Cautela, J. R., & Kearney, A. J. (1986). *The covert conditioning handbook.* New York: Springer.

Cautela, J. R., & Wisocki, P. A. (1977). The thought-stopping procedure: Description, application, and learning theory interpretations. *The Psychological Record, 1,* 255–264.

Cervone, D. (1989). Effects on envisioning future activities on self-efficacy judgements and motivation: An availability heuristic interpretation. *Cognitive therapy and research, 13,* 247–262.

Condry, J. (1977). Enemies of exploration: Self-initiated versus other-initiated learning. *Journal of Personality and Social Psychology, 35,* 459–477.

Davison, G. C. (1973). Counter-control in behavior modification. In L. A. Hamerlynck, L. C. Handly, & F. J. Mash (Eds.), *Behavior change: Methodology, concepts and practice* (pp. 153–167). Champaign, IL: Research Press.

Deci, E. L., & Ryan, R. M. (1985). *Intrinsic motivation and self-determination in human behavior.* New York: Plenum Press.

Deci, E. L., & Ryan, R. M. (1987). The support of autonomy and the control of behavior. *Journal of Personality and Social Psychology, 53,* 1024–1037.

DiClemente, C., & Prochaska, J. (1982). Self-change and therapy change of smoking behavior: A comparison of processes of change in cessation and maintenance. *Addictive Behaviors, 7,* 133–142.

DiMatteo, M. R., & DiNicola, D. D. (1982). *Achieving patient compliance.* Elmsford, NY: Pergamon Press.

Elkins, R. L. (1980). Covert sensitization treatment of alcoholism: Contributions of successful conditioning to subsequent abstinence maintenance. *Addictive Behaviors, 5,* 67–89.

Ellis, A. (1985). *Overcoming resistance: Rational-emotive therapy with difficult clients.* New York: Springer.

Emmelkamp, P. M. G. (1974). Self-observation versus flooding in the treatment of agoraphobia. *Behaviour Research and Therapy, 12,* 229–237.

Ewart, C. K. (1978). Self-observation in natural settings: Reactive effects of behavior desirability and goal setting. *Cognitive Therapy and Research, 2,* 39–56.

Ferster, C. B., Nurnberger, J. L., & Levitt, E. B. (1962). The control of eating. *Journal of Mathetics, 1,* 87–109.

Fisk, A. D., & Schneider, W. (1984). Memory as a function of attention, level of processing and automatization. *Journal of Experimental Psychology: Learning, Memory and Cognition, 10,* 181–197.

Försterling, F. (1988). *Attribution theory in clinical psychology*. New York: John Wiley & Sons.

Foreyt, J. P., & Hagan, R. L. (1973). Covert sensitization: Conditioning or suggestion? *Journal of Abnormal Psychology, 82*, 17–23.

Frank, J. D. (1982). Therapeutic components shared by all psychotherapies. In J. H. Harvey & M. M. Parks (Eds.), *Psychotherapy research and behavior change* (Master Lecture Series, Vol. 1, pp. 9–37). Washington, DC: American Psychological Association.

Fremouw, W. J., & Brown, J. P. (1980). The reactivity of addictive behaviors to self-monitoring: A functional analysis. *Addictive Behaviors, 5*, 209–217.

Frijda, N. H. (1986). *The emotions*. Cambridge, England: Cambridge University Press.

Gartner, A., & Riessman, F. (Eds.). (1984). *The self-help revolution*. New York: Human Sciences Press.

Glasgow, R. E., & Rosen, G. M. (1978). Behavioral bibliotherapy: A review of self-help behavior therapy manuals. *Psychological Bulletin, 85*, 1–23.

Glasgow, R. E., & Rosen, G. M. (1979). Self-help behavior therapy manuals: Recent developments and clinical usage. *Behavior Therapy Review, 1*, 1–20.

Goldfried, M. R. (1982). On the history of therapeutic integration. *Behavior Therapy, 13*, 572–593.

Goldfried, M. R., & Robins, C. (1982). On the facilitation of self-efficacy. *Cognitive Therapy and Research, 6*, 361–380.

Goldstein, A. P., & Kanfer, F. H. (Eds.). (1979). *Maximizing treatment gains: Transfer enhancement in psychotherapy*. New York: Academic Press.

Green, L. (1978). Temporal and stimulus dimensions of self-monitoring in the treatment of obesity. *Behavior Therapy, 9*, 328–341.

Greenberg, L. S., & Safran, J. D. (1987). *Emotion in psychotherapy*. New York: Guilford Press.

Greiner, J. M., & Karoly, P. (1976). Effects of self-control training on study activity and academic performance. An analysis of self-monitoring, self-reward and systematic planning components. *Journal of Counseling Psychology, 23*, 495–502.

Grimm, L. G. (1980). The evidence for cue-controlled relaxation. *Behavior Therapy, 11*, 283–293.

Halish, F., & Kuhl, J. (Eds.). (1987). *Motivation, intention and volition*. New York: Springer Verlag.

Hayes, S. C., & Nelson, R. C. (1983). Similar reactivity produced by external cues and self-monitoring. *Behavior Modification, 7*, 183–196.

Heckhausen, H., & Gollwitzer, P. M. (1987). Thought contents and cognitive functioning in motivational versus volitional states of mind. *Motivation and Emotion, 2*, 101–120.

Heckhausen, H., & Kuhl, J. (1985). From wishes to action: The dead end and short cuts on the long way to action. In M. Frese & J. Sabini (Eds.), *Goal-directed behavior: Psychological theory and research on action* (pp. 134–159). Hillsdale, NJ: Lawrence Erlbaum Associates.

Heffernan, T., & Richards, C. S. (1981). Self-control of study behavior: Identification of natural methods. *Journal of Counseling Psychology, 28*, 361–364.

Herzberg, A. (1945). *Active psychotherapy*. New York: Grune & Stratton.

Holroyd, K. A., & Creer, T. L. (Eds.). (1986). *Self-management of chronic disease*. Orlando, FL: Academic Press.

Homme, L. E. (1965). Perspectives in psychology—XXIV. Control of coverants: The operants of the mind. *Psychological Record, 15*, 501–511.

Isen, A. M. (1984). Toward understanding the role of affect in cognition. In R. S. Wyer & T. K. Srull (Eds.), *Handbook of social cognition* (pp. 179–236). Hillsdale, NJ: Lawrence Erlbaum Associates.

Jacobson, N. S. (1977). Problem-solving and contingency contracting in the treatment of marital discord. *Journal of Consulting and Clinical Psychology, 45,* 92–100.

Jacobson, N. S. (1983). Clinical innovations in behavioral marital therapy. In K. D. Craig & R. J. McMahon (Eds.), *Advances in clinical behavior therapy* (pp. 74–98). New York: Brunner/Mazel.

Jeffrey, R. W., Gerber, W. M., Rosenthal, B. S., & Lindquist, R. A. (1983). Monetary contracts in weight control: Effectiveness of group and individual contracts of varying size. *Journal of Consulting and Clinical Psychology, 51,* 242–248.

Johnson, M. K., & Raye, C. L. (1981). Reality-monitoring. *Psychological Review, 88,* 67–85.

Johnson, M. K., Raye, C. L., Wang, A. Y., & Taylor, T. H. (1979). Fact and fantasy: The roles of accuracy and variability in confusing imaginations with perceptual experiences. *Journal of Experimental Psychology: Human Learning and Memory, 5,* 229–240.

Johnson, S. M., & Martin, S. (1973). Developing self-evaluation as a conditioned reinforcer. In B. Ashem & E. G. Poser (Eds.), *Behavior modification with children* (pp. 69–78). Elmsford, NY: Pergamon Press.

Johnson, S. M., & White, G. (1971). Self-observation as an agent of behavioral change. *Behavior Therapy, 2,* 488–497.

Jones, E. E., & Nisbett, R. E. (1971). *The actor and observer: Divergent perceptions of the causes of behavior.* New York: Silver Burdett, General Learning Press.

Jones, R. T., Nelson, R. E., & Kazdin, A. E. (1977). The role of external variables in self-reinforcement: A review. *Behavior Modification, 1,* 147–178.

Kanfer, F. H. (1970a). Self-monitoring: Methodological limitations and clinical applications. *Journal of Consulting and Clinical Psychology, 35,* 148–152.

Kanfer, F. H. (1970b). Self-regulation: Research, issues and speculations. In C. Neuringer & J. L. Michael (Eds.), *Behavior modification in clinical psychology* (pp. 178–220). New York: Appleton-Century-Crofts.

Kanfer, F. H. (1971). The maintenance of behavior by self-generated stimuli and reinforcement. In A. Jacob & L. B. Sachs (Eds.), *The psychology of private events* (pp. 39–57). New York: Academic Press.

Kanfer, F. H. (1977). The many faces of self-control, or behavior modification changes its focus. In P. B. Stuart (Ed.), *Behavior self-management* (pp. 1–48). New York: Brunner/Mazel.

Kanfer, F. H. (1985). Target behavior selection for clinical change programs. *Behavioral Assessment, 7,* 7–20.

Kanfer, F. H. (1986). Implications of a self-regulation model of therapy for treatment of addictive behaviors. In W. R. Miller & N. Heather (Eds.), *Treating addictive behaviors: Processes of change* (pp. 29–47). New York: Plenum Press.

Kanfer, F. H. (1987). Self-regulation and behavior. In H. H. Heckhausen, P. M. Gollwitzer, & F. E. Weinert (Eds.), *Jenseits des Rubikons: Der Wille in den Humanwissenschaften.* (Beyond the Rebicon: The will in the social sciences.) Heidelberg, West Germany: Springer-Verlag.

Kanfer, F. H., & Busemeyer, J. P. (1982). The use of problem-solving and decision-making in behavior therapy. *Clinical Psychology Review, 2,* 239–266.

Kanfer, F. H., Cox, L. E., Greiner, J. M., & Karoly, P. (1974). Contracts, demands characteristics and self-control. *Journal of Personality and Social Psychology, 30,* 605–619.

Kanfer, F. H., & Duerfeldt, P. H. (1967). Motivational properties of S-R. *Perceptual and Motor Skills, 25,* 237–246.

Kanfer, F. H., & Grimm, L. G. (1978). Freedom of choice and behavioral change. *Journal of Consulting and Clinical Psychology, 46,* 873–878.

Kanfer, F. H., & Grimm, L. G. (1980). Managing clinical change: A process model of therapy. *Behavior Therapy, 4*, 419–444.

Kanfer, F. H., & Hagerman, S. (1981). The role of self-regulation. In L. P. Rehm (Ed.), *Behavior therapy for depression: Present status and future directions* (pp. 143–179). New York: Academic Press.

Kanfer, F. H., & Phillips, J. S. (1970). *Learning foundations of behavior therapy.* New York: John Wiley & Sons.

Kanfer, F. H., & Schefft, B. K. (1988). *Guiding the process of therapeutic change.* Champaign, IL: Research Press.

Kanfer, F. H., & Seidner, M. L. (1973). Self-control: Factors enhancing tolerance of noxious stimulation. *Journal of Personality and Social Psychology, 25*, 381–389.

Karoly, P. (in press). Models and methods of self-management in health care and illness prevention. In C. R. Snyder & D. R. Forsyth (Eds.), *Handbook of social and clinical psychology: The health perspective.* Elmsford, NY: Pergamon Press.

Karoly, P., & Kanfer, F. H. (Eds.). (1982). *Self-management and behavior change: From theory to practice.* Elsmford, NY: Pergamon Press.

Karoly, P., & Steffen, J. J. (Eds.). (1980). *Improving the long-term effects of psychotherapy.* New York: Gardner Press.

Kazdin, A. E. (1974). Self-monitoring and behavior change. In M. J. Mahoney & C. E. Thoreson (Eds.), *Self-control: Power to the person* (pp. 218–246). Monterey, CA: Brooks/Cole.

Kazdin, A. E. (1977). Research issues in covert conditioning. *Cognitive Therapy and Research, 1*, 45–58.

Kazdin, A. E. (1979). Imagery elaboration and self-efficacy in the covert modeling treatment of assertive behavior. *Journal of Consulting and Clinical Psychology, 47*, 725–733.

Kazdin, A. E., & Mascitelli, S. (1982). Covert and overt rehearsal in homework practice in developing assertiveness. *Journal of Consulting and Clinical Psychology, 52j*, 250–258.

Kelly, G. A. (1955). *The psychology of personal constructs.* New York: W. W. Norton.

Kirschenbaum, D. S. (1987). Self-regulatory failure: A review with clinical implication. *Clinical Psychology Review, 7*, 77–104.

Kirschenbaum, D. S., & Flanery, R. C. (1983). Behavioral contracting: Outcomes and elements. In M. Hersen, R. M. Eisler, & P. M. Miller (Eds.), *Progress in behavior modification* (Vol. 15, pp. 217–275). New York: Academic Press.

Kirschenbaum, D. S., Sherman, J., & Penrod, J. D. (1987). Promoting self-directed hemodialysis: Measurement and cognitive-behavioral intervention. *Health Psychology, 6*, 373–385.

Kirschenbaum, D. S., & Tomarken, A. J. (1982). On facing the generalization problem: The study of self-regulatory failure. In P. C. Kendall (Ed.), *Advances in cognitive-behavioral research and therapy* (Vol. 1, pp. 119–200). New York: Academic Press.

Klinger, E., Barta, S. G., & Maxeiner, M. E. (1979). Current concerns: Assessing therapeutically relevant motivation. In P. C. Kendall & S. D. Hollon (Eds.), *Assessment strategies for cognitive-behavioral interventions* (pp. 161–196). New York: Academic Press.

Koberg, D., & Bagnall, J. (1976). *The polytechnic school of values: Values Tech.* Los Altos, CA: William Kaufmann, Inc.

Komaki, J., & Dore, B. K. (1978). Self-recording: Its effects on individuals high and low in motivation. *Behavior Therapy, 9*, 65–72.

Kopel, S., & Arkowitz, H. (1975). The role of attribution and self-perception in behavior change: Implications for behavior therapy. *Genetic Psychology Monographs, 92*, 175–212.

Kuhl, J., & Beckmann, J. (Eds.). (1985). *Action control: From cognition to behavior*. New York: Springer-Verlag.

Kuhn, T. S. (1977). *The essential tension*. Chicago, IL: University of Chicago Press.

Lakein, R. (1973). *How to get control of your time and your life*. New York: New American Library, Signet.

Lambert, M. J. (Ed.). (1983). *A guide to psychotherapy and patient relationships*. Homewood, IL: Dow-Jones-Irwin.

Lamontagne, Y., & Lesage, A. (1986). Private exposure and covert sensitization in the treatment of exhibitionism. *Journal of Behavior Therapy and Experimental Psychiatry, 17*, 197–201.

Langer, E. J., Janis, I. L., & Wolfer, J. A. (1975). Reduction of physiological stress in surgical patients. *Journal of Experimental Social Psychology, 11*, 155–165.

Langer, E. J., & Rodin, J. (1976). The effect of choice and enhanced personal responsibility for the aged: A field experiment in an institutional setting. *Journal of Personality and Social Psychology, 34*, 191–198.

Lanyon, R. I. (1986). Theory and treatment in child molestation. *Journal of Consulting and Clinical Psychology, 54*, 176–182.

Lee, C. (1983). Self-efficacy and behaviour as predictors of subsequent behaviour in an assertiveness training program. *Behaviour Research and Therapy, 21*, 225–232.

Lehr, B. K. (1986). A comparative study of self-management and cognitive-behavioral therapies in the treatment of cardiac rehabilitation. Unpublished Ph.D. dissertation, University of Wisconsin–Milwaukee, Milwaukee, WI.

Liem, G. R. (1975). Performance and satisfaction as affected by personal control over salient decisions. *Journal of Personality and Social Psychology, 31*, 232–240.

Little, L. M., & Curran, J. P. (1978). Covert sensitization: A clinical procedure in need of some explanations. *Psychological Bulletin, 85* (3), 513–531.

Litrownik, A. J. (1982). Special considerations in the self-management of training of the developmentally disabled. In P. Karoly & F. H. Kanfer (Eds.), *Self-management and behavior change: From theory to practice* (pp. 315–352). Elmsford, NY: Pergamon Press.

Lovitt, T. C., & Curtiss, K. A. (1969). Academic response rate as a function of teacher and self-imposed contingencies. *Journal of Applied Behavioral Analysis, 2*, 49–53.

Mackie, D. M., & Worth, L. T. (1989). Processing deficits and the mediation of positive affect in persuasion. *Journal of Personality and Social Psychology, 57*, 27–40.

Mahoney, M. J. (1971). The self-management of covert behavior: A case study. *Behavior Therapy, 2*, 575–578.

Mahoney, M. J., Moura, N. G. M., & Wade, T. C. (1973). Relative efficacy of self-reward, self-punishment, and self-monitoring techniques for weight loss. *Journal of Consulting and Clinical Psychology, 40*, 404–407.

Marlatt, G. A., & Gordon, J. R. (Eds.). (1985). *Relapse prevention: Maintenance strategies in the treatment of addictive behaviors*. New York: Guilford Press.

McFall, R. M. (1977). Parameters of self-monitoring. In P. B. Stuart (Ed.), *Behavior self-management: Strategies, techniques and outcomes* (pp. 196–214). New York: Brunner/Mazel.

Meichenbaum, D., & Turk, D. C. (1987). *Facilitating treatment adherence: A practitioner's guide*. New York: Plenum Press.

Miller, W. R., & Dougher, M. J. (1984). Covert sensitization: Alternative treatment approaches for alcoholics. *Alcoholism: Clinical Experimental Research, 8*, 108.

Montgomery, G. T., & Parton, D. A. (1970). Reinforcing effect of self-reward. *Journal of Experimental Psychology, 84*, 273–276.

Nelson, R. O. (1977). Methodological issues in assessment via self-monitoring. In J. D. Cone & R. P. Hawkins (Eds.), *Behavioral assessment: New directions in clinical psychology* (pp. 217–240). New York: Brunner/Mazel.

Nelson, R. O., Hayes, S. C., Spong, R. T., Jarret, R. B., & McKnight, D. L. (1983). Self-reinforcement: Appealing misnomer or effective mechanism? *Behaviour Research and Therapy, 21,* 557–566.

Nelson, R. O., Lipinski, D. P., & Black, J. L. (1976). The reactivity of adult retardates' self-monitoring: A comparison among behaviors of different valences, and a comparison with token reinforcement. *Psychological Record, 26,* 189–201.

Nicassio, P. M., & Buchanan, D. C. (1981). Clinical application of behavior therapy for insomnia. *Comprehensive Psychiatry, 22,* 512–521.

O'Banion, D., Armstrong, B. K., & Ellis, J. (1980). Conquered urge as a means of self-control. *Addictive Behaviors, 5,* 101–106.

Perri, M. G., Richards, C. S., & Schultheis, K. R. (1977). Behavioral self-control and smoking reduction: A study of self-initiated attempts to reduce smoking. *Behavior Therapy, 8,* 360–365.

Posner, M. I., & Snyder, C. R. R. (1975). Attention and cognitive control. In R. L. Solso (Ed.), *Information-processing and cognition: The Loyola symposium* (pp. 55–85). Hillsdale, NJ: Lawrence Erlbaum Associates.

Prochaska, J. D., & DiClemente, C. O. (1982). Transtheoretical therapy: Toward a more integrative model of change. *Psychotherapy: Theory, Research, and Practice, 19,* 276–288.

Prochaska, J. O., DiClemente, C. O., Velicer, W. F., Ginpil, S., & Norcross, N. C. (1985). Predicting change in smoking status for self-changers. *Addictive Behaviors, 10,* 395–406.

Rehm, L. P., & Kaslow, N. J. (1984). Behavioral approaches to depression: Research results and clinical recommendations. In C. M. Franks (Ed.), *New developments in behavior therapy: From research to clinical application* (pp. 155–230). New York: Haworth Press.

Rehm, L. P., & Kornblith, S. J. (1979). Behavior therapy for depression: A review of recent developments. In M. Hersen, R. M. Eisler, & P. M. Miller (Eds.), *Progress in behavior modification* (Vol. 7, pp 277–318). New York: Academic Press.

Richards, C. S. (1975). Behavior modification of studying through study skills advice and self-control procedures. *Journal of Counseling Psychology, 22,* 431–436.

Richards, C. S., & Perri, M. G. (1977). Do self-control treatments last? An evaluation of behavioral problem solving and faded counselor maintenance strategies. Paper presented at the 11th annual meeting of the Association for Advancement of Behavior Therapy, Atlanta, GA.

Rodin, J. (1982). Biopsychosocial aspects of self-management. In P. Karoly & F. H. Kanfer (Eds.), *Self-management and behavior change: From theory to practice* (pp. 60–92). Elmsford, NY: Pergamon Press.

Rodin, J. (1987). Weight change following smoking cessation: The role of food intake and exercise. *Addictive Behaviors, 12,* 303–317.

Rodin, J., & Langer, E. J. (1977). Long-term effects of a control-relevant intervention with the institutionalized aged. *Journal of Personality and Social Psychology, 35,* 897–902.

Romanczyk, R. G. (1974). Self-monitoring in the treatment of obesity: Parameters of reactivity. *Behavior Therapy, 5,* 531–540.

Rosen, G. M. (1982). Self-help approaches to self-management. In K. R. Blankstein & J. Polivy (Eds.), *Self-control and self-modification of emotional behavior* (pp. 183–199). New York: Plenum Press.

Rosenbaum, M. (1980). A schedule for assessing self-control behaviors: Preliminary findings. *Behavior Therapy, 11,* 109–121.

Rosenbaum, M. (1988). Learned resourcefulness, stress and self-regulation. In S. Fisher & J. Reason (Eds.), *Handbook of life stress, cognition and health* (pp. 483–496). Chichester, England: John Wiley & Sons.

Rosenbaum, M., & Merbaum, M. (1984). Self-control of anxiety and depression: An evaluative review of treatments. In C. M. Franks (Ed.), *New developments in practical behavior therapy: From research to clinical application* (pp. 105–154). New York: Howarth Press.

Rosenbaum, M., & Palmon, N. (1984). Helplessness and resourcefulness in coping with epilepsy. *Journal of Consulting and Clinical Psychology, 52*, 244–253.

Rosenbaum, M., & Rolnick, A. (1983). Self-control behaviors and coping with seasickness. *Cognitive Therapy and Research, 7*, 93–98.

Rothbaum, F., Weisz, J. R., & Snyder, S. S. (1982). Changing the world and changing the self: A two process model of perceived control. *Journal of Personality and Social Psychology, 42*, 5–37.

Schefft, B. K., & Kanfer, F. H. (1987). The utility of a process model in therapy. A comparative study of treatment effects. *Behavior Therapy, 2*, 113–134.

Schneider, W., & Shiffrin, R. M. (1977). Controlled and automatic human information processing: I. Detection, search and attention. *Psychological Review, 84*, 1–66.

Schwarz, N. (in press). Feelings as information: Informational and motivational functions of affective states. In R. Sorrentino & E. T. Higgins (Eds.), *Handbook of motivation and cognition: Foundations of social behavior* (Vol. 2). New York: Guilford Press.

Seligman, M. E. P. (1970). On the generality of the laws of learning. *Psychological Review, 77*, 406–418.

Seltzer, L. F. (1986). *Paradoxical strategies in psychotherapy: A comprehensive overview and guidebook*. New York: John Wiley & Sons.

Shelton, J. L. (1979). Instigation therapy: Using therapeutic homework to promote treatment gains. In A. P. Goldstein & F. H. Kanfer (Eds.), *Maximizing treatment gains* (pp. 225–245). New York: Academic Press.

Shelton, J. L., & Levy, R. L. (1981). *Behavioral assignments and treatment compliance: A handbook of clinical strategies*. Champaign, IL: Research Press.

Sherman, T. R., & Anderson, C. A. (1987). Decreasing premature termination from therapy. *Journal of Social and Clinical Psychology, 5*, 298–312.

Spring, F. L., Sipich, J. F., Trimble, R. W., & Goeckner, D. J. (1978). Effects of contingency and noncontingency contracts in the context of a self-control-oriented smoking modification program. *Behavior Therapy, 9*, 967–968.

Stanley, M. A., & Maddux, J. E. (1986). Self-efficacy theory: Potential contributions to understanding cognitions in depression. *Journal of Social and Clinical Psychology, 4*, 268–278.

Stiles, W. B., Shapiro, D. A., & Elliott, R. (1986). Are all psychotherapies equivalent? *American Psychologist, 41*, 165–180.

Stock, G. (1987). *The book of questions*. New York: John Wiley & Sons.

Stotland, E., & Blumenthal, A. L. (1964). The reduction of anxiety as a result of the expectation of making a choice. *Canadian Journal of Psychology, 18*, 139–145.

Stuart, R. B., & Davis, B. (1972). *Slim chance in a fat world: Behavioral control of obesity*. Champaign, IL: Research Press.

Suinn, R. M., & Richardson, R. (1971). Anxiety management training: A nonspecific behavior therapy for anxiety control. *Behavior Therapy, 2*, 498–510.

Surwit, R. S., Feingloss, M. N., & Scovern, A. N. (1983). Diabetes and behavior: A paradigm for health psychology. *American Psychologist, 38*, 255–262.

Susskind, D. J. (1970). The idealized self-image (ISI): A new technique in confidence training. *Behavior Therapy, 1*, 538–541.

Sweet, A. A. (1984). The therapeutic relationship in behavior therapy. *Clinical Psychology Review, 4*, 253–272.

Taylor, S. E., & Schneider, S. K. (1989). Coping and the simulation of events. *Social Cognition, 7*, 174–194.

Tearman, B. H., Lahey, B. B., Thompson, J. K., & Hammer, D. (1982). The role of coping self-instructions combined with covert modeling in specific fear reduction. *Cognitive Therapy and Research, 6,* 185–190.

Thoreson, C. E., & Mahoney, M. J. (1974). *Behavioral self-control.* New York: Holt, Rinehart & Winston.

Tressler, D. P., & Tucker, R. D. (1980, November). *The comparative effects of self-evaluation and self-reinforcement training in the treatment of depression.* Paper presented at the meeting of the Association for Advancement of Behavior Therapy, New York, NY.

Tulving, E. (1972). Episodic and semantic memory. In E. Tulving & W. Donaldson (Eds.), *Organization of memory* (pp. 382–403). New York: Academic Press.

Turkewitz, H., O'Leary, K. D., & Ironsmith, M. (1975). Generalization and maintenance of appropriate behavior through self-control. *Journal of Consulting and Clinical Psychology, 43,* 577–583.

Wachtel, P. L. (Ed.). (1982). *Resistance: Psychodynamic and behavioral approaches.* New York: Plenum Press.

Wills, T. A. (Ed.). (1978). *Basic processes in helping relationships.* New York: Academic Press.

Wing, R. R., Epstein, L. H., Nowalk, M. P., & Lamparski, D. M. (1986). Behavioral self-regulation in the treatment of patients with diabetes mellitus. *Psychological Bulletin, 99,* 78–89.

Wuertele, S. K. (1986). Self-efficacy and athletic performance: A review. *Journal of Social and Clinical Psychology, 4,* 290–301.

9
Cognitive Behavior Modification

Peter Salovey
Jefferson A. Singer

Although therapies emphasizing cognitive restructuring have been practiced for about 30 years (Beck, 1963; Ellis, 1962), cognitive behavior therapies as described by Meichenbaum (1977), Mahoney (1974), Goldfried and Davison (1976), and Kanfer (1975) heralded what in retrospect can be considered a new movement in the practice of psychotherapy, a movement that emphasized the reciprocal relationship of cognition and behavior. As a new decade begins, cognitive behavior therapy has moved into a phase of its life where it is widely accepted and applied to a diverse array of psychological problems. Systematic cognitive behavioral approaches have been employed in the treatment of unipolar depression (e.g., Dobson, 1989), intractable phobias (e.g., Williams, Dooseman, & Kleifield, 1984), social anxieties (e.g., Shaffer, Shapiro, Sank, & Coghlan, 1981), academic anxieties (e.g., Salovey & Haar, in press), eating disorders (e.g., Agras, Schneider, Arnow, Raeburn, & Telch, 1989; Fairburn, 1985), substance abuse (e.g., Marlatt & Gordon, 1985; Stevens & Hollis, 1989), chronic pain (e.g., Turk, Meichenbaum, & Genest, 1983), coping with medical procedures (e.g., Jay, Elliott, Katz, & Siegel, 1987), and conduct disordered children (e.g., Kazdin, 1987a).

Underlying these assorted interventions is a common core of (a) theoretical assumptions regarding the relationship of cognition to behavior, and (b) practical

Preparation of the manuscript was partially supported by NIH Biomedical Research Support Grant S07 RR07015, National Cancer Institute Grant P01 CA42101, and National Center for Health Statistics contract 200-88-7001 to the first author.

361

assumptions concerning the best ways to help people change. In the present chapter, we will first describe these sets of assumptions. While discussing these assumptions, we will devote attention to a less well developed aspect of cognitive behavior therapy, the importance of affective processes in the relationship between cognition and action. What then follows is a discussion of the application of cognitive behavior therapy to an anxiety-ridden adult and to a conduct disordered child. We will conclude with some thoughts about clinical judgment in cognitive behavior therapy, especially focusing on affective processes in this domain.

THE BASIS OF COGNITIVE BEHAVIOR THERAPY

Theoretical Assumptions of Cognitive Behavior Therapy

Behavior Change Is Mediated by Cognitive Activities

Perhaps the most fundamental assumption in CBT, but one that may not be unique to it, is that behavior can best be understood by examining its cognitive antecedents. The cognitive mediation of behavior is thought to account for the etiology of most dysfunctional behaviors as well as the adoption of more healthy responses. For example, Lazarus and his colleagues have described how stress responses result from individuals' *interpretations* or *appraisals* of external events rather than directly from the external events themselves (Lazarus, 1977; Lazarus & Folkman, 1984). Similarly, Ellis's rational-emotive therapy has long emphasized the primary importance of cognition and evaluative beliefs in accounting for maladaptive behavior (Dryden & Ellis, 1988).

Textbook definitions of cognitive behavior therapy emphasize this cognitive mediation of behavior as well as two additional assumptions (e.g., Dobson & Block, 1988). One assumption concerns the idea that cognitive activities are available for explicit monitoring by either clients or therapists. Another assumption is that systematically altering maladaptive cognitions will produce desired behavioral changes. However, the theoretical foundations of cognitive behavior therapy (Bandura, 1977a; Mischel, 1973) have described a more complex view of causation than one centered solely on cognitive activities. It is to this view of causality, called reciprocal determinism (Bandura, 1978, 1986), that we now turn.

Reciprocal Determinism

Consider the case of Paula, a 34-year-old woman who is married to an officer in the Coast Guard, stationed at a base connected to the mainland by a long suspension bridge. Over the past several years, Paula has developed strong phobic reaction to driving over bridges. She reports increased anxiety—sweating, hyperventilating, racing heart, and thoughts about fatal car accidents—every time she approaches the bridge to cross to the mainland. These thoughts and reactions have become so severe that Paula has begun to call in sick to her job more frequently and regularly cancels social engagements with friends.

A traditional, cognitive mediational view of Paula's case (e.g., Ellis) might emphasize the specific thoughts in Paula's mind associated with anxiety as she considered crossing the bridge. Intervention might involve systematically changing these thoughts by, for example, challenging their irrational nature (Ellis) or developing and rehearsing a new set of appraisals regarding the safety of bridges and her personal competencies about crossing them (Meichenbaum).

Although these techniques, which are centered on examining and altering cognitive antecedents of the maladaptive behavior, produce desired change, a greater number of potentially effective treatment alternatives are suggested by a slightly more complex conceptualization of Paula's difficulties. Bandura's (1978, 1986) model of causality, called reciprocal determinism, describes the mutual interactions among person variables (e.g., cognitions), observable behaviors, and environmental cues and reinforcers. Each of these variables—person, behavior, environment—is both affected by and in turn affects each other variable. Thus, six causal pathways can be delimited: the influence of person variables on behavior and behavior on person variables; the influence of person variables on the environment and the environment on person variables; and the influence of environment on behavior and behavior on environment. It is illustrative to examine Paula's case from each of these vantage points. We should mention, however, that these causal pathways in the model of reciprocal determinism can be considered part of a larger system of personality that is reorganized in the course of psychotherapy (see Hollandsworth, 1986, and Kanfer & Schefft, 1988, for applications of such a general systems approach to clinical practice).

Paula's exaggerated thoughts about disasters on bridges represent cognitions (i.e., person variables) that result in an avoidant behavior pattern. Because these thoughts produce unpleasant sensations of anxiety, Paula is likely to take actions that minimize these feelings. One strategy for minimizing anxiety about bridges is to avoid situations that might elicit her dysfunctional thoughts about bridges. In turn, subsequent thoughts are shaped by her observing her own (lack of) behavior. Noting the incredible lengths to which she goes to avoid bridges, Paula concludes that, indeed, bridges must be especially scary, and, more importantly, that she is the type of person who has neither bridge-crossing skills nor control over her emotions. In addition, her physiological reactions (e.g., sweating, racing heart) elicit further thoughts about being out of control and panicky. Soon, she finds herself becoming anxious about the possibility of a bridge-induced panic attack. Her self-confidence is undermined, and her self-esteem suffers.

In addition to this reciprocal link between thoughts and behavior, links between thought and the external environment are important. For example, because Paula's phobic thoughts prevent her from crossing the bridge to visit her friends, they increase the frequency with which they visit Paula and no longer invite her to come to their homes. This change in her social environment reinforces Paula's belief that crossing the bridge is in fact beyond her capacities. Further, she finds that she enjoys staying home, socializing in her own place, and receiving the attention and sympathy of her friends. In turn, Paula develops a new set of cognitions concerning the desirability of organizing her work life to be home-based as well.

Connections between Paula's behavior and the environment follow from these cognition-environment links. Paula's increased absence from work causes her boss to FAX her work home to her with the demand that Paula bring her paperwork up to date. This change in her occupational environment enables Paula to conduct her work, in addition to her social life, without crossing the bridge. With diminished occupational and social reasons to cross the bridge to the mainland, Paula has lost behavioral opportunities that could demonstrate the irrationality of her thoughts or modify her maladaptive self-beliefs.

We have come full circle in exploring the reciprocally determined causes of Paula's bridge phobia. Ultimately, the conditions that are "enabling" to her phobia—solicitous friends and flexible bosses—may fade such that Paula is faced with social isolation and unemployment if she continues her maladaptive ways. At such a point, Paula's perceived competencies might be at their lowest ebb and felt anxieties at their zenith. We should mention that Paula successfully conquered her phobias through a treatment program that emphasized direct exposure to fearful situations and the development of behavioral and cognitive coping strategies.

A model of reciprocal determinism is a useful framework for cognitive behavioral therapists because it suggests multiple points of intervention. For example, Paula's therapist might provide her with graded mastery experiences in which she confronted the objects of her fears and could develop thoughts about her actual competencies (a behavioral intervention). Further, environmental contingencies, the actions of her friends and boss, could be managed so that they do not reinforce avoidant behavior (an environmental intervention). Adaptive coping self-statements could be rehearsed to replace maladaptive thoughts (a cognitive intervention). Treatment strategies such as these will be discussed later in the chapter.

Some Cognitions are More Important Than Others

Although cognitive behavior therapy is based on the assumption that cognitive processes and products mediate behavior, adaptive and maladaptive, certain types of cognitions have been thought to be critical for both the genesis of problems and their resolution. A shared aspect of these cognitions is their relevance to the self. Cognitions about the self are widely believed to be more complexly organized, more affect-laden, and more likely to motivate behavior than other thought processes (Cantor, Markus, Niedenthal, & Nurius, 1986; Greenwald & Pratkanis, 1984; Salovey & Rodin, 1985).

Mischel (1973) described several self-relevant cognitions that are instrumental to how individuals construe and respond to their environment. First there are individuals' thoughts regarding their *competencies,* which are beliefs about their capacity to respond appropriately to a variety of environmental stimuli. Second, individuals display characteristic styles of *encoding and categorizing* events in their lives. Third, individuals generate *expectations* about both desired and unwanted outcomes. Fourth, the behavior of individuals follows a set of *self-regulatory plans.* An example of a self-regulatory plan is the *life task* (Cantor, Markus, Niedenthal, & Nurius, 1986). Life tasks are problems faced by individuals at particular times in their lives that serve to organize their goals and actions. Life tasks are closely tied to developmental challenges that give focus to an individual's activities over time. When accomplished, they signify substantial change or growth for the individual. For instance, one of the most significant life tasks that individuals face is the transition from the home environment of the high school years to life on one's own in a college or university (Cantor, Norem, Niedenthal, Langston, & Brower, 1987).

Another important set of cognitions that powerfully influence adaptive and maladaptive behavior concerns expectations about one's capacities. Bandura (1977b) termed these expectations *self-efficacy* beliefs and defined them as "judgment[s] of one's capability to accomplish a certain level of performance . . . People tend to avoid tasks and situations they believe exceed their capabilities, but they undertake and perform assuredly activities they judge themselves capable of handling" (Bandura, 1986, pp. 391, 393). Recall the perils of Paula, the phobic individual discussed earlier. Paula very likely believed that she was incapable of crossing the bridge to the mainland without experiencing considerable distress. In other words, her perceived self-efficacy concerning bridge crossing was quite low. Not surprisingly, she initiated few attempts to cross bridges. However, in the security of her own living room, Paula felt perfectly capable of carrying out social and occupational behaviors.

Not only do self-efficacy expectations influence the choice of behaviors in which to engage, but they in part determine expenditure of energy and persistence in pursuit of goals (Bandura & Cervone, 1983; Schunk, 1984), stress experienced in the face of challenges (Lazarus & Launier, 1978), and attributions for the causes of successes and failures (Collins, 1982). Clinically, improving self-efficacy expectations by providing people with success experiences, coping models, or verbal persuasion has been linked to the successful treatment of chronic pain problems (Litt, 1988; Turk et al., 1983), phobias (Bandura & Adams, 1977; Bandura, Adams, Hardy, & Howells, 1980; Williams & Watson, 1985), difficulties with assertiveness (Kazdin, 1979), health damaging behaviors (DiClemente, 1981; O'Leary, 1985), recovery from chronic illnesses (Bandura, 1982), and many other conditions.

A final set of important self-cognitions involves what Singer (1984) has termed the "private personality." These thoughts include extended autobiographical memories, pleasant and unpleasant fantasies, expectations for the future, ruminations about dreams, and other highly personal aspects of the stream of consciousness. These kinds of higher order cognitions may be organized thematically and termed *schemas* (Singer & Salovey, in press; Turk & Salovey, 1985), *core organizing principles* (Meichenbaum & Gilmore, 1984), or *core conflictual relationship themes* (Luborsky, 1977). Organized sets of temporally stable, repetitive images and beliefs such as these may provide the basis for individual differences in perceptions of capacities and self-efficacy expectations.

For example, Klos and Singer (1981) demonstrated that individuals are more likely to have repetitive thoughts about unresolved conflicts if the conflict shares themes with long-standing unresolved psychological issues. These unresolved issues function as a "background of latent emotionality" (Lazarus, 1977) that makes the individual more susceptible to current stressors relevant to the long-standing issue. Predisposing features of the personality can take the form of repetitive memories or imagery that intensify emotional responses in new situations. The therapist needs to be vigilant to these subtler background issues that might slow or undermine interventions based on current concerns. In fact, recent findings suggest that individuals who deliberately attempt to suppress thinking about such long-standing conflicts may suffer from intensive and debilitating obsessions about them (Wegner, 1989; Wegner, Schneider, Carter, & White, 1987).

Connecting Emotion to Thought and Behavior

Recall that the model of reciprocal determinism on which cognitive behavior therapy draws discusses three points for intervention: person variables, environmental contingencies, and actual behavior. Traditionally, in social learning theory, person variables have been construed as the *cognitive* activities of the individual. Yet, an examination of the cognitive constructs that we discussed as especially important reveals that they include emotion. How can one think coldly about life tasks, personal competencies, goals, expectations, autobiographical memories, and fantasies without being aware of associated affect (Salovey & Rodin, 1985)? The therapist must be alert to emotions that color the maladaptive cognitions that are traditionally the focus of treatment. Even though feelings often also arise as a consequence of cognition, it still may be possible to alter maladaptive cognitions by first assessing and then intervening at the level of feelings.

Emotional arousal has specifiable cognitive consequences. Its influence spans from memory encoding and retrieval, to thoughts about oneself, to social decision-making and problem-solving strategies. The influence of emotion on encoding and retrieval has been reviewed extensively elsewhere (Blaney, 1986; Ellis & Ashbrook, 1989; Gilligan & Bower, 1984; Isen, 1987; Mayer & Salovey, 1988; Singer & Salovey, 1988). Essentially, new material that shares the same emotional tone as one's current mood is easier to learn (encoding congruency). Moreover, individuals tend to recall more readily from memory information that is congruent with their current mood (recall congruency). For example, Nasby and Yando (1982) found that children in a pleasant mood found it easier to learn positive adjectives than children in a neutral mood. Recall congruency is demonstrated in studies showing that individuals are more likely to recall the pleasant events from the past couple of weeks when happy and more likely to recall the unpleasant ones when sad (Salovey & Singer, 1989; Snyder & White, 1982).

Imagine a depressed patient being treated by a cognitive behavior therapist. In didactic and constructive ways, the therapist might provide the patient with feedback about progress during the past week. After listing a long string of positive achievements, the therapist might note a single area needing further improvement. The patient may leave the session having attended to and thus remembering only the bit of negative feedback. His depressed mood created a filter that screened out positive information and was especially sensitive to potential criticism. Similarly, if the depressed patient was asked to describe significant events from his life, distressing memories may be much more easily brought to mind. In this case, it might have been appropriate for the therapist to have pointed explicitly to the possibility that the depressed client might attend only to the negative feedback in order to deactivate the client's automatic tendencies in this regard.

Emotional states also influence the kinds of self-relevant thoughts that are especially important to social learning theorists and cognitive behavior therapists. For example, mood has a systematic influence on self-efficacy expectations. Correlational work by Kanfer and Zeiss (1983) suggests that depressed individuals have lower self-efficacy expectancies in a variety of situations than normals. Experimental work has demonstrated similar links between induced moods and self-efficacy in domains such as athletics and romance (Kavanagh & Bower, 1985), helping (Salovey, 1986; Salovey & Rosenhan, 1989), and beliefs about one's health (Salovey & Birnbaum, 1989). In general, positive affect leads individuals to form optimistic expectations about future performances, while negative affect has the opposite effect on expectations (Wright & Mischel, 1982). Moreover, estimates of the likelihood of future events appear to be influenced by mood. When happy, individuals believe that positive events (e.g., winning the lottery) are more likely. When sad, they believe that negative events are more probable (e.g., dying at a young age; Isen & Patrick, 1983; Johnson & Tversky, 1983; Mayer & Bremer, 1985; Mayer & Volanth, 1985).

Emotion also systematically influences social problem solving and decision making (reviewed by Isen, 1987). For example, happy individuals may be more likely to rely on intuitive and heuristically based strategies when solving problems (Isen, Means, Patrick, & Nowicki, 1982) but also exercise greater creativity (Isen, Daubman, & Nowicki, 1987). The depressed patient whose mood has improved may find himself or herself able to generate many more potential solutions to interpersonal difficulties that had at one time seemed insurmountable.

Affect-Action Sequences

So far we have described the kinds of cognitions (or person variables) that have been important to cognitive behavior therapists. We have also noted that these thoughts are likely to be influenced by mood. What is similar about all of these thoughts is that their object is often the self. Emotional reactions often motivate adaptive and maladaptive social behaviors, and it appears that the link between these feelings and behaviors is self-relevant thought (Salovey & Rodin, 1985).

It seems that feelings, especially negative ones, first tend to cause attention to shift away from the environment and on to the self (Ingram & Smith, 1984; Pyszczynski & Greenberg, 1987; Pyszczynski, Holt, & Greenberg, 1987; Salovey, 1986; Wegner & Giuliano, 1980). While focused on the self after mood is aroused, one is likely to have thoughts congruent with the mood (Bower, 1981; Isen, 1987); these thoughts may concern self-efficacy expectations, perceived competencies, goals, and images of past performance, just the sort of person variables that are most closely linked to behavior (Bandura, 1986). Subsequent behaviors in turn feed back to and affect the original mood, often prolonging it, if positive, and repairing it, if negative, at least among nondepressed individuals (Salovey & Rosenhan, 1989; Salovey, Mayer, & Rosenhan, in press). This feedback system affects mood in two ways. It provides the individual with knowledge about what kinds of behaviors will prolong a positive mood state or end a negative one. At the same time, it gives the individual *affective* knowledge about the intensity and quality of the feelings that the behaviors produce. Individual differences in the ability to appreciate and make use of these sources of information have been termed *emotional intelligence* (Salovey & Mayer, 1990).

Therapists can work with clients to help them develop skills in emotional self-regulation. Clients can learn to initiate behaviors that maintain positive moods or improve negative ones. For example, therapists might give a depressed individual the following homework assignment—choose a positive activity, such as listening to a favorite song, and engage in this behavior when starting to feel down. The idea behind such a directive is to prescribe a behavior that breaks a pattern of depressive self-absorption and to provide the client with an experience that demonstrates their capacity to control their own emotions.

Therapists might also choose to intervene at the level of mood-related cogni-tions themselves. Individuals differ in their ability to monitor, evaluate, and therefore regulate their own moods (Mayer & Gaschke, 1988). Therapists can help clients develop these skills through the use of mood diaries in which clients monitor the thoughts associated with a particular mood state. Once they have learned to identify characteristic patterns of thought, they can work with the therapist to generate alternative and more adaptive mood-regulating thoughts.

Practical Assumptions of Cognitive Behavior Therapy

Therapeutic Change Is Affected by Altering Dysfunctional Thoughts

Implicit in our discussion of Paula's case and a model of reciprocal determinism are several practical assumptions about how cognitive behavior therapy with a client such as Paula might proceed. First, the therapist assumes that dysfunctional thoughts are at the heart of the client's maladaptive behavior and that these thoughts must be identified by both client and therapist. Assessment of irrational ideas, overgeneralizations, self-defeating beliefs, and so on is integral to any cognitive behavior therapy. Cognitive behavior therapists use a variety of techniques to assess maladaptive cognitions including asking clients for daily logs of thoughts occurring prior to the undesired behavior, engaging clients in imagery exercises in which they describe their thoughts and feelings, and even role-playing situations with clients that would be likely to elicit the dysfunctional thoughts.

Behind the therapist's emphasis on the dysfunctional thoughts is the realistic knowledge that of the three components of reciprocal determinism (person, behavior, and environment), person variables, such as thoughts and feelings, are the most accessible in the therapeutic hour and provide insight into how clients understand their behaviors and their effects on the environment. Since the therapist is interested in the specific connection of dysfunctional thoughts to clients' maladaptive behaviors, assessment of thought processes is not as open-ended and wide-ranging as the psychoanalytic procedure of free association might be. Rather, the therapist zeroes in on cognitions relevant to the behaviors causing the client distress. Ultimately, observable change in these behaviors is seen as evidence that underlying cognitive processes have been successfully modified. In contrast to more insight-oriented therapies, the time-frame of the therapy is relatively brief and the scope of therapy is problem focused. We turn to these practical assumptions next.

Therapy is Time Limited and Problem Focused

For many reasons, cognitive behavior therapists emphasize the value of therapy that is focused on specific problems (often the original presenting problem) and that is delimited in time. Most therapies last from 8 to 25 sessions, although even briefer and, occasionally longer term, approaches exist. Perhaps the initial impetus for brief therapy was Ellis and others' frustration with the inefficiency of long-term psychoanalytic approaches. These individuals sensed that mental health care was not being delivered to the vast numbers of people in need of treatment. But, in addition to this economic argument, there are therapeutic reasons why a focused, short-term intervention might be especially efficacious.

For one, the short-term approach keeps the focus of therapy sessions on modifiable aspects of clients' current concerns. This focus on the "here and now" prevents therapy from moving into a deliberate exploration of past experiences that minimizes pressure on clients to experiment with specific change strategies. While much value can be gained from retrospective analysis, this process can often induce a reduction in clients' resolve to take action. It is not that cognitive behavior therapists believe that insight about problems is irrelevant. Rather, insight is seen almost as the reward of having made successful changes in maladaptive behaviors and ways of thinking as opposed to the required antecedent to such changes.

Finally, the time-limited nature of psychotherapy motivates the client and therapist to set specific goals through which progress can be measured. The client knows from the start that time is of the essence and is thus less inclined to use sessions unproductively. This "action orientation" reinforces the strong value placed on self-control in cognitive behavior therapy. Clients early on realize that they must take personal responsibility, in collaboration with the therapist, if they are to make the most of the limited time allotted. Although the number of sessions is limited, clients are provided with strategies that they may rehearse and employ long after treatment has ended. Clients are discouraged from thinking about the therapist in a dependent way; emphasis is placed on their own abilities to maintain and generalize from gains made in treatment. Before discussing this issue in more detail, we will turn to the nature of the therapeutic relationship in cognitive behavior therapy.

Therapeutic Relationship is Collaborative and Educative

Perhaps the most compelling difference between cognitive behavior therapy and more traditional approaches is the nature of the therapeutic alliance. Therapists of nearly any orientation understand that effective interventions require the establishing of rapport and the development of a therapeutic relationship characterized by warmth, authenticity, and empathy (Frank, 1985; Rogers & Truax, 1967). However, therapies do differ in the specific ways in which therapists interact with clients. Cognitive behavior therapists see themselves as working with clients collaboratively to solve problems. For example, after helping clients to reconceptualize their problems in terms of dysfunctional thoughts and maladaptive behaviors, they might then make a menu of potentially helpful interventions available to the client. The client, in turn, might make suggestions to the therapist regarding which interventions could be tried first. In this sense, the therapist might best be viewed as a consultant with an expertise in the linkages among thoughts, feelings, and behaviors.

The collaborative nature of the therapeutic relationship is possible because cognitive behavior therapists do not share one of the fundamental assumptions of the psychodynamic approach: that analysis of the relationship that emerges between the client and therapist is essential for therapeutic success. Certainly cognitive behavior therapists will use the way in which clients interact with them as a source of information about potentially maladaptive thoughts and behaviors. These interactions, however, do not become the focal point of therapy and instead remain as but one source of therapeutic data.

Because the cognitive behavior therapist sees clients' thoughts and behaviors as the subject matter for therapy (rather than the nature of the therapist's relationship with the client), such therapists are freer to take an active role in encouraging change. For example, therapists can prod, exhort, use humor, role-play, model, give specific advice and recommendations, and provide didactic information (e.g., books, lectures, handouts) in order to promote change without undue concern about the ways in which these behaviors might be interpreted by the client or affect the therapeutic relationship.

Ongoing Assessment is an Integral Aspect of Therapy Itself

Unlike other forms of therapy in which assessment is often defined as the initial phase of treatment and may be conducted by someone other than the therapist, cognitive behavior therapy employs an ongoing assessment of clients' thoughts and behaviors throughout the duration of therapy. The first phase of cognitive behavior therapy involves three major goals. First, the therapist identifies those thoughts, feelings, behaviors, and environmental conditions critical to clients' presenting problems. Second, the therapist forms hypotheses about how these variables interact leading to clients' psychological distress. Third, the therapist determines aspects of the clients' thoughts, feelings, behaviors, and situations that are accessible to modification (Lehman & Salovey, 1990).

However, unlike other forms of therapy, assessment is ongoing and an integral part of the cognitive behavior therapy itself. Clients are asked to monitor dysfunctional thoughts and behaviors between sessions and to discuss them in therapy in order to identify successes and failures in the change process. The therapy actively builds on this feedback, making clients' responses to homework assignments one focus of therapy sessions.

Skills Should be Maintained Following Termination

As we mentioned earlier, the collaborative nature of cognitive behavior therapy should motivate clients to become active agents of their own change processes following therapy termination. Because the skills learned in therapy are tangible and teachable, clients can continue to work on them after therapy has ended. Sometimes "booster" sessions are offered at monthly or bimonthly intervals so that clients can report on their self-directed progress and review change strategies as necessary. Booster sessions would unlikely be provided in more psychodynamic therapies because they might be construed as evidence of continuing dependence on the therapist. However, because the cognitive behavior therapist is viewed as a consultant, reinvolvement with the therapist is seen as the clients' decision to sharpen skills that ultimately foster independence.

AN OVERVIEW OF COGNITIVE BEHAVIOR THERAPY TECHNIQUES

Now that we have established a grounding in the theoretical and practical assumptions of cognitive behavior therapy, let us zero in more specifically on exactly what cognitive behavior therapy is. The major techniques that fall under the rubric of cognitive behavior therapy are: (a) cognitive restructuring methods,

(b) coping skills training programs such as stress inoculation and anxiety management, (c) self-control and self-instructional training methods, and (d) problem-solving skills training.

Cognitive Restructuring Methods

Most cognitive restructuring methods trace their roots to the cognitive therapy of Beck and Ellis's rational-emotive therapy (Beck, Rush, Shaw, & Emery, 1979; Ellis & Grieger, 1977). The general goal of these therapies is to identify long-standing styles of thinking that are based on the misapplication of rules or unwavering belief in irrational assumptions and challenge them directly. It is maintained that these dysfunctional cognitive styles are often the source of unhappiness rather than the actual external situations in which clients find themselves. These cognitive styles often take the form of organized sets of expectations about oneself and the world called *schemas* (Hollon & Kriss, 1984; Singer & Salovey, in press; Turk & Salovey, 1985).

Especially important are schemas concerning inferences in emotionally arousing situations. For example, a man might see his wife laughing with an attractive man at a party and begin to experience jealousy (see Salovey & Rodin, 1989). He immediately assumes his wife is having an affair, drawing an *arbitrary inference* in the presence of minimal evidence to support this conclusion. He ignores the fact that the man is the host of the party and may have simply been making cordial small talk; this focus only on their laughing exchange rather than the context in which it occurs is called a *selective abstraction*. When the man thinks to himself that his wife should not laugh and smile at any other man but him, he is *thinking dichotomously,* placing experiences in one of two rigid categories (DeRubeis & Beck, 1988).

Maladaptive schemas may also be based on tenacious irrational assumptions about one's self-worth or capacity to be loved. For example, the jealous husband just described may subscribe to the irrational belief that he must be the center of his wife's attention at all times or otherwise she must not love him. Through logical analysis the therapist challenges the basis for this assumption and encourages the client to confront the unrealistic expectations the assumption engenders. The client can then see that his emotional responses are due more to expectations based on an irrational belief rather than evidence provided by the actual event (Dryden & Ellis, 1988).

In some ways, cognitive restructuring may be considered the first step in any of the cognitive behavioral therapies we will discuss. Before the client can learn more adaptive thoughts and coping strategies to rehearse and practice, characteristic patterns of thought that derail effective coping must be identified. Since these thought patterns are considered quite general by cognitive therapists, they play a role in how the client responds to many different kinds of stressful situations. Changing general patterns will make the therapist's and client's work on specific problems much easier. The effectiveness of these treatment procedures for depression has been long established (e.g., Kovacs, Rush, Beck, & Hollon, 1981; Simons, Murphy, Levine, & Wetzel, 1986).

Coping Skills Training Programs

Whereas cognitive restructuring methods involve the identification and challenging of general belief systems, coping skills training programs elicit the specific content of thoughts generated in a given stressful situation. One commonly implemented set of techniques for teaching coping skills to individuals experiencing anxieties and phobias is Stress Inoculation Training (SIT; Meichenbaum, 1985). SIT proceeds in three phases—in the first, educational phase, therapists and clients discuss a reconceptualization of the clients' dysphoric emotions. Clients learn that their own maladaptive thoughts play a role in determining their emotional reactions to external stressors. Further, by discussing the coping strategies that clients already implement, the therapist underscores the idea that clients have the competence to control their emotional responses by monitoring their thoughts and substituting adaptive ones for maladaptive ones. The situations that produce anxiety are divided into several phases: (a) preparing for the stressor; (b) confronting the stressor; (c) becoming overwhelmed by the stressor; (d) reinforcing oneself for having coped.

The essential ingredient of SIT is the tracking of self-statements (what clients say to themselves) at each of the four phases. Once statements that exacerbate anxiety (e.g., "This is too much for me!") are identified, new coping self-statements can be substituted (e.g., "I know I can handle it"). In the second phase of therapy, clients rehearse these new more adaptive self-statements during therapy and through homework assignments. Once mastery of coping statements is attained, the third phase of therapy, practice, can begin. Therapists may provide clients with graded stressful situations that provide clients with realistic feedback about the effectiveness of their new-found coping skills. The efficacy of SIT has been reported in recent studies concerning the treatment of social anxiety (Emmelkamp, Mersch, Vissia, & van der Helm, 1985; Jerremalm, Jansson, & Öst, 1986), chronic pain (Turk et al., 1983), and writer's block (Salovey & Haar, in press), to name just a few.

Self-Control/Self-Instructional Training

As a part of many kinds of cognitive behavior therapy, clients are often taught methods by which they can direct and control their own behaviors outside the context of therapy. These *self-management* techniques emphasize the development of control over internal and external cues and reinforcers. Drawing on principles of learning and information processing, the goal of self-management therapy is to teach clients how to manipulate their own thoughts and feelings, as well as environmental contingencies, to increase desired behaviors and decrease harmful ones.

Kanfer's self-management model (Kanfer, 1970) is the dominant approach in this area. He and his colleagues (Kanfer & Karoly, 1972a, 1972b) proposed a model that offered an alternative set of processes to individuals whose current behaviors were not yielding desired consequences. These processes are of three types: self-monitoring, self-evaluation, and self-reinforcement. For example, a woman has had little success in losing weight. Perhaps, her problem is with self-monitoring. She may not be aware of how prone to external cues about food she is; she may have little sense of her actual caloric intake. She may have difficulties with self-evaluation, especially in deciding what an appropriate standard of comparison should be. For example, if she always compares herself to extremely thin models from television, she may easily become frustrated and give up on her diet.

A final way in which individuals may fail to manage themselves optimally involves appropriate self-reinforcement. For example, individuals expect immediate reward from their behaviors and are unable to recognize there may be delays between an action and its positive consequence. Moreover, they may not have developed internally generated rewards to keep them motivated during this gap. For example, the woman who sets out on her diet must be prepared to see slow progress toward her desired body image and be able to reward herself internally through self-praise for meeting her dietary goals in the absence of obvious external results.

One example of a self-management therapy used primarily with children is self-instructional training (Meichenbaum, 1977). The assumption here is that control over behavior can be regulated by talking silently to oneself. So, for example, a child with attention deficit hyperactivity disorder might be taught specific self-instructions (e.g., "I am a slow turtle," "Now, just walk very slowly back to my seat") in order to manage impulsive behaviors. Self-instructional training can be taught within the same three-phase context as Stress Inoculation Training (Rehm & Rokke, 1988). The efficacy of this approach is well documented, especially for dealing with conduct disordered children (Kendall & Wilcox, 1980), learning disabled children (Harris, 1986; Harris & Graham, 1985), mentally retarded children (Whitman, Burgio, & Johnston, 1984), and anxious children (Graziano & Mooney, 1980).

Problem-Solving Training

A final cognitive behavior therapy technique is problem-solving skills training (PSST), discussed in more detail by Haaga and Davison in chapter 7. PSST involves learning how to size up the different characteristics of problems, gather data about them, and clarify their severity. Then, skills are developed concerning formulating reasonable problem-solving goals, generating alternative solutions, and selecting from among these alternatives. Finally, solutions must be implemented and the consequences of this choice for oneself and others evaluated (D'Zurilla, 1988).

Problem-solving training has been applied to an impressive array of clinical problems (see D'Zurilla, 1986; D'Zurilla & Nezu, 1982). It appears to be effective in promoting social skills among psychiatric patients (Bedell, Archer, & Marlow, 1980), and treating alcohol abuse (Chaney, O'Leary, & Marlatt, 1978), depression (Hussian & Lawrence, 1981), anxiety disorders (Jannoun, Munby, Catalan, & Gelder, 1980), difficult adolescents (Spivack, Platt, & Shure, 1976), and preventing conduct disorder among school children (Weissberg & Allen, 1986).

COGNITIVE BEHAVIOR THERAPY: TWO CASE STUDIES

In what follows, we will discuss first how cognitive restructuring and stress inoculation techniques can alleviate anxiety-related sexual dysfunction. After discussing treatment of this anxious adult, we will then turn to the treatment of a chronically angry and conduct disordered child.

Cognitive Behavior Therapy With an Anxious Adult

A Cognitive Behavioral View of Anxiety

Historically, researchers working within a cognitive behavioral framework have viewed anxiety as the consequence of dysfunctional thoughts stimulated by the presence of fear-arousing cues in the environment. Often, these thoughts are the automatic cognitions provoked by situations demanding performance or social interaction. Mandler and Watson (1966) suggested that beliefs about not being in control were the central cognition in anxiety states. Social learning theorists view anxiety as the result of situations in which the individual believes that his or her capacities are exceeded, that is, lacks a sense of self-efficacy.

Anxiety states promoted by dysfunctional thoughts are aggravated by their tendency to focus attention on to the self (for a review of this literature, see Ingram, in press). Self-focused attention, a construct that has promoted a great deal of research in social psychology (see Buss, 1980; Carver & Scheier, 1981, for reviews), is a state of enhanced awareness of one's physical self, what one is doing, and the content of one's thoughts and feelings (Carver, 1979). As Ingram (1990) has reviewed, chronic self-focusing seems to be associated with a variety of psychopathological states, including alcohol abuse (Hull, 1981), depression (Pyszczynski & Greenberg, 1987), and anxiety (Buss, 1980; Carver & Scheier, 1986).

Although self-focused attention is not by definition maladaptive (indeed it is required to adjust one's behavior to situational demands), when chronic and uncontrollable, it leads to a restricted ability to respond to the outside world, a loss of empathy with others, and an intensification of one's anxious feelings. A painful trap can ensue: Dysfunctional thoughts of poor performance and social inadequacy create anxiety; anxiety engenders self-attending; excessive self-preoccupation only intensifies anxiety until the individual is so self-conscious that his or her worst fears of social failure are fulfilled. This debilitating cycle has been well researched in the areas of test anxiety (Deffenbacher, 1978; Slapion & Carver, 1981) and social anxiety (Hope & Heimberg, 1985), yet this model seems equally applicable to anxiety-related sexual dysfunction.

The primary cause of sexual dysfunction in both men and women when there is no organic basis for it is anxiety. Anxiety may be elicited by a lack of knowledge about sexual behavior, an overly moralistic belief system, fear-engendering early experiences with sex (e.g., about caught or becoming pregnant), tensions in the romantic relationship, or self-imposed demands for performance that must exceed the exploits of James Bond. Sex therapists and investigators have long noted the tendency among individuals with various sexual dysfunctions to experience sexual activities not as times of intense pleasure, but rather as periods of intense monitoring of their own bodily sensations and private thoughts (Kaplan, 1974). This preoccupation with the body's response rather than with the pleasure associated with sexual activity has been termed "spectatoring" (Masters & Johnson, 1970). It should be clear that the tendency for anxiety to arouse self-focused attention can play a role in sexual dysfunctions of all kinds (e.g., inhibited sexual excitement, inhibited orgasm, premature ejaculation, or dyspareunia). The sexually nervous individual approaches an opportunity for intimacy with thoughts of worry and helplessness that evoke considerable anxiety. The self-focus promoted by the anxiety inhibits sexual enjoyment and fulfills the individual's worst fears about sexual encounters.

The Case of Greg

Greg was a 54-year-old man with a history of treatment for anxiety and a mild heart condition, who reported to the psychological clinic at the county hospital. His primary presenting complaint was that for many years he had not had satisfactory sexual relations with his wife. Their present pattern was that he would watch television late into the evening in his study, generally fall asleep in an easy chair, only to be found there the next morning by his wife. When his wife persuaded him to sleep with her, her attempts to initiate sexual relations were met by Greg's anxiety-ridden ruminations and worries. Nevertheless, he would attempt to become aroused but usually could not maintain an erection long enough to permit intercourse.

Greg was a successful insurance salesman, accustomed to being among the sales leaders of the region. Used to working hard and playing hard, Greg found the adjustment to later middle age difficult and became increasingly self-conscious that he was finally starting "to slow down." These self-absorbed concerns with his aging readily transferred to his evaluation of his sexual performance. Noting a longer period of time before he became aroused and achieved an erection, Greg grew increasingly worried that his lovemaking days were over. He obsessively monitored the fullness of his erections, often making mental estimates of the percentage of full erection he had been able to attain. Not surprisingly, this kind of scrutiny was associated with further delays in arousal and increased anxiety for Greg. With increased anxiety, Greg found his mind filled with memories of previous failed sexual attempts, somatic concerns, and even worries about his work performance.

Directly Modifying Dysfunctional Cognitions

An attempt was made to modify Greg's dysfunctional cognitions using stress inoculation training. The purpose of this intervention was to identify Greg's habitual self-statements that occurred during sexual encounters. Then, collaboratively, the therapist and Greg considered how these self-statements interfered with sexual arousal and contributed to anxiety. Greg and the therapist next jointly generated alternative self-statements that might be part of a more adaptive coping process. On his own, Greg was encouraged to personalize these statements so that they felt comfortable to him (Meichenbaum, 1985).

Greg's habitual thoughts around sexual activities were assessed first. He was asked to monitor his thoughts during four different phases: (a) when considering sexual relations with his wife (preparing for the stressor); (b) when actually initiating sexual relations (confronting and handling the stressor); (c) when self-doubts about sexual performance become overwhelming (coping with feelings of being overwhelmed); (d) after the sexual experience has ended (evaluating coping efforts and self-rewards). When considering sexual relations, Greg reported a fear that this might be the time where his body would finally quit on him and he would not be able to become aroused ("I've become too old for this"). When he and his wife began to be intimate with each other, he would often monitor his progress toward erection and become quickly frustrated ("It's taking too long, it's never going to happen. She's going to get bored.") At this point he would experience intense anxiety and give up rather than face further humiliation ("I can't stand this anymore. Why do I even bother?"). When later reflecting on the entire episode, he would become self-critical and depressed ("It really is over for me. I'm finished as a lover.").

In the early sessions of therapy with Greg, the therapist sought to substitute self-statements that Greg could invoke to replace his dysfunctional ideas. Some examples of these coping self-statements were "How nice to share this time with my wife. It isn't some test of my power," when considering intimacy; "Whatever happens, happens. There are lots of ways to be loving," when initiating intimacy; "There will be many more chances," when overwhelmed by self-doubts; and "It was wonderful to be close with my wife," when reflecting on the experience.

Reducing Anxiety-Driven Self-Consciousness

While Greg practiced his self-statements, the therapist designed a more behavioral intervention to increase Greg's comfort with intimacy, and to break the cycle of anxiety-induced self-preoccupation. Following the basic prescriptions of Masters and Johnson's sensate focusing exercises (Masters & Johnson, 1970), a series of graded homework assignments involving gradually increasing degrees of intimacy was initiated. These steps are as follows:

- Week 1: sleep in same bed with wife; no sleeping in study
- Week 2: prior to sleep, hold each other while being verbally affectionate
- Week 3: nongenital physical contact (e.g., sensual massage)
- Weeks 4–6: touching and stroking involving genitals, but no intercourse
- Weeks 7–8: intercourse initiated by the wife

For each of these graduated steps, Greg was encouraged to relax as much as possible and accept whatever happened with his body. He was reminded that the goal was not necessarily a full erection, but rather a regaining of enjoyment and pleasure in his intimate moments with his wife. For each week, Greg repeated the prescription assigned until he no longer felt anxiety. By the end of the week, he would determine whether he was ready to move on to the next level of intimacy. During the course of this intervention, Greg accumulated mastery experiences that served to bolster his self-confidence and provide a source of new coping self-statements ("It's worked so far. There is no need to worry."). In addition to extinguishing Greg's anxiety reactions, these exercises served to shift his attentional focus away from the mechanics of his body and on to feelings of enjoyment and appreciation of his partner. When recontacted several years later, Greg reported more frequent and enjoyable sexual experiences with his wife. Although he still occasionally has difficulties maintaining erections (especially when there are other stressors in his life), he is less anxious about these situations and enjoys the wider range of intimate behaviors that he and his wife have learned.

The case of Greg provides a good example of how dysfunctional affective reactions can be modified both by altering cognitions and behaviors. Moreover, Greg's change in affect from anxiety to pleasure served to generate new cognitions that were much more adaptive and provided him with the confidence to initiate new behaviors. By engaging in new more positive behaviors and adopting new coping statements, Greg was also able to disengage from the self-preoccupation that often accompanies negative mood states.

Cognitive Behavior Therapy With Angry and Conduct Disordered Children

Conduct disorder in children refers to a pattern of antisocial behavior that significantly disrupts everyday functioning either at school or home and where the behaviors are considered uncontrollable (Kazdin, 1987b). The diagnosis is generally reserved for children who exhibit problem behaviors that exceed the boundaries of normal functioning. For example, conduct disordered children may be involved in deliberate fire setting, substance abuse, multiple acts of aggression toward peers, repeated thefts, and destruction of property. Nearly half of all referrals to child and adolescent clinics are for conduct problems of these kinds.

Despite the prevalence of conduct disorder, investigators in this area (e.g., Kazdin, 1987b) have noted that it has been remarkably resistant to diverse interventions ranging from residential treatment programs, pharmacotherapy, work with families, to individual psychodynamically oriented therapy. However, because conduct disordered children evidence considerable deficits in interpersonal cognitive problem-solving skills, impulsivity, impaired moral reasoning, and maladaptive cognitive strategies and plans, cognitive behavioral interventions appear promising (Arbuthnot & Gordon, 1986; Kazdin, 1987a; Kazdin, Bass, Siegel, & Thomas, 1989; Kendall & Braswell, 1982, 1985; but see Gresham, 1985, or Tisdelle & St. Lawrence, 1986, for criticisms).

A Cognitive Behavioral View of Conduct Disorder

Although the diagnostic criteria for conduct disorder emphasizes observable behavior, recall that the model of reciprocal determinism that underlies cognitive behavior therapy recognizes the importance of person variables (affects and cognitions) and environmental contingencies as antecedents to abnormal behavior. The cognitive behavioral approach is especially concerned with the child's appraisals of external events and other people. Maladaptive behavior is thought to result from incorrect attributions about the intents of others (Dodge, 1985), misperceiving external cues as necessitating aggressive responses, failure to empathize with or take the perspective of others (Ellis, 1982), and a poor approach to problem solving that focuses on ends rather than means, fails to generate sufficient alternatives, and is insensitive to the needs of others (Spivack & Shure, 1982).

Although traditionally they have not been the focus of treatment, it should be obvious that affect-related person variables are implicated in all of these cognitive difficulties. Children whose anger is easily triggered may find that this emotion causes them to attend selectively to hostile cues from others and to ignore environmental events that might reinforce prosocial behaviors. In laboratory studies, children who are angry when learning new positive and negative material are less likely to recall later the positive information and more likely to recall the negative information (Nasby & Yando, 1982, Exp. 2). Similarly, dysphoric moods may impair normal problem-solving strategies by constraining the number of solutions generated, limiting creativity, and omitting decision-making rules (See Isen, 1987, for review). Negative emotional states may also inhibit prosocial behavior; for example, depressed and anxious children are less likely to help others in need (see Eisenberg, 1986, for review).

Cognitive behavior therapy for conduct disordered children generally focuses on such cognitive deficits and their emotional underpinnings. For example, Kazdin et al. (1989) developed a multifaceted intervention for such children that included:

> cognitive and behavioral techniques to teach problem-solving skills (e.g., generating alternative solutions, means-ends and consequential thinking, and taking the perspective of others) that the child can use to manage interpersonal situations. Training began by teaching the child to use the problem-solving steps on academic tasks and games, which became increasingly complex over the course of sessions. The bulk of treatment was devoted to enacting interpersonal situations through role-play, where the child applied the steps. In each session . . . , practice, modeling, role-playing, corrective feedback, and social reinforcement [were used] to develop problem-solving skills. [Also used was] response cost (loss of chips) for errors in carrying out the problem-solving approach (e.g., skipping a step). Children could exchange the chips provided at the beginning of each session for small toys and prizes at the end of each session. (Kazdin et al., 1989, pp. 525, 527)

This kind of careful training of the child in more adaptive problem-solving skills is often accompanied by training of the parents to be effective models and consistent administrators of reinforcers (e.g., parent management training, Patterson, 1986). In order to understand how these techniques actually work, let us turn to a case study of the treatment of a conduct disordered child.

The Case of Jack

Jack is a 13-year-old boy living with his divorced mother in a small Midwestern town. He was brought to therapy by his mother because of his persistent refusal to go to school and his powerful temper tantrums when forced to go. Initial sessions with Jack revealed that this was not a simple case of school phobia because he was able to enter the school for tutoring and for baseball team practice. Moreover, Jack exhibited symptoms that were more consistent with a diagnosis of conduct disorder. He threatened his mother physically, and verbally abused the truant officer who made a home visit. During the previous school year, he had clashed with other students on several occasions and been suspended once for pulling the fire alarm. During his sessions with the therapist, he presented a hostile demeanor, often suspecting the therapist of trying to trip him up or prove him wrong. His mother had reinforced his negative behavior by spending excessive time with him each morning in arguments rather than leaving for her own work.

Rationale for Treatment

Given Jack's negative attitude, the prognosis for therapy appeared to be poor, as it seemed unlikely he would be engaged in therapy and cooperate with the therapist's requests. However, Jack knew that his participation on the school baseball team was contingent on his school attendance and was willing begrudgingly to overcome his aversion to school. The therapist set the following goals for

Jack's treatment: (a) identifying and changing dysfunctional cognitions; (b) modifying his problem-solving skills; (c) changing the reinforcement contingencies provided by his mother. We will describe the therapeutic techniques involved in implementing each of these three goals. Then, a brief discussion will illustrate how modification of affect would play an important role in Jack's treatment.

Modifying Dysfunctional Cognitions

Jack's thoughts tended to be impulsive and antisocial reactions to situations in which his self-esteem was threatened. He was especially sensitive to instances in which he was singled out for poor academic performance. The therapist asked Jack to describe what went through his mind when he anticipated critical feedback from his teacher. Jack listed the following thoughts:

"She's picking on me."
"She didn't like me from the start."
"I can't do anything right."
"I'm dumb and she's rubbing my nose in it."
"How'd she like a punch in the face."

To modify these dysfunctional thoughts, Jack was taught self-instruction techniques for four specific stages in dealing with these kinds of situations (Kettlewell & Kausch, 1983; Meichenbaum, 1977; Meichenbaum & Goodman, 1971). The first stage involved getting ready for the critical situation. Jack would typically prepare for feeling humiliated and responding with aggression. Instead, he was instructed to say to himself, "What am I going to do?" and then pause for a moment and do nothing. In the next stage, he was taught to make a specific plan ("I am going to tell myself that whatever she says, I can handle it. The important thing is to stay calm"). The third stage dealt with remaining calm and inhibiting aggressive tendencies ("This is making me angry, but I don't have to show it"). Finally, Jack learned to reward himself for successfully coping with these difficult situations ("I did OK. Now I can play baseball. No one is mad at me. I'm in control").

Modifying Problem-solving Skills

Once Jack had learned better control over his automatic cognitions, a self-instructional training approach that focused on learning a new problem-solving style could be implemented. The primary focus of problem-solving skills training (PSST) is on the cognitive processes by which problems are appraised and acted on rather than on the ultimate outcome (Kendall & Braswell, 1985; Spivack et al., 1976). First, the therapist evaluated Jack's approach to problems by asking him to describe situations at school that had made him feel unhappy. Though Jack was reluctant to answer the therapist at first, he gradually listed three or four situations that unnerved him. One of them was a fear that his math teacher would ridicule him in front of the class for not knowing the right answer. The therapist encouraged

Jack to describe a specific instance in which he felt ridiculed. Jack talked about a time that he was asked to provide the answer to a word-problem in his math class. When he became confused, the teacher stood over his desk and pointed out to the class that Jack's confusion was due to his not having done his homework. Jack was asked to describe how this incident made him feel and what he was thinking about at the time. Jack said that he could feel his face turning red, that he wanted either to run away or to punch the teacher in the stomach. The next day when Jack's mother woke him for school, he refused to go, and then threw a temper tantrum.

Jack's therapist used role-playing and think-aloud techniques (cf. Camp, Blom, Hebert, & van Doorninck, 1977) to model a new way of confronting these kinds of situations. Jack was asked to play his teacher while the therapist acted as if he were Jack, describing his thoughts and feelings in the situation. The therapist modeled a problem-solving process that was similar to the self-instruction procedures but was more focused on generating solutions. It emphasized: (a) pausing for a moment and getting ready ("What is it that I have to do? Stay calm"); (b) thinking about how he is feeling ("I am angry and embarrassed"); (c) generating alternative behaviors ("I could run away, or I could punch the teacher, or I could let her say what ever she wants and prove to her that I'm not a screw-up"); (d) choosing an alternative ("She can say whatever she wants, and I can take it, and besides if I punch her or run away I won't be able to play on the baseball team"); and (e) rewarding himself for successful problem solving ("I pulled it off, it wasn't as hard as I thought it would be, and now my mom is off my back and I can play baseball"). After modeling several such problem-solving episodes for Jack, the therapist asked Jack to try this out himself, first in the context of the therapy session where corrective feedback was possible, then on his own during the ensuing week, for discussion later during the session.

It took Jack some time to be able to transfer the problem-solving skills he learned in therapy to situations at home and in school. There was an incident in which he threatened a teacher but was able to calm himself by standing outside in the hall. Slowly, he learned to combine his new skills at self-instruction and problem solving and apply them to situations not like those rehearsed in therapy.

Altering Reinforcement Contingencies Provided by Mother

Parents of conduct disordered children may inadvertently find themselves caught in a "reinforcement trap" (Kazdin, 1987b; Patterson, 1986). This was the case with Jack's mother. Jack's belligerence in the mornings around going to school would be ignored initially by his mother, forcing him to escalate into more histrionic displays. His mother would then argue and plead with Jack to go to school. Finally, realizing she would be late for her job, she would give in, allowing him to stay home from school, and reinforcing his tantrum. At the same time, she is negatively reinforced for giving in: Her acquiescing to his demands terminated his aversive tantrums and allowed her to go to work.

Working with Jack's mother, the therapist pointed out this reinforcement pattern. Then he collaborated with her to establish specific rules regarding courses of action to take with Jack in the morning. The night before, she and Jack would write out a contract that would specify the rewards Jack would receive for going to school and the punishments for refusal. The mother also contracted to encourage Jack once and only once to get ready for school so that there was no chance she would be late for work. It would be up to Jack to get ready on his own. If Jack got ready on his own, his mother would make him his favorite food for breakfast. If he attended school, he would then be able to play baseball. Failure to attend school resulted in his not being able to attend baseball practice in the afternoon nor leave his room during the following weekend. This contract freed the mother from indirectly rewarding Jack's escalating tantrums.

Modification of Affect

One theme of this chapter is to emphasize the emotional underpinnings of dysfunctional cognitive processes. Jack experienced anger, embarrassment, shame, and, perhaps, sadness and anxiety on a daily basis. These emotions likely colored the content of his cognitions and his ability to take into account others' perspectives. As we described earlier, the process of mood-congruent recall might have operated so that in situations where Jack was about to experience shame, he was likely to recall previous experiences with shame more readily than more positive experiences. This created what has been called "a cognitive loop" (Isen, Shalker, Clark, & Karp, 1978) in that dysphoric affect facilitated the accessibility of negative thoughts that in turn strengthened these feelings. In addition, his ability to generate alternative problem-solving strategies was compromised by his intense negative feelings.

A byproduct of Jack's training in self-instruction and problem solving was an increased capacity to overcome his negative feelings and their effects on his thought process. Both techniques offered Jack material to consider that took his mind away from self-absorbed negative rumination. They broke his negative loop by initiating steps of planning, solution generation, and self-reward. This constructive problem-solving focus gave Jack both practical suggestions and a sense of hope about his problem (Frank, 1961).

A FINAL NOTE ON CLINICAL JUDGMENT

We would like to conclude with a word of caution. In this chapter, we have emphasized some of the ways in which feelings influence thought and behavior in typical clients of cognitive behavior therapists. But various aspects of clinicians' behavior are also susceptible to influence by feelings and other sources of bias, and so we would like to note some of these here (these biases have been reviewed more systematically by Salovey & Turk, 1988; Salovey & Turk, in press; Turk &

Salovey, 1986). In particular, feelings influence therapists' (a) initial impressions of clients, (b) remembering of information about clients, and (c) clinical decisions.

Initial Impressions

Moods and emotions experienced by clinicians may influence their initial impressions of clients. For example, in a set of now classic studies, pleasant moods were induced in observers by allowing them to succeed on a skill task (Lerner, 1965), receive a prize (Lott & Lott, 1968), view a joyful film (Gouaux, 1971), or experience warm sunshine (Griffitt, 1970). In all cases, other people were judged more attractive and desirable by these happy observers than by those who were assigned to conditions thought to evoke sad moods.

When the information we know about someone else is ambiguous, moods may be especially likely to bias initial impressions. For instance, happy individuals are more likely to rate an illustration on a TAT card as containing pleasant content than are angry individuals (Bower, 1981), and they are more likely to interpret ambiguous written material consistently with their moods (Clore, Schwarz, & Kirsch, 1983). In general, judgments about others follow a mood-congruent pattern: When people are in good moods, their judgments of others are positive, and when in bad moods, negative (Forgas & Bower, 1988; Mayer & Bremer, 1985; Mayer & Volanth, 1985).

Remembering of Information

As mentioned earlier, there are two ways in which moods and emotions influence what is remembered that have received fairly substantial empirical support: (a) feelings affect what information is attended to and encoded into memory such that information consistent in valence with one's feelings is learned better; and (b) feelings affect what information is recalled from memory such that information consistent in valence with one's feelings is more likely retrieved (see Blaney, 1986; Singer & Salovey, 1988, for reviews). The first of these phenomena has been labeled mood-congruent encoding, and the second, mood-congruent recall (taken together, they are often called mood-congruent memory, see Bower, 1981).

Mood-congruent encoding has been demonstrated in studies where subjects must read a story involving several characters while they experience a happy or sad mood. Later, once mood has dissipated, subjects are better able to recall information about the character in the story whose affect was most similar to their own (Bower, Gilligan, & Monteiro, 1981). This effect of mood seems to hold for both happy (Nasby & Yando, 1982) and sad (Bower et al., 1981) moods, but it has been difficult to replicate using naturally occurring rather than artificially induced moods (Hasher, Rose, Zacks, Sanft, & Doren, 1985).

The tendency to recall information consistent with mood has been demonstrated using a variety of laboratory mood induction procedures (e.g., Natale & Hantas, 1982; Salovey & Singer, 1989; Teasdale & Fogarty, 1979) as well as clinically depressed subjects (Lloyd & Lishman, 1975). The problem for clinicians created by mood-congruent recall is that in preparing for a session, clinicians may be more likely to recall and therefore inquire about issues consistent with their own current moods, likely eliciting mood-congruent responses from clients.

Clinical Decisions

Finally, clinicians' moods may influence their ultimate decision making. When the outcome of a decision is not especially important, positive moods tend to instigate riskier decisions. But, when there is a potential for great loss, individuals actually become more conservative in their decisions when feeling good (Arkes, Herren, & Isen, 1988; Isen & Geva, 1987; Isen & Patrick, 1983). It is as if individuals want to maintain their happiness at all costs, so they avoid risks that are seen as threatening to their existing positive mood state (Isen, Nygren, & Ashby, 1985). In general, moods influence perceptions of the probability of positive and negative outcomes such that the likelihood of future calamities seems much higher when we are sad rather than happy (Johnson & Tversky, 1983; Salovey & Birnbaum, 1989).

The decision-making strategies of clinicians may vary depending on their ongoing moods. It appears that when happy, individuals use more intuitive, quick, and simple strategies rather than more taxing and logical ones. Happy individuals seem more likely to go with gut instincts rather than to make careful decisions (Isen & Daubman, 1984; Isen et al., 1982). This may be yet another instance where sadness reduces rather than inflates judgmental bias (Taylor & Brown, 1988).

Other Sources of Bias

In this section, we have emphasized biases in clinical judgment rooted in affective processes primarily because the influence of emotion on thought and action is a theme developed in various contexts in this chapter. At this point, however, we should note that many of the difficulties clinicians have making accurate judgments and "rational" decisions emanate from biases in information processing that are not affectively based. These have been reviewed elsewhere (Kanfer & Schefft, 1988; Salovey & Turk, in press), and so they will not be discussed in detail here. In brief, (a) our expectations often determine what we observe and remember so that we tend to confirm a priori hypotheses rather than seek disconfirming evidence, (b) we often estimate how likely an event is by how easily it can be brought to mind, (c) we ignore frequently base-rate information and instead become overly impressed with single case examples or single instances of behavior, especially if they are vivid, and (d) we have great difficulty assessing covariation, that is, the likelihood that two events (e.g., a diagnostic sign and future behavior) are or are not related to each other.

Reducing Judgmental Bias

At times, articles on biases in clinical judgment have taken a rather derogatory tone, scolding clinicians for their inattention to variables biasing judgment. We have no intention of doing that here. Rather, our closing message is simply that clinicians, like other humans trying to make sense of a barrage of information, are limited in the capacity to remain unbiased. As a result, we should embrace research on techniques that reduce these biases. Unfortunately, such research is scant; greater attention has been focused on identifying biases than on reducing them. However, a few thoughts about reducing bias (what we once termed *bias inoculation,* Turk & Salovey, 1986) follow.

Although it is important to become aware of sources of bias, mere awareness of them or even direct training in reasoning skills have not been especially effective ways of reducing them. Rather, if we were to make a single debiasing suggestion it would be: Minimize reliance on memory. Many judgmental biases are the result of limitations of our cognitive systems to deal simultaneously with multiple bits of information. Thus, the use of external aids— from pencil and paper to sophisticated computer programs—can reduce uncertainty. Often, however, clinicians have been reluctant to use such aids, preferring to rely on memory and clinical intuition. Unfortunately, such intuitive judgments are likely to result in worse prediction (Arkes, Dawes, & Christensen, 1986). There are a multitude of creative solutions to reducing the load on memory during judgmental tasks. Arnoult and Anderson (1988) have suggested using multiple judges, role-playing, videotape, rating scales, balance sheets, and graphics. By not burdening working memory, we are less likely to rush to choose a seemingly satisfactory but, perhaps, wrong-headed solution to a clinical problem.

Kanfer and Schefft (1988) provide a very useful list of other recommendations for minimizing bias in clinical judgment and decision making (see also Arkes, 1981; Faust, 1986; Salovey & Turk, in press). Among others, they suggest that clinicians (a) seek out learning experiences in which the validity of inferences can be evaluated (e.g., discussions with colleagues, case conferences), (b) generate alternative hypotheses and evaluate incoming evidence against this multiplicity of possibilities (i.e., rather than just a single hypothesis), (c) deautomatize inferences by thinking about them in a step-by-step rather than automatic, "snap judgment" manner, (d) identify counterarguments to one's own hypotheses, and (e) identify missing information that needs to be garnered prior to making inferences. In general, the more clinicians challenge their initial impressions and the less they rely on remembering information about clients or making quick judgments, the greater the likelihood that judgments and inferences will prove valid in the long run.

At various points in this chapter, we emphasized the important role played by affective processes in psychopathology and cognitive behavior therapy. It is our hope that this final section will cause a bit of therapist self-preoccupation; it is often profitable to reflect on how the thought processes of clinicians may be influenced by the same variables as those of our clients. As Meehl (1954) remarked many yeas ago, "psychologists should be sophisticated about errors of observing, recording, retaining, and recalling to which the human brain is subject. We, of all people, ought to be highly suspicious of ourselves. We have no right to assume that entering the clinic has resulted in some miraculous mutation and made us singularly free from ordinary errors" (pp. 27–28).

REFERENCES

Agras, W. S., Schneider, J. A., Arnow, B., Raeburn, S. D., & Telch, C. S. (1989). Cognitive-behavioral and response-prevention treatments for bulimia nervosa. *Journal of Consulting and Clinical Psychology, 57*, 215–221.

Arbuthnot, J., & Gordon, D. A. (1986). Behavioral and cognitive effects of a moral reasoning development intervention for high-risk behavior-disordered adolescents. *Journal of Consulting and Clinical Psychology, 54*, 208–216.

Arkes, H. R. (1981). Impediments to accurate clinical judgment and possible ways to minimize their impact. *Journal of Consulting and Clinical Psychology, 49*, 323–330.

Arkes, H. R., Dawes, R. M., & Christensen, C. (1986). Factors influencing the use of a decision rule in a probabilistic task. *Behavior and Human Decision Processes, 37*, 93–110.

Arkes, H. R., Herren, L. T., & Isen, A. M. (1988). The role of potential loss in the influence of affect on risk-taking behavior. *Organizational Behavior and Human Decision Processes, 42*, 181–193.

Arnoult, L. H., & Anderson, C. A. (1988). Identifying and reducing causal reasoning biases in clinical practice. In D. C. Turk & P. Salovey (Eds.), *Reasoning, inference, and judgment in clinical psychology* (pp. 209–232). New York: Free Press.

Bandura, A. (1977a). *Social learning theory.* Englewood Cliffs, NJ: Prentice-Hall.

Bandura, A. (1977b). Self-efficacy: Toward a unifying theory of behavioral change. *Psychological Review, 84*, 191–215.

Bandura, A. (1978). The self system in reciprocal determinism. *American Psychologist, 33*, 344–358.

Bandura, A. (1982). Self-efficacy mechanism in human agency. *American Psychologist, 37*, 122–147.

Bandura, A. (1986). *Social foundations of thought and action: A social cognitive theory.* Englewood Cliffs, NJ: Prentice-Hall.

Bandura, A., & Adams, N. E. (1977). Analysis of self-efficacy theory of behavioral change. *Cognitive Therapy and Research, 1*, 287–308.

Bandura, A., Adams, N. E., Hardy, A. B., & Howells, G. N. (1980). Tests of the generality of self-efficacy theory. *Cognitive Therapy and Research, 4*, 39–66.

Bandura, A., & Cervone, D. (1983). Self-evaluative and self-efficacy mechanisms governing the motivational effects of goal systems. *Journal of Personality and Social Psychology, 45,* 1017–1028.

Beck, A. T. (1963). Thinking and depression. *Archives of General Psychiatry, 9,* 324–333.

Beck, A. T., Rush, A. J., Shaw, B. F., & Emery, G. (1979). *Cognitive therapy of depression: A treatment manual.* New York: Guilford Press.

Bedell, J. R., Archer, R. P., & Marlow, H. A. (1980). A description and evaluation of a problem solving skills training program. In D. Upper & S. M. Ross (Eds.), *Behavioral group therapy: An annual review* (pp. 3–35). Champaign, IL: Research Press.

Blaney, P. H. (1986). Affect and memory: A review. *Psychological Bulletin, 99,* 229–246.

Bower, G. H. (1981). Mood and memory. *American Psychologist, 36,* 129–148.

Bower, G. H., Gilligan, S. C., & Monteiro, K. P. (1981). Selectivity of learning caused by affective states. *Journal of Experimental Psychology: General, 110,* 451–473.

Buss, A. (1980). *Self-consciousness and social anxiety.* San Francisco: W. H. Freeman.

Camp, B. W., Blom, G. E., Hebert, F., & van Doorninck, W. J. (1977). Think aloud: A program for developing self-control in young aggressive boys. *Journal of Abnormal Child Psychology, 5,* 157–169.

Cantor, N., Markus, H., Niedenthal, P., & Nurius, P. (1986). On motivation and the self-concept. In R. M. Sorrentino & E. T. Higgins (Eds.), *Handbook of motivation and cognition: Foundations of social behavior* (pp. 96–121). New York: Guilford Press.

Cantor, N., Norem, J. K., Niedenthal, P. M., Langston, C. A., & Brower, A. M. (1987). Life tasks, self-concept ideals, and cognitive strategies in a life transition. *Journal of Personality and Social Psychology, 53,* 1178–1191.

Carver, C. S. (1979). A cybernetic model of self-attention processes. *Journal of Personality and Social Psychology, 37,* 1251–1281.

Carver, C. S., & Scheier, M. F. (1981). *Attention and self-regulation: A control theory approach to human behavior.* New York: Springer-Verlag.

Carver, C. S., & Scheier, M. F. (1986). Functional and dysfunctional responses to anxiety: The interaction between expectancies and self-focused attention. In R. Schwarzer (Ed.), *Self-related cognitions in anxiety and motivation.* Hillsdale, NJ: Lawrence Erlbaum Associates.

Chaney, E. F., O'Leary, M. R., & Marlatt, G. A. (1978). Skills training with alcoholics. *Journal of Consulting and Clinical Psychology, 46,* 1092–1104.

Clore, G. L., Schwarz, N., & Kirsch, J. (1983). *Generalized mood effects on evaluative judgments.* Paper presented at the meeting of the Midwestern Psychological Association, Chicago.

Collins, J. L. (1982, March). *Self-efficacy and ability in achievement behavior.* Paper presented at the annual meeting of the American Educational Research Association, New York.

Deffenbacher, J. L. (1978). Worry, emotionality, and task-generated interference in test anxiety: An empirical test of attentional theory. *Journal of Educational Psychology, 70,* 248–254.

DeRubeis, R. J., & Beck, A. T. (1988). Cognitive therapy. In K. S. Dobson (Ed.), *Handbook of cognitive-behavioral therapies* (pp. 273–306). New York: Guilford Press.

DiClemente, C. C. (1981). Self-efficacy and smoking cessation maintenance: A preliminary report. *Cognitive Therapy and Research, 5,* 175–187.

Dobson, K. S. (1989). A meta-analysis of the efficacy of cognitive therapy for depression. *Journal of Consulting and Clinical Psychology, 57,* 414–419.

Dobson, K. S., & Block, L. (1988). Historical and philosophical bases of the cognitive-behavioral therapies. In K. S. Dobson (Ed.), *Handbook of cognitive-behavioral therapies* (pp. 3–38). New York: Guilford Press.

Dodge, K. A. (1985). Attributional bias in aggressive children. In P. C. Kendall (Ed.), *Advances in cognitive-behavioral research and therapy* (Vol. 4, pp. 73–110). Orlando, FL: Academic Press.

Dryden, W., & Ellis, A. (1988). Rational-emotive therapy. In K. S. Dobson (Ed.), *Handbook of cognitive-behavioral therapies* (pp. 214–272). New York: Guilford Press.

D'Zurilla, T. J. (1986). *Problem-solving therapy: A social competence approach to clinical intervention.* New York: Springer.

D'Zurilla, T. J. (1988). Problem-solving therapies. In K. S. Dobson (Ed.), *Handbook of cognitive-behavioral therapies* (pp. 85–135). New York: Guilford Press.

D'Zurilla, T. J., & Nezu, A. (1982). Social problem-solving in adults. In P. C. Kendall (Ed.), *Advances in cognitive-behavioral research and therapy* (Vol. 1, pp. 202–274). New York: Academic Press.

Eisenberg, N. (1986). *Altruistic emotion, cognition, and behavior.* Hillsdale, NJ: Lawrence Erlbaum Associates.

Ellis, A. (1962). *Reason and emotion in psychotherapy.* Secaucus, NJ: Lyle Stuart.

Ellis, A., & Grieger, R. (Eds.). (1977). *Handbook of rational-emotive therapy.* New York: Springer.

Ellis, N. C., & Ashbrook, P. W. (1989). The "state" of mood and memory research: A selective review. *Journal of Social Behavior and Personality, 4,* 1–21.

Ellis, P. L. (1982). Empathy: A factor in antisocial behavior. *Journal of Abnormal Child Psychology, 10,* 123–134.

Emmelkamp, P. M. G., Mersch, P. P., Vissia, E., & van der Helm, M. (1985). Social phobia: A comparative evaluation of cognitive and behavioral interventions. *Behaviour Research and Therapy, 23,* 365–369.

Fairburn, C. (1985). Cognitive-behavioral treatment of bulimia. In K. S. Dobson (Ed.), *Handbook of cognitive-behavioral therapies* (pp. 214–272). New York: Guilford Press.

Faust, D. (1986). Research on human judgment and its application to clinical practice. *Professional Psychology, 17,* 420–430.

Forgas, J., & Bower, G. H. (1988). Affect in social and personal judgments. In K. Fiedler & J. Forgas (Eds.), *Affect, cognition, and social behavior* (pp. 183–208). Toronto: C. J. Hogrefe.

Frank, J. D. (1961). *Persuasion and healing.* New York: Schocken.

Frank, J. D. (1985). Therapeutic components shared by all psychotherapies. In M. J. Mahoney & A. Freeman (Eds.), *Cognition and psychotherapy* (pp. 49–79). New York: Plenum Press.

Garner, O. M., & Garfinkel, P. (Eds.) (1985). *Handbook of psychotherapy for anorexia nervosa and bulimia.* New York: Guilford Press.

Gilligan, S. C., & Bower, G. H. (1984). Cognitive consequences of emotional arousal. In C. Izard, J. Kagen, & R. Zajonc (Eds.), *Emotions, cognition, and behavior* (pp. 547–588). New York: Cambridge University Press.

Goldfried, M. R., & Davison, G. C. (1976). *Clinical behavior therapy.* New York: Holt, Rinehart & Winston.

Gouaux, C. (1971). Induced affective states and interpersonal attraction. *Journal of Personality and Social Psychology, 20,* 37–43.

Graziano, A. M., & Mooney, K. C. (1980). Family self-control instructions for children's nighttime fear reduction. *Journal of Consulting and Clinical Psychology, 48,* 206–213.

Greenwald, A. G., & Pratkanis, A. R. (1984). The self. In R. S. Wyer & T. K. Srull (Eds.), *Handbook of social cognition* (pp. 111–150). Hillsdale, NJ: Lawrence Erlbaum Associates.

Gresham, F. M. (1985). Utility of cognitive-behavioral procedures for social skills training with children: A critical review. *Journal of Abnormal Child Psychology, 13,* 411–423.

Griffitt, W. B. (1970). Environmental effects of interpersonal affective behavior: Ambient effective temperature and attraction. *Journal of Personality and Social Psychology, 15,* 240–244.

Harris, K. R. (1986). The effects of cognitive-behavior modification on private speech and task performance during problem-solving among learning disabled and normally-achieving children. *Journal of Abnormal Child Psychology, 14,* 63–67.

Harris, K. R., & Graham, S. (1985). Improving learning disabled students' composition skills: Self-control strategy training. *Learning Disabilities Quarterly, 8,* 27–36.

Hasher, L., Rose, K. C., Zacks, R. T., Sanft, H., & Doren, B. (1985). Mood, recall, and selectivity effects in normal college students. *Journal of Experimental Psychology: General, 114,* 104–118.

Hollandsworth, J. G. (1986). *Physiology and behavior therapy.* New York: Plenum Press.

Hollon, S. D., & Kriss, M. R. (1984). Cognitive factors in clinical research and practice. *Clinical Psychology Review, 4,* 35–76.

Hope, D. A., & Heimberg, R. G. (1985). *Public and private self-consciousness in a social phobic sample.* Paper presented at the annual meeting of the Association for the Advancement of Behavior Therapy.

Hull, J. G. (1981). A self-awareness model of the causes and effects of alcohol consumption. *Journal of Abnormal Psychology, 90,* 586–600.

Hussian, R. A., & Lawrence, P. S. (1981). Social reinforcement of activity and problem-solving training in the treatment of depressed institutional elderly patients. *Cognitive Therapy and Research, 5,* 57–69.

Ingram, R. E. (1990). Self-focused attention in clinical disorders: Review and a conceptual model. *Psychological Bulletin, 107,* 156–176.

Ingram, R. E., & Smith, T. W. (1984). Depression and internal versus external focus of attention. *Cognitive Therapy and Research, 8,* 139–152.

Isen, A. M. (1987). Positive affect, cognitive processes, and social behavior. In L. Berkowitz (Ed.), *Advances in experimental social psychology* (Vol. 20, pp. 203–253). San Diego: Academic Press.

Isen, A. M., & Daubman, K. A. (1984). The influence of affect on categorization. *Journal of Personality and Social Psychology, 47,* 1206–1217.

Isen, A. M., Daubman, K. A., & Nowicki, G. P. (1987). Positive affect facilitates creative problem solving. *Journal of Personality and Social Psychology, 52,* 1122–1131.

Isen, A. M., & Geva, N. (1987). The influence of positive affect on acceptable level of risk: The person with a large canoe has a large worry. *Organizational Behavior and Human Decision Processes, 39,* 145–154.

Isen, A. M., Means, B., Patrick, R., & Nowicki, G., (1982). Some factors influencing decision-making strategy and risk-taking. In M. S. Clark & S. T. Fiske (Eds.), *Affect and cognition: The Carnegie symposium on cognition* (pp. 243–261). Hillsdale, NJ: Lawrence Erlbaum Associates.

Isen, A. M., Nygren, T. E., & Ashby, F. G. (1985). *The influence of positive affect on the subjective utility of gains and losses: It's not worth the risk.* Paper presented at the meeting of the Psychonomic Society, Boston, MA.

Isen, A. M., & Patrick, R. (1983). The effect of positive feelings on risk-taking: When the chips are down. *Organizational Behavior and Human Performance, 31,* 194–202.

Isen, A. M., Shalker, T., Clark, M., & Karp, L. (1978). Affect, accessibility of material in memory, and behavior: A cognitive loop? *Journal of Personality and Social Psychology, 36,* 1–12.

Jannoun, L., Munby, M., Catalan, J., & Gelder, M. (1980). A home-based treatment program for agoraphobia: Replication and controlled evaluation. *Behavior Therapy, 11,* 294–305.

Jay, S. M., Elliott, C. H., Katz, E., & Siegel, S. E. (1987). Cognitive behavioral and pharmacological interventions for children's distress during painful medical procedures. *Journal of Consulting and Clinical Psychology, 55*, 860–866.

Jerremalm, A., Jansson, L., & Öst, L. G. (1986). Cognitive and physiological reactivity and the effects of different behavioral methods in the treatment of social phobia. *Behavior Research and Therapy, 24*, 171–180.

Johnson, E. J., & Tversky, A. (1983). Affect, generalization, and the perception of risk. *Journal of Personality and Social Psychology, 45*, 20–31.

Kanfer, F. H. (1970). Self-regulation: Research, issues, and speculations. In C. Neuringer & J. L. Michael (Eds.), *Behavioral modification in clinical psychology* (pp. 178–220). New York: Appleton-Century-Crofts.

Kanfer, F. H. (1975). Self-management methods. In F. H. Kanfer & A. P. Goldstein (Eds.), *Helping people change: A textbook of methods* (pp. 309–356). Elmsford, NY: Pergamon Press.

Kanfer, F. H., & Karoly, P. (1972a). Self-control: A behavioristic excursion into the lion's den. *Behavior Therapy, 2*, 398–416.

Kanfer, F. H., & Karoly, P. (1972b). Self-regulation and its clinical application: Some additional conceptualizations. In R. C. Johnson, P. R. Dokecki, & O. H. Mowrer, (Eds.), *Socialization: Development of character and conscience* (pp. 428–437). New York: Holt, Rinehart & Winston.

Kanfer, F. H., & Schefft, B. K. (1988). *Guiding the process of therapeutic change.* Champaign, IL: Research Press.

Kanfer, R., & Zeiss, A. M. (1983). Depression, interpersonal standard setting, and judgments of self-efficacy. *Journal of Abnormal Psychology, 92*, 319–329.

Kaplan, H. S. (1974). *The new sex therapy.* New York: Brunner/Mazel.

Kavanagh, D. J., & Bower, G. H. (1985). Mood and self-efficacy: Impact of joy and sadness on perceived capabilities. *Cognitive Therapy and Research, 9*, 507–525.

Kazdin, A. E. (1979). Imagery elaboration and self-efficacy in the covert modeling treatment of unassertive behavior. *Journal of Consulting and Clinical Psychology, 47*, 725–733.

Kazdin, A. E. (1987a). Treatment of antisocial behavior in children: Current status and future directions. *Psychological Bulletin, 102*, 187–203.

Kazdin, A. E. (1987b). *Conduct disorder in childhood and adolescence.* Newbury Park, CA: Sage.

Kazdin, A. E., Bass, D., Siegel, T., & Thomas, C. (1989). Cognitive-behavioral therapy and relationship therapy in the treatment of children referred for antisocial behavior. *Journal of Consulting and Clinical Psychology, 57*, 522–535.

Kendall, P. C., & Braswell, L. (1982). Cognitive-behavioral self-control therapy for children: A components analysis. *Journal of Consulting and Clinical Psychology, 50*, 672–689.

Kendall, P. C., & Braswell, L. (1985). *Cognitive-behavioral therapy for impulsive children.* New York: Guilford Press.

Kendall, P. C., & Wilcox, L. E. (1980). A cognitive-behavioral treatment for impulsivity: Concrete vs. conceptual training in non-self-controlled problem children. *Journal of Consulting and Clinical Psychology, 48*, 80–91.

Kettlewell, P. W., & Kausch, D. F. (1983). The generalization of the effects of a cognitive behavioral treatment program for aggressive children. *Journal of Abnormal Child Psychology, 11*, 101–114.

Klos, D. S., & Singer, J. L. (1981). Determinants of the adolescent's ongoing thought following simulated parental confrontations. *Journal of Personality and Social Psychology, 41*, 975–987.

Kovacs, M., Rush, A. J., Beck, A. T., & Hollon, S. D. (1981). Depressed outpatients treated with cognitive therapy or pharmacotherapy: A one year follow-up. *Archives of General Psychiatry, 38,* 33–39.

Lazarus, R. S. (1977). Cognitive and coping processes in emotion. In A. Monat & R. S. Lazarus (Eds.), *Stress and coping* (pp. 145–158). New York: Columbia University Press.

Lazarus, R. S., & Folkman, S. (1984). *Stress, appraisal, and coping.* New York: Springer.

Lazarus, R. S., & Launier, R. (1978). Stress-related transactions between person and environment. In L. A. Pervin & M. Lewis (Eds.), *Perspectives in interactional psychology* (pp. 287–327). New York: Plenum Press.

Lehman, A. K., & Salovey, P. (1990). An introduction to cognitive-behavior therapy. In V. Giannetti (Ed.), *The handbook of brief psychotherapies* (pp. 239–259). New York: Plenum Press.

Lerner, M. J. (1965). The effect of responsibility and choice on a partner's attractiveness following failure. *Journal of Personality, 33,* 178–187.

Litt, M. D. (1988). Self-efficacy and perceived control: Cognitive mediators of pain tolerance. *Journal of Personality and Social Psychology, 54,* 149–160.

Lloyd, G. G., & Lishman, W. A. (1975). Effect of depression on the speed of recall of pleasant and unpleasant experiences. *Psychological Medicine, 5,* 173–180.

Lott, A. J., & Lott, B. E. (1968). A learning theory approach to interpersonal attitudes. In A. G. Greenwald, T. C. Brock, & T. M. Ostrom (Eds.), *Psychological foundations of attitudes* (pp. 67–88). New York: Academic Press.

Luborsky, L. (1977). Measuring a pervasive psychic structure in psychotherapy: The core conflictual relationship theme. In N. Freedman & S. Grand (Eds.), *Communicative structures and psychic structures* (pp. 367–395). New York: Plenum Press.

Mahoney, M. (1974). *Cognition and behavior modification.* Cambridge, MA: Ballinger.

Mandler, G., & Watson, D. L. (1966). Anxiety and the interruption of behavior. In C. D. Spielberger (Ed.), *Anxiety and behavior* (pp. 263–288). New York: Academic Press.

Marlatt, G. A., & Gordon, J. R. (1985). *Relapse prevention.* New York: Guilford Press.

Masters, W. H., & Johnson, V. E. (1970). *Human sexual inadequacy.* Boston: Little, Brown & Co.

Mayer, J. D., & Bremer, D. (1985). Assessing mood with affect-sensitive tasks. *Journal of Personality Assessment, 49,* 95–99.

Mayer, J. D., & Goschke, Y. N. (1988). The experience and meta-experience of mood. *Journal of Personality and Social Psychology, 55,* 102–111.

Mayer, J. d., & Salovey, P. (1988). Personality moderates the interaction of mood and cognition. In K. Fiedler & J. Forgas (Eds.), *Affect, cognition, and social behavior* (pp. 87–99). Toronto: C. J. Hogrefe.

Mayer, J. D., & Volanth, A J. (1985). Cognitive involvement in the emotional response system. *Motivation and Emotion, 9,* 261–275.

Meehl, P. E. (1954). *Clinical versus statistical prediction.* Minneapolis: University of Minneapolis Press.

Meichenbaum, D. (1977). *Cognitive-behavior modification: An integrative approach.* New York: Plenum.

Meichenbaum, D. (1985). *Stress inoculation training.* Elmsford, NY: Pergamon Press.

Meichenbaum, D. (1986). Self-instructional methods. In F. H. Kanfer & A. P. Goldstein (Eds.), *Helping people change: A textbook of methods* (pp. 357–392). Elmsford, NY: Pergamon Press.

Meichenbaum, D., & Gilmore, J. B. (1984). The nature of unconscious processes: A cognitive-behavioral perspective. In K. Bowers & D. Meichenbaum (Eds.), *The unconscious reconsidered* (pp. 273–298). New York: John Wiley & Sons.

Meichenbaum, D., & Goodman, J. (1971). Training impulsive children to talk to themselves: A means of developing self-control. *Journal of Abnormal Psychology, 77*, 115–126.

Mischel, W. (1973). Toward a cognitive social learning reconceptualization of personality. *Psychological Review, 80*, 252–283.

Nasby, W., & Yando, R. (1982). Selective encoding and retrieval of affectively valent information: Two cognitive consequences of children's mood states. *Journal of Personality and Social Psychology, 43*, 1244–1253.

Natale, M., & Hantas, M. (1982). Effect of temporary mood states on selective memory about the self. *Journal of Personality and Social Psychology, 42*, 927–934.

O'Leary, A. (1985). Self-efficacy and health. *Behaviour Research and Therapy, 23*, 437–451.

Patterson, G. R. (1986). Performance models for antisocial boys. *American Psychologist, 41*, 432–444.

Pyszczynski, T., & Greenberg, J. (1987). Self-regulatory perseveration and the depressive self-focusing style: A self-awareness theory of depression. *Psychological Bulletin, 102*, 122–138.

Pyszczynski, T., Holt, K., & Greenberg, J. (1987). Depression, self-focused attention, and expectancies for future positive and negative events for self and others. *Journal of Personality and Social Psychology, 52*, 994–1001.

Rehm, L. P., & Rokke, P. (1988). Self-management therapies. In K. S. Dobson (Ed.), *Handbook of cognitive-behavioral therapies* (pp. 136–166). New York: Guilford Press.

Rogers, C. R., & Truax, C. B. (1967). The therapeutic conditions antecedent to change: A theoretical view. In C. R. Rogers (Ed.), *The therapeutic relationship and its impact: A study of psychotherapy with schizophrenics* (pp. 3–27). Madison: University of Wisconsin Press.

Salovey, P. (1986). The effects of mood and focus of attention on self-relevant thoughts and helping intention. *Dissertation Abstracts International, 1987–88, 48*(10), 3121-B.

Salovey, P., & Birnbaum, D. (1989). Influence of mood on health-relevant cognitions. *Journal of Personality and Social Psychology, 57*, 539–551.

Salovey, P., & Haar, M. D. (in press). The efficacy of cognitive-behavior therapy and writing process training for alleviating writing anxiety. *Cognitive Therapy and Research*.

Salovey, P., & Mayer, J. D. (1990). Emotional intelligence. *Imagination, Cognition, and Personality, 9*, 185–211.

Salovey, P., Mayer, J. D., & Rosenhan, D. L. (in press). Helping and the regulation of mood. *Review of Personality and Social Psychology*.

Salovey, P., & Rodin, J. (1985). Cognitions about the self: Connecting feeling states to social behavior. *Review of Personality and Social Psychology, 6*, 143–166.

Salovey, P., & Rodin, J. (1989). Envy and jealousy in close relationships. *Review of Personality and Social Psychology, 10*, 221–246.

Salovey, P., & Rosenhan, D. L. (1989). Mood states and prosocial behavior. In H. Wagner & A. Manstead (Eds.), *Handbook of social psychophysiology* (pp. 371–391). Chichester: John Wiley & Sons.

Salovey, P., & Singer, J. A. (1989). Mood congruency effects in recall of childhood versus recent memories. *Journal of Social Behavior and Personality, 4*, 99–120.

Salovey, P., & Turk, D. C. (1988). Some effects of mood on clinicians' memory. In D. C. Turk & P. Salovey (Eds.), *Reasoning, inference, and judgment in clinical psychology* (pp. 107–123). New York: Free Press.

Salovey, P., & Turk, D. C. (in press). Clinical judgment and decision making. In C. R. Snyder & D. R. Forsyth (Eds.), *Handbook of social and clinical psychology: The health perspective*. Elmsford, NY: Pergamon Press.

Schunk, D. H. (1984). Self-efficacy perspective on achievement behavior. *Educational Psychologist, 19,* 48–58.

Shaffer, C. S., Shapiro, J., Sank, L. I., & Coghlan, D. J. (1981). Positive changes in depression, anxiety, and assertion following individual and group cognitive behavior therapy intervention. *Cognitive Therapy and Research, 2,* 149–157.

Simons, A. D., Murphy, G. E., Levine, J. L., & Wetzel, R. D. (1986). Cognitive therapy and pharmacotherapy for depression: Sustained improvement over one year. *Archives of General Psychiatry, 43,* 43–48.

Singer, J. A., & Salovey, P. (1988). Mood and memory: Evaluating the network theory of affect. *Clinical Psychology Review, 8,* 211–251.

Singer, J. L. (1984). The private personality. *Personality and Social Psychology Bulletin, 10,* 7–30.

Singer, J. L., & Salovey, P. (in press). Organized knowledge structures and personality: Person schemas, self-schemas, prototypes, and scripts. In M. Horowitz (Ed.), *Person schemas and maladaptive interpersonal behavior patterns.* Chicago, IL: University of Chicago Press.

Slapion, J. J., & Carver, C. S. (1981). Self-directed attention and facilitation of intellectual performance among persons high in test anxiety. *Cognitive Therapy and Research, 5,* 323–331.

Snyder, M., & White, E. (1982). Moods and memories: Elation, depression, and remembering the events of one's life. *Journal of Personality, 50,* 149–167.

Spivack, G., Platt, J. J., & Shure, M. B. (1976). *The problem-solving approach to adjustment.* San Francisco: Jossey-Bass.

Spivack, G., & Shure, M. B. (1982). The cognition of social adjustment: Interpersonal cognitive problem solving thinking. In B. B. Lahey & A. E. Kazdin (Eds.), *Advances in child clinical psychology* (Vol. 5, pp. 323–372). New York: Plenum Press.

Stevens, V. J., & Hollis, J. F. (1989). Preventing smoking relapse, using an individually tailored skills-training technique. *Journal of Consulting and Clinical Psychology, 57,* 420–424.

Taylor, S. E., & Brown, J. D. (1988). Illusion and well-being: A social psychological perspective on mental health. *Psychological Bulletin, 103,* 193–210.

Teasdale, J. D., & Fogarty, S. J. (1979). Differential effects of induced mood on retrieval of pleasant and unpleasant events from episodic memory. *Journal of Abnormal Psychology, 88,* 248–257.

Tisdelle, D. A., & St. Lawrence, J. S. (1986). Interpersonal problem-solving competency: Review and critique. *Clinical Psychology Review, 6,* 337–356.

Turk, D. C., Meichenbaum, D., & Genest, M. (1983). *Pain and behavioral medicine.* New York: Guilford Press.

Turk, D. C., & Salovey, P. (1985). Cognitive structures, cognitive processes, and cognitive-behavior modification: I. Client issues. *Cognitive Therapy and Research, 9,* 1–17.

Turk, D. C., & Salovey, P. (1986). Clinical information processing: Bias inoculation. In R. E. Ingram (Ed.), *Information processing approaches to clinical psychology* (pp. 305–323). Orlando, FL: Academic Press.

Wegner, D. M. (1989). *White beans and other unwanted thoughts.* New York: Viking.

Wegner, D. M., & Giuliano, T. (1980). Arousal-induced attention to self. *Journal of Personality and Social Psychology, 38,* 719–726.

Wegner, D. M., Schneider, D. J., Carter, S., & White, T. (1987). Paradoxical effects of thought supression. *Journal of Personality and Social Psychology, 53,* 5–13.

Weissberg, R. P., & Allen, J. P. (1986). Promoting children's social skills and adaptive interpersonal behavior. In B. Edelstein & L. Michelson (Eds.), *Handbook of prevention* (pp. 153–175). New York: Plenum Press.

Whitman, T., Burgio, L., & Johnston, M. B. (1984). Cognitive-behavioral intervention with mentally retarded children. In A. W. Meyers & W. E. Craighead (Eds.), *Cognitive behavior therapy with children* (pp. 193–227). New York: Plenum Press.

Williams, S. L., Dooseman, G., & Kleifield, E. (1984). Comparative effectiveness of guided mastery and exposure treatments for intractable phobias. *Journal of Consulting and Clinical Psychology, 52,* 505–518.

Williams, S. L., & Watson, N. (1985). Perceived danger and perceived self-efficacy as cognitive mediators of acrophobic behavior. *Behavior Therapy, 16,* 136–146.

Wright, J., & Mischel, W. (1982). Influence of affect on cognitive social learning person variables. *Journal of Personality and Social Psychology, 43,* 901–914.

10
Utilization of Community and Social Support Resources

Michael T. Nietzel
Pamela R. Guthrie
David T. Susman

The search for the history of any therapeutic technique or principle often begins with Freud. Freud is where we started, and we learned that his enthusiasm for using natural, community resources to help people change was restrained, to say the least. Should patients be encouraged to extend their "working through" with supportive others? No, said Freud (1913), to do so would be to spring a "leak which lets through just what is most valuable." How about attempting new behaviors in contexts selected to maximize the chances for success? Forget it; "it is the analyst's task to detect these by-paths and to require him every time to abandon them, however harmless the performance which leads to satisfaction may be in itself" (Freud, 1919). Could we supplement our insights with a little self-help reading? Hardly. Not only did Freud proscribe analytical writings for his patients because he required "them to learn by personal experience," he also warned against "any attempt to engage the confidence or support of parents or relatives by giving them psychoanalytical books to read" because such literature would only have the "effect of evoking prematurely the natural and inevitable opposition of the relatives to the treatment . . ." (Freud, 1912).

While we begin with Freud, we need not end with him. Psychotherapists are now much more pluralistic on the question of whether or how to use naturally occurring, community resources to facilitate client change. Freud's advice to insulate therapy from natural supports is even challenged within the psychoanalytic ranks. For example, data from the long-term Menninger Psychotherapy Research Project has confirmed both the frequent and effective use by psychoanalysts of what Wallerstein (1989) termed the "transfer of the transference." With this strategy, transference needs and dependencies are gratified in part by psychological support from "outside" providers like Alcoholics Anonymous, church groups, or even sublimating social-cultural activities. While at one extreme we still find opposition to these strategies, it is phrased not so much as an outright injunction against naturalized change methods as it is caveats against the limits and risks of methods whose injection into therapy might immunize clients against the power of "the real thing." A more charitable, but still limited, endorsement comes from therapists who see these methods as "adjuncts" to therapy, boosting the length or strength of effects beyond that otherwise achieved. Finally, we find therapists who believe that naturalized change strategies are sturdy enough to stand alone, promoting client changes that might not have otherwise been realized or maintained.

In this chapter we review the rationale and methods for using community and social network resources for helping people change. We provide examples of these techniques from clinical lore and the professional literature as well as review their empirical status. Finally, we discuss some limitations and ethical concerns that surround the therapeutic use of natural, community resources.

THEORETICAL FOUNDATIONS

Several theoretical perspectives point toward the wisdom and necessity of therapists broadening their vision to include the natural and social contexts in which their clients' lives are embedded. We have chosen to summarize four theoretical traditions that have consistently emphasized the importance of context, in one way or another, for adequately understanding and producing meaningful therapeutic change.

Systems Theory and Cybernetics

The 20th century has witnessed an explosion of knowledge in all fields of science. This explosion is fueled by advances in computers and technology that have given us the ability to process vast amounts of information as well as the capability to dissect natural events into their smallest component parts. One result of these abilities has been increased specialization and narrowness of interest in all disciplines, a regrettable trend when it leads scientists to become isolated from others in their own field as well as from researchers in other disciplines. While we have more and more technical capability to explore intricate relationships between components of large slices of nature, we instead tend to concentrate on individual processes and minute mechanisms. Individual phenomena always take place within a larger panorama of ongoing events, but the increasing specialization among scientists carries the potential for limiting the view of bigger pictures if glimpsed only through small windows.

As one response to the dangers of narrow perspectives, von Bertalanffy (1956, 1968a, 1968b) developed a theoretical framework known as general systems theory. Defining systems as "sets of elements standing in interaction," the theory has been applied to a multitude of phenomena including several topics within clinical psychology. It has played a particularly prominent role in theories of family dysfunction and family intervention, although it is also relevant to the psychological processes of individuals.

In systems theory, there are both closed and open systems. A closed system is isolated from its environment. While its components are dynamically related to one another, there is a state of equilibrium, which, once reached, is not affected by incoming changes. Psychology is seldom concerned with closed systems. On the other hand, open systems, with which psychology is often concerned, maintain themselves in relatively steady, but never inert, states by constantly adjusting to input from the environment. von Bertalanffy (1968a, p. 39) states, "every living organism is essentially an open system."

von Bertalanffy (1968a) also believed that to explain a system and its workings, it is necessary to know not only what all the constituent parts are, but also what the interactions between the parts involve. Knowing both the elements and the nature of their interactions allows predictions about the behavior of the entire system.

An additional important concept of a system approach to human behavior is cybernetics and its concern with how a system becomes self-regulatory. A cybernetic view of human behavior concentrates on the self-regulatory components in human systems, similar to homeostatic components in biology. If there are mechanisms inherent within human systems intended to preserve balance, then changes in an individual will upset the system of which that person is a part, and other persons in the system will respond in an effort to maintain equilibrium. For example, an individual in therapy may intitiate changes in personal behavior that affect the person's family or co-workers. The system may not tolerate these changes because of threatened equilibrium, and it reacts with pressure for the individual to maintain an arguably unhealthy, but system-sustaining, posture. Therapists frequently encounter situations in which a client's behavioral changes are sabotaged by a spouse who is threatened by the new possibilities now available to the client. For example, the formerly overweight spouse who loses weight often faces a mixture of distrust and resentment from a partner who suddenly fears the positive attention that the spouse begins to attract.

In any discipline, the phenomenon being studied defines the larger system of which it is necessarily a part. Thus, in the case of psychotherapy, the individual client can be seen as a system or as an element within a system. To the psychophysiologically oriented therapist treating a client with a stress-related disorder, the individual might be viewed as the system, with the organs of respiration, circulation, and regulation being key elements interacting within the system. To a more interpersonally oriented psychotherapist treating the same client, the person might be understood as part of a larger system—an environment made up of ever-changing situational factors and people within which and with whom a stream of interactions flows. Which view is correct? Both, of course, because each of us is simultaneously a physiological system and a part of several psychosocial systems. Systems theory, with its recognition of how individuals are embedded in reciprocally influential contexts, highlights one of the central issues facing the psychotherapist: how to balance attempts at fostering autonomy, personal efficacy, and responsible independence in clients with a sensitive recognition of the constraints, pushes and pulls, and dependence inherent in their daily lives.

Social Learning Theory

In addition to its emphasis on diverse learning processes by which personality characteristics are forged, social learning theory stresses the contingent relationships between new behaviors and the social-environmental conditions of which the behaviors are to be displayed. The terminology for this type of contingency varies with certain theoretical enclaves within the social learning camp. For example, predominantly operant types talk of "stimulus control" to describe the fact that specific responses occur predominantly in the presence of specific stimuli. Their more cognitively oriented colleagues stress that behaviors are influenced by the way persons construe or anticipate social-environmental contingencies. Although these expectations are sometimes distorted, they also tend to capture the reality of past, if not always present, environments. Distorted cognitive constructions of environmental contexts are often modified most effectively by exposing the person to a tailored sequence of planned interactions with these contexts.

Social learning therapists stress the importance of the client's context for two phases of intervention: instigation of behavior change and maintenance of therapeutic gains. The client's environment provides a natural laboratory where the client can be encouraged to test out new behaviors. Adler's frequent question, "Would you be interested in seeing what difference this type of change would make in your life?" is an adroitly phrased invitation to behavior change that takes advantage of those aspects of a client's context that are likely to reinforce new behavior. The therapist still must correctly discern the availability of these reinforcers and formulate "homework" that will earn them, but having done so, he or she can help the client capitalize on the corrective experiences that a supportive interpersonal environment has to offer.

Concerns about maintenance of change also lead the social learning therapist to consider the client's social-environmental context from the perspective of the damage it can do. In fact, any reasonable assessment of psychotherapy must recognize that the positive changes it promotes can be reduced, if not eliminated, by chronic adversities and major stressful life events. This understanding has led some therapists (Jacobson, 1989) to recommend that treatment regularly include a follow-up phase where periodic check-ups (which might involve one-to-one sessions or might take the form of self-help meetings with a group of similar clients) are provided to the client in order to prevent loss of treatment gains. This routine extension of treatment would be the psychotherapeutic equivalent to the protective undercoating applied to new cars, and it is recommended for the same reason: Stormy weather can erode and corrode even the most sturdy structures.

Interpersonal Theory

Following Sullivan, interpersonally oriented therapists have concentrated on the influence of context, defined primarily as the repeated interpersonal relationships in which their clients are involved. In this view, interpersonal relationships provide both the crucible in which disturbed behavior begins and the arena in which it is then maintained. To be successful, psychotherapy must result in clients exploring new styles of interacting with important persons in their lives in order to discover that old ways of behaving may no longer be necessary.

The interpersonal approach focuses on how the client "pulls" desired behaviors from others by enacting a limited, even rigid, interpersonal style. This style is motivated by a desire to insure security and prevent anxiety. It becomes problematic when the person becomes locked into a rigid, extreme form of behavior rather than a flexible range of behavior as warranted by different social situations.

Leary's (1957) interpersonal circumplex has been the most influential system for describing characteristic interpersonal sequences although several other models have shown remarkable convergence with Leary's ideas (see Wiggins & Broughton, 1985 for a review). Circumplex models are usually organized around two dimensions—a vertical axis defined by dominance at one pole and submissiveness at the other, and a horizontal axis anchored by love at one extreme and hate at the other. Around the perimeter of the circle are octants representing various blends of power (dominance–submission) and affiliation (love–hate); furthermore, as one moves from the center of the circle to the perimeter, the intensity of the behaviors increases. Octants adjacent to one another are maximally positively correlated. Octants lying directly opposite each other on the circle should be negatively correlated.

Certain sequences of interpersonal actions are more common than others. The rule of *complementarity* predicts that along the power dimension, dominant behavior will be reciprocated by submissiveness and vice versa. The rule of *correspondence* suggests that along the affiliative dimension, love will evoke love and hate will evoke hate. These principles point to some ideas about how therapists should respond to clients' standard interpersonal maneuve.s. Because clients tend to perpetuate maladaptive behavior by evoking complementary behaviors from others, one goal for a therapist is to adapt a noncomplementary stance toward clients' usual gambits. The therapist tries to respond antidotally to the client in order to induce new behaviors. For example, an antisocial client's hostile dominance pulls hostile submissiveness from others (including the therapist). The therapist, however, could try to act in a friendly dominant manner toward the client in an attempt to "swing him around the circle" toward increased friendly submissiveness.

The importance of interpersonal context emerges after the therapist has been successful in inducing new behavior in the session. Now it becomes crucial to see if these new behaviors can be maintained in the natural environment. If clients are able to display even a few examples of friendly submissiveness, any reasonably benign interpersonal environment is likely to reinforce the change and help strengthen it. The therapist can promote this effect by sensitizing clients to look for the effects their new behavior has on people around them. However, clients often do not enjoy a reasonably benign interpersonal context. Therefore, the therapist has the added burden of finding ways to prompt the environment to support the fledgling changes that have been nurtured within therapy. Supplemental family consultation (Bernheim, 1989; Wynne, Weber, & McDaniel, 1986) or couple therapy can be used in this way to bolster the changes introduced in individual psychotherapy (see Jacobson, Holtzworth–Munroe, & Schmaling, 1989, for a review of spouse involvement in treatments of depression, anxiety disorders, and alcoholism). Encouraging clients to join mutual-help groups or organizations can also solidify positive changes by increasing the probability of social reinforcement for new interpersonal behaviors.

How a client's therapy affects the client's spouse, lover, or other close acquaintances is an important question not only because of the facilitative role that relatives and loved ones can play for clients but also because significant others can be affected by their partners' therapy in both positive and negative ways. To examine the effects of individual therapy on the significant others in a client's life, Brody and Farber (1989) interviewed 20 "significant others" whose partners were currently in therapy. Results indicated that most of these people held conflicted feelings about their partners' therapy. While they all perceived improvements in areas such as communication and in better understanding both themselves and their partner's needs, the majority of significant others also reported negative feelings about the therapy. Prominent among these negative feelings were (1) feelings of inadequacy because their partners found it necessary to confide in someone else, (2) resentment and jealousy over the privacy and closeness of the therapeutic relationship, and (3) displeasure with the expense of treatment. Partners who were less aware of the nature of the therapy tended to be more disturbed by it.

We believe there are two implications of these findings. First, the context-sensitive therapist should recognize the possibility of these complications and be prepared to discuss them with clients. Second, within the boundaries of confidentiality and informed consent, there may be advantages to conducting at least one "consulting" session jointly with the client and his or her most significant other to ease anxieties the partner may have about the therapeutic relationship and to promote the partner's cooperation with therapeutic homework experiments the client will be attempting.

Empowerment Theory

Introduced originally for the purpose of suggesting an alternative to primary prevention as a social policy agenda for community psychologists, Rappaport's (1981) ideology of empowerment is also relevant to the strategies and behaviors of psychotherapists. The idea of empowerment stems in part from deliberate divergent thinking about social problems so as to avoid the possible dangers of one-sided interventions:

> Partly because institutions have a tendency to become one-sided many social problems are ironically and inadvertently created by the so-called helping systems . . . and often "solutions" create more problems than they solve (p. 8). That social institutions and professions create as well as solve problems is *not* a call for working harder to find the single best technique or lamenting the failure of our best minds to be creative. Quite the opposite. *It is a problem to be understood as contained in the basic nature of the subject matter of our field.* It will always be this way. There can never be a now and for all time single discipline "breakthrough" which settles and solves the puzzles of our discipline. Today's solution must be tomorrow's problem. (Rappaport, 1981, p. 9; italics in original)

The dangers of a one-sided commitment to prevention include paternalistic and patronizing programs that ignore or obscure the personal resources of recipients, and "overreach" of professionals into problems of so-called high-risk people whether the people want the services or not. The practice of empowerment seeks to avoid these problems by enhancing the possibilities for people to control their own lives. As Rappaport (1981) states, "We will, should we take empowerment seriously, no longer be able to see people simply as children in need or as only citizens with rights, but rather as human beings who have both rights and needs. We will confront the paradox that even the people most incompetent, in need, and apparently unable to function, require, just as you and I do, more rather than less control over their own lives" (p. 15).

We believe there is an analogy to the practice of psychotherapy in Rappaport's concept. Psychotherapy can breed dependency especially if it deters clients from being open to nonexpert sources of help. The implications of empowerment for therapists is that they should help their clients become attuned and responsive to the natural mediating and supportive opportunities that the environment can provide. The family, the neighborhood, the church, friends, and voluntary organizations all provide numerous lessons on how problems in living can be handled successfully. This is the context in which people live their lives, and the more control therapy helps them acquire over it, the better.

At the meta-theoretical level, the preceding ideas point us in a direction increasingly appreciated in the social sciences and the helping professions. Rosnow and Rosenthal (1989) summarize this direction as follows: "There is a growing awareness is psychology that just about everything under the sun is context dependent in one way or another" (p. 1280). "Helping people change" is no exception. Just as the beauty of a painting is not destroyed by the frame that surrounds it, our therapeutic efforts will not be strengthened by ignoring the contexts of our clients' lives. Therapists' respect for and use of natural contexts can lead to fuller and more empathic understanding of clients and, at the same time, extend their psychotherapeutic influences.

USE OF CLIENT CONTEXT AND COMMUNITY RESOURCES

Facilitating Social Support

Conceptualizations of social support, originally anthropological in nature, made early inroads into the field of sociology, were then taken up by social psychologists, and recently have activated a strong push toward intervention policy changes in community mental health and clinical psychology. This push is understandable in light of the fact that, intertwined with research on stress and coping, the study of social support appeals to those interested in both therapeutic and preventive responses to emotional problems (Lieberman, 1986). This appeal is different from the pre-1960 attitude of many psychologists that one's social environment consisted strictly of demands which strained the individual rather than of some positive factors that could potentially alleviate stress and strain (Heller, Swindle, & Dusenbury, 1986).

The current push for applications appears to be outstripping our understanding of basic theoretical issues and underlying mechanisms of support. There is considerable disagreement in the social support literature about the definition of support, and the terms *social support* and *social network* are often used interchangeably, despite important differences in them (Vaux, 1988). Because of this confusion, we begin this section with some explication of important concepts. Following this discussion, we delineate essential common factors between psychotherapy and social support as helping activities. Finally, we discuss implications for the practice of psychotherapy.

Social Networks

A social network has been defined by Mitchell (cited in Powell, 1987, p. 88) as, "a specific set of linkages among a defined set of persons with the additional property that the characteristics of these linkages as a whole may be used to interpret the social behavior of the persons involved." A social network is an intermediate range of social ties between one's intimate relationships and one's standing in the community at large (Vaux, 1988). The size, reachability, and density of one's social network are important properties of how it functions. Vaux (1988) distinguishes between the support network as one facet of the construct of support and the perception of support as another facet. In other words, tangible support resources and subjective appraisals of support are distinct concepts and the relationships between them are important to an overall understanding of social support.

Social Support

Vaux (1988) defines social support as a meta-construct made up of support networks, supportive behavior, and subjective appraisals of support. There are eight mechanisms by which support functions:

1. protective direct action (best exemplified by protection of children by parents);
2. inoculation (through promotion of a general sense of well-being);
3. primary appraisal guidance;
4. secondary appraisal guidance;
5. reappraisal guidance (through all types of appraisal guidance other people, immediately or in an ongoing manner, provide alternative explanations of events that later alter one's appraisals of what has taken place);
6. diversion (by taking one's mind off problem situations);
7. supportive direct action (in which one is helped with problem-solving approaches to the situation); and
8. palliative emotional support (in which support is of a purely emotional, sustaining, and containing nature).

Heller et al. (1986, p. 467) define social support as "a social activity . . . perceived by the recipient . . . as esteem enhancing or [involving] stress-related interpersonal aid (emotional support, cognitive restructuring, or instrumental aid)." *Perceived support,* on the other hand, is a belief in being cared for and valued and does not necessarily require other parties to be involved in any overt helping activities. The mechanisms whereby perceived support is experienced are still unknown, but many researchers believe its positive effects are achieved because it enhances self-esteem and feelings of efficacy in dealing with potential problems.

Thoits' (1982, 1986) view of social support as coping assistance is a currently popular perspective. According to Thoits (1986, p. 417), social support can best be understood as "the active participation of significant others in an individual's stress-management efforts." Social support can buffer the effects of stress by serving as an additional resource in which a persons' individual attempts at managing problems are guided and aided by the help and participation of others. Although there is a body of evidence for a buffering effect (Cohen & Syme, 1985), more exacting research methods need to be applied to the study of how received and perceived social support achieve their positive effects.

Continued study of social support has led to discoveries that not all attempts at supportiveness produce positive results. Under some circumstances, networks or activities intended to be helpful actually produce adverse consequences (Schradle & Dougher, 1985). Sometimes networks can be too large, creating a burden for the recipient to be sufficiently reciprocal in helping efforts, or diffusing the responsibility across helpers so that each individual actually reduces his or her assistance (Shumaker & Brownell, 1984). Social ties often carry conflicts with them that complicate helping efforts, especially when recipients feel as if their expectations for assistance have gone unmet (Barrera, 1981). When helping efforts become too one-sided, recipients may come to feel resentful, indebted, or less capable. When the recipient is not able to reciprocate helping efforts, he or she may feel reduced freedom or control in interactions with the donor. In some instances, potential helpers may behave in misguided ways leading the recipient to feel rejected and guilty (Wortman & Lehman, 1985).

Common Factors in Therapy and Social Support

Several investigators discuss links between social support and psychotherapy. Thoits (1986) suggests that effective support is most likely to come from socially similar others who are empathically understanding, who have faced the same stressor, and who have done so more calmly than the distressed individual. However, she goes on to say there might be an exception in the case of psychotherapists because "the client's faith in the authority and expertise of the therapist may override dissimilarities in background and experience" (Thoits, 1986, p. 421).

Winefield (1987) argues that a fine-grained look at the crucial aspects of beneficial social interactions, referred to as "events level analysis" in psychotherapy, and "disaggregation" in social support research, might yield similar findings. Both these terms refer to studying specific, moment-to-moment interactions to learn how they contribute to desired results. To the extent that each provides "opportunities for adaptive learning, by the intended beneficiary, within the context of a feeling of being personally valued" (Wortman & Conway, 1985, p. 632), both should be helpful.

As we noted at the beginning of this chapter, Wallerstein (1989), commenting on the results of the Menninger Psychotherapy Research Project, identified a pervasive presence of supportive elements in therapy, even within traditional psychoanalysis, where the success of therapy often appeared to depend on a shift of support from the therapist to a person within the patient's social network. Therapeutic benefits depended "not only on the effectiveness and self-consciousness of the therapeutic work within ongoing treatment but also on the capacity and willingness of the chosen individual to carry this transferred burden indefinitely" (Wallerstein, 1989, p. 201).

Implications for Therapists

Within the framework of individual psychotherapy, how can social support be facilitated to enhance the functioning of a client? We discuss three general issues in this regard.

A first step necessary for increasing social support is to enhance the ways a client offers, elicits, and accepts supportive behaviors from available providers. How might this step take place? Exploring the general themes of mistrust, clingy dependence, and excessive independence is often necessary. Some clients place such a premium on maintaining an image of sturdy independence that they regard turning to others for help as reflecting a moral weakness that will cause others to lose respect for them or reject them. This attitude can sometimes be countered by asking clients to reflect on how they feel when others solicit help from them. Generally, clients acknowledge feeling closer to people who occasionally look to them for assistance. The therapist then can ask clients to consider whether the same positive feelings might not accompany their own openness to others' assistance.

Clients often decide to keep their problem, whether it be a fear, an impending divorce, or discouragement with a specific area of life, a secret from important people in their lives. Initially, keeping this secret begins with a desire to spare others extra trouble, but it soon becomes an emotional burden clients feel they must maintain. Directly encouraging the client to consider disclosing the secret to one trusted confidant can be therapeutic in at least two ways: (1) The client learns that others care enough about him or her to help, and (2) the burden of keeping the secret is lifted.

Second, some potential providers of social support are good at providing practical, tangible aid in times of need; they extend a helping hand. Others are effective at listening with patience and understanding to a person's expressions of worry, doubt, or anger; they provide a sympathetic ear. Likewise, some problems require material support while others call for opportunities to ventilate feelings to an empathic listener. Therapists can help clients experiencing a crisis diagnose what kind of support a given problem most requires and who is available to best provide that kind of support.

Finally, we have learned enough about the potential negative effects of some forms of social support that we can help clients understand and accept their own ambivalent feelings about the well-intentioned, but unhelpful, assistance that is sometimes offered to them. Clients may feel guilty, resentful, criticized, coerced, or burdened by others' attempts to help them. They need to understand that such feelings are legitimate and common reactions to activities by others that are too controlling, judgmental, or overprotective or to actions that overload the recipient with responsibilities "to get better" or be appreciative. Normalizing these feelings should also be accompanied by two other therapeutic objectives. First, clients can be encouraged during a crisis to distance themselves temporarily from associates whose intended helpfulness is upsetting because of its implied messages. (Of course, if the negative effects are due to intentionally harmful acts, different strategies are merited.) Second, clients can be helped to understand that unhelpful social support often stems from the anxieties and strong feelings of compassion potential providers feel when interacting with people in need rather than from uncaring or demeaning feelings about the recipient (Lehman, Ellard, & Wortman, 1986).

Self-Help Groups

Self-help groups (SHGs) are an important community resource either in lieu of professional intervention or in addition to traditional psychotherapy. The prevalence of SHGs is difficult to estimate accurately because many groups have no formal membership rolls, and those that do often prefer to keep the names of members anonymous. Although estimates of SHG members in the U.S. range as high as 15 million persons, Jacobs and Goodman (1989) used a well-reasoned multifactorial approach to arrive at an estimate of approximately 6.25 million individuals, or 3.7% of all American adults, who are currently participants in SHGs. This number rivals the number of clients currently in psychotherapy and suggests that SHGs will become a major method of mental health care in the 1990s. Projections for SHG membership are 10 million persons by 1999. Other clinicians predict that SHGs will be *the* major treatment modality in the coming decade (Prochaska & Norcross, 1982).

Characteristics of Self-Help Groups

SHGs have been compared to miniature mental health democracies (Jacobs & Goodman, 1989) that share the following major defining characteristics:

1. Group members have a relatively well-defined, common problem and/or share a common life experience.
2. Groups meet for the purpose of exchanging information and social support, discussing mutual problems, and improving psychological functioning.
3. Groups charge small or no fees.
4. Groups are largely member-governed, but may use professionals as consultants.
5. Groups rely on fellow members (typically unpaid volunteers) as the primary caregivers.

As can be seen from these characteristics, SHGs are not professional caregiving systems, but they are more structured than informal social networks. They place more emphasis on experiential wisdom than on technical expertise, and all members try to help one another.

Types of Self-Help Groups

SHGs range in size and scope from specialized groups in a single locality serving only a handful of people to large national or international organizations with memberships of well over 100,000. Powell (1987) offers a typology of SHGs organized by five basic structural missions. First, *habit disturbance* organizations emphasize a specific behavioral change, typically to reduce or eliminate a maladaptive habit. Representative organizations include Alcoholics Anonymous (AA), Gamblers Anonymous, Weight Watchers, Narcotics Anonymous, and Smokestoppers. These organizations are some of the largest and most widely known SHGs. Second, *general purpose* organizations address a wide range of difficulties, such as dealing with the death of a child (Compassionate Friends), coping with troubling emotions of anxiety, depression, and anger (Emotions Anonymous), child abuse and neglect (Parents Anonymous), and helping nervous and former mental patients (Recovery, Inc.). Third, *lifestyle organizations* support individuals who are often the object of discrimination, such as single parents (Parents Without Partners), gays and lesbians (National Gay and Lesbian Task Force), and the elderly (Gray Panthers). Fourth, many *significant other organizations* provide advocacy, education, support, and partnership for relatives of troubled or disturbed individuals. These groups include the National Alliance for the Mentally Ill, Al-Anon (relatives of alcoholics), and Gam-Anon (relatives of compulsive gamblers). Finally, a multitude of *physical handicap organizations* support individuals with distress or disorders like epilepsy (Epilepsy Foundation), emphysema (Emphysema Anonymous), cerebral palsy (Cerebral Palsy Association), and open-heart surgery patients (Mended Hearts).

Mechanisms of Change in Self-Help Groups

In examining the processes which foster changes in SHG members, Levy (1979) identified four broad behaviorally oriented processes occurring in SHGs. Members receive both direct and vicarious social reinforcement for maintaining desirable behaviors and eliminating maladaptive behaviors. Training, indoctrination, and support in a number of self-control behaviors are given. Additionally, members are exposed to modeling of methods of coping with stress and changing behavior. Finally, members are provided with an agenda of actions to change their social environment.

Levy (1979) discusses a survey of 72 SHG members representing seven different organizations who were asked which help-giving activities they used most frequently. The nine *most* common activities were empathy, mutual affirmation, explanation, sharing, morale building, self-disclosure, positive reinforcement, personal goal setting, and catharsis. The nine *least* frequent activities were confrontation, punishment, requesting feedback, behavioral rehearsal, offering feedback, extinction, modeling, reference to group norms, and behavioral prescription. Therefore, the general atmosphere of these SHGs appears more safe and supportive, as opposed to controlling or threatening.

Similarly, Levy identified several cognitively oriented processes in SHGs, including demystifying the disturbing, frightening, and alienating experiences members share, increasing members' expectancies for change by providing them with a rationale for their problems, offering normative information and advice, providing support for changes in attitudes about oneself and others, and introducing social comparison and consensual validation to reduce members' uncertainty and isolation.

Further understanding of SHG dynamics is given by Riessman's (1965) "helper-therapy" concept, or simply put, those who help are helped most themselves. A primary benefit from the group experience may come from helping another member in the group. Skovholt (1974) noted the following potential benefits from helping: increased interpersonal competence from making an impact on another person's life; a feeling of equality in giving and receiving with others; receiving valuable information about one's own problems; and receiving social approval. Finally, Gartner and Riesmann (1984) add that helpers may feel less dependent on others, observe their own problems at a greater distance, and feel socially useful.

Effectiveness of Self-Help Groups

Empirically based outcome studies of SHGs are severely lacking. Levy (1984) notes that SHGs historically have not questioned their own effectiveness and have consequently seen no need for scientific evaluation. Also, most SHGs have operated outside the formal health care delivery system, and have not had to be officially accountable for the effectiveness of their programs. SHG outcome research is difficult for several reasons. Definition of the appropriate criteria for group evaluation is thorny; individual group members, the group as a whole, and the researcher may each define goals for improvement in different ways. Generalization of results is limited in many instances because of the great heterogeneity among different chapters of an organization. A related problem is self-selection of members, which can result in groups comprised of individuals displaying a great range of problems of markedly diverse levels of severity and chronicity.

Keeping these methodological difficulties in mind, there are a limited number of outcome studies showing somewhat mixed results on the benefits of participation in SHGs. For example, Lieberman, Bond, Solow, and Reibstein (1979) noted that participants in a women's consciousness-raising group showed increased self-esteem and reduced distress on various self-identified problems which were targeted at the beginning of the group. Videka (1979) studied Mended Hearts, a SHG for heart surgery patients and their spouses. There were very few significant differences in psychosocial adaptation to heart surgery between members and nonmembers; members did seem to benefit psychologically from visiting other prospective heart surgery patients. Lieberman & Gourash (1979) studied SAGE (Senior Actualization and Growth Explorations), a SHG for the elderly, and found that group members had fewer psychiatric symptoms (e.g., anxiety and depression) and greater increases in self-esteem than a control group. However, fears about illness were not reduced, and frequency of health-related behaviors did not change.

Additional studies indicate that SHG participants have shown better postpartum adjustments than nonmembers (Gordon, Kapostins, & Gordon, 1965), improvements in communication ability following laryngectomy (Katz, 1981), reduced feelings of hopelessness (Levens, 1968), and higher "quality of life" ratings (Raiff, 1982). A group of acutely bereaved widows showed no benefit from participation in a SHG for the newly widowed (Bankoff, 1979), but widows' groups have been credited with increasing social interactions and self-esteem (Barrett, 1978). Powell (1987) concluded that SHG members who actively participate on a long-term basis show "moderately positive" improvement; more passive members find lesser benefits from the group.

Collaboration Between Self-Help Groups and Practitioners

Many SHGs were established to combat the lack of professional services for a number of mental health problems. A notable example was the founding of the National Alliance for the Mentally Ill (NAMI) in 1979, which started as a network of support groups for families of the chronically mentally ill in response to deinstitutionalization and the concomitant lack of adequate community resources for the mentally ill. NAMI has since expanded into a nationwide advocacy and education organization representing more than 70,000 families (Backer & Richardson, 1989). As Levy (1979) stated, "one might well look to those areas where self-help groups have developed as the points where it [society] has failed in one or more of its functions" (p. 235).

There is some evidence that several SHGs have a bias against professional help (Barish, 1971) and distrust professionals (Back & Taylor, 1976). However, experienced professionals were involved in the founding and support of several SHGs, and many SHGs regularly use professionals in a consultative capacity. Finally, most SHG members use professional help *more* than do nonmembers (Borman & Lieberman, 1979). Therefore, the view that all SHGs are antiprofessional is a misconception. As for professionals' views toward SHGs, some SHGs are almost universally accepted and frequently utilized by professional therapists. Alcohol abusers are *routinely* referred to AA as a part of their treatment program, and many mental health facilities even have their own chapter of AA on the grounds of the institution. In contrast, many SHGs are virtually unknown to mental health professionals; others may be publicly visible but viewed indifferently by practitioners.

Opportunities for collaboration between SHGs and professional clinicians exist that could be beneficial to both parties. For example, Wollert, Knight, and Levy (1980) collaborated with Make Today Count, a SHG for people adjusting to life-threatening illnesses. The researchers studied the group intensely and suggested numerous organizational changes to improve the group, which were well received by the members. Based on their experience, the authors offer a model for collaboration between mental health professionals and SHGs: First, professionals should obtain an adequate knowledge of the workings of the SHG. Second, effective rapport between the group and the professional should be achieved. Third, an appropriate model for consultation is that it be long-term, nonevaluative, and group centered. In short, professionals should view themselves as organizational consultants.

Guidelines for Practitioners

One particular advantage of referring clients to SHGs as an adjunct to psychotherapy is to provide support in areas that may not necessarily be the primary focus of psychotherapy, but are distressing to the client nonetheless. For example, a depressed client is likely to seek psychotherapy to combat depressive feelings. However, this same individual may also have chronic emphysema, which contributes to the depression in specific ways, as the disease is stressful and often fatiguing. Referral, in this case, to a local Emphysema Anonymous group would afford the individual the support of others who are coping with a similar experience. Loss of a job because of general economic conditions is another example where referral to a SHG might lead to appropriate social support than would be possible with psychotherapy alone.

˹ Additionally, participation in SHGs can provide clients with a direct complement to the content of psychotherapy sessions. Lieberman et al. (1979) noted that many women in consciousness-raising SHGs were also receiving professional psychotherapy concurrently. Some of these women noted the SHG brought out material for later therapy sessions, and bolstered changes initiated in therapy.

SHGs provide support, reinforcement, sanctions, norms, and feedback to their members about a broad array of problems. Evidence that SHGs are typically more task oriented, more structured, and more devoted to practical problem solving than traditional psychotherapy groups (Toro, Rappaport, & Seidman, 1987) suggests that they might be particularly useful in helping clients set limits on undesirable, acting-out behaviors. This goal happens to be one with which many psychotherapists, who are often oriented toward helping clients become more expressive and socially extraverted, are not entirely comfortable nor adroit in addressing.

Powell (1987) lists six strategies for professionals to make effective referrals to SHGs:

1. Confer with contact persons in the SHG.
2. Discuss the rationale for the recommendation with the client.
3. Make self-help literature and brochures available to the client.
4. Discuss the option of selective participation in SHG activities rather than overcommitting by trying to take part in the entire program.

5. Develop a joint plan with the client to explore the SHG.
6. Discuss the client's first contacts and later experiences with the SHG.

Much more systematic evaluation of SHGs effectiveness is needed. This task will be difficult from a methodological standpoint, because SHGs do not lend themselves readily to typical research designs or questions. However, because SHGs will continue to be a valuable resource in the total spectrum of mental health care, practitioners should become more familiar with the functions, variety, and potential benefits of SHGs.

Other Self-Help Aids

Self-help books have attained boom status in the publication industry. Thousands of titles are now available for a gamut of problems spanning educational, intellectual, emotional, sexual, marital, interpersonal, developmental, occupational, and existential issues. Clinicians have been prolific in writing bibliotherapeutic materials especially on such bread-and-butter problems as depression (Lewinsohn, Munoz, Youngren, & Zeiss, 1986), obesity (Epstein & Squires, 1988), phobias (Wolpe, 1981), sexual dysfunction (Zeiss & Zeiss, 1978), shyness (Zimbardo, 1977), and insomnia (Coates & Thoresen, 1977). Rosen (1987) reports there are more than 150 published self-help programs written from a behavioral perspective alone. The popularity of these materials suggests that "Read a self-help book and call me in the morning" will soon become the psychotherapist's equivalent to the physicians's well-known aspirin prescription. The only constraint on the growth of self-help books may be technological; self-help autiotapes, videos, cassettes, and discs threaten to make written materials obsolete. Radio talk shows hosted by mental health professionals are another form of self-help and advice that have the advantages of ready availability and no expense, and have some preliminary empirical support for their helpfulness (Levy, 1989).

Practicing clinicians generally view self-help materials favorably. In a survey of 121 psychologists in Boston/Cambridge and San Diego, Starker (1988) found that over 65% believed self-help books were helpful to clients, and more than 60% of these therapists had encouraged their clients to read them at some point. Very few therapists believed that self-help books harmed clients. The most frequent areas for recommended reading were parenting (54.8% of the therapists had prescribed a reading on this topic), personal growth (39.7%), and relationship problems (38.4%).

The widespread acceptance of self-help books, along with the interesting finding that psychodynamically oriented therapists were less positive about their use in treatment (Starker, 1988), points to some intriguing trends about psychotherapy. First, an emphasis on active coping, personal choice, and client responsibility rather than unconscious dynamics, historical determinants, and transference issues is consistent with a rational/educational approach to therapy in which the client is included as an informed decision maker rather than a passive recipient of services. Self-help materials fit well within a rational/educational perspective on therapy.

Second, self-help materials can extend the therapy process by focusing clients on issues that can be carefully contemplated and then discussed at subsequent sessions. For example, a mother who is concerned about the aggressiveness, noncompliance, and sassiness of her grade-school son could be assigned chapters 11 and 12 in Gerald Patterson's (1975) *Families* and asked to think about how the events described therein compare to her own experiences. The subsequent session could then be devoted to developing and tailoring an intervention that was appropriate to the specific needs of her family.

Third, self-help materials can sometimes introduce clients to sensitive or threatening topics (e.g., sexual or marital problems) that they would otherwise postpone or avoid discussing with their therapist. This facilitative effect is promoted when the assigned material reassures clients that their problems are common ones at the same time that it convinces them that treatment can be helpful. Finally, bibliotherapy offers the possibility of greater cost effectiveness, no small consideration in this age of capped coverage for mental health treatment benefits.

Critics of self-help materials have decried the lack of empirical research evaluating their effectiveness and have warned against the ethical problems presented by commercial promoters who make extravagant promises about these products (Rosen, 1976, 1987). Rosen (1989) even organized "the First Annual Golden Fleece Awards for Do-It-Yourself Psychotherapies" to be presented at the APA convention as part of a program to call attention to the possible dangers of such materials. The call for evaluative research has not gone unanswered, however. Recent self-help formats have consistently been shown to be as effective as therapist-directed treatment, at least for problems such as insomnia (Morawetz, 1989) and moderate depression in the elderly (Scogin, Hamblin, & Beutler, 1987). Of course, these studies are evaluating a more "extreme" version of self-help materials than that used by most therapists who typically integrate bibliotherapeutic material into ongoing personal therapy and carefully monitor their clients' interpretation of assigned material. To our knowledge, the effects of supplemental bibliotherapy on the process and outcome of therapy have not been rigorously tested.

Although the risks of therapist-guided bibliotherapy appear to be minimal, we would urge caution in two areas. First, some clients tend to be compulsive readers of self-help books, approaching each new publication as a panacea which, if studied diligently enough, will be their salvation. Inevitably, they are demoralized when the promised changes do not occur or do not last, and they lose some faith that durable change will ever be possible for them. Second, advice books sometimes lead clients to self-diagnose their problems, often with faddish labels that seem to "explain everything about me" but which actually discourage clients from a more careful examination of their lives. As with all therapeutic inputs, self-help information should be processed in the context of an ongoing therapeutic relationship where the client feels free to examine and explore its full meaning.

Contexts for Change

A therapist who uses natural community and network resources is aiming for one of two broad goals. First, the therapist is interested in helping the client learn about new alternatives in behavior, lifestyle, relationships, beliefs, or activities. For any of several reasons—misinformation, limited experience, practical constraints, or false assumptions—clients may not be aware of their alternatives. Natural resources may make the best teachers of these lessons, but it is the therapist's responsibility to help the client become accessible to them. The second goal when using community and network resources is to help the client become involved in activities that will be esteem enhancing. By facilitating new social interactions for the client, the therapist increases opportunities for the client to derive better self-esteem as a result of reflecting both on new accomplishments and the positive appraisals provided by others (Heller et al., 1986). Recalling William James's (1890) formula for self-esteem as our successes divided by our pretensions, the therapist realizes it is usually easier to increase the client's numerator than decrease the denominator.

How best to promote these goals is a major question, currently unanswered on empirical grounds. However, there are several clinical intuitions that can provide guidance about the best ways to tap natural therapeutic resources (see chapter 8 of this volume for more discussion of these techniques). First, the techniques of diary-keeping, contracting, and role-playing are primary vehicles for transporting the client back-and-forth between therapy sessions and the natural context. Diaries are excellent tools for helping clients perform detailed and accurate assessments of important events in their personal lives and for communicating spontaneous interpretations of their life context to therapists. "Contracting the context" involves forging agreements with the client about "homework" or "experiments" the client will be willing to conduct in order to see what differences might result from changes in his or her own behavior. The rationale given for homework is crucial. If the client is led to believe that contracted changes will improve the behavior of another person, enhance a relationship, or win the boss over, the most probable outcomes are disappointment and reduced enthusiasm for the next contract to be proposed. Homework should be presented as a chance for clients to learn something about themselves. It is everyday empiricism at work, aimed not at changing others but at revealing new knowledge to the client. It enables the client to explore the benefits of uncertainty. If others should also change as a result of the experiment, that is an extra benefit.

George Kelly's (1955) practice of *fixed-role therapy* is unsurpassed as an example of how to foster a spirit of collaborative curiosity and experimentation with a client. After contemplating and rehearsing new behaviors or plans in therapy sessions with clients, Kelly would encourage his clients to try them out in real life, just once or for a short while, in order to see whether clients' existing constructs or anticipations were correct. An additional tactic was to challenge clients to make a prediction about the outcomes of various tests because Kelly believed that clients would be unable to resist trying an experiment if they had made a specific prediction about it (Phares, 1988).

How much preparation/rehearsal is necessary before a client attempts assigned homework is a question that requires careful assessment by the therapist. Three dimensions need to be addressed: the general skills required to perform the skills; the level of competence in these skills the specific client possesses; and how supportive of new and uncertain performance by the client the environment is likely to be. In general, a structuring of tasks along desensitization-hierarchy principles is advised. Start with the easiest tasks in front of the most charitable audience and then gradually increase the level of difficulty. One does not want to send out the meek, shy client to begin practicing assertion skills with a bully when there is a gentle soul in the neighborhood.

Clinical experience suggests that there are several contexts where the therapist can prescribe homework to promote new learning and boost self-esteem. Obsessive-compulsive clients find novel tasks involving the use of leisure time to be particularly challenging and instructive (see DiLorenzo, Prue, & Scott, 1987, for a discussion of "leisure therapy"). Introverted clients often find it easiest to practice and hone social skills in structured environments such as work or church groups. Neurotically perfectionistic clients are usually willing to commit deliberate, small mistakes in the privacy of their home and thereby discover the pleasure of a little less super-ego; paradoxically orchestrated errors in a more public forum such as one's job are much riskier. Substantial improvements in self-concept, particularly among depressed clients, have been linked to involvement in a regular exercise regimen (Doyne, Chambless, & Beutler, 1983; Ossip–Klein et al., 1989).

One general way in which the therapist can consider the role of the client's overall context is to help the client learn to solicit helpful advice, interactions, and support from the people with whom the client has regular contact. A reasonable goal of psychotherapy is to increase clients' ability to attract and maintain social support for themselves (Winefield, 1987). In fact, it is possible that this result is an important, but neglected, mediator of therapeutic change. In a preliminary investigation of this issue, Cross, Sheehan, and Khan (1980) compared the extent to which clients receiving different types of psychotherapy sought informal advice or counsel from sources other than the therapist. Fifteen clients receiving short-term, insight-oriented therapy were matched on demographic variables and compared to 15 clients receiving behavior therapy and 12 no-treatment controls in terms of how much outside-of-therapy, alternative advice they sought, how much advice was offered to them by others, and how much of this advice they accepted. The results indicated that both treatment groups sought more informal advice from others (friends and neighbors were the most popular sources) by the end of therapy than did the control subjects. Recipients of behavior therapy sought more informal contacts than did participants in insight-oriented treatment. The amount of alternative advice offered to treated clients increased over the course of therapy, but not significantly so. While both treatment groups tended to accept more advice than controls by the end of therapy, behavior therapy participants accepted more advice than did the insight-oriented group.

Two implications of these data merit special attention for our concerns here. First, the positive association between being in therapy and making increased use of alternative sources of advice and counsel suggests that therapy might achieve some of its positive effects by facilitating clients' openness to the helpful influences of others in their lives. Perhaps therapy primes clients to become more receptive to the untutored, anti-neurotic experiences that everyday life provides. Second, the greater use of alternative advice by behavioral versus insight-oriented clients is intriguing. Are the different styles or goals of these treatments linked to this outcome? Possibly the teacher-student version of the therapeutic relationship championed by many behavior therapists carries over to other interactions, allowing clients to have more positive expectations about their encounters with others. Alternatively, the more exclusive nature of the therapeutic relationship in psychodynamic treatment might foster a greater sense of independence in clients. These possibilities need empirical study.

LIMITATIONS AND ETHICAL CONCERNS

Although many of the hidebound, doctrinaire objections to the methods discussed in this chapter have gradually yielded to a more balanced acceptance of using natural supports and community resources, obstacles do remain. We discuss a few of these obstacles in this last portion of this chapter.

Therapists are very accustomed to clients expressing their misgivings and ambivalence about beginning therapy because of the implication that, having failed to "solve" their problems on their own, they are weaker, less capable, and/or more disturbed than persons not seeking professional help. Therapists also understand the importance of normalizing this fear at the same time they help clients arrive at an alternative view of the process—the decision to seek professional help is a courageous one taken by people prepared to look at how they want to change their lives. Is it possible that a counterpart to this view, held by therapists rather than by clients, deters therapists from considering the use of community resources and sources of mutual help? Perhaps therapists sometimes feel that changes brought about through a combination of in-session techniques and extra-therapy experiences is a diminished or second-rate accomplishment in comparison to changes crafted entirely within the therapy session proper. Of course, the antidote for this feeling is understanding that good therapy prepares the soil for new ideas to grow. Who plants the seed is less important than making sure the conditions for growth are maintained.

A second complication in the full therapeutic use of natural resources and supports is the tension that exists between context theories of behavior and the clinical principle that clients need to take individual responsibility for their own behavior. How does one help clients understand the multiple, interrelated, reciprocal influences in their lives without discouraging them from taking active, relatively autonomous steps toward change? Can too much insight cause the client to think that personal changes are not possible because their past behavior is so complexly determined? Clinical experience suggests that such "paralysis" is not likely when the therapist and client continue to focus on learning what effects changes made by the client will have on the context.

A third problem, related at least in part to therapists' sometimes ambivalent feelings about the use of self-help organizations or support groups, is that the groups themselves may be suspicious of the therapist, reluctant to work collaboratively with the therapist, or sabotaging of certain therapy strategies. In practice, such problems prove to be rare when the therapist remains committed to the value of integrating naturalized help efforts with the therapy. In those rare instances where problems of collaboration do arise, they can usually be resolved successfully if the therapist processes the issues fully with the client during therapy.

A fourth potential difficulty concerns ethics, particularly the area of confidentiality. The therapeutic use of context will sometimes require information to be shared with others that would otherwise not be shared. As one obvious example, family members may be consulted and included in some therapy sessions. Such a step requires that the client and therapist always carefully discuss it first so that the client can make an informed decision about how the matter is to be handled.

We also believe it is important to recognize that the clinical consideration and use of context can carry some distinctive ethical advantages. For example, the ethical practice of psychotherapy obligates psychologists to "recognize the boundaries of their competence and the limitations of their techniques" (APA, "Ethical Principles of Psychologists," 1990). While this section of Principle 2 is often interpreted as meaning that psychologists should not offer services for which they do not have proper training, it also implies that psychologists should understand the limits of those techniques even in which they have superb training. Psychotherapy can produce positive changes, but the size and durability of those changes depend on the overall context in which a client must function. A realization that psychotherapy, by itself, has inherent limits to its power is necessary on both ethical and empirical grounds. However, such a view is not a reason for apology or discouragement, when coupled with a therapist's willingness to explore ways in which natural supports and community resources can complement the therapy process.

REFERENCES

American Psychological Association. (1990). Ethical principles of psychologists. *American Psychologist, 45,* 390–395.

Back, K. W., & Taylor, R. C. (1976). Self-help groups: Tool or symbol? *Journal of Applied Behavioral Science, 12,* 295–309.

Backer, T. E., & Richardson, D. (1989). Building bridges: Psychologists and families of the mentally ill. *American Psychologist, 44,* 546–550.

Bankoff, E. A. (1979). Widow groups as an alternative to informal social support. In M. A. Lieberman & L. D. Borman (Eds.), *Self-help groups for coping with crisis: Origins, members, processes, and impact* (pp. 181–193). San Francisco: Jossey-Bass.

Barish, H. (1971). Self-help groups. In *The Encyclopedia of Social Work* (Vol. 2, pp. 1163–1169). New York: National Association of Social Workers.

Barrera, M. (1981). Social support in the adjustment of pregnant adolescents: Assessment issues. In B. H. Gottlieb (Ed.), *Social networks and social support* (pp. 69–96). Beverly Hills, CA: Sage.

Barrett, C. J. (1978). Effectiveness of widows' groups in facilitating change. *Journal of Consulting and Clinical Psychology, 46,* 20–31.

Bernheim, K. F. (1989). Psychologists and families of the severely mentally ill: The role of family consultation. *American Psychologist, 44,* 561–564.

Borman, L. D., & Lieberman, M. A. (1979). Conclusion: Contributions, dilemmas, and implications for mental health policy. In M. A. Lieberman & L. D. Borman (Eds.), *Self-help groups for coping with crisis: Origins, members, processes, and impact* (pp. 406–430). San Francisco: Jossey-Bass.

Brody, E. M., & Farber, B. A. (1989). Effects of psychotherapy on significant others. *Professional Psychology: Research and Practice, 20,* 116–122.

Coates, T., & Thoresen, C. E. (1977). *How to sleep better: A drug-free program for overcoming insomnia.* Englewood Cliffs, NJ: Prentice-Hall.

Cohen, S., & Syme, S. L. (Eds.). (1985). *Social support and health.* Orlando, FL: Academic Press.

Cross, D. A., Sheehan, P. W., & Khan, J. A. (1980). Alternative advice and counsel in psychotherapy. *Journal of Consulting and Clinical Psychology, 48,* 615–625.

DiLorenzo, T. M., Prue, D. M., & Scott, R. R. (1987). A conceptual critique of leisure assessment and therapy: An added dimension to behavioral medicine and substance abuse treatment. *Clinical Psychology Review, 7,* 597–610.

Doyne, E. J., Chambless, D. L., & Beutler, L. E. (1983). Aerobic exercise as a treatment for depression in women. *Behavior Therapy, 14,* 434–440.

Epstein, L. H., & Squires, S. (1988). *The stop-light diet for children.* Boston: Little, Brown.

Freud, S. (1912). Recommendations for physicians on the psychoanalytic method of treatment. In P. Reiff (Trans. & Ed.), *Freud: Therapy and technique* (pp. 117–126). New York: Collier Books (1963).

Freud, S. (1913). Further recommendations in the technique of psychoanalysis. In P. Reiff (Trans. & Ed.), *Freud: Therapy and technique* (pp. 135–156). New York: Collier Books (1963).

Freud, S. (1919). Turnings in the ways of psychoanalytic therapy. In P. Reiff (Trans. & Ed.), *Freud: Therapy and technique* (pp. 181–190). New York: Collier Books (1963).

Gartner, A., & Riessman, F. (1984). Introduction. In A. Gartner & F. Riessman (Eds.), *The self-help revolution* (pp. 17–23). New York: Human Sciences Press.

Gordon, R. D., Kapostins, E. E., & Gordon, K. K. (1965). Factors in post-partum emotional adjustment. *Obstetrical Gynecology, 25,* 156–166.

Heller, K., Swindle, R. W., Jr., & Dusenbury, L. (1986). Component social support processes: Comments and integration. *Journal of Consulting and Clinical Psychology, 54*, 466–470.

Jacobs, M. K., & Goodman, G. (1989). Psychology and self-help groups: Predictions on a partnership. *American Psychologist, 44*, 536–545.

Jacobson, N. S. (1989). The maintenance of treatment gains following social learning-based marital therapy. *Behavior Therapy, 20*, 325–336.

Jacobson, N. S., Holtzworth–Munroe, A., & Schmaling, K. B. (1989). Marital therapy and spouse involvement in the treatment of depression, agoraphobia, and alcoholism. *Journal of Consulting and Clinical Psychology, 57*, 5–10.

James, W. (1890). *The principles of psychology.* New York: Holt, Rinehart & Winston.

Katz, A. H. (1981). Self-help and mutual aid. *Annual Review of Sociology, 7*, 129–155.

Kelly, G. A. (1955). *The psychology of personal constructs* (Vols. 1 & 2). New York: W. W. Norton.

Leary, T. F. (1957). *Interpersonal diagnosis of personality.* New York: Ronald Press.

Lehman, D. R., Ellard, J. H., & Wortman, C. B. (1986). Social supports for the bereaved: Recipients' and providers' perspectives on what is helpful. *Journal of Consulting and Clinical Psychology, 54*, 438–446.

Levens, H. (1968). Organizational affiliation and powerlessness: A case study of the welfare poor. *Social Problems, 16* (October), 18–32.

Levy, D. A. (1989). Social support and the media: Analysis of responses by radio talk show hosts. *Professional Psychology: Research and Practice, 20*, 73–78.

Levy, L. H. (1979). Processes and activities in groups. In M. A. Lieberman & L. D. Borman (Eds.), *Self-help groups for coping with crisis: Origins, members, processes, and impact* (pp. 234–271). San Francisco: Jossey-Bass.

Levy, L. H. (1984). Issues in research and evaluation. In A. Gartner & F. Riessman (Eds.), *The self-help revolution* (pp. 155–172). New York: Human Sciences Press.

Lewinsohn, P., Munoz, R., Youngren, M. A., & Zeiss A. (1986). *Control your depression.* Englewood Cliffs, NJ: Prentice-Hall.

Lieberman, M. A. (1986). Social supports—the consequences of psychologizing: A commentary. *Journal of Consulting and Clinical Psychology, 54*, 461–465.

Lieberman, M. A., Bond, G. R., Solow, N., & Reibstein, J. (1979). Effectiveness of women's consciousness raising. In M. A. Lieberman & L. D. Borman (Eds.), *Self-help groups for coping with crisis: Origins, members, processes, and impact* (pp. 387–405). San Francisco: Jossey-Bass.

Lieberman, M. A., & Gourash, N. (1979). Effects of change groups on the elderly. In M. A. Lieberman & L. D. Borman (Eds.), *Self-help groups for coping with crisis: Origins, members, processes, and impact* (pp. 387–405). San Francisco: Jossey-Bass.

Morawetz, D. (1989). Behavioral self-help treatment for insomnia: A controlled evaluation. *Behavior Therapy, 20*, 365–380.

Ossip–Klein, D. J., Doyne, E. J., Bowman, E. D., Osborn, K. M., McDougall–Wilson, I. B., & Neimeyer, R. A. (1989). Effects of running or weight lifting on self-concept in clinically depressed women. *Journal of Consulting and Clinical Psychology, 57*, 158–161.

Patterson, G. R. (1975). *Families: Applications of social learning to family life.* Champaign, IL: Research Press.

Phares, E. J. (1988). *Introduction to personality* (2nd ed.). Glenview, IL: Scott, Foresman.

Powell, T. J. (1987). *Self-help organizations and professional practice.* Silver Spring, MD: National Association of Social Workers.

Prochaska, J. D., & Norcross, J. C. (1982). The future of psychotherapy: A Delphi poll. *Professional Psychology, 13*, 620–627.

Raiff, N. R. (1982). Self-help participation and quality of life: A study of the staff of Recovery, Inc. *Prevention in Human Services, 1,* 79–89.

Rappaport, J. (1981). In praise of paradox: A social policy of empowerment over prevention. *American Journal of Community Psychology, 9,* 1–25.

Riessman, F. (1965). The "helper-therapy" principle. *Social Work, 10,* 27–32.

Rosen, G. M. (1976). The development and use of nonprescription behavior therapies. *American Psychologist, 31,* 139–141.

Rosen, G. M. (1987). Self-help treatment books and the commercialization of psychotherapy. *American Psychologist, 42,* 46–51.

Rosen, G. M. (1989). Call for nominations. *The Clinical Psychologist, 42,* 71.

Rosnow, R. L., & Rosenthal, R. (1989). Statistical procedures and the justification of knowledge in psychological science. *American Psychologist, 44,* 1276–1284.

Schradle, S. B., & Dougher, M. J. (1985). Social support as a mediator of stress: Theoretical and empirical issues. *Clinical Psychology Review, 5,* 641–662.

Scogin, F., Hamblin, D., & Beutler, L. E. (1987). Bibliotherapy for depressed older adults: A self-help alternative. *The Gerontologist, 27,* 383–387.

Shumaker, S. A., & Brownell, A. (1984). Toward a theory of social support: Closing conceptual gaps. *Journal of Social Issues, 40,* 11–36.

Skovholt, T. M. (1974). The client as helper: A means to promote psychological growth. *Counseling Psychologist, 4,* 58–64.

Starker, S. (1988). Do-it-yourself therapy: The prescription of self-help books by psychologists. *Psychotherapy, 25,* 142–146.

Thoits, P. A. (1982). Conceptual, methodological, and theoretical problems in studying social support as a buffer against life stress. *Journal of Health and Social Behavior, 23,* 145–149.

Thoits, P. A. (1986). Social support as coping assistance. *Journal of Consulting and Clinical Psychology, 54,* 416–423.

Toro, P. A., Rappaport, J., & Seidman, E. (1987). Social climate comparison of mutual help and psychotherapy groups. *Journal of Consulting and Clinical Psychology, 55,* 430–431.

Vaux, A. (1988). *Social support: Theory, research and intervention.* New York: Praeger.

Videka, L. (1979). Psychosocial adaptation in a medical self-help group. In M. A. Lieberman & L. D. Borman (Eds.), *Self-help groups for coping with crisis: Origins, members, processes, and impact* (pp. 362–386). San Francisco: Jossey-Bass.

von Bertalanffy, L. (1956). General system theory. *General Systems, 1,* 1–10.

von Bertalanffy, L. (1968a). *General system theory.* New York: George Braziller.

von Bertalanffy, L. (1968b). *Organismic psychology and systems theory.* Barre, MA: Clark University Press.

Wallerstein, R. S. (1989). The psychotherapy research project of the Menninger Foundation: An overview. *Journal of Consulting and Clinical Psychology, 57,* 195–205.

Wiggins, J., & Broughton, R. (1985). The interpersonal circle: A structural model for the integration of personality research. In R. Hogan & W. H. Jones (Eds.), *Perspectives in personality* (pp. 1–47). Greenwich, CT: JAI Press.

Winefield, H. R. (1987). Psychotherapy and social support: Parallels and differences in the helping process. *Clinical Psychology Review, 7,* 631–644.

Wollert, R. W., Knight, B., & Levy, L. H. (1980). Make Today Count: A collaborative model for professionals and self-help groups. *Professional Psychology, 1,* 130–138.

Wolpe, J. (1981). *Our useless fears.* Boston: Houghton-Mifflin.

Wortman, C. B., & Conway, T. L. (1985). Social support and recovery from illness. In S. Cohen & S. L. Syme (Eds.), *The role of social support in adaptation and recovery from physical illness* (pp. 281–302). Orlando, FL: Academic Press.

Wortman, C. B., & Lehman, D. R. (1985). Reactions to victims of life crises: Support attempts that fail. In I. G. Sarason & B. R. Sarason (Eds.), *Social support; Theory, research, and applications* (pp. 463–489). Dordrecht, The Netherlands: Martinus Nijhoff.

Wynne, L., Weber, T. T., & McDaniel, S. H. (Eds.). (1986). *Systems consultation: A new perspective for family therapy*. New York: Guilford Press.

Zeiss, R. A., & Zeiss, A. (1978). *Prolong your pleasure*. New York: Pocket Books.

Zimbardo, P. G. (1977). *Shyness*. New York: Berkley.

11
Group Methods
Sheldon D. Rose
Craig Winston LeCroy

The group consisted of five women and three men in their late 20s and 30s. All were unmarried or separated. This was the fifth session of the group designed to help singles cope more effectively with their unique stresses. As the group settled into places on the floor or on chairs, Harriet, the group therapist, welcomed them and asked each member to review what he or she had done throughout the week to complete the assignment of the previous week. One at a time, members described their social achievements, their success in coping with anxiety, and the frequency with which they used the relaxation exercise. Several also related unusually stressful situations they had experienced during the week.

After each had summarized her or his experiences, amid a great deal of praise and support from group members for achievements, Delores volunteered to describe in some detail her situation, in which her ever-present feelings of helplessness were intensified. Her supervisor at her office, she stated, was always giving her instructions on the least little thing. "It was as if she thought I was stupid and, frankly, I'm beginning to believe it." The other members inquired as to the nature of her job, which was quite complicated. They noted that she did receive good feedback from her peers, who often consulted with her with various problems. She also noted that in a previous job no one gave her more than the briefest instructions, and she did fine. Charles wondered whether she couldn't conclude that there was a problem between her and her supervisor and not with her as a person. There was just no evidence that she was dumb in any way; in fact, she appeared to be uniquely qualified to do the job. The others agreed.

Delores said she guessed they were right, but she didn't know what to do about it, and it was making her miserable. She had thought about quitting, but it was in other ways a good job; and besides, she added, "good jobs were hard to get these days."

After careful questioning by the other clients in order to have a clear picture of what was going on, they then provided her with a number of strategies she could employ to deal with the situation and suggested what she could specifically say to herself and to her supervisor. She evaluated and selected several from among these for practice in the group.

This excerpt is taken from the beginning of a cognitive-behavioral group therapy session. Such therapy within the context of the group focuses on the development of cognitive, affective, and social coping skills necessary to improve the quality of each client's relationships with others and to help group members cope more effectively with the numerous stress and problematic situations with which they are confronted. Through various highly specific procedures, a client is helped to learn not only a wide variety of verbal and nonverbal coping behaviors and cognitive skills, but also to differentiate among those situations that require the application of such skills. Essential in this process is the mutual support, teaching, demonstrations, and feedback that group members give each other. Cognitive-behavioral group therapy draws on a number of specific techniques, many of which are described elsewhere in detail in this volume. For example, modeling theory and procedures are the major themes of chapter 4. Cognitive methods, such as restructuring and problem solving, are covered in chapter 7. Finally, role-playing and homework are well represented in chapter 8. In this chapter, we will emphasize how these very same procedures are administered in a group. Cognitive behavioral group therapy can be looked on as a continuum from short-term training to intensive long-term therapy (Shoemaker, 1977). At the training end of the continuum, groups focus on teaching a narrow range of highly specific behaviors such as assertion, parenting skills, marital communication, and stress reduction. The tools are brief lecture, specific social interactive exercises, and cognitive-behavioral techniques applied in a group, especially social skill training. Because of the restricted number of sessions, a highly specific agenda at each meeting is used, and only limited flexibility is permitted. Most research on small group therapy has evaluated this type of program.

At the intensive therapy end of the continuum, all the interventions mentioned may be used, but individualization is greater. Group problems and processes are dealt with as learning experiences, and the structured exercises used in training are also included if the group members reveal a common need. Moreover, the problems are usually more complex and more varied in therapy groups than in the training groups. Because of greater individualization, more attention is also given to pregroup assessment in the long-term therapy groups than in short-term training groups. Although both groups are at different extremes of the continuum, they follow many of the same principles described in this chapter.

What kinds of clients are seen in cognitive-behavioral group therapy? Most group members present at least one and often several of the following problems: social skill deficits, depression, phobias, anxiety, stress, sexual disorders, pain management, anger or violence control, obesity or weight control, alcohol and drug abuse, and child management. In the short-term groups, most members are referred or refer themselves for one of these problems in response to a group specifically available for that given problem, for example, a parent-training group, an assertiveness group, a weight loss group. Because all members have similar problems, the assumption is that one can work more quickly on the specific area if everyone has similar goals. In the longer term groups, a more heterogeneous composition in terms of presenting problems is possible.

What all these groups of clients hold in common is the use of the group as the context of therapy. This context provides a number of unique possibilities that the group therapist assumes can enhance (but can also hinder) the therapeutic process. The approach described in this chapter emphasizes how the more common behavioral and cognitive-behavioral strategies can be uniquely applied in the group context and how an assortment of strategies unique to the group can be incorporated into the approach.

THE GROUP CONTEXT

The most crucial aspect of group therapy is the context in which it takes place. A number of advantages and limitations of the group are assumed that both guide and constrain the therapist's role. The most fundamental assumption is that the presence of other clients provides a unique opportunity for practicing new social interactional skills with peers in a protected setting.

The group provides clients with an opportunity to recognize and change many behaviors and cognitions as the clients respond to the constantly changing group demands and challenges. The group structure encourages clients to offer other clients feedback about their behavior and to offer advice about behaviors more appropriate to their situations. By helping others, clients are also afforded practice in the skills required to help themselves.

As clients interact with each other, norms (informal agreements among members as to preferred modes of action and interaction in the group) are developed to which members pressure each other to conform. If protherapeutic norms are introduced and effectively maintained by the group therapist, these norms serve as efficient therapeutic tools. For example, group norms regarding honest self-disclosing, regular attendance, mutual peer reinforcement, and systematic problem analysis would serve to encourage members who manifest deviant behaviors to conform. Of course, antitherapeutic norms might also be generated in groups, as indicated by such behaviors as erratic attendance, noncompletion of agreed-on assignments, and excessive criticism of other group members.

To prevent or resolve such problems, the therapist can draw on a modest body of basic research about norms and other group phenomena in which individual behavior both influences and is influenced by the various attributes of the group (see Cartwright & Zander, 1968, for an extensive summary). In addition to establishing protherapeutic norms, therapists can facilitate the attainment of both individual and group treatment goals by using group strategies, for example, increasing the cohesiveness of the group or to redistributing patterns of communication from narrow to broad participation. However, if negative group attributes are not dealt with effectively, much of the unique power of group therapy is harnessed to the service of defeating change.

Another unique characteristic of therapy in groups is the opportunity for mutual reinforcement. Each person is afforded ample opportunity to learn or to improve his or her ability to mediate rewards for others in social interactive situations (with family, friendship groups, the work group). The therapist can structure a therapeutic situation in which each person has frequent opportunities, instructions, and even rewards for reinforcing others in the group. Reinforcement is a valued skill in our society. Research suggests that, as a person learns to reinforce others, he or she is reciprocally reinforced by others, and mutual liking increases (Lott & Lott, 1961).

Opportunity for more precise assessment is another advantage of group therapy. As group members assess an individual's report about a situation, many aspects of that situation that would escape even the most sensitive therapist are often clearly revealed during the intensive group discussion. This is helpful, especially when clients cannot readily pinpoint what is problematic in their behavior. The group, more effectively than a single therapist, provides clients with a major source of feedback about what in their behavior is annoying to others and what makes them attractive to others. Furthermore, feedback from peers is often more readily accepted than from the therapist.

The group makes available a variety of models, coaches, and role-players for behavioral rehearsal, personpower for monitoring, and partners for use in a buddy system or pairing off of one client with another for work between sessions. These supportive roles are learned as part of the therapeutic process.

Because the group offers simultaneous treatment to a number of people, this type of therapy appears to be less costly than individual treatment in terms of staff and money. Almost all research has shown that group therapy is at least as effective as, and less expensive than, individual treatment (see the discussion of relevant research).

Finally, the group serves as a check to keep the group therapist from imposing his or her values on individual clients. Clients in groups appear to be less accepting of the arbitrary values proposed by therapists than clients in dyads. A group of people can readily support each other in their disagreement with the therapist. The group therapist is constantly forced by group members to make his or her values explicit.

Several disadvantages of groups have also been noted. First, as already mentioned, antitherapeutic norms can develop, especially in highly cohesive groups. This atmosphere could work against effective treatment. If identified early, however, it is possible to examine the norms and work together to change them.

When the group is highly structured, as it is in behavioral group therapy, additional disadvantages can be noted. Although a group contract might prevent excessive wandering to irrelevant topics, it could also serve to deter exploration of the idiosyncratic needs of any one individual. Each person needs to be allotted some time at every meeting to discuss unique problems. Therefore, no one or two persons can be permitted to dominate an entire session. For the clients whose needs are pressing, it might be difficult to wait a turn.

Another potential disadvantage of the group is the difficulty of guaranteeing confidentiality. Although all clients are urged to hold in confidence any discussion of individual problems in the group, they are not necessarily committed to the professional ethics of the therapist. The limits of any guarantee of confidentiality can also restrict the degree to which some clients are willing to self-disclose. It could even restrict the degree to which the therapist should urge the members to self-disclose in the group. However, it should be noted that in the author's and his colleagues' experience, actual breaches of confidentiality have been rare.

The disadvantage for those few clients whose anxiety in social situations is so great that they cannot function in a group without panic is that the group is not the preferred context of therapy for them.

Now that we have reviewed the major advantages and disadvantages of groups, let us examine what therapists actually do in cognitive-behavioral group therapy to facilitate the learning of social and cognitive skills by the clients within the constraints of the assumptions just discussed.

THERAPIST FUNCTIONS

At least 10 major categories of functions can be identified in cognitive-behavioral group therapy. Although there is considerable overlap, each category is sufficiently unique to describe separately. These categories include organizing the group, orienting the members to the group, building group attraction, assessing the problem and the possibilities for resolving it, monitoring the behaviors determined as problematic, evaluating the progress of treatment, planning for and implementing specific change procedures, assessing group problems, modifying group attributes, and establishing transfer and maintenance programs for behavior changes occurring in the group. Each functional category consists of a series of still more specific activities, some of which will be described. These leader functions occur throughout the group although most are predominantly found in one or another of the group phases.

Beginning the Group

In the initial phase of group therapy, the therapist focuses on three major activities: organizing the group, orienting the clients, and building group attraction.

Organizational activities involve discussion and decision making about type of group, duration of group, length of meetings, number of therapists, location of meetings, nature of fees or deposits, and similar structural concerns. In the pregroup interview, clients decide whether the therapist's description of the group's focus adequately meets what they perceive to be their needs. Most intensive therapy groups involve a pregroup interview, 14 to 18 full-length weekly 1 1/2–2 hour sessions, and several "booster" sessions at 1- to 6-month intervals. Short-term training groups are 8 to 12 sessions, with one booster session 1 to 3 months after treatment. Most groups require a pregroup interview as well. Some therapists have successfully used open-ended groups for intensive therapy. In open-ended groups, clients terminate when they achieve treatment goals or no longer feel the need for group support. New members are added as old members terminate, usually one at a time. The more experienced members orient the new members, which provides experienced clients an opportunity for leadership.

Orientation refers to those activities in which the therapist informs the client of the group's purposes and content and of the responsibilities of the clients to themselves and to the others. It also involves the process of negotiating the content of the general treatment contract. As part of this function, the group is oriented toward the philosophy of treatment and its empirical foundations. In the orientation process, the therapist is the major contributor, who provides information and case studies as examples. The major therapist activities of the pretreatment interview and the first session are, to a large degree, concerned with orientation and development of initial group structure, that is, rules for the group.

In particular in the pregroup interview, the leader attempts to set positive expectations about the group experience. Group members are better prepared when (1) they believe they can do what is expected of them in the group, (2) they understand what their role will be in the group, and (3) they expect that their involvement will lead to positive outcomes for them (this last assumption is extrapolated from Bandura's self-efficacy concept, 1977).

To achieve the aforementioned expectations, the prospective client is provided a rationale for the treatment group. For example, the leader points out that people experience difficulties primarily due to learned patterns of interactions. The group members are told that the group is a special place to learn about oneself because of the opportunity to interact with others and that they will obtain feedback about their interactional patterns. Additionally, group members have the opportunity to learn and practice new patterns of behavior. Group members are then given examples of what typically takes place in the group, and the various ways of being a productive group member are illustrated.

Building group attraction focuses on increasing the positive attitudes of the group members toward each other, the therapist, and the content of the program. Initially, the group is merely an assembly of strangers who often are quite frightened of one another. There are many advantages to building group attraction (or cohesion) in the early stages.

High group cohesion has been found to be positively associated with group effectiveness (Flowers & Booraem, 1980; Liberman, 1970). Flowers and Booraem (1980) have found that increasing the following factors is correlated with cohesion: attending to the speaker, problem disclosure, negative feedback, role flexibility, client-client interactions, and number of group members trusted. Also included as a correlate is decreased frequency of group members in negative input or output roles. Research by Liberman (1970) demonstrated that a group therapist can directly influence the level of group cohesion by shaping, modifying, and facilitating verbal behavior reflecting cohesiveness.

Other strategies employed to increase group cohesion include providing food at meetings, varying the content of meetings, providing audiovisual aids, providing incentives for attendance, using humor judiciously, using interactive group exercises, employing goal-oriented interactive games, and providing sociorecreational activities for adolescents and children.

Assessment, monitoring, and evaluation are also a part of the beginning phase of the group, but because these activities continue throughout treatment and require distinct activities, they are discussed under a separate section.

Assessment, Monitoring, and Evaluating

As defined earlier, assessment is the group activity concerned with defining problem situations and the behavior and cognitions utilized by the client in coping with those situations. The resources of the individual and his or her environment that facilitate remediation of the problem situations are also explored in the course of group discussions.

The assessment process in group therapy is continuous throughout therapy. Preliminary information and initial complaints are first used to decide whether the group is appropriate for a given individual and, if appropriate, to ascertain the particular kind of group that is appropriate; for example, a stress management group, a long-term group therapy, or an assertiveness training program. Later, this information and other facts that come up in group sessions are used to determine the interventions most likely to be successful, the types of goals the client selects while in the group, and the evaluation process. Effective assessment is facilitated by pregroup interviews in which the therapist explores with the client the unique problematic situations clients are experiencing with their behavioral, cognitive, and affective responses to those situations. From these interviews and subsequent contacts, information is obtained about resources for and barriers to effective treatment. Interviews are often supplemented by role-play tests, behavioral inventories, checklists, and observations in and out of the group, as a means of zeroing in on specific target areas. These same tests may be used, if administered again at termination or at some period after termination, in evaluating the effectiveness of the group.

Although pregroup interviews by the therapist and tests are useful, most of the needed data are obtained in group discussions, after the group is formed, as members bring to the group descriptions of problematic or stressful situations. The members, by interviewing each other, help spell out the relevant details of situations before going on to problem solving or other treatment approaches. To facilitate this process, clients are asked to keep a diary containing a concrete description of all critical or stressful events.

Group members also serve as observers and judges of each other's role-plays and give feedback to each other. Such involvement not only increases the relevance of the assessment process, because it provides multiple perceptions, but it also increases interpersonal attraction.

Also included in group assessment is the collection of group data such as the distribution of participation, the level of satisfaction, the rate of attendance, and the rate of assignment completion. These rates provide a basis for evaluating whether group problems exist and whether group goals are being attained. For example, if the average rate of satisfaction at a given meeting is 2.2 on a five-point scale, and the average assignment completion is 30%, a group problem exists that needs to be dealt with in the group (for greater detail on this subject, see Rose, 1984). In addition, such data as participation, satisfaction, attendance, and assignment completion are used in an overall group or program evaluation.

Although assessment begins in the pregroup interview, it constantly shifts emphasis throughout treatment. In the pregroup interview and in the initial group sessions, members are encouraged to present problem situations, complaints, and reasons why they have come to the group. Clients are later taught how to define their problems in terms of specified criteria (discussed later in this chapter).

One of the most crucial steps in ongoing assessment is the analysis of situations that are viewed as problematic or stressful by the client. In this analysis, an attempt is made to define a time-limited event in terms of what was happening, who was involved, and where it occurred. Additionally, clients are asked which moment in time was the most difficult for them. This is referred to as the *critical moment*.

In response to the critical moment, clients are asked to describe their behavior or affective responses. Following this, clients are asked to describe their satisfaction with their behavioral responses or their affective rating of anxiety or anger. If the client is not at least somewhat dissatisfied with the response, the problem might not warrant targeting for change. Once the clients become familiar with these criteria, they are encouraged to interview each other for these data.

Once defined, behaviors, and the situations in which they occur, are systematically observed and measured in some way. The clients, and occasionally others, serve as recorders. Only after such assessment is an explicit change procedure started. For example, in anxiety management groups, clients first rate their anxiety levels three to four times a day. After treatment is begun, data collection is continued until the follow-up interview. The group therapist uses the data as it is collected to evaluate the effectiveness of specific treatment procedures, the group meetings, and the course of therapy. Effectiveness is determined on the basis of whether the goals of a given technique, a given meeting, or a given therapy have, indeed, been achieved. If it is discovered that the format of a given session has been partially or totally unsuccessful (because of the high frequency of critical comments on the session's evaluation, low participation in the meeting, and failure of most members to complete their weekly assignments), the format can be changed. Thus, changes are initiated on the basis of a review of data, not on intuitive hunches. Moreover, the members are involved in the decision as to what changes should take place. Because of the abundance of data and the regularity of feedback, change procedures can be designed and carried out as soon as a specific problem has been identified. As a consequence of assessment, the therapist and the clients as a group can also evaluate the degree to which each individual's treatment goals are achieved.

To plan for the kind of individualized intervention to be used in a way which involves the group, a review of the assessment data is first required for all the members during a group session. Where possible, common treatment goals are established which permit common intervention plans. For example, if many of the members have some problems with agoraphobia, then group exposure could be the appropriate strategy, because empirical support exists for its use in groups (Emmelkamp, 1982). Similarly, if all or most of the members have difficulty talking with members of the opposite sex, social situations could be created in which members must observe, then practice, a variety of common conversations. If the group is homogeneous in reference to a problem, common intervention strategies are possible. Even when the specific complaints are quite diverse, there are a number of common skills that must be taught in order to mediate the achievement of solutions to the diverse problems. For example, most programs contain exercises which train the clients in the giving and receiving of feedback, in systematic problem solving, in systematic relaxation, and in role-playing. Once these skills are learned, clients bring in problematic situations that require a range of interventions.

In one instance, one client, having first undergone the aforementioned training programs with the other group members, brought in the question of what he could say to a garage owner who had inadequately serviced the client's car and what the client could say to himself to keep himself calm while confronting the garage owner. Because the group members had been trained in the aforementioned procedures, they were able to participate in systematic problem solving and to recommend strategies such as relaxation plus cognitive restructuring of the client's cognitive distortions. In this way, much of the leadership of the session could be carried out by the members themselves.

PLANNING FOR AND IMPLEMENTING SPECIFIC CHANGE PROCEDURES

Because social skills training, cognitive restructuring, problem solving, and group intervention are the major intervention strategies used, let us continue the preceding example into the planning phase. The group first helped the client to generate ideas as to what he could say. The situation required both social skill training to practice the words he was to use to the garage owner, and cognitive restructuring to change his self talk. It could have also been necessary in that situation for the client to use relaxation or avoidance strategies as a means of coping with the situation. In this example, we see a meshing of the common and the individualized intervention plan.

Now let us examine the specific procedures commonly used in groups.

Social Skills Training

To survive in a group and in social situations in general, a minimum of social skills is necessary. For these reasons, in almost every type of behavioral group therapy, some form of social skill training is required. For those clients who have social skill deficiencies, social skill training could represent the major intervention strategy.

Combs and Slaby (1977) defined social skills as "the ability to interact with others in a given social context in specific ways that are societally acceptable or valued and at the same time personally beneficial, mutually beneficial, or beneficial primarily to others" (p. 162).

Social skills training has received widespread application in the last 15 years to numerous client groups. Application has moved beyond the early efforts of assertiveness training (Wolpe & Lazarus, 1966) to include: children (Cartledge & Milburn, 1980; Ladd, 1984), adolescents (Goldstein, Sprafkin, Gershaw, & Klein, 1983; LeCroy, 1983), psychiatric clients (Goldsmith & McFall, 1975), older women (Engels & Poser, 1987), adult caregivers (Robinson, 1988), and spouse abusers (Hamberger & Hastings, 1988), to name only a few.

Social skills development involves several critical assumptions (Bellack & Hersen, 1978). The first is that interpersonal behavior is based on a distinct set of skills that are primarily learned behaviors. Thus, how one behaves in an interpersonal situation depends on the individual's repertoire of effective social behaviors. The second aspect is that socially skilled behavior is situationally specific. It is important to recognize that cultural and situational factors determine social norms or what is expected of an individual. Third, effective functioning (e.g., carrying on a conversation with a new acquaintance) depends on whether an individual's repertoire of social skills provide a source of reinforcement. Effective social skills should facilitate receiving reinforcement and avoiding punishing responses from significant others.

Research on social skills training has revealed no specific components that are universally effective across different subject populations and difficult problems. It appears that different training components are effective in producing different aspects of social skills (Edelstein & Eisler, 1976; Hersen, Eisler, Miller, Johnson, & Pinkston, 1973), and that results have different effects, depending on the subject population (Eisler, Frederiksen, & Peterson, 1978). Some research suggests that the combined effects of using both overt and covert rehearsal in skills training may be better than the effects of either alone (Kazdin, 1985). In general, a group approach to teaching social skills appears particularly effective in groups that target assertion skills, conversational skills, heterosocial or dating skills, and job interview skills (Kelly, 1985). Furthermore, it appears that a comprehensive treatment package is important when teaching complex response patterns. For example, Marzillier & Winter (1983), in their investigation of social anxiety, found that social skills training alone is limited in its effectiveness. In fact, several studies have not been able to detect a social skills deficit in socially anxious clients (Curran, Wallander, & Aschetti, 1977; Newton, Kindness, & McFudyen, 1983). Such studies suggest the need for a more comprehensive approach to treatment. Although we discuss separately social skills training, cognitive restructuring, and coping skills training, in practice many of these approaches are combined.

Social skills training in groups involves orientation to the approach, development of problem situations, goal setting, intervention planning, the application of modeling, and the application of rehearsal, feedback, and homework. Because few of the above steps refer uniquely to group therapy, let us look at each of these procedures as it is applied in a group context.

Orientation

Prior to the initiation of social skills training, the therapist discusses with members the rationale of the procedures and provides examples. Kazdin & Krouse (1983) suggest that an adequate rationale consists of a reason for the procedure and a brief overview of its components. When possible, the therapist draws on those members who have used the procedures to share their experiences with the group.

If the members have had no previous experience with role-play or other simulation procedures, the group therapist might have to train them in the technique. Prepared situations are presented to the group in which the therapist and an experienced member or a member from a previous group demonstrate how to role-play. The group is divided into pairs. Each pair role-plays the same or a similar situation in one corner of the room. Later, each pair demonstrates their role-play to the entire group, and each person receives positive feedback on what she or he role-played well. Group leaders should give clients doing the role-play the first opportunity to assess their own performance. If clients are responsible for giving feedback to each other, it is more likely that they will make the desired change.

Developing Problem Situations

Once the group members have demonstrated role-play skills, they are trained to develop situations that lend themselves to social skills training. As already mentioned in the section on assessment, these situations should be brief with a clear-cut beginning and end; the place, the persons involved, the content of the interaction, and the time the situation took place are clearly delineated; the client should be dissatisfied with what she or he did or said in the situation; and finally, each event should have a critical moment, that is, a point in time in which the client is expected to respond or expects herself or himself to respond. An example of a situation which meets the aforementioned criteria is the following:

> The client, when he was at work the day before the session, was unable to complete the assignment his employer had given him because he simply did not understand the instructions. When his boss asked him how it was going he said, "fine," even though he wanted to ask for help. In this example we know when it occurred, where, and with whom. It is interactive, and the critical moment occurred when the boss asked how it was going and the client was dissatisfied with his response.

The therapist provides, first, a number of examples of situations, such as the one just given, that meet the criteria. The group then discusses these situations. Later, the therapist might provide situations that do not meet the criteria and let the group modify them to meet the criteria. Then, the members are asked to develop in pairs or larger subgroups at least one new situation of their own that meets the criteria. Each of the situations is evaluated in terms of whether the criteria have been met.

Ongoing Monitoring

Once the group is trained in the development of problem situations, they keep a diary of such situations as they occur in the course of the week. Each week, one or more such situations by each member is handled in the group.

Goal Formulation

When the situation is presented, the member either states her or his goals, or is helped by the group to develop goals for the situation. In the situation given earlier, the goals at the critical moment were to explain in a clear voice, with good eye contact, that the client had not understood the original instructions and to ask whether the supervisor might not explain them again.

Intervention Planning

Once the goals are agreed on and evaluated in terms of potential risk and reasonableness, the major thrust of assessment is ended and intervention begins. The members are asked to propose the exact things the client could do or say to achieve the determined goals. Effective problem-solving techniques prohibit evaluation of suggestions until after all suggestions have been presented. The group then helps the client evaluate the list of suggestions in reference to relative risk, appropriateness, compatibility with personal style, and probable effectiveness. Ultimately, it is the client with the problem situation who decides on an overall strategy.

Modeling

Usually, the therapist or another group member models the desired verbal and nonverbal behavior in a brief role-played demonstration. The given client evaluates how realistic the modeled situation was and states what he or she finds useful in the performance of the model. The client may also ask for another modeling trial with the same or a different model.

Rehearsal

The client then practices or rehearses her or his own role in the situation, utilizing the agreed-on behaviors. In subsequent rehearsals, the difficulty and complexity of the situation can be increased gradually. When the client has difficulty carrying out the strategy in the rehearsal, she or he can be coached or assisted by the therapist or another member, or even through the use of cue cards. In *coaching,* the coach usually stands behind the role-playing client and whispers suggestions as to what to say or how to say it. Coaching is usually eliminated in subsequent rehearsals.

Feedback

Following each rehearsal, the client receives feedback from the group as to what was done well and what might be done differently. Prior to the modeling sequence, clients will have been trained and have the opportunity to practice how to deliver constructive feedback in the group and outside of the group. Feedback is an essential skill both in treatment and the real world. Feedback is also used in problem solving and cognitive restructuring exercises.

Homework

After several increasingly difficult rehearsals, the client assigns to himself or herself a homework assignment, to try out some of the new behaviors learned in the group. Homework is an essential part of this approach and is used as a means of increasing time spent on therapeutic endeavors, as well as for transferring therapeutic activities to the real world. In a study on the use of homework, Kazdin and Mascitelli (1982) found that homework was needed to maintain treatment gains at the conclusion of the intervention. In designing the homework assignment, the group members provide each other suggestions and evaluation of the alternatives, but the final decision is in the hands of the given client. Homework is used following all interventions, not only the social skills sequence.

An Example of the Sequence

Let us look briefly at the sequence of these procedures as they applied in a group.

> Evelyn had been upset when her colleague gave her advice whether she asked for it or not. Evelyn did nothing about it except get upset. Her goal was to ask Annie politely and firmly to stop it. In the group, the members recommended a number of things she could say. The particular suggestion Evelyn liked best was to say in a firm tone that she appreciated all the help she had been given, but now it was important for her to do everything on her own. Whenever she needed help, she'd be sure to ask. Otherwise, please, no help needed! When Evelyn was asked about what risk she

might incur if she was assertive with her colleague, Annie, she thought the risk was far greater if she did nothing. Sticking up for herself, she added, wasn't her style, but it was a style, she said, she would like to acquire. Karin demonstrated in a role-play how Evelyn might say it (modeling). Evelyn role-played the situation herself in her own role (behavioral rehearsal), with Janet playing the role of the colleague. Most group members thought she was quite impressive and pointed to specific things she did well. Glenda and Jean added that she might speak a little more slowly and emphatically (group feedback). After a second rehearsal, Evelyn said she couldn't wait for her real colleague to give her advice, so she could try out what she had just learned; but, just in case, she'd practice a half dozen more times with her buddy, Karin, during the week.

Cognitive Change Procedures

Most of the same procedures, such as modeling, rehearsal, and homework, are used in the modification of cognitions. In addition, a number of specific adaptations and uniquely cognitive procedures are used.

Cognitive Restructuring

In describing their cognitive responses during stress or problem situations, clients often reveal self-defeating thoughts or severely distorted beliefs about themselves in relation to the world about them. For example, in the excerpt just cited, Evelyn implied that some catastrophe might befall her if anyone became angry or upset with her. In some cases, these cognitions seem to generate so much anxiety for an individual that she or he is unable to make use of social skills training in developing and trying out specific alternatives for coping with stress as it occurs in the real world. Under these conditions, some form of restructuring of cognitions could be necessary. Cognitive restructuring refers to the process of identifying and evaluating one's own cognitions, recognizing the deleterious effect of maladaptive cognitions, and replacing these cognitions with more appropriate ones (Beck, 1976).

The role of cognitions is becoming increasingly recognized as an important factor in developing effective treatments. In the past, a highly anxious client might have been assumed to need only to learn appropriate social skills. However, recent research has found that such individuals are more likely to underestimate their own level of interpersonal skills in social situations (Edelmann, 1985). Furthermore, such individuals generate a high frequency of negative cognitions in stressful situations (Swartz & Gottman, 1976) and have been found to have more irrational beliefs when compared with matched controls (Monti, Zwick, & Warzak, 1986). Such negative cognitions interfere with performance regardless of the available social skills. Lucock & Salkovskis (1988) found that anxious clients overestimate the probability that unpleasant social events will occur and that cognitive therapy could remediate such appraisals. Widespread recognition of the significance of such cognitive factors has led to cognitive therapy procedures being applied to a broad range of problems.

Cognitive restructuring has been used to help clients with such problems as speech anxiety (Fremouw & Zitter, 1978; Thorpe, Amatu, Blakey, & Burns, 1976), social interaction anxiety (Glass, Gottman, & Shmurak, 1976; Lucock & Salkovskis, 1988), depression (Beck, Rush, Shaw, & Emory, 1979; Taylor & Marshall, 1977), anger control (Benson, Rice, & Miranti, 1986; LeCroy, 1988), pain-related stress (Langer, Janis, & Wolfer, 1975; Turk, 1975), women experiencing divorce (Graff, Whitehead, & LeCompte, 1986), and eating disorders (Garner & Bemis, 1982; Lee & Rush, 1986; Roth & Ross, 1988). This procedure also is used in conjunction with other therapeutic strategies when the client's belief system becomes part of the change target. The major steps in cognitive restructuring are the following: orientation, identifying distorted cognitions, developing coping statements, cognitive modeling, cognitive rehearsal, feedback, and homework.

Orientation. Just as in social skills training, offering a rationale for cognitive restructuring is an imperative first step (Meichenbaum, 1977). As a part of this step, clients are provided with examples, evidence of effectiveness, and an overview of the major steps. Members are encouraged to provide others with their own examples of the relationship between cognitions, anxiety, and behavior.

Determining distorted cognitions. The following serves to identify each client's particular self-defeating or irrational cognitions through analysis of logical inconsistencies and long-range consequences of pervasive cognitions. In order to analyze cognitive responses to stress, situations are brought in by the clients, who are interviewed by the other members of the group. The group provides each participant feedback on the accuracy of her or his cognitions. This step of identifying self-defeating statements is exemplified in the group's work with Karl in an early session.

> Karl had told about a situation in which he had wanted to ask a girl in his class for a date. He knew what to say, but he failed to say it because, as he thought, "She'll never go out with a slob like me, and, if she says no, I'll not be able to stand it!" The group members pointed out to Karl two apparent self-defeating cognitions. The first implied "if she refused him he would be devastated" and the second that he considered himself a socially inept individual. Janine (therapist) had the group deal with each cognition, one at a time. The members interviewed Karl. Terry asked Karl if he had had any successes at all in approaching and talking to women. Karl gave a couple examples. Janine asked if the women in the group had experienced Karl as a slob. "To the contrary," Ellie said, "you make me feel quite comfortable." (The discussion continued with both Karl and the group providing evidence inconsistent with Karl's self-description.)

Developing coping statements. Group exercises can be used first to teach clients to differentiate between self-defeating and coping statements (see Rose, Tolman, Hanusa, & Tallant, 1984, exercise 26). Additional exercises are sometimes used to encourage clients to learn how to identify and analyze their own cognitions.

Group participants provide each other not only with feedback but also with repeated and varied models of a cognitive analysis.

Often, repeated recognition that one is consumed by a given set of self-defeating cognitions is sufficient to warrant change (Beck, 1976; Ellis, 1970), but more often, further steps must be employed. The subsequent step is to solicit ideas from the client and from other group members as to potential self-enhancing or coping cognitions that facilitate problem solving or effective actions. The following is a continuation of Karl's group interview:

> *Janine:* What else might Karl say in a similar situation to himself that would accurately portray his response, instead of, "I'm such a slob that she would never go out with me"?
>
> *Gerard:* I've got to admit lots of people don't view me as a slob, and maybe she won't either.
>
> *Analisa:* Everyone's a slob once in a while, and in the group I'm learning how to approach people. Let's try it out now. The worst that can happen is that she'll say, no, and that's not so terrible.
>
> *Sylvia:* What do you think about . . . "So what if I feel slobby. I can do something about it, like asking her for a date."

Cognitive modeling. After the client decides on a set of accurate and comfortable cognitive statements, cognitive modeling is used in which the client imagines the stressful situation, experiences the initial self-defeating statements, stops herself or himself, and replaces the self-defeating statement with a coping statement, as the previous example continues:

> *Janine:* Gerard, would you demonstrate to Karl how he might handle himself in that situation? I'll help you if you get stuck.
>
> *Gerard:* OK, I imagine I see this girl in the library, OK? She seems real nice. I know her from class. There's a movie tonight at the student union. I'd really like to ask her to go with me. Got the picture? But I think Oh, she'd never go out with a slob like me. Wait a minute! (note the shift statement) I feel like a slob sometimes, but other people find me attractive. (Gerard seems at a loss so Janine coaches him at this time.) Oh yes, and I have been working on making friends in the group so, damn it, I'll ask her for a date. If she says no, she says no, it's not so awful.
>
> *Janine:* OK, Karl, how does that sound?

Cognitive rehearsal. With this procedure the client goes through the same steps as the model but adapts these steps to her or his own style. Afterward the client gets feedback from the group. The client might need to be coached during the first few trials. Finally, when feeling comfortable, the client practices the entire process silently. After the example just given, Karl duplicated in a cognitive rehearsal much of what Gerard had said. Now Janine asks the group for positive feedback.

> *Janine:* Well, what did Karl say to himself or how did he say it in ways that should prove useful to him?
>
> *Theresa:* He sounded like he believed it.
>
> *Sparky:* He was really into the situation.
>
> *Gerard:* For sure, he improved on my version. I especially liked the way he switched from the self-defeating statements.

Janine: (After a pause) What might he have done or said differently?
Karl: I forgot to say, "After all, plenty of people don't think I'm a slob."

It should be noted that Janine focused first on positive feedback, before asking for ways of improving. Now, after several practices, Janine shifts to a silent rehearsal.

Janine: OK, let's try again, only this time let's do it silently. All of you might practice your own situation at the same time.

Homework. Usually, after several trials in the group, an assignment to practice a number of times at home is developed at the end of one session and is monitored at a subsequent session. Assignments are usually developed in pairs and discussed in larger groups. Homework is developed at successive levels of difficulty each week. For example, it might initially focus on learning to discriminate in general between self-defeating and self-enhancing or coping cognitions. Later, the focus might be on identifying and evaluating the clients' cognitive responses to their own situations or shifting from the practice of self-defeating responses to coping skills, with the addition of praise to one's self for one's achievements. Homework can be carried out with "buddies" from the group, with a friend, or with a family member.

Stress Inoculation

Of course, with most problems, just learning to perceive or evaluate oneself differently in a situation is probably not enough. Social skills training might be necessary to help Karl with the actual words he needed to talk with women. And additional coping skills such as relaxation (or deep breathing) might be necessary to create an internal state that facilitates thinking or speaking appropriately. The entire package of all these skill training procedures has been referred to as *stress inoculation*. This procedure is quite similar to cognitive restructuring but goes beyond it in teaching physical, as well as cognitive and social coping skills. Designed by Meichenbaum and Cameron (1973), stress inoculation aims to provide a client with a set of skills to deal with future stress situations. Stress inoculation works on situations in each of three important phases: prior to, during, and immediately following a stressful situation. This approach has been used to aid abusive clients and law enforcement personnel with anger control (Novaco, 1975, 1977) and to teach others how to manage anxiety, stress, tension, headaches, and pain (for a review of this research, see Mahoney & Arnkoff, 1978).

Because most of these procedures have already been explained, except physical or coping skills training, let us look briefly at these skills.

Coping skills training. In addition to overt interactive responses, which are usually taught through social skills training procedures, a number of other more general behavioral strategies have been found effective in coping with both specific stress, for example, coping with cancer (Telch & Telch, 1986) and general stress situations (Horan, Hackett, Buchanan, Stone, & Demchik–Stone, 1977).

The treatment procedures include relaxation, deep breathing, inquiry, and (in some cases) avoidance of the stress situation and problem solving. (See Barrios & Shigetomi, 1979, for a review of the research on coping skill training.)

Relaxation and deep breathing are taught in groups in which anxiety-related problems are prominent. The skills are demonstrated, and members then practice the skills in pairs and give each other feedback. Finally, with the help of instructional tapes, they practice the skills at home. Once learned, the group discusses when and where such procedures should be used.

Avoidance, too, is often looked on as one alternative response in every stress situation. However, the question is usually discussed in the group of whether the costs or risks of avoidance are greater than the risks of a more confrontative or cognitive coping or physical coping strategy.

Systematic Problem Solving

All of the strategies thus far discussed can be integrated within a problem-solving framework. Within the framework, the client learns to work through a set of steps systematically for analyzing a problem, discovering new approaches, evaluating those approaches, and developing strategies for implementing those approaches in the real world, and finally validating the effectiveness of the strategies employed. In groups, problem solving is taught through exercises in which each person brings a problem to the group, and the group goes through the various steps explicitly. For example, one member introduced the problem of his not being able to find a baby-sitter so that he could attend the session. After discussing his limited resources for paying a baby-sitter and the importance to him of attending the meetings, a number of ideas were generated with care being taken not to evaluate any of them until all had been disclosed. Among the ideas generated were the following: to bring the baby to the meeting, drop the baby at the home of his estranged wife, rotate the members of the group as baby-sitters, charge everyone a baby-sitting fee to be drawn only by those who need it, and ask the agency which sponsored the group to provide a fund out of the fees from the group for baby-sitters. After examining the risks and benefits attached to each suggestion, the group and the member thought meeting at his house, which was centrally located, was the best idea. It was noted that group attendance improved after this discussion not only for the given member but for the rest of the group.

Problem solving is also demonstrated when group problems arise and must be dealt with. (For group examples, see the following section on solving group problems.) Moreover, a review of both social skills training and cognitive restructuring reveals that group members participate in the major steps of the problem-solving process. For further information and a review of empirical support for the efficacy of the problem-solving process, see D'Zurilla (1986). Thus, behavior group therapy, as it is described here, permits the integrated use of (a) social skills training; (b) cognitive therapy, especially cognitive restructuring and stress inoculation; and (c) systematic problem solving. An additional set of procedures are derived from group therapy as a means of enhancing client social functioning. These techniques unique to group therapy are called group procedures.

Group Procedures

Group procedures involve dividing the group into subunits and/or involving the group in interactive exercises in which the members must communicate in prescribed ways. The purposes of such group procedures are to increase the interaction, modify the general pattern of interaction, increase responsibility to members, provide leadership opportunities, and/or provide greater opportunities for autonomous functioning. Let us examine the commonly used group procedures in more detail.

Recapitulation is a group technique used to slow down the pace of interaction and increase listening to others. With this procedure, a participant summarizes what the previous speaker has said before he or she expresses his or her own opinion. The problem with the procedure is that the discussion often loses its spontaneity, and some members are afraid to speak at all. We have found it useful only when the activity is limited to several 5-minute exercises throughout the group meeting. As persons appear to be listening more effectively, the technique is eliminated.

A case study can be presented to the group for discussion whenever the therapist wants the group members to discuss an issue without first talking directly about themselves. In early sessions, when the group is hesitant to self-disclose, this technique is especially useful. In the first session, the author and his colleagues often present the group with two cases of persons who are similar to, but not the same as, a composite of several persons in the group. We ask the members to describe how each feels he or she is different for one or both of the cases.

A *fishbowl procedure* can be used in groups of 10 or more. Half the group is placed in a tight inner circle, and the remainder are seated in an outer circle surrounding the others. The inner circle usually discusses an issue while the outer circle observes. The outer circle is not permitted to interact until the inner circle is finished. At that time, the outer circle provides feedback to the members of the inner circle. The two circles may be reversed and the exercise repeated.

The *buddy system* was mentioned earlier in this chapter. The members select partners for mutual monitoring during the week between sessions. Contacts can be in person or by telephone. They are usually quite brief. This arrangement provides members the opportunity to be helper as well as client and to practice their newly learned leadership skills. The assignments for the partners are highly specific and limited in scope, so that clients will not deal with areas for which they are not prepared. Contact outside the group also serves to extend treatment into everyday life. It should be noted that, in contrast with our suggestions, some authors do not recommend extragroup contact among members (e.g., Lawrence & Sundell, 1972).

Small group exercises are also used when the group addresses specific topics. For example, clients are taught feedback by having members write down one feedback statement to the group therapist about their behavior. Then, each statement is evaluated in terms of a specific set of criteria, its content, and the way it was delivered. Finally, each member does the same thing with the person on his or her right, who in turn gives him or her feedback on the feedback.

An additional small group exercise that we use a lot is having members work on self-defeating statements. Clients are given a list of self-defeating statements and asked to clarify why each statement is self-defeating and then change it to a coping or self-enhancing statement. Members then discuss each of the statements in the group. Following this part of the exercise, members describe to the group their own self-defeating statements, and the group suggests alternative coping thoughts. Other exercises are described in an exercise manual (Rose et al. 1984).

Group Problems

Because of the diversity of clients who make up any given group, there are diverse patterns of interaction, varied norms, differing levels of group cohesion, and unique patterns of conflict among groups. Some of these patterns or structures facilitate the achievement of treatment goals, whereas others interfere with them. One of the unique characteristics of group therapy, in contrast with individual therapy, is the possibility of modifying group structure or resolving group problems in such a way as to enhance problem-solving and feedback skills and to provide practice in a protected setting for the members to deal with complex social situations. These particular conditions often function as interactive barriers to goal attainment.

Instead of group problems being viewed as limitations of group therapy, they should be considered therapeutic opportunities. In the identification of a problem, in discovering each individual's contribution to that problem, in planning for and carrying out intervention to resolve a problem, and in evaluating the outcome of the entire process, the group worker models and gives members multiple occasions to practice a systematic problem-solving approach around a significant common issue. Members have the opportunity to view their own unique patterns of behavioral, cognitive, and affective response to interactive events of the group. In the group, the individual can evaluate with the help of the others those responses to problems that are ineffective. In the group, members design together new strategies of remediation for group problems and observe and evaluate the consequences of their plans in terms of problem remediation.

Athough, in the case of a group problem, no one person in the group can escape partial responsibility, no one should assume sole responsibility for it. Since blame can be avoided, members are more readily able to participate openly and actively in the process. In the world outside the group, responsibility for most communication problems is shared with others. Learning to deal with mutual problems is an important task in its own right.

Assessing Group Interactive Problems

Group interactive problems occur in almost all groups. If not identified and dealt with, such problems often interfere with the achievement of treatment goals. However, if identified they may serve as opportunity for immediate problem solving and observing oneself in the problem-solving process. In most forms of group therapy, the leader draws unsystematically on personal observations to decide whether or not a group problem exists. One of the major characteristics of the approach advocated in this chapter is the reliance on data in determining whether or not a problem exists. Data are obtained from postsession questionnaires administered at the end of every session and from systematic observations from observers. The data, of course, must be interpreted by the therapist and the group, as is exemplified later in this chapter. Such data make it possible to define group problems in quantifiable terms.

The postsession questionnaire. A major source of group data can be derived from a postsession questionnaire (see Rose, 1984) that is administered at the end of every meeting. This questionnaire has proven valuable in ascertaining a number of different group problems. Some of the questions asked are related to usefulness of the session, the degree to which the client self-disclosed, the strength of feelings experienced during the session, the effectiveness of the session, the actions the leader could take to improve the quality of the session, and the actions the client could take to improve the quality of the session. If limited to 10 questions, the entire questionnaire takes about 2 minutes to fill in. The time for the leaders to analyze the data is somewhat longer, but the method is extremely valuable for revealing general group problems and specific member concerns.

Observations of group interaction. The second set of data can be derived from direct observations. One simple method that is not too costly in terms of observer training and data analysis is the quantity of interaction schema. Data is collected every 10 seconds on who is speaking. This method provides an estimate of who is participating and how much. One can use former members, present members, visitors, or students as the observers. Because the method is simple, observers can be reliably trained in about 10 minutes. The reader is referred to Mash and Terdal (1976, pp. 261–352) for a critical review and detailed presentation of still more elaborate systems. Because these usually are too costly for the practitioner to train observers, carry out the data analysis, and interpret in the typical clinical group program, they are not included here.

The rate of assignment completion. This also has been shown to correlate with behavioral change on a role-play test (Rose, 1981) and is a good index of ongoing productivity. Low productivity is a major group problem and requires dramatic action as soon as it is detected. One way it can be assessed is to collect data on all assignments agreed on at the end of one meeting and completed by the beginning of the next. The rate is computed by the number of assignments completed, divided by the number of assignments given. One problem with this index is that all assignments are assumed to be equal. An assertive task, such as talking to a new person, might be far more important than describing in writing a stressful situation. Some leaders give more weight to the completion of such tasks. Others consider only the completion of tasks in ascertaining productivity, because these assignments alone represent transfer of learning to the real world.

Attendance. Based on the assumption that the more time spent in treatment the more likely that treatment goals will be achieved, attendance and promptness data can also be collected without intruding into the group interaction. Irregular attendance may be a better indicator of cohesion than verbal report on the attractiveness of the group. However, it should be noted that attendance was not significantly correlated with outcome in the aforementioned study.

Resolving Group Problems

Based on data collected with the aforementioned instruments, group problems can be identified. If members are dissatisfied with the group meeting, if some people are dominating the interaction while others are left out, if members are often absent or late, if homework is not being completed, a group problem can be said to exist. As we mentioned earlier, if these problems are not dealt with they may interfere with the achievement of group goals. Modification of a group problem is illustrated in the following example.

> The data revealed that 2 to 6 members spoke about 60% of the time and one person less than 5% of the time. Average satisfaction had dropped from 4.5 to 3.5 on a 5-point scale. After the data were presented to the group, they agreed that the uneven distribution of participation was a problem, and they developed a plan through systematic problem solving, which they agreed to implement at that meeting. The more active members stated they would reformulate the previous speaker's position before making a point of their own (recapitulation), whereas the less active members agreed to write down any thoughts they had relevant to each subject. The group therapist would then call upon them to review their notes, if they had not spoken. The group practiced the complex plan for the following 5 minuters and decided to use it only twice per meeting for 20 minutes because it was somewhat disruptive. They also agreed to end it once the distribution of participation was somewhat more even. Thus, the plan utilized problem solving, recapitulation, self-monitoring, cueing by the leader, and rehearsal.

Another group with a similar problem utilized primarily cognitive procedures, which they had recently been working on in the group.

> The members decided to analyze their thinking whenever they were expected to participate, and, in a later discussion, the group helped each member to determine whether a given thought was individually and group self-enhancing. Other proce- dures commonly used have been verbal reinforcement of inactive participants for even brief contributions and role-play practice with a buddy prior to a meeting regarding what might be said at that meeting. (For further examples, see Rose, 1989 for adults and Rose & Edleson, 1987 for children and adolescents.)

As clients respond to the unique and often complex group problems, the group therapist often discusses with the group the typical responses of each of the members and how each has learned to respond in more flexible and appropriate ways. By looking at the general pattern, the group therapist facilitates the generalization of changes learned in the group to situations outside the group. Teaching the general pattern is only one approach to facilitating generalization. The following section discusses other ways in which the group can increase the likelihood of generalization and maintenance of learning.

Generalization and Maintenance of Behavioral Changes

Generalization strategies involve the application of those procedures designed to facilitate the transfer of learning occurring in the treatment situation to the real world of the client. There are two major types of procedures for generalization. The first type comprises intragroup procedures such as behavioral rehearsal, which simulates the real world and represents a preparatory step toward performance outside the group. The second type are extragroup procedures, such as the behavioral assignment or homework in which the client tries out the rehearsed behavior in the community. Other extragroup techniques include meeting in the homes of the clients and using the buddy system outside the group.

Some strategies involve procedures oriented toward maintaining the goal level of quality of behavior achieved during the course of group therapy for a significant period after treatment is terminated. Several techniques uniquely designed for the purpose are used. Among them are gradual fading of the treatment procedures and thinning of the reinforcement schedules, that is, reducing frequency and regularity of rewards. Overlearning the new behavior through frequent trials has been used but probably is not sufficient by itself. It is also necessary to review summary rules or cognitive strategies so that the more complex patterns of functioning may be maintained (Rosenthal & Bandura, 1978). In groups, this review is often carried out at the end of each meeting, and the members are asked to participate.

In preparing for termination, the attraction of other groups is increased relative to the therapy groups. Clients are encouraged to join nontherapeutic groups in order to practice their newly learned skills under less controlled conditions. Greater reliance is placed on the decisions of the clients as they increasingly perform the major leadership tasks in the group. The role of the therapist shifts from direct therapist to consultant. These activities not only serve to make termination easier on the clients, but they also permit clients to function independently of a therapist. This independence is necessary not only for the maintenance of changes beyond the end of the group, but also for making the client more comfortable in dealing with new problems as they occur.

Clients are prepared for potential setbacks, unsympathetic relatives and friends, and unpredicted pressure through role-play of situations simulating these conditions. It should be noted that preparation for generalization and maintenance of change is found throughout treatment. As early as the third or fourth meeting, partners are working with each other outside the group, rehearsals are occurring within the group, and behavioral assignments are given for practicing the desired behavior outside of the group (See Rose, 1989, for further discussion of these principles).

RELEVANT RESEARCH

Throughout this chapter, we have reported on some of the empirical support for each of the behavioral components of group therapy. In putting a behavioral and cognitive behavioral group package together for various problems, a large number of experimental studies can be identified. All of the students have components of the package developed in this chapter, but no two packages appear to be exactly the same. Most of the studies have been on homogeneous groups of clients with a common major problem such as social skills deficits, depression, anxiety and stress, agoraphobia, and sexual disorders. Most of the studies failed to mention group conditions such as group cohesion or group structure as a concern of the experimenter. Several studies compared the effectiveness of group behavioral intervention strategies with individual ones. However, very few studies have attempted to measure the effects of group process or have attempted to manipulate the group process. Yet most clinicians working with groups would usually view the group as a variable as important as the major intervention strategies in behavioral change.

Comparing Different Approaches

Several studies have attempted to examine the relative efficacy of different approaches to group work. Linehan, Goldfried, and Goldfried (1979) found that a combined behavioral and cognitive restructuring approach in groups was superior to behavioral rehearsal alone, cognitive-behavioral alone, relationship therapy, and a waiting list control in the development of social skills. In a 1-year follow-up study of cognitive-relaxation and social skills treatment for anger, Deffenbacher (1988) found subjects in both groups reported less anger on several measures. Resnick, Jordan, Girelli, Hutter, & Marhoefer–Dvorak (1988) compared three types of group treatment: stress inoculation, assertion training, and supportive psychotherapy for treating rape victims. Assessment included multiple measures such as SCL-90, fear survey, self-concept, and impact of event scale. Analysis indicated that there were no interactions or group effects. The authors did find significant improvement on all of the measures. LaPointe and Rimm (1980) compared Beck's cognitive-behavioral group approach with both an assertiveness training group and an insight-oriented group. All three treatments resulted in significant improvements in depression, rationality, and assertiveness measures.

Unexpectedly, the insight group and the assertiveness group made significantly more gains in rationality regarding self than the cognitive-behavioral approach. These studies suggest that no particular behavioral approach (e.g., social skills versus cognitive restructuring) has been found more effective. Studies have also not been able to consistently find cognitive-behavioral groups to be superior to non-behavioral groups (Hodgson, 1981; Shaffer, Shapiro, Sank, & Coghlen, 1981; Shaw, 1977; Shipley & Fazio, 1973). Interpretation of these mixed findings is difficult. However, one cannot underestimate the importance of the group as a component, even in the absence of the behavioral or cognitive-behavioral intervention package. In many studies, it is not clear if and how the experiments made use of the unique characteristics and potential of the group. Perhaps with more research, practitioners will be able to match the best treatment with the most salient aspect of the client's problem, but for the present, no general conclusions can be reached.

Group Therapy Preparation

Research (France & Dugo, 1985) supports the importance of properly preparing individuals for group therapy. France & Dugo found that individuals who experienced a pretherapy orientation for group treatment had greater attendance ratings than individuals who did not experience the pregroup orientation.

Group Versus Individual Therapy

Another important area of research concerns the relative effectiveness of group therapy and individual therapy. Several studies compared a group cognitive-behavioral approach to an individual one. When the psychoeducational group model of Brown and Lewinsohn (1984) was compared with individual tutoring, Teri and Lewinsohn (1981) found that both the group and the individual approaches were equally effective but that the individualized treatment requires 12 contact hours per client, the group only 3 contact hours per client.

In a comprehensive study of time-limited individual and group therapy, Budman et al. (1988) found that the two therapies show nearly identical effects. Budman et al. randomly assigned 98 subjects to group or individual treatment provided by experienced therapists and used multiple measures of outcome. Both treatments were found to be effective, and there were only small differences. However, Budman et al. did find that clients had a clear preference for individual treatment. On a subjective measure of outcome, individual therapy subjects claimed to benefit more from treatment than those in the group. The implication of these findings suggests the need to "make group therapy more palatable" (Budman et al., 1988, p. 83). Perhaps the use of a pregroup therapy interview could have mediated some of the negative reactions to the group approach. As Budman et al. point out, group therapy is probably, at least initially, more difficult for clients to tolerate than individual therapy.

In a review of research that examined the relative effectiveness of individual and group therapy, Toseland & Siporin (1986) report that in 24 of 32 studies, no significant differences in effectivenss were found between individual and group treatment formats. Furthermore, in the remaining eight studies, group treatment was found superior to individual treatment, leading Toseland & Siporin (1986, p. 194) to conclude that "group treatment was more effective than individual treatment in 25 percent of the studies reviewed and in no study was individual treatment found to be more effective." The authors also report that group treatment was found to be more efficient than individual treatment. With the exception of the Beck approach (see, e.g., Rush & Watkins, 1981), most approaches lean toward supporting the use of group in comparison with individual methods.

Unfortunately, in most of the studies cited, the group seemed to be used merely as a convenience for dealing with a large number of clients at the same time rather than a therapeutic tool in its own right. In a review of the literature on cognitive behavioral group therapy, Rose, Tolman, & Tallant (1985) examined the use of the group as the means and the context of cognitive-behavioral therapy. The authors report that most studies did not attend to group processes as relevant to the outcome. In most studies, group therapy appeared to be the context of therapy because it was a convenient and cost-effective method for delivering the treatments being studied. It is suggested that this lack of attention to the group may limit the development of knowledge about effective group therapy.

Fortunately, some researchers have attempted to examine the contribution of the group in exploratory parts of their studies. D'Alelio and Murray (1981) compared 8-week groups to 4-week groups in the treatment of anxiety. They found that 8 weeks of group behavioral treatment was consistently superior to 4 weeks on the self-report component of anxiety. The study went further in exploring group process by asking each client at the end of therapy what each thought was most useful in treatment. Specifically, 73% reported "seeing that others were going through the same thing" was the most important component. Only 45% thought that the behavioral learning techniques were of equal importance. A similar questionnaire with groups of depressives was used by Roth, Bielski, Jones, Parker, and Osborn (1982) with similar client responses that emphasized the importance of the group in contributing to outcome.

In an examination of client-perceived curative factors in group therapy, Goldberg, McNeil, & Binder (1988) found clients rated cohesion, instillation of hope, and altruism as the most helpful factors. Couch & Childers (1987) discuss some strategies for instilling hope, including pregroup interviews for prospective group members, giving information about the goals of group therapy, and validating the group's common fears about such issues as confidentiality, self-disclosure, and uncertainty about norms. A key research issue is on identifying what factors in the group context are therapeutic factors and then identifying the means by which to specify these behaviors and motivate clients to engage in them.

In some instances, the group method is being recognized as having distinct advantages over individual treatment. For example, recent research in the area of eating disorders has found group treatment an effective therapy method (Laessle, Waadt, & Pirke, 1987; Lee & Rush, 1986; Reed & Sech, 1985; Roth & Ross, 1987; Schneider & Agras, 1985; Wolchik, Weiss, & Katzman, 1986). Roth and Ross (1988) argue that the group is important for eating disordered clients because it can address the interface between irrational cognitions, maladaptive social skills, disordered interpersonal relationships, and eating disordered behaviors. Roth and Ross (1988, p. 496) believe a cognitive group format offers advantages not readily available in individual cognitive therapy: "The fact that interpersonal interactions are directly observable in the group gives the therapist a powerful therapeutic tool. Connections between cognitive distortions, maladaptive interactions, and symptomatic behavior can be examined *in vivo* . . . the interpersonal milieu of the group can provide adequate safety and support for experimenting with new and risky international styles, beliefs, and coping skills."

Antonuccio, Lewinsohn, and Steinmetz (1982) attended to several group process variables. The authors studied 106 subjects in eight groups, all of which followed a Brown and Lewinsohn (1984) cognitive-behavioral or psychoeducational model for the treatment of depression. Although they did not control for group process, they did examine homework compliance rates, rates of attendance, participation levels of each individual, and level of group cohesion. Leadership behavior, style, and leadership characteristics were also assessed. Not only did all groups improve on Beck's Depression Inventory after twelve 2-hour sessions, but there were also significant effects on participation levels, group cohesiveness, leadership style differences, and differences on several other group dimensions. However, these differences had no effect on outcome.

In a more direct examination of group process, Piccinin, McCarrey, and Chislet, (1988) examined two group methods for teaching social skills training. Subjects were assigned to a facilitative condition, stressing individualized attention, informality, and emotional understanding and support with attention to the personal needs of each member, or didactic condition, which was more leader centered, more formal, and less focused on personalizing the content. The results found neither self-report nor behavioral outcome to differ between the approaches. Both approaches produced gains that were maintained 1–2 years later.

In conclusion, although there is growing empirical support for the utility of various components of a behavioral and cognitive-behavioral group therapy, only modest evidence exists on the advantage of integrating various behavioral techniques and group methods. Although most authors and clients believe that the group itself is a significant component of group therapy, few authors have attempted to investigate this dimension within the context of the therapeutic group. This may become increasingly important—as Dies (1985), in discussing the future of group work, suggests, there is a growing demand for focused, short-term group interventions. He believes this will stimulate greater collaboration between researchers and practitioners with an increasing documentation of the value of time-limited group treatment. Group therapy, thus far, has been demonstrated to be at least as effective as individual treatment and, in most cases, much less costly. Obviously, further research is necessary, not only on comparative outcome of different approaches and on who can use what kind of treatment best, but also on the contribution of group process to outcome.

REFERENCES

Antonuccio, D. O., Lewinsohn, P. M., & Steinmetz, J. (1982). Identification of therapist differences in a group treatment for depression. *Journal of Consulting and Clinical Psychology, 50,* 433–435.

Barrios, B. A., & Shigetomi, C. C. (1979). Coping skills training for the management of anxiety: A critical review. *Behavior Therapy, 10,* 491–522.

Beck, A. T. (1976). *Cognitive therapy and the emotional disorders.* New York: International Universities Press.

Beck, A. T., Rush, A. J., Shaw, B. F., & Emery, G. (1979). *Cognitive therapy of depression.* New York: Guilford Press.

Bellack, A. S., & Hersen, M. (1978). Chronic psychiatric patients and social skills training. In M. Hersen & A. S. Bellack (Eds.), *Behavior therapy in the psychiatric setting* (pp. 128–168). Baltimore, MD: Williams & Wilkins.

Benson, B. A., Rice, C. J., & Miranti, S. V. (1986). Effects of anger management training with mentally retarded adults in group treatment. *Journal of Consulting and Clinical Psychology, 54,* 728–739.

Brown, R., & Lewinsohn, P. M. (1984). A psycho-educational approach to the treatment of depression: Comparison of group, individual, and minimal contact procedures. *Journal of Consulting and Clinical Psychology, 52,* 774–783.

Budman, S. H., Demby, A., Redondo, J. P., Hannan, M., Feldstein, M., Ring, J., & Springer, T. (1988). Comparative outcome in time-limited and group psychotherapy. *International Journal of Group Psychotherapy, 38,* 63–85.

Cartledge, G., & Milburn, J. F. (1980). *Teaching children social skills.* Elmsford, NY: Pergamon Press.

Cartwright, D., & Zander, A. (Ed.). (1968). *Group dynamics: Research and theory.* New York: Harper & Row.

Combs, M. L., & Slaby, D. A. (1977). Social skills training with children. In B. B. Lahley & A. E. Kazdin (Eds.), *Advances in clinical child psychology* (Vol. 1). New York: Plenum Press.

Couch, R. D., & Childers, J. H. (1987). Leadership strategies for instilling and maintaining hope in group counseling. *Journal of Specialists in Group Work, 12,* 138–143.

Curran, J. P., Wallander, J. L., & Aschetti, M. (1977). *The role of behavioural and cognitive factors in the maintenance of heterosexual social anxiety.* Paper presented to the Psychological Convention, Chicago, IL.

D'Alelio, W. A., & Murray, E. J. (1981). Cognitive therapy for test anxiety. *Cognitive Therapy and Research, 5,* 299–307.

Deffenbacher, J. L. (1988). Cognitive-relaxation and social skills treatments of anger: A year later. *Journal of Counseling Psychology, 35,* 234–236.

Dies, R. R. (1985). Research foundations for the future of group work. *Journal of Specialists in Group Work, 10,* 68–73.

D'Zurilla, T. J. (1986). *Problem solving therapy: A social competence approach to clinical intervention.* New York: Springer.

Edelmann, R. J. (1985). Dealing with socially embarassing events: Socially anxious and non-socially anxious groups compared. *British Journal of Clinical Psychology, 24,* 281–288.

Edelstein, B. A., & Eisler, R. M. (1976). Effects of modeling and modeling with instructions and feedback on the behavioral components of social skills. *Behavior Therapy, 7,* 382–389.

Eisler, R. M., Frederiksen, L. W., & Peterson, G. L. (1978). The relationships of cognitive variables to the expression of assertiveness. *Behavior Therapy, 9,* 419–427.

Ellis, A. C. (1970). *The essence of rational psychotherapy: A comprehensive approach to therapy.* New York: Institute for Rational Living.

Emmelkamp, P. M. G. (1982). *Phobic and obsessive-compulsive disorders.* New York: Plenum Press.

Engels, M. L., & Poser, E. (1987). Social skills training with older women. *Clinical Gerontologist, 6,* 70–73.

Flowers, J. V., & Booraem, C. D. (1980). Three studies toward a fuller understanding of behavioral group therapy: Cohesion, Client flexibility and outcome generalization. In D. Upper & S. M. Ross (Eds.), *Behavior Group Therapy.* Champaign, IL: Research Press.

France, D. G., & Dugo, J. M. (1985). Pretherapy orientation as preparation for open psychotherapy groups. *Psychotherapy, 22,* 256–261.

Fremouw, W. J., & Zitter, R. E. (1978). A comparison of skills training and cognitive restructuring-relaxation for the treatment of speech anxiety. *Behavior Therapy, 9,* 248–259.

Garner, D., & Bemis, J. (1982). A cognitive-behavioral approach to anorexia nervosa. *Cognitive Therapy and Research, 6,* 123–150.

Glass, C. R., Gottman, J. M., & Shmurak, S. H. (1976). Response-acquisition and cognitive self-statement modification approaches to dating-skills training. *Journal of Counseling Psychology, 23,* 520–525.

Goldberg, F. S., McNiel, D. E., & Binder, R. L. (1988). Therapeutic factors in two forms of inpatient group psychotherapy: Music therapy and verbal therapy. *Group, 12,* 145–156.

Goldsmith, J. B., & McFall, R. M. (1975). Development and evaluation of an interpersonal-skill training program for psychiatric inpatients. *Journal of Abnormal Psychology, 84,* 51–58.

Goldstein, A. P., Sprafkin, R. P., Gershaw, N. J., & Klein, P. (1983). *Skillstreaming the adolescent.* Champaign, IL: Research Press.

Graff, R. W., Whitehead, G. I., & LeCompte, M. (1986). Group treatment with divorced women using cognitive-behavioral support-insight methods. *Journal of Counseling Psychology, 33,* 276–281.

Hamberger, L., & Hastings, J. (1988). Skills training for treatment of spouse abusers: An outcome study. *Journal of Family Violence, 3,* 121–130.

Hersen, M., & Barlow, D. H. (1976). *Single case experimental designs.* Elmsford, NY: Pergamon Press.

Hersen, M., Eisler, R. M., Miller, P. M., Johnson, M. B., & Pinkston, S. G. (1973). Effects of practice, instructions and modeling on components of assertive behavior. *Behaviour Research and Therapy, 11,* 443–451.

Hodgson, J. (1981). Cognitive versus behavioral interpersonal approaches to the group treatment of depressed college students. *Journal of Counseling Psychology, 28,* 243–249.

Horan, J. J., Hackett, G., Buchanan, J. D., Stone, C. I., & Demchik–Stone, D. (1977). Coping with pain: A component analysis of stress inoculation. *Cognitive Therapy and Research, 1,* 211–221.

Kazdin, A. E. (1985). The separate and combined effects of covert and overt rehearsal in developing assertive behavior. *Behaviour Research and Therapy, 20,* 17–25.

Kazdin, A. E., & Krouse, R. (1983). The impact of variations in treatment rationales on expectancies for therapeutic change. *Behavior Therapy, 14,* 657–671.

Kazdin, A. E., & Mascitelli, S. (1982). Behavioral rehearsal, self-instructions, and homework practice in developing assertiveness. *Behavior Therapy, 13,* 346–360.

Kelly, J. A. (1985). Group social skills training. *The Behavior Therapist, 8,* 93–95.

Ladd, G. W. (1984). Social skills training with children: Issues in research and practice. *Clinical Psychology Review, 4,* 317–337.

Laessle, R. G., Waadt, S., & Pirke, K. M. (1987). A structured behaviorally oriented group treatment for bulimia nervosa. *Psychotherapy and Psychosomatics, 48,* 141–145.

Langer, E. J., Janis, I. L., & Wolfer, J. A. (1975). Reduction of psychological stress in surgical patients. *Journal of Experimental Social Psychology, 11,* 155–165.

LaPointe, K., & Rimm, D. (1980). Cognitive, assertive, and insight-oriented group therapies in the treatment of reactive depression in women. *Psychotherapy: Theory, Research, and Practice, 17,* 312–321.

Lawrence, H., & Sundell, M. (1972). Behavior modification in adult groups. *Social Work, 17,* 34–43.

LeCroy, C. W. (1983). Social skills training with adolescents: A review. In C. W. LeCroy (Ed.), *Social skills training for children and youth.* New York: Haworth Press.

LeCroy, C. W. (1988). Anger management or anger expression: Which is most effective? *Residential Treatment for Children and Youth, 5,* 29–40.

Lee, M. F., & Ruth, A. J. (1986). Cognitive-behavioral group therapy for bulimia. *International Journal of Eating Disorders, 5,* 595–616.

Liberman, R. P. (1970). A behavioral approach to group dynamics: I. Reinforcement and prompting of cohesiveness in group therapy. *Behavior Therapy, 1,* 141–175.

Linehan, M. M., Goldfried, M. R., & Goldfried, A. P. (1979). Assertion therapy skill training or cognitive restructuring. *Behavior Therapy, 10,* 372–388.

Lott, A. J., Lott, B. E. (1961). Group cohesiveness, communication level and conformity. *Journal of Abnormal and Social Psychology, 62,* 408–412.

Lucock, M. P., & Salkovskis, P. M. (1988). Cognitive factors in social anxiety and its treatment. *Behaviour Research and Therapy, 26,* 297–302.

Mahoney, M. J., Arnkoff, D. (1978). Cognitive and self-control therapies. In S. L. Goldfried & A. E. Bergin (Eds.), *Handbook of psychotherapy and behavior changes* (2nd ed.). New York: John Wiley & Sons.

Marzillier, J. S., & Winter, K. (1983). Limitations in the treatment of social anxiety. In E. B. Foa & P. M. G. Emmelkamp (Eds.), *Failures in behavior treatment.* New York: John Wiley & Sons.

Mash, E. J., & Terdal, L. G. (Eds.). (1976). *Behavior-therapy assessment: Diagnosis, design, and evaluation.* New York: Springer.

Meichenbaum, D. (1977). *Cognitive behavior modification.* New York: Plenum Press.

Meichenbaum, D., & Cameron, R. (1973). Training schizophrenics to talk to themselves: A means of developing attentional controls. *Behavior Therapy, 4,* 515–534.

Monti, P. M., Zwick, W. R., & Warzak, W. J. (1986). Social skills and irrational beliefs: A preliminary report. *Journal of Behavior Therapy and Experimental Psychiatry, 17,* 11–14.

Newton, A., Kindness, K., & McFudyen, M. (1983). Patients and social skills group: Do they lack social skills? *Behavioral Psychotherapy, 11,* 116–126.

Novaco, R. W. (1975). *Anger control: The development and evaluation of an experimental treatment.* Lexington, MA: D. C. Heath.

Novaco, R. W. (1977). Stress inoculation: A cognitive therapy for anger and its application to a case of depression. *Journal of Consulting and Clinical Psychology, 45,* 600–608.

Piccinin, S., McCarrey, M., & Chislett, L. (1985). Assertion training outcome and generalization effects under didactic vs. facilitative training conditions. *Journal of Clinical Psychology, 41,* 753–762.

Reed, G., & Sech, E. P. (1985). Bulimia: A conceptual model for group treatment. *Journal of Psychosomatic Nursing, 23,* 16–21.

Resick, P. A., Jordan, C. G., Girelli, S. A., Hutter, C. K., & Marhoefer–Dvorak, S. (1988). A comparative outcome study of behavioral group therapy for sexual assault victims. *Behavior Therapy, 19,* 385–402.

Robinson, K. M. (1988). A social skills training program for adult caregivers. *Advances in Nursing Science, 10,* 59–72.

Rose, S. D. (1981). How group variables relate to outcome in behavior group therapy. *Social Work Research and Abstracts, 17,* 25–29.

Rose, S. D. (1984). Assessment in groups. *Social Research and Abstracts, 17,* 29–37.

Rose, S. D. (1989). *Working with adults in groups: A cognitive-behavioral and small groups approach.* San Francisco: Jossey-Bass.

Rose, S. D., & Edleson, J. (1987). *Working with children and adolescents in groups: A multimethod approach.* San Francisco: Jossey-Bass.

Rose, S. D., Tolman, R., Hanusa, P., & Tallant, R. (1984). *Leader's manual for stress management training.* University of Wisconsin, Madison, WI: School of Social Work.

Rose, S. D., Tolman, R., & Tallant, S. (1985). Group process in cognitive-behavioral therapy. *The Behavior Therapist, 8,* 71–75.

Rosenthal, T., & Bandura, A. (1978). Psychological modeling: Theory and practice. In S. L. Garfield & A. E. Bergin (Eds.), *Handbook of psychotherapy and behavior changes* (2nd ed.). New York: John Wiley & Sons.

Roth, D., Bielski, R., Jones, M., Parker, W., & Osborn, G. (1982). A comparison of self-control therapy and combined self-control therapy and anti-depressant medication in the treatment of depression. *Behavior Therapy, 13,* 133–144.

Roth, D. M., & Ross, D. R. (1987). Short-term cognitive-behavioral group therapy for eating disorders. Unpublished manuscript.

Roth, D. M., & Ross, D. R. (1988). Long-term cognitive-interpersonal group therapy for eating disorders. *International Journal of Group Psychotherapy, 38,* 491–510.

Rush, J., & Watkins, J. (1981). Group versus individual cognitive therapy: A pilot study. *Cognitive Therapy and Research, 1,* 95–103.

Schneider, J. A., & Agras, W. W. (1985). A cognitive behavioural group treatment of bulimia. *British Journal of Psychiatry, 146,* 66–69.

Shaffer, C., Shapiro, J., Sank, L., & Coghlen, D. (1981). Positive changes in depression, anxiety, and assertion following individual and group cognitive-behavior therapy intervention. *Cognitive Therapy and Research, 5,* 149–157.

Shaw, B. (1977). Comparison of cognitive therapy and behavior therapy in the treatment of depression. *Journal of Consulting and Clinical Psychology, 45,* 543–551.

Shipley, C., & Fazio, A. (1973). Pilot study of a treatment for psychological depression. *Journal of Abnormal Psychology, 2,* 372–376.

Shoemaker, M. E. (1977). Developing assertiveness: Training or therapy? In R. E. Alberti (Ed.), *Assertiveness innovation, applications, issues.* San Luis Obispo, CA: Impact.

Swartz, R. M., & Gottman, J. M. (1976). Toward a task analysis of assertive behavior. *Journal of Consulting and Clinical Psychology, 44,* 910–920.

Taylor, F. G., & Marshall, W. L. (1977). Experimental analysis of a cognitive-behavioral therapy for depression. *Cognitive Therapy and Research, 1,* 59–72.

Telch, C. F., & Telch, M. J. (1986). Group coping skills instruction and supportive group therapy for cancer patients: A comparison of strategies. *Journal of Consulting and Clinical Psychology, 54,* 802–808.

Teri, L., & Lewinsohn, P. M. (1985). Group intervention for unipolar depression. *The Behavior Therapist*, 8, 109–111.

Thorpe, G. L., Amatu, H. I., Blakey, R. S., & Burns, L. E. (1976). Contributions of overt instructional rehearsal and "specific insight" to the effectiveness of self-instructional training: A preliminary study. *Behavior Therapy, 7,* 504–511.

Toseland, R. W., & Siporin, M. (1986). When to recommend group treatment: A review of the clinical and research literature. *International Journal of Group Psychotherapy, 36,* 171–201.

Turk, D. (1975). *Cognitive control of pain: A skills training approach for the treatment of pain*. Unpublished master's thesis, University of Waterloo, Waterloo, Ontario, Canada.

Wolchik, S. A., Weiss, L., & Katzman, M. A. (1986). An empirically validated, short-term approach to the treatment of bulimiarexia. *Psychotherapy: Theory, Research, and Practice, 18,* 21–34.

Wolpe, J., & Lazarus, A. A. (1966). *Behavior therapy techniques: A guide to the treatment of neuroses*. Oxford: Pergamon Press.

Author Index

Gilligan, S.C., 366, 384
Gilmore, J.B., 366
Gino, A., 231
Ginpil, S., 320
Girelli, S.A., 445
Gladstein, G., 28
Glaros, A.G., 286
Glaser, E.M., 104
Glasgow, R.E., 151, 184, 349
Glass, C.R., 263, 284, 285, 436
Glass, D.R., 288
Glass, G.V., 3, 12
Glassock, S.T., 152
Glick, P., 33
Glover, J.H., 235
Göeckner, D.J., 330
Goins, C., 83
Goldberg, F.S., 447
Goldfried, 13
Goldfried, A.P., 185, 253, 445
Goldfried, M.R., 171, 172, 185,
    248–249, 252, 253, 270, 276, 280,
    283, 290, 306, 321, 361, 445
Goldiamond, I., 229
Goldin, J.C., 268
Goldsmith, J.B., 431
Goldstein, A.J., 191
Goldstein, A.P., 3, 13, 24, 25, 33–34,
    39, 44, 48, 63, 64, 172, 317,
    431
Goldstein, G., 13
Gollwitzer, P.M., 313, 325
Gomes-Schwartz, B., 64
Good, B., 32
Goodman, G., 407
Goodman, J., 381
Gordon, A., 192
Gordon, D.A., 379
Gordon, J.R., 313, 317, 361
Gordon, K.K., 410
Gordon, R.D., 410
Gordon, W.A., 153
Gossard, D., 80
Gotlib, I.H., 268
Gottman, J.M., 285, 435, 436
Gouaux, C., 384
Gourash, N., 409
Gouvier, W.D., 153
Graff, R.W., 436
Graham, S., 374
Graziano, A.M., 374

Greco, F.A., 89
Green, L., 333
Greenberg, J., 368, 375
Greenberg, L.S., 4, 287, 326
Greenberg, P.D., 104
Greenberg, R.L., 259, 270, 271,
    272
Greenwald, A.G., 364
Greer, J.H., 272
Greiner, J.M., 310, 313
Gresham, F.M., 379
Grieger, R.M., 250, 372
Griffiths, R., 330
Griffitt, W.B., 384
Grimm, L.G., 3, 13, 164, 219, 306,
    320, 349, 351
Grohns, C., 224
Gross, A.M., 223, 240
Grove, W.M., 269
Groves, G.A., 191
Guerney, B.G., 48, 63
Guess, D., 202–203
Guiliano, T., 368
Guise, B.J., 109
Gumprez, J.J., 30
Gurman, A.S., 65

Haaga, D.A.F., 253, 254, 257, 269,
    283, 284, 285, 288, 374
Haar, M.D., 361, 373
Haavik, S., 132
Hackett, G., 438
Hadley, S.W., 64, 65, 268
Hagan, R.L., 346
Hagerman, S., 310
Haley, J., 37
Halisch, F., 314
Hall, R.V., 331
Hall, S.M., 104, 233
Halmi, K.A., 152
Halpern, S., 92
Hamberger, L., 431
Hamblin, D., 413
Hamilton, D.I., 163
Hammen, C.L., 253, 284
Hammer, D., 347
Hampe, 162
Hannan, M., 446
Hantas, M., 385
Hanusa, P., 436, 441, 442

Subject Index

About the Editors and Contributors

ABOUT THE EDITORS

Frederick H. Kanfer (PhD, Indiana University) is professor of psychology and director of clinical training at the University of Illinois. His primary interest is in developing the necessary conceptualizations and methods to provide a broad behavioral framework for application to personal and social problems.

He was awarded a Diplomate in Clinical Psychology from the American Board of Examiners in Professional Psychology. He is a Fellow of the American Psychological Association and has held office in the Division of Clinical Psychology and in the Association for the Advancement of Behavior Therapy.

Dr. Kanfer has taught at Washington University, St. Louis; at Purdue University; in the Department of Psychiatry at the University of Oregon Medical School; and at the University of Cincinnati. (He is currently Professor of Psychology at the University of Illinois.) He was a Fulbright Scholar to Europe, and received the Alexander V. Humboldt Senior Scientist Award and the Gold Medal of Honor from the city of Vienna for his contributions to the advancement of clinical psychology in Europe. He has been visiting professor and consultant to various agencies dealing with psychological problems, both in the United States and in Europe. In addition, he has served on editorial boards of several psychological journals and has published over 120 articles. He is co-author of *Learning Foundations of Behavior Therapy* and of *Guiding the Process of Therapeutic Change,* and co-editor of *Maximizing Treatment Gains* and of *Self-Management and Behavior Change.* His experimental work is primarily in the area of self-regulation, self-control, and altruism.

Arnold P. Goldstein (PhD, Pennsylvania State University) is professor of special education and director of the Center for Research on Aggression at Syracuse University. His primary interest is behavior modification, juvenile delinquency, and interpersonal skill training. He is a Fellow of the American Psychological Association and a member of the International Society for Research on Aggression and the Correctional Education Association.

Dr. Goldstein has taught at the University of Pittsburgh Medical School and served as a research psychologist at the VA outpatient research laboratory in Washington, DC. He was a visiting professor at the Free University of Amsterdam, Holland, in 1970, and at the University of Hawaii in the summer of 1972. He has published over 75 articles and is author, co-author, or editor of *Therapist-Patient Expectancies in Psychotherapy; Psychotherapy and the Psychology of Behavior Change; The Investigation of Psychotherapy; Psychotherapeutic Attraction; The Lonely Teacher; Structured Learning Therapy; Changing Supervisor Behavior; Skill Training for Community Living; Prescriptive Psychotherapies; Prescriptions for Child Mental Health and Education; Police Crisis Intervention; Hostage; Police and the Elderly; Maximizing Treatment Gains; Skillstreaming the Adolescent; In Response to Aggression; Youth Violence; Aggression in Global Perspective; Aggression Replacement Training; Reducing Delinquency; Intervention in the Community; and The Prepare Curriculum.*

ABOUT THE CONTRIBUTORS

Gerald C. Davison, Ph.D., is Professor of Psychology at the University of Southern California. His major professional interests are in cognitive assessment, cognitive behavior therapy, and integration of the psychotherapies.

Lisa Gaelick-Buys, Ph.D., is a psychologist at the Alberta Hospital in Edmonton. She is involved in the application of self-management therapy models in inpatient populations.

Pamela R. Guthrie is a graduate student in the Psychology Department at the University of Kentucky. Forensic psychology and community mental health are her major interests.

David A. F. Haaga, Ph.D., is Assistant Professor of Psychology at the American University, Washington, D. C. His areas of particular interest are depression, addictive behaviors, cognitive assessment, and psychotherapy outcome research methodology.

H. Nick Higginbotham, Ph.D., is Senior Lecturer in Health and Social Science at the Faculty of Medicine, University of Newcastle, in Newcastle, Australia. His professional focus has been on the social psychology of health with special attention to problems of international health development.

Paul Karoly, Ph.D., is Professor of Psychology at Arizona State University. Health psychology, assessment, and human self-regulation are his major professional interests.

Craig Winston LeCroy, Ph.D., is Associate Professor of Social Work at Arizona State University. His major works concern social skills training and evaluating interventions designed for adolescents.

Richard J. Morris, Ph.D., is Professor of Educational Psychology and Director of the School of Psychology Training Program at the University of Arizona. Fear reduction procedures and the management of aggressive behavior are his primary professional interests.

Carol J. Nemeroff, Ph.D., is Assistant Professor of Psychology at Arizona State University. Her current work focuses on "magical" thinking, the concept of contagion, examination of public reactions to Aids, and the etiology of eating disorders.

Michael T. Nietzel, Ph.D., is Professor of Psychology and Director of Clinical Training at the University of Kentucky. Forensic psychology, intervention outcome research, and social learning theory are his primary professional interests.

Sheldon D. Rose, Ph.D., is Professor of Social Work at the University of Wisconsin—Madison. His career focus and research interests concern group interventions for both adults and children.

Ted L. Rosenthal, Ph.D., is Professor, Department of Psychiatry at the University of Tennessee College of Medicine. His major professional concerns are the measurement and alleviation of stress, anxiety, and affective disorders.

Peter Salovey, Ph.D., is Assistant Professor of Psychology at Yale University. His primary research interests are the psychological consequences of moods and emotions for cognitive processes, social behavior, and interpersonal relationships.

Jack Sandler, Ph.D., is Professor of Psychology at the University of South Florida. His major research emphasis is in the domain of applied behavior analysis.

Jefferson A. Singer, Ph.D., is Assistant Professor of Psychology at Connecticut College. His main research focus is in the interrelationships of emotion, memory, and personality.

Holly Steele is a graduate student in the Psychology Department at the University of South Florida. Her primary areas are applied behavior analysis, developmental disabilities, and interventions directed toward two populations, Vietnam veterans and juvenile offenders.

Bruce D. Steffek is a graduate student in clinical psychology at the State University of New York in Albany. His major research interests are in stress disorders and marital therapy.

David T. Susman is a graduate student in the Psychology Department at the University of Kentucky. His primary professional focus is in forensic psychology, and ethical issues in psychotherapy.

Pergamon General Psychology Series

Editors: **Arnold P. Goldstein,** Syracuse University
Leonard Krasner, Stanford University &
SUNY at Stony Brook

*Out of print in original format. Available in custom reprint edition.